READINGS
FOR A
COGNITIVE
THEORY
OF
PERSONALITY

READINGS FOR A COGNITIVE THEORY OF PERSONALITY

Edited with Commentary by

JAMES C. MANCUSO
State University of New York at Albany

HOLT, RINEHART AND WINSTON, INC.
New York   Chicago   San Francisco   Atlanta
Dallas   Montreal   Toronto   London   Sydney

To the contributing authors ...
for their dedication to ideas.

PREFACE

We often hear complaints about the niggardly yield that has been derived from the productive efforts of psychologists. Nevertheless, one can achieve a strong sense of satisfaction from having engaged in the development of concepts to explain behavior, especially if he traces a particular line of thought through the last fifty years of psychological writing. The continuous cyclic process of the introduction of a concept, the entrenchment of the concept by research activity, the attack on the inadequacy of the concept, and the substitution of a more attractive concept reflects a pattern of worthy progress. In the realm of study known as *personality theory* this process is clearly apparent; satisfying changes have occurred, particularly during the past twenty years.

Twenty years ago one who enrolled in a graduate course in personality theory could fully expect to be provided with a unifying theory to guide his thinking about the totally functioning organism. The most common approach to obtaining a guiding system involved an "objective" review of the theories of various writers. Inspired instructors would buttress their objectivity by requiring an evaluation of a theoretical position in terms of the empirical research that could be marshaled to validate the theory's concepts. Many personality theorists, then, developed an allegiance to consistent research efforts that were aimed at clarifying the emerging concepts. Gradually, the study of personality theory has become a matter of reviewing the research that is directed to the total functioning of an organism, particularly the human organism. And as research questions have become more and more pointed, the researchers have given more and more of their time to the study of assumptions underlying the research efforts. No longer is the personality theorist content with an investigation of the association of castration anxiety to the punitiveness of the father figure. Instead, we find more attention being given to the motivational assumptions that underlie concepts about the development of "Oedipal relationships." One now finds that a course in personality theory can make use of textbooks that investigate the "core considerations" of existing theories, or that give extensive attention to the philosophical underpinnings of the theoretical venture.

One effect of the trends toward careful analysis of assumptive structure and greater reliance on empirical verification is that some of the theories that were once the cornerstones of personality study are showing serious signs of decay. It is our view that personality theorists recognize the decay of previously respected grand theories and that they have been borrowing their concepts directly from formal academic psychology. Studies that have been carried out in laboratories to clarify the nature of learning, or of perceptual processes, or of cognitive processes are becoming the basis for the development of key concepts in currently produced theories of behavior. As we make these assertions, we are aware that we can be accused of rampant optimism. There are still many textbooks that treat personality theory as a realm separate from general psychology. And there are still more than enough psychologists who proceed to study personality theory as though there would be little gain from looking into the concepts in formal psychology.

This text reflects our wish to meet current trends in personality theorizing. Our first aim is to show that one can draw together, from a vast available selection, a series of studies that can be coalesced into a unitary approach to the study of an organism's total behavioral functioning. Our second goal is to show that a theory which focuses on cognitive function can serve as an extremely valuable general theory of behavior. While we have attempted to provide an integrated comprehensive theory, based on cognitive functioning, we have been cautious about presenting *the* cognitive theory of behavior. The use of principles of behavior based on cognitive function reflects an *approach* to theory—an approach we believe to be a fruitful one. We would not be satisfied with proposing *the* cognitive theory of behavior, for the approach of structuring behavior in terms of cognitive processes will surely continue to yield a variety of contestable principles to describe behavior. Our third aim has been to gather a set of interesting, interrelated papers which can be used by someone attempting to direct students as they work to gain a comprehensive view of behavior. It is our view that these papers serve to clarify the most significant questions that can be asked about behavior. We try to focus on these significant questions and to explicitly state the assumptions on which we build answers to these questions.

An effort to assemble an integrated collection of papers provokes many problems. The most troublesome problem is being unable to include the many other papers of great value and significance. The second problem is that of avoiding a serious time lag. Preparing this text compares with taking care of a home lawn. Having trimmed the back yard, one must return to the front. The kind responses of those authors from whom we requested reprint permissions frequently increased our discomfort by reminding us of more recent and more representative papers. The process of reassembling could go on interminably. Our final selection and organization therefore reflects only an interim report in the busy course of developing concepts.

It is our hope that the serious student will help us to augment possible deficiencies that may arise from these conditions. Once the reader has become involved with the frame of reference this book is intended to provide, he can readily locate current discussions in the psychological literature. He can also pursue the material cited in the reference sections of the articles in this text. And most of the authors whose work is reproduced in this text are actively contributing to professional publications, so refinements of their positions will continue to appear.

It has been our experience that the papers we have assembled can be used in courses of personality study to elucidate a particular approach to comprehensive behavior theory—specifically, a theory that considers the individual's cognitive structures to be the core concept in considering the unitary person. We have found these readings to be valuable as a research-based "summation" for an undergraduate course in personality study. We have also made use of these (and other) papers in a first-level graduate course in personality theories, where they serve as a contrast to research with other approaches.

As is evident from the table of contents, we have tried to select the most relevant and central problems one encounters in an effort to construct a total theory of behavior, and to locate research-oriented attacks on these problems. Although we know that the salient questions of today can become the trivia of tomorrow, we had no choice but to commit ourselves to the ones we deem most current and valuable.

Before proceeding to the text itself, we want to give credit and thanks to a number of colleagues. First, the students who cooperated with our sometimes fumbling efforts to derive the organizational scheme that has finally emerged; we hope they gained something from the experience. Naturally we are grateful to the numerous psychologists who produced the provocative work from which this book's content has grown; primary among these, of course, are the authors who prepared the articles herein reproduced. Of special importance has been the contribution of Professor T. R. Sarbin, whose early suggestions about organization and content have been most valuable. We also offer praise to the staff of the library of the State University of New York at Albany, who, despite the immense problems occasioned by their own extremely rapid growth, pursued the hundreds of articles from which we made this final selection. To the graduate students, particularly Thomas Lickona and Lawrence Weitz, who chased down leads and came up with valuable references, we offer recognition of their contributions. All the typists who translated disconnected parcels of script into a continuous text should be given special awards; Mrs. Donna Urban, who tolerated the idiosyncrasies of a dozen psychologists and still managed to know where to locate our manuscripts, deserves a distinguishing medal. During the final phases of preparing this manuscript we were fortunate to have Mrs. Elizabeth G. Holmberg capably serving as typist and unofficial editor. And a last note of thanks to the hundreds of people who work in the publisher's world, taking care of the myriad problems presented to them by readers and writers.

J. C. M.

Albany, New York
January, 1970

CONTENTS

I
INTRODUCTION

1
THE RE-EMERGENCE
OF COGNITIVE CONCEPTS
IN COMPREHENSIVE
THEORIES OF BEHAVIOR
JAMES C. MANCUSO

Psychologists use a two-poled construct along which they rank their fellow psychologists. They also tend to judge their own professional identities on the same bipolar construct. Cronbach (1957) identifies the poles as *experimental psychologist* and *correlational psychologist*. Some students speak of *clinical psychologists* as one end of the dichotomy and of *experimental psychologists* as the other. An analysis of these beliefs and attitudes would undoubtedly reveal that individual psychologists, or groups of psychologists, use significantly different subconstructs to develop their major categories. Some psychologists construct a dichotomy on the basis of preferences for research methodologies. Other psychologists use dichotomies that have emerged from differences in subject matter. Other psychologists assume that the location of a psychologist's place of work— that is, a university as opposed to a clinic—allows his placement within a significant dichotomy. The validity of all these constructs, of course, is open to debate.

We propose an addition to these classificatory schemas, a dichotomy that distinguishes between scientifically-oriented, formal, academic psychologists and comprehensive personality theorists. One could take several routes toward testing incipient hypotheses that would help to demonstrate the utility of the suggested dichotomy. In order to test a hypothesis that *formal, experimental psychologists* are not identifiable as *comprehensive personality theorists,* we would first define our poles. When we refer to personality theorists we are speaking of the people whose work is found discussed in current, standard textbooks on personality theory (Sahakian, 1965; Hall and Lindzey, 1957; Maddi, 1968). The names of these theorists are familiar: Freud, Rogers, Lewin, Jung, Fromm, Miller, Dollard, Allport,

3

Cattell, etc. When we speak of formal, academic psychologists we have in mind those persons who carry on laboratory or experimental work, or who use this kind of work to advance concepts about the nature of behavior.

To demonstrate that our proposed dichotomy has a distinguishing value we might ask psychologists to draw up lists of highly esteemed psychologists of the past who could be placed at one end or the other of our dimension. The simple prediction would be that few of the names on one list would appear on the other. When Thorndike (1954) had psychologists rate well-known psychology leaders he was able to extract two bi-polar factors that defined the nature of the psychological work that engendered the esteem of other psychologists. One of the factors was a *verbal-quantitative* factor, and the other was a *laboratory data-field data* factor. Global theorists were very much at the verbal end of the first factor and toward the field data end of the second factor. This kind of study clearly helps to encourage the use of the classification we have proposed.

There is another source of support for the validity of differentiating between the global personality theorist and the formal, experimental psychologist. A student could select from the shelves of the library a current basic psychology textbook (for example, Vinacke, 1968), and turn to the sections dealing with personality and personality disorder. He would discover that the materials in these sections are practically irrelevant to other parts of the book. The references in the sections on motivation, emotion, sensation, perception, learning, forgetting, conceptual behavior, creative thinking, intelligence, or development, and the references in the sections on personality are two remote sets of items. The names of the important scholars in one of the areas are not to be found in the discussions of the other area. The study of personality appears to be more related to psychiatry, psychoanalysis, and social philosophy than it is to formal psychology. The references in the personality sections are more likely to be found in the literature of medicine than in the literature of psychology. It is even more startling to find that textbooks which bear the term "abnormal psychology" in their titles take their theoretical base almost exclusively from medical literature.

Undergraduate students, of course, are aware of the nature of the dichotomy and quickly learn to identify the placement of their psychology professors. Depending on their own inclinations, then, the students will choose to take courses from professors who are identified with their own personal orientation and will avoid professors whom they place at the opposite pole. An advisor of undergraduates finds that a sizeable amount of pressure must be exerted to convince a student who is interested in personality theory that he might profit from a course in perception or learning. This writer, as he was preparing to give a lecture on thinking processes to a class studying psychological development, was chagrined to overhear one of the students tell another that she would certainly enjoy the course on personality—"Real psychology, you'll study Freud and all that." And graduate students are convinced of the validity of the formal psychologist versus personality theorist dichotomy. When the majority of graduate students think of personality theory they hardly think of the dry-as-dust notions, such as *response hierarchy,* from a learning theory course, or of the *phi-phenomena* discussed in a perception course. There are psychology departments in which a person could complete an advanced degree program without taking a course in personality theory if he did take a perception course; or, conversely, if he were interested in perception he would not need to take a course on theory of personality.

Having accepted the value of recognizing a dichotomy between comprehensive behavior theorists and formal, academic psychologists, one might wish to understand the events that have led to the establishment of the dichotomy. One could begin by proposing that formal psychology has not produced personality theorists because a formal psychologist, by the very fact that he has chosen such a life venture, is aware that there simply is an insufficient conceptual base on which to build such a comprehensive theory. He will therefore devote his life to accumulating concepts rather than to seeking what he would regard as a premature amalgamation of ill-defined principles. On the other hand, the person who enters psychology to pursue a profession that is charged with managing behavior change or conduct reorganization cannot avoid taking an all-inclusive view about personal behavior. With behavior change as his responsibility, a professional cannot divide a person according to the chapter titles of a first-year psychology textbook: Motivation, emotion, learning, perception, social behavior, and development cannot remain as neat and separate divisions of behavior. This categorization of behavior is pointless to one who is faced with the task of altering the behavior of an adolescent who has been arrested five times for breaking and entering. The nature of the basic commitment made by these different groups of students of behavior—the formal psychologist being committed to the precise development of concepts and the applied psychologist being committed to behavior change—leads them toward their respective attitude regarding the value of developing comprehensive theory.

Though the foregoing formulation might explain why personality theorists emerge from one or another particular professional pool, ramifications of the separation of interests call for further clarification. What has prevented the appearance of personality theorists who draw heavily from the concepts which have been developed by the formal psychologists? Why have those who demand a comprehensive personality theory generally neglected the concepts that have been provided by the formal psychologists? Here we have a question that would require analysis on a grand scale. We must recount the whole history of psychology and analyze while recounting, deep philosophical divisions by which groups of psychologists are separated. But this analysis will not be developed here. Rychlak (1968) has presented a well documented set of arguments as to why personality theorists have not borrowed from current formal psychology.

The broad thesis of this short discussion is that the positions espoused by the formal psychologists of the past four decades have been philosophically incompatible with the objectives of psychologists who labor to construct comprehensive personality theories. We will highlight two of Rychlak's points, and will then proceed from these points toward elaborating our view that there is a growing consensus among formal psychologists and personality theorists. This blossoming rapprochement, we maintain, is taking place around a re-emerging cognitive personality theory.

The first of Rychlak's propositions illumines the point that formal psychology has espoused a position of realism. The psychologist who adopts a position of realism assumes "that the world (sometimes phrased 'external world') of perception and cognition has an immutable existence all its own, entirely independent of the perceiver. Man looks out onto a world that has an independent existence. Abstractions map a reality—maybe not in a one-to-one sense at all times, but such one-to-one mapping is possible" (Rychlak, 1968, p. 17). In contrast to the realist, let us point out, is the psychologist who would claim that one is pursuing an unattainable goal when he seeks to "map reality." The idealist is one who tends to believe that: "Man looks out on a world of his own making. Knowledge is primarily an act of creation, of actively tying together rather than passively mapping certain of the many variables that play before our eyes" (Rychlak, 1968, p. 17). In its effort to emulate the success of the physical sciences, psychology has worked to create a model of man that would exclude the possibility that external variables would be transmuted within the organism. If the psychologist was one who would gain his knowledge about behavior through "mapping the reality" of behavior, then his subjects had best be seen as "mappers of reality." Watson's (1913) smarting attack on introspectionalism advocated an approach to psychology which would eliminate any need to deal with the interpretations that an organism might make of stimuli. This approach was superfluous to the development of the science of behavior. Psychology had become so enmeshed in speculation about the nature of the "mind" and "consciousness" that its references to these entities might best be discarded. It was Watson's belief that one could evolve a psychology that would be stated entirely in terms of stimulus, response, and habit formations. In his landmark article, Watson also showed his admiration for the success of biology, physics, and chemistry. He believed that psychology would become a matter of structures, and that its principles would one day be reducible to physiochemical terms. The effect of this highly influential article was to purge internal psychological mechanisms from psychological theory. The "mind" was banished from psychology, and with it went references to notions that spoke of the "interpretations" that an organism placed on stimuli. The explanations of an organism's responses were to be made entirely in terms of antecedent stimuli.

As formal psychologists struggled to develop methods that would allow them to abide by the stringent proscriptions which Watson so admirably laid down, they gradually reached the theoretical point where they could erect a very suitable theoretical framework by grafting Pavlov's (1960) conditioning model to associationism, which was then best represented in psychology by Thorndike's (1913) connectionalism. With an associationistic approach, and using Pavlov's principles of reinforcement by contiguous presentation of stimuli, one could demonstrate the acquisition of sets of responses. In the conditioning model the antecedent stimulus and variables associated with it, as well as the resultant response with its associated variables, would be neatly specified. Nothing could be more suitable to the demands for scientific order that Watson had laid down. In time, as Rychlak (1968, p. 137) so aptly points out, the stimulus is seen as "controlling" the response, and it becomes the independent variable in precise hypotheses statements. The philosophical position of the realists led them to a point where they could not propose motivational principles that gave the individual organism control of its own behavior. The control resided in the stimulus, the independent variable of the hypothesis statement.

Formal psychology, having first ejected concepts that spoke of internal organization, then moved to assert its scientific identity by insisting that experimentation be carried on through stating symmetrical hypotheses where the stimulus becomes the independent variable while the response served as the dependent variable. Thorndike's connectionalism, elaborated into Hull's (1943) drive reduction theory, and Skinner's (1938) operant conditioning, became the height of scientific respectability in psychology. The aims of psychology as a science which could "predict and control" behavior could readily be met by discovering the laws, laws which are waiting "out there" to be discovered, which relate the antecedent stimuli to the consequent response.

The achievement of an acceptable solution to the problem of control of behavior was a major advance for formal psychologists. By using drive reduction as a central motivational concept, an investigator could place the motivational variable at the stimulus end of the stimulus-response sequence. Drive was a matter of the organism being deprived of the satisfaction of a basic biological need. Behavior was instigated by the arousal of a drive, and that behavior which led to the reduction of the drive would be reinforced; that is, it would reappear when similar stimulus conditions reappeared. This proposition, of course, required a great deal of clarification and elaboration; but it had a huge appeal, within the system that was being advocated, for it allowed one to describe drive and drive reduction in quantitative and mathematical formulations. Drive reflected a state of bodily deficit. Thus, deprivation of bodily requirements could be seen as inducing drive. The supplementing of substances which filled bodily requirements would be regarded as drive reduction. Both drive arousal and drive reduction, then, could be stated as stimulus variables, while the response that produced drive reduction could be seen as being dependent upon drive state. Furthermore, experiments easily attest to the validity of this theory. An organism in high drive state will arrive at a criterion of satisfactory performance in a learning study more rapidly than will an organism which is relatively satiated in all its known needs. Also, if an animal in a high drive state is presented with substances which reduce its drive, this presentation being contingent upon performance of a particular response, the animal will reach a criterial performance more rapidly than if it is presented with substances relating to needs which are irrelevant to those which the animal is presumedly seeking to satisfy.

In addition to subscribing to the value of a scientifically sound methodology, the use of the drive concept carried another aura that made it highly valued in a discipline that was struggling to establish its scientific identity. The concept of drive could be shown to have a direct link to Darwinian evolutionary theory. Organisms which were impelled into action by a bodily deficit could be neatly shown to be organisms which would have a higher probability of maintaining life in the bloody struggle for survival. An organism which could be "signaled" of its lack of proper internal chemical balances, and could then be driven into action which could result in a reduction of deficits, or in the expelling of toxic substances, would surely gain a survival edge over organisms that were not equipped with this biologically valuable adaptability. Darwinism, then, could be related to the behavioral sciences, which, after all, are a branch of the biological sciences. In this way, all the high prestige accorded to the biologists, who were neatly ordering the living world, could be accumulated by the behavioral scientists, who were trying to order the behavior of the living world.

Darwin gave the movement a significant impetus. His book on emotions, and their evolutionary character (Darwin, 1873), represented an influential effort to show that large segments of man's behavior were derived from the self-preservative and defensive behavior of the lower animals. His easy use of the concept of "instinct" provided the model that led to the theory that vast amounts of human behavior are directed by instinct. McDougall (1908) is the most representative of these theorists. He saw instincts underlying huge segments of human behavior, and borrowed very directly from Darwin's conception that instinct prepared the organism to act in ways that gave it a greater probability of surviving. The concept of instinct, however, had a simplicity that was dangerous to the existence of the idea. It reached a point where its explanatory power was so great that the concept became useless. If an instinct theorist were pressed to explain a particular behavior, then he could simply explain every minute function as the expression of an instinct. One writes psychological theory because one has an instinct to write psychological theory!

This major objection to instinct theory gave a more refined drive theory a greater attractiveness. If one spoke of drive, rather than of instinct, one needed to specify a deficit which could be registered by the organism, and one could also be required to show how the deficit would be replenished by the behavior that was associated with a particular stimulus. In this form of motivational statement the organism would be assumed to be motivated to pursue a particular behavior only after that behavior had been instrumental in attaining drive reduction. A particular behavior was not the automatic consequent of a bodily deficit.

The ultimate in this line of theorizing was finally achieved by Skinner. In his theory, wherein reinforcement is the central concept, one does not attempt to specify the basic nature of reinforcement (Skinner, 1968). One simply assumes that if a behavior is repeated in the presence of a particular stimulus, then one has sufficient evidence that the particular stimulus-response sequence had been reinforced. This kind of proposition has high appeal to Skinner, who shows a particular fondness for his own ability to avoid "vestigial cognitive theories" (Skinner, 1968, p. 707). One can work completely outside the organism. One need never enter the organism. There is no need to flirt with the danger of engaging in the use of a mentalistic concept, even at the point where one might want to clarify the nature of the internal functioning which accompanies the powerful activity of reinforcement. So long as a particular stimulus-response sequence retains the high probability of appearing in an organism's response repertoire, then we can be satisfied that the stimulus-response sequence has been reinforced. Having reached this point in methodology and theory, we have arrived at the epitome of "empty organism" theorizing. Everything that is done to this organism and his resulting actions are assumed to be describable in terms of external, quantifiable variables.

Formal psychology, then, has been intent upon producing theory that could be scientifically respectable. This respectability was to be found, the philosophers of the science maintained, by staying outside of the organism. Borrowing heavily from Adam Smith's economic theories, psychologists found that they could talk about controlling the organism; that is, motivating him, by directing his drive state. Comprehensive behavior theorists were not prepared to adopt this constricted approach to describing their behaving subject.

Furthermore, the course of the development of a suitable way to treat the behavior of organisms did not flow in as neat and orderly a line as our condensed account would suggest. Other students of behavior continued to introduce disrupting matters into the way of the researchers who were trying to develop a conception of an organism whose only contents were some kind of meter which could indicate that a comfortable, steady state had been achieved. The most persistent disruptions came from investigators who kept pointing out that the organism somehow transformed stimuli. Simply, one could devise demonstrations that "absolutely objective" stimuli would produce responses that did not coincide with the measurable physical properties of the stimulus. The first important experimental demonstrations of this kind of event, of course, were those that emerged from the work of Wertheimer; and these led to the development of the Gestalt school of psychology. Wertheimer's work with the phi-phenomenon raised the question of what variables accounted for the subject's report that he saw light "moving across" an unlighted space when a light at point A was switched off and a light at point B, separated from A by a measurable distance, was switched on. There was no light "in the empty space." The subject was apparently "doing something" to the two stimuli, the light at A and the light at B. Similar studies continue to be reported, and there has been greater precision in measuring the variations involved in the subject's imposition of his "interpretations" on a stimulus configuration. Let us briefly note two standard studies which induce the hypotheses that subjects impose internal interpretation on external stimuli. Wallach (1963) reports a series of studies in which subjects viewed an arrangement of light stimuli and reported what they "saw." The arrangement was such that a disc of light was surrounded by a ring of light. The brightness, or intensity, of the outer ring could be varied in intensity. The brightness of the inner disc remained the same. Thus, the outer ring could be less bright, as bright as, or brighter than the inner disc. Subjects were asked to determine the brightness of the inner disc. When the ratio of the ring intensity to that of the disc intensity was 1:3, the disc was reported to be very bright. When the ratio of the intensity of the ring to the intensity of the disc was changed to 8:1, the disc was seen as being quite dim. In both cases the intensity of the disc remained the same. The judgment of its intensity, however, changed markedly. Why should subjects "see" something that was not there? Apparently "seeing" a stimulus is not simply a matter of that stimulus being recorded on one's sensory apparatus. In this case the relationship of one level of intensity to another level of intensity altered the judgment of the disc's intensity level.

In another simple experiment Sherif (1935) neatly demonstrated how subjects can "see something that isn't objectively present." Subjects were placed in a totally dark room and were asked to make judgments about the nature of the movement of a pinpoint of light. Though the light was stationary, subjects reported that the light moved. Here we see that movement, as Wertheimer suggested in his work, is not simply a matter of physical properties of the external, physical world. In Sherif's terms, it appears that subjects develop *frames of reference* within which they anchor or locate stimuli. His study suggests that the external referents of the frame of reference in which subjects spatially locate objects are removed by putting the person in a darkened room. In the absence of these referents, the spatial world becomes difficult to interpret. Thus, when a single tiny spot of light is introduced into the undifferentiated world, the subject will organize it within whatever internal systems he has available to anchor this stimulus. The "movement" of the light spot could well be a consequence of his own head or eye movement, which would change the location of the light stimulus on his retina.

In addition to this evidence that the subject transforms stimuli, the second matter that continually emerged to confound the picture of an externally directed, empty organism was that organisms would continue to develop new behaviors in conditions in which one could not find an observable bodily deficit. If an organism is placed into a relatively stimulus-free environment after having been satiated for its physiological needs, it will adopt a response that will allow it access to varied stimulation (Butler, 1953). The course of behavior that creates access to stimulation is similar to the course of performance improvement that accompanies the "reinforcement" which is provided by supplying primary need satiation. In other studies it has been shown that animals that have been deprived of satiation in some of their "primary" needs will deflect their activity from their search for the "primary need reducer" in order to investigate novel stimuli, that is, "to explore" (Dennis, 1939).

Faced with data of this kind, theorists who tried to specify the variables associated with behavior strictly in terms of external stimuli formulated an "exploratory drive." The instigation of the exploratory drive could be treated in terms that are identical to those used to treat other biologically based drives. Depriving an animal of access to novel stimuli would be assumed to raise the exploratory drive. High drive would be associated with more vigorous behavior; and more effective learning would be hypothesized to be the result of reduction of higher drive levels. This strategy would once again put the matter of motivation into "externalized" language, and the researcher would again have control over the variables.

The strategy of inventing new drives, however, placed the investigator in the same dilemma that faced the instinct theorist. Once we allow ourselves to simply add drives to a growing list, we reach a point where the concept of drives loses its explanatory power—one can explain anything through expediently calling it a new drive. Further, it again becomes difficult to locate the biological mechanisms which might underlie the exploratory drive. Where is the sensory mechanism that is activated when the organism faces a shortage of stimuli? What blood chemistry is altered when the organism is again exposed to appropriate, and therefore satisfying, levels of stimulation?

At least two major lines of difficulty kept placing insistent pressure on theorists to look into the internal structures of the organism. First, there was the evidence that subjects would alter stimuli. Second, there was evidence that all motivation was not a matter of the external world withholding or supplying materials that were necessary for the biological survival of the organism. The organism seemed to have some control of what it "wanted to do."

Formal psychology, having nothing to say about how the organism transformed stimuli or about motivation as a matter of something that the organism "wanted to do," could not serve as a source of principles that would be useful in developing a comprehensive theory of personality. Professionals who were charged with altering the behavior of persons could find little help in theories that ignored these matters.

In this setting the stimulating work of Sigmund Freud proved to be attractive. The theory had a striking appeal to those who could be influenced by scientific prestige. This set of propositions, generated directly out of a prestigious medical ambience, had consistent ties to Darwinian evolutionary theory. It offered a powerful motivational position, serving to explain the instigation and alteration of behavior in terms of the organism trying to live out its biological existence. It clearly dealt with the matter of an individual's internal transformation of stimulus events. The theory assimilated large segments of morality and social interaction. And, not the least of its values, the theory was presented in a highly literate form.

In proposing that the basic motivational force of an organism's psychological functioning is to be found in its id-derived impulses, Freud was working along a line that did not differ greatly from the concept of drive having its basis in biological deficit. The impulses that surged toward expression had the aim of achieving a biological homeostasis, and once this homeostasis was achieved the organism was put into closer harmony with the world in a way that would contribute to its continued existence. The organism had little choice in the matter of goals. A biological deficit automatically produced an impulse which sought expression in order to achieve organism-preserving goals. It was necessary, of course, to expand this formulation somewhat to include sexual impulses, those titillating strivings that were so important in creating world-wide interest in Freud's theory. This could be done by recognizing that Darwinian theory called for biological mechanisms that served to preserve not only the individual organism, but also the species. In this way, sexual impulse would be seen as having the altruistic function of preserving the species. Ultimately, the source of all behavior is to be found in these life instincts. All behaviors represent a transformation of id impulses into behaviors that allow impulse expression in the face of society's proscriptions against rampant gratification of these impulses. Within the Freudian system one could explain the organism's transformations of stimulus situations by viewing them as the individual's efforts to do what it "wants to do." The organism always "wants to" express its impulses, so that if the organism's response is not a reflection of the "reality" of an event, then the organism is reverting to operating on the "pleasure principle," by which it expresses "primary processes" rather than "secondary processes." If the individual tries to look into his personal functioning to seek out the basic motivations for his behavior he will be unable to do so, for these transformations take place in his unconscious, and they take place there so that the person *cannot* look into them. In the course of his life he has become aware of, and ashamed of, his impulses. He has come to know that they are the "sins" of Judeo-Christian theology, and that his "conscience" will not treat him favorably if he were to indulge in "sin." Under these circumstances he is fortunate to have a mechanism like his unconscious to work out for him the means of living out his sins. The psychoanalyst is also economically fortunate that there is a function like the unconscious. Otherwise, each individual would be able to look into his own personal "hang-ups" in impulse expression, and he would not need the skilled services of the professional analyst.

By achieving this amalgamation of scientific credibility, Darwinian evolutionary theory, Judeo-Christian theology, spicy sexuality, deep mystery, and dramatic metaphors, Freud won international attention to his personality theory. Even today, his theory, with its innumerable variants, provides the framework for many conceptualizations on the total functioning of the individual. It becomes almost impossible for a theorist, regardless of his divergence from a basic Freudian position, to exclude the notion of biologically based drives. And if theorists are firmly in the grasp of this concept, the general public is virtually strangled by it. The majority of educated people in our culture find it extremely difficult to conceive of a theory of motivation that excludes notions of individuals striving to preserve their biological selves. The concept of self-preservation is in the public domain.

At any rate, a theory such as Freud's could explain why the organism did not continue to do what it had been "taught" to do (in the straightforward stimulus-response associationistic sense of the meaning of "teaching"). Something is happening inside the organism, and that something is clearly aimed at accomplishing what the person most basically wants to accomplish. When one tries to teach an individual, in a complex life situation, that person cannot be taught to carry out an activity in precisely the way that he has been instructed to do it, for his impulse life encroaches on the desired behavior and distorts it into another form. No matter how hard you try to teach a juvenile thief that he must adopt other means of obtaining personal goods, he could continue to steal. His "oral" impulses would seek to expend themselves, and he would express this orality by appropriating those gifts that he perceived as being withheld from him. Or, since psychoanalytic theory is as flexible as one wishes to make it, one could hypothesize that the stealing reflects distorted "aggressive" impulses that are being diverted from direct expression upon his mother. Once one has allowed the assumption of a psychological function like the psychoanalytic *unconscious,* his theory takes on magnificent possibilities for explaining innumerable phenomena.

The pervasiveness of the pessimism of the Freudian message, with all its superexplanatory power, is now a matter of record. Freud established the trend in his later writings (Freud, 1930). The theme that man's primeval past will continue to be reflected in his behavior through the transformation of "reality" into expressions of his instincts, is now constantly used to explain why society has difficulty in teaching its members to refrain from those behaviors that the community judges to be unacceptable. Aggression is a basic part of man's heritage. Repression of sexual expression will lead one into the most unhappy of neurotic conditions. Slum-reared children are delinquent, in the broad society's terminology, because they have been deprived of oral gratifications. Straightforward training of nonaggressive means of resolving personal conflicts is deemed to be futile. Parentless children must be placed into foster homes, even inadequate homes, rather than into expensive institutions, or the children will be deprived of oral gratifications and thus become distorted subhumans. And if this kind of

indiscriminate application of psychoanalytic theory does not have sufficient scientific credibility to explain our social ills, we can turn to the
ethologists (Lorenz, 1966; Tinbergen, 1968) to gain greater support. These
investigators have recently done the interesting double-turn of borrowing
from psychoanalytic theory to explain their observations of aggression and
sexuality in animals. Some of them (particularly Tinbergen, 1968) seem to
be convinced that psychologists have worked only within the psychoanalytic framework. Studies of aggression that have followed other models
(Kuo, 1960; Bandura and Walters, 1964) are completely ignored. This,
again, reflects our major thesis: that formal psychology has not been
regarded as the source of comprehensive theories of personality.

Freudian psychoanalytic theory, then, has become the touchstone of
general personality theory. The concepts from this theory have infused the
thought and art of all manner of commentators on human behavior. Being
free to speculate, free to enter the organism's internal structures, free to
talk of the organism "doing what it wants to do" and transforming the
data that is fed into its sensorium, this kind of comprehensive theory could
win the approval of those concerned with the total functioning of a person.
Does formal academic psychology offer a promise of producing a more
systematic, less slippery, comprehensive behavior theory than that which
was supplied by Freud and his followers?

THE RETURN TO INTERNAL STRUCTURES

In the last fifteen years we have seen increasing interest in a return to a
once-respectable position in formal psychology. Formal psychology has
recognized that variables representing internal psychological functioning
of organisms must be included in comprehensive theories of behavior, and
this recognition has led to vitalized efforts to develop principles that
provide an understanding of cognitive functions. Studies in cognitive
functioning have proliferated, and recent comprehensive theories of
behavior consider these functions to be the major focus of interest. This
revived concern in internal processes has been accompanied by another
major theoretical shift, one which again reflects a reversion to a concept
that once had, but lost, scientific respectability. Motivational principles are
being cast in terms of the organism's effort "to know." Numerous current
writings are devoted to the motivational value of novel, personally
complex stimuli. The concepts of "cognitive strain," "arousal," or "activation" are fast achieving the status of all-inclusive motivational terms.

Though the Watsonian dictum of avoiding discussion of internal psychological mechanisms was overtly heeded by investigators, even those who strove to pursue a most pure course found that their systems could achieve greater explanatory power by injecting some kind of statement about internal functioning. Hull, whose work provided the most adhered-to model of stimulus response associationism, began to speak of the "anticipatory goal response" (Hull, 1931). The presentation of a stimulus activated mechanisms within the organism which represented behavior anticipatory to achieving the final goal. The anticipatory goal response (r_g) was conceptualized as part of the total external response, and could be regarded as stimuli to the ensuing r_g's. In that the $r_g \longrightarrow s_g \longrightarrow r_g$ chain would begin to "run off" when the organism was first placed into the stimulus situation, the sequence could be regarded as the basis of the animal's "expectancy." "Thinking processes" could also be conceived as chainings of these r_g's. The concept of anticipatory goal responses became particularly attractive in the hands of Osgood, with whom r_g's became the mechanism for explaining the development of *meaning* in language operations (Osgood, Suci, Tannenbaum, 1957). This intriguing use of the concept of anticipatory goal responses led to vast amounts of research, all of which served to emphasize the utility of notions that spoke of internal psychological functioning.

Staats (1968) represents the most active of the investigators who use the stimulus-response associationistic approach to discussing cognitive functioning. Staats regards motivation as an entity that must be supplied, at least initially, from the outside. He assumes, as Skinner makes explicit (Skinner, 1968), that reinforcement that is supplied by outside forces is the most effective, if not basically the only, kind of motivation. Staats says, "It is frequently said in the context of cognitive learning that 'learning is (or should be) its own reward.' This general expectation for example, appears to be generally accepted in the field of education. The author's own work with cognitive learning that has employed extrinsic rewards has at times been questioned on the basis of the expectation, when extrinsic rewards are used to produce cognitive learning, that some individuals will label the process bribery although it is a misuse of the term."

"The conception that learning must be self-reinforcing can be criticized for impracticality, as well as on the grounds that there is no biological structure in man that makes learning reinforcing in and of itself" (Staats, 1968, p. 441). In this formulation Staats reflects the reluctance of stimulus-response associationistic theorists to adopt a principle of motivation that allows the organism to "want to know." The reinforcement must be seen as emanating, basically, from the outside. Later in its life the organism might be intrinsically motivated to learn, but this will reflect "imitation" of socially reinforced behaviors.

Berlyne is another theorist who has found concepts about internal organizations to be highly useful, and who continues to try to treat them within a theory that regards drive as motivation (Berlyne, 1966). He has adopted a position of regarding curiosity as a drive, and sees the acquisition of information as a drive reducer. In his discussion of an organism's reactions to novelty, Fowler (1965) also tries to hold to the concept of exploration, or curiosity, as a drive. He feels, however, that to speak strictly of exploration as a drive is unsatisfactory, for doing so creates a basic dilemma. If one is to speak of *lack* of novel stimuli as producing a curiosity drive, then how does one explain the fact that an organism will continuously approach novel stimuli even if they are presented serially? If curiosity drive is seen as something that accumulates in the absence of novel stimuli, then it should diminish when there is a serial presentation of novel stimuli, and each novel stimulus should add to the satiation of the drive. In practice, this does not happen. As long as a new stimulus is introduced the animal will be diverted to exploring it. This now places us in the position of saying that novel stimuli themselves produce a drive, and this formulation disagrees with the drive concept. Drive theory would postulate that drive is a result of a biological deficit, and in this case should be produced by a deficit of, not a presence of, novel stimuli. Fowler attempts to resolve this dilemma by taking recourse to the useful concept of r_g. He introduces what he calls the incentive aspect of curiosity: ". . .the incentive motivational concept is operationally defined in terms of the magnitude—for example, size, weight, or amount— of the food object, because it is this feature of the incentive that influences the strength and vigor of the goal response, its r_g–s_g component, and hence the strength and vigor of the instrumental response" (Fowler, 1965, p. 42). Novel stimuli will continue to attract an organism because the novel stimuli will evoke the r_g–s_g sequences that have been associated with drive satiation in previous novel situations. "Specifically, the drive motivation (boredom) may be defined in terms of the animal's length of exposure to or 'familiarity' with a relatively unchanging stimulus condition, or conversely, in terms of the animal's length of deprivation of a change in stimulation. Incentive motivation (curiosity), on the other hand, may be defined in terms of the magnitude of the exploratory incentive—that is, the magnitude of the change in stimulation that the animal experiences upon performing some instrumental response for stimuli that are novel, unfamiliar, and so on" (Fowler, 1965, p. 42f).

In these efforts, then, we see the work of investigators who try to remain within the stimulus-response associationistic framework to explain internal functioning and the matter of the motivation that causes this functioning to proceed along certain dimensions. These writers reflect a position that has become traditional in psychology, and they insist that the resolutions of the serious questions will be answered by using variables that are externalizable. If one maintains the format of stimulus-response associationism, even though the stimuli and responses have now gone underground, one is working with an assumedly purer concept. And we must persist in seeing the motivation as being external to the organism, else we will lose an important arm of the dual purpose of the scientific study of behavior: to predict and control behavior. Giving an organism a mechanism through which its behavior is directed from within will remove the organism from the control of the scientist. If one wishes to break out of the convincing hold that these proscriptions have on the behavioral scientist, he would need to produce convincing evidence of the utility of other approaches to viewing the organism.

A major step in providing convincing evidence of the utility of other approaches was taken by Hebb in his book, *Organization of Behavior* (1949). Hebb was intent on reintroducing a useful concept to cover important internal events in psychological functioning. "The image has been a forbidden notion for twenty years, particularly in animal psychology, but the fiend was hardly exorcised before 'expectancy' had appeared instead. What is the neural basis of expectancy, or of attention, or interest? Older theory could use these words freely, for it made no serious attempt to avoid interactionist philosophy. In modern psychology such terms are an embarrassment; they cannot be escaped if one is to give a full account of behavior, but they still have the smell of animism; and must have, until a theory of thought is developed to show how 'expectancy' or the like can be a physiologically intelligible process" (Hebb, 1949, p. xviii).

Hebb proposed the concepts of "cell assembly" and "phase sequence" to provide the "physiologically intelligible process" which can be used to treat the internal psychological variable of expectancy. Arguing that the internal representations of stimuli could be seen as massive interconnections of neural networks, Hebb shows how this conceptualization can be related to a wide variety of phenomena. Expectancy, for example, is a matter of providing a set of stimuli that initiate the running off of an established cell assembly. His discussion of the stability of perceptual organizations is cast mainly in terms of organization of visually produced perceptions. He describes, for example, the old problem of how one comes to regard three dots, which are located in space in positions that would place them at the points of a triangle, as representing the triangle itself. In his discussion he argues that the motor movements associated with looking at angles A, B, and C, come to develop cell assemblies a, b, and c. With continued use, these assemblies become integrated into a phase sequence. The total assembly, t, then becomes interspersed with the assemblies a, b, and *c* to become *a, t, b, c, t.* At this point any activation of the motor movements *A, B,* and *C* will trigger the assemblies *a, b,* and *c,* along with the total integration "triangle." The individual then has an expectancy which he then proceeds to impose upon external stimuli. He thus "sees things that aren't there," just as Wertheimer's subjects saw the light moving across the space intervening between two alternately lighted spots.

Does the development of these cell assemblies and phase sequences depend on external motivation? Or can the organism achieve shifts in these organizations on the basis of internal events? Is all behavior determined by external sensory stimulation? The experimenter who wants to achieve external control of the organism must, in some way, "achieve control of the phase sequence" (Hebb, 1949, p. 181). The usual notion of biological deficit as the source of drive, which when reduced provides the reinforcement of a response, is discarded. Instead of speaking simply of drive in talking about biological deficits, Hebb chose to speak of stimuli caused by these biological deficits. When an animal became hungry, it also experienced a variety of internal stimuli. Upon reaching sufficient intensity these stimuli could disrupt ongoing cell assemblies, and the organism had to be diverted toward building cell assemblies that would be associated with these incessantly impinging stimuli. Building on a position which he had proposed in an earlier article (Hebb, 1946), Hebb proposed that any disruption of a cell assembly whose action had been initiated would produce "fear," a form of activation. In later work (Hebb, 1955), the concept of fear became retranslated into the notion of arousal. Arousal is simply a matter of cognitive processes. Any stimulation that is not immediately integrated into existing cortical structures produces a set of impulses to the cortex which are not "messages" but "serve, instead, to tone up the cortex, with a background supporting action that is completely necessary if the messages proper are to have their effect" (Hebb, 1955, p. 249). These "toning" impulses emanate from the ascending reticular arousal system and represent diffuse discharges that are instigated by the inflow of any stimulation. The ascending reticular arousal system, in turn, is deactivated by feedback from the cortex.

Having achieved this point in his thinking, Hebb has completed the circle that returns the formal psychologist to central processes and that also gives the organism an internal mechanism to guide the formation of cell assemblies, the central processes. By linking the motivational system to the neural mechanisms involved with the reticular arousing system, Hebb ties his theory, which states that the formation of cell assemblies is learning, to a meaningful series of biological studies. One can take issue with Staats contention (see above) that there is no biological structure in man that would account for learning, itself, being reinforcing. One can work on the hypothesis that reduction of "cognitive strain," i.e., the achievement of integrating cell assemblies, provides feedback which decreases the stimulation of the reticular arousal system to the cortex and to the autonomic system. In this way, "the achievement of knowledge" would represent the prototype of all reinforcement.

We would venture to say that the most valuable aspect of Hebb's theory is that it satisfied the formal psychologist while, at the same time, its philosophical underpinnings—its basic assumptions—can satisfy the theorist who is trying to develop a picture of the comprehensive functioning of the individual. Since the basic philosophical position is phenomenological and idealistic, in that there is no effort to say that the internal structures need to correspond to an external reality, the theorist can avoid becoming mired in the issue of the nature of reality. The theorist does not worry with the question of the person transforming reality. He is concerned only with the ways in which cell assemblies develop. The form of the position allows a motivational statement which puts the control of instigation and alteration of behavior within the organism. The "goal" of psychological activity is to conserve the continual, uninterrupted functioning of cell assemblies and phase sequences. So long as the environment "fits" the organism's existing structures, all is well. If there is a lack of "fit," then the structure can be changed, or the stimulus can be "cognitively altered." One can either "learn"—that is, develop new structures—or one can interpret the stimulus in terms of structures he already has available. In short, the theory allows us to speak about the organism translating stimuli into what it "wants" them to be.

In choosing Hebb as one of the leading figures in the return to central process, we do not intend to ignore other investigators who focused their attention on this type of concept. Our hypothesis is that Hebb stands out in the development of what we will call *cognitive theory of behavior* because of his approach of anchoring his concepts securely to physiological and perceptual concepts. The studies that Hebb and his productive students derived from Hebb's theory were readily accepted by other research-oriented psychologists. If psychologists accepted Hebb's concepts, they could feel more secure in turning to other studies of cognition and perception to develop comprehensive theories of behavior.

If one were to attempt to select other important contributors to the development of cognitively based, comprehensive behavior theory, he would quickly come across the volume of work that has been produced by Muzafer Sherif. His imaginative demonstration of the use and development of "frames of reference" (Sherif, 1935), internal guides to judgment, along with his continued study and clarification of judgmental processes, has provoked a constant stream of thought and research. His work with

Hadley Cantril (Sherif and Cantril, 1947) remains an important model of an attempt to amalgamate cognitive and perceptual principles into a total theory of behavior.

The fact that Sherif is generally regarded as a social psychologist points up a significant aspect of the development of comprehensive cognitive theory. Somehow, investigators who were identified as social psychologists persisted in using concepts that reflected an organism's internal mechanisms. Sherif's consistent use of the concept of frame of reference has already been mentioned. Kurt Lewin, whose effort to develop a comprehensive behavior theory is commonly cited as the model of cognitively oriented personality theory, came to be identified primarily as a social psychologist. His contributions to recent cognitively based theories of behavior were greatly extended by the work of his students and their collaborators, who also were originally identified as social psychologists. Festinger, one of Lewin's students, and his co-workers produced an excellent treatise on the group as a confirmer of the reality of a person's cognitive organizations (Festinger, Schachter, and Back, 1950). Another instance of social psychologists persisting in the use of cognitive concepts is found in the highly influential social psychology text written by Krech and Crutchfield (1948). Without the background of studies these so-called social psychologists provided, the current infusion of cognitive constructs into comprehensive behavior theory would not have nearly the vigor that is now apparent. We would suggest that this tendency for social psychologists to persist in using cognitive concepts reflects their inability to escape the influence of the great sociologists who used notions like "role" in their writings (Durkheim, 1951; Thomas and Znaniecki, 1918; Mead, 1934).

Other theorists also helped to reintroduce cognitive concepts into comprehensive behavior theory. Tolman tried to show that one could use cognitive constructs and still remain a behaviorist by tying his "intervening variables" firmly to the experimental operations which would allow one to determine their presence and absence, as well as their relationship to independent and dependent variables (Tolman, 1951). Snygg and Combs prepared a comprehensive theory of behavior that was firmly in the phenomenological tradition, focusing strongly on the individual's perceptual organizations (Snygg and Combs, 1949). Rogers, in his effort to formulate an approach to helping people to alter their behavior via the use of face-to-face counseling, reflected a personality theory that had strong phenomenological and cognitive orientations (Rogers, 1951). Tolman, who had established his credentials as a careful, formal psychologist, was taken seriously by other formal psychologists, despite the small effect he had on comprehensive behavior theory. Rogers and Snygg and Combs were widely influential among general personality theorists, although they did not influence formal psychologists. These latter writers did not draw on the extensive literature of perception and cognition, and they did not generate experimental study of the basic concepts related to their theory. Their theory, however, carried the tradition of cognitively based principles, and provided a superstructure to which one could amalgamate formally developed concepts.

Our final comment on psychological theorists who persisted in the use of cognitive concepts is devoted to a theorist whose professional life is a mirror-image of the fortunes of cognitive concepts in psychology. Jean Piaget appeared on the professional psychological scene early in the 1920's. This, of course, was a point in psychology's history when cognitive concepts were given very little attention in psychology, particularly in the United States. For the first ten years of his career, Piaget barely stirred a ripple in American psychological thought. By the 1930's his highly prolific theoretical imagination had produced a quality and quantity of work which at least forced his recognition by the mainstream of psychology. The reaction to his studies and theory, however, was generally negative. A group of studies was quickly produced to invalidate his conclusions. He was constantly criticized for his poor experimental and data-treatment techniques. By the 1940's Piaget's work had declined into near obscurity in general psychological thought. Fortunately for modern psychology, Piaget did not desist from his efforts to understand the adaptability of individual human organisms in terms of the organism's cognitive functioning. In the later part of the 1950's, as cognitive theorizing again became scientifically respectable, psychologists could find a wealth of significant concepts in the publications of Piaget and his numerous collaborators. In recent years Piaget has been threatened with a cult that is as avid as that which surrounded Freudian theory.

The development of comprehensive, cognitively based theories of behavior began in the latter part of the 1950's. Some of the publication landmarks that marked this beginning are identified as: Osgood, Suci, and Tannenbaum's (1957) monograph on meaning; Festinger's (1957) treatise on the motivation involved in the organism's experience of cognitive dissonance; Bruner, Goodnow, and Austin's (1956) investigation of the nature of concept development and use; and Miller, Galanter, and Pribram's (1960) analysis of problem solving. Since this auspicious initial effort, the significant work on cognitive theories has rapidly multiplied. Here we will cite only a few of the provocative ventures into the use of cognitive concepts to discuss general behavior. References to other important writers will appear in later sections of the book.

Sarbin, Taft, and Bailey (1960) guaranteed that "clinical diagnosis" of behavior will never revert to the simplistic kind of categorizing that preceded their analysis of the cognitive processes which guide the behavior of the clinical psychologist. J. McV. Hunt (1961) has reminded intelligence testers that they could profitably refer to the extensive work that has been done on perceptual and cognitive processes. Hunt's book has been a major force in reviving interest in the work of Piaget. Shortly thereafter Flavell (1963) masterfully synthesized the enormous quantity of work that has been done around the theory and methods of Piaget, putting Piaget's work into a form easily accessible. Harvey, Hunt, and Schroder (1961) contemporaneously issued a monograph that discusses personality in terms of an individual's conceptual systems.

While formal psychologists were "rediscovering" cognitive concepts, Sherif and Piaget continued to produce the kind of outstanding studies that marked their professional careers (Inhelder and Piaget, 1958; Piaget, Inhelder, and Szeminska, 1960; Sherif and Sherif, 1964; Sherif, Sherif, and Nebergall, 1965). One could cite other valuable work (much of which will be noted in later discussion) which served to reintroduce cognitive concepts into the comprehensive behavior theory. But one more salient landmark is George Kelly's theory of personal constructs (Kelly, 1955). A summary of his theory of personal constructs is the first reading in this study.

Kelly's theory is regularly used as a model of a comprehensive cognitively based theory of behavior. Kelly clearly, intended that his theory be a complete one. His theory is neatly ordered; it provides a succinct focus for testing the validity of building a comprehensive theory of behavior on principles of cognitive functioning. Kelly's theory also has a sound empirical base. However, as Bruner points out in his review of Kelly's book (see below), Kelly did not document the experimental and theoretical sources of his assumptions and postulates. The research readings included in this study are chosen to demonstrate systematic approaches to the issues that Kelly sought to resolve by stating his corollaries. Although the research does not completely clarify the issues, the selected studies do suggest that Kelly's resolutions are quite reasonable and acceptable. And at points where there may be questions about the validity of his assumptions, this theory provides useful guides for the direction of further research.

The re-entry of cognitive concepts suggests that comprehensive personality theorizing and formal psychology will once again become a unitary effort. We look forward to having future introductory psychology textbooks include a chapter on personality theory which is a logical extension of the material presented in other chapters in that text. For those who in the future venture to prepare a personality theory should feel the work of formal psychologists, and to cite their carefully conducted experimental studies.

We could discuss the kinds of criticisms that are leveled against cognitively-based theories. Maddi, for example, points out that cognitive theory does not make a good case for how perception and cognition are translated into motor action (Maddi, 1968, p. 122). Bruner, as we shall see, feels that cognitive theory does not deal with the "passions" of human behavior. But we will let the readings that follow illuminate these issues.

REFERENCES

BANDURA, A., & WALTERS, R. H. *Social Learning and Personality Development.* New York: Holt, Rinehart, and Winston, 1964.

BERLYNE, D. E., KOENIG, J. D. V., & HIROTA, T. "Novelty, Arousal, and the Reinforcement of Diversive Exploration in the Rat." *Journal of Comparative and Physiological Psychology,* 1966, *62,* 222–226.

BRUNER, J. S., GOODNOW, J. J., & AUSTIN, G. A. *A Study of Thinking.* New York: Wiley, 1956.

BUTLER, R. A. Discrimination Learning by Rhesus Monkeys to Visual-Exploration Motivation. *Journal of Comparative and Physiological Psychology,* 1953, *46,* 95–98.

CRONBACH, L. J. "The Two Disciplines of Scientific Psychology." *American Psychologist,* 1957, *12,* 671–684.

DARWIN, C. *The Expressions of the Emotions in Man and Animals.* New York: Appleton-Century-Crofts, 1873.

DENNIS, W. Spontaneous Alternation in Rats as an Indicator of the Persistence of Stimulus Effects. *Journal of Comparative Psychology,* 1939, *28,* 305–312.

DURKHEIM, E. *Suicide.* Glencoe, Ill.: Free Press, 1951.

FESTINGER, L. *A Theory of Cognitive Dissonance.* Stanford, Calif.: Stanford University Press, 1957.

FESTINGER, L., SCHACHTER, S., & BACK, K. *Social Pressures in Informal Groups.* New York: Harper and Row, 1950.

FOWLER, H. *Curiosity and Exploratory Behavior.* Macmillan, 1965.

FREUD, S. *Civilization and Its Discontents.* London: Hogarth Press, 1930.

HALL, C. S., & LINDZEY, G. *Theories of Personality.* New York: Wiley, 1957.

HARVEY, O. J., HUNT, D. E., & SCHRODER, H. M. *Conceptual Systems and Personality Organization.* New York: Wiley, 1961.

HEBB, D. O. On the Nature of Fear. *Psychological Review,* 1946, *53,* 259–276.

HEBB, D. O. *The Organization of Behavior.* New York: Wiley, 1949.

HEBB, D. O. Drives and the C. N. S. (Conceptual Nervous System). *Psychological Review,* 1955, *62,* 243–254.

HULL, C. L. Goal Attraction and Directing Ideas Conceived as Habit Phenomena. *Psychological Review,* 1931, *38,* 487–506.

HULL, C. L. *Principles of Behavior.* New York: Appleton-Century-Crofts, 1943.

HUNT, J. McV. *Intelligence and Experience.* New York: Ronald Press, 1961.

INHELDER, B. & PIAGET, J. *The Growth of Logical Thinking from Childhood to Adolescence.* New York: Basic Books, 1958.

KELLY, G. A. *The Psychology of Personal Constructs.* New York: Norton, 1955.

KRECH, D., & CRUTCHFIELD, R. S. *Theory and Problems of Social Psychology.* New York: McGraw-Hill, 1948.

KUO, Z. Y. Studies on the Basic Factors in Animal Fighting: VII. Inter-species Coexistence in Animals. *Journal of Genetic Psychology,* 1960, *97,* 211–225.

LORENZ, K. *On Aggression.* New York: Harcourt, Brace, and World, 1966.

MADDI, S. *Personality Theories: A Comparative Analysis.* Homewood, Ill.: Dorsey Press, 1968.

MCDOUGALL, W. *Introduction to Social Psychology.* London: Metheun, 1908.

MEAD, G. H. *Mind, Self, and Society.* Chicago: Chicago Press, 1934.

MILLER, G. A., GALANTER, E., & PRIBRAM, K. H. *Plans, and the Structure of Behavior.* New York: Holt, Rinehart, and Winston, 1960.

OSGOOD, C. E., SUCI, G. J., & TANNENBAUM, P. H. *The Measurement of Meaning.* Urbana, Ill.: University of Illinois Press, 1957.

PAVLOV, I. P. *Conditioned Reflexes.* New York: Dover, 1960.

PIAGET, J., INHELDER, B., & SZEMINSKA, A. *The Child's Conception of Geometry.* New York: Harper and Row, 1964.

ROGERS, C. *Client-centered Therapy: Its Current Practice, Implications, and Theory.* Boston: Houghton-Mifflin, 1951.

RYCHLAK, J. F. *A Philosophy of Science for Personality Theory.* Boston: Houghton-Mifflin, 1968.

SAHAKIAN, W. S. (Ed.) *Psychology of Personality: Readings in Theory.* Chicago: Rand McNally, 1965.

SARBIN, T. R., TAFT, R., & BAILEY, D. E. *Clinical Inference and Cognitive Theory.* New York: Holt, Rinehart, and Winston, 1960.

SHERIF, C. W., SHERIF, M., & NEBERGALL, R. E. *Attitude and Attitude Change.* Philadelphia: Saunders, 1965.

SHERIF, M. A Study of Some Social Factors in Perception. *Archives of Psychology,* 1935, *27,* No. 187.

SHERIF, M., & CANTRIL, H. *The Psychology of Ego-Involvements.* New York: Wiley, 1947.

SHERIF, M. & SHERIF, C. W. *Reference Groups.* New York: Harper and Row, 1964.

SKINNER, B. F. *The Behavior of Organisms.* New York: Appleton-Century-Crofts, 1938.

SKINNER, B. F. Teaching Science in High School—What is Wrong. *Science,* 1968, *159,* 704–710.

SNYGG, D. & COMBS, A. W. *Individual Behavior.* New York: Harper and Row, 1949.

STAATS, A. W. *Learning, Language, and Cognition.* New York: Holt, Rinehart, and Winston, 1968.

THOMAS, W. I. & ZNANIECKI, F. *The Polish Peasant in Europe and America.* Boston: Badger, 1918.

THORNDIKE, E. I. *Educational Psychology: The Psychology of Learning.* New York: Columbia University Press, 1913.

THORNDIKE, R. L. The Psychological Value Systems of Psychologists. *American Psychologist,* 1954, *9,* 787–790.

TINBERGEN, N. On War and Peace in Animals and Man. *Science,* 1968, *160,* 1411–1418.

TOLMAN, E. C. The Intervening Variable. In M. H. Marx (Ed.), *Psychological Theory.* New York: Macmillan, 1951, 87–102.

VINACKE, W. E. *Foundations of Psychology.* New York: American Book, 1968.

WALLACH, H. The Perception of Neutral Colors. *Scientific American,* 1963, *208,* 107–118.

WATSON, J. B. Psychology as the Behaviorist Views It. *Psychological Review,* 1913, *20,* 158–177.

2

A SUMMARY STATEMENT
OF A COGNITIVELY-ORIENTED
COMPREHENSIVE
THEORY OF BEHAVIOR

GEORGE A. KELLY

Who can say what nature is? Is it what now exists about us, including all the tiny hidden things that wait so patiently to be discovered? Or is it the vista of all that is destined to occur, whether tomorrow or in some distant eon of time? Or is nature, infinitely more varied than this, the myriad trains of events that might ensue if we were to be so bold, ingenious, and irreverent as to take a hand in its management?

Personal construct theory neither offers nor demands a firm answer to any of these questions, and in this respect it is unique. Rather than depending upon bedrock assumptions about the inherent nature of the universe, or upon fragments of truth believed to have been accumulated, it is a notion about how man may launch out from a position of admitted ignorance, and how he may aspire from one day to the next to transcend his own dogmatisms. It is, then, a theory of man's personal inquiry—a psychology of the human quest. It does not say what has or will be found, but proposes rather how we might go about looking for it.

1. PHILOSOPHICAL POSITION

Like other theories, the psychology of personal constructs is the implementation of a philosophical assumption. In this case the assumption is that whatever nature may be, or howsoever the quest for truth will turn

Unpublished manuscript: Brandeis University, 1966. Published by kind permission of Mrs. Gladys Kelly; copyright, Gladys Kelly.

out in the end, the events we face today are subject to as great a variety of constructions as our wits will enable us to contrive. This is not to say that one construction is as good as any other, nor is it to deny that at some infinite point in time human vision will behold reality out to the utmost reaches of existence. But it does remind us that all our present perceptions are open to question and reconsideration, and it does broadly suggest that even the most obvious occurrences of everyday life might appear utterly transformed if we were inventive enough to construe them differently.

This philosophical position we have called *constructive alternativism,* and its implications keep cropping up in the psychology of personal constructs. It can be contrasted with the prevalent epistemological assumption of *accumulative fragmentalism,* which is that truth is collected piece by piece. While constructive alternativism does not argue against the collection of information, neither does it measure truth by the size of the collection. Indeed it leads one to regard a large accumulation of facts as an open invitation to some far-reaching reconstruction which will reduce them to a mass of trivialities.

A person who spends a great deal of his time hoarding facts is not likely to be happy at the prospect of seeing them converted into rubbish. He is more likely to want them bound and preserved, a memorial to his personal achievement. A scientist, for example, who thinks this way, and especially a psychologist who does so, depends upon his facts to furnish the ultimate proof of his propositions. With these shining nuggets of truth in his grasp it seems unnecessary for him to take responsibility for the conclusions he claims they thrust upon him. To suggest to him at this point that further human reconstruction can completely alter the appearance of the precious fragments he has accumulated, as well as the direction of their arguments, is to threaten his scientific conclusions, his philosophical position, and even his moral security. No wonder, then, that in the eyes of such a conservatively minded person, our assumption that all facts are subject—are wholly subject—to alternative constructions looms up as culpably subjective and dangerously subversive to the scientific establishment.

2. FACTS AND CONCLUSIONS

But wherein does responsibility lie? Can we ever make facts, even facts that turn out as predicted, responsible for conclusions? I think not. Whatever the world may be, man can come to grips with it only by placing his own interpretations upon what he sees. While his ingenuity in devising suitable constructions may be limited, and many misfortunes therefore come to pass, still it is he, not facts, who holds the key to the ultimate future. This, it seems to me, makes him responsible, and suggests that it is quite inappropriate for him ever to claim that his conclusions have been dictated by any nature other than his own.

This, of course, is how I construe it; and in this undertaking I, too, have chosen to bear responsibility for where my constructive alternativism is leading me. So, also, my reader, if he accepts this invitation to join me, will, like any other Adam or Eve who chooses to understand for himself, be held responsible for his choice—though no more so than I should think him responsible for any other choice he might make, including the choice of *not* accepting this invitation.

None of this is a denial that men customarily share each other's insights and prejudices. Our ingenuity in devising alternative constructions is limited by our feeble wits and our timid reliance upon what is familiar. So we usually do things the way we have done them before or the way others appear to do them. Moreover, novel ideas, when openly expressed, can be disruptive to ourselves and disturbing to others. We therefore often avoid them, disguise them, keep them bottled up in our minds where they cannot develop in the social context, or disavow them in what we believe to be loyalty to the common interest. And often, against our better judgment, we accept the dictates of authority instead, thinking thus to escape any personal responsibility for what happens.

But though our devices for interpreting circumstances are still meager, and the human adventure continues to be fraught with dire uncertainties, it does not follow that facts ever dictate our conclusions, except by the rules we impose upon our acts. Events do not tell us what to do, nor do they carry their meanings engraved on their backs for us to discover. For better or worse we ourselves create the only meanings they will ever convey during our lifetime. The facts of life may even be brutal, but they are nonetheless innocent of any evil intent, and we can scarcely accuse them of taking sides in our epistemological disputes. Our ever present task is to devise ways of anticipating their occurrences, and thus to prepare ourselves for assuming a more and more responsible role in the management of the universe.

3. THE MEANING OF EVENTS

Constructive alternativism stresses the importance of events. But it looks to man to propose what the character of their import shall be. The meaning of an event—that is to say, the meaning we ascribe to it—is anchored in its antecedents and its consequents. Thus meaning displays itself to us mainly in the dimension of time. This is much more than saying that meanings are rehearsals of outcomes, a proposition implicit in behavioristic theory, or that the ends justify the means—the ethical statement of the same proposition.

Besides including anticipated outcomes, meaning includes also the means by which events are anticipated. This is to suggest that different meanings are involved when identical events are correctly anticipated by different sets of inferences. It suggests also the implication of quite different meanings when the basic assumptions are different, even when the chains of inference are otherwise more or less similar.

In all of this we look to events to confirm our predictions and to encourage our venturesome constructions. Yet the same events may confirm different constructions, and different, or even incompatible, events may appear to validate the same construction. So, for each of us, meaning assumes the shape of the arguments which lead him to his predictions, and the only outside check on his personal constructions are the events which confirm or disconfirm his expectations. This is a long way from saying that meaning is revealed by what happens, or that meaning is something to be discovered in the natural course of events, or that events shape men and ideas. Thus in constructive alternativism events are crucial, but only man can devise a meaning for them to challenge.

When we place a construction of our own upon a situation, and then pursue its implications to the point of expecting something to happen, we issue a little invitation to nature to intervene in our personal experience. If what we expect does happen, or appears to happen, our expectation is confirmed and we are likely to think that we must have had a pretty good slant on the trend of affairs, else we would have lost our bet. But if we think the matter over carefully we may begin to have doubts. Perhaps a totally different interpretation would have led to an equally successful prediction; and it may, besides, have been more straightforward, or more consistent with our conscience. Or perhaps our vivid expectations overlaid our perception of what actually happened.

So, on second thought, even when events are reconciled with a construction, we cannot be sure that they have proved it true. There are always other constructions, and there is the lurking likelihood that some of them will turn out to be better. The best we can ever do is project our anticipations with frank uncertainty and observe the outcomes in terms in which we have a bit more confidence. But neither anticipation nor outcome is ever a matter of absolute certainty from the dark in which we mortals crouch. And, hence, even the most valuable construction we have yet contrived—even our particular notion of God Himself—is one for which we shall have to continue to take personal responsibility—at least until someone turns up with a better one. And I suspect he will! This is what we mean by *constructive alternativism*. Our view might even be called a philosophical position of *epistemological responsibility*.

4. THE CONDUCT OF INQUIRY

One of the most exciting aspects of constructive alternativism is its bearing upon the conduct of human inquiry. According to the canons of logic a statement, if meaningful, is either true or not true. Indeed, the logical positivists have reversed the logic and argued that the criterion for meaningfulness is whether or not a statement can be proved true or not true. This means, I take it, that we should not ask a question until we have answered it. But constructive alternativism suggests that the canon itself is not fruitful, or at least that it tends to stultify fruitful endeavor. Besides, I note that most of the members of the famous Vienna Circle abandoned their extreme position—bursting with unanswerable questions, no doubt.

Since ultimate truth is such a long way off, it seems as inappropriate to try to capture it by, say, five o'clock on Tuesday as it is to claim we already have it in our grasp. Thus any proposition we contrive must be regarded as a crude formulation of a question which, at best, can serve only as an invitation to further inquiry, and one that can be answered only through personal experience and in terms of the *ad interim* criterion of anticipated events. Indeed, the answer we get is not likely to be exactly an answer to our question at all, but an answer to some other question we have not yet thought to ask.

To this way of thinking the verbs in all significant statements a man makes are implicitly cast in an 'invitational mood,' rather than in the indicative mood, or in one of the other moods recognized by English grammar. "What," he says, "would happen if . . .?" We suspect, furthermore, that this is psychologically characteristic of man whenever he is not in a defensive posture, and that it characterizes his unspoken impulses as well as his articulate sentences. "Please," he means to say, "join me in pursuing the implications of this pose I have assumed."

In this light, then, it is not necessary to disprove one proposition before entertaining alternatives to it. In certain situations, as in psychotherapy for example, it may even be disastrous to start with disproof, at least until we know what alternatives will drop into place once the disproof is taken seriously. Constructive alternativism is therefore an invitation to immediate adventure. By not insisting on disproof as a precondition for initiative it saves a lot of wear and tear on nerves and it should release a great deal of scholarly manpower for more productive and less disputatious occupations.

So, under constructive alternativism, even the appearance of some objective certainty may be taken as a flagrant challenge to throw—without waiting for the courage that disillusionment provides—a new light on the very circumstances that make it seem so obvious. Yet constructive alternativism tells us also that the reconstructive enterprise may be forestalled even earlier in the sequence. If one cautiously insists that truth must be compiled and cross-validated in fragments before he ever ventures further in the human quest, he may never reach the point where he can sense the challenge of upending smug certainties. He will be so eager to nail down his bits of truth once and for all that he will never back off and treat himself to a fresh look.

Generally, propositions cannot be effectively refuted unless we accept their terms of reference. But unless the terms are better stated than they usually are, it may be more appropriate to discard an old proposition than to go through the contortions necessary to disprove it. This seems to be mostly what we do with old propositions anyway! In any case, constructive alternativism suggests that we need not become bogged down in tedious refutations and that audacious proposals, including some that are badly put, may well serve as springboards for novel inquiry—even while we still retain a preference for their traditional alternatives.

5. GENERATING PSYCHOLOGICAL THEORY

But now, since we are already on the threshold of psychological theorizing, we might as well get on with it, even though there is much more that could be said about the philosophical position of constructive alternativism. So let us talk about personal construct theory itself. We can come back to philosophy later if necessary.

The question of just how a theory is generated is about as complicated as the whole of human psychology. Since theories—so far, at least—are devised by men, it seems unreasonable to claim that they are shaped by any process other than a psychological one. Yet for a long time we have been saying that one moves from old propositions to new ones by the logical procedures of induction or deduction, as if this could happen independently of the personal disposition of man. Indeed, I have come to doubt that the notions of induction and deduction tell us very much about what goes on. In the one case I suppose it means we listen to ourselves making a clutter of assertions only to end up trying to say them all in one mouthful. In the other we let loose with a high-sounding remark and then, like a four-year-old child trying to "read" his own "writing," struggle to figure out what we meant by it.

In formulating the theory I have called *the psychology of personal constructs* I cannot say that I actually launched out deductively from the assumption of constructive alternativism as I have phrased it here, though now I can see how, with the help of a certain amount of idiosyncratic bias along the way, one could start with constructive alternativism and end up with personal construct theory. And I believe I can see how the clutter of events I experienced was important. Now that I think of it, I can remember a lot of relevant things that happened over the years. But not for one moment would I claim that these events converged to shape my theory. They seemed only to keep challenging it—and not always to be very constructive about it either. It may even be that I can remember these incidents now only because, on hindsight, they seem to confirm what my present formulation would forecast. And I am sure that I found myself perplexed and aggravated by many circumstances I have long since forgotten, and that what I came to think as a psychologist was what, over the years, I had jury-rigged as a man to cope with what was going on.

So let us not be hasty. Perhaps constructive alternativism was my basic assumption all along. I may only have delayed putting it into words. I recall that I have often felt that personal construct theory was as much an account of what had long been running through my noggin as it was the outcome of my labored thinking after I told myself to go ahead and dare to write a theory.

All of this is to suggest that the psychological postures—mine included—that we accent with words, or dignify in philosophical terms, may be quite personal and may considerably antedate our verbal statements about them. There is even reason to dread bringing such nascent constructions to light lest they betray us as foolish or even crazy. And I must say, at some risk to myself I suppose, that to propose a statement of such sweeping proportions as constructive alternativism is to flirt with grandiosity—a symptom more often associated with psychosis than with genius. But just as good cannot be accomplished without risking evil, so enlightenment cannot be sought wholeheartedly without approaching the brink of what may turn out to be insanity. There is no such thing as adventure with safety guaranteed in advance, not even when sitting alone with a typewriter. Not that I have ever lost any sleep over the matter!

6. SCIENTIFIC BEHAVIOR AS A PARADIGM OF HUMAN BEHAVIOR

Legend has it that many theories originated with simple observations, often occuring under the most commonplace of circumstances. Archimedes is supposed to have been dallying in his bath when he made the observation that led to the notion of specific gravity. And there is the story about Newton napping under the apple tree. Then there is Bernoulli. I have long had my suspicions about what Bernoulli was doing.

Not to be outdone in fictionalizing itself, personal construct theory also can lay claim to an initial anecdote. In this case it is an observation of an amusing human, and even better than that, a psychologist's foible—which happily lowers it, I think, to the level of a caricature. So let us say that personal construct theory is a bit of humor that examined its own implications. And what, may I ask, could be more candidly psychological than that?

Psychologists are likely to be very much in earnest about making their discipline into a science. (Unfortunately, not many are as concerned as they might be about making science into something.) And they are never more deadly serious about staking a claim to scientific respectability than they are when they are writing elementary textbooks. It struck me rather suddenly one day that all the elementary texts I had read contained at least two theories of personality—one covert, lucid, and facile, and the others labeled, abstruse, and labored.

"Psychology is a science," each author would say as soon as he had finished his initial exhortation to his young readers to stop relying upon common sense, "and a scientist is one who observes, construes relationships, articulates theories, generates hypotheses, ventures predictions, experiments under controlled conditions, and takes candid account of outcomes." This is to say that if the student is to understand a psychologist's commitment to life, here is the way to make sense out of it. Not bad! It gives us a pretty clear picture of what it is like to be a psychologist. Altogether it is a most penetrating and perceptive theory of personality, albeit one reserved for the scientifically elite.

Later on in the book, after the writer has explained that the eye really sees things upside down, that dogs' mouths water when they hear the dinner bell, and that the child's confrontation with the school system at age sixteen turns out about the same way it did when he was six (proving that it is *the child's* intelligence that does not change) he takes up the matter of personality theories, making it clear that he is really talking about organisms and being careful not to anthropomorphize his explanations—even his explanations of man. And how do organisms, such as human organisms (still being careful to avoid the use of such a compromising term as *persons*), behave? Why, they are *conditioned* (meaning that learning is something they must have had done to them—probably when they weren't looking), they are propelled by drives (anyone can see that otherwise they would just sit and do nothing at all), deluded by their motives (why else would they disagree with us?), and stalked by the ghosts of their childhood fantasies (note how they read the comic strips in the newspaper).

But what would happen if one were to envision all human endeavor in those same terms the psychologists have found so illuminating in explaining themselves to their students? And, indeed, might it not be that in doing so one would see the course of individual life, as well as human progress over the centuries, in clearer perspective? Scientists are men, and, while it does not follow that men are scientists, it is quite appropriate to ask if it is not their human character that makes scientists what they are. This leads us to the question of how that human character can better be construed so as to account for scientists, and whether our construction can still explain as well the accomplishments that fall far short of what we, at this transient moment in our history, think good science is.

This is not a question of whether or not men do, in fact, live by the canons of science. That, except to an accumulative fragmentalist, is not even an appropriate question. We are not in search of such a neat conclusion, but of a strategic advantage in the long term quest for understanding. No theory can offer us more than that. The issue, then, is what this constructive alternative of seeing man as an incipient scientist will contribute at the present state of the search for a psychological understanding of him. Who knows—a by-product of this venture may be new light on scientific endeavor itself. In fact, I think I can see such a by-product emerging as personal construct theory suggests ways in which psychological processes we have hitherto spurned may enliven the scientific enterprise.

7. BASIC POSTULATE

A person's processes are psychologically channelized by the ways in which he anticipates events. This is what we have proposed as a fundamental postulate for the psychology of personal constructs. The assumptions of constructive alternativism are embedded in this statement, although it may not be apparent until later in our exposition of the theme just how it is that they are.

We start with a *person*. Organisms, lower animals, and societies can wait. We are talking about someone we know, or would like to know—such as you, or myself. More particularly, we are talking about that person as an event—the processes that express his personality. And, since we enter the system we are about to elaborate at the point of a process—or life—rather than at the point of a body or a material substance, we should not have to invoke any special notions, such as dynamics, drives, motivation, or force to explain why our object does not remain inert. As far as the theory is concerned, it never was inert. As we pursue the theoretical line emerging from this postulate I think it becomes clear also why we do not need such notions to account for the direction of movement—any more than we need them to explain the movement itself.

This is to be a psychological theory. Mostly this is a way of announcing in the basic postulate that we make no commitment to the terms of other disciplines, such as physiology or chemistry. Our philosophical position permits us to see those other disciplines as based on man-made constructions, rather than as disclosures of raw realities, and hence there is no need for the psychologist to accept them as final, or to limit his proposals to statements consistent with them. In addition, I think the theory sounds more or less like the other theories that are known as psychological. This gives me an inclusive, as well as an exclusive reason for calling it a psychological theory, although this is more or less a matter of taste rather than of definition. Certainly I have no intention of trying to define psychology; there are just too many things called psychological that I do not care to take responsibility for.

Some have suggested that personal construct theory not be called a psychological theory at all, but a metatheory. That is all right with me. It suggests that it is a theory about theories, and that is pretty much what I have in mind. But I hope that it is clear that it is not limited to being a metatheory of formal theories, or even of articulate ones.

There is also the question of whether or not it is a cognitive theory. Some have said that it was; others have classed it as existential. Quite an accomplishment; not many theories have been accused of being both cognitive and existential! But this, too, is all right with me. As a matter of fact, I am delighted. There are categorical systems in which I think the greater amount of ambiguity I stir up, the better. Cognition, for example, strikes me as a particularly misleading category, and, since it is one designed to distinguish itself from affect and conation, those terms, too, might well be discarded as inappropriately restrictive.

Personal construct theory has also been categorized by responsible scholars as an emotional theory, a learning theory, a psychoanalytic theory (Freudian, Adlerian, and Jungian—all three), a typically American theory, a Marxist theory, a humanistic theory, a logical positivistic theory, a Zen Buddhistic theory, a Thomistic theory, a behavioristic theory, an Apollonian theory, a pragmatistic theory, a reflexive theory, and no theory at all. It has also been classified as nonsense, which indeed, by its own admission, it will likely some day turn out to be. In each case there were some convincing arguments offered for the categorization, but I have forgotten what most of them were. I fear that no one of these categorizations will be of much help to the reader in understanding personal construct theory, but perhaps having a whole lap full of them all at once will suggest what might be done with them.

The fourth term in the postulate—*channelized*—was chosen as one less likely than others to imply dynamics. This is because there is no wish to suggest that we are dealing with anything not already in motion. What is to be explained is the direction of the processes, not the transformation of states into processes. We see states only as an *ad interim* device to get time to stand still long enough for us to see what is going on. In other words, we have assumed that a process can be profitably regarded as more basic than an inert substance. We have had to do this notwithstanding the commitments of the centuries to quite another kind of language system. There are some disadvantages that come with this notion of what is basic, but we are willing to accept them for the time being in order to explore the heraclitean implications more fully than psychologists have ever done before.

In specifying *ways of anticipating events* as the directive referent for human processes we cut ourselves free of the stimulus-response version of nineteenth century scientific determinism. I am aware that this is a drastic step indeed, and I suspect that others who claim to have taken similar steps have not always seriously taken stock of the difficulties to be encountered. For one thing the very syntax of the language we must employ to voice our protest is built on a world view that regards objects as agents and outcomes as the products of those agents.

In our present undertaking the psychological initiative always remains a property of the person—never the property of anything else. What is more, neither past nor future events are themselves ever regarded as basic determinants of the course of human action—not even the events of childhood. But one's way of anticipating them, whether in the short range or in the long view—this is the basic theme in the human process of living. Moreover, it is that events are anticipated, not merely that man gravitates toward more and more comfortable organic states. Confirmation and disconfirmation of one's predictions are accorded greater psychological significance than rewards, punishments, or the drive reduction that reinforcements produce.

There are, of course, some predictions we would like to see disconfirmed, as well as some we hope will indeed materialize. We should not make the mistake of translating personal construct theory back into stimulus-response theory and saying to ourselves that confirmation is the same as a positive reinforcement, and that disconfirmation nullifies the meaning of an experience. Disconfirmation, even in those cases where it is disconcerting, provides grounds for reconstruction—or of repentance, in the proper sense of that term—and it may be used to improve the accuracy and significance of further anticipations. Thus we envision the nature of life in its outreach for the future, and not in its perpetuation of its prior conditions or in its incessant reverberation of past events.

Personal construct theory is elaborated by a string of eleven corollaries which may be loosely inferred from its basic postulate. Beyond these are certain notions of more limited applicability which fall in line with personal construct thinking—notions about such matters as anxiety, guilt, hostility, decision making, creativity, the strategy of psychological research, and other typical concerns of professional psychologists. These latter notions need not be considered part of the formal structure of the theory, although our theoretical efforts may not come to life in the mind of the reader until he has seen their applicability to the daily problems he faces.

8. CONSTRUCTION COROLLARY

A person anticipates events by construing their replications. Since events never repeat themselves, else they would lose their identity, one can look forward to them only by devising some construction which permits him to perceive two of them in a similar manner. His construction must also permit him to be selective about which two are to be perceived similarly. Thus the same construction that serves to infer their similarity must serve also to differentiate them from others. Under a system that provides only for the identification of similarities the world dissolves into homogeneity; under one that provides only for differentiation it is shattered into hopelessly unrelated fragments.

Perhaps it is true that events, as most of us would like to believe, really do repeat aspects of previous occurrences. But unless one thinks he is precocious enough to have hit upon what those aspects will ultimately turn out to be, or holy enough to have had them revealed to him, he must modestly concede that the appearance of replication is a reflection of his own fallible construction of what is going on. Thus the recurrent themes that make life seem so full of meaning are the original symphonic compositions of a man bent on finding the present in his past, and the future in his present.

9. INDIVIDUALITY COROLLARY

Persons differ from each other in their constructions of events. Having assumed that construction is a personal affair, it seems unlikely that any two persons would ever happen to concoct identical systems. I would go further now than when I originally proposed this corollary and suggest that even particular constructions are never identical events. And I would extend it the other way too, and say that I doubt that two persons ever put their construction systems together in terms of the same logical relationships. For myself, I find this a most encouraging line of speculation, for it seems to open the door to more advanced systems of thinking and inference yet to be devised by man. Certainly it suggests that scientific research can rely more heavily on individual imagination than it usually dares.

10. ORGANIZATION COROLLARY

Each person characteristically evolves, for his convenience in anticipating events, a construction system embracing ordinal relationships between constructs. If a person is to live actively within his construction system it must provide him with some clear avenues of inference and movement. There must be ways for him to resolve the more crucial contradictions and conflicts that inevitably arise. This is not to say that all inconsistencies must be resolved at once. Some private paradoxes can be allowed to stand indefinitely, and, in the face of them, one can remain indecisive or can vacillate between alternative expectations of what the future holds in store for him.

So it seems that each person arranges his constructions so that he can move from one to another in some orderly fashion, either by assigning priorities to those which are to take precedence when doubts or contradictions arise, or by arranging implicative relationships, as in boolean algebra, so that he may infer that one construction follows from another. Thus one's commitments may take priority over his opportunities, his political affiliations may turn him from compassion to power, and his moral imperatives may render him insensitive to the brute that tugs at his sleeve. These are the typical prices men pay to escape inner chaos.

11. DICHOTOMY COROLLARY

A person's construction system is composed of a finite number of dichotomous constructs. Experience has shown me that this is the point where many of my readers first encounter difficulty in agreeing with me. What I am saying is that a construct is a "black and white" affair, never a matter of shadings, or of "grays." On the face of it, this sounds bad, for it seems to imply categorical or absolutistic thinking rather than any acceptance of relativism or conditionalism. Yet I would insist that there is nothing categorical about a construct.

When we look closely the initial point of difficulty in following personal construct theory usually turns out to lie in certain unrecognized assumptions made earlier while reading the exposition, or even carried over from previous habits of thought. Let us see if we can get the matter straightened out before any irreparable damage is done.

Neither our constructs nor our construing systems come to us from nature, except, of course, from our own nature. It must be noted that this philosophical position of constructive alternativism has much more powerful epistemological implications than one might at first suppose. We cannot say that constructs are essences distilled by the mind out of available reality. They are imposed *upon* events, not abstracted *from* them. There is only one place they come from; that is from the person who is to use them. He devises them. Moreover, they do not stand for anything or represent anything, as a symbol, for example, is supposed to do.

So what are they? They are reference axes, upon which one may project events in an effort to make some sense out of what is going on. In this sense they are like cartesian coordinates, the x, y and z axes of analytic geometry. Events correspond to the points plotted within cartesian space. We can locate the points and express relations between points by specifying x, y and z distances. The cartesian axes *do not represent* the points projected upon them, but serve as guidelines for locating those points. That, also, is what constructs do for events, including ones that have not yet occurred. They help us locate them, understand them, and anticipate them.

But we must not take the cartesian analogy too literally. Des Cartes' axes were lines or scales, each containing in order an infinite number of imaginary points. Certainly his x- or y-axis embodied well enough the notion of shadings or a succession of grays. Yet a construct is not quite such an axis.

A construct is the basic contrast between two groups. When it is imposed it serves both to distinguish between its elements and to group them. Thus constructs refer to the nature of the distinction one attempts to make between events, not to the array in which his events appear to stand when he gets through applying the distinction between each of them and all the others.

Suppose one is dealing with the construct of good versus bad. Such a construct is not a representation of all things that are good, and an implicit exclusion of all that are bad. Nor is it a representation of all that are bad. It is not even a representation of all things that can be called either good or bad. The construct, of itself, is the kind of contrast one perceives and not in any way a representation of objects. As far as the construct is concerned there is no good-better-best scale, or any bad-worse-worst array.

But, while constructs do not represent or symbolize events, they do enable us to cope with events, which is a statement of quite a different order. They also enable us to put events into arrays or scales, if we wish. Suppose, for example, we apply our construct to elements, say persons, or to their acts. Consider three persons. One may make a good-bad distinction between them which will say that two of them are good in relation to the third, and the third is bad in relation to the two good ones. Then he may, in turn, apply his construct between the two good ones and say one of them is good with respect to the other formerly "good" one and the one already labeled "bad."

This, of course, makes one of the persons, or acts, good in terms of one cleavage that has been made and bad in relation to the other. But this relativism applies only to the objects; the construct of good versus bad is itself absolute. It may not be accurate, and it may not be stable from time to time, but, as a construct, it has to be absolute. Still, by its successive application to events one may create a scale with a great number of points differentiated along its length. Now a person who likes grays can have them—as many as he likes.

But let us make no mistake: A scale, in comparison to a construct, is a pretty concrete affair. Yet one can scarcely have himself a scale unless he has a construct working for him. Only if he has some basis for discrimination and association can he get on with the job of marking off a scale.

Now note something else. We have really had to fall back on our philosophical position of constructive alternativism in order to come up with this kind of an abstraction. If we had not first disabused ourselves of the idea that events are the source of our construct, we would have had a hard time coming around to the point where we could envision the underlying basis of discrimination and association we call the construct.

12. THE GEOMETRY OF PSYCHOLOGICAL SPACE

While we are at it, let us keep on going with this kind of abstract thinking and envision an equally abstract construction system made up of many constructs. If we can hold on we shall be well on our way to understanding personal construct theory's underlying mathematics or metaphysics. But we dare not fall back on our cartesian analogy, once we have reached this point in the argument, lest we find ourselves envisioning systems of lines intersecting at common points. That may be all right for dimensioning physical space—though I am not so sure—but certainly it will not do for structuring psychological space.

To catch a glimpse of psychological space we may imagine a system of planes, each with two sides or aspects, slicing through a galaxy of events. One does not measure distances on these planes, he notes only, at any one instant of application, which side of each plane faces which events when the set is suspended in the galaxy. The set, or construct system, can, of course, be moved around in the galaxy in the manner I have described when a single construct is used to devise a scale. If the set is moved into all possible positions it generates a paracartesian hyperspace with its relatively concrete scalar axes. But that is a rather large undertaking, and one likely to fall through because man is inventive enough to keep thinking of new constructs he would like to add to the system. Another way of saying this is to suggest that even the simplest personal construct system can hardly get around to putting all events in order, and, unless the man is pretty unimaginative, he will have to keep starting over each time he thinks of a new way to discriminate or associate.

One thing more has to be said. In order to make the point, I have had to talk about constructs in such an explicit manner that I have probably given the impression that a construct is as highly articulate and cognitive as my discussion has had to be. If I had been able to say what I have said in metaphor or hyperbole I might have left the impression that a construct had something to do with feeling or with formless urges too fluid to be pinned down by labels. But personal construct theory is no more a cognitive theory than it is an affective or conative one. There are grounds for distinction that operate in one's life that seem to elude verbal expression. We see them in infants, as well as in our own spontaneous aversions and infatuations. These discriminative bases are no less constructs than those the reader may have been imagining during the reading of the preceding paragraphs. Certainly it is important not to consider a construct as another term for a concept, else a major sector of the arena in which constructs function will be obscured from view.

13. CHOICE COROLLARY

A person chooses for himself that alternative in a dichotomized construct through which he anticipates the greater possibility for the elaboration of his system. It seems to me to follow that if a person makes so much use of his constructs, and is so dependent upon them, he will make choices which promise to develop their usefulness. Developing the usefulness of a construction system involves, as far as I can see, two things: defining it and extending it. One defines his system, by extension at least, by making it clear how its construct components are applied to objects or are linked with each other. He amplifies his system by using it to reach our for new fields of application. In the one case he consolidates his position and in the other he extends it.

Note that the choice is between alternatives expressed in the construct, not, as one might expect, between objects divided by means of the construct. There is a subtle point here. Personal construct theory is a psychological theory and therefore has to do with the behavior of man, not with the intrinsic nature of objects. A construct governs what the man does, not what the object does. In a strict sense, therefore, man makes decisions which initially affect himself, and which affect other objects only subsequently—and then only if he manages to take some effective action. Making a choice, then, has to do with involving oneself, and cannot be defined in terms of the external object chosen. Besides, one does not always get the object he chooses to gain. But his anticipation does have to do with his own processes, as I tried to say in formulating the basic postulate.

So when a man makes a choice what he does is align himself in terms of his constructs. He does not necessarily succeed, poor fellow, in doing anything to the objects he seeks to approach or avoid. Trying to define human behavior in terms of the externalities sought or affected, rather than the seeking process, gets the psychologist pretty far off the track. It makes more of a physicist of him than a psychologist, and a rather poor one, at that. So what we must say is that a person, in deciding whether to believe or do something, uses his construct system to proportion his field, and then moves himself strategically and tactically within its presumed domain.

Men change things by changing themselves first, and they accomplish their objectives, if at all, only by paying the price of altering themselves—as some have found to their sorrow and others to their salvation. The choices that men make are choices of their own acts, and the alternatives are distinguished by their own constructs. The results of the choices, however, may range all the way from nothing to catastrophe, on the one hand, or to consummation, on the other.

14. RANGE COROLLARY

A construct is convenient for the anticipation of a finite range of events only. A personal construct system can hardly be said to have universal utility. Not everything that happens in the world can be projected upon all the dichotomies that make up a person's outlook. Indeed I doubt that anyone has ever devised a construct that could cover the entire range of events of which he was aware. There are patches of clouds in every man's sky. This is to say that the geometry of the mind is never a complete system. The lines of reference here and there become lost in irrelevancies and make it practically impossible to write formulas that are universally applicable.

The classical notion of a *concept* is that it embraces all elements having a common property, and excludes all others. But this kind of notion will not do for *constructs*. A construct is a distinction which has the effect of distributing objects tentatively into two associations. If one says that a man is tall he does more than exclude all objects that are not tall. He denies that the man is short. He asserts that there are other objects that are both not tall and are short. And he excludes only those objects which are outside his range of concern.

Logicians, accustomed to thinking about concepts and not yet altogether clear about what I mean by constructs, might take issue with me at this point. They might say that all one has disclaimed is the possiblilty that the man is not tall. But we must remind ourselves that here we are talking about the psychology of man's actions and intents, and we can be sure that if the person who makes the remark has nothing more on his mind that what formal logic suggests, he will keep his mouth shut. Psychologically, the only point in commenting on the man's being tall is to deny some alternative that needed denying. What is excluded, therefore, includes some pretty important considerations, as well as some irrelevancies.

If we are to understand a person's statement we had better take into account just what it was he felt he must negate, as well as what he used as the subject or the predicate of his sentence. This, again, is a way of saying that the construct is a basis of making a distinction and, by the same act, creating an association, as one does when saying that a man is tall and implying thereby that he is like some other objects in that respect. Especially, one must keep in mind that a construct is not a class of objects, or an abstraction of a class, but a dichotomous reference axis.

A construct has its *focus of convenience*—a set of objects with which it works especially well. Over a somewhat larger range it may work only reasonably well; that is its *range of convenience*. But beyond that it fades into uselessness and we can say the outer array of objects simply lies beyone that range of convenience.

It would be nice, mathematically, if every event in a man's world could be projected onto every construct he had. Then we might hope to check out the whole system and all its internal relationships. It would be even nicer if every event could be projected upon every construct of every man. Then we could check one man's outlook precisely against another's—hoping that neither would change his mind before the wallpaper came out of the computer. But I don't think this is very likely to happen, at least not during the natural life of personal construct theory.

15. EXPERIENCE COROLLARY

A person's construction system varies as he successively construes the replications of events. Here again our analytic geometry model does not quite fit the mathematics of psychological space. Rather than remaining altogether fixed, as the axes of analytic geometry do when points are plotted within them, the tendency is for personal constructs to shift when events are projected upon them. The distinctions they implement are likely to be altered in three ways: (1) The construct may be applied at a different point in the galaxy, (2) it may become a somewhat different kind of distinction, and (3) its relations to other constructs may be altered.

In the first of these shifts it is a matter of a change in the location of the construct's application, and hence not exactly an intrinsic change in the construct itself. In the second case, however, it is the abstraction itself which is altered, although the change may not be radical enough for the psychologist to say a new construct has been substituted. Finally, in the third case, the angular relations with other constructs are necessarily affected by the transition, unless, by some chance, the construct system were rotated as a whole. But that is not a very likely contingency.

The first kind of shift might be observed when a person moves to an urban community. Some of the actions he once regarded as aloof and unneighborly he may come to accept as relatively friendly in the new social context. But he may also rotate the axis of his construct as he gains familiarity with city life, and, as a result, come to see "aloofness" as a neighborly respect for his privacy, something he had never had very clearly in mind before. This would be an example of the second kind of shift. The third kind of shift comes when he alters his notion of respect as a result of the experience, perhaps coming to sense it not so much a matter of subservience or adulation but more a matter of empathy and consideration. As a matter of fact, we might regard the whole transition as leading him in the direction of greater maturity.

Keeping in mind that events do not actually repeat themselves and that the replication we talk about is a replication of ascribed aspects only, it begins to be clear that the succession we call experience is based on the constructions we place on what goes on. If those constructions are never altered, all that happens during a man's years is a sequence of parallel events having no psychological impact on his life. But if he invests himself—the most intimate event of all—in the enterprise, the outcome, to the extent that it differs from his expectation or enlarges upon it, dislodges the man's construction of himself. In recognizing the inconsistency between his anticipation and the outcome, he concedes a discrepancy between what he was and what he is. A succession of such investments and dislodgements constitutes the human experience.

A subtle point comes to light at this juncture. Confirmation may lead to reconstruing quite as much as disconfirmation—perhaps even more. A confirmation gives one an anchorage in some area of his life, leaving him free to set afoot adventuresome explorations nearby, as, for example, in the case of a child whose security at home emboldens him to be the first to explore what lies in the neighbor's yard.

The unit of experience is, therefore, a cycle embracing five phases: anticipation, investment, encounter, confirmation or disconfirmation, and constructive revision. This is followed, of course, by new anticipations, as the first phase of a subsequent experiential cycle gets underway. Certainly in personal construct theory's line of reasoning experience is not composed of encounters alone.

Stated simply, the amount of a man's experience is not measured by the number of events with which he collides, but by the investments he has made in his anticipations and the revisions of his constructions that have followed upon his facing up to consequences, A man whose only wager in life is upon reaching heaven by immunizing himself against the miseries of his neighbors, or upon following a bloody party-line straight to utopia, is prepared to gain little experience until he arrives—either there, or somewhere else clearly recognized as not the place he was looking for. Then, if he is not too distracted by finding that his architectural specifications have been blatantly disregarded, or that the wrong kind of people have started moving in, I suppose he may begin to think of some other investments he might better have been making in the meantime. Of course, a little hell along the way, if taken more to heart than most heaven-bound people seem to take it, may have given him a better idea of what to expect, before it was too late to get a bit of worthwhile experience and make something out of himself.

16. MODULATION COROLLARY

The variation in a person's construction system is limited by the permeability of the constructs within whose ranges of convenience the variants lie. While the Experience Corollary suggests that a man can revise his constructions on the basis of events and his invested anticipations of them, there are limitations that must be taken into account. He must have a construct system which is sufficiently open to novel events to let him know when he has encountered them, else the experience cycle will fail to function in its terminal phases. He must have a system which also will admit the revised construct that emerges at the end of the cycle. If the revised construct is left to stand as an isolated axis of reference it will be difficult for him to chart any coordinated course of action that takes account of it; he therefore can do little with respect to it except vacillate.

Perhaps it is clear from these remarks that what is meant by permeability is not a construct's plasticity, or its amenability to change within itself, but its capacity to be used as a referent for novel events and to accept new subordinate constructions within its range of convenience. A notion of God, for example, which includes an unabridged dictionary of all things holy is likely to be impermeable. Anything new that turns up—such as an unbiblical event or idea—is likely to be excluded from the construct's realm of concern. Unless the novelty can fit elsewhere into some more permeable part of the construct system, it is likely to be ignored.

17. FRAGMENTATION COROLLARY

A person may successfully employ a variety of construction subsystems which are inferentially incompatible with each other. We must be careful not to interpret the Modulation Corollary to mean that a construct system has to be logically intact. Perhaps in any proximate transition in the human process there is an inferential relationship between antecedent and consequent at some constructive level in the person's system. But persons move from *a* to *b*, and on to *c* without always taking into account the fact that their overview of *c* cannot be inferred from their overview of *a*. A man may move from an act of love to an act of jealousy, and from there to an act of hate, even though hate is not something that would be inferred from love, even in his peculiar system. This is the kind of psychological fact to which the Fragmentation Corollary calls particular attention.

Perhaps I should add that I do not see this kind of "irrationality" as necessarily a bad thing. For man logic and inference can be as much an obstacle to his ontological ventures as a guide to them. Often it is the un-inferred fragment of a man's construction system that makes him great, whereas if he were an integrated whole—taking into account all that the whole would have to embrace—the poor fellow would be no better than his "natural self."

18. COMMONALITY COROLLARY

To the extent that one person employs a construction of experience which is similar to that employed by another, his processes are psychologically similar to those of the other person.[1] On the face of it, this corollary appears to assert pretty much what personal construct theory seems to stand for: The notion that behavior is governed by constructs. But there is more to it than what such a simplified statement might be taken to imply.

---

[1]To my mild dismay I have only now realized that the word "psychological" was misplaced in my original phrasing of this corollary. Instead of modifying "processes," as I originally had it, the term should modify "similar," as constructive alternativism would suggest. Sorry about that!

If we do as most behavioristically influenced psychologists do, and use behavior as a synonym for all human process, we then might, I suppose, substitute the term "behaviors" for "processes" in stating this corollary. But what thoughtful behaviorists have in mind when they make behavior the focus of their concern is the logical positivist position that anything that cannot be identified as behavior is untestable and therefore a scientific distraction. If we were to take this stand—as I would prefer not—we would be concerned only with that phase of the experiential cycle I have called "personal investment." Personal construct theory would lead us, I think, to be concerned with the whole experiential cycle and the process which it represents, rather than with the behavioral phase only.

There is something more. I have used the expression, "construction of experience," rather than "construction of events." I wanted it to be clear that the construction would have to cover the experience itself, as well as the external events with which experience was ostensibly concerned. At the end of an experiential cycle one not only has a revised construction of the events he originally sought to anticipate, but he has also a construction of the process by which he reached his new conclusions about them. In launching his next venture, whatever its concern might be, he will have reason to take account of the effectiveness of the experiential procedures he employed in his last.

To be sure, in writing this corollary it would have been literally correct to say simply, "construction of events," a phrase that appears so frequently in this exposition. This would have included "experience," since an experience, once it has been enacted, is itself an event. But experience is such an important event in charting what comes next, it seemed important to single it out for special mention. Besides, since experience, as I have defined it, already embraces the events with which the experiencing person has involved himself, the term is sufficiently inclusive, as well as exclusive, to pinpoint what needs to be said. What I especially want to make clear is that the extent of the psychological similarity between the processes of two persons depends upon the similarity of their constructions of their personal experiences, as well as upon the similarity in their conclusions about external events.

But let us also be especially clear about something this corollary does not say, and what that means for the psychology of man in motion. It does not say that the two persons must have experienced "the same" events and it does not say their two experiential cycles have to be "the same." And, to go further, it does not even say they must have experienced "similar" events or that the two experiential cycles must actually have been similar in some way. What has to be similar, in order for their processes to be similar in the same degree, is their construction of experience. And that includes similarity of the construction of events that emerges in the terminal phase of the experiential cycle.

The reason for this being so important is that the outcome of an experience is not merely a tendency to repeat or to avoid it thereafter, as reinforcement theory presumes, but that the conclusions reached through experience are likely to be in the form of new questions which set the stage for new ventures. One does not fully understand human behavior, or human processes, except as he understands also the flashes of ingenuity that intersperse human monotonies. While novel undertakings can be construed in ways which show replications, as the Construction Corollary suggests, it is not behavior or process itself which is concretely re-enacted. But in construing replications, rather than in claiming he has seen concrete repetitions, one may project a view of man engaged in ventures, rather than always repeating concretely what has been reinforced.

This corollary makes it possible to say that two persons who have confronted quite different events, and who might have gone through experiential cycles which actually seem to us to be quite different, might nevertheless end up with similar constructions of their experiences, and, because of that, thereafter pursue psychologically similar processes of further inquiry. Thus personal construct theory further releases psychology from assumptions about the identity of events and man's dependence upon them. It leaves us free to envision man coping with "familiar" events in new ways and cooperating with other men to produce novelities which make their world a different place to live in. Neither behaviorism nor phenomenology, as I see them, provides a psychological basis for this kind of forward movement in man.

19. SOCIALITY COROLLARY

To the extent that one person construes the construction processes of another, he may play a role in a social process involving the other person. The implications of this corollary are probably the most far reaching of any I have yet attempted to propound. It establishes grounds for understanding *role* as a psychological term, and for envisioning thereupon a truly psychological basis for society. As far as I can see, the term has only extra-psychological meaning elsewhere. This view offers, moreover, an approach to certain puzzling aspects of psychopathy, and it permits one to understand guilt in far more intimate terms than are possible within more conventional "personality" theories, or within current theological doctrines. It leads us also to a position from which we can distinguish personality theories from others.

Perceptive psychologists are keenly aware that there must be some important relationship between what they call "role," "guilt," and "psychopathic personality" on the one hand, and the viability of society on the other. Yet there is little in the stimulus-response kind of theorizing that throws psychological light on what the relationship may be. There is scarcely more to be found in the so-called dynamic theories, although the literature associated with them richly documents a vaguely disquieting awareness of what may be transpiring in the community of man.

Let me start by trying to differentiate two levels at which I may try to understand another person—say, my reader. It is not hard for me to imagine him—*you*, I mean—at this moment a figure bending over a book. It—the figure—is skimming the paragraphs with the right forefinger in a position to turn to the pages that follow. The eye movements zigzag down the page and quickly the next leaf is flipped, or perhaps a whole section—a chapter or more—is lifted with the left thumb and drawn horizontally aside.

What I am envisioning is a moving object, and whether or not I am correctly describing the movements that are taking place can be reasonably well confirmed—or disconfirmed—by an observer who has been watching you for the past few moments, or if he saw a motion picture film of what has been taking place. This is to say I have couched my picture of you in the terms of "objective" psychology. I have offered a hypothesized description of a "behaving organism."

Ordinarily, if I wanted to play the game by the rules of objectivity, I would not stoop to ask you outright whether or not my description of your actions was correct; the noises you might make in reply could be taken in so many different ways I can be sure of being "a scientist" only if I stick to what can be confirmed. Being a "scientist" may be so important to me that I dare not risk sullying myself with your delusions. I shall therefore play my part and retain my membership in Sigma Xi by referring to your reply as a "vocal response" of a "behaving organism." *Hello there, Behaving organism!*

But now let me say it quite another way. There you are, my reader, wondering, I fear, what on earth I am trying so hard to say, and smiling to yourself as the thought crosses your mind that it all might be put in a familiar phrase or two—as indeed it may. You are hunched uncomfortably over the book, impatiently scanning the paragraphs for a cogent expression or poignant sentence that may make the experience worth the time you are stealing from more urgent duties. The right forefinger is restlessly poised to lift the page and go on to discover if perhaps anything more sensible follows.

Let me confess that I feel at this moment like urging you not to try so hard. While it has taken me hours to write some of these paragraphs—the four preceding ones, for example—and I would like to think the outcome has been worth some of your time too, they were not meant to be hammered into your consciousness. They are intended, instead, to set off trains of thought. And, in following them, I earnestly hope we shall find ourselves walking along the same paths.

There now, isn't that the way it really is? It isn't? Then, tell me, what *are* you doing? And while we are at it, tell me also how my efforts strike you—I mean, what do you think I am trying to do, not merely whether I am making sense or not. Only please do not tell me that all I am really doing is pounding a typewriter in an effort to keep my wife awake; I have other psychoanalytically oriented friends who are only too happy to offer me that kind of "interpretation."

Although these two descriptions of my view of the reader both represent a wide departure from accepted literary style, I hope they will make clear the contrast between construing the construction processes of another person and construing his behavior merely. In the first instance, I construed only your behavior. There is nothing wrong with that, as far as it goes. In the second case I went further and placed a construction upon the way in which I imagined you might be thinking. The chances are that I was more or less mistaken in both instances, particularly in the second. But the point I want to make lies in the difference in my mode of construing you. In both formulations I was indeed concerned with your behavior, but only in the second did I strive for some notion of the construction which might be giving your behavior its form, or your future behavior its form. If immediate accuracy is what I must preserve at all costs, then I had better stick to the first level of construction. But if I am to anticipate you I must take some chances and try to sense what you are up to.

One does not have to be a psychologist to treat another person as an automaton, though training in "experimental psychology" may help. Conversely, treating him that way does not make one into a scientist—though some of my colleagues may wish to dispute this. It is easy enough to treat persons we have never met as behaving organisms only, and many of us think that is the sophisticated way to go about secondary human relations. We may even treat our neighbors that way, expecially if there are more of them than we care to know. I have even observed parents who go so far as to treat their children so, and they sometimes come to me for psychological advice on how to do it. I sometimes suspect it is because they have more children than they care to know. To be very frank about it, my construction of you, while writing some of these passages, has often lapsed into no more than that. And, if you are like me in this respect, there must have been moments when you regarded me as a disembodied typewriter, or as an Irish name on the title page of a book, or as a kind of animated sentence ejector.

20. POINTS ABOUT ROLES TO BE EMPHASIZED

I know from past experience in attempting to explain this notion of role that two things need especially to be made clear, particularly if I am trying to explain it to a thoroughly trained fellow psychologist. First, my construing of your construction processes need not be accurate in order for me to play a role in a social process that involves you. I have seen a person play a role, and do it most effectively—even in a manner quite acceptable to his colleagues—when he grossly misperceived their outlooks, and they knew it. But because he did what he did on the basis of what he thought they understood, not merely on the basis of their overt acts, he was able to play a collaborative role in a social process whose experiential cycle led them all somewhere. Experiential cycles which are based on automaton-like constructions do not, I think, generate social processes, though they may lead to revisions of the manipulative devices by which men try to control each other's actions.

The second point that experience has led me to stress is that my construction of your outlook does not make me a compliant companion, nor does it keep us from working at cross purposes. I may even use my construction of your view as a basis for trying to undo your efforts. But there is something interesting about this; there is still a good chance of a social process emerging out of our conflict, and we will both end up a good way from where we started—in my case, because the experiential cycle will reflect back upon my construction of your outlook, not of your behavior only, and, in your case, because you would find that something beyond your overt behavior was being taken into account, and you might revise your investments accordingly.

There is a third point that sometimes needs mentioning. What I have proposed is a psychological definition of role, and therefore it does not lean upon sociological assumptions about the nature of society or economic assumptions about the coordination of human labor. Being psychological, it attempts to derive its terms from the experience of the individual, though, once the derivations have been made, there are no necessary restrictions on pursuing implications on out into the world of the sociologist, or even into that of the mathematician.

What comes out, then, is a definition that permits us to say that roles are not necessarily reciprocal; you may indeed enact a role based on your construction of my outlook, but my failure to construe you as anything more than a "behaving organism" may prevent me from enacting a role in relation to you. The social process that results from such an exchange stems from you but not from me. It involves you because your behavior tests out a version of my outlook, and the experiential cycle in which you invest yourself leads you to a reinterpretation of our social relationship. It does not involve me because the only hypotheses to which I have made an experiential commitment are hypotheses about your overt behavior.

21. ROLE AND EXPERIENCE

If I fail to invest in a role, and relate myself to you only mechanistically, then the only thing that disconfirmation can teach me is that the organism I presumed you to be is not wired up to produce the behaviors I thought it would—just as my typewriter does not always behave in the way I expect it to. When my typewriter behaves unpredictably I look to see if there isn't a screw loose, or if something hasn't gotten into the works. Sometimes I find I have struck the wrong key; I'll strike a different one next time.

And if I insist on construing you as I do my typewriter, I shall probably take my predictive failures as an indication only that I should look to see if there isn't "a screw loose somewhere" in you. Or perhaps I shall wonder if I haven't "struck the wrong key," or if something hasn't "gotten into your works," like a "motive" or a "need," for example. I may even conclude that you are a brand of "typewriter" that has been badly put together. Certainly if this is the way I go about concluding my experiential cycle, I can scarcely claim that I have engaged myself in a social process. Mine might be the kind of experience that gets the commonwealth's work done, but it would not be the sort that builds viable societies.

When one construes another person's outlook, and proceeds to build an experiential cycle of his own upon that construction, he involves himself, willy nilly, in an interesting way. He can test his construction only by activating in himself the version of the other person's outlook it offers. This subtly places a demand upon him, one he cannot lightly reject if his own experience is to be completed. He must put himself tentatively in the other person's shoes. Only by enacting that role can he sense the impact of what happens as a result of taking the point of view he thinks his friend must have.

This means making a behavioral investment of his own, following the hypothesized lines, and experiencing the consequences. The enactment by which he pursues this experiential venture comes close to what is popularly regarded as role-taking. While not all enactments constitute roles in the personal construct sense, and not all role enactments culminate in completed experiential cycles, these brief comments may serve to suggest why the term *role* has been given such a salient part in the development of this theory.

22. GUILT

It is in the context of the Sociality Corollary that one can begin to develop a truly psychological definition of *guilt*. This is not to say that such a definition has to be at odds with ecclesiastical or legal definitions, though it may indeed suggest quite different courses of human action where misdemeanor is involved. We shall be speaking, of course, about the experience of guilt and what it is like, psychologically.

Most psychological theories, both "mechanistic" ones and "dynamic" ones, regard the experience of guilt as a derivative of punishment. One feels guilty because he thinks he has made himself eligible for punishment. But suppose one does not see punishment as the appropriate treatment of wrong-doing, only as revenge by injured persons serving simply to make clear that they have been hurt. Or suppose one does not see wrong-doing as something for which he has been systematically punished. Can he still feel guilty? I think he can. I think Jesus thought so too, though very few ecclesiastics appear to agree with either of us on this point. Even the term "repentance," which I think might better be taken to mean rethinking or reconstruing, as its etymology suggests, has come to stand for undertaking something irrelevantly unpleasant or punitive in compensation for disobedience, rather than doing something which will throw light on past mistakes.

As far as I can see, both from what I have observed and what I have figured out for myself, a person who chronically resorts to this kind of penitence to bring his guilt feelings back into comfortable equilibrium, or to write off his wrong-doing, ends up as a well-balanced sanctimonious psychopath. His only possible virtue is obedience and the society he perpetuates has no purpose except to uphold its own laws. I suspect, furthermore, that this is the net effect of any stimulus-response-reinforcement kind of theory, whether in psychology, religion or politics. And I have been moved to say, on occasion, that a psychopath is a stimulus-response psychologist who takes it seriously—a remark I find does not endear me to all of my colleagues.

From the standpoint of personal construct theory, guilt is the sense of having lost one's core role structure. A core structure is any one that is maintained as a basic referent of life itself. Without it a person has no guidelines for staying alive. To the extent that one's core structure embodies his role also, as we have defined role, he is vulnerable to the experience of guilt. He has only to perceive himself dislodged from such a role to suffer the inner torment most of us know so well.

To feel guilty is to sense that one has lost his grasp on the outlook of his fellow man, or has unwittingly played his part in a manner irrelevant to that outlook by following invalid guidelines. If the role is based on one's construction of God's outlook, or The Party's, he has only to fail to play it or to find that in playing it he has grossly misinterpreted its principal dimensions, to experience a religious sense of guilt. With this goes a feeling of alienation from God, or man, or from both. It is not a pleasant experience, and if the perception of excommunication is extensive or the core role deeply disrupted, it may be impossible for life to continue. Indeed, among primitive people, life may be extinguished within a few days, and, among more civilized ones, it may be abandoned by suicide.

A person who has never developed a role, or who has never allowed his life to depend on it, need not experience guilt. Guilt follows only from the loss of such a central part in the affairs of man. Persons who have always lacked a sense of role, such as psychopaths are said to be, may become confused or even anxious, as they contemplate the disconfirming outcomes of their experiences, but what they display is usually clinically distinguishable from guilt. But, then, neither do such persons play any substantial part in the development by which societies emerge. Guilt is thus a concomitant risk in any creative social process by which man may seek to transcend blind obedience. The author of the Book of Genesis seems to have perceived this a good deal more clearly than his readers have.

23. HOSTILITY

At this point let us turn back to the Experience Corollary and examine its contribution to our understanding of another puzzling matter—hostility. The experience cycle described in that section included a terminal phase embodying an assessment of the construction in terms of which the initial anticipation had been cast and the behavioral commitment had been made. If outcomes emerging successively from ventures based on the same construction continue to leave a trail of disconfirmations behind, it becomes increasingly clear, even to the most dim-witted adventurer, that something is wrong with his reference axes.

Of course, all he has to do when this happens is to start revising his constructs. But, if he procrastinates too long or if his core constructs are involved, this may prove to be a major undertaking. Constructs which are in the process of revision are likely to be pretty shaky, and if he has a great deal of importance resting of one of them, with no others nearby to take up the load, he may find himself on the verge of confusion, or even guilt.

Ordinarily one can loosen his constructs by falling back on more permeable constructions, as suggested by the Modulation Corollary. But if his superordinate constructs are impermeable he will find himself unable to range any new constructions under them. He will then be confronted with a far more extensive revision of his system than he would if he had more open-ended constructions to fall back upon. The upshot of all this may be that he will find himself precariously poised between the minor chaos that his recent disconfirmations have disclosed, and the major chaos that might engulf him if he attempted to make the needed repairs in his reference axes. In this predicament he may look for some way to avoid both.

One way to avoid the immediate chaos is to tinker with the validational evidence which has recently been giving trouble. There are several ways of doing this. One is to stop short of completing one's experiments. Graduate students are quick to catch on to this one. Another is to loosen up one's construction of outcomes, though this is likely to invite charges of being unrealistic. Still another is to claim rewards as valid substitutes for confirmations, the way doting parents and reinforcement theorists do. One does this by exploiting his dependency on people who are over eager to be helpful.

But there is still another way. That is to force the circumstances to confirm one's prediction of them. A parent who finds that his child does not love him as much as he expected may extort tokens of affection from the helpless youngster. A nation whose political philosophy has broken down in practice may precipitate a war to draft support for its outlook. A meek and trembly spinster, confronted at last by the fact that it is her impregnable posture that renders her unmarriageable, may "prove" the validity of her stand by enticing one of the male brutes to victimize her. A child, unwilling to concede his parents' better judgment because of its far-reaching implications for himself, may seize upon the first opportunity to engage in spiteful obedience by following their advice legalistically in a situation to which it obviously does not apply.

Each of these illustrates an instance of hostility. What personal construct theory has to offer in this matter differs radically from what conventional psychological theory implies. As with other topics with which it deals, personal construct theory attempts to define psychological constructs in terms of the personal experience of the individual to which they are to be applied. Thus, in defining hostility, we do not say that it is essentially an impulse to destroy—even though that may be its consequence—for that sounds more like a complaint of the victim than a prime effort of the hostile person. Instead, hostility is defined as the continued effort to extort validational evidence in favor of a type of social prediction which has already proved itself a failure.

24. FURTHER IMPLICATIONS OF PERSONAL CONSTRUCT THEORY

Since this presentation is intended to be a brief introduction to personal construct theory, rather than a condensation of it, much has had to be omitted. The important decision cycles and creativity cycles which the theory envisions remain unmentioned until this moment, as does a radically different view of dependency. There are strictly psychological definitions of threat, impulsivity, anxiety, transference, preemption, constellatoriness, and propositionality. There is a linguistic system called the language of hypothesis, an ontology exemplified in orchestrated approaches to psychotherapy, and a methodology of psychological research. The notions of motivation, needs, and psychodynamics vanish under the light of the Basic Postulate which accepts man as alive to begin with, and the principle of the elaborative choice which takes care of the directionality of man's moves without invoking special motivational agents to account for each of them.

The concept of learning evaporates. The boundary between cognition and affect is obliterated, rendering both terms meaningless. Fixed role therapy illustrates one of the variety of psychotherapeutic approaches which, at first glance, appear to violate most accepted canons of mental treatment by recognizing man as his own scientist. A new view of schizophrenia emerges, as well as fresh interpretations of "the unconscious," depression, and aggression.

But this is enough to mention now. All it has been possible to accomplish in these pages is to state the basic propositions from which hypotheses may be drawn, to illustrate a few of the lines of inference that may be pursued, and to encourage the more impatient readers to seek out the theory's most exciting implications for themselves.

3

TWO CRITICAL COMMENTS ON THE PSYCHOLOGY OF PERSONAL CONSTRUCTS, BY G. A. KELLY, 1955

A Cognitive Theory of Personality

Jerome S. Bruner

These excellent, original, and infuriatingly prolix two volumes [Kelly, 1955] easily nominate themselves for the distinction of being the single greatest contribution of the past decade to the theory of personality functioning. Professor Kelly has written a major work.

The book is an effort to construct a theory of personality from a theory of knowledge: how people came to know the world by binding its diverse appearances into organized construct systems which vary not only in organization but in their goodness of fit to the bricks and mortar of reality. The point of view that dominates the work—the author labels it "constructive alternativism"—is one that the author applies both to himself as a science-maker and to his troubled clients. In a deep sense, the book reflects the climate of a generation of nominalistic thinking in the philosophy of science.

Let me summarize the major theoretical elements of the work—a task made somewhat easier than usual by the author's admirable use of a Fundamental Postulate and a set of elaborating corollaries. The Fundamental Postulate is that "A person's processes are psychologically channelized by the ways in which he anticipates events." In short, man's effort is to gain prediction and control over his environment—much as a scientist. Does not man "have his theories, test his hypotheses, and weigh his experimental evidence"—and each in his own way? The author contrasts

Jerome S. Bruner, review of George A. Kelly's The Psychology of Personal Constructs, *Vol. I and II, in* Contemporary Psychology, I *(1956), pp. 355–357. Reprinted by permission of the author and the American Psychological Association.*

this point of view with one that he feels is prevalent among personality theorists: "I, being a *psychologist* and therefore a *scientist,* am performing this experiment in order to improve the prediction and control of certain human phenomena; but my subject, being merely a human organism, is obviously propelled by inexorable drives welling up within him." If it was Freud's genius to cut through the rationalistic cant of nineteenth-century Appolonianism, George Kelly's talent is to outstare the fashionable Dionysianism of the twentieth.

The Eleven Corollaries provide ways of describing or chronicling the vicissitudes of man's fumbling efforts at predicting and controlling his world. The first, or Construction Corollary, has to do with the process of cognitive working-through: "A person anticipates events by construing their replications." It is not from experience but from its reconstruing that we learn. The next two corollaries deal with the idiosyncratic nature of each man's construct world and man's construing acts.

The next corollary leads to some highly original and striking ideas about psychodiagnostic testing. It is the notion of dichotomization that has proved so fruitful in communication theory and in modern structural linguistics. "A person's construction system is composed of a finite number of dichotomous constructs." The dichotomized construct is inferred from triadic judgments. That is to say, given events A, B, and C, A and B are judged similar to each other in the same respect in which C is in contrast to both of them. A construct is not understood unless one grasps the two construct poles that form it, one of which may often be unrecognized by the construing person.

The Choice Corollary gets the author, I think, into a conceptual trap. "A person chooses for himself that alternative in a dichotomized construct through which he anticipates the greater possibility for extension and definition of his system." That is to say, an event is construed or "placed" at one or the other alternative poles of a construct ("good" or "bad," "healthy" or "hostile," or whatever) depending upon "which seems to provide the best basis for anticipating the ensuing events." One object of categorizing the world in terms of a construct system is to minimize the disruptive surprises that it can wreak on us. This, I think, is the principal doctrine of "motivation" in the book—an implicit one, but one stamped on every page. It is the author's counterproposal to the Law of Effect, to the Pleasure Principle, to the watered-down hedonisms and tension reductions of such various Yale thinkers as Neal Miller, John Dollard, and David McClelland. But must event-construing or categorizing always be guided by the need to extend cognitive control over one's environment? Need man be viewed *either* as the pig that reinforcement theory makes of him *or* the professor that Kelly implies as a model? I think not: in categorizing events, there is more to be maximized than predictiveness. Here is an example of the folly. "No matter how obvious it may be that a person would be better off if he avoided a fight . . ., such a course of action would seem to him personally to limit the definition and extension of his system as a whole." I rather suspect that when some people get angry or inspired or in love, they couldn't care less about their "system as a whole." One gets the impression that the author is, in his personality theory, overreacting against a generation of irrationalism.

The next four corollaries have to do with what might be called the dynamics of construct utilization and change. Any given construct anticipates only a finite range of events, and effective action depends upon recognizing this "range of convenience." Construct systems change with time, experience, and the reconstruing of replicates, and they vary in their permeability to the influence of new events. As he goes through life, a person may develop a construct system with high or low degrees of integration, fragmentation, or imcompatibility.

So much, then, for the axiomatic apparatus in terms of which Professor Kelly construes the world. What does he make of it?

For one thing, and a very considerable thing, I believe, he has found a way of ungluing the eye of psychology from the keyhole of projective techniques. His REP test (Role Construct Repertory Test) is a simple and elegant way of determining the manner in which significant figures in the person's life are fitted into a construct system. Take a list of the significant kinds of people with whom a person interacts: parents, boy friends, teachers, sweethearts, bosses, "a person who dislikes you," etc. The client thinks of specific people who fill these roles in his life. He is then given triads of these and asked to indicate which two are most alike, in what respects, and how the third differs from these: the method of getting at the dichotomized contrast poles of the construct. The constructs that emerge from the sorting of the triads are then reduced mathematically and intuitively to get at the nature of general constructs used, the range they comprise, their degree of preemptiveness, etc.

The author then sets forth a subtle and interesting set of dimensions for describing the constructs of patients: looseness-tightness, constriction-dilation, level of cognitive awareness, and then proceeds to redefine some classic concepts in terms of these. He redefines *anxiety* as awareness that events to be coped with lie outside the range of convenience of one's construct system, and *hostility* as an effort to extort validational evidence for an anticipatory prediction already recognized as failing.

I have said nothing about Professor Kelly's approaches to therapy, nor am I particularly qualified to do so. One point I must make, however, for it is at the core of his theoretical approach. The effort in therapy is not to give the patient "insight" which, according to the author, too often means getting the patient's construct system to conform to that of the therapist. Rather the process of therapy is considered as an occasion for learning—for testing the fit of one's own (not the therapist's) construct system to the world. To do this, a kind of role-playing approach is employed, much in the spirit of characters in a Pirandello or O'Neill play who learn of themselves partly through the experience of contrasting or confusing (or both) what they are with the mask they are wearing in different life situations.

Where does the book succeed and where fall down? Who are the ancestors? What is portended by the appearance of this extraordinary and original work? The book succeeds, I think, in raising to a proper level of dignity and importance the press that man feels toward cognitive control of the world. It succeeds too in recognizing the individuality and "alternativeness" of the routes to mental health. It succeeds in providing a diagnostic device strikingly in keeping with its presuppositions.

The book fails signally, I think, in dealing convincingly with the human passions. There was a strategy in Freud's choice of Moses or Michelangelo or Little Hans. If it is true that Freud was too often the victim of the dramatic instance, it is also true that with the same coin he paid his way to an understanding of the depths and heights of *la condition humaine.* By comparison, the young men and women of Professor Kelly's clinical examples are worried about their dates, their studies, and their conformity. If Freud's clinical world is a grotesque of *fin de siècle* Vienna, Kelly's is a gloss on the post-adolescent peer group of Columbus, Ohio, who are indeed in the process of constructing their worlds. Which is more "real"? I have no idea. I wish Professor Kelly would treat more "most religious men in their most religious moments," or even just Nijinsky or Gabriel d'Annunzio.

With respect to ancestry, Professor Kelly seems to care little for it. One misses reference to such works as Piaget's *The Child's Construction of Reality,* the early work of Werner, and the writings of Harry Stack Sullivan, Lewin, and Allport—all of whom are on his side and good allies to boot.

The book is a theory of cognition extrapolated into a theory of personality—a genuine new departure and a spirited contribution to the psychology of personality.

REFERENCE

KELLY, G. A. *The Psychology of Personal Constructs.* New York: Norton, 1955.

Intellectualized Psychotherapy

Carl R. Rogers

This [Kelly, 1955] is a man's life work. In this enormous outpouring of 1200 pages (broken into two volumes only because of its bulk) George Kelly has endeavored to express the thinking which has grown out of twenty years of clinical experience, teaching, and supervision of research. Here is his philosophical base, the theory of personality which has emerged in his thinking, a new diagnostic instrument he has developed, a new therapeutic method, plus his extended views on all phases of psychodiagnosis and psychotherapy. In these half million words he is saying "Here I am." It is a good solid figure which emerges, even if the question grows ever stronger as one reads on, whether any man has 1200 pages to express at one time.

In Kelly's view the framework of the book is provided by his theory of personality and behavior, largely presented in the first three chapters. To this reviewer these 183 pages were much the freshest, most original, most valuable. Kelly takes off from no current theory, but solely from the distillation of his own informed experience with individuals. He attempts to build a theoretical system which looks forward, not backward—which sees behavior as anticipatory not reactive. He is attempting to hold persons as processes, not objects. He emphasizes phenomenological information, but his theory superimposes normative thinking upon the phenomenological data.

His basic concept is that the individual's behavior is channelized by the way he anticipates events, and that the individual anticipates events by the constructions (interpretations, meanings) he has placed upon his experience. The careful, rigorous logic with which Kelly works out the way in which these constructs are formed, the implications which flow from their mode of organization, and the ways in which they may change, make stimulating and thought-provoking reading. There emerges a picture of man as being not "a victim of his past, only the victim of his construction of it." This view, in Kelly's opinion, allows for the "determinism" which is a part of science, yet permits a concept of "constructive alternativism," or choice, in the way in which the individual construes his world. It is gratifying to learn that this carefully formulated theory, presented in terms which can be given operational definition, is already being tested in small

Carl R. Rogers, review of George A. Kelly's The Psychology of Personal Constructs, *Vol. I and II, in* Contemporary Psychology, *I (1956), pp. 357–358. Reprinted by permission of the author and the American Psychological Association.*

ways by a very considerable number of doctoral researches at Ohio State University (most of them unfortunately unpublished).

Since the space limits of this review severely restrict the reviewer, he must omit many areas of the book to comment on Kelly's views on psychotherapy.

It is in his chapter on *Fixed-Role Therapy* that the author becomes most personally expressive. It is clear that in this new method he has found an approach congenial to his personality, which is perhaps the basic aim of every therapist. Essentially, a diagnosis is made of the client's psychological constructs as they operate in his most significant interpersonal relationships. Then a number of clinicians (to avoid the bias of any one) develop a sketch of a new person, one that this client might become if his constructs were altered constructively. The aim is to get him to "play-act" this role for several weeks, without any notion that it represents a goal for him. The hope is that by shaking loose the organization of his psychological constructs, by giving him a new role, he will be more able to choose a role for himself built around an altered set of personal hypotheses, which will be confirmed or disconfirmed in his continuing experience.

Kelly shows real zest in his description of the way the client is kept from knowing the purpose of this "play-acting," and the enthusiastic manner in which he coaches the client in his new role, playing the parts, one after another, of the individuals with whom the client will interact. Kelly's statement that the therapist needs "a great deal of enthusiastic momentum" and "some measure of verbal fluency and acting skill" to succeed in this effort seems a decided understatement, but it is clear that Kelly enjoys it. He describes his clinical experience with the use of this method both in individual and in group therapy (where a role sketch is devised for each person), but there are as yet no research studies of its effectiveness. One point which is unmentioned by Kelly is that this method could not be used with any client who had read about it or heard about it, since it is very important that the client regard the new role initially as simply an exercise, not in any sense as a possible pattern for his personality.

There are many other chapters, including the last five of Volume II, which deal with Kelly's psychotherapeutic observations. It is impossible to do more than indicate briefly some reactions to them.

An overwhelming impression is that for Kelly therapy is seen as almost entirely an intellectual function, a view which should be comforting to many psychologists. He is continually thinking about the client, and about his own procedures, in ways so complex that there seems no time or room for entering into an emotional relationship with the client. One small example. There are ten types of weeping to be differentiated. In dealing with one of them or with some other problem the client is expressing, there are nine techniques for reducing anxiety, twelve techniques (in addition to role playing) for encouraging the client to move or experiment in therapy, fifteen criteria to consider regarding the client's readiness to explore new areas, etc., etc. One has the impression of an incredibly "busy" therapist. This reviewer cannot help but wonder about the relation between "busyness" and effectiveness in therapy.

This approach to therapy is also highly eclectic. The therapist in appropriate situations manipulates the transference, prescribes activities, gives interpretations, uses "non-directive reflecting," confrontation, the discussion of dreams, the playing back of previous recorded interviews, etc. What the effect will be of setting this enormous cookbook of therapy before students who are preparing to undertake therapy is problematical. Certainly they will find almost every problem of therapy mentioned in its pages, but what a student should do about a particular problem with a particular client will depend upon whether he construes the difficulty as "controlling guilt feelings" or "loosening constructs." The recipes are very different. Kelly believes that his views on therapy are given unity by his initial theory, but such unity consists largely in the fact that anything done to the client affects his psychological constructs in some way.

In the beginning of the theoretical presentation Kelly pays tribute to the strength of each individual as a private "scientist" who tests out hypotheses in his own behavior. In the chapters on therapy, however, the wisdom all lies in the mind of the therapist. Since the client's perceptions of therapy and therapist are mostly false, therapy can only reach its proper goal if the therapist carefully chooses the role which should be played with this client at this time and appropriately manipulates the multitudinous aspects of the therapeutic process as suggested above. Confidence in the client as the "scientist" of his own life does not here find much operationl expression.

Another disappointing element in this clincan, who has undoubtedly been of help to many individuals, is the lack of any sense of depth in his discussions of therapy. The chapters on theory clearly show an author who has thought deeply about his experience. The chapters on therapy seem to present meager evidence that he has lived deeply with his clients, and the bulk of the anecdotal examples seem to describe but superficial change. This reviewer had the feeling that perhaps Kelly was not doing justice to this phase of his experience. Actually the work might have a stronger impact if much of the last section were omitted.

However any one reader may see their strengths and weaknesses, these two volumes are clearly the measure of a man. They are written with modesty, with occasional humor, with brilliance in the theoretical sections, with earnestness and essential openmindedness in the diagnostic and therapeutic sections. In spite of being too wordy, they show a person who is not afraid to launch out on his own in the development of theory, who looks to his experience rather than to authority for the source and the confirmation of his ideas. They show a man who believes deeply in the scientific method and who expects his views to be changed much by research findings. Psychologists, perhaps especially young ones, will profit greatly from reading these chapters because they will find their own psychological constructs loosened by the experience. And, while any reader will find a great many pages which seem to him of dubious value, that still leaves many pages, ample enough to constitute highly rewarding reading.

REFERENCE

KELLY, G. A. *The Psychology of Personal Constructs.* New York: Norton, 1955.

II
THE BASIC
DESCRIPTIVE UNITS
OF BEHAVIOR
IN COGNITIVE THEORY

1

OVERVIEW

In what terms shall the personality theorist describe his data? With what aspects of the person is the theorist concerned? In the history of personality theory the focus of theorists has varied greatly. Persons have been described in terms of their humors, their zodiac signs, their guiding goals, their central factors, their libidinal balances, their body-types, or their stimulus-response bonds. Each of these concepts has been explored to achieve the greatest possible understanding of the person being studied. Many notions have been invented, explored, and then abandoned as being sheer nonsense; others remain tentatively in the repertoire of the personality theorist. Ultimately the concepts must be related to observable behavior.

In the early part of this century the observables of behavior became so important that psychologists, as a general group, tended to offer allegiance to John B. Watson, who demanded that *only* observable behavior be regarded as the province of psychology. Watson's vigorous attack (1913) on concepts that had a mentalistic quality won the support of psychologists who were ready to abandon, in despair, the glib efforts of psychologists to use internal, unobservable mechanisms to explain human functioning. The psychologists who might have accepted mentalistic concepts as being scientifically useful were unprepared, philosophically or methodologically, to defend their position against behaviorism. Proponents of theories that stressed concepts about internal events were regarded as "soft-headed," and theorists who used such concepts were put into a defensive position.

Researchers, in the past several decades, have produced a series of studies that show the procedures by which inferred internal organizations can be tied to overt behaviors. A most effective research strategy has been one by which the experimenter infers, from the subject's behavior, something about the subject's cognitive organization. The subject is then exposed to stimulation which is hypothesized to produce a predictable change in the subject's cognitive organizations. The change, it is further predicted, should systematically lead to a particular behavior. Typically, this strategy first assesses the form of a subject's orientation toward a set of stimulus events. He might, for example, be asked to report his views on governmental involvement in economic affairs. Following this assessment of his views, which are regarded as the cognitive structures he takes into events, he is asked to read material attributed to a person who is reputed to disagree, or agree, with his initial attitudes. Predictions are then made about how he will assimilate or reject the material he has read. The predictions can be hypothesized to be related to such variables as the nature of his original position, the extremeness of his basic position, and so on.

Another strategy is similar in that there is an assessment of the subject's initial cognitive structure. Again the subject is given stimulation of a particular sort, which, it is predicted, he will perceive in a particular way. In its simplest form, this strategy speaks of *set*. The subject's set is determined or assumed, and he is then presented a stimulus pattern. The nature of his set will predictably influence his report of the nature of the stimulus. For example, three dots located in positions which correspond to the points of a triangle are presented to a subject. He reports that the figure represents a triangle. His set to see a triangle influences what he reports. The psychologist who has the propensity to use these research approaches feels more comfortable in developing explanations of behavior that stress the person's role in "organizing" stimulus input.

Even during the zenith of the advocacy of the behavioristic approach there were theorists who could not abandon a position that made the person's cognitive organizations the key function to be explained (Lewin, 1935; Snygg and Combs, 1949; Piaget, 1952; Rogers, 1951). As perceptual and cognitive studies increase, in scope and sensitivity, personality theories based on cognitive concepts become more bold and imaginative (Kelly, 1955; Harvey, Hunt, and Schroder, 1961; Heider, 1958).

In these theories the central organization is regarded as the basic unit of study. All behavior is referred to the central cognitive organization. Piaget (1952) and Bartlett (1932) follow the practice of Sir Henry Head by using the term *schema* when they refer to the internal organization. Many writers refer simply to *cognitive organization* or to *perceptual organization*. Others used the term *concept,* as in *self-concept.* Luchins (1959) has consistently used the terms *set* or *einstellung.* During his thirty years of work on behavior Sherif has referred to the central organizational feature as *attitude* or *frame of reference* (Sherif and Sherif, 1964). Bruner and his associates (Bruner, Goodnow, and Austin, 1956) speak of *categories,* a term associated with Kant's (1952) classic use of the term.

M. Sherif, with H. Cantril, provided an example of an early effort to amalgamate the work on attitudes into a comprehensive theory of behavior (Sherif and Cantril, 1945, 1946, 1947). They argued for the value of using *attitudes* as the core construct in behavior. They stressed two points which currently retain their theoretical value. First, they argue for a position that the *attitude* can be taken as a main unit of psychological study. "Attitudes are among those components of the psychological make-up of the individual which determine that he shall react not in a passive or neutral way, but in a selective and characteristic way especially in relation to certain specific stimulus situations" (Sherif and Cantril, 1945, p. 300). "Various terms such as 'set,' 'stereotype,' 'prejudice,' and 'opinion' may all be regarded as attitudes with particular characteristics which have been given certain labels by common users" (Sherif and Cantril, 1945, p. 306). ". . . Any final adequate psychology of attitude will someday be linked closely with the psychology of learning or conditioning, especially in accounting for the more or less enduring character and for the range of attitudes" (Sherif and Cantril, 1945, p. 307).

Their second point is that a valuable source for understanding the nature of attitudes is to be found in studying the nature of judgmental (cognitive) or perceptual processes. "When characterized psychologically and traced from the point of view of its formation, it becomes evident that the psychology of attitudes is intimately related to the psychology of perception and judgments" (Sherif and Cantril, 1945, p. 307). In this set of papers Sherif and Cantril support their argument with laboratory studies of judgment and perception that help to establish the value of the concept of cognitive organization. Their point of departure is that, "A frame of reference is involved in perceptual and judgmental activity. It is an established fact in psychology that stimuli do not have an absolute stimulating value. A stimulus is experienced, perceived, judged, and reacted to in relation to other stimuli, present or past, to which it is *functionally* related. In perception this relative character of a stimulus emerges from its relationship in the organized whole; in judgments from its relationship to other stimuli (present and past) which are operative at the moment" (Sherif and Cantril, 1945, p. 309).

Thus, we owe Sherif and Cantril a large intellectual debt for formulating a cogent statement on internal organizing processes as a central feature of psychological theory. They also deserve a large share of the credit for demonstrating that the nature of *judgments* made in the most rigorous laboratory studies and the nature of *judgments* made in the most loosely structured social and interpersonal situations follow the same laws. This kind of pioneering work allows us to feel comfortable when we extend the principles developed from psychophysical studies of sensation, perception, and judgment, toward explaining cognitive functioning in one's general personal and social world.

Kelly, whose extended work is summarized in Section I as a model of a cognitive personality theory, calls his set of principles "the psychology of personal constructs." Kelly defines personal constructs as the central organizations through which any and all incoming stimuli are filtered. They are the "templates" which are imposed on the stimuli so that the stimuli "make sense." The construct "shapes" what the subject "sees." Stimuli are classed, categorized, or grouped in ways that are consonant with structures that the subject has developed. Kelly's position as a cognitive theorist is emphasized by his *Construction Corollary* (the first of his eleven corollaries): A person anticipates events by construing their replications.

REFERENCES

BARTLETT, F. C. *Remembering*. Cambridge: Cambridge University Press, 1932.

BRUNER, J. S., GOODNOW, J. J., & AUSTIN, G. A. *A Study of Thinking*. New York: Wiley, 1956.

HARVEY, O. J., HUNT, D. E., & SCHRODER, H. M. *Conceptual Systems and Personality Organization*. New York: Wiley, 1961.

HEIDER, F. *The Psychology of Interpersonal Relations*. New York: Wiley, 1958.

KANT, I. *The Critique of Pure Reason*. In R. M. Hutchins (Ed.), *Great Books of the Western World*. Chicago: Encyclopedia Britannica, 1952, *42,* 1–250.

KELLY, G. A. *The Psychology of Personal Constructs*. New York: Norton, 1955.

LEWIN, K. *A Dynamic Theory of Personality*. New York: McGraw-Hill, 1935.

LUCHINS, A. S. *Rigidity of Behavior*. Eugene, Oregon: University of Oregon Press, 1959.

PIAGET, J. *The Origins of Intelligence in Children*. New York: International Universities Press, 1952.

ROGERS, C. *Client-Centered Therapy: Its Current Practice, Implications, and Theory*. Boston: Houghton-Mifflin, 1951.

SHERIF, M. & CANTRIL, H. The Psychology of Attitudes. Part I. *Psychological Review,* 1945, *52,* 295–319.

SHERIF, M. & CANTRIL H. The Psychology of Attitudes. Part II. *Psychological Review,* 1946, *53,* 1–24.

SHERIF, M. & CANTRIL, H. *The Psychology of Ego-Involvements*. New York: Wiley, 1947.

SHERIF, M. & SHERIF, C. W. *Reference Groups*. New York: Harper and Row, 1964.

SNYGG, D. & COMBS, A. W. *Individual Behavior*. New York: Harper and Row, 1949.

WATSON, J. B. Psychology as the Behaviorist Views It. *Psychological Review,* 1913, *20,* 158–177.

2

THE FUNCTIONS
OF SCHEMATA IN PERCEIVING
M. D. VERNON

Vernon advocates that the "schema" be given a central position in the study of behavior. Her position is that schemata reflect internalized organizations of repeated stimulus events, that they are "persistent, deep-rooted and well-organized classifications of ways of perceiving, thinking, and behaving." The schema, in short, is the psychological manifestation of organism-environment interaction. Vernon is careful, however, to phrase her enthusiasm for the concept in an interrogatory format. Her article is a call for research: How is the concept of schema related to previous research in perception? How are motivational principles related to schema function? Vernon points out some of the trends she observed and suggests directions for future research. In other sections of this text we will see that Vernon's questions on construct change, construct organization, and motivation have concerned other researchers who regard cognitive function to be the core of behavior.

*　　*　　*

THE DEVELOPMENT OF SCHEMATA

There has been a striking tendency among psychologists in recent years to stress the importance of motivational factors in determining our perceptions of the outside world. Perception has even been regarded as "an approach to personality" (see Blake and Ramsey, 5), as though a study of the individual's percepts would throw some light upon the nature of his individual personality characteristics. These psychologists appear to underestimate the importance of the cognitive aspects of perception; of the

Reprinted from Psychological Review, *1955, 62, 180–192, by permission of the author and the American Psychological Association.*

parts played by thought and reasoning in building up our understanding of the world; and of the functions of our background of knowledge[1] in determining our immediate percepts. At the same time, these psychologists seem to overestimate the influence of the factors of immediate need, and especially of the relatively transient and unimportant influences they exert upon most of the simpler and more straightforward of our perceptions. It is possible to hold the view that percepts are constructed from sensory data though not wholly a function of them; and at the same time to maintain that the construction is determined by cognitive activities as much as by individual need and interest. I shall proceed to discuss this view.

It is clear to all that at the basis of our perceptions of the external world there are a series of effects in the sense organs produced by external stimulation which vary in an orderly way, both temporally and spatially. And, as Gibson (12) has pointed out, our percepts vary also in gradients which correspond closely to the gradients of stimulation. Moreover, there is an orderly continuity of sensory impression between one moment and the next; and there is also a consistency and correspondence between the types and variations of effect in the different sense organs. From these patterns of sensory impressions are constructed our percepts of the external world. We assume that our percepts represent accurately what is "really there." We believe that certain visual impressions represent solid objects of particular shapes, which continue to exist indefinitely; and this probably because we can repeatedly check the fact of their solidity and identity by touching and manipulating them. For most practical purposes, tactile and kinesthetic data can be relied upon to be consistent.

It seems fairly clear from the evidence of Piaget and others (discussed in Vernon, 44) that the infant is not at first aware either of the orderly repetition and continuity of sensory data, or of the association between such data from different sense organs. Neither does he allocate such impressions to sources in a more or less permanently existing external environment. He gradually acquires the processes of constructing his percepts of the external world through manipulation and experiment. It may well be that the tendency to do so is innate and develops through maturation; but the infant does require specific individual practice and experience before he arrives at the concept of the world around him as permanently existing outside himself and independent of himself. Indeed, the notion of the complete independence and objectivity of the external world seems not to be fully established until many years after birth.

Now is it not obvious that this view of the external world must be

---

[1] "Knowledge" is used throughout this paper in its widest sense, to include not only verbally formulated knowledge and ideas, but also our background of knowledge of how to behave appropriately in the widely varying range of situations we normally encounter in our everyday life.

constructed by the individual for himself, since it cannot be directly "given" by the sensory impressions coming from the sense organs? And since, sooner or later, our perceptions and ideas about the world do become in general coherent and consistent, is it not probable that they are coordinated in accordance with some system of classification of percepts and ideas about them? If the infant is to be impressed by the repetition, coherence, and consistency of certain combinations of sensory data, he must adopt some organized procedure of retaining, coordinating, and classifying these data in an orderly manner. The earliest classifications of data may be formed in relation to the satisfaction of the needs common to all children; they center upon the mother, who is the supplier of food, warmth, and comfort. But, also, the infant and the young child are intensely interested in the appearance of the phenomena they experience, and make every effort to study and understand them. Thus data are classified in terms of the appearance and behavior of external objects and situations. These classifications supplement and are substituted for the classifications in terms of need satisfaction. As language develops, it forms a tool of increasing value in assisting the former type of classification.

I suggest that to this type of classification we may usefully apply Bartlett's concept of the "schema" (3). Bartlett defines the schema[2] as follows:

> "Schema" refers to an active organization of past reactions or of past experiences, which must always be supposed to be operating in any well-adapted organic response. That is, whenever there is any order or regularity of behavior, a particular response is possible only because it is related to other similar responses which have been serially organized, yet which operate, not simply as individual members coming one after another, but as a unitary mass (3, p. 201).

Thus we may regard schemata as persistent, deep-rooted, and well-organized classifications of ways of perceiving, thinking, and behaving. They are based upon the individual's knowledge of "what sort of thing to do in, and about, certain kinds of situations." Thus they involve the classification of (a) situations of related kinds; and (b) kinds of behavior appropriate in these situations. But the behavior and its results react back upon the classification of situations. If the results prove unsatisfactory, the classifications of both situations and behavior may be modified until they appear to be more realistic and more appropriate. Thus schemata are not in themselves stereotyped habit systems, though in certain circumstances it may be that they will degenerate into such habit systems.[3] There is no

[2]For a fuller discussion of this definition, and of its relation to other uses of the term "schema," see Oldfield and Zangwill (26).

[3]Recently H. Kay has, in an unpublished thesis, given evidence that old people's behavior shows signs of such deterioration.

doubt, however, that the individual's motivational tendencies will operate in such a way as to build up and strengthen schemata which lead to behavior that satisfies need and to modify or suppress those which do not.

The essential point to note is that the use of a concept such as that of the schema reflects the fact that our percepts, thoughts, and behavior are on the whole consistent and orderly—reasonably appropriate though not necessarily logical—and that they are consistently related to previous acts of perceiving, thinking, and behaving. Thus, in investigating the operation of schemata, we must endeavor to find if the observer shows some consistent method of classifying perceptual situations in a realistic and meaningful manner. Furthermore, we must note if there is evidence that this type of classification has been built up through individual personal experience or interest, in which case there may be considerable individual differences in perceiving the same situation (such as the responses I have quoted elsewhere [44, pp. 262–263] to a reproduction of Sickert's picture, "Brighton Pierrots"). Or if the systems of classification are shared by members of a group having, for instance, a common culture or type of education, we may expect that the percepts of these people will be alike but will differ from those of other groups. Lastly, there are many schemata related to the spatial and temporal relationships of objects in the external environment which are probably acquired by almost everyone in the course of his ordinary everyday life. It is not always easy to detect the manner in which perception is determined schematically, since often we are unaware of the background of knowledge and experience to which our present perceptual behavior is related. But it is, I think, quite essential to the understanding of our immediate perceptual reactions to take into account these organized classifications of knowledge about the physical and social environment which guide and inform us as to "what is the sort of thing to do about the sort of thing we now see."[4]

OPERATION OF SCHEMATA IN
EXPERIMENTS ON PERCEPTUAL AND FORM QUALITIES

Although the sensory data are accurately recorded at some level in the central nervous system, nevertheless, it does not seem that we are ever directly or consciously aware of anything corresponding to the sensations of Titchenerian theory. Instead, we perceive stable solid objects, enduringly located in the world around us. This "visual world" is perceived, and we react to it, in accordance with the schemata we have built up for ourselves from infancy upwards. But we do also perceive that certain

[4]This appears to correspond to Postman's views (31) on the categorization of "perceptual response dispositions."

aspects of the external world do at times vary independently of one another, and that they cannot, and must not, always be determined by our ideas of the general nature of the external world and the objects which it contains. Perhaps only the sophisticated Westerner has gone to much trouble to distinguish these particular aspects and their inherent differences and variations. For it is only by a considerable effort of differentiation and abstraction from his total perceptual experience that he can perceive them at all. Moreover, this abstraction is never complete. What is perceived is always affected to some extent by the global schematized perception of the total field; and other aspects of the field are always liable to slip in and distract the observer.

Now it seems that most of the *experimental* work which has been carried out on perception depends on the ability of the observer to abstract more or less completely certain aspects of the perceived field from the total global impression. In particular, all so-called "sensory" experiments are of this nature. They indicate that the trained and sophisticated observer can analyze his perceptual field, and differentiate certain parts of it from the remainder, with considerable finesse. Furthermore, it seems to be true that the degree of possible differentiation is fairly consistent, both in the same observer from time to time, and also between different observers with the same degree of training. It has been assumed that in such experiments, the abilities of the sense organs to respond to and discriminate stimuli are being measured. It would be more correct to say that when the situation is arranged in such a way that the physical stimulus is varying in one way only, and all other stimulus qualities are maintained constant, then the variations in what is perceived are largely a function of that stimulus variable. But appropriate schemata are nevertheless operating in the construction of the percepts. For they will vary greatly between different observers with different degrees of sophistication and training, and those who have built up appropriate schemata of observation and response will react differently from those who have not. Furthermore, in situations which are not limited in this way, other schemata will operate, and the percepts will be differently constructed from the sensory impressions.

Again, in many experiments on perception, as Gibson (13) has stressed, the observer is required to abstract from his total experience small differences in the outlines of two-dimensionally projected shapes, shown to him momentarily. He learns by experience to construct some percepts of this type with considerable facility. Whether all children learn to recognize representations of objects from their outlines is impossible to say. Certainly children brought up in Western civilizations acquire this facility at an early age, presumably by coordinating together visual impressions of brightness gradients and tactually perceived "edges." But when it is a matter of perceiving nonrepresentational outline drawings, of the kind so frequently used by the gestalt psychologists, the individual has little previously acquired experience to assist him. Then his percepts may be characterized by the failure to differentiate the parts from the whole, as is shown in many of the gestalt figures and in the visual illusions.

OPERATION OF SCHEMATA
IN "CONSTANCY" EXPERIMENTS

In experiments on the "constancies," the observer is required to differentiate and abstract aspects of his total experience in a way that is quite unfamiliar to him. The child has learned in the course of his development that objects may retain their identity, and hence their "real" shape and size, although the visual aspects of their shape and size vary as their spatial position varies. This he learns at a comparatively early age with objects which he can reach and handle, but at a much later age, as Piaget (27, 28) has shown, with distant objects which he cannot manipulate. In the end, however, he can make this act of identification even when, for instance, distant objects appear actually as little more than dots on the landscape. Furthermore, on the basis of impressions of projected size and shape, he can and does make fairly accurate estimates of the distance and spatial orientation of the objects. What he is never required to do, and cannot do with any accuracy, under normal conditions, is to estimate their projected size and shape. (Piaget and Lambercier [30] have shown that this is done more accurately by younger children, aged 7–8, whose percepts are less closely linked to the spatial framework, than by older children, aged 9–10; after that, the ability improves somewhat as they become more capable of making abstract judgments.) Yet this is what the observer is required to do in experiments on size and shape constancy. The unsophisticated observer naturally finds this task difficult. In estimating or matching the size of distant objects, he is apt to choose the size which the object would appear to have if it were close to him. He uses both his knowledge of the size of the object as such, and also schematized knowledge relating this size to the retinal projections of objects at distances which can be judged from other criteria. But suppose that, instead of being required to estimate the perceived size of the object, he is asked to estimate what fraction or segment of the total field of view it covers. Then, as Joynson (17) has shown, the estimated size approaches that of the retinal projection of the object. Much the same procedure must be adopted by anyone who attempts to make a landscape drawing. He must try to estimate the size of the spaces between objects, as well as of the objects themselves; otherwise the latter will be drawn too big to fit into his drawing. Thus the object is judged to be of one size if it is regarded "figurally," as an object in itself, and of another size if it is perceived as part of the "ground."

A somewhat different situation seems to arise in experiments on shape constancy. Here the observer rarely judges the shape of the inclined object to be exactly the same as that of the object in the frontal parallel position, unless the angle of inclination is very small. Thus if the object is a circle, his judgments become more and more elliptical as the angle of inclination is increased. It is possible that in the course of our upbringing we learn to perceive two-dimensional shape as such, and apart from the object concerned, with a fair amount of accuracy. The observer attempts, in the experiment, to apply this schematic perceptual category to the estimation of projected three-dimensional shapes. In effect, he says to himself, "This tilted circle looks elliptical." But he cannot judge very accurately how elliptical.

It is not justifiable, I consider, to compare the processes of estimation which occur under normal conditions with those which operate when the object is exposed in such a way that only its projected shape is visible. Such estimates are made when the object is viewed monocularly, with no variations of lighting or surface texture, and with all surroundings concealed. The normal schemata are not brought into action, and the variations of the percept are determined by the only variation perceptible—that of projected shape. In the experiments of Ittelson (15), however, the observer perceived a single shape continually varying in size. His schematized ideas as to the persistent nature of objects, which frequently change their distance but not their size, suggested to him that, when the area of retinal stimulation varied, the object was in fact moving rather than expanding or contracting; and that was what he perceived. Again, in the experiments of Langdon (20), a circular outline shape made of wire was rotated about a vertical axis, in such a way that its projected shape varied continuously. The shape of the object was then estimated as somewhere between that of the circle and the projected shape, thus approaching the estimate that would have been made under normal conditions of perception. Possibly, once more, the continuity of experience was the important factor; and the rotating outline was perceived in somewhat the same way as a stationary solid object whose spatial orientation was clearly visible.[5]

A rather different schematic determination of perception again appears to operate in brightness—or "whiteness"[6]—and in color constancy. Here

[5]Langdon states that it often appeared to the observers that the wire shape was being squeezed in and out, rather than rotated, but that this made no difference to their estimates. It is possible that they developed a procedural "set" in matching which was too well-established to be disrupted.

[6]In accordance with the usage of Thouless (42) and of Koffka (18).

also it is true that what we are concerned with in ordinary everyday life is the intrinsic or normal whitenesses and colors of objects—those which appear in ordinary daylight. Over a wide range of brightness and hue in general illumination, we do ignore changes in perceived whiteness and color of objects. At the same time, if an observer is asked to match the whiteness or color of white objects exposed in dim or colored light, against gray or colored objects exposed in bright white light, it will appear that his perceptions of the former have become appreciably modified—that is to say, they are less white or are tinted with color. Now it may be that although we can accurately differentiate between two whitenesses or two colors placed side by side, we have no schematic categories appropriate to the remembering of absolute degrees of whiteness or color. Anyone who has tried to remember the exact hue of a fabric in order to match it against another, even in white light, will confirm the difficulty of this task. We have, it is true, developed some schematic knowledge of the changes in whiteness and color of objects with changes in brightness and hue of the light falling upon them. It may be, as Wallach argues (47), that we have learned to assess the proportion of incident light which is reflected to us, rather than the absolute amount. Thus whiteness constancy is perceived as long as the proportion or ratio remains approximately constant. But this judgment is not completely accurate, and constancy of whiteness and color is in general less than constancy of shape and size.

I do not of course claim that this discussion of the "constancies" has covered exhaustively all the phenomena they exhibit. This argument merely advances a new approach to the subject, which might suggest a somewhat different type of experimental investigation, for instance, studies of the relation of constancy judgments made in different types of naturalistic surroundings, and with different types of experimental instructions. Those of Gibson (12) constitute a valuable beginning which needs to be followed up. Above all, it is important that the observers should attempt to report in some detail the nature of the phenomena as they actually perceive them, and thus demonstrate the individual differences in their perceptions.

RELATION OF SCHEMATA
TO MOTIVATIONAL FACTORS

I have argued that we perceive certain aspects of the perceptual field in accordance with the schematic category of events to which at the moment they seem to appertain. Since these schemata develop differently according to different individual experience, it cannot be assumed that percepts which may be claimed to be, logically and objectively, of the same kind—for instance, the "constancies"—will in fact follow the same logical principles or "laws." Furthermore, the operative schemata can up to a point be varied by the intentions of the observer—by his concern with certain aspects of the field, and his lack of interest in others. The individual can choose to some extent what he will perceive. But it has generally been found that in carrying out skilled perceptual tasks, for instance, the observer cannot perform satisfactorily, however strong his motivation, merely by intending from moment to moment to concentrate on particular aspects of the field. He must be instructed beforehand where and how to direct his awareness, and he must acquire facility in this by repeated practice. In other words, he must build up the appropriate schemata for the selection, assimilation, and interpretation of the appropriate sensory data. The formation of the schemata is strongly motivated and stimulated by interest, but the actual percepts are not directly determined by the motivation. The construction of such schemata is a necessary part of the training of aircraft spotters, radar and Asdic operators; and in a variety of industrial tasks of inspection and of grading materials.

The schemata operating in perception perform two functions: (a) They produce a condition of expectation in which the observer is not merely on the *qui vive,* but also knows what to look for—what particular sensory data to select from the incoming flood. (b) He then knows how to deal with these data—how to classify, understand, and name them, and draw from them the inferences that give the meaning to the percepts. We are sufficiently familiar with the case of the unsophisticated student who does not even see the minute details of, for instance, biological specimens, from which the expert can derive the most important information. An interesting study of such cases by Johnson (16) demonstrated the manner in which students could be directed to observe the essential points of specimens, etc. seen under the microscope, which they had hitherto overlooked, and not to make incorrect inferences about them. Another instructive example of this phenomenon occurred in an experiment by Fox (11), who showed pictures of armor to students, and required them afterwards to report what they remembered of the pictures. He found that if he gave the students some preliminary instruction on technical details, and if they thoroughly understood and assimilated this information, then subsequent performance was superior to that of the uninstructed. But if, on the other hand, they did not fully assimilate the instruction—that is to say, it had not been fully absorbed and schematized—then it did not assist them at all, but merely confused them.

Now it might be argued that such highly skilled perceptual tasks were characteristic only of the expert, and had little relationship to the perceptions of ordinary everyday life. The distinction seems to be one of degree rather than of kind. It was pointed out above that young children were, in general, intensely interested in and curious about the external world and the objects and events within it. It is not probable that for many of them the same features of the environment are important and interesting, and that therefore they build up similar schemata on which to base their subsequent perceptions? Thus Piaget has described the development of schematized ideas and corresponding perceptions of movement (29), casual phenomena (27), distance and space (28), and many others. Though his observations covered only small numbers of children in one particular environment, it seems probable that all children must develop such schemata sooner or later in order to adjust themselves to the surrounding world. But insofar as their environments differ, for instance, as between town and country dwellers, then different schemata are also developed.

Such differences in individual experience also seem to operate in what is called "social perception." It is a subject too wide to discuss here in detail. But I would include in it both the ability to perceive and act upon fine shades of behavior and emotional expression in others; and also differences in the construction of percepts from given sensory characteristics. There is little doubt that particular interests and sentiments affect the ability to develop schemata for classifying and responding appropriately to what we perceive in the behavior of others. As regards the selection of particular sensory data, it appeared in the experiments of Marks (24) that individuals with pro-Negro sentiments had developed schemata which enabled them to perceive and remember in greater detail than those without those sentiments the characteristic facial differences between different Negroes. In the experiment of Seeleman (41), Negroes themselves seemed to have established schematized scales of facial color, which in part determined the estimates of color which they made in the experiment.

It is possible that some long-term schema based upon the interests of a particular social class was operating to cause the overestimation of size of the more valuable coins in the famous experiment of Bruner and Goodman (6). However, the dust of controversy has not settled upon the methods and results of this experiment. It seems fairly certain that, as in the experiments described by Ansbacher (1) and Postman and Page (37), there was an inability to isolate a single aspect from a global percept. But one would need to know more about the poor children to decide why their overestimation was greater than that of the well-to-do.

However, in these and other cases the schemata were very complex, and the factors which brought different schemata into operation from moment to moment are obscure. Although it seems probable that in prolonged and continuous perceptual activity, highly developed and motivated schemata will tend to operate, it can by no means be assumed that any particular schema will function at any particular moment, particularly in somewhat ambiguous and indeterminate situations. In some experiments, such as those on tachistoscopic perception, there may be nothing to inform the observer as to which, if any, of his schemata are appropriate to the particular material presented to him. In such circumstances, schematic determination of the perceptual response may be weak and unclear; no one schema can function very effectively, and the observer may be quite uncertain what to look for and to select from the visual field. He is then prone to develop, as a reaction to the experimental situation, a cognitive "set" which causes him to expect and hence to perceive the type of material indicated by the instructions or the conditions of the experiment. Thus in one experiment (43), I presented tachistoscopically to a number of airmen a series of rather bizarre pictures, terminating in a simple picture of an airman in a cockpit. Several of them failed to recognize the picture, and it seemed that this failure was due to a set established by the preceding pictures to perceive "something queer." In this situation they had no reason to suppose that any particular schema, for instance one related to their professional interests, would be appropriate; thus their perceptions were determined by the short-term cognitive set. Of course, had this type of situation been indefinitely repeated, and had they been satisfied that their responses were appropriate to the situation, the set might in time have developed into a schema related to this situation. Such schemata, as was noted above, may be built up by observers who have had prolonged training and experience in experiments on sensory qualities.

We may now proceed to examine some of the experiments which have purported to demonstrate the direct effects of short-term need states upon perception. It must be noted that in many of these experiments, also, there may have been no schema available to direct, in a clear and unambiguous manner, the observer's expectations of what would appear, or his selection from the sensory data presented. But, indeed, in some of these experiments it hardly seems that we are dealing with perception based upon external stimulation; but rather with the projection of internal imagery upon the external situation. The latter process appears to have occurred in the experiments of Levine, Chein, and Murphy (21) and of McClelland and Atkinson (22) on the reporting of "food objects" by hungry observers in response to subliminal stimulation, or to no stimulation at all. Yet Postman and Crutchfield (36) have since shown that even a temporary cognitive set established by instructions to expect to see words connected with food was more effective in stimulating the perception of such words than was actual hunger. After all, why should a hungry individual expect to see words connected with food, or even pictures of food, in a tachisto-scope? Why should he wish to do so? But there is nothing to be gained by confusing processes which are initiated by sensory stimulation with those for which there is no known sensory basis. This applies also to the Rorschach responses, for instance, which consist of imagery that the observer himself can differentiate from the immediate percepts (cf. data reported in the chapter by Dennis in Blake and Ramsey, 5). Indeed, it is probably true of all situations in which the sensory data are so scanty that the individual is forced to construct something imaginatively. Even if it is impossible to draw a hard and fast line between these situations and those of normal everyday perception, it is still undesirable to extend conclusions based upon the former to cover the latter also.

In many of the genuine perceptual experiments employing the perception of words, it appears that perception was determined by the long-term schemata which direct this extremely subtle and highly skilled activity. In particular, the effect of familiarity, a function of these schemata, is always great. No accurate compensation for individual differences in familiarity can be provided by the use of the Thorndike-Lorge word count, since highly educated individuals vary greatly in their familiarity with the more uncommon words, and it is impossible to measure this variation. Familiarity, however, is probably at least in part a function of schemata built up in accordance with individual interests. The individual develops particular sets of ideas, and words to express them, which are related to his interests. This indeed appeared in the experiments of Postman, Bruner, and McGinnies (35) and of Postman and Schneider (38). Here the tendency was for observers to perceive most readily words, and especially unusual words, which were related to their prevailing interests.

In another type of experiment, for instance, those of Verville (45) and of Verville and Cameron (46), the observer's ability to perceive incomplete pictures appeared to be inhibited as the result of certain frustrating experiences which they had received not long before. The same effect upon the reading of words was demonstrated by Postman and Bruner (34). It seems probable that in these experiments the observer became accustomed to the occurrence of a task which was too difficult for him to accomplish, and in most cases resigned himself to failure. However, Eriksen (10) reported that observers who forgot their previous failures were slower than those who did not, to perceive words which were likely to affect them emotionally—those to which they gave a long reaction time in a free association test. Thus it may be that in some cases an experience of failure may stimulate the observer and set up an increased concentration of attention.

But most of the experiments on the so-called "perceptual defense" have probably been affected by differences in familiarity with the "taboo" words presented. Again the Thorndike-Lorge word count seems singularly inadequate for equating the familiarity of these words with the familiarity of the "neutral" control words. Familiar acquaintance with "rude" words, the readiness to report them without hesitation, and the whole complex of emotions tied up with them, are likely to vary enormously among different individuals. Indeed, considerable variability in these respects was indicated in the experiments of Bruner and Postman (7) and of Cowen and Beier (8); though Bruner and Postman provided a control on individual differences by measuring the reaction times in free association. That many of the observers did dislike saying the taboo words out loud was clearly shown in the comments quoted by Bitterman and Kniffin (4) of observers whose susceptibilities had obviously been outraged! However, it seems that this effect wore off as the observers became accustomed to the situation, according to the results of Lacy, Lewinger, and Adamson (19). That it could be removed by allowing the observers to write the words, and by giving them special instructions to do so, appeared from the experiment of Postman and Gropper (32). Once these difficulties had been overcome it seemed that, in general, the taboo words were perceived *more* easily than the neutral words, rather than more slowly, as McGinnies (23) originally suggested. Thus it may be that in certain circumstances the ease of perception may be increased by emotional excitement. However, the conclusions drawn from these experiments are of doubtful import, because of the effects of differences in familiarity; and the same may also be true of experiments carried out with pictures, such as those of Eriksen (9). It would be difficult to conclude that these emotional factors determined the actual nature of what was perceived.

We come now to experiments in which it did appear that what the observers perceived was in part a function of motivation set up during the experiment. In the experiments of Proshansky and Murphy (39) and of Schafer and Murphy (40) the observers were found to accentuate certain aspects of what they perceived and to reject others, insofar as the former were presented in conjunction with a "reward," and the latter in conjunction with a "punishment." For the reward money was given them; and for the punishment the money was taken away from them. The experimenters satisfied themselves that the observers did not become consciously aware of the connection between the particular aspects of the field, and the reward or punishment, so that they did not deliberately choose the former and reject the latter. But it is important to note that in the experiment of Schafer and Murphy, the rewarded aspect was favored by contrast with the punished only over a limited period. After about sixteen responses, the observers developed cognitive sets based upon the nature of the experimental material, which thereafter completely determined what they perceived and eliminated the effects of the reward and punishment. Thus, in these experiments the reward and punishment situation did for a time affect the observers' selection of certain aspects of the field. But the effects were apparently unstable; and there was a tendency for the observer to develop a cognitive set which was more stable and effective. This result parallels that of Postman and Crutchfield (36) with the food words. Haggard and Rose (14) tried to show that the amount of additional activity carried out by the observer in connection with his perceptual activity was also a factor of importance; and it may be that such activity would be related to the establishment of sets. But the evidence was obtained from experiments on the "auto-kinetic effect," a phenomenon which cannot be termed wholly perceptual since it is at least partly illusory.

Stronger evidence of the direct effect of motivation upon perception is given by the experiment of Postman and Brown (33). They found that observers who had been told that they had "succeeded" (surpassed their level of aspiration) in certain tasks were relatively quicker than those told they had "failed" (fallen short of their level of aspiration) to perceive words related to success (excellent, succeed, perfection, winner); whereas those told they had failed were quicker than those told they had succeeded to perceive words related to failure (failure, unable, defeat, obstacle). Here it seems unlikely that the results could be attributed to differences in familiarity with the different words. Moreover, the experiences of success and failure were set up in the experimental situation and did not reflect any inherent individual tendencies to optimism or defeatism. There is at present no evidence as to how this effect upon ease of reading these particular words would compare in extent or permanence with that of a cognitive set or established schema. But the motivation had at least a temporary effect upon the observer's selection from the sensory data supplied to him.

The fundamental criticism of the experiments designed to show the direct effects of motivation upon perception is that they do not appear to take into account what this motivation might make the observer expect to see. As we have noted, in situations closely linked to an established interest, and those in which the observer received some specific training, he is on the lookout for certain aspects of the field of view and thus perceives them readily. But in the experimental situations, he may not know what to expect; and he has no reason, in most cases, to expect that anything related to the satisfaction of his needs will appear. Thus sets are readily established by the experimental conditions to perceive certain phenomena which are stressed by these conditions. To determine more clearly the effect of motivation, further thought and experiment are required to work out what are the aspects of a complex perceptual field which an observer in a state of unsatisfied need might look for and select. It may then appear that those features are the ones which have become schematically related to the need state and to the behavioral responses to the field which tend to satisfy the need.

CONCLUSIONS

It is true that we cannot at the moment predict the exact mode of operation of the schemata of any given individual in any particular set of circumstances. Neither can we hypothesize as to their neurological basis; although Oldfield (25) has recently advanced a suggestion as to how they might be explained in terms of the circuital storage devices of modern computing machines. But even in default of such an explanation, I would argue that the concept of schemata and their functions is of value in systematizing the following observations:

1. Percepts of the surrounding world, the objects it contains and their interrelationships, are not infinitely variable, sporadic, and inconsistent. Neither do the percepts vary in a one-to-one relationship with the sensory impression produced by external stimulation, although there is obviously a close correspondence.

2. Percepts are consistent; they have a continuity of meaning and make sense. The meaning and the sense are established by the coordinated knowledge of the observer about the external world and its happenings, and about the types of behavior appropriate and satisfactory in different perceived situations.

3. The percepts of different observers of the same situation may in certain circumstances differ greatly from one another. But these variations do not appear to be purely random ones; there is some correspondence between the modes of perceiving of any given observer. Different observers have built up different schemata in accordance with their differing individual experience and the interests which lead them to seek this experience. Their expectations and their selection of what they perceive are in part determined schematically. But far more experimental evidence is required to work out these relationships in detail; evidence which must be obtained by a careful study of individual cases, their particular knowledge and interests.

4. In many of the experiments on perception, the observer is presented with a situation in which his existent schemata cannot operate freely, nor tell him what to look for. The sensory data are transient or ambiguous, and cannot be readily fitted into existing categories of experience. In these circumstances, the observer is rather readily influenced by short-term cognitive sets based upon the actual conditions of the experiment. In suitable conditions, such sets may ultimately develop into long-term schemata. His perceptions may also be affected by temporary need states, though I have argued that these effects have not been as clearly established as some experimenters have maintained. Particularly, we have little evidence as to what an observer in such states of need might look for or wish to perceive in any particular experimental situation. It is therefore

difficult to draw any conclusions from these experiments which throw light on the fundamental relations between perception and motivation. In contrast, in the perceptions of everyday life, schemata established by previous experiences are available to direct us in perceiving certain aspects of the environment and reacting to them appropriately. It would, therefore, be most valuable to study the consistent modes of perceptual behavior which are shown by different individuals in situations more like those of everyday life than the situations encountered in so many perceptual experiments.

REFERENCES

1. ANSBACHER, H. Perception of Number as Affected by the Monetary Value of Objects. *Arch. Psychol., N. Y.,* 1937, No. 215.
2. ASCH, S. E. *Social Psychology.* New York: Prentice-Hall, 1952.
3. BARTLETT, F. C. *Remembering.* Cambridge, England: Cambridge University Press, 1932.
4. BITTERMAN, M. E., & KNIFFIN, C. W. Manifest Anxiety and Perceptual Defense. *J. Abnorm. Soc. Psychol.,* 1953, *48,* 248–252.
5. BLAKE, R. R., & RAMSEY, G. V. *Perception: An Approach to Personality.* New York; Ronald, 1951.
6. BRUNER, J. S., & GOODMAN, C. C. Value and Need as Organizing Factors in Perception. *J. Abnorm. Soc. Psychol.,* 1947, *42,* 33–44.
7. BRUNER, J. S., & POSTMAN, L. Emotional Selectivity in Perception and Reaction. *J. Pers.,* 1947, *16,* 69–77.
8. COWEN, E. L., & BEIER, E. G. The Influence of Threat Expectancy on Perception. *J. Pers.,* 1950, *19,* 85–94.
9. ERIKSEN, C. W. Perceptual Defense as a Function of Unacceptable Needs. *J. Abnorm. Soc. Psychol.,* 1951, *46,* 557–564.
10. ERIKSEN, C. W. Defense against Ego-Threat in Memory and Perception. *J. Abnorm. Soc. Psychol.,* 1952, *47,* 230–235.
11. FOX, C. A Study in Pre-Perception. *Brit. J. Psychol.,* 1924, *15,* 1–16.
12. GIBSON, J. J. *The Perception of the Visual World.* Boston: Houghton Mifflin, 1950.
13. GIBSON, J. J. What Is Form? *Psychol. Rev.,* 1951, *58,* 403–412.
14. HAGGARD, E. A., & ROSE, G. J. Some Effects of Mental Set and Active Participation in the Conditioning of the Autokinetic Phenomenon. *J. Exp. Psychol.,* 1944, *34,* 45–59.
15. ITTELSON, W. H. Size as a Cue to Distance: Radial Motion. *Amer. J. Psychol.,* 1951, *64,* 188–202.
16. JOHNSON, M. L. Discussion Methods in Pre-Clinical Teaching. *Lancet,* 1950, *259,* 313–317.
17. JOYNSON, R. B. The Problem of Size and Distance. *Quart. J. Exp. Psychol.,* 1949, *1,* 119–135.
18. KOFFKA, K. *Principles of Gestalt Psychology.* London: Kegan Paul, 1935.

19. LACY, O. W., LEWINGER, N., & ADAMSON, J. F. Foreknowledge as a Factor Affecting Perceptual Defense and Alertness. *J. Exp. Psychol.*, 1953, *45,* 169–174.

20. LANGDON, J. Further Studies in the Perception of a Changing Shape. *Quart. J. Exp. Psychol.*, 1953, *5,* 89–107.

21. LEVINE, R., CHEIN, I., & MURPHY, G. The Relation of Intensity of a Need to the Amount of Perceptual Distortion. *J. Psychol,* 1942, *13,* 283–293.

22. MCCLELLAND, D. C., & ATKINSON, J. W. The Projective Expression of Needs. I. The Effect of Different Intensities of the Hunger Drive on Perception. *J. Psychol,* 1948, *25,* 205–222.

23. MCGINNIES, E. Emotionality and Perceptual Defense. *Psychol. Rev.,* 1949, *56,* 244–251.

24. MARKS, E. S. Skin Color Judgments of Negro College Students. *J. Abnorm. Soc. Psychol.,* 1943, *38,* 370–376.

26. OLDFIELD, R. C., & ZANGWILL, O. L. Head's Concept of the Schema and its Application in Contemporary British Psychology. Part I. Head's Concept of the Schema. Part II. Critical Analysis of Head's Theory. Part III. Bartlett's Theory of Memory. Part IV. Wolters' Theory of Thinking. *Brit. J. Psychol.,* 1942, *32,* 267–286; *33,* 58–64; 113–129; 1943, *33,* 143–149.

27. PIAGET, J. *La Construction du Réel Chez l'Enfant.* Neuchâtel: Delachaux et Niestlé, 1937.

28. PIAGET, J. *La Formation du Symbole Chez l'Enfant.* Neuchâtel: Delachaux et Niestlé, 1945.

29. PIAGET, J. *Les Notions de Mouvement et de la Vitesse Chez l'Enfant.* Paris: Presses Universitaires de France, 1946.

30. PIAGET, J., & LAMBERCIER, M. La Comparaison des Grandeurs Projectives Chez l'Enfant et Chez l'Adulte. *Arch. de Psychol.,* 1951, *33,* 81–130.

31. POSTMAN, L. Perception, Motivation and Behavior. *J. Pers.,* 1953, *22,* 17–31.

32. POSTMAN, L., BRONSON, W. C., & GROPPER, G. L. Is There a Mechanism of Perceptual Defense? *J. Abnorm. Soc. Psychol.,* 1953, *48,* 215–224.

33. POSTMAN, L. & BROWN, D. R. The Perceptual Consequences of Success and Failure. *J. Abnorm. Soc. Psychol.,* 1952, *47,* 213–221.

34. POSTMAN, L., & BRUNER, J. S. Perception under Stress. *Psychol. Rev.,* 1948, *55,* 314–323.

35. POSTMAN, L., BRUNER, J. S., & MCGINNIES, E. Personal Values as Selective Factors in Perception. *J. Abnorm. Soc. Psychol.,* 1948, *43,* 142–154.

36. POSTMAN, L., & CRUTCHFIELD, R. S. The Interaction of Need Set and Stimulus Structure in a Cognitive Task. *Amer. J. Psychol.,* 1952, *65,* 196–217.

37. POSTMAN, L., & PAGE R. Retroactive Inhibition and Psychophysical Judgment. *Amer. J. Psychol.,* 1947, *60,* 367–377.

38. POSTMAN, L., & SCHNEIDER, B. H. Personal Values, Visual Recognition and Recall. *Psychol. Rev.,* 1951, *58,* 271–284.

39. PROSHANSKY, H., & MURPHY, G. The Effects of Reward and Punishment on Perception. *J. Psychol,* 1942, *13,* 295–305.

40. SCHAFER, R., & MURPHY, G. The Role of Autism in a Visual Figure-Ground Relationship. *J. Exp. Psychol.,* 1943, *32,* 335–343.

41. SEELEMAN, V. The Influence of Attitude upon the Remembering of Pictorial Material. *Arch. Psychol., N. Y.,* 1940, No. 258.

42. THOULESS, R. H. Individual Differences in Phenomenal Regression. *Brit. J. Psychol.,* 1932, *22,* 216–241.
43. VERNON, M. D. Different Types of Perceptual Ability. *Brit. J. Psychol.,* 1947, *38,* 79–89.
44. VERNON, M. D. *A Further Study of Visual Perception.* New York: Cambridge University Press, 1952.
45. VERVILLE, E. The Effect of Emotional and Motivational Sets on the Perception of Incomplete Pictures. *J. Genet. Psychol,* 1946, *69,* 133–145.
46. VERVILLE, E., & CAMERON, N. Age and Sex Differences in the Perception of Incomplete Pictures by Adults. *J. Genet. Psychol.,* 1946, *68,* 149–157.
47. WALLACH, H. Brightness Constancy and the Nature of Achromatic Colors. *J. Exp. Psychol.,* 1948, *38,* 310–324.

3

BIAS IN POSTDICTION
FROM PROJECTIVE TESTS[1]
WILLIAM F. SOSKIN

One could hardly doubt, if he approached psychology as a matter of the study of constructs, that clinical psychologists also develop constructs. Soskin's paper examines the origin and nature of the clinical psychologist's construct systems, and their development and use. First, it is obvious that one's personal constructs will have considerable influence on how the external world is "shaped." Second, we see that the personal constructs derive from one's reference groups and the authority associated with those groups. Third, in ambiguous situations, the stimulus situation is interpreted in a way that makes it consistent with the individual's total construct system. To the subjects in this study, who are persons who hope to become, or have become, experts on "mental illness," the stimulus situation becomes consistent with the view of the subjects that they can identify "mental illness" in places where others would tend to see "health." It requires intense training, they seem to say, to put aside naive impressions of the nature of behavior and to see the pathology that is hidden under every act. Could "pathology" be an equally naive dimension? For our purposes, this study nicely illustrates that the central variable to be studied, even when we are studying psychologists, is the person's construct system.

*   *   *

In a preceding investigation (1, 2) an effort was made to study the rater bias or set found in personality appraisals based on projective tests and other types of personal documents by comparing such appraisals with others based on more extensive information and observation. In this

Reprinted from Journal of Abnormal and Social Psychology, *1954, 49, 69–74, by permission of the author and the American Psychological Association.*
   [1]Grateful acknowledgement is hereby expressed to Drs. William E. Henry and Donald W. Fiske at the University of Chicago, Dr. E. L. Kelly at the University of Michigan, and Dr. Julian Pathman of Downey Veterans Administration Hospital, Downey, Illinois, for obtaining the participation of the several groups involved in this study.

earlier study the criterion consisted of a series of trait ratings arrived at be a three-man team after five days of study of the individual through objective and projective tests, interviews, various personal documents, and observations of behavior in standard situations. However, inasmuch as the criterion ratings consisted of a series of judgments of traits, i.e., of certain abstractions currently familiar in personality studies, the validity of the appraisals which were investigated and pointed out to be a "relative validity" contingent upon the validity of the judgments of the team making the criterion ratings. Since the consensus of "experts" may or may not correlate satisfactorily with an external criterion of validity, an effort was made to conduct an analogous investigation in which the appraisals could be evaluated against a more rigorous criterion, viz., a criterion test dealing more directly with specific behaviors of the subject which had occurred in the past rather than with the appraisal of so-called traits. The present report deals with this effort.

METHOD

Criterion test. As the criterion for this study a post-diction test was constructed consisting of an array of multiple-choice items which were built primarily around incidents known to have happened in the recent past history of a single subject *(S)*, hereafter called "Linda." Although the majority of items concerned specific situational behaviors, some items were developed from commonly shared characterizations of *S* provided by several intimate acquaintances. Several examples of the items are:

4. In the immediate neighborhood she *(a)* has a wide circle of casual friends who frequently "drop in"; *(b)* is the confidant of several young mothers; *(c)* has one intimate friend, and has only fleeting contacts with others; *(d)* is considered a gossip, hence not too popular.

5. As a housekeeper she is *(a)* meticulous and tidy, rather intolerant of toys, clothes, etc. not in their proper places; *(b)* rather untidy—doing about as much as needs to be done; *(c)* spends a considerable amount of time adding new feminine touches to the interior; *(d)* so incompetent that on two occasions neighbors have complained to the Board of Health.

8. Last summer the family went on a long trip to visit Linda's parents-in-law. Linda *(a)* was rather excited about the trip since she likes her husband's parents better than her own parents; *(b)* privately felt a little bitter about spending the money this way, when it would be no vacation for her to have to take care of the children as usual; *(c)* was opposed to taking the trip because the money would have to be taken out of savings they were accumulating to buy a house; *(d)* induced her husband to fly instead of driving—to get the maximum thrill out of the trip.

The information on which these items are based was collected in the following manner:

Through friends with contacts in social circles different from his own, the investigator obtained a list of several persons previously unknown to him but judged by these informants as likely candidates for this type of investigation. The S, was the first and only one contacted from this list. After the nature of the project had been carefully explained to both the S and her husband, the investigator conducted three private interviews with S, each lasting one and one-half to two hours. The interviews were not unlike those carried on in the initial stages of psychotherapy. The S was given maximum freedom to talk about her present, her past, etc.; the interviewer only occasionally interposed a question when it seemed that certain areas might not be touched on spontaneously. During the same interval of several weeks the investigator also interviewed privately the husband and several of S's closest friends. The latter informants, persons in virtually daily contact with S were designated by S herself upon request of the investigator.

From the information gathered in this total of approximately 15 to 20 hours of interviewing three general types of questions were developed: *(a)* items involving factual material reported by S, e.g., that she attended college for a specified period of time; *(b)* items involving S's expressed attitudes and feelings, e.g., that she was never very close to her mother and that even today she feels her mother's relation to her is an exploitative one; *(c)* items in which S met a certain situation in a manner that was presumed to be fairly characteristic of her. The material for these latter items was taken largely from situations reported spontaneously and independently by several informants. The material thus collected was developed into multiple-choice items of the type shown above, the three distractor alternatives in each instance being sheer inventions designed to present a range of plausible choices suitable to the item under consideration.

After the first interview Linda was given the Rorschach and the TAT, both administered by the interviewer. The verbatim record of the 20 TAT stories of the adult female series was duplicated so that each judge had his own copy. Similarly the Rorschach was reproduced in detail along with an appropriately marked location chart. This report is primarily concerned with postdictions based on the blind interpretation of these protocols.

Clinical judges. The Linda test, consisting of 24-multiple-choice items, was administered to three different groups. The first, hereafter referred to as Group N or "novices," consisted initially of 42 graduate students taking their first course in TAT interpretation, a one-quarter, regularly scheduled graduate course which met for 12 two-hour sessions. This group worked only with the TAT. Group E_{Stereo} consisted of 12 advanced trainees and three supervisory-level clinical psychologists; Group E_{Proj} consisted of three advanced trainees at a large mental hospital and two supervising psychologists in the hospital's diagnostic service. Individuals in the E groups had from two to five or more years of experience in use of projective tests, whereas the majority of students in Group N had no previous experience or training in the use of projective tests.

Procedure for Group N. At the conclusion of the second meeting of the introductory TAT course Group N was given a general explanation of the nature of the investigation, i.e., that it concerned a study of postdiction of specific behaviors by means of blind interpretation of projective devices. Then copies of the Linda test were circulated and student judges were provided the following basic information about S: that she had had some college training, that her father was a moderately successful businessman, that she was a white married woman, 26 years of age, mother of two children, etc. This information, incidentally, with the exception of her age, was also stated as facts contained in the headings of one or another of the test items. Given only this basic information (*before* they were permitted to see Linda's TAT protocol), the judges were asked to study the entire postdiction test carefully and to try to guess the correct answers. The purpose of this procedure was threefold: *(a)* to have every individual thoroughly familiar with the specific postdictions he would be called on to make after studying the TAT, *(b)* to determine this group's pretest stereotype for a person like Linda, and *(c)* to obtain from the stereotype profile an additional base besides the true answers against which to evaluate the postdictions.

After completing the stereotype scoring (hereafter called stage S), judges were given the TAT protocol and asked to rescore the postdiction test after careful study of the TAT. (This stage is hereafter referred to as T-1.) Neither the judges nor the instructor of the course was given any information about the true answers at any stage of the investigation. At the conclusion of the course the test was administered once more, although this time no pretest stereotype was asked for. (This stage is hereafter referred to as T-2.)

Procedure for E Group. Group E_{Proj} participants took the test individually. No attempt was made to determine the stereotype of this group. Each person who volunteered to participate in the investigation was provided with a packet of materials which included *(a)* a copy of the Linda test, *(b)* a sealed envelope containing the Rorschach protocol, summary, location chart, and a standard IBM answer sheet, and *(c)* a second sealed envelope containing a typed copy of the 20 TAT stories, and a second answer sheet.

Judges were provided with both written and oral directions explaining that they were first to answer the Linda test on the basis of the Rorschach alone. Then, after returning their answer sheets to the supervisor they were to open the second envelope, study the TAT protocol, and complete the test a second time using the combined resources of the Rorschach and TAT.

Judges were permitted to do this work on paid time, and those who cared to do so were invited to code their answer sheets so the test scores could be made available at a later time.

Group E_{Stereo} had *no* projective test data; they were provided only with the basic information initially available to Group N, and were asked to guess the correct answers.

RESULTS

The procedure followed with Group N yielded three different sets of scores, one for each of the conditions under which the Linda test was taken. The first of these, stage S, was the set of answers selected when the judges were asked merely to guess the correct answers before having seen the TAT. The second, T-1, was the set of answers selected after the first exposure to Linda's TAT protocol, at the end of the second meeting of the course. The third, T-2, was the final set, the responses made at the conclusion of the course.

The general character of the performance of Group N under each condition is summarized in Table 1. For stages S and T-1 only those judges were studied who completed all items satisfactorily on both administrations. For stage T-2 only those judges were studied who completed all items on all three stages.

The comparison of before-and-after accuracy scores suggests a very slight change from the first to the third test administration; while this is undoubtedly interesting in so far as number of correct postdictions is concerned, the comparison fails to suggest at all one of the more striking findings of the investigation. As a crude measure of the amount of shift that occurred from S to T-1 to T-2, the 24 items were ranked for each stage in terms of the frequency with which the item was answered correctly. The rho for each of the several combinations is reported in Table 2, where it will be seen that the relative difficulty of items in the pre-TAT stage (S) is negatively correlated with the relative difficulty of these same items in the two post-TAT stages (T-1 and T-2). From inspection of the data it is evident that items which were correctly answered by a considerable number of judges on the basis of only basic information were less often answered correctly when the TAT was made available; conversely, those items most often answered correctly with the aid of the TAT were relatively difficult to answer correctly with the basic information

TABLE 1   Mean and Range of Scores Obtained by Group N
on Three Different Administrations of Postdiction Test.

Stage	N	Mean	Range
S	24	7.32	4–16
T-1	24	8.48	5–12
T-2	19	9.42	6–14

TABLE 2   Rho between Ranks of Postdiction Test Items
Ordered in Terms of Difficulty at Each Stage.

Stage	Rho
S–T-1	−.23
1–T-2	−.15
T-1–T-2	.90

alone. The negative correlation between S on the one hand and T-1 and T-2 on the other suggests that a marked shift in orientation occurred after initial study of the TAT, a shift which did not alter substantially even at the conclusion of the course.

Examination of individual records helped reveal the nature of this shift. The characterization of Linda that emerged from a compilation of most-frequently-chosen alternatives under condition S suggested a pre-TAT stereotyping of Linda as a well-adjusted, fun-loving young woman, a happy wife, and a good mother. By contrast, the stereotype suggested by most-frequently-chosen alternatives in the two post-TAT administrations characterized her as severely maladjusted, an irritable, moody person, one dissatisfied with her lot both as wife and as mother, etc.

In order to obtain a better understanding of this shift, weights on an adjustment-maladjustment continuum were determined for each of the alternatives in the test. Three persons not involved in the postdiction tasks independently ranked the four alternatives for each item on the contin-uum, and the mean of the three ranks was assigned as the weight for a particular alternative. (Several items which did not lend themselves to such ranking were omitted from further consideration.) The stereotype profile for each condition, determined by computing the mean weight for each item, is presented in Figure 1. The items are arranged in terms of the mean weight assigned to the correct answer: items at the top of the figure are those for which the correct answer was judged to constitute relatively adjustive behavior; those at the bottom are items for which the correct answer was judged to constitute relatively maladjustive behavior. The fact

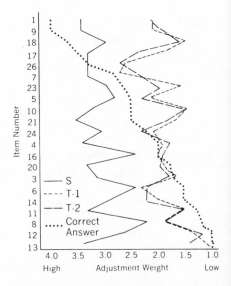

FIG. 1

Shift in group N mean by item for stages S, T-1, and T-2 when alternatives are weighted on adjustment-maladjust-ment scale.

that there is no overlap between the S profile and the profiles obtained from T-1 and T-2 is strikingly evident.

To test the significance of the shifts revealed in Figure 1, a score was determined for each judge by summing the adjustment weights assigned to each alternative he selected in the postdiction test and performing t tests between groups of judges for the several administrations of the test. Between S and T-1, $t = 2.807$ ($df = 46$); between S and T-2, $t = 3.617$ ($df = 36$). Both are significant beyond the .01 level. The t of .708 ($df = 36$) between T-1 and T-2 is not significant. It is clear that a rather marked change in stereotype developed as a consequence of exposure to the TAT protocol; in effect, the group as a whole tended to shift from a stereotype of an essentially healthy person to that of a quite maladjusted one. Furthermore, the shift was somewhat extreme within the limits permitted by the nature of the alternatives. Although Linda, as known to the investigator and to his informants, was neither perfectly adjusted nor unusually disturbed emotionally, the tendency among students was to see her first as one, then as the other.

No claim can be made for the representativeness of the items sampled. It is not known, for example, what proportion of the total of Linda's behaviors over a three- or four- month period might be judged as adjustive or maladjustive. But the items were not intentionally selected to give the balance suggested by the profile of correct answers in Figure 1. In this study all behavior or events which seemed amenable to clear statement in the form of a multiple-choice item were utilized. The weights for correct answers were not determined until after the judges' responses had been collected.

The negative rho reported in Table 2 between items ranked for difficulty under conditions S and under conditions T-1 and T-2 suggested what was verified by inspection, viz., that although mean accuracy scores changed very little before and after TAT, the items answered correctly by Group N judges under the two circumstances were by and large *different sets of items*. Under condition S, since the group initially entertained a stereotype of a well-adjusted person, they appear to have guessed correctly items for which the correct answer conformed to the stereotype and erred on those items in which the correct answer did not conform to that stereotype. Conversely, when, after studying the TAT, the group's stereotype shifted to a conception of an extremely maladjusted person and selections tended rather consistently to favor the alternative most characteristic of maladjustment, the group tended to err on those items in which, so far as is known, Linda's behavior was actually characteristic of good adjustment.

Effect of experience. To explore the possible effects of further training and experience in the use of projective techniques on ability to make accurate postdictions in this type of setting, and also to study the contributions of different kinds of projective information to postdiction, the Linda test was administered to the two E groups, persons more experienced than the students in Group N. Essentially two kinds of comparisons were desired, viz., comparison of stereotype scores and comparison of scores based on analysis of projective test data.

Unfortunately, circumstances under which the cooperation of the more experienced workers was secured did not permit for the collection from a single group of the kinds of data necessary for the two comparisons mentioned above. Rather, the stereotype data were collected from one group and the postdiction data from another. Group E_{Stereo}, as was mentioned earlier, was comprised of 12 advanced trainees in the clinical psychology program of a large Midwestern university and three supervisory-level clinical psychologists, whereas Group E_{Proj} consisted of three advanced trainees and two supervisory-level psychologists at a large mental hospital.

The stereotype was based on essentially the same procedure as that utilized with Group N. Group E_{Stereo} was given the same basic information regarding Linda's age, marital status, etc., and was then asked to read through the entire set of questions and alternatives before attempting to

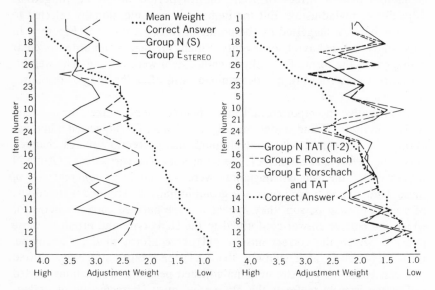

FIG. 2   *Profile of mean weight for the stereotype scores of novices (group N) and for more experienced users of projective tests (group E_{Stereo}) as compared with the profile of weighted correct answers.*

FIG. 3   *Group weighted mean by item for group N (T-2) and for group E (Rorschach) and group E (Rorschach and TAT).*

guess the answers. Scores were weighted in the manner described earlier. The comparison of weighted means for each item is presented in Figure 2 along with the stereotype curve of Group N. It is evident from the figure that the more experienced individuals—even though they had no different or additional data about her—tended at the very outset to select a higher proportion of maladjustive responses than did the novices. In 18 out of 21 items Group E_{Stereo} deviated from Group N in the direction of the maladjustive pole. By the sign test the direction of difference is significant at the .01 level. However, the t between adjustment-weight scores of the two groups is only 1.719 ($df = 37$; .05 – p – .10).

A second comparison was made between the Group N score with the TAT at the conclusion of its course of training (T-2) and the scores of Group E_{Proj} first with the Rorschach alone, then with Rorschach plus TAT. Group E_{Proj} was provided with the same basic information initially available to Group N and, in addition, had available a typed Rorschach protocol with a rather detailed inquiry and location chart, and, later, typed manuscripts of the entire 20 TAT stories.

As Table 3 indicates, there was no significant difference between mean scores of novice judges and this small sample of more experienced judges. Furthermore, two different tests were not significantly better than one test alone as aids to this type of postdiction. The group means of adjustment-weight scores for N_{T-2} and E_{R+TAT}, or between the two E_{Proj} groups are not significantly different according to t tests. This is best revealed in Figure 3 where the stereotype profiles for Group E_{Proj} using Rorschach alone and then Rorschach plus TAT are compared with the profiles obtained for Group N under condition T-2 (TAT at end of course). With minor variations, the three profiles show a striking similarity. They suggest that within the limits of variation permitted by the Linda test items, individuals with from two to five years more experience in the use of projective techniques tended, for the purpose of postdiction, to conceptualize the subject in more or less the same way as did the novices. Both Group E_{Proj} and Group N, after study of the projective devices, tended in a majority of items to pick alternatives more suggestive of maladjustment than adjustment.

TABLE 3 Comparison of Scores of Group N Using TAT and
of Group E_{Proj} Using Both Rorschach and TAT.

Group	N	Mean	Range
Group N on T-2	19	9.42	6–14
Group E_{Proj} on Rorschach	5	10.00	7–13
Group E_{Proj} on Rorschach	5	9.60	6–13

DISCUSSION

While the results are in certain respects quite clear, their limitations should be made explicit, since both the accuracy of postdictions and the tendency toward bias are here studied within the context of a difficult and somewhat uncommon task. For one thing, users of projective tests are not often called upon to postdict specific situational behaviors. Furthermore, it may be argued that projective devices of the sort employed in this study were not designed to supply the information requisite for such postdictions. Nevertheless, it would appear that neither unfamiliarity with the task, nor shortcomings in the criterion, nor claims for the specialized nature of projective devices should vitiate certain of the results. When novices and more experienced persons used the Rorschach and/or TAT as the basis for conceptualizing a subject they appear to have been predisposed to anticipate more maladjustive tendencies and, hence, in fitting this conceptualization to the alternatives of the criterion test, were led to select alternatives more indicative of maladjustment. It seems reasonable to assume that if the conceptualization were translated into a diagnostic report rather than postdictions, a similar distortion would have maintained, although in less measurable form.

Whether this tendency toward distortion is a function of the selective information conveyed by the projective instruments or is attributable to characteristics of the users of the information is not unequivocally established in this study. It might well be, for example, that novices characteristically develop distorted conceptualizations, whereas among more experienced persons some continue to be relatively undiscriminating while others gradually learn more accurately to integrate signs of adjustment with those of maladjustment. The population available for this study was too small to permit investigation of this possibility. The results indicate merely that both experts and novices are subject to this distortion.

As the foregoing implies, these results cannot be taken to indicate that there is no difference between novices and more experienced persons in their ability to use projective devices accurately. It seems sounder to assume that which is most in accord with observation, viz., that some people learn with experience while others do not, and that among more experienced users of these instruments there will be both "good" and "poor" predictors. Neither the size of the population nor the sophistication of the criterion test warrants attempting to investigate this question from the available data, however.

SUMMARY

A postdiction test consisting of 24 multiple-choice items pertaining to behaviors deemed characteristic of an adult female by the investigator and by informants well acquainted with the S was administered for comparative purposes to a group of graduate students taking their first course in TAT interpretation and to two groups of workers more experienced in the use of projective techniques. The following trends were observed:

1. Novices, at the beginning of the course, provided with only a few basic items of information such as age, race, marital status, etc., tended to characterize the S as well-adjusted.

2. Although novices held an initially favorable stereotype of S, a marked change occurred immediately after reading her TAT—before training in interpretation had begun—and the group's characterization shifted in the direction of maladjustment.

3. After completion of the training course, the novices' characterization of S remained essentially as it stood at the beginning of the course, on their first exposure to the TAT protocol, and there was no significant improvement in accuracy scores.

4. A group of more experienced users of projective techniques using either Rorschach alone or Rorschach plus TAT earned postdiction accuracy scores not significantly different from those earned by the novices at the end of their course, and showed the same tendency to postdict preponderantly maladjustive behaviors after study of the projective tests.

These results, within the limitations imposed by the particular array of test items and by the generalizability of results obtained from the study of a single person, suggest that the data of projective tests predispose toward an overestimation of maladjustive trends in postdiction situations.

REFERENCES

1. KELLY, E. L., & FISKE, D. W. *The Prediction of Performance in Clinical Psychology.* Ann Arbor: University of Michigan Press, 1951.
2. SOSKIN, W. F. *A Study of Personality Ratings Based on Brief Observation of Behavior in Standard Situations.* Unpublished doctor's dissertation, University of Michigan, 1948.

4

JUDGMENTAL PHENOMENA
AND SCALES
OF ATTITUDE MEASUREMENT[1]
CARL I. HOVLAND AND MUZAFER SHERIF

Hovland and Sherif, in their approach to the effects of a subject's internal cognitive organizations, first assess the subject's original position on the issue of accepting Negroes. Knowledge of this position allows them to predict, using their theory of judgmental processes in attitudinal functioning, other features of the subject's responses to the stimuli. Individual items on a scale of attitudes toward Negroes are viewed differently by persons who hold different personal views. Those who hold strong positions on this issue will judge "neutral" items as being extreme judgments, whereas subjects who hold moderate views will judge these same items as being neutral. In other studies Sherif and his co-workers (see Section VIII) related the findings of this study to the phenomena they describe as "assimilation" and "contrast." In psychophysical studies of judging weight, for example, where a contrasting

Reprinted from Journal of Abnormal and Social Psychology, *1952, 47, 822-832, by permission of Muzafer Sherif and the American Psychological Association.*

[1]The present study, the first of several on the topic of judgmental phenomena and scales of attitude measurement, was done as part of a coordinated program of research on opinion and attitude change being conducted at Yale under a grant from the Rockefeller Foundation to whom acknowledgement is gratefully made (cf. Hovland, C. I. Changes in attitude through communication. *J. Abnorm. Soc. Psychol.,* 1951, *46,* 424-437). The writers wish to express their appreciation to the following: Prof. E. D. Hinckley, for supplying us with the statements used in his original study; Dr. Bennett B. Murdock, Jr., for supervision of the extensive coding operation; Dr. William Bevan, Jr., for making arrangements for securing *S*s in five different Georgia colleges; O. J. Harvey, Johnnie Davis, and Charles Shedd, for assistance in the administration of schedules; Harvey Davis, for help in the preparation of the stimulus materials; Miss Lorraine Scrivenor, for assistance in tabulations; and Drs. L. W. Doob, I. L. Janis, H. H. Kelley, and F. D. Sheffield, for editorial suggestions during the preparation of the manuscript. The warm cooperation of Dean Laurence Snyder in facilitating administrative arrangements is also gratefully acknowledged.

weight was noticeably different from the rest of the judgment series, the subject would tend to compress the series toward the end of the scale in a direction away from the deviant weight. This kind of behavior is analogous to the behavior of a subject who holds an extreme position, on an attitude measurement scale, and proceeds to judge all other positions to be in extreme contrast to his own. His position acts as a deviant contrast weight. In short, this study illustrates that knowledge of the subject's existing cognitive organizations allows us to predict other features of his performance. Knowing that a person views himself as strongly accepting or strongly rejecting toward Negroes, we also know that he will categorize moderately accepting or rejecting behaviors on a polar opposite to his own behavior.

*   *   *

In his influential study *The Measurement of Attitude,* Thurstone states as a major requirement for attitude scales that the scale values of statements be independent of the position held by the judges who do the initial categorization:

> If the scale is to be regarded as valid, the scale values of the statements should not be affected by the opinions of the people who help to construct it. This may turn out to be a severe test in practice, but the scaling method must stand such a test before it can be accepted as being more than a description of the people who construct the scale. At any rate, to the extent that the present method of scale construction is affected by the opinions of the readers who help to sort out the original statements into a scale, to that extent the validity or universality of the scale may be challenged (19, p. 92).

The first research study of the Thurstone assumption was carried out by Hinckley (8) on attitudes toward Negroes. Opinion statements were categorized by two groups of white judges, one with anti-Negro attitudes and the other with pro-Negro attitudes, and by a group of Negro judges. Scale values were determined by the method of equal-appearing intervals. Hinckley found that the average scale values for the two white groups were highly correlated ($r = .98$) despite their difference in attitude of the issue and that the scale values for the anti-Negro white judges were also closely correlated with those for the Negro judges ($r = .93$). On the basis of these results Hinckley concluded that "the scale which we have constructed for measuring attitude toward the social position of the Negro is not influenced in its measuring function by the attitudes of the subjects used in the construction" (8, p. 293). Substantially similar results were obtained in a later study by Pintner and Forlano (14), who used the Attitude toward Patriotism scales which had also been derived by the method of equal-appearing intervals.

That the attitudes and opinions of the judges have no effect on the placement of items is in sharp conflict with the results of studies in the fields of perception and judgment. These studies indicate that judgments *are* greatly influenced by motivational and attitudinal factors operative at the time. Thus in studies by Asch, Block, and Hertzman (2) where subjects judged photographs, political figures, professions, and slogans along such dimensions as intelligence, honesty, and social usefulness, judgments were made "in accordance with an underlying attitude of acceptance or rejection." Other studies indicate that category intervals are directly affected by attitudinal factors. As long ago as 1914 Fernberger (7) showed that changes in attitude bring about changes in the range of judgments of equality, hence in the size of category intervals. A series of studies by Volkmann (20), Rogers (16), and McGarvey (13) showed that category intervals are caused to expand or shrink by the experimental introduction of anchoring agents beyond or within the scale and that "anchoring can be achieved by appropriate verbal instructions, without the use of anchoring stimuli" (21, p. 287).

Displacement of judgments along a scale seems a general phenomenon when the stimuli carry strong social and personal values. For example, Cartwright found that the *S*'s estimation of equivalence of statements was affected by his own position. "The size of the range of equivalence related to a 'radical' and to a 'conservative' differed, depending upon *S*'s own political attitudes" (3, p. 195). "For the radical *S*, the judgments of 'radical' extend 7.5 units while the judgments of 'conservative' extend 10 units. For the conservative *S*, on the other hand, the judgments of 'radical' extend 8.5 units, while the judgments of 'conservative' extend only 5.2 units" (3, p. 198).

In studying the response of Negro youth to the social value placed on light skin color, Johnson (10) found a tendency for self-ratings to be a shade or more lighter than they appear to the tester. This was shown even more definitively in the study by Marks (12) who matched each Negro *S*'s skin color with an objective hue. The tendency was to displace one's own coloring as much as objective fact allowed in the direction of the desired norm of light brown. A dark individual, rating himself close to average, would displace individuals lighter than himself to lighter than average categories. In contrast, a light individual would judge the majority of the group as dark. While the relative position of each *S* is kept the same by different raters, the absolute position varies from rater to rater.

It is interesting to note that in Cartwright's study the *S*s were more discriminating in accepting items at their own end of the scale, and lumped together items at the extreme opposite to their own stand, while in the study of Marks the displacements of items (skin color) were in the direction of the desired skin color. It is apparent that the direction of item displacement will depend upon both the stimulus material and the *S*'s motivation in relation to it.

More recently Hinckley himself, in collaboration with Rethlingshafer, added further substantiating evidence of the effect of the judge's own attitude upon his judgments. Starting with the general assumption that "men judging heights of men on a scale of short to tall would be influenced in their scale of values by their own heights" (9, p. 257), these investigators found that "the judgment of the average height of all men is influenced by the height of the man making the judgment. The 'meaning' of the social value terms of 'short' and 'tall' is in part determined by the height of the judge. The 'egocentric' influence is also controlled by the objective facts, particularly in judging the extreme heights" (9, p. 262).

Thus we have the paradox that some leading texts in social psychology say in the chapter on perception and judgment that judgments are greatly affected by the individual's attitudes and motives, while in the chapter on scaling methods they state that judgments of the meaning of items are unaffected by the position of the judges who do the sorting. Analysis of prior attitude scale studies suggests a possible explanation for the discrepancy: the utilization of too narrow a range of individuals, with the consequent elimination of the extreme Ss who would show variation and displacement of judgments most clearly. In the Pintner and Forlano study, the question may be raised as to whether intense personal involvement was achieved on the issue of patriotism during the thirties, and the authors report that "No group could be called unpatriotic" (14, p. 41). In the Hinckley study (8), on the other hand, considerable personal involvement in the issue would be expected, particularly on the part of the Negro judges. But the report suggests that here again the range may have been unintentionally narrowed by the procedure he intended only to eliminate "careless" subjects:

> One tendency which revealed itself in the sorting of the subjects was the bunching of statements in one or more piles to the apparent detriment of the other piles. This phenomenon of bunching at the extremes was noticed in the case of *certain* of the *white subjects,* but was *especially noticeable* in the Negro subjects. Since the 114 statements are distributed with fair uniformity over the entire scale, *marked bunching is a sign of careless sorting.* If more than a fourth of the statements are assigned to any one pile, it will leave less than three-fourths to distribute over the remaining ten piles. Furthermore, the individual who sorts the statements in this fashion often ignores some of the piles completely. *On the assumption that this bunching was due to poor discrimination and carelessness every case having 30 or more statements in any one pile was automatically eliminated from consideration, and the results were not recorded* (8, p. 283).[2]

From the studies of judgment cited above it would be predicted that this piling up of statements in certain categories by some of the white Ss and,

[2] Italics ours.

in a more noticeable way, by the Negro *S*s may be due to the effect of the *S*s' strong attitudes on the topic. It may be that by eliminating these *S*s the investigator eliminated, at the same time, those who had the most accentuated attitudes on the issue. It is interesting, in connection with this hypothesis, that even after all *S*s placing 30 or more statements in any category were eliminated, there was still "a slight tendency for Group I which is prejudiced against the Negro, to judge a given statement to be more favorable to the Negro than Group II [favorable to the Negro] judged it" (8, p. 293).

PROBLEM

The previous studies of the Thurstone scale do not appear to the writers to have fully settled the issue of whether or not scale values are affected by the attitude of the judges, since there does not appear to be sufficient evidence that adequate representation was made of *S*s at the extremes, with intense involvement in the issues being judged. We were, therefore, interested in reinvestigating the problem under conditions which would provide the maximum opportunity for the operation of the types of factors which have been found important in the field of perception and judgment. It is hoped that such a study will be a contribution to a *rapprochement* between the areas of judgment and of attitude measurement.

Accordingly, the Hinckley experiment was duplicated using attitudes toward Negroes, but with means of insuring that the Negro and pro-Negro white judges were not selected in any way which might exclude those with the strongest attitudes on the issue, as we thought possible with the Hinckley procedure of eliminating individuals who placed 30 or more items in any one category. Moreover, checks were incorporated to evaluate his inference that such individuals were "careless."

On the assumption that the set of 114 statements used by Hinckley represents a wide range of positions, with some clearly *pro* and others clearly *con,* and that a large number are of a neutral character, a favorable situation exists for studying how internal factors such as motives and attitudes affect the placement of the rather unstructured and ambiguous middle-position statements. The literature on judgment and perception cited earlier clearly suggests the general hypothesis that the position of a judge on an issue in which he has strong personal involvement will constitute an "anchor" for his judgments, whether or not his attitude is specifically called for in the instructions. The specific hypotheses for the present study may be stated in summary form as follows:[3]

I. Judges with extremely pro or con attitudes will show a tendency to concentrate their placement of items into a small number of categories.

II. Judges with an extreme position and strong personal involvement will be highly discriminating in accepting items at their own end of the scale. They will correspondingly display a strong tendency to lump together statements at the end of the scale which they reject. The former tendency can be described as a raised *threshold of acceptance* and the latter as a lowered *threshold for rejection*.

III. A greater degree of displacement will occur for the "neutral" items and a smaller degree for the sharply defined pro and con statements at the extremes.

In less technical terminology these hypotheses state that individuals with strong personal involvement will tend to see issues pretty much "in all black or white" rather than with fine distinctions, and that statements even mildly critical of their position will be judged to be more hostile by them than by more neutral individuals.

METHOD

Procedure. The problem presented above requires a design satisfying the following: *(a)* a topic which has strong personal involvement for Ss chosen to represent the *pro* or *con* stand on the issue, *(b)* clear differentiation of Ss with respect to their position on the issue, *(c)* administration of the judging task without giving any hints that an attitude study is involved, and *(d)* checks to determine whether heavy concentration of statements in any category is due to "carelessness." For these reasons, the Attitude Toward Negro scale was considered to be the most appropriate topic, and through the kindness of Professor Hinckley we were able to secure the original 114 statements he used concerning the social position of Negroes. These statements had been selected to include the entire range from very favorable to very unfavorable on the issue and to be distributed in a fairly representative way over the range.

[3]These hypotheses are formulated in relation to the placement of items in categories along a scale prescribed by the experimenter. Such scales and categories may be referred to as "imposed" scales and "imposed" categories. We have also extended these hypotheses by allowing each S to define his own scale by choosing the number of categories he personally considered necessary to distinguish the different positions in the issue. Results using these methods, obtained in conjunction with the present experiment, will be reported in a separate paper.

Studies in addition to those already cited which bear on our hypotheses include 1, 4, 11, 15 and 17.

The prime consideration in each step of the procedure was that all means be taken to insure careful and uniform administration to relatively small groups of Ss in each session and to be certain that Ss understood the instructions at each point. In every case the experiment was administered by graduate assistants who had been thoroughly briefed concerning the procedure, who had themselves carried out the instructions under close supervision, and who had in most cases practiced the procedure on a trial group. A special point was made to select administrators who would appear to Ss to be "one of them." The groups were kept small in number whenever possible in order that administrators could easily but unobtrusively observe Ss while instructions were being carried out. On the whole the sorting was administered in large rooms, chiefly in laboratory space, in order to give each S ample room to spread out the statements before him.

Categorization of items. The first task for the Ss consisted of sorting the statements into piles. Each of the 114 statements was mimeographed on a 3×5 in. card. To facilitate later tabulation, an arbitrary code number unrelated to the content of the item was assigned to each statement and stamped on the back of the card. No S asked a question concerning any possible connection between the statement and the code number. As a further precaution, the cards were shuffled beforehand so that S would not be able to get an idea about the exact number of statements. It was thought that the knowledge of the exact number of statements might tempt him to divide the total number of cards by the number of categories to give him a fixed guide for the number to be assigned to each category.

Deliberately, no mention of attitude measurement was introduced in the instructions until the sorting phase was completed. It was only after sorting was completed by S that instructions aiming to tap his attitude on the issue were introduced. To insure this, the instructions pertaining to sorting and those requiring the checking of S's particular stand on the issue were put on different sheets, and those relating to the attitudinal aspect were not passed out until the sortings were completed. This temporal sequence was employed in line with our basic hypothesis that, whether or not the attitude of Ss was explicitly activated, the Ss would reveal it in their behavior when faced with appropriate stimuli.

After receiving the envelope containing the 114 statements, Ss were given the appropriate instructions for sorting. The instructions for the actual procedure of sorting were identical with those used by Thurstone and Chave (19), Hinckley (8), and others. The S,s were given 3 to 4 minutes to read the instruction sheet. The administrator then read the following instructions aloud.

You are given a number of statements expressing opinions in regard to the social position of Negroes. These cards are to be sorted into different piles.

You will find it easier to sort them if you look over a number of cards, chosen at random, before you begin to sort.

You are given eleven cards with roman numbers on them: I, II, III, IV, V, VI, VII, VIII, IX, X, XI. Please arrange these before you in regular order. Under Card I, put those statements which are most *unfavorable* in regard to the social position of Negroes. Under Card XI, put those statements which are most *favorable* in regard to the social position of Negroes. Under each of the other 9 cards, between I and XI, put those statements which correspond to that step in the 11 piles.[4]

This means that when you are through sorting you will have 11 piles of statements arranged in order from I, the *lowest,* to XI, the *highest.*

Use your judgment as to where each statement should be placed in the 11 piles. Do not be concerned about the number of cards in each pile.

When you are through sorting, please put a rubber band around each of the 11 piles of cards, placing the numbered card on top of each pile.

If you complete the sorting before others, please remain quietly in your seat until final announcements are made by the experimenter.

After the appropriate instructions for sorting were read aloud, the administrator answered any questions concerning the sorting to be sure that instructions were understood. Administrators were, however, cautioned not to use examples relating to Negroes to clarify the instructions. For example, as an instance of a very unfavorable statement on an issue, administrators used "Organized religion is the greatest single detriment to the advancement of civilization in the world today"; or, as an example of a very favorable statement on an issue, "Organized religion is the only hope for the salvation of the world."

When the instructions for sorting were clear to the Ss, the sorting began. During this time, the administrator distributed rubber bands to each S and performed other tasks so that he would be in a position to see that each S was conscientiously performing the task according to instructions, without seeming to be observing the placement of specific cards. The sorting process consumed about 55 minutes. The Ss were reminded to remain in their seats and keep their cards with them until all Ss had finished sorting.

Obtaining the judges' own attitudes. The second instruction sheet, which concerned the Ss' agreement and disagreement with the piles of statements they had had sorted, was then distributed. After sorting, the following instructions were given for the purpose of tapping Ss' attitudes on the issue.

Now that you have completed the sorting of cards into piles, pick up that pile of cards which comes closest to your view on the issue (that is, the social position of Negroes). On the numbered card on top of that pile, please write the word "agree." After writing the word "agree" on this pile, please write *one* of the following to indicate the degree of agreement with that pile: *(a)* "very strongly," *(b)* "strongly," or *(c)* "mildly."

Now pick up that *pile* of cards which is most objectionable from your point of view. On the numbered card on top of that pile, please write the word

[4]Probably for this issue, it would have been preferable to use I as the favorable and IX as the unfavorable end. The few sortings done by Negro Ss under individual supervision showed a tendency to switch I to the favorable end unless reminded that I represented the unfavorable end. Therefore, special care was taken in the experimental sessions (especially with Negro Ss) to repeat several times that I was the unfavorable, XI the favorable end of the scale. To provide maximum comparability we conformed to Hinckley's use of I as the most unfavorable end. A small number of Ss consistently reversed the two extremes and these data were recopied in the standard direction.

"disagree." After writing the word "disagree" on this pile, please write *one* of the following to indicate the degree of disagreement with that pile: *(a)* "very strongly," *(b)* "strongly," or *(c)* "mildly."

When you have completed the above, please replace the 11 piles of cards, each carefully separated by its rubber band, in the envelope.

This is part of a scientific research project. The results of each person's sorting will be treated as scientific data and will be confidential.

Check on the "carelessness" hypothesis. The chief purpose of the next procedural step was to have the Ss estimate the proportion of statements which they judged to be "very unfavorable," "unfavorable," "neutral," "favorable," and "very favorable" to Negroes to determine whether or not there would be general correspondence between actual proportions of cards sorted into various piles and the Ss' estimates of these proportions when the cards were out of sight. This step is critical for the problem at hand. If there is a general correspondence between the patterns of these percentages filled in by S without the actual sight of the objective piles he has made and the actual proportions into which he sorted the cards, the explanation for disproportionately large piles (of 30 or more statements) as due to "carelessness" appears inadequate. Correspondence between the actual proportions in the piles and the percentages filled in by Ss at a later time would indicate a consistency in evaluation of the stimulus material at two time intervals which would not be expected if the sorting were casual and random.

The estimates of sortings were obtained after all Ss had replaced the statements in their envelopes. The administrator passed out a 3×5 in. card to each S *individually* so that he could check to be sure that the sorted piles were in the envelopes. The administrator explained the task orally as follows:

Now that you have sorted the statements into piles in terms of their stand regarding Negroes, please estimate the percentage of statements which in your judgment were "very unfavorable" to Negroes, "unfavorable" to Negroes, "neutral," "favorable" to Negroes, and "very favorable" to Negroes. Write the percent for each of these stands printed on the card from "very unfavorable" to "very favorable" in the appropriate space under the column headed "% of statements regarding Negroes." The five percentages which you write should add up to 100%. You will note that there is a question at the bottom of the card to be answered on the back. I believe the other items are self-explanatory.

Supplementary attitude measurement with white judges. It was important to have a clearer differentiation of groups than that afforded by the rather crude list of six statements used for this purpose by Hinckley. In the case of Negro Ss the intensity of agreement and disagreement with the piles of statements they had sorted and the obvious attitude of Negro Ss sufficed. But for the white Ss, a further check on their attitudes was obtained by administration of the Likert Negro Scale[5] as the final step in the session. The scale was not administered to the Negro Ss because discussion with Negro pretest Ss revealed a strong animosity toward filling out a form prepared entirely from the white

[5]See Likert, R. A Technique for the Measurement of Attitudes. *Arch. Psychol., N. Y.,* 1932, No. 140.

point of view. In fact, some Negro *S*s spontaneously remarked that the statements to be sorted were prepared from the white standpoint.

Subjects. The final procedure presented above was decided upon after pretesting on both white and Negro *S*s ($N = 100$). Ten *S*s made the sortings individually under close supervision with the view of getting detailed hints for the procedure.

The main concern in the selection of the final experimental *S*s was to insure groups of *S*s who would represent differentiated segments on the scale ranging from an extremely favorable position to an extremely unfavorable position in regard to the issue of the social position of Negroes. For this purpose, groups and institutions were selected which would insure a likelihood of obtaining such differentiated positions on the scale.

Negro groups. It followed that Negro *S*s should be used, to represent the pro end of the scale. A total of 103 were used. Fifty-four were enrolled as graduate students or were attending the summer session at the University of Oklahoma. These more mature Negroes may be taken as the most self-consciously pro group in this study. Since these individuals were attending the University in the year following the Supreme Court decision ending segregation at the University, they had a sense of mission and an accentuated identification as members of their group. Many were brought to the university by the National Association for the Advancement of Colored People, which has encouraged Negroes on the campus to form active social groups. As a group, these students had had more actual contact with discrimination practices than the younger Negro *S*s.

The younger group of Negro *S*s was made up of 49 undergraduates at a state university for Negroes; hence, their age and educational level are lower than that of the University of Oklahoma group. While segregation and awareness of anti-Negro feeling had been a part of their life, they had grown up largely in a Negro environment. Since this university is also located in a Negro community, this relatively "sheltered" condition is continued in academic life.

White groups: 1. Pro-Negro. Because validity derived from the stands taken in actual life was the desired criterion governing selection of subject groups, two small groups of white *S*s who had actually participated in pro-Negro activities were chosen. Members of these groups, totaling 19, had been among the leaders in local campaigning at the University of Oklahoma (by student polls, newspaper work, etc.) for an end to segregation. One group was selected by the director of the YMCA as among those individuals who were thus active. Another group had been organized around this issue. Thus, for these very pro-Negro white *S*s, personal information as well as details of the stand of their groups were available.

2. "Average" subjects. Here results from a number of different colleges throughout the South were secured. These included two in an area in southeastern Oklahoma popularly known as "Little Dixie." In general, students attending these schools are from a lower socioeconomic level than those attending the state university. The educational level of the area is relatively low. Affiliation with fundamentalist religious groups is common. The students in these colleges are, for the most part, preparing to become teachers. From one, 53 *S*s were chosen from classes in elementary English. From the other, 58 students, who had not been exposed to courses in either psychology or sociology, were used.

Three colleges and universities from the state of Georgia were also secured. Sixty-four *S*s were obtained, distributed about equally through the three institutions. In all, 194 white judges were used.

3. Anti-Negro subjects. It was hoped to secure a group of strongly anti-Negro *S*s. The major difficulty in finding strongly anti-Negro *S*s lay in the fact that no groups organized strictly around such a stand were available. Further, pretesting revealed a strong tendency on the part of college students to express more liberal attitudes than would probably have been expressed at the time of the original Hinckley study. A number of such *S*s who were believed to be somewhat less liberal on this issue were obtained from living units at the University of Oklahoma. But it finally appeared necessary to use the *S*s in the total white sample who expressed the most anti-Negro attitudes on the evaluation cards and on the Likert questionnaires.

RESULTS

Categorization of statements by various groups. One method of analyzing any differences between the major groups of *S*s in the degree to which items are displaced is to determine the number of statements placed in each of the eleven categories. Results on these distributions are shown in Fig. 1 for *(a)* Negro *S*s, *(b)* strongly pro-Negro white *S*s (leaders in the anti-segregation movement), and *(c)* "average" white *S*s from six Southern colleges. To permit comparison of the results for the last group with those obtained by Hinckley, his procedure of eliminating all individuals placing 30 or more statements into any single category was also studied. Data are also presented for a group of 17 *S*s who appeared to have the most anti-Negro attitudes within the white group. These 17 *S*s had indicated disagreement with the pile of statements most favorable to Negroes and had markedly anti-Negro Likert scale scores (below 50).

It will be observed that the Negro group shows a heavy piling up of statements in the extreme categories, indicating displacement of neutral statements to the extreme position. This displacement is particularly noticeable for category I at the anti-Negro end, a position with which these *S*s strongly disagree. The distribution of responses of the pro-Negro white group is similar to that for Negroes but a little less extreme. The dotted line at 30 indicates the frequency which Hinckley used to eliminate *S*s. Over three-fourths of the Negro *S*s and two-thirds of the pro-Negro white *S*s would be eliminated by applying the Hinckley criterion.

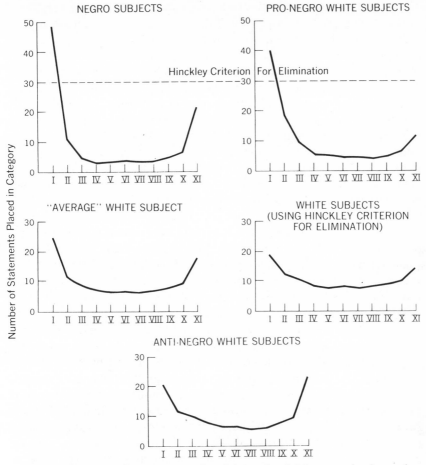

FIG. 1 *Number of statements placed in each of 11 categories by each group of judges.*

The data for the average white group show considerably less piling up at the ends. When the Hinckley elimination procedure is followed the distribution is relatively flat. The differences in the distributions for the Negro and average white are highly significant statistically.

The results for the anti-Negro *S*s are not strikingly different from those for the average white *S*s. But it will be noted that as compared with the white *S*s they tend to show a slightly greater tendency to concentrate items at the *positive* end of the scale.

Scale values for the various criterion subgroups. Another method of studying displacement of items is to investigate the distributions of scale values obtained for the various subgroups. These are the data on which

Thurstone, Hinckley, and others base their main case for the validity of their scaling procedure. Inspection of the original 114 items reveals that all of the statements are not equally appropriate for white and Negro *S*s. For example, items like "I would not patronize a hotel that accomodates Negroes" or "My lack of contact with the Negro makes it impossible for me to pass judgment as to his social position" are not as relevant to Negro *S*s as to whites. But it was possible to find 11 items which seemed equally appropriate for the Negro and white populations, and which were approximately equidistant in the original Hinckley scaling. Scale values were then found for each of these items for each of the present groups, using the conventional Thurstone procedure. The eleven items were all used in the final forms of the Scale of Attitude toward the Negro.[6] They are numbered 5, 6, 10, and 16 in Scale A, and 1, 2, 3, 5, 8, 9, and 15 in Scale B.

The distributions of scale values for these eleven items derived from the responses of the various groups are presented graphically in Fig. 2. For comparison, the scale values reported by Hinckley are given. It will be seen that there is considerable similarity in the scale values for the average white *S*s (with the Hinckley procedure of eliminating those with 30 or more statements in any category) and the scale values originally found by Hinckley. The correlation between the two sets of scale values is .96 (11 items). But the values for the strongly pro-Negro white judges and for the Negro judges do not correspond at all to those obtained by Hinckley. The distributions of the Negro groups show the majority of the items bunched up at the extreme anti-Negro end of the scale (in line with the results of Fig. 1). The items which are neutral for Hinckley's group and for our "average" white *S*s are displaced by the Negro judges to the extremes, principally to the anti-Negro end. The distribution of scale values for the pro-Negro white *S*s is similar to that for the Negro *S*s but again not quite as extreme. The results for the anti-Negro *S*s also show a tendency for neutral items to be displaced toward the extremes, but in their case some displacement is also noticeable toward the pro-Negro end.

"Carelessness" as an explanation for the results. It will be recalled that *S*s who placed 30 or more statements in any single pile were discarded by Hinckley on the grounds of carelessness. To obtain a check on this explanation for the large number of our *S*s who placed this number of statements in the extreme position piles, after the sorting was completed and the cards placed in their envelope, a question was asked concerning the *S*s' impressions of the percentage of the statements which were "very unfavorable," "unfavorable," "neutral," "fairly favorable,"

[6]Hinckley, E. D. *Attitude Toward the Negro,* Scale No. 3, Forms A and B. (L. L. Thurstone, Ed.) Chicago: University of Chicago Press, 1930.

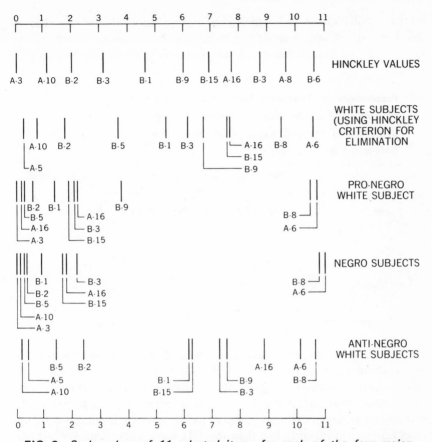

FIG. 2 *Scale values of 11 selected items for each of the four major groups.*
[Values obtained for these items by Hinckley (8) are included for comparison. Number of Ss in each group is the same as in Fig. 1.]

'and "very favorable" to the Negro. From these data we have evidence that the Ss who placed a large number of their cards in the extremely unfavorable categories may really have perceived the statements in that way and did not place them there through carelessness. The data are presented in Table 1 to show the difference in the evaluations of the number of unfavorable statements in the list among Ss who placed less than 30 statements at the anti-Negro end of the scale, among those who placed between 30 and 59, and among those who placed 60 or more in this category. The Ss who placed a greater number of statements in the anti-Negro category were definitely more inclined to believe that there were a high number of unfavorable statements in the list. The chi-square value for the distributions is 43.3, which gives a probability value of considerably less than .001. A very high degree of relationship is not to be expected in view of the fact that Ss had not been given any prior intimation that they

TABLE 1 Percentages of statements considered "very unfavorable" or "unfavorable" to Negroes by individuals placing varying numbers of statements in Category I (anti-Negro).

Per cent of items judged "very unfavorable" or "unfavorable"	Percentages making various estimates of unfavorableness of items among individuals who placed		
	Less than 30 items in Cat. I (N = 119)	30 to 59 items in Cat. I (N = 105)	60 or more items in Cat. I (N = 34)
60 or over	22.7	51.5	79.4
40–59	55.5	39.0	17.7
Less than 40	21.8	9.5	2.9

$$\chi^2 = 43.3$$
$$p = <.001$$

would be required to make such a judgment. For the entire group of 258 Ss on whom the relevant information was available, a correlation of .32 was obtained between the percentage of statements considered "very unfavorable" and "unfavorable" and the number of cards placed in the extreme anti-Negro category. This correlation is significantly different from zero at considerably less than the .001 level. These data suggest that Ss who put a large number of statements into the extreme category do so not because of carelessness but because they actually perceive the statements differently.

DISCUSSION

The results just presented clearly support the three principal hypotheses investigated. Even though judges are not asked to state their own attitudes, the position of the judge on the issue does influence in a significant way his categorization of the items. The displacements are away from the individual's own position, supporting the notion that those with extreme positions are more selective in the statements they will accept at their own end of the scale (their "threshold of acceptance" is *raised*), and more inclined to reject items which are at variance with their position (their "threshold of rejection" is *lowered*). The degree of displacement is greatest for the items in the middle of the scale, in line with the hypothesis that "neutral" items are more ambiguous[7] and less well structured, and hence are more readily subject to the personal interpretations of the judges.

The present data do not indicate whether the distortions and displacements are caused by the fact that individuals with extreme positions lack the ability to discriminate between adjacent items at the opposite extreme, and hence place them in the same category, or whether they reflect variations in the judge's interpretation of the total scale and the magnitude of category intervals. On the surface, the second alternative is supported by the study of Ferguson (6) who found no differences in the distributions of paired comparisons for judges with differing attitudes toward war. But in the light of the present results a question is again raised as to the magnitude of differences in attitudes of his contrasted groups of judges and in the degree of their involvement in the issue. During the thirties, when the study was done, it is likely that variation in attitude toward war may not have been very pronounced, and Ferguson himself states that it was impossible "to secure any groups favorable toward war" (p. 116). The data of the present experiment suggest that it is quite likely that the effects are specific to methods of absolute scaling (the second alternative), since the rank orders of the items for the pro and con judges are very similar. An experiment is currently underway specifically on this problem, in which the Attitude toward the Negro issue is again used with Negro *S*s in an attempt to see whether the items which are bunched together with the equal-appearing interval method are clearly differentiated with the method of paired comparison.

On the basis of the present study it appears quite likely that the startling difference between the present results and those of Hinckley is due to his elimination of the extreme cases. When his elimination procedure is followed and the sample restricted to white *S*s, there is a close correspondence in results even though 20 years have elapsed since his original study.

Evidence against the explanation of the results as due to "carelessness" comes from several sources. The data already presented indicate that those who placed a large number of the statements in the extreme anti categories judged at a later time that more of the items had been unfavorable to Negroes. Further evidence comes from another study done in conjunction with the present one in which *S*s were allowed to use as many or as few categories for sorting as they deemed necessary to

---

[7]Edwards (5) has called attention to "lower Q values at both extremes of the scale and higher Q values toward the center of the scale" (p. 163). On the basis of this tendency Edwards concluded "Clearly, then, we have evidence to indicate that the scale and Q values of items sorted by the method of equal-appearing-intervals are not independent, that *"neutral" items are relatively more ambiguous than items at either extreme of the continuum."* (Italics ours.)

distinguish among the items on the issue. The *S*s who placed a large number of items in the extreme categories under the present instructions used fewer categories to express shades of opinion and again placed a large number in the extreme categories. A different type of evidence is the lawful nature of the phenomenon. It is the very subgroups with extreme positions (determined either by their own attitude statements or by their assignment to a criterion group) who place the large number at the extremes, and the items they displace are those in the middle of the scale (the more ambiguous items).

Our results do, as Thurstone (19) had clearly anticipated, raise serious questions as to the use of the method of equal-appearing intervals on issues where strong attitudes are involved. Further research is needed to determine whether under these conditions a single scale is involved for the different groups of judges or whether distinctive scales will be required. A Guttman or Lazarsfeld type of analysis will be required to answer this question (18). Even if a single scale is involved, great care will be required in the selection of judges, since their position may influence the scale values obtained. Obtaining an unbiased sampling of positions may constitute a difficult practical problem, since on many issues attitudes are related to educational and socioeconomic status. It may therefore be very difficult to secure representatives of all positions among those who are well enough educated and have sufficient sophistication to carry out the difficult task of categorizing the items.

From the present results there emerges an interesting possibility for developing a behavioral, "projective" method of attitude assessment through study of the way an individual sorts statements on an issue. If the tendencies found in the present experiment for individuals with extreme positions to bunch up the statements at the extremes are found for other issues, it may be possible to assess the attitude of an individual without ever asking him his opinion but by relying entirely on the way he distributes his judgments. Individuals with more or less neutral attitudes would be expected to space their judgments rather evenly over the entire range, those at the pro end would tend to reject neutral items and hence pile them up at the anti end, and those with anti attitudes would place them at the opposite end of the scale. As indicated previously, one may even carry this technique a step further by not using a fixed number of categories, but by deliberately letting the individual establish a scale of his own with whatever number of categories he sees fit. Then the extension or constriction of the scale he establishes, the number of categories he uses, the crowding or neglecting of certain categories, and the direction of concentration of items may all provide useful indices for analysis of the way the individual "perceives" the issue. In such a technique one would obviously want to insure the inclusion of a large number of ambiguous and unstructured items, since these will be the ones which are more conducive to displacement. In another study done in conjunction with the present experiment, investigation has been carried out along these lines and the results will be reported in a forthcoming paper.

SUMMARY

1. Investigation was made of the apparent discrepancy between studies in the field of judgment, where the position of the individual on an issue affects the nature of his judgments, and those in the field of attitude scaling, where it has been reported that the scaling of statements is independent of the judges's stand on the issue.

One possible hypothesis for the discrepancy, based on an analysis of the original studies, was that prior experiments had not employed Ss who would be most likely to show the distortions and displacements typically obtained in the field of perception and judgment. Accordingly, every effort was made to secure samples of Ss who were deeply involved in the issue about which the items to be judged were written. Attitudes toward the social position of the Negro furnished an issue on which strong personal involvement could be secured, particularly on the part of Negro Ss. The materials to be judged were the 114 statements originally used by Hinckley (8), and his instructions and procedures were duplicated. In addition to Negro judges, groups of white Ss with known pro-Negro attitudes, "average" white Ss, and a small group of anti-Negro whites, were employed as judges.

2. It was found that Negro Ss and militantly pro-Negro white Ss tended to place a disproportionate number of statements in the extreme categories, in line with the predictions from judgment theory that individuals with strong attitudes tend to see issues in "black and white" and displace neutral statements to the extremes. The numbers of statements assigned to the various categories by "average" white Ss are much more uniform.

3. Scale values for 11 statements spaced rather evenly over the entire scale in Hinckley's study were compared for each of the major groups. The distributions of scale values for the Negro and pro-Negro white Ss were compressed at the anti-Negro end of the scale, with a small number at the other extreme. Those for the "average" white Ss were spaced more evenly throughout the range in a manner closely approximating the distribution found by Hinckley. Anti-Negro Ss tended to displace neutral statements to the extremes, particularly toward the pro-Negro end.

4. The results support the notion that part of the discrepancy in results between the present study and those of previous experimenters may be

attributable to the representation of a greater range of attitudes. In the experiment of Pintner and Forlano (14) on attitude toward patriotism it is likely that there was considerable homogeneity in position and perhaps insufficient personal involvement. In Hinckley's study the procedure of eliminating *S*s who placed 30 or more statements in any category may have eliminated the individuals with the strongest attitudes on the issue. His procedure would eliminate the majority of our Negro *S*s and many of our pro-Negro white *S*s.

5. The disproportionately large number of sortings in the extreme position does not appear to be due to carelessness, as thought by Hinckley. Evidence against this explanation is the fact that *S*s who put a large number of statements in the extreme anti-Negro categories expressed the opinion on a questionnaire after the cards were removed that a high proportion of the statements were unfavorable to Negroes. Further evidence is the lawful regularity of the phenomenon obtained.

6. The implications of the present results for procedures used in the construction of attitude scales are discussed.

REFERENCES

1. ANSBACHER, H. Number Judgment of Postage Stamps: A Contribution to the Psychology of Social Norms. *J. Psychol.,* 1938, *5,* 347–350.
2. ASCH, S. E., BLOCK, H., & HERTZMAN, M. Studies in the Principles of Judgment and Attitude: I Two Basic Principles of Judgment. *J. Psychol.,* 1938, *5,* 219–251.
3. CARTWRIGHT, D. Relation of Decision-Time to the Categories of Response. *Amer. J. Psychol.,* 1941, *54.* 174–196.
4. COFFIN, T. E. Some Conditions of Suggestion and Suggestibility. *Psychol. Monogr.,* 1941, *53,* No. 4 (Whole No. 241).
5. EDWARDS, A. L. A Critique of "Neutral" Items in Attitude Scales Constructed by the Method of Equal Appearing Intervals. *Psychol. Rev.,* 1946, *53,* 159–169.
6. FERGUSON, L. W. The Influence of Individual Attitudes on Construction of an Attitude Scale. *J. Soc. Psychol.,* 1935, *6,* 115–117.
7. FERNBERGER, S. W. The Effect of the Attitude of the Subject Upon the Measure of Sensitivity. *Amer. J. Psychol.,* 1914, *25,* 538–543.
8. HINCKLEY, E. D. The Influence of Individual Opinion on Construction of an Attitude Scale. *J. Soc. Psychol.,* 1932, *3,* 283–296.
9. HINCKLEY, E. D., & RETHLINGSHAFER, D. Value Judgments of Heights of Men by College Students. *J. Psychol.,* 1951, *31,* 257–262.
10. JOHNSON, C. S. *Growing Up in the Black Belt.* Washington: American Council on Education, 1941.
11. LUCHINS, A. S. On Agreement With Another's Judgment. *J. Abnorm. Soc. Psychol.,* 1944, *39,* 97–111.
12. MARKS, E. Skin Color Judgments of Negro College Students. *J. Abnorm. Soc. Psychol.,* 1943, *38,* 370–376.

13. MCGARVEY, H. R. Anchoring Effects in the Absolute Judgment of Verbal Materials. *Arch. Psychol.,* 1943, No. 281.
14. PINTNER, R., & FORLANO, G. The Influence of Attitude Upon Scaling of Attitude Items. *J. Soc. Psychol.,* 1937, *8,* 39–45.
15. PROSHANSKY, H., & MURPHY, G. The Effect of Reward and Punishment on Perception. *J. Psychol.,* 1942, *13,* 295–305.
16. ROGERS, S. The Anchoring of Absolute Judgments. *Arch. Psychol.,* 1941, No. 261.
17. SHERIF, M. A Study of Some Social Factors in Perception. *Arch. Psychol.,* 1935, No. 187.
18. STOUFFER, S. A., GUTTMAN, L., et al. *Measurement and Prediction.* Princeton: Princeton University Press, 1950.
19. THURSTONE, L. L., & CHAVE, E. J. *The Measurement of Attitude.* Chicago: University of Chicago Press, 1929.
20. VOLKMANN, J. The Anchoring of Absolute Scales. *Psychol. Bull.,* 1936, *33,* 742–743.
21. VOLKMANN, J. Scales of Judgment and Their Implications for Social Psychology. In J. Rohrer and M. Sherif (Eds.), *Social Psychology at the Crossroads.* New York: Harper, 1951. Pp. 273–294.

III
WHAT EVENTS
INITIATE AND ALTER
THE COURSE
OF BEHAVIOR

1
OVERVIEW

More professional energy of psychologists has been expended on the question of motivation than on any other single concept about the nature of behavior. What instigates an organism to develop and alter behaviors? What is the nature of the variables that guarantees a stable performance in the next situation in which similar stimuli appear? These questions frequently appear in discussions of behavior. With different theorists they take different forms, and they sometimes become far enough removed from their basic form that they become unrecognizable. At other times the answers to the questions become reified to the point where the theorist replaces the questions with part of the answers he has already given. It is easy, for example, for the theorist who has totally accepted fear avoidance as a basic motivational principle never again to ask, "Why is an organism instigated to develop and alter behaviors?" He spends his professional life asking questions about intervals between the onset of the stimulus and the onset of pain withdrawal and their effect on response strength. He becomes concerned with associating the "emotional" state of the organism to the stimulus. The emotion has then developed a "life" of its own. The motivational issue is dissolved into the framework of the theory that was proposed to explain it, and questions emerge only within the structure of that theory.

When an adult human in Western culture sets out to ask the "why" of instigating and altering behavior he can readily fall into an introspective analysis and come up with the concept of "willing" to adopt a behavior. He sees people adopting behaviors because they "want to" do something. This, after all, is why they see themselves engaging in a particular behavior. The behavior has a goal; it is "end-directed." If this view of motivation is transposed to infants, or to other organisms, they will also be seen as striving toward an end. The infant begins to use words because it "wants to" obtain something from its environment. The rat explores a maze because it "wants to" find food. This motivational concept can be recognized as the "willing" faculty of the great tripartite division of

125

psychological function that was formulated by the faculty psychologists. The concept still exists in "naive theory" (Heider, 1958).

When the early developmental psychologists tried to describe the nature of the goals of the developing infant they derived the concept of *instinct*. The infant "wanted to" live, it "wanted to" eat, it "wanted to" reproduce. The emptiness of this approach soon became apparent. The infant was being given an *a priori* goal for every action in which it engaged. When dissatisfaction with this approach to motivation began to mount, it was not surprising that the psychologists should turn to one of the other "faculties" for an explanatory principle. At a later point in theory development, the basic motivation was seen as being located in the *emotional* faculty. An organism was motivated to alter its behavior because it was in a displeasing hedonic state, and would repeat a particular action because it had previously engaged in that same action with pleasing results. This formulation of motivation placed the emphasis on what *had happened* to the organism rather than on what the organism *wanted to do*.

Current cognitive theory attempts to achieve a position that thoroughly integrates the three "faculties," and would reject a view that separates emotion, cognition, and motivation for other than purely heuristic purposes. Motivation, which is frequently subsumed under the general term of *activation* (Duffy, 1962), is regarded as being "intrinsically" involved with cognition (Hunt, 1965). A shorthand statement of a view of motivation within a cognitive theory would be that the organism strives to maintain the integrity of its already developed cognitive system. The organism is constantly motivated by its effort "to know," "to recognize."

Perhaps the most formal statement of a motivational position that can be adapted to cognitive principles is one offered by Fiske and Maddi (1961). After having, in effect, defined activation as being a direct function of the novelty of a stimulus situation, they state their fifth proposition: "*V*." The behavior of an organism tends to modify its activation level toward the optimal zone for the task at hand" (Fiske and Maddi, 1961, p. 35). If a stimulus is a highly "novel" stimulus it produces high "activation" which the organism tends to modify toward an optimal zone. The most effective means of reducing an excessive amount of activation is to reduce the "novelty" of a stimulus—that is, to develop a construction system that can integrate the stimulus. In short, the basic motivation of an organism is the maintenance of an optimum level of arousal through its development of constructs that allows the successful integration of incoming stimuli.

This position is further elaborated by considering the psychological events associated with a low degree of novelty. Low novelty would be associated with low arousal. This, too, is seen as deviation from an optimal level of arousal. Again, the organism is expected to modify its activation level toward the optimal zone. This is achieved through a search for "interesting" stimuli, i.e., optimally novel stimuli. Berlyne (1960) and Fowler (1965) offer excellent discussion and reviews on the phenomena of curiosity and exploratory behavior. They consider the question of why an organism initiates and alters behavior in situations where stimuli produce activation below an optimal level. Sufficient evidence has been accumulated to support the validity of the statement that the organism seeks novel stimuli. Within the framework which we are constructing, we would extrapolate this assumption to state that the organism seeks to maintain an optimal level of activation, which is produced by the organism's participation in cognizing novel stimuli.

A number of theorists employ a "deviation" notion as a primary motivational principle, although each imposes his own particular variation on the general position. Cofer and Appley (1964), after a thorough review of motivational concepts, propose that the most comprehensive theoretical position is one which speaks of the organism's effort to maintain *expectancies*. McClelland (McClelland, Atkinson, Clark, and Lowell, 1953) has woven a similar principle into his extensive work on achievement motivation. Haber (1958) initiated research efforts to show that particular deviations from adaptation level, a concept extensively investigated by Helson (1964) and his students, produce varied levels of affect. Among the most thoroughly discussed concepts of deviation from optimally arousing novelty, and one that speaks directly of the effort to maintain *cognitive* structures, is Festinger's concept of *cognitive dissonance* (Festinger, 1957). Piaget (1952) writes of the infant being "forced" to accommodate when schema that are available to him do not match external events in a way that will allow immediate assimilation. Another valuable set of related materials is found in the study of Russian psychologists devoted to the "orienting reflex" (Razran, 1961). These studies present evidence for a variety of physiological concommitants to the organism's exposure to stimuli that are novel to the organism's response systems. And, finally, Sarbin (1967) has been writing about the concept of "cognitive strain" as a key concept in the development of "abnormal" behavior. An excellent and stimulating review of the voluminous research on concepts of activation is to be found in a comprehensive article by Berlyne (1967).

If we return to Kelly's theoretical structure (see chapter I), we find that he regarded the organism's effort to maintain a successfully functioning construct system to be the fundamental quality of a living organism. He states as his fundamental postulate, in order to totally encompass his theory within his motivational principle, that "A person's processes are psychologically channelized by ways in which he anticipates events." We find it difficult to accept the "goal-directed" quality of this postulate. Our inclination is to move toward a position that is more akin to Fiske and Maddi's fifth proposition, quoted above. In this statement, the organism is seen as having first established an optimum arousal state. One can propose that optimum, for the newborn, is the state to which it had adapted as it developed in its mother's uterus. Only *after* having experienced deviation from this optimum state can the organism's behavior patterns become established through returning it to an optimal level of activation. We do not view the person as engaging in a preordained search for cognitive order. Only after it has had experience with successful integration will it repeat integrative efforts in order to "remove" novel stimuli.

Freud (1959, pp. 135–137) presented us with a literate and delightful description of "the birth trauma" as a prototype of the condition of deviation from optimal arousal through exposure to unusual new stimulation. His constant reference to this inundation of stimuli as a sign of danger retains a flavor which says that the danger is to the biological being of the organism. His position on this reflects his efforts to weld faculty psychology solidly to Darwinian evolutionary theory. The organism that could attach the mobilizing emotion of fear to novel stimuli would stand a better chance of surviving in a hostile world where novel stimuli frequently meant physical harm.

One further issue demands attention: Can we sensibly speak of neurophysiological correlates in a theory which proposes that the organism's principal motivation is to maintain its cognitive functioning at an optimal level? Hebb, who repeatedly warns us of the danger of developing psychological theory that cannot be structured into physiological counterpart (Hebb, 1949), has also been a central figure among those who have been working to provide a proper physiological model. In his outstanding paper, *On the Nature of Fear* (Hebb 1947), he posed and offered his resolution to a series of central questions relating to emotion. Essentially, he argues for a view that would speak of singular arousal rather than a variety of "emotions"; and then states that "the fundamental source of either emotion (fear or rage) is of the same kind, a disruption of coordinated cerebral activity. Flight and aggression are two different modes of reaction tending to restore the dynamic equilibrium, or stability, of cerebral processes" (Hebb, 1947, p. 273). In later work, Hebb (1949) extensively elaborated his notions of "cerebral organization" by demonstrating the explanatory utility of the concept of "cell assembly," which is readily regarded as the physiological counterpart of the "cognitive structure." Emotionality, in Hebb's theory, was related to an interference with the "running off" of a phase sequence.

Hebb's position was given particular impetus when physiological researchers (Moruzzi and Magoun, 1949; Lindsley, 1957; Jouvet and Michel, 1958) accumulated evidence of an arousal control mechanism. Clarification of the functions of the reticular arousal system gave credence to the position that there is a direct physical link between the organism's effort to integrate novel stimulus input and its arousal state. Further extensive research and discussion will be required to integrate the psychological variables of "novelty" or "stimulus complexity" with the physiological variables of "arousal."

We are willing to assume, at this point, that an amalgamation of cognitive constructs with the motivational constructs being discussed within "arousal theory" allows a most satisfactory approach to the issue of why an organism initiates and alters behavior. In short, behavior is instigated and altered by the organism's constant efforts to maintain a level of cognizing activity that is optimally arousing. Bruner, et al (1956) and Sarbin (1967) might paraphrase this to state that the organism strives to achieve optimum "cognitive strain." Emotional activity, with all its neurophysiological counterparts; motivational activity, which reflects the functioning of the organism's emotional neurophysiology; and cognitive processes, are regarded as totally and inseparably intertwined. The readings included in this section reflect efforts to clarify these interrelationships.

REFERENCES

BERLYNE, D. E. Arousal and Reinforcement. In D. Levine (Ed.), *Nebraska Symposium on Motivation.* Lincoln, Nebraska: University of Nebraska Press, 1967, pp. 1–110.

BRUNER, J. S., GOODNOW, J. J., & AUSTIN, G. A. *A Study of Thinking.* New York: Wiley, 1956.

COFER, C. N., & APPLEY, M. H. *Motivation: Theory and Research.* New York: Wiley, 1964.

DUFFY, E. *Activation and Behavior.* New York: Wiley, 1962.

FESTINGER, L. *A Theory of Cognitive Dissonance.* Stanford, Calif.: Stanford University Press, 1957.

FISKE, D. W., & MADDI, S. R. *Functions of Varied Experience.* Homewood, Ill.: Dorsey, 1961.

FOWLER, H. *Curiosity and Exploratory Behavior.* New York: Macmillan, 1965.

FREUD, S. Inhibitions, Symptoms, and Anxiety. In Strachey, J. (Ed.) *The Complete Psychological Works of Sigmund Freud.* London: Hogarth Press, 1959, pp. 77–175.

HABER, R. N. Discrepancy from AL as a Source of Affect. *Journal of Experimental Psychology,* 1958, *56,* 370–375.

HEBB, D. O. *The Organization of Behavior.* New York: Wiley, 1949.

HEIDER, F. *The Psychology of Interpersonal Relations.* New York: Wiley, 1958.

HELSON, H. *Adaptation Level Theory.* New York: Harper and Row, 1964.

HUNT, J. MCV. Intrinsic Motivation and Its Role in Psychological Development. In David Levine, *Nebraska Symposium on Motivation.* Lincoln, Nebraska: University of Nebraska Press, 1965, pp. 189–282.

JOUVET, M., & MICHEL, F. Recherches sur l'Activité Electrique Cérébrale au Cours du Sommeil. *Comptes Rendus Société de Biologie,* 1958, *152,* 1167–1170.

LINDSLEY, D. B. Psychophysiology and Motivation. In M. R. Jones (Ed.), *Nebraska Symposium on Motivation.* Lincoln, Nebraska: University of Nebraska Press, 1957, pp. 44–105.

MᶜCLELLAND, D. C., ATKINSON, J. W., CLARK, R. A., & LOWELL, E. L. *The Achievement Motive.* New York: Appleton-Century-Crofts, 1953.

MORUZZI, G., & MAGOUN, H. W. Brain Stem Reticular Formation and Activation of the EEG. *EEG Clinical Neurophysiology,* 1949, *1,* 455–473.

PIAGET, J. *The Origins of Intelligence in Children.* New York: International Universities Press, 1952.

RAZRAN, G. The Observable Unconscious and the Inferable Conscious in Current Soviet Psychophysiology. *Psychological Review,* 1961, *68,* 99–119.

SARBIN, T. R. Notes on the Transformation of Social Identity. In N. S. Greenfield, M. H. Miller, and L. M. Roberts (Eds.). *Comprehensive Mental Health: The Challenge of Evaluation.* Madison, Wisconsin: University of Wisconsin, 1967.

2

THE NEW LOOK
IN MOTIVATION
WILLIAM N. DEMBER

Dember's paper is a lucid demonstration of how a sound research orientation leads from one experiment to another in order to test the predictive power of a concept. Starting the discussion with the early studies by Dennis, which showed that animals seem to "explore," Dember proceeds to a statement of his Theory of Choice: ". . . every object can be assigned an information value, or a 'complexity value' . . . [and] if an individual is free to choose, he will prefer to encounter objects of a complexity level that matches his own [ideal complexity level]." This statement is parallel to Fiske and Maddi's Fifth Proposition (see Overview, above). The organism seeks to maintain an optimum level of arousal by approaching "pacer" stimuli—that is, those stimuli that have a level of complexity which allows a rapid assimilation into the organism's existing response repertoire. The organism is in a satisfying state at that time when it is called on to construe stimuli that demand slight alteration in its existing cognitive organizations. Dember does not attempt to postulate the theory of choice as a replacement for other types of motivation. Rather, he seems to regard the concept he is developing as an addition to other motivational concepts. We need to looks elsewhere for the possibility of thinking of the stimuli that are produced by biological deficit as being "pacer" stimuli.

* * *

About a decade and a half ago, when I began graduate training in psychology, one of the most exciting research topics concerned the effects on perception of motivational and cognitive variables. For example,

Reprinted from American Scientist, *1965, 53, 409–427, by permission of the author and the Society of Sigma Xi. The article is based on a lecture given by the author on the occasion of his receipt of the fourth annual Distinguished Scientist Award, presented by the University of Cincinnati Chapter of Sigma Xi. The ideas presented are the product of close collaboration between the author and Dr. Robert W. Earl.*

evidence was presented that showed recognition thresholds for words to be affected by the motivational significance of the words; thus, words with positive or pleasant connotations might have lower thresholds—that is, be correctly recognized at a shorter presentation duration—than neutral words, whereas the recognition of negatively toned or taboo words required longer durations of presentation than those needed for the recognition of neutral words. Other research showed the perceived size of an object to be related to its value. Thus, children tended to overestimate the size of coins relative to discs of neutral value, and poor children were more subject to this type of error than were rich children. By now, a host of such studies has been conducted; with each passing year the methodology employed gets a little more sophisticated and the results a little more equivocal. But that is a different story.[1] The point for the present purpose is to note that this approach to the study of perception—which became known as the New Look in Perception—emphasized the interaction between processes which psychologists had in general hitherto been careful to keep in separate conceptual categories, and, in the textbooks, in separate chapters.

To speak of a New Look implies an "old look." In the case of perception the old look was one in which the variables influencing perception were thought to reside in two sources: (1) the physical stimulus and (2) the sensory system, consisting of receptor organ, afferent nerve and subcortical and cortical sensory projection areas. The New Look in perception was not antineurophysiology; rather, it postulated kinds of interactions within the nervous system that were more elaborate and diffuse than those allowed for in the classical neurophysiology and neuroanatomy of the nineteenth century. Interestingly enough, direct evidence for some of the neural mechanisms consistent with the New Look has been reported, as, for example, in the discovery of the cortical priming function of the reticular arousal system.[2]

Let me make one last remark about the New Look in Perception before I turn to its analogue in motivation. And that is to note that the New Look was not entirely new. Similar ideas had been proposed earlier by such diverse theorists as Freud and John Dewey. What made the New Look novel was its attempt at empirical verification of its postulates.

THE NEW LOOK IN MOTIVATION

What about the New Look in Motivation? From the sense of my previous remarks you might anticipate, first of all, that the New Look in Motivation will be characterized by an emphasis on *interaction* between

[1]For a review of this literature, see December (1960).
[2]See, for example, Samuels (1959).

motivational and perceptual and cognitive processes. Secondly, you might expect to hear something about the "old look" in motivation. Finally, you should not be surprised to learn that the New Look in Motivation has a long history of its own, and that what might better be called the "latest new look" is characterized not so much by its theoretical postulates as by its attempts at empirical verication.

Now, rather than elaborate on these ideas at this point, I would prefer to defer their discussion until later, and launch immediately into a description of some of my own research experience in this area.

ALTERNATION BEHAVIOR

Let me begin where I began—with a phenomenon called "alternation behavior." This behavior has been studied almost exclusively in rats, but has also been observed in other species, including man. It can be described very simply with the aid of the first figure.

Figure 1 depicts in plan view a piece of apparatus that is popular among those who investigate the behavior of rats. It is called a T-maze, and consists of: a starting alley; a choice-point region; and two goal arms. Frequently, guillotine doors are located at the juncture of the goal arms and the choice-point so that once the rat has entered an arm it can be prevented from leaving that arm until the experimenter is ready to remove it from the maze. Depending on the purpose of a particular experiment, the goal arms may be kept identical in stimulus properties, or specific differences between them may be introduced, as, for example, by painting one arm black and the other white. For the experiments which I will first describe, let us assume that the left arm is black and the right arm is white.

The T-maze is typically used in studying *learning* in the rat, and usually in the following manner. The rat is first deprived of some commodity to establish a state of physiological need and a concomitant state of "psychological drive"; for example, a schedule of food deprivation might be instituted in order to make the rat hungry. Then the rat is introduced

FIG. 1

The T-maze, consisting of (A) starting alley, (B) choice-point, and (C) goal arms. The dashed lines indicate guillotine doors, which can be lowered to prevent retracing.

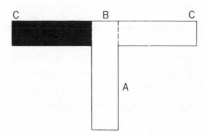

into the T-maze; at the end of one of the goal arms a bit of food is located. If the rat enters that arm, it is allowed to eat the food and is then removed from the maze. Such "trials" are repeated until the rat has reached a criterion performance level—perhaps entering the proper arm on 10 successive trials.

Such a problem, though it may seem simple to us, will usually not be solved immediately by the rat. Indeed, it may take 20 or 30 trials before criterion is reached. The gradual improvement in performance that occurs over trials, as evidenced by the behavior of a large group of rats, is considered to reveal the gradual establishment of a habit. One can then study the variables that influence habit acquisition; for example, strength of hunger drive during training, amount and quality of the drive-reducing commodity (i.e., the reward or reinforcement), the distribution of training trials, and a host of other variables, limited only by the imagination and ingenuity of the experimenter.

Now, in pursuing such an experiment about 30 years ago, Wayne Dennis (1935) noticed something unexpected. He had assumed along with other researchers, that the acquisition of the habit—say, of always turning right in the maze—was superimposed on an initially random process. That is, the rat's behavior on the first few trials at least was expected to be unsystematic. But Dennis found it to be quite the contrary. In particular, on examining the records of the early trials, he discovered the phenomenon of *alternation:* that is, if a rat made a right turn, for example, on the first trial, the probability was high that it would turn left on the second trial. Incidentally, this will happen, on the early trials, even if the rat finds food on the first trial. Thus, the behavioral stereotypy which emerges during the course of learning is superimposed on an already existing and strong tendency toward behavioral variability, and variability that is *systematic,* not random.

What Dennis did next, as any good scientist would, was to put aside his investigation of learning and to explore the alternation phenomenon. I have reviewed his and other work on alternation elsewhere (Dember and Fowler, 1958; Dember, 1961) and will not burden you with the details of all those investigations. What is significant for this presentation is the assumption that Dennis made about *what* the rat was alternating with respect to. According to Dennis, the rat was alternating with respect to the *maze arms.*

What other possibilities might there be? When an animal is observed entering the black goal arm, one could describe that bit of behavior by reference to the arm, as Dennis did, by saying that the rat entered the *black* arm, or the arm on the left, or perhaps the arm oriented toward the west. All such statements focus on the part of his environment with which the rat's behavior brings him into contact. A different kind of assertion would focus on the behavioral act itself, and say that the animal made a left-turning *response*.

If, on the next trial, the rat alternates, one could say, again with Dennis, that the rat was alternating with respect to maze arms (he went into the black arm on the first trial, and into the white arm on the second). Or, from the other point of view, one could say that having made a left-turning response on the first trial (which happened to bring the rat into the black arm), the rat alternated by way of a right-turning response on the second trial (which happened to bring him into the white arm).

Dennis's view, which sees alternation as stimulus-alternation, not only has historical priority; it also would seem the more natural of the two accounts. Strangely enough, however, the response-alternation point of view was the one that prevailed.

This happened, and quite obviously to one who is familiar with American psychology, because there existed a dominant behavior theory which had the concepts available to allow the deduction of response-alternation, i.e., Hull's (1943) learning theory. Within Hull's theory is contained the concept of "reactive inhibition"; it is the function of the concept of reactive inhibition[3] to account for the process of experimental extinction and related phenomena—that is, the process whereby the animal stops making a learned response when that response is no longer followed by reward. In essence, reactive inhibition is a hypothetical quantity which grows each time a particular response is made. The size of the increment to reactive inhibition is a direct function of the amount of effort required to make the response and also a function of how many times the response has been made. An additional property of reactive inhibition is that it spontaneously dissipates over time. The behavioral effect of reactive inhibition is to decrease the tendency to make the response that gave rise to it. If you think of reactive inhibition as a fatigue-like state, its properties and effects may become more readily apparent.

The application of Hull's reactive inhibition concept to the case of alternation behavior is straightforward. Whenever a response is made—say, a left turn in a T-maze—a certain quantity of left-turning, reactive inhibition is built up. Given a second trial, the animal will be somewhat less inclined than previously to make that response, and given no other compelling tendency to turn left, it will turn right by default, and thus will alternate. In these terms, alternation reflects the animal's attempt to minimize the aversive consequences of its own responding. At this point, one might wonder why an animal behaves at all—why make that first left turn or the second right turn? Why not stay put in the starting alley? The answer, I believe, from the Hullian point of view is that the animal *would*

---

[3] An additional concept, conditioned inhibition, is necessary for a complete account of the extinction process.

be entirely quiescent were it not for the behavior-arousing physiological drives. That answer, by the way, expresses the essence of the "old look" in motivation, whether it be the version of the animal psychologists, such as Hull, or of the classical Freudian psychoanalysts.[4]

To continue with the alternation story, recall that two accounts of alternation have been proposed, which we will refer to as the *stimulus-alternation* hypothesis and the *response-alternation* hypothesis. The response-alternation hypothesis was for several decades the generally accepted account, largely because of its nice fit within Hullian theory, but also because it allowed for some testable derivations that were empirically confirmed. For example, the response-alternation hypothesis predicts decreasing probability of alternation with increasing time between the two trials; it predicts increasing probability of alternation with increases in the number of forced turns to one side of the maze prior to a free-choice trial. These and other predictions were confirmed, lending additional credence to the response-alternation hypothesis, but also additional impact to the experiments next to be described.

Since the conflicting hypotheses were designed to account for the same phenomenon—i.e., alternation in the T-maze—any attempt to choose between them must necessarily be based on some variation from the standard procedure. A beautiful set of experiments were finally conducted by Murray Glanzer (1953a; 1953b) that permitted a clear choice between the opposing hypotheses.

Glanzer's theoretical position was derived from Dennis's. It asserted that alternation occurred with respect to environmental stimuli, not to the rat's own prior responses. According to the theory, any time an organism is exposed to a stimulus, a quantity, called "stimulus satiation," is built up which has the effect of decreasing the probability that the organism will respond to that stimulus on future occasions. Note that this postulate is *formally* just like the reactive inhibition postulate in Hullian theory. Indeed, Glanzer has endowed stimulus satiation with all the properties of reactive inhibition; for example, it accumulates with increasing exposure to a stimulus; it spontaneously dissipates in time, and so forth. As a result, Glanzer's theory can predict equally as well as Hull's the outcome of the experiments mentioned earlier relating to the interval between trials, number of forced turns in the goal arm, and so on.

Beyond this, Glanzer devised some situations for which the two theories make opposing predictions. One of these situations made use of a cross-shaped maze, as depicted in Figure 2. On a given trial, the maze is used as a T, with one of the two possible starting alleys blocked off at the choice-point. The two trials which any animal runs, however, are made from

[4]Robert White (1959) has most clearly drawn the parallel between motivational concepts, old and new, in academic psychology and psychoanalytic theory.

FIG. 2

*The cross-maze. The solid arrow repre-
sents the behavior of an animal on
trial-one. Behavior predicted on trial-
two is represented by broken arrows,
one for the reactive-inhibition prediction, the other for the satiation prediction.*

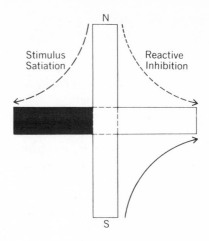

opposite starting alleys. For example, if on trial-1 a rat is started from the
south starting alley, it will start its second trial from the north.

Now, consider the rat, who, starting from the south, turns right on the
first trial. According to reactive inhibition theory it should make a left-
turning response on the second trial, regardless of the alley into which that
response takes it. But, to alternate responses in the cross-maze, the animal
must repeat maze arms.

According to satiation theory, that same animal, having been exposed to
the white arm on the first trial, should avoid that arm on the second trial,
and therefore should enter the black arm, even though that means
repeating its previous right-turning response. The experiment suggested by
these arguments was done and clearly confirmed Glanzer's prediction. The
rats were stimulus alternaters, not response alternaters.

A second, and equally elegant experiment, was conducted, based on the
following argument. According to the Hullian theory, reactive inhibition
following a response dissipates over time. Thus, if a rat makes a right turn
and is then confined in the maze arm instead of being immediately
removed, the reactive inhibition generated on the first trial should
decrease in amount. A second trial, following a long delay in the maze
arm, should be less likely to exhibit the alternation tendency than an
immediate second trial. In addition, it should not matter where the rat
spends its time during the delay. A long wait between trials outside the
maze should have the same effect on propability of alternation as a long
delay within the maze arm.

From the point of view of satiation theory, it matters considerably where
the rat spends its time, but matters little how it got there. Indeed, a long
delay in a maze arm is really a longer than usual exposure to the to-be-
satiated stimulus; the longer the exposure, the greater the satiation; the

greater the satiation, the greater the probability of alternation. Thus, rats delayed in the maze arm should alternate more than rats given an immediate second trial, and rats delayed in the maze arm should alternate more than rats given an equally long delay outside the maze. Again, the data clearly confirmed Glanzer's predictions. Rats are stimulus alternaters, not response alternaters.

The dramatic success of Glanzer's satiation theory made it worthy of further inspection and test. One such test, the first of the studies in which I was directly involved, examined the validity of the assumption that exposure to a stimulus *per se* is a sufficient condition for inducing alternation behavior (Walker, *et al.,* 1955). For these experiments a simple modification was made in the standard procedure: instead of walking into one of the goal arms on the "exposure" trial, rats were *placed* in the arm by the experimenter. After an appropriate length of exposure, the animals were removed from the arm and given an immediate free-choice trial. Several variations of this procedure were run, but in no case was there any evidence that this "passive exposure" to the goal arm stimuli had an effect on the rats' subsequent behavior. At that point it looked as though alternation depended on the rats' making an active choice on the first trial.

Several years after those initial failures to find alternation following passive exposure, the effect was obtained in experiments by Glanzer, by myself, and by others. Why those earlier studies did not reveal the effect remains a mystery.[5] In a way, however, that failure was fortunate, for it led to a pair of new experiments which are of great significance, at least for purposes of this presentation.

RESPONSE TO CHANGE

The first of the pair was based on the following argument. In the previous passive exposure experiments the animals were not in direct contact with the stimuli at the juncture of the choice-point and the goal arm. But that is the place at which the choice was to be made on the second trial. Thus, it would seem a fairer test of satiation theory if the first trial were so designed that the rat's exposure to the goal arm stimuli occurred within a context that included the choice-point region.

That argument was translated into an experiment (Kivy, Earl, and Walker, 1956) for which the standard T-maze was modified slightly by employing transparent glass doors instead of the usual opaque doors to block off the goal arms from the choice-point. These glass doors were

---

[5]The mystery may have been cleared up, and indeed the whole problem of alternation behavior reopened, by an exciting group of experiments recently reported as a doctoral dissertation by Robert Douglas (1964).

already in place when the exposure trial began. When the rats were introduced into the starting alley, they could wander up to the choice-point and peer through the glass doors into the goal arms, but could not enter either arm on that trial. What the rat saw on the exposure trial was two goal arms of the same brightness, either both black or both white. The animals were given lengthy exposure trials to assure adequate satiation; they were then taken out of the maze, the glass doors were removed, and one of the goal arms was changed in brightness.

The design of the experiment is given in Figure 3. It was expected that if Glanzer's theory were correct, and if this version of the passive exposure procedure were the appropriate one, then those rats exposed to black goal arms on the first trial would enter the white arm on the second trial, and *vice versa*. And that is exactly what happened.

Before discussing the second experiment of this pair, let me recall a comment I made earlier about Glanzer's theory—that it was formally identical with the reactive inhibition theory, with the exception of the assumed source of the alternation tendency. The formal identity that I referred to was related to the postulates about the growth and decay of the inhibiting quantity. But there is another way in which the two theories are identical: for both, alternation behavior represents an *avoidance* response. For both, the animal does what it does on trial-two because it cannot do what it did on trial-one. Hull's rat turns left because, in some sense, it is "tired of making right turns"; Glanzer's rat enters the black arm because it "can't stand seeing whiteness," not because it finds the black arm attractive.[6]

Now, during the time when we were working on these studies with Professor Walker, Robert Earl and I were beginning to develop some theoretical ideas about motivation which I intend to discuss more fully a little later. These ideas were stimulated in large part by the work I have been describing, but they also derived from a variety of other sources, including our own introspections. One notion we had was that it was

FIG. 3

Design of the Kivy, Earl, and Walker experiment. On the exposure trial, the arms of the T-maze are both black or both white and the rat views them through glass partitions; on the test trial, the animal can choose between a black and a white arm.

	Maze Arm	
	left	right
Exposure	W(B)	W(B)
Test	B(W)	W(B)

[6]For a newer and more sophisticated analysis of alternation theories than the one offered here, see O'Connell (1965).

inappropriate to consider the choices an animal or a person makes to be determined exclusively by avoidance tendencies. This might prevail in some instances, but there must also be cases in which an alternative is chosen because it has positive valence, and positive in an absolute, not just a relative sense.

To develop this idea further, it was necessary to specify the properties of a stimulus object that would make it attractive to a given individual. In somewhat different language, our task was to specify the properties of what the learning theorists variously called "goal objects," "incentives," or "rewards." Within classical motivation theory, such objects were characterized either by their ability to reduce a physiological need or by their having been associated with such need-reducing objects. The former class constituted the so-called *primary rewards,* the latter, the *secondary* or *acquired* rewards. Between them, the primary and secondary rewards comprised the entire set of goal objects.

Now, it was our notion—and not ours alone, of course[7]—that this conceptualization of motivation and reward was incomplete; that there were goal objects other than those that reduced physiological need states. Moreover, we believed that the slack could not adequately be taken up by reference to a vaguely specified set of acquired rewards.

Let me postpone completion of this level of discussion and return temporarily to the real world of rats and mazes, beginning with another brief look at Figure 3, in which the Kivy experiment is diagrammed. While that experiment was designed as a test of Glanzer's satiation theory and the results fit the satiation prediction, an alternative interpretation of what was going on in that experiment could be offered. It was my thought that what the rat was doing when it entered the white arm, after having been exposed to two black arms, was not avoiding further exposure to blackness; rather, on approaching the choice-point and noting a marked change in one of the goal arms—for example, the one changed from black to white—the rat responded to the change by entering the changed arm and exploring it. I refer to this interpretation as the *response-to-change* hypothesis.

But an alternative interpretation is not worth much if all it can do is predict experimental results that have already been obtained. To be taken seriously it must make unique predictions and preferably predictions that are opposite to those derived from the original theoretical position. What can the response-to-change hypothesis predict that will differentiate it from the satiation hypothesis?

As so often happens, the answer to that question came by way of a

---

[7]We were working within a tradition begun in recent decades by, among many others, Berlyne (1954, 1960), Harlow (1953), and Nissen (1954) and continued most recently by Munsinger and Kessen (1964), and Walker (1964).

mistake I made while describing the Kivy experiment to a psychology class. What I did, in effect, was to reverse the stimulus conditions that prevailed in the Kivy experiment; my erroneous description would be represented by the diagram in Figure 4. Here, on the exposure trial the two arms are different—one black and one white, and on the test trial they are of the same brightness, both black or both white. My initial response to the error in presentation was to apologize to the class, erase the mistake from the blackboard, and do it properly. Several hours later, while I was perseverating on this error, it struck me that my erroneous diagram provided the design for an experiment that would answer the question: how can the response-to-change hypothesis be differentiated from the satiation hypothesis? What would each of the two hypotheses predict were the experiment diagrammed in Figure 4 actually run?

First consider the satiation hypothesis. On the exposure trial, the animal is satiated for black and for white; on the test trial it is offered a choice between, say, two black arms. The satiation induced on the exposure trial would not bias it against either the black arm on the left or the black arm on the right. In short, the choices made by a group of rats should be distributed independently of the rats' satiation experience.

The response-to-change hypothesis makes a different prediction. The rat which saw black on the left and white on the right on the exposure trial and is then faced with two black arms on the test trial should be attracted to the *changed* arm—in this case the black arm that used to be white; that is, the arm on the right.

The experiment suggested by this analysis was run (Dember, 1956), using the Kivy apparatus and generally following his procedures except for the configuration of the stimuli on the two trials. The rats' behavior conformed to the response-to-change prediction, and this result has since been replicated by other investigators.

The outcome of this experiment greatly encouraged Robert Earl and me to pursue the theoretical developments that we had been working on. Rather than dwell further on the details of where the ideas came from, I propose at this point to sketch the product of this thinking, which took the form of both some general hypotheses about motivation (that we called the Theory of Choice) and some specific experimental tests of these hypotheses.

FIG. 4

Design of the Response-to-Change experiment. Conditions are just the reverse of those in the Kivy, et al., experiment.

Maze Arm

	left	right
Exposure	B(W)	W(B)
Test	W(B)	W(B)

THE THEORY OF CHOICE[8]

From the experiments that I have described, from many that I do not have time to mention, and from the set of observations which form the base of those nonexperimental approaches to knowledge about man and his motives—such as philosophy and art—it is clear that the direction of an individual's behavior is at least partly under the control of the stimulus objects and events surrounding him. It is clear also that one need not be suffering from physiological imbalance, or anticipating that state, to become interested in those external objects; it is clear that these objects of interest need not be potential restorers of physiological balance, nor even associated with such servants of the homeostatic process, in order to exert powerful impact on the individual's behavior.

What are these objects and events? For a rat, a change in the brightness of a goal arm in a T-maze; for a monkey, a toy railroad train running on a table top; for a human baby, a rattle, its own fingers, plastic birdies swinging on a mobile over its crib; for the human adult, a painting, a puzzle, a pin-ball machine, a poem (I am tempted to add "a partridge in a pear tree," perhaps to preserve the alliteration, but maybe also because it typifies a class of objects, characterized by incongruity, that has considerable impact on the direction of behavior).

I have used the word incongruity, the items in the preceding list call to mind other terms, such as novelty, complexity, movement, uncertainity, ambiguity, and so on. There are specific objects and events, impinging on specific individuals at particular moments which might best be labeled by one of these terms, rather than another. For example, the rat entering the changed goal arm is responding to novelty; the toy railroad train is characterized, for the monkey, by movement; the puzzle by uncertainty, and so on. Rather than dwell on these fine distinctions, the Theory of Choice seizes on what they appear to have in common, as objects or events, and on the way that they influence behavior.

As objects or events, the items in the list share the property of being bearers of *information*. I use the word in the technical sense of Information Theory; these are objects or events which are unexpected, nonredundant, and which, when they occur, therefore reduce uncertainty. With regard to the perceiving individual, these highly informative objects or events have the effect of arousing his interest, directing his attention, consuming his time and energy—at least if he is free to let them.

The Theory of Choice asserts, then, that every object (let us drop the

[8]The theory is presented more formally and in greater detail in Dember and Earl (1957), Earl (1957, 1961), and Musselman (1963).

word, event, for convenience) can be assigned an information value, or a "complexity value," as the theory was originally proposed; moreover, the theory asserts that the complexity of an object is a motivationally crucial property of that object, so long as that object is functioning as a goal object, and not simply as a means to another end.

The next step in the development of the theory is hard to convey clearly without a lot of attendant discussion. It asserts that each individual can also be assigned a "complexity value." What we have in mind here is that for each individual there is some highest level of complexity, in the range of objects that he might encounter, which he is equipped to deal with comfortably and effectively. The individual's complexity level is called his "ideal."

Some objects would *for him* be excessively complex; some would be too simple; some would be just right, as the baby bear's bed was for Goldilocks. Objects that are too simple elicit boredom if they are unavoidable; objects that are too complex elicit fear, anger, and sometimes rage if one is forced to maintain contact with them.

Quite obviously, then, if the individual is free to choose, he will prefer to encounter objects of a complexity level that matches his own. He will *select* them from among others if they are made available to him; he will *seek* them out if they are absent; he will *work* for them; and he will even *learn* what he must do in order to obtain them, all of these (select, seek, work, learn) behaviors that in classical motivation theory serve as indicators of the presence of a primary or secondary reward.

While the theory expects that the individual will maintain considerable contact with objects of ideal complexity in preference to objects of much lower or higher complexity, it also recognizes that nonideal objects will also be sampled by the individual. Indeed, it seems to be the case, as evidenced by some results that Earl (1957) obtained in his doctoral dissertation, that the modal amount of time goes not to the ideal stimulus, but to one that is just a little more complex than the ideal.

We refer to that object as a "pacer," and attribute to it a special function. It is the pacer, if one is available, that enables the individual to change his ideal. As he maintains active contact with the pacer and eventually masters it, his own level of complexity grows, and he is ready for a new pacer and eventually a still higher ideal.

Of course pacers are not always available, and there are probably some neurophysiological limits to perceptual and cognitive growth, but, in general, the theory takes the optimistic position that under the proper circumstances an individual's complexity level can keep increasing and that learning can be achieved neither as a boring chore nor as a fearful burden. Indeed, the New Look in Motivation—of which the Theory of Choice is but a glance—has already invaded the classroom, or so I gather from a recent article by Robert Gross published in the *New York Times Magazine*, for Sunday, September 6, 1964. The article is about innovations in teaching techniques, and in one brief paragraph the author says

> ". . . Another element is a new consensus on motivation. Cumulative evidence from many sources—animal experiments, studies of how children learn, everyday observations of the way they really behave—has shown up the inadequacies of old notions of motivation, based on reward and punishment, by demonstrating that human beings are born with the desire to know, the urge to explore and to master their environment, to achieve. . ."

The ideas contained within the Theory of Choice are not especially novel. As I implied earlier, they can be found in the writings of many authors. For example, I was both dismayed and delighted to discover some very similar notions in the works of Herbert Spencer and Thomas Brown, two nineteenth-century philosopher-psychologists. The major innovation provided by the theory—I said this also about the New Look in Perception—is its attempt at empirical verification, which in turn implies an attempt at operational definition of its concepts, such as complexity, pacer, etc., and a related concern for measurement.

SOME TESTS OF THE THEORY

A brief account of two experiments will serve to illustrate both the problem of measuring the concepts of the theory and the beginning steps that have been taken to solve that problem. In addition, the two experiments will reveal how the theory can be generalized to cover the phylogenetic range from rats to college students and stimulus materials ranging from visual patterns to poetry.

The theory was first tested in an experiment with rats (Dember, Earl, and Paradise, 1957). A new piece of apparatus was constructed, the figure-8 maze, as illustrated in Figure 5. The rat, after several days of taming, was introduced into the maze and then left there for about an hour. One loop of the figure-8 was lined with horizontal black and white stripes; the other loop was lined with vertically oriented stripes. The two loops were equal in total brightness. However, as the rat moved through the vertically striped loop, it experienced more changes in illumination than it did when moving through the horizontally striped loop. We assumed that, for the rat, the greater the number of illumination changes, the greater the perceptual complexity. Note that our assessment of the relative complexity of the two alternatives was based on intuitive judgment, and though derived from many years of intimate contact with rats, our judgment is ideally no substitute for a more direct measurement.

FIG. 5

The figure-S maze. The rat is placed in one of the boxes at the juncture of the two loops and enters the maze by pushing through the one-way café doors.

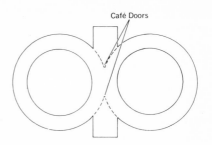

Café Doors

Now, the theory enabled the following prediction: any change in the rat's preference for one of the loops, as indexed by the amount of time it spent in each loop over two consecutive daily one-hour sessions, would be in the direction *from less complex to more complex*. The basis of this prediction can be shown with the help of Figure 6. The rat that enters the maze with an ideal at C would have an initial preference for the more complex, i.e., the vertically striped loop, and would maintain that preference, as long as it kept behaving in the situation. Rats entering at A would initially prefer the less complex loop; in the course of sampling both loops, however, their ideals might grow until they are close enough to the complexity of the vertically striped alternative so that it became preferred. Once that happened, if it did, a fixed preference for the more complex loop would be evidenced. Rats entering with ideals at B might initially prefer either H or V, depending on which of the two they were closer to, but if their preference changed, once again the change could occur only from H to V.

The data collected from 17 rats conformed very well to the prediction, but the sample was small and the procedure somewhat informal, to be excused on the grounds that this was a "pilot study." Therefore, a second experiment was conducted, with a neater procedure—for example, 5 daily sessions were conducted rather than just 2—and with a change in the patterns lining the two loops. In this case, the horizontally striped loop was contrasted with a plain black loop for half the rats and a plain white loop for the other half. Here the intuitive judgment about which was the more complex seemed less equivocal; clearly the horizontally striped loop was now functioning as the more complex alternative. The same prediction was made—any change in preference would be from the less to the more complex loop, i.e., from plain to horizontally striped, but not vice versa—and again was convincingly verified in the data.

The theory so far has been successful with rats, but what about people? I have already mentioned Earl's doctoral dissertation, in which the subjects were 12-year-old children, and the stimulus materials were puzzles which

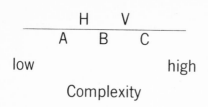

FIG. 6

Two stimuli, H and V, and three hypothetical rats, arranged according to their complexity values. See text for explanation.

the children were allowed to work on. I am also aware of an attempt by some colleagues at the University of Chicago to run (literally) children in a human-size version of the figure-8 maze, complete with horizontally and vertically striped loops. There the results were a bit messy, but they probably should have been.

Closer to home is an experiment conducted by Richard Kammann (1966) as his doctoral dissertation at the University of Cincinnati. This is the study in which the stimulus material was poetry.

I think it is clear that the physiological-need approach to motivation would be hard pressed to predict which of a set of poems would be preferred by college students. What can the Theory of Choice, as a representative of the New Look in Motivation, contribute to this problem?

A poem, like any other stimulus, has a complexity value, which is the resultant of a whole set of formal, or structural properties of the elements of the poem—for example, its meter, rhyme scheme, etc.—as well as semantic properties, relating to the meanings of individual words and phrases. Also contributing to the complexity of a poem is the ambiguity of its total message—the meanings of the individual words may be clear, but the poet's intent may not. In addition to these formal and nonformal sources of complexity is the factor of familiarity. It seems reasonable to anticipate that even the initially most complex poem would lose in complexity as it became more and more familiar to, and better and better understood by, a particular reader. "A rose is a rose is a rose" is a very unlikely sequence of words, but not to someone who has heard that line a few times. This last consideration suggests that it might be futile to attempt an assessment of the complexity of a given poem without interposing the intended reader of that poem. In short, he is the one who should, in effect, tell us how complex that poem is for him. But how might that be done?

One could try a direct approach and simply ask subjects to rate poems according to their complexity. This seemed too simple-minded, however, and while it might work, its usefulness would appear limited. A somewhat less direct approach to measuring poem complexity was sought by Dr. Kammann and found in what is referred to as the Cloze technique.

Suppose I show you the letters CINCINNAT-, with a blank space for a final letter, and I ask you to guess what single letter belongs in that space.

I believe you would have little difficulty in correctly guessing the appropriate letter. It is really terribly redundant, and I am sure that a piece of mail addressed to the city of "Cincinnat" would not be delayed any longer than ususal.

Suppose, however, at the opposite extreme, I randomly selected a sequence of 9 letters and asked you what the 10th should be; the redundancy of that last letter, and hence its predictability by you, would be greatly reduced.

We could play the same game with sequences of words, deleting say every fourth word in a passage and asking people to fill in the blanks. Their ability to make correct guesses surely would reflect the internal redundancies within the word sequence. This, in essence, is the Cloze technique. It was developed, incidentally, as a measure of readability to compete with the popular Flesch count.

Dr. Kammann saw in the Cloze technique a possible way of measuring the complexity of a poem. He argued that the higher the Cloze score associated with a given poem—the greater the number of blanks properly filled in by a subject, or group of subjects—the less complex it was as a total stimulus object.

The rest should now be obvious. A set of 15 poems was selected, which seemed *a priori* to cover a wide range of complexity values. Every fourth word was deleted from each of the poems, beginning with the second word, and these "unclozed" poems were given to college students, whose task it was to guess what word belonged in each blank space. One such fragmented poem is shown in Figure 7.

On the basis of the subjects' performance, the poems could then be ranked according to their complexity. At a later date, these same subjects were given the intact poems and asked, among other tasks, to rate them on a good-bad scale and to indicate which they would like to have the opportunity to memorize, to hear discussed by an expert, etc.

Among the many interesting results that were obtained, the two most pertinent were that the poems of intermediate complexity were given the highest "goodness" ratings and that the subjects' own ability to guess the missing words in all the poems—what one might call the subjects' "clozability" score—was highly correlated with the complexity of the poems they said they would prefer to memorize and hear discussed by an expert.

This brief description fails to do justice to a very complex and clever piece of work, but it does indicate a promising approach to the measurement of the concepts in the theory. In addition, it may suggest the scope of coverage that the theory is seeking. In this latter respect, the theory is quite representative of those that comprise the New Look in Motivation.

A _____, a ringing health, _____ the king
of _____ our hearts to-day! _____ what proud song
_____ follow on the _____, nor do him _____?
Unless the sea _____ harp, each mirthful _____
Woven of the _____ of the nights _____ Spring,
And Dawn _____ lonely listener, glad _____ grave
With colours _____ the sea-shell _____ the wave
In _____ eye and cheek, _____ is none to _____!
Drink to him, _____ men upon an _____ peak
Brim one _____ cup of crimson _____,
And into it _____ one pure cold _____ of snow,
Then _____ it up, too _____ to speak
And _____ -to the mountains, _____ on glittering line,
_____ away into the _____ -glow.

FIG. 7 *One of the un-clozed poems (for the Eightieth Birthday of George Meredith) used in the poetry experiment. The deleted words, in order, are: health, unto, all, But, should, thought, wrong, were, string, lightning, of, the, and, of, and, brightening, there, sing, as, Alpine, immortal, wine, drop, crust, hold, rapturously, drink, line, surging, sunset.*

REFERENCES

BERLYNE, D. E. A Theory of Human Curosity. *Brit. J. Psychol.,* 1954, *45,* 180–191.

BERLYNE, D. E. *Conflict, Arousal, and Curiosity,* New York: McGraw-Hill, 1960.

DEMBER, W. N. Response by the Rat to Environmental Change. *J. Comp. Physiol. Psychol.,* 1956, *49,* 93–95.

DEMBER, W. N. *The Psychology of Perception.* New York: Henry Holt, 1960.

DEMBER, W. N. Alternation behavior. In D. W. Fiske and S. R. Maddi (Eds.), *Functions of Varied Experience.* Homewood, Illinois: The Dorsey Press, Inc., 1961.

DEMBER, W. N., & EARL, R. W. Analysis of Exploratory, Manipulatory, and Curiosity Behavior. *Psychol. Rev.,* 1957, *64,* 91–96.

DEMBER, W. N., EARL, R. W., & PARADISE, N. Response by Rats to Differential Stimulus Complexity. *J. Comp. Physiol. Psychol.,* 1957, *50,* 514–518.

DEMBER, W. N., & FOWLER, H. Spontaneous Alternation Behavior. *Psychol. Bull.,* 1958, *55,* 412–428.

DENNIS, W. A Comparison of the Rat's First and Second Explorations of a Maze Unit. *Amer. J. Psychol.,* 1935, *47,* 488–490.

DOUGLAS, R. J. An Analysis of Spontaneous Alternation Cues. Unpublished doctoral dissertation, University of Michigan, 1964.

EARL, R. W. Problem Solving and Motor Skill Behaviors Under Conditions of Free-Choice. Unpublished doctoral dissertation, University of Michigan, 1957.

EARL, R. W. *A Theory of Stimulus Selection.* Human Factors Section, Hughes Ground Systems, Special Document SD 61-132, 1961.

GLANZER, M. Stimulus Satiation: An Explanation of Spontaneous Alternation and Related Phenomena. *Psychol. Rev.,* 1953 (a), *60,* 257-268.

GLANZER, M. The Role of Stimulus Satiation in Spontaneous Alternation. *J. Exp. Psychol.,* 1953 (b), *45,* 387-393.

HARLOW, H. F. Mice, Monkeys, Men, and Motives. *Psychol. Rev.,* 1953, *60,* 23-32.

HULL, C. L. *Principles of Behavior.* New York: Appleton-Century-Crofts, 1943.

KAMMANN, R. Verbal Complexity and Preferences in Poetry. *Journal of Verbal Learning and Verbal Behavior,* 1966, *5,* 536-540.

KIVY, P. N., EARL, R. W., & WALKER, E. L. Stimulus Context and Satiation. *J. Comp. Physiol. Psychol.,* 1956, *49,* 90-92.

MUNSINGER, H., & KESSEN, W. Uncertainty, Structure, and Preference. *Psychol. Monographs,* 1964, *78* (No. 9, Whole No. 586).

MUSSELMAN, D. R. Free Choice Behavior as a Function of Stimulus Changes Along Three Dimensions of Complexity. Unpublished doctoral dissertation, Claremont Graduate School, 1963.

NISSEN, H. W. The nature of the Drive as Innate Determinant of Behavioral Organization. In M. R. Jones (Ed.), *Nebraska Symposium on Motivation.* Lincoln, Nebraska: University of Nebraska Press, 1954.

O'CONNELL, R. H. Trials With Tedium and Titillation. *Psychol. Bull.,* 1965, *63,* 170-179.

SAMUELS, INA. Reticular Mechanisms and Behavior. *Psychol. Bull.,* 1959, *56,* 1-25.

WALKER, E. L. Psychological Complexity as a Basis for a Theory of Motivation and Choice. In D. Levine (Ed.), *Nebraska Symposium on Motivation,* 1964. Lincoln: University of Nebraska Press, 1964.

WALKER, E. L., DEMBER, W. N., EARL, R. W., FLIEGE, S. E., & KAROLY, A. J. Choice Alternation: II. Exposure to Stimulus or Stimulus and Place Without Choice. *J. Comp. Physiol. Psychol.,* 1955, *48,* 24-28.

WHITE, R. W. Motivation Reconsidered: The Concept of Competence. *Psychol. Rev.,* 1959, *66,* 297-333.

3

ACTIVATION:
A NEUROPSYCHOLOGICAL
DIMENSION[1]
ROBERT B. MALMO

What kinds of physiological functioning can be associated with the concept of arousal as a function of novel stimuli? A better understanding of the central nervous system mechanisms which appear to be associated with arousal would be of great value in clarifying the relationship between varied stimulation and physical activation. In his paper, Malmo proceeds from the work of Lindsley and Hebb to go on to spell out the nature of the relationships between activation and other variables. The ascending reticular arousal system (ARAS) becomes a focus of attention in developing the concept of general activation. Malmo discusses the determinant of activation level, suggesting that it is a function of deprivation of biological needs on which is superimposed environmental stimulating conditions. We would suggest that the biological need deficit is one means of producing stimuli, and that the greater deficit is essentially a more novel (or intense) internal stimulus which results in a more aroused organism. After continued exposure to intense internal stimuli the organism will "adapt" to this high level of stimuli—that is, this high level of internal stimulation will be cognitively integrated. At this point—that is, after adaptation—the researcher can

Reprinted from Psychological Review, 1959, 66, 367–368, by permission of the author and the American Psychological Association.

[1]Support for some of the research reported herein has come from the following sources: National Institute of Mental Health, National Institutes of Health, United States Public Health Service: Grant Number M-1475; Medical Research and Development Division, Office of the Surgeon General, Department of the United States Army: Contract Number DA-49-007-MD-626; Defence Research Board, Department of National Defence, Canada: Grant Number 9425-04; and National Research Council of Canada: Grant Number A. P. 29.

Grateful acknowledgement is made to A. Amsel, R. C. Davis, S. M. Feldman, P. Milner, M. M. Schnore, R. G. Stennett, D. J. Ehrlich and L. R. Pinneo for constructive criticism of the manuscript.

The main parts of this paper were presented in a Symposium entitled, "Experimental Foundations of Clinical Psychology," under the chairmanship of Arthur J. Bachrach, at the University of Virginia, April 1–2, 1959. To Ian P. Stevenson, who was the discussant of my paper on that Symposium, I owe a debt of gratitude for his very helpful comments.

get overt measures of high activation only by introducing other stimuli that must be integrated. This issue is not yet ready for resolution. Nevertheless, the continuing work on the ARAS suggests that its function is a physiological counterpart for the psychological phenomena of motivation. Malmo's discussion is a quest for the explanation of the relationship of ARAS to general motivation.

Professor Malmo in his recent writings has underscored his earlier emphasis on the importance of research that yields direct information concerning central nervous system functions. A recent experiment by Goodman (1968) provides a prime example of this kind of research.

REFERENCE:

GOODMAN, S. J. *Visuo-Motor Reaction Times and Brain Stem Multiple Unit Activity.* Experimental Neurology, 1968, *22*, 1367–1378.

*   *   *

There have been three main lines of approach to the problem of activation: *(a)* through electroencephalography and neurophysiology, *(b)* through physiological studies of "behavioral energetics," and *(c)* through the learning theorists' search for a satisfactory measure of drive. Before attempting a formal definition of activation, I shall briefly describe these three different approaches to the concept.

Neurophysiological approach: Lindsley's Activation Theory.[2] The neurophysiological approach to activation had its origin in electroencephalography (EEG). Early workers in the EEG field soon discovered that there were distinctive wave patterns characterizing the main levels of psychological functioning in the progression from deep sleep to highly alerted states of activity (Jasper, 1941). In deep sleep large low-frequency waves predominate. In light sleep and drowsy states the frequencies are not as low as in deep sleep, but there are more low-frequency waves than in the wakeful states. In relaxed wakefulness there is a predominance of waves in the alpha (8–12 c.p.s.) range that gives way to beta frequencies (approximately 18–30 c.p.s.) when the *S* is moderately alert. Under highly alerting and exciting conditions beta waves predominate. In addition to the

[2] I am using neuropsychology in a rather broad sense, meaning to include the work often referred to by the term "psychophysiology." This usage implies that the chief problems being studied are psychological ones, and it also stresses the importance of neurophysiological techniques. It is true that, strictly speaking, many of the physiological techniques in use are not neurophysiological ones; yet our main interest lies in the central neural control of the physiological functions under study rather than in the peripheral events themselves.

Later on in the paper I shall attempt a formal definition of activation. For the first section of the paper, I believe that it will be sufficient to say that in using the term "activation" I am referring to the intensive dimension of behavior. "Arousal" is often used interchangeably with activation; and level of drive is a very similar concept. For instance, a drowsy *S* is low, an alert *S* is high in activation.

increased frequency of the waves under these conditions of heightened alertness there is also a change from a regular synchronized appearance of the tracing to an irregular desynchronized tracing, usually of reduced amplitude.

For Lindsley's theory, desynchronization (called "activation pattern") became the single most important EEG phenomenon. My use of the term "desynchronization" is purely descriptive. Desynchronization or "flattening" in the EEG tracing was consistently found associated with increased alertness in a large variety of experiments with animal and human Ss. The consistency and generality of this phenomenon suggested the existence of mechanisms in the brain mediating behavioral functions having to do with levels of alertness, although at the time that the original observations were made it was not at all clear what these neural mechanisms were.

With the discovery of the ascending reticular activating system (ARAS), however, there was rapid and very significant advance in theory and experimentation. Some of the most important general findings have been as follows: *(a)* Lesions in the ARAS abolished "activation" of the EEG and produced a behavioral picture of lethargy and somnolence (Lindsley, 1957). *(b)* The "activation pattern" in the EEG was reproduced by electrical stimulation of the ARAS. Furthermore, in the monkey, Fuster (1958) recently found that concurrent ARAS stimulation of moderate intensity improved accuracy and speed of visual discrimination reaction. He also found that higher intensities had the opposite effect, producing diminution of correct responses and increase of reaction times. Interpretation of these latter findings is complicated by the fact that they were obtained with stimulation intensities higher than the threshold for the elicitation of observable motor effects such as generalized muscular jerks. It is not stated whether intensity of stimulation was systematically studied. In any event, these observations of deleterious effect from high intensity stimulation are of considerable interest because they are what might be expected according to the activation theory.

The activation theory as first stated by Lindsley (1951)—although introduced in the handbook chapter on emotion—was from the outset, conceived by him to be broader than an explanatory concept for emotional behavior. The theory was elaborated by Hebb (1955) in an attempt to solve the problem of drives. With the continuous flow of new experimental data on the ARAS (Lindsley, 1957), this area of neuropsychological investigation appears to be heading toward an important breakthrough. I shall attempt to state very briefly the main points of the current theory, drawing upon the ideas of several authors. According to

[3]The expression "excited states" is frequently used to refer to the upper end of the activation continuum. In using this term I do not wish to imply increased overt activity. In fact, overt activity may be reduced to a very low level at the high end of the continuum, when—for example—a person is immobolized by terror.

this theory, the continuum extending from deep sleep at the low activation end to "excited states"[3] at the high activation end is very largely a function of cortical bombardment by the ARAS, such that the greater the cortical bombardment the higher the activation. Further, the relation between activation and behavioral efficiency (cue function or level of performance) is described by an inverted **U** curve. That is, from low activation up to a point that is optimal for a given function, level of performance rises monotonically with increasing activation level, but beyond this optimal point the relation becomes nonmonotonic: further increase in activation beyond this point produces a fall in performance level, this fall being directly related to the amount of the increase in level of activation.

Principles of neural action that could account for the reversal in the effects of nonspecific neural bombardment of the cortex by the ARAS have long been known (Lorente de Nó, 1939, p. 428). Circulation of neural impulses in a closed chain of neurons (or "cell assembly" to use Hebb's [1949] term) may be facilitated by impulses arriving outside the chain (e.g. from the ARAS). According to Lorente de Nó's schema, such extraneous impulses have the effect of stimulating certain neurons subliminally thus making it possible for an impulse from within the chain to finish the job, that is make it fire at the appropriate time in the sequence, when alone, without the prior hit, it would have failed to fire it.

Again, according to the same account by Lorente de Nó (1939, p. 428), the deleterious effects of overstimulation from impulses outside the chain can be explained. A neuron in the chain may fail to respond to stimulation if owing to repeated activity it acquires a high threshold, and this failure to transmit the circulating impulses would mean cessation of activity in a cell assembly. I proposed this kind of explanation previously (1958) to account for the downturn in the inverted **U** curve as an alternative to Hebb's suggestion that "the greater bombardment may interfere with the delicate adjustments involved in cue function, perhaps by facilitating irrelevant responses (a high D arouses conflicting sH_R's?)" (Hebb, 1955, p. 250).

It seems reasonable to suppose that as diffuse bombardment from the ARAS greatly exceeds an amount that is optimal for some simple psychological function being mediated by a particular cell assembly, the operation of that cell assembly will be impaired, and that the performance being mediated by it will suffer accordingly. This line of reasoning suggests that the inverted **U** relation should be found in quite simple psychological functions. Present evidence appears to support this suggestion. A recent (unpublished) experiment by Bélanger and Feldman, that I shall describe later in this paper, indicates that in rats the inverted **U** relation is found with simple bar-pressing performance, and an experiment by Finch (1938) suggests that even such a simple response as the unconditioned salivary response yields the inverted **U** curve when plotted against activation level.

It may be noted that according to a response competition hypothesis, the inverted **U** relation should appear most prominently in complex functions where opportunities for habit interference are greater than they are in the case of simple functions. According to the response competition hypothesis, in the limiting case where response is so simple that habit interference is negligible, the relation between response strength and activation level should be monotonic. Therefore, finding the nonmonotonic relation in such simple responses as bar pressing and salivation raises strong doubts that the habit interference explanation can account for the seemingly pervasive phenomenon of the inverted **U** curve.

Principle of activation growing out of work on behavioral intensity. Even before the EEG work on desynchronization, the behavioral evidence had suggested the existence of some brain mechanism like the ARAS. The writings of Duffy (1951, 1957), Freeman (1948), and others of the "energetics" group have long stressed the importance of an intensity dimension in behavior.

In an attempt to obtain a measure of this intensity variable, Duffy relied mainly on records of muscular tension (1932) while Freeman's favorite indicator was palmar conductance (1948). These workers concluded from their experiments that there was a lawful relationship between a state of the organism, called "arousal," "energy mobilization," "activation," or simply "intensity" and level of performance. Moreover they suggested that the relationship might be described by an inverted **U** curve (Duffy, 1957). This suggestion has proved heuristic as indicated by the current experimental attack on the inverted **U** hypothesis (Stennett, 1957a; Bindra, 1959; Cofer, 1959; Kendler, 1959).

The inverted **U** shaped curve has been shown to hold in numerous learning and performance situations where the amount of induced muscle tension was varied systematically (Courts, 1942). It is tempting to conclude that tension induction is simply one of the many ways to increase activation level, but as Courts' (1942) discussion suggests this conclusion would be premature. It is possible that squeezing on a dynamometer, a typical means of inducing tension in these experiments, may produce generalized activation effects as some data from Freeman indicate (1948, p. 71). But Freeman's data are insufficient to establish this point, and there are alternative explanations for the relationship between the performance data and induced tension (Courts, 1942). By repeating the induced-tension experiments with simultaneous recordings of EEG and other physiological functions it would be possible to determine how general the effects of inducing tension actually are. Such direct tests of the activation hypothesis are very much needed.

Drive and activation. A third approach to the activation principle was made by learning theorists, especially those of the Hull school. I have argued elsewhere (Malmo, 1958) that general drive *(D)*, without the steering component, became identical in principle with activation or arousal. Set aside for the moment the attractive possibility of using ARAS as a neural model for mediation of *D*, and consider only the methodological advantages of physiological measures in the quantification of *D*. It seems that none of the other attempts to measure *D* have been really satisfactory, and that physiological indicants where applied have been surprisingly effective. Learning theorists up to the present time have made only very occasional use of physiological measures. For instance, in arguing that a previously painful stimulus had lost its drive properties, Brown (1955) cited the absence of physiological reaction when the stimulus was applied. More recently, Spence (1958) has reported some success with physiological measures in his studies of "emotionally-based" drive.

In keeping with traditional views concerning the place of physiological measures in psychology, on those few occasions that they were employed at all they were applied to aversive or emotionally based drive. According to the activation principle, however, it should be possible to use physiological measures to gauge appetitionally based as well as aversively based drive. This means, for instance, that in a water deprivation experiment there should be close correspondence between number of hours of deprivation and physiological level. That is, heart rate, for example, should be higher in an animal performing in a Skinner box after 36 hours of deprivation than after 24, higher still after 48 hours of deprivation and so on. In my Nebraska Symposium paper I stated that, so far as I was aware, this kind of experiment had not been reported (Malmo, 1958, p. 236).

Bélanger and Feldman in Montreal have recently completed such an experiment, and, as can be seen by inspecting Fig. 1, the results were as predicted by the activation hypothesis. Heart rate in rats showed progressive change corresponding with increasing hours of water deprivation. Although there were only seven rats in the group, this change in heart rate was highly significant. Deprivations were carried out serially on the same group of animals, commencing at 12 hours and proceeding to 24, 48 hours and so on with sufficient hydration (four to seven days) between deprivation periods to prevent any cumulative effects from affecting the experiments. Heart rate was picked up by means of wire electrodes inserted in the skin of the animals and was amplified and registered graphically by means of a Sanborn electrocardiograph. Particular care was taken to record heart rate under nearly the same conditions of stimulation each time, that is, when the animal was pressing on the lever in the Skinner box or during drinking from the dispenser immediately after pressing. Under

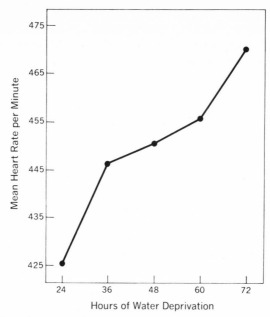

FIG. 1   *Data from Bélanger and Feldman showing relation between water deprivation and heart rate in rats (N=7). See text for explanation.*

these conditions it was not possible to obtain sufficient heart-rate data at the 12-hour deprivation interval. Testing the animal under constant stimulating conditions is a very important methodological consideration. Some exploratory observations indicated that heart-rate measurements taken in a restraining compartment did not agree with those taken under the carefully controlled stimulus conditions provided by the Skinner box. I shall return to this finding later on because, aside from its methodological importance, I believe that it has considerable theoretical significance as well.

Figure 2 presents the behavioral data which are again in remarkably good agreement with prediction from the activation hypothesis. Up to the 48-hour deprivation interval there is an increasing monotonic relationship between number of bar presses and hours of deprivation which is strictly in accordance with Hullian theory. The accompanying rise in heart rate suggests that for this part of the curve, hours of deprivation and the physiological indicant are roughly equivalent as measures of drive. But after the 48-hour point on the curves, the combined heart rate and behavioral data support predictions previously made from activation theory (Malmo, 1958) and suggest that the Hullian position requires revision. This kind of downward turn in the response curve has usually

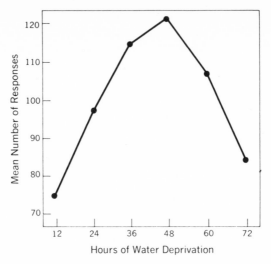

FIG. 2 *Data from Bélanger and Feldman showing relation between water deprivation and Skinner box performance in rats (N=7). See text for explanation.*

been attributed to a physical weakening of the animal due to the deprivation of food or water. In the absence of physiological data such an assumption appeared reasonable in many cases, although it did not account for response decrement in certain experiments where physical weakening seemed to be ruled out (Finan, 1940; Freeman, 1940; Fuster, 1958; Kaplan, 1952; Stennett, 1957a). Attack on this problem with physiological methods should soon provide a definitive answer concerning the main determinants of this response decrement. The present experiment represents an important first step in a program of animal studies that should go a long way towards solving this problem. It is not claimed that this one experiment demolishes the inanition hypothesis, but it does seem that the results are opposed to it. Heart rate in the Minnesota starvation experiments was found lowered in the weakened individuals (Malmo, 1958, p. 252) whereas heart rate in the present experiment was markedly increased during the period when number of responses was declining. Moreover, Bélanger was careful to record the weights of the animals all through the experiments, and he observed only very slight changes in weight, even at the 72-hour deprivation interval. Again, it should be stressed that all through the experiment the animals received four to seven days of hydration between conditions. Furthermore, it is interesting to note that the animals continued to press the bar at fairly regular intervals in the high deprivation conditions (with response decrement). That is, their behavior did not appear as though they had "given up." The acts of pressing continued to occur regularly, only they were separated by longer temporal intervals than under more optimal conditions of deprivation.

The increasing monotonic curve for heart rate did not seem to be simply due to the physical conditions of exertion associated with the act of bar pressing. It is true that up to the peak of the performance curve increasing heart rate was accompanied by increasing frequency of bar pressing, but past this point, heart rate continued to show rise despite the decline in exertion due to bar pressing. One might conjecture that exercise may have had greater effect on heart rate under extreme deprivation, but this would be counterbalanced—to some extent, at least—by the reduced number of presses.

To control for possible serial effects in this experiment there were two checks. First, he obtained similar findings from a second group of rats in which the order of deprivation conditions was reversed, commencing with the 72-hour deprivation condition, and finishing with the 12-hour condition. Second, the group of rats that had the ascending order of deprivation intervals were tested one week after the end of the experiment under the 60-hour deprivation condition. Mean number of responses was 96.7 and mean heart rate was 458.9 beats per minute, thus providing good agreement with the results that were obtained in the main experiment.

Finally, it is possible to speculate along various lines about how the heart rate data could be accounted for without involving the concept of activation. Obviously, further experimentation is need, but it is encouraging nonetheless that the first animal experimentation specifically designed to explore the relation between appetitional drive and activation turned out according to prediction.

CHARACTERISTICS OF ACTIVATION

The three approaches described in the previous section appear to lead to the same fundamental concept of activation. It will, of course, be difficult to state a precise definition of activation that will satisfy everyone. Neurophysiologically oriented workers will maintain a healthy scepticism concerning the so-called "peripheral" indicants of activation. The "energetics" group while welcoming the extended use of what is essentially their own methodology will in company with some learning theorists look askance at theoretical models that verge on neurologizing. Despite differences in point of view, however, it seems worthwhile to attempt to deal with certain major characteristics of activation on which we may expect a large measure of agreement.

Activation level a product of multiple factors. When a man is deprived of sleep for some 60 hours his activation level appears higher than it was before he had suffered sleep loss. Physiological indicants reveal an upward shift in activation level that is gradual and progresseive throughout the vigil (Malmo, 1958). Having once demonstrated these physiological changes it is tempting to dispense with physiological recording in further work, assuming that 60 hours of deprivation will invariably produce a heightened state of activation. Such an assumption, however, cannot be made. An example will make clear why this assumption is untenable. A sleep-deprived S requires constant stimulation to prevent him from going to sleep. It is a general finding in such studies that despite the best intentions of the S to remain awake he will "catnap" if left alone. When he is working at a task trying to keep his efficiency from falling, the effect of major sleep loss is to produce a large increase in activation level. The important point to see here, however, is that the higher activation level is a combined product of the stimuli and their demands on him plus the condition of sleep loss. Without such stimulation, the S would surely fall asleep and we know from our studies of sleep that physiological levels drop very rapidly as one drifts into sleep. It is obvious, therefore, that in the absence of the task, physiological indicants at 60 hours' deprivation would show lower, not higher, activation in comparison with the rested condition.

That the "drive state" is in large part determined by environmental stimulating factors is indicated also by the observations of Bélanger and Feldman in their water deprivation experiments. Incidental observations suggested that, in addition to being more variable, heart rates recorded from the animal in a restraining compartment seemed to be consistently lower than those that were recorded when the animal was pressing the lever or drinking. In the restrainting compartment the animal could view the lever through glass so that apparently mere sight of the lever was insufficient stimulation to produce the full effect upon heart rate that was produced by the acts of pressing on the lever and drinking. It thus appeared that, with deprivation time approximately the same, activation level differed appreciably depending upon the conditions of external stimulation. These observations were merely incidental ones in the experiment, and they should be repeated; but they encourage the point of view that activation level is in large part a function of environmental stimulation conditions. The experiments of Campbell and Sheffield (1953) seem to point in the same direction. In the absence of sufficient environmental stimulation, food deprived rats are no more active than satiated ones, but with stimulation they are much more active than the satiated controls.

Returning to the example of the water deprived rat in the Skinner box, the two major factors determining the level of activation in that situation are *(a)* the internal conditions produced by deprivation and *(b)* the environmental stimulating conditions. To restate a point previously made, level of activation does not seem to be simply determined by the condition of deprivation alone. This would mean that depriving an animal of water per se could not produce some direct effect on motor mechanisms such as a simple discharge into the cardiac accelerating mechanism, leading to increased heart rate. Instead of some direct effect of this kind leading immediately over to some observable effector action, deprivation appears to have a sensitizing effect that is undetectable (or latent). According to this view, when appropriate stimulation does occur, the previously latent effect of deprivation will show itself in the heart rate: within limits, the longer the period of deprivation the higher the heart rate. Furthermore, according to activation theory, the same central mechanism that increases heart rate also acts to increase bombardment of the cerebral cortex. As previously stated, this central mechanism is presumed to be the ARAS.[4]

What could be the means of sensitizing cells in the ARAS by a condition such as deprivation of water or food? If some hormone like epinephrine were released by deprivation, it is conceivable that this hormone could act to sensitize the ARAS cells in degree proportional to the amount of time that the animal had been deprived. As a matter of fact, hormonal sensitization of neural mechanisms is a currently active area of research (Saffran, Schally & Benfey, 1955; Dell, 1958).

There are some real difficulties in defending the position that the ARAS is a unitary intensity-mediating mechanism, because the ARAS does not appear to be a homogeneous anatomical system. Indeed, as Olszewski (1954) has shown, these central brain-stem structures appear very complex and highly differentiated. This unreassuring fact must not be forgotten, but neither should it be accepted as precluding the unitary function. As Lashley points out in the discussion of Olszewski's paper, structural differences are not reliable indices of function when unsupported by other evidence.

As a matter of fact, there is some important functional evidence which encourages the unitary view despite the structural complexity of the ARAS. Dell (1958) has found that: "Epinephrine does not activate selectively mammillothalamocingular systems, . . . but instead activates the ascending reticular system *en masse,* thus leading to a generalized cortical arousal" (p. 370). Control experiments showed that the activation effect was due to a direct action of the epinephrine at the reticular level and not to an effect on the cerebral cortex. Similar results have been obtained by Rothballer (1956).

---

[4] It is very likely that the descending reticular activating system is involved here too, but, at the present stage of knowledge in this field, it does not seem wise to introduce further complications into the neuropsychological model.

Another kind of difficulty for the quantitative view would be posed by showing that patterned discharge from the ARAS to the cortex (not merely total quantity of discharge) was the crucial factor in supporting some behavioral action. Don't the effector patterns of standing, walking, and righting pose just such a difficulty? The relation of midbrain mechanisms to posture seems to be clearly one in which patterns of discharge from the midbrain are important. But the decorticate mammal (guinea pig, rabbit, cat, dog,) in which the cortex of both hemispheres have been removed shows approximately normal postural and progressional activities (Dusser de Barenne, 1934, p. 229). Since the activation concept under review deals with bombardment of the cerebral cortex, it appears that these noncortically mediated response patterns fall outside of phenomena under present consideration.

I should add, finally, that my admittedly speculative suggestion concerning hormonal sensitization is by no means essential to the main point which is that the behavioral evidence clearly shows the effects of deprivation to be latent (i.e. unobservable) under certain conditions. Moreover, this stress placed on the latent effects of deprivation is not mere hairsplitting. In addition to being required for an explanation of the Montreal experiments, this concept of latent deprivation effects appears to account in large measure for the findings of Campbell and Sheffield (1953), and more generally for the failure of random activity to adequately serve as a measure of drive or activation (Malmo, 1958).

Activation and the S–R framework. As the product of interaction between internal (perhaps hormonal) conditions and external stimulating ones, activation cannot be very reasonably classified as either stimulus or response. This means that the physiological measurements that are used to gauge level of activation do not fit very well into the S–R formula. It is perhaps useful to think of these physiological conditions as part of O in the S-O-R formula (Woodworth & Schlosberg, 1954, p. 2).

The momentary physiological reaction to a discrete stimulus like the sudden rise in palmar conductance accompanying pin-prick is not of primary concern to us in our study of activation. This kind of S–R reaction, important as it undoubtedly is for investigating other problems, is of little relevance for the study of activation, compared with the longer lasting changes. As Schlosberg has put it to me in personal communication, in employing skin conductance to gauge level of activation, one observes the "tides" and not the "ripples." I do not mean to disparage studies that use physiological reactions as R terms in the strict S–R sense. It is just that in this paper I am concerned with physiological functions only insofar as they are related to activation.

It may be queried whether we are dealing with a needless and hairsplitting distinction by saying that activation is not a response.

However, the kind of difference I have in mind appears quite distinct and useful to keep in mind, though it should not be stressed unduly. Basically, it is the same distinction which Woodworth and Schlosberg (1956) make when they draw particular attention to the difference between slow and rapid changes in skin conductance. As examples of rapid changes in skin conductance, there are the "GSRs" as R terms in conditioned responses, and in free association tests. Examples of slow skin conductance changes, on the other hand, are the gradual downward drifts that occur over hours during sleep (see Fig. 4), the slow downward changes in skin-conductance in Ss as they become gradually habituated to an experimental situation (Davis, 1934; Duffy & Lacey, 1946), and (going up the activation scale) the progressive upward changes in conductance during a vigil (Malmo, 1958).

I would not deny that there are stimuli and responses going on in the physiological systems, but at the present time I see no way of identifying and handling them. It should be added, however, that this does not give one license to completely disregard the antecedents of physiological changes. For instance, if the hand of a sleeping S becomes hot by being covered with heavy bedclothing the local thermal sweating induced thereby will bring about a sudden rise in palmar conductance which has nothing to do with activation. Or sleep may be induced by certain drugs which have a specific stimulating effect on respiration, such that respiation rate will not fall during sleep as it usually does (see Fig. 5 for curve obtained under nondrug conditions). Furthermore, artifacts due to movement and postural shifts may prevent muscle potentials from serving as reliable indicants of activation level.

Limitations of the activation concept. I am not attempting to solve the problem of selection, i.e., the problem of finding the neurophysiological mechanisms that determine which cues in the animal's environment are prepotent in the sense of winning out over other cues in triggering off a pattern of effector action. This point seems clear enough, especially when it is stressed that activation has no steering function; and yet there is still the risk that some critics may misunderstand and state as one shortcoming of this theory that it does not adequately handle the problem of selection. The theory may be open to criticism on the grounds that it is limited, but it should not be criticized for failing to do something which it was not intended to do.

It will be noted that in general an attempt is made to raise theoretical questions that stand a good chance of being answered by available experimental techniques. Schematically, the experimental paradigm is as follows:

Activation level: Low   Moderate   High
Expected performance level: Low   Optimal   Low

It is important to stress that the measure denoted by "moderate activation level" has meaning only in relative (not in absolute) terms. That is, the level is "moderate" because it is higher than that of the low activation condition, and lower than the level of the high activation condition. Comparisons are invariably of the within-individual, within-task kind, which means that the level of activation which is found to be optimal for one task is not directly compared with the level of activation which is found to be optimal for a different task. Thus, at the present stage of theorizing, no attempt is made to deal with the question of whether tasks which differ in complexity, for example, also differ with respect to the precise level of activation which is optimal for each one. However, I have dealt elsewhere (Malmo, 1958) with the related question of response competition, suggesting an alternative to the response competition explanation for decrement in performance with increased activation (or D).

Again, the theoretical formulations may be criticized for being too narrow. But it must be kept in mind that their narrowness is due to the close nexus between theory and experiment in this program. These formulations may also be criticized for an unjustifiable assumption in the postulation of a communal drive mechanism. One may well ask where the evidence is that proves the existence of a state of general drive. In dealing with this kind of question, it is essential to refer back to the outline of the experimental paradigm. The experimental induction of the three discriminable activation levels referred to in the outline depends upon the controlled variation of certain conditions in the S's environment. The fact that by varying conditions as dissimilar as appetitional deprivations and verbal incentives it is possible to produce similar shifts in physiological indicants provides a sound basis for introducing the operationally defined concept of activation level that cuts across traditional demarcation lines of specific drives. All this, of course, does not constitute final proof for a communal drive mechanism. Certainly further data are required before it is even safe to conclude equivalence of drive conditions in the alteration of physiological levels, to say nothing of proving the existence of a communal drive mechanism.

INTERRELATIONS BETWEEN PHYSIOLOGICAL INDICANTS OF ACTIVATION

Criticism directed against physiological measures as indicants of activation usually involves one or both of the following points. The first objection is that intercorrelations between physiological measures are so low that it is unreasonable to consider their use for gauging a single dimension of behavior. A second objection is that activation properly refers to events in the brain and that the correspondence between these central events and what may be observed in such peripheral functions as heart rate, respiration, muscle tension and the like is not close enough to permit valid inferences from the peripheral events to the central ones. In the following section, I shall attempt to answer these criticisms.

Intra- and interindividual correlations among physiological indicants of activation. In an unpublished paper, Schnore and I have discussed certain misconceptions that have confused some critics of physiological methods. The most serious misunderstanding concerns correlations among physiological measures. It is true that *inter*-individual correlations are low, but this fact is actually irrelevant insofar as using these measures to gauge activation is concerned. The important question is whether significant *intra*-individual correlations are found in a sufficiently high proportion of individuals, and the answer appears to be yes (Schnore, 1959).

What the low *inter*individual correlations mean, of course, is that an individual in any given situation may have a heart rate that is high relative to the mean heart rate for the group, and at the same time have a respiration rate or a blood pressure that is low relative to the group mean. These findings are in line with the principle of physiological specificity that is now supported by several lines of evidence.[5] Physiological specificity is a separate problem that is in no way crucial for the activation hypothesis. An illustration will make this clear. Take a rather extreme example of an individual with a very *high* heart rate (say 95 when the mean for his group under specified conditions is 75) and very *low* palmar conductance (50 microhms when the group mean is 100). In an experiment with varied incentive, in going from a low incentive to a high incentive condition this *S* will likely show an increase in heart rate from 95 to say 110 and an increase in palmar conductance from 50 to say 60 microhms. The main point is that even though the *S*'s heart rate is already high compared with the mean for his group, it goes still higher (concordantly with palmar conductance) when the stimulating situation increases the level of activation. This is the kind of intraindividual correlation between physiological measures[6] that is required for gauging

---

[5] The general principle of physiological specificity states that under significantly different conditions of stimulation individuals exhibit idiosyncratic but highly stereotyped patterns of autonomic and somatic activation. I use the term *physiological specificity* as a generic reference to autonomic-response stereotypy (Lacey & Lacey, 1958) to symptom specificity (Malmo & Shagass, 1949), and to stereotypy of somatic and autonomic activation patterns (Schnore, 1959).

[6] It is not claimed, however, that all physiological measures are equally useful for the purpose of gauging activation level. On the contrary, as Schnore's experiments have suggested, some measures appear superior to others, and eventually we may be able to select the most discriminating ones and thus improve our measurement (Schnore, 1959).

the dimension of activation and, to repeat, the evidence strongly indicates that the intraindividual correlations are sufficiently high for this purpose.

RELATIONS BETWEEN CENTRAL
AND PERIPHERAL INDICANTS OF ACTIVATION

As previously noted, the pioneer EEG workers observed definite changes in EEG pattern accompanying major shifts in the conscious state of the *S*. Moreover, they recognized a continuum of increasing activation usually referred to as the sleep-waking-excitement continuum, just as other workers like Freeman (1948) and Duffy (1957) employing peripheral measures of palmar sweating and muscular tension recognized it. Among the early workers in this field, Darrow (1947) studied EEG and other measures simultaneously, but only very recently have techniques been made available that can provide the kind of quantitative EEG measurements required for critical comparisons along the activation continuum. That is, from simple inspection of the raw EEG tracing it is possible to see gross differences between sleeping and waking, or between a drowsy, relaxed state and one of extreme alertness. But for experiments on activation it is necessary to have an instrument that will reveal measureable differences for "points" lying closer to each other on the activation continuum. For example, it is essential to have a measure that will discriminate reliably between a moderately alert and a highly alert state. For such discriminations the method of inspection will not do, and a device for objective quantification of the wave form is required.

Because of its complexity the EEG tracing has been difficult to quantify, and although gross differences in activation level could be detected by simple inspection of the tracing, this method was too crude for more detailed work. However, with the advent of EEG frequency analysers, quantification of the EEG looked promising because these analysers were designed to provide quantified EEG data for each of many different narrow frequency bands. Unfortunately, these instruments have not proved useful because of insufficient stability. In our laboratory we have been trying band-pass filters to provide stable quantification of various selected frequency bands in which we are primarily interested (Ross & Davis, 1958). Results thus far appear highly encouraging.

Data indicating relationships between EEG and other physiological functions. In a recent sleep deprivation experiment, we found that palmar conductance and respiration showed progressive rise during the vigil, indicating increasing activation with deprivation of sleep. In the same experiment we recorded EEG and, by means of a band-pass filter, obtained a quantified write-out of frequencies from 8–12 per second, in the alpha range. It will be recalled that the classical picture of activation is reduction in the amount of alpha activity. Therefore, what we might expect to find in this experiment is progressive decrease in the amount of alpha activity. As a matter of fact, this is exactly what was found (Malmo, 1958, p. 237).

As Stennett (1957b) has shown, however, the relationship between EEG alpha activity and other physiological variables is sometimes curvilinear. In the sleep deprivation experiments physiological measurements were taken under highly activating conditions and at this high end of the continuum further increase in activation seems invariably to decrease the amount of alpha activity. But at the lower end of the continuum with the S in a drowsy state, increased activation has the opposite effect on alpha activity. An alerting stimulus, instead of producing a flattening of the EEG tracing, will actually produce an augmentation of the alpha activity. This has sometimes been referred to as a "paradoxical" reaction, although it seems paradoxical only when it is assumed that the relation between activation level and alpha amplitude is a decreasing monotonic one throughout the entire activation continuum. But Stennett (1957b) has shown that the relationship is not monotonic. From his data he plotted a curve which has the shape of an inverted **U**. From this curve it would be predicted that with a drowsy S, stimulation should *increase* alpha amplitude. From the same inverted **U** curve it would also be predicted that an S whose activation level was sufficiently high (past the peak of the curve) before stimulation would show a *decrease* in alpha amplitude. Actually, some unpublished experiments on startle by Bartoshuk fit these predictions very well.

Recent data indicate the usefulness of a 2–4 c.p.s. band-pass filter in experiments on sleep. The data in the figures that follow represent mean values from three men who slept all night in our laboratory after serving as Ss in our sleep deprivation experiments.

Bipolar sponge electrodes, soaked in electrode jelly and attached to the S by Lastonet bands, were used for the parietal EEG placement (two thirds of the distance from nasion to inion, and 3 cm. from the midline on each side). The primary tracing was recorded by an Edin Electroencephalograph, and the two secondary tracings were integrations of the EEG potentials that were passed through band-pass filters for selective amplification of signals in the 2–4 and 8–12 c.p.s. frequency bands. Measurements on the secondary tracings were carried out with special rulers, and these measurements were converted to microvolt values by reference to calibration standards.

Method of recording and measuring palmar conductance was similar to that described by Stennett (1957a).

Electrocardiograms were picked up from electrodes placed on contralateral limbs, and heart rates were determined from measurements of electrocardiotachometric tracings. Respiration rates were obtained by means of a Phipps and Bird pneumograph.

All three Ss slept well throughout the night (approximately from 10 P.M. to 9 A.M. after some 60 hours without sleep). Physiological recordings were carried out continuously during the whole period of sleep in each case, and except for occasional attention to electrodes (e.g., application of electrode jelly and saline to electrodes) the Ss were undisturbed.

Four pairs of cellulose sponge electrodes were attached to the four limbs (to the pronator teres muscles of the arms and the peroneal muscles of the legs) for the purpose of recording muscle potentials. Primary muscle-potential tracings were recorded on the chart of a custom built Edin electromyograph (EMG). Electronic integrators (employing the condensor charge–discharge principle, like those used for the secondary EEG tracings), attached in parallel across the galvanometer of this EMG unit, integrated the muscle potentials over successive 4-second periods.

These muscle-potentials tracings were used to record movements and periods of restlessness during sleep. Five-minute periods free from muscle-potential activity and preceded by at least 5 minutes of movement-free tracings were chosen for measurement in order to provide the values plotted in Fig. 3–5. The actual times plotted on the baseline represent the medians for the three Ss. In each instance the three times were close to one another.

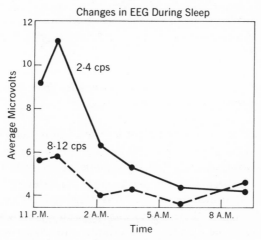

FIG. 3   *Mean EEG values from three healthy young male Ss during a night's sleep. Subjects had been sleep-deprived. Band-pass filters were used in connection with electronic integrators to provide quantitative data in the two different frequency bands.*

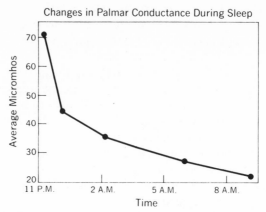

FIG. 4 *Mean palmar conductance values from the same Ss, at the same times during sleep as in Fig. 3.*

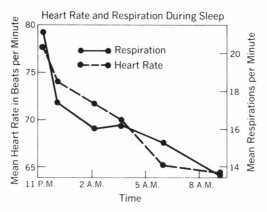

FIG. 5 *Mean values for heart rate and respiration from the same Ss at the same times during sleep as in Figs. 3 and 4.*

In Fig. 3 observe that following a brief rise early in sleep the upper curve for 2–4 c.p.s. falls continuously during the entire period of sleep. This curve is consistent with published accounts of changes in EEG during sleep noted by inspection of the raw tracings (Lindsley, 1957, p. 68). Early in sleep there is an increase in slow waves around 2-4 cycles per second, but as sleep continues these waves are replaced by even slower ones. As far as I am aware, the data in Fig. 3 represent the first use of a 2–4 band-pass filter to quantify the EEG. The curve for 8–12 c.p.s. EEG also shows some fall, and the voltage is low in accordance with the well-known disappearance of alpha waves from the raw tracings during sleep.

Figures 4 and 5 show data for palmar conductance, heart rate, and respiration, that were recorded at the same time as the EEG data. From the second plotted point on, there is rather close resemblance between these curves and the one for 2–4 c.p.s. EEG. It seems likely that a band-pass filter for fast frequencies in the beta range might yield a continuously falling curve commencing with drowsiness and continuing through the onset and early stages of sleep. There are serious technical difficulties in quantifying the next step of frequencies above the alpha band, but we are hopeful that a band-pass filter that has recently been constructed in our laboratory will overcome these difficulties.

Direct alteration of ARAS activity by means of electrical stimulation and related animal experimentation. The most relevant experiment on direct stimulation of the ARAS is, as far as I know, the one by Fuster (1958) that was mentioned earlier. By stimulating in the same part of the ARAS that produces the EEG picture of activation, Fuster was able to produce improved discrimination performance in the monkey. Presumably, this effect was achieved by causing a larger number of impulses from the ARAS to bombard the cortex. The assumption would be that before the onset of electrical stimulation the cortex was not receiving sufficient bombardment for optimal performance (Hebb, 1955) and that ARAS stimulation brought total bombardment in the cortex closer to the optimal value. The situation may not be as simple as this, but the success of the Fuster experiment encourages further experimentation along these same lines. Finding that level of performance can be altered by electrical stimulation of the ARAS opens up the exciting possibility that if amount of neural activity in the ARAS can be measured, we might find a direct correlation between a central measure of activity and level of performance. For instance, the Bélanger and Feldman experiment described earlier might be repeated with the addition of recordings from the ARAS. The aim of such an experiment would be to determine whether the continuous rise in the heart rate curve with increasing deprivation times could be matched by a similar rise in amplitude of deflections from recording in the ARAS with implanted electrodes. Recent neurophysiological experiments appear encouraging with respect to the feasibility of such an approach (Li & Jasper, 1953, pp. 124–125; Magoun, 1958, p. 68).

EFFECTS OF INCREASED ACTIVATION ON LOCALIZED SKELETAL-MUSCLE TENSION IN PSYCHIATRIC PATIENTS

The implication of activation theory for various clinical phenomena might very well be the topic of a separate paper. Certainly there is not space to deal at length with the topic here. I have chosen, therefore, to present a few recent observations, chiefly in order to suggest how level of activation may be studied in relation to a clinical phenomenon.

The graph in Fig. 6 illustrates what appears to be a general finding in patients complaining of tensional discomfort in a localized muscular site. The data for the curves plotted in the figure were obtained from a psychiatric patient, a 42-year old woman who complained of muscular discomfort localized in the left thigh. In the session when these data were taken electromyograms (EMGs) were recorded from various muscles over the body; those from the left and right thighs are shown in the figure. The patient was engaged in pursuit tracking using an apparatus similar to the one employed by Surwillo (1955, 1956). Figure 6 shows that when a loud distracting noise, of the kind described by Schnore (1959), was presented during tracking, the tension in the left thigh was very much higher than that of the right thigh. When tracking was carried out under distraction free conditions this tensional difference between thighs was not observed.

Interpretation of these data seems quite straightforward. When level of activation was increased by presenting a loud distracting noise the effect was shown entirely in one muscle group, the left thigh, which was the symptom area in this patient. Simultaneous recordings of tension from other parts of the body showed that the tension was specific to the left

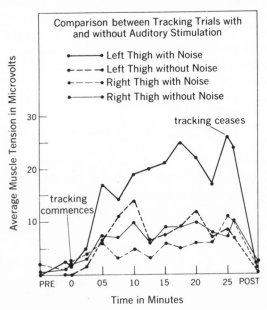

FIG. 6 *Mean muscle tension from left thigh and right thigh from patient with complaint of tensional discomfort in the left thigh. Note that when patient was performing the tracking task under distraction (loud noise), tension rose in the left thigh but not in the right. See text for explanation.*

thigh and was not merely increased on the whole left side of the body. The specificity of the left thigh in indicating the higher activation is quite clear. Observe that tension in the thigh muscles on the opposite side of the body actually fell slightly under the activating conditions.

The same procedure was carried out with a second patient, a young girl of 28, who complained of a distressing feeling of tightness in the neck on the right side. Results were similar to the ones obtained in the previous case, with activation again showing its effect specifically in the symptom area. When the loud distracting noise was turned on during tracking, tension in this area showed marked increase whereas tension in the muscles on the left side of the neck showed no rise whatever.

Very similar results were obtained from two additional patients whose areas of tensional discomfort were localized in still different parts of the body. One woman with complaint of tension on the left side of her neck served as a useful control for the patient previously described with tension localized in the opposite side of the neck. No tracking experiment was carried out with this patient. Apparently the sight of the EMG recording room for the first time was itself sufficient to increase the amplitude of muscle potentials from the symptom area so that they become appreciably higher than those on the opposite side of her neck. The other woman (fourth patient in this series) complained of tensional discomfort that appeared to originate in the left shoulder. EMGs were recorded from the left and right shoulders of this patient while she lay in bed listening to the playback of a recorded interview. During the first part of the playback, tension was about the same on the two sides of the body. But when the topic concerning her dead sister commenced to come over the speaker, tension in the left shoulder became much greater than that in the right.

As far as could be determined, the EMG data from all these patients were consistent in suggesting that for skeletal-muscle tension in patients with well-developed tensional symptoms, increasing the activation level up to a certain point has the effect of raising muscle tension in one localized muscle group, the one in which the patient complained of tensional discomfort. It was not necessary for the patient to actually feel the discomfort during the experimental session for this differential result to appear. I have been using the term "symptom area" to refer to the muscle group when the discomfort was localized when present.

Interesting findings that appear to parallel those from the patients were obtained from three young male nonpatient Ss in our recent investigation of sleep deprivation. As previously mentioned, evidence from EEG, palmar conductance, and respiration indicated that activation during tracking increased progressively with hours of sleep deprivation. In addition to these other physiological tracings, EMGs from various areas over the body were also recorded. One muscle area, a different one for each S, showed significant rise in tension over the vigil. It was the neck muscles in one *S*, the forehead in another, and the biceps muscle of the right arm in the third. In each case the one muscle showed statistically significant rise in tension, and in none of the *S*s was there significant tensional rise in any other muscle. In fact, there was regularly progressive and very significant fall in the tension of the left forearm in all three *S*s. As far as I know, none of the men actually complained of tensional discomfort in the areas showing rise in tension during the vigil.

Where high level activation is long continued as in a vigil or in certain psychoneurotic patients, it appears that skeletal tension may become localized to a single muscle group. The discomfort associated with this tension in some patients can become extremely severe. It should be noted that in one-session experiments, where rise in activation was for relatively short intervals of time, tensional rise occurred in more than one muscle group (Surwillo, 1956; Stennett, 1957a).

Methodologically, these results are important because they reveal a difference between EMGs and some other physiological measures with respect to gauging activation. Unlike heart rate or respiration rate that invariably yields one measure no matter how it is recorded, there are as many measures of muscle tension as there are muscles that can be recorded from. It appears that when sufficient care is taken, EMGs may be very valuable in helping to gauge activation, but that considerable caution is required in the interpretation of results, and especially in the interpretation of negative results.

From the clinical point of view it seems an interesting speculation that the patient's localized muscle tension may itself actually increase the general activation level. (I do not mean the level of muscle tension all over the body.) Two main assumptions are involved in this suggestion. The first one is that the area of localized muscle tension in the patient acts like tension that is induced, for example, by having an *S* squeeze on a dynamometer. From the generalized effects of tension induction on learning and performance it is clear that the effects of increased muscle tension are quite general ones. Though crucial physiological data are missing in these experiments, as previously menitioned, one very likely explanation of these results is that the local increase in muscle tension somehow produces an increase in the general level of activation, with rise in heart rate and blood pressure, with fall in level of EEG alpha, and so on. This is the second assumption. The results of two recent experiments are in line with this assumption. Meyer and Noble (1958) found that induced tension interacted with "anxiety" in verbal-maze learning ("anxiety" measured by means of the MAS [Taylor, 1953], while Kuethe and Eriksen (1957) in a study of stereotypy likewise reported a significant interaction between these two variables when "anxiety" was experimentally produced by means of electric shocks. The MAS appears to select individuals who are significantly above the mean in activation, and from the results of Schnore (1959) and Feldman (1958) it seems safe to conclude that anticipation of shock also leads to increased levels of physiological activity. In short, generalizing from the induced tension experiments, it seems reasonable to suppose that a patient's muscular tension in a small focal area might have the general effect of increasing activation. If such is the case symptomatic treatment might have significant general as well as specific effects. Although based on only one patient, Yates' (1958) results from symptomatic treatment of tics seems encouraging with respect to the feasibility of research in this general area.

SUMMARY

The neuropsychological dimension of activation may be briefly described as follows: The continuum extending from deep sleep at the low activation end to "excited" states at the high activation end is a function of the amount of cortical bombardment by the ARAS, such that the greater the cortical bombardment the higher the activation. The shape of the curve relating level of performance to level of activation is that of an inverted **U**: from low activation up to a point that is optimal for a given performance or function, level of performance rises monotonically with increasing activation level; but past this optimal point the relation becomes nonmonotonic: further increase in activation beyond this point produces fall in performance level, this fall being directly related to the amount of the increase in level of activation.

Long before the discovery of the ARAS the behavioral evidence of Duffy, Freeman, and others of the "energetics" group had suggested the existence of some such brain mechanism. Moreover, learning theorists of the Hull school have in their concept of the general drive state come very close to the activation principle. Up to the present time they have employed physiological measures only sparingly and have restricted their use to the aversive aspects of drive. But with evidence that such measures may also be applied to nonaversive (appetitional) drive, it seems likely that the present rather unsatisfactory measures of drive may eventually be replaced by physiological indicants.

Activation has a number of main characteristics that may be listed as follows: *(a)* Activation has no steering function in behavior. *(b)* It is considerably broader than emotion. *(c)* Activation is not a state that can be inferred from knowledge of antecedent conditions alone, because it is the product of an interaction between internal conditions such as hunger or thirst, and external cues. *(d)* Activation does not fit very well into the S-R formula. It is a phenomenon of slow changes, of drifts in level with a time order of minutes (even hours) not of seconds or fractions thereof. *(e)*

Activation is a quantifiable dimension and the evidence indicates that physiological measures show a sufficiently high intraindividual concordance for quantifying this dimension.

It is suggested that activation is mediated chiefly through the ARAS which seems, in the main, to be an intensity system. Neurophysiological findings strongly suggest that it may be possible to achieve more precise measurement of activation through a direct recording of discharge by the ARAS into the cerebral cortex. Research on this problem is urgently needed.

The concept of activation appears to have wide application to phenomena in the field of clinical psychology. As one illustration, in this paper, activation was applied to clinical phenomena of tensional symptoms.

REFERENCES

BINDRA, D. *Motivation. A Systematic Reinterpretation.* New York: Ronald, 1959.

BROWN, J. S. Pleasure-Seeking Behavior and the Drive-Reduction Hypothesis. *Psychol. Rev.,* 1955, *62,* 169–179.

CAMPBELL, B. A., & SHEFFIELD, F. D. Relation of Random Activity to Food Deprivation. *J. Comp. Physiol. Psychol.,* 1953, *46,* 320–326.

COFER, C. N. Motivation. *Annu. Rev. Psychol.,* 1959, *10,* 173–202.

COURTS, F. A. Relations Between Muscular Tension and Performance. *Psychol. Bull.,* 1942, *39,* 347–367.

DARROW, C. W. Psychological and Psychophysiological Significance of the Electroencephalogram. *Psychol. Rev.,* 1947, *54,* 157–168.

DAVIS, R. C. Modification of the Galvanic Reflex by Daily Repetition of a Stimulus. *J. Exp. Psychol.,* 1934, *17,* 504–535.

DELL, P. C. Humoral Effects on the Brain Stem Reticular Formations. In H. H. Jasper, L. D. Proctor, R. S. Knighton, W. C. Noshay, & R. T. Costello (Eds.), *Reticular Formation of the Brain.* Toronto: Little, Brown, 1958. Pp. 365–379.

DUFFY, ELIZABETH. The Measurement of Muscular Tension as a Technique for the Study of Emotional Tendencies. *Amer. J. Psychol.,* 1932, *44,* 146–162.

DUFFY, ELIZABETH. The Concept of Energy Mobilization. *Psychol. Rev.,* 1951, *58,* 30–40.

DUFFY, ELIZABETH. The Psychological Significance of the Concept of "Arousal" or "Activation." *Psychol. Rev.,* 1957, *64,* 265–275.

DUFFY, ELIZABETH, & LACEY, O. L. Adaptation in Energy Mobilization: Changes in General Level of Palmar Skin Conductance. *J. Exp. Psychol.,* 1946, *36,* 437–452.

DUSSER DE BARENNE, J. G. The Labyrinthine and Postural Mechanisms. In C. Murchison (Ed.), *A Handbook of General Experimental Psychology.* Worcester, Mass.: Clark University Press, 1934. Pp. 204–246.

FELDMAN, S. M. Differential Effect of Shock as a Function of Intensity and Cue Factors in Maze Learning. Unpublished doctoral dissertation, McGill University, 1958.

FINAN, J. L. Quantitative Studies of Motivation. I. Strength of Conditioning in Rats Under Varying Degrees of Hunger. *J. Comp. Psychol.*, 1940, *29*, 199–134.

FINCH, G. Hunger as a Determinant of Conditional and Unconditional Salivary Response Magnitude. *Amer. J. Physiol.*, 1938, *123*, 379–382.

FREEMAN, G. L. The Relationship Between Performance Level and Bodily Activity Level. *J. Exp. Psychol.*, 1940, *26*, 602–608.

FREEMAN, G. L. *The Energetics of Human Behavior.* Ithaca, N. Y.: Cornell University Press, 1948.

FUSTER, J. M. Effects of Stimulation of Brain Stem on Tachistoscopic Perception. *Science*, 1958, *127*, 150.

HEBB, D. O. *The Organization of Behavior.* New York: Wiley, 1949.

HEBB, D. O. Drives and the C.N.S. (Conceptual Nervous System). *Psychol. Rev.*, 1955, *62*, 243–254.

JASPER, H. H. Electroencephalography. In W. Penfield & T. C. Erickson (Eds.), *Epilepsy and Cerebral Localization.* Springfield, Ill.: Charles C. Thomas, 1941, 380–454.

KAPLAN, M. The Effects of Noxious Stimulus Intensity and Duration During Intermittent Reinforcement of Escape Behavior. *J. Comp. Physiol. Psychol.*, 1952, *45*, 538–549.

KENDLER, H. H. Learning. *Annu. Rev. Psychol.*, 1959, *10*, 43–88.

KUETHE, J. L., & ERIKSEN, C. W. Personality, Anxiety, and Muscle Tension as Determinants of Response Sterotypy. *J. Abnorm. Soc. Psychol.*, 1957, *54*, 400–404.

LACEY, J. I., & LACEY, BEATRICE C. Verification and Extension of the Principle of Autonomic Response-Stereotypy. *Amer. J. Psychol.*, 1958, *71*, 50–73.

LI, C. L., & JASPER, H. H. Microelectrode Studies of the Electrical Activity of the Cerebral Cortex in the Cat. *J. Physiol.*, 1953, *121*, 117–140.

LINDSLEY, D. B. Emotion. In S. S. Stevens (Ed.), *Handbook of Experimental Psychology.* New York: Wiley, 1951. Pp. 473–516.

LINDSLEY, D. B. Psychophysiology and Motivation. In M. R. Jones (Ed.), *Nebraska Symposium on Motivation, 1957.* Lincoln: University of Nebraska Press, 1957. Pp. 44–105.

LORENTE DE NO, R. Transmission of Impulses Through Cranial Motor Nuclei. *J. Neurophysiol.*, 1939, *2*, 402–464.

MAGOUN, H. W. *The Waking Brain.* Springfield, Ill.: Charles C. Thomas, 1958.

MALMO, R. B. Measurement of Drive: An Unsolved Problem in Psychology. In M. R. Jones (Ed.), *Nebraska Symposiom on Motivation, 1958.* Lincoln: University of Nebraska Press, 1958, 229–265.

MALMO, R. B., & SHAGASS, C. Physiologic Study of Symptom Mechanisms in Psychiatric Patients Under Stress. *Psychosom. Med.*, 1949, *11*, 25–29.

MEYER, D. R., & NOBLE, M. E. Summation of Manifest Anxiety and Muscular Tension. *J. Exp. Psychol.*, 1958, *55*, 599–602.

OLSZEWSKI, J. The Cytoarchitecture of the Human Reticular Formation. In J. F. Delafresnaye (Ed.), *Brain Mechanisms and Consciousness.* Springfield, Ill.: Charles C. Thomas, 1954. Pp. 54–76.

ROSS, W. R. D., & DAVIS, J. F. Stable Bandpass Filters for Electroencephalography. *IRE Canad. Convention Rec. 1958*, Paper No. 860, 202–206.

ROTHBALLER, A. B. Studies on the Adrenaline-Sensitive Component of the Reticular Activating System. *EEG Clin. Neurophysiol.,* 1956, *8,* 603–621.

SAFFRAN, M., SCHALLY, A. V., & BENFEY, B. G. Stimulation of the Release of Corticotropin From the Adenohypophysis by a Neurohypophysial Factor. *Endocrinology,* 1955, *57,* 439–444.

SCHNORE, M. M. Individual Patterns of Physiological Activity as a Function of Task Differences and Degree of Arousal. *J. Exp. Psychol.,* 1959, *58,* 117–128.

SPENCE, K. W. Theory of Emotionally Based Drive (D) and Its Relation to Performance in Simple Learning Situations. *Amer. Psychologist,* 1958, *13,* 131–141.

STENNETT, R. G. The Relationship of Performance Level to Level of Arousal. *J. Exp. Psychol.,* 1957, *54,* 54–61. (a)

STENNETT, R. G. The Relationship of Alpha Amplitude to the Level of Palmar Conductance. *EEG Clin. Neurophysiol.,* 1957, *9,* 131–138. (b)

SURWILLO, W. W. A Device for Recording Variations in Pressure of Grip During Tracking. *Amer. J. Psychol.,* 1955, *68,* 669–670.

SURWILLO, W. W. Psychological Factors in Muscle-Action Potentials: EMG Gradients. *J. Exp. Psychol.,* 1956, *52,* 263–272.

TAYLOR, JANET A. A Personality Scale of Manifest Anxiety. *J. Abnorm. Soc. Psychol.,* 1953, *48,* 285–290.

WOODWORTH, R. S., & SCHLOSBERG, H. *Experimental Psychology.* New York: Holt, 1954.

YATES, A. J. The Application of Learning Theory to the Treatment of Tics. *J. Abnorm. Soc. Psychol.,* 1958, *56,* 175–182.

4

THE USE OF REFLEXES
JEAN PIAGET

Since our basic argument is that a comprehensive personality behavior theory needs to develop from general psychology, we would argue that Piaget's extended theory is, indeed, a "personality" theory. Anyone who has evolved a theory as extensive as Piaget's should be required to provide an answer to the question: "What initiates and alters behavior?"

The following selection is unequivocally a motivational statement. It would be of added value for the reader to check the observations to which Piaget refers. The observations of succinct recordings of the behavior of infants excellently illustrate Piaget's points. Checking these references will give an even more thorough understanding of many of Piaget's original, and somewhat complex, concepts. However, the selection given here does indicate Piaget's view on what instigates the application and alteration of reflexes.

In short, reflexes, which are regarded as prototypes of schemata, must be repeated; under conditions of repetition, assimilation, a basic fact of life, may occur. Piaget goes on: "The tendency of the reflex being to reproduce itself, it incorporates into itself every object capable of fulfilling the function of the excitant." When the infant incorporates an object into its sucking reflex, does it do so because the object provides milk, a reducer of a biological deficit, *per se*?

"The object sucked is to be conceived, not as nourishment for the organism in general, but so to speak, as an aliment for the very activity of sucking." The sucking schema has "meaning." Its implementation, though strictly a matter of simple motor recognitions, does bring a cessation of the excitation that accompanies the arousal of the schema in the absence of the conditions that allow the exercise of the previously-developed totality of the sucking schema. ". . . Need is thus the expression of a totality momentarily incomplete and tending toward reconstituting itself . . ." When a stimulus is presented, the infant is motivated to assimilate that stimulus into an appropriate schema. "Furthermore, the more the intelligence develops and strengthens, the more the assimilation of reality to functioning itself is transferred into real comprehension. The principle of motive power of intellectual activity becoming the need to incorporate things into the subject's schemata." To state Piaget's motivational position succinctly, the basic motivation of an organism is to preserve its capacity to avoid nonapplicability of its schemata—that is, to reconstitute its schema in the face of a "totality momentarily incomplete."

*   *   *

Concerning its *adaptation,* it is interesting to note that the reflex, no matter how well endowed with hereditary physiological mechanism, and no matter how stable its automatization, nevertheless needs to be used in order truly to adapt itself, and that it is capable of gradual accommodation to external reality.

Let us first stress this element of *accommodation.* The sucking reflex is hereditary and functions from birth, influenced either by diffuse impulsive movements or by an external excitant (Obs. 1); this is the point of departure. In order that a useful function may result, that is to say, swallowing, it often suffices to put the nipple in the mouth of the newborn child, but, as we know (Obs. 1), it sometimes happens that the child does not adapt at the first attempt. Only practice will lead to normal functioning. That is the first aspect of accommodation: contact with the object modifies, in a way, the activity of the reflex, and, even if this activity were oriented hereditarily to such contact, the latter is no less necessary to the consolidation of the former. This is how certain instincts are lost or certain reflexes cease to function normally, due to the lack of a suitable environment.[1] Moreover, contact with the environment not only results in developing the reflexes, but also in coordinating them in some way. Observations 2, 3, 5 and 8 show how the child, who first does not know how to suck the nipple when it is put in his mouth, grows increasingly able to grasp and even to find it, first after direct touch, then after contact with any neighboring region.[2]

[1]Thus Larguier des Brancels (*Introduction à la Psychologie,* 1921, p. 178). after recalling Spalding's famous experiments concerning the decline of instincts in newly hatched chickens, adds: "The sucking instinct is transitory. A calf which has been separated from its mother and fed by hand for a day or two and then is taken to another cow, more often than not refuses to nurse. The child behaves somewhat similarly. If he is first spoon-fed, he subsequently has great difficulty in taking the breast again."

[2]See Preyer (*L'Ame de L'Enfant,* translated by Variguy, 1887, pp. 213-217), in particular the following lines: "To be sure, sucking is not as fruitful the first as the second day and I have often observed in normal newborn children (1869) that attempts at sucking were completely vain in the first hours of life: when I made the experiment of putting an ivory pencil in their mouth, they were still uncoordinated" (p. 215). Also: "It is well known that newborn children, when put to the breast do not find the nipple without help; they only find it by themselves a few days later (in one case only on the eighth day), that is to say, later than animals" (pp. 215-216). And: "When the child is put to the breast the nipple often does not enter his mouth and he sucks the neighboring skin; this is still evident in the third week . . ." (p. 216).

How can such accommodations be explained? It seems to us difficult to invoke from birth the mechanism of acquired associations, in the limited sense of the term, or of "conditioned reflexes," both of which imply systematic training. On the contrary, the examining of these behavior patterns reveals at once the respects in which they differ from acquired associations: Whereas with regard to the latter, including conditioned reflexes, association is established between a certain perception, foreign to the realm of the reflex, and the reflex itself (for example, between a sound, a visual perception, etc., and the salivary reflex), according to our observations, it is simply the reflex's own sensibility (contact of the lips with a foreign body) which is generalized, that is to say, brings with it the action of the reflex in increasingly numerous situations. In the case of Observations 2, 3, 5 and 8, for example, accommodation consists essentially of progress in the continuity of the searching. In the beginning (Obs. 2 and 3) contact with any part of the breast whatever sets in motion momentary sucking of this region, immediately followed by crying or a desultory search, whereas after several days (Obs. 5), the same contact sets in motion a groping during which the child is headed toward success. It is very interesting, in the second case, to see how the reflex, excited by each contact with the breast, stops functioning as soon as the child perceives that sucking is not followed by any satisfaction, as is the taking of nourishment (see Obs. 5 and 8), and to see how the search goes on until swallowing begins. In this regard, Observations 2 to 8 confirm that there is a great variety of kinds of accommodation. Sucking of the eider-down quilt, of the coverlet, etc., leads to rejection, that of the breast to acceptance; sucking of the skin (the child's hand, etc.) leads to acceptance if it is only a matter of sucking for the sake of sucking, but it leads to rejection (for example when it involves an area of the breast other than the nipple) if there is great hunger; the paternal index finger (Obs. 6) is rejected when the child is held against the breast, but is accepted as a pacifier, etc. In all behavior patterns it seems evident to us that learning is a function of the environment.

Surely all these facts admit of a physiological explanation which does not at all take us out of the realm of the reflex. The "irradiations," the "prolonged shocks," the "summations" of excitations and the intercoordination of reflexes probably explains why the child's searching becomes increasingly systematic, why contact which does not suffice to set the next operation in motion, does suffice in doing so a few days later, etc. Those are not necessarily mechanisms which are superposed on the reflex such as habit or intelligent understanding will be, later. But it remains no less true that the environment is indispensable to this operation, in other words, that reflex adaptation is partly accommodation. Without previous contact with the nipple and the experience of imbibing milk, it is very likely that the eider-down quilt, the wool coverlet, or the paternal index finger, after setting in motion the sucking reflex, would not have been so briskly rejected by Laurent.[3]

But if, in reflex adaptation, allowances must be made for accomodation, accommodation cannot be dissociated from progressive *assimilation,* inherent in the very use of the reflex. In a general way, one can say that the reflex is consolidated and strengthened by virtue of its own functioning. Such a fact is the most direct expression of the mechanism of assimilation. Assimilation is revealed, in the first place, by a growing need for repetition which characterizes the use of the reflex (functional assimilation) and, in the second place, by this sort of entirely practical or sensorimotor recognition which enables the child to adapt himself to the different objects with which his lips come in contact (recognitory and generalizing assimilations).

The need for repetition is in itself alone very significant; in effect, it is a question of a behavior pattern which shows a history and which proceeds to complicate the simple stimuli connected with the state of the organism considered at a given moment in time. A first stimulus capable of bringing the reflex into play is contact with an external object. Preyer thus set in motion the sucking movements of a newborn child by touching his lips, and Observation 1 shows us that children suck their hand a quarter of an hour or half an hour after birth. In the second place, there are internal stimuli, connected with the somato-affective states: diffuse impulsive movements (Obs. 1) or excitations due to hunger. But to these definite excitations, connected with particular moments in the life of the organism, there is added, it seems to us the essential circumstance that the very repetition of the reflex movements constitutes a cynamogeny for them. Why, for instance, does Lucienne suck her fingers soon after birth for ten minutes in succession? This could not be because of hunger, since the umbilical cord had just been cut. There certainly is an external excitant from the moment the lips touch the hand. But why does the excitation last, in such a case, since it does not lead to any result except, precisely, to the use of the reflex? It therefore seems that, from the start of this primitive mechanism, a sort of circular process accompanies the function, the activity of the reflex having augmented due to its own use. If this interpretation remains doubtful, in so far as the point of departure is concerned, it obtains increasingly, on the other hand, with regard to subsequent behavior patterns. After the first feedings one observes, in Laurent (Obs. 2), sucking-like movements, in which it is difficult not to see a sort of autoexcitation. Besides, the progress in the search for the breast in Observations 2–5 and 8 seems also to show how much the function itself

[3]In animals every slightly complicated reflex mechanism occasions reactions of the same kind. The beginnings of copulation in the mollusks, for example, give way to very strange gropings before the act is adapted.

strengthened the tendency to suck. The counterproof of this is, as we have seen, the progressive decay of reflex mechanisms which are not used. How to interpret these facts? It is self-evident that "circular reaction," in Baldwin's sense of the term, could not yet be involved, that is to say, the repetition of a behavior pattern acquired or in the process of being acquired, and of behavior directed by the object to which it tends. Here it is only a matter of reflex and not acquired movements, and of sensibility connected with the reflex itself and not with the external objective. Nevertheless the mechanism is comparable to it from the purely functional point of view. It is thus very clear, in Observation 9, that the slightest excitation can set in motion not only a reflex reaction but a succession of seven reactions. Without forming any hypothesis on the way of conserving this excitation, or *a fortiori,* without wanting to transform this repetition into intentional or mnemonic behavior, one is compelled to state that, in such a case, there is a tendency toward repetition, or, in objective terms, cumulative repetition.

This need for repetition is only one aspect of a more general process which we can qualify as assimilation. The tendency of the reflex being to reproduce itself, it incorporates into itself every object capable of fulfilling the function of excitant. Two distinct phenomena must be mentioned here, both equally significant from this particular point of view.

The first is what we may call "generalizing assimilation," that is to say, the incorporation of increasingly varied objects into the reflex schema. When, for example, the child is hungry but not sufficiently so to give way to rage and to crying, and his lips have been excited by some accidental contact, we witness the formation of this kind of behavior pattern, so important due to its own future developments and the innumerable analogous cases which we shall observe in connection with other schemata. Thus, according to chance contacts, the child, from the first two weeks of life, sucks his fingers, the fingers extended to him, his pillow, quilt, bedclothes, etc.; consequently he assimilates these objects to the activity of the reflex.

To be sure, we do not claim, when speaking of "generalizing" assimilation, that the newborn child begins by distinguishing a particular object (the mother's breast) and subsequently applies to other objects the discoveries he has made about the first one. In other words, we do not ascribe to the nursling conscious and intentional generalization with regard to transition from the particular to the general, especially as generalization, in itself intelligent, never begins by such a transition but always proceeds from the undifferentiated schema to the individual and to the general, combined and complementary. We simply maintain that, without any awareness of individual objects or of general laws, the newborn child at once incorporates into the global schema of sucking a number of increasingly varied objects, whence the generalizing aspect of this process of assimilation. But is it not playing on words to translate a fact so simple into the language of assimilation? Would it not suffice to say "the setting in motion of a reflex by a class of analoguous excitants?" And, if one sticks to the term assimilation, must the conclusion then be reached that the nonhabitual excitants of any reflex (for example the aggregate of objects capable of setting in motion the palpebral reflex when they approach the eye) give rise to an identical phenomenon of generalizing assimilation? There is nothing to it. What does present a particular and truly psychological problem, in the case of the sucking reflex, is that the assimilation of objects to its activity will gradually be generalized until, at the stage of acquired circular reactions and even at the stage of intentional movements, it gives birth to a very complex and strong schema. From the end of the second month the child will suck his thumb systematically (with acquired coordination and not by chance), then at nearly five months his hands will carry all objects to his mouth and he will end by using these behavior patterns to recognize bodies and even to compose the first form of space (Stern's "buccal space"). It is thus certain that the first assimilations relating to sucking, even if they reveal a lack of differentiation between contact with the breast and contact with other objects, are not simple confusion destined to disappear with progress in nutrition, but constitute the point of departure for increasingly complex assimilations.

How to interpret this generalizing assimilation? The sucking reflex can be conceived as a global schema of coordinated movements which, if it is accompanied by awareness, certainly does not give rise to perception of objects or even of definite sensorial pictures but simply to an awareness of attitudes with at most some sensorimotor integration connected with the sensibility of the lips and mouth. Now this schema, due to the fact that it lends itself to repetitions and to cumulative use, is not limited to funcioning under compulsion by a fixed excitant, external or internal, but functions in a way for itself. In other words, the child does not only suck in order to eat but also to elude hunger, to prolong the excitation of the meal, etc., and lastly, he sucks for the sake of sucking. It is in this sense that the object incorporated into the sucking schema is actually assimilated to the activity of this schema. The object sucked is to be conceived, not as nourishment for the organism in general, but, so to speak, as aliment for the very activity of sucking, according to its various forms. From the point of view of awareness, if there is awareness, such assimilation is at first lack of differentiation and not at first true generalization," but from the point of view of action, it is a generalizing extension of the schema which foretells (as has just been seen) later and much more important generalizations.

But, apart from this generalizing assimilation, another assimilation must be noted from the two first weeks of life, which we can call "recognitory assimilation." This second form seems inconsistent with the preceding one; actually it only reveals progress over the other, however slight. What we have just said regarding the lack of differentiation which characterizes generalizing assimilation is, in effect, true only with respect to states of slight hunger or of satiety. But it is enough that the child be very hungry for him to try to eat and thus to distinguish the nipple from the rest. This search and this selectivity seem to us to imply the beginning of differentiation in the global schema of sucking, and consequently a beginning of recognition, a completely practical and motor recognition, needless to say, but sufficient to be called recognitory assimilation. Let us examine, from this point of view, the way in which the child rediscovers the nipple. Ever since the third day (Obs. 3), Laurent seems to distinguish the nipple from the surrounding teguments; he tries to nurse and not merely to suck. From the tenth day (Obs. 4), we observe the alacrity with which he rejects the eider-down quilt or the coverlet which he began to suck, in order to search for something more substantial. Furthermore, his reaction to his father's index finger (Obs. 6) could not be more definite: disappointment and crying. Lastly, the gropings on the breast itself (Obs. 5 and 8) also reveal selectivity. How is this kind of recognition to be explained?

Of course there could be no question, either here or in connection with generalizing assimilation, of the recognition of an "object" for the obvious reason that there is nothing in the states of consciousness of a newborn child which could enable him to contrast an external universe with an internal universe. Supposing that there are given simultaneously visual sensations (simple vision of lights without forms or depth), acoustic sensations and a tactile-gustatory and kinesthetic sensibility connected with the sucking reflex, it is evident that such a complexus would in no way be sufficient to constitute awareness of objects: the latter implies, as we shall see,[4] characteristically intellectual operations, necessary to secure the permanence of form and substance. Neither could there be a question of purely perceptive recognition or recognition of sensorial images presented by the external world, although such recognition considerably precedes the elaboration of objects (recognizing a person, a toy, or a linen cloth simply on "presentation" and before having a permanent concept of it). If, to the observer, the breast which the nursling is about to take is external to the child and constitutes an image separate from him, to the newborn child, on the contrary, there can only exist awareness of attitudes, of emotions, or sensations of hunger and of satisfaction. Neither sight nor hearing yet gives rise to perceptions independent of these general reactions. As H. Wallon has effectively demonstrated, external influences

[4] Volume II, *La Construction du Réel chez l'Enfant.*

only have meaning in connection with the attitudes they arouse. When the nursling differentiates between the nipple and the rest of the breast, fingers, or other objects, he does not recognize either an object or a sensorial picture but simply rediscovers a sensorimotor and particular postural complex (sucking and swallowing combined) among several analogous complexes which constitute his universe and reveal a total lack of differentiation between subject and object. In other words, this elementary recognition consists, in the strictest sense of the word, of "assimilation" of the whole of the data present in a definite organization which has already functioned and only gives rise to real discrimination due to its past functioning. But this suffices to explain in which respect repetition of the reflex leads by itself to recognitory assimilation which, albeit entirely practical, constitutes the beginning of knowledge.[5] More precisely, repetition of the reflex leads to a general and generalizing assimilation of objects to its activity, but, due to the varieties which gradually enter this activity (sucking for its own sake, to stave off hunger, to eat, etc.), the schema of assimilation becomes differentiated and, in the most important differentiated cases, assimilation becomes recognitory.

In conclusion, assimilation belonging to the adaptation reflex appears in three forms: cumulative repetition, generalization of the activity with incorporation of new objects to it, and finally, motor recognition. But, in the last analysis, these three forms are but one: The reflex must be conceived as an organized totality whose nature it is to preserve itself by functioning and consequently to function sooner or later for its own sake (repetition) while incorporating into itself objects propitious to this functioning (generalized assimilation) and discerning situations necessary to certain special modes of its activity (motor recognition). We shall see—and this is the sole purpose of this analysis—that these processes are again found, with the unwedging accounted for by the progressive complexity of the structures, in the stages of acquired circular reactions, of the first voluntary schemata and of truly intelligent behavior patterns.

The progressive adaptation of the reflex schemata, therefore, presupposes their *organization*. In physiology this truth is trite. Not only does the reflex arc as such presuppose an organization but, in the animal not undergoing laboratory experimentation, every reflex system constitutes in itself an organized totality. According to Graham Brown's theories, the simple reflex is, in effect, to be considered as a product of differentiation.

[5]Let us repeat that we do not claim to specify the states of consciousness which accompany this assimilation. Whether these states are purely emotional or affective, connected with the postures accompanying sucking, or whether there exists at first conscious sensorial and kinesthetic discrimination, we could not decide by studying behavior of the first two or three weeks. What this behavior simply reveals is the groping and the discernment which characterizes the use of the reflex, and these are the two fundamental facts which authorize us to speak of psychological assimilation at this primitive stage.

From the psychological point of view, on the other hand, there is too great a tendency to consider a reflex, or even a complex instinctive act such as sucking, to be a summation of movements with, eventually, a succession of conscious states juxtaposed, and not as a real totality. But two essential circumstances induce us to consider the sucking act as already constituting psychic organization: The fact that sooner or later this act reveals a meaning, and the fact that it is accompanied by directed searching.

Concerning the meanings, we have seen how much sucking acts vary according to whether the newborn child is hungry and tries to nurse, or sucks in order to calm himself, or whether in a way he plays at sucking. It seems as though they have a meaning for the nursling himself. The increasing calm which succeeds a storm of crying and weeping as soon as the child is in position to take nourishment and to seek the nipple is sufficient evidence that, if awareness exists at all, such awareness is from the beginning awareness of meaning. But one meaning is necessarily relative to other meanings, even on the elementary plane of simple motor recognitions.

Furthermore, that organization exists is substantiated by the fact that there is directed search. The precocious searching of the child in contact with the breast, in spite of being commonplace, is a remarkable thing. Such searching, which is the beginning of accommodation and assimilation, must be conceived, from the point of view of organization, as the first manifestation of a duality of desire and satisfaction, consequently of value and reality, of complete totality and incomplete totality, a duality which is to reappear on all planes of future activity and which the entire evolution of the mind will try to abate, even though it is destined to be emphasized unceasingly.

Such are, from the dual point of view of adaptation and organization, the first expressions of psychological life connected with hereditary physiological mechanisms. This survey, though schematic, we believe suffices to show how the psyche prolongs purely reflex organization while depending on it. The physiology of the organism furnishes a hereditary mechanism which is already completely organized and virtually adapted but has never functioned. Psychology begins with the use of this mechanism. This use does not in any way change the mechanism itself, contrary to what may be observed in the later stages (acquisition of habits, of understanding, etc.). It is limited to strengthening it and to making it function without integrating it to new organizations which go beyond it. But within the limits of this functioning there is room for a historical development which marks precisely the beginning of psychological life. This development undoubtedly admits of a physiological explanation: if the reflex mechanism is strengthened by use or decays through lack of use, this is surely because coordinations are made or unmade by virtue of the laws of reflex activity. But a physiological explanation of this kind does not exclude the psychological point of view which we have taken. In effect, if, as is probable, states of awareness accompany a reflex mechanism as complicated as that of the sucking instinct, these states of awareness have an internal history. The same state of awareness could not twice reproduce itself identically. If it reproduces itself it is by acquiring in addition some new quality of what has already been seen, etc., consequently some meaning. But if, by chance, no state of awareness yet occurred, one could nevertheless speak of behavior or of behavior patterns, given, on the one hand, the *sui generis* character of their development and, on the other, their continuity with those of subsequent stages. We shall state this in precise terms in our conclusion.

The true character of these behavior patterns involves the individual utilization of experience. In so far as the reflex is a hereditary mechanism it perhaps constitutes a racial utilization of experience. That is a biological problem of which we have already spoken (Introduction, §3) and which, while of highest interest to the psychologist, cannot be solved by his particular methods. But, inasmuch as it is a mechanism giving rise to use, and consequently a sort of experimental trial, the sucking reflex presupposes, in addition to heredity, an individual utilization of experience. This is the crucial fact which permits the incorporation of such a behavior pattern into the realm of psychology, whereas a simple reflex, unsubordinated to the need for use or experimental trial as a function of the environment (sneezing for example) is of no interest to us. Of what does this experimental trial consist? An attempt can be made to define it without subordinating this analysis to any hypothesis concerning the kinds of states of consciousness which eventually accompany such a process. Learning connected with the reflex or instinctive mechanism is distinguished from the attainments due to habits or intelligence by the fact that it retains nothing external to the mechanism itself. A habit, such as that of a 2- or 3-month-old baby who opens his mouth on seeing an object, presupposes a mnemonic fixation related to this object. A tactile-motor schema is formed according to the variations of the object and this schema alone explains the uniformity of the reaction. In the same way the acquisition of an intellectual operation (counting, for instance) implies memory of the objects themselves or of experiments made with the objects. In both cases, therefore, something external to the initial mechanism of the act in question is retained. On the other hand, the baby who learns to suck retains nothing external to the act of sucking; he undoubtedly bears no trace either of the objects or the sensorial pictures on which later attempts have supervened. He merely records the series of attempts as simple acts which condition each other. When he recognizes the nipple, this does not involve recognition of a thing or of an image but rather the assimilation of one sensorimotor and postural complex to another. If the experimental trial involved in sucking presupposes environment and experience, since no functional use is possible without contact with the environment, this is a matter of a very special kind of experimental trial, of an autoapprenticeship to some extent and not of an actual acquisition. This is why, if these first psychological behavior patterns transcend pure physiology—just as the individual use of a hereditary mechanism transcends heredity—they still depend on them to the highest degree.

But the great psychological lesson of these beginnings of behavior is that, within the limits we have just defined, the experimental trial of a reflex mechanism already entails the most complicated accommodations, assimilations and individual organizations. Accommodation exists because, even without retaining anything from the environment as such, the reflex mechanism needs the environment. Assimilation exists because, through its very use, it incorporates to itself every object capable of supplying it with what it needs and discriminates even these objects thanks to the identity of the differential attitudes they elicit. Finally, organization exists, inasmuch as organization is the internal aspect of this progressive adaptation. The sequential uses of the reflex mechanism constitute organized totalities and the gropings and searchings apparent from the beginnings of this period of experimental trial are oriented by the very structure of these totalities.

But if these behavior patterns transcend pure physiology only to the very slight extent in which individual use has a history independent of the machine predetermined by heredity (to the point where it could seem almost metaphorical to characterize them as "behavior patterns" as we have done here), they nevertheless seem to us to be of essential importance to the rest of mental development. In effect, the functions of accommodation, of assimilation and of organization which we have just described in connection with the use of a reflex mechanism will be found once more in the course of subsequent stages and will acquire increasing importance. In a certain sense, we shall even see that the more complicated and refined intellectual structures become, the more this functional nucleus will constitute the essence of these very structures.

ASSIMILATION: BASIC FACT OF PSYCHIC LIFE

In studying the use of reflexes we have ascertained the existence of a fundamental tendency whose manifestations we shall rediscover at each new stage of intellectual development: the tendency toward repetition of behavior patterns and toward the utilization of external objects in the framework of such repetition. This assimilation—simultaneously reproductive, generalizing, and recognitory—constitutes the basis of the functional use which we have described with respect to sucking. Assimilation is therefore indispensable to reflex accommodation. Moreover, it is the dynamic expression of the static fact of organization. From this double point of view it emerges as a basic fact, the psychological analysis of which must yield genetic conclusions.

Three circumstances induce us to consider assimilation the fundamental fact of psychic development. The first is that assimilation constitutes a process common to organized life and mental activity and is therefore an idea common to physiology and psychology. In effect, whatever the secret mechanism of biological assimilation may be, it is an empirical fact that an organ develops while functioning (by means of a certain useful exercise and fatigue). But when the organ in question affects the external behavior of the subject, this phenomenon of functional assimilation presents a physiological aspect inseparable from the psychological aspect; its parts are physiological whereas the reaction of the whole may be called psychic. Let us take for example the eye which develops under the influence of the use of vision (perception of lights, forms, etc.). From the physiological point of view it can be stated that light is nourishment for the eye (in particular in primitive cases of cutaneous sensibility in the lower invertebrates, in whom the eye amounts to an accumulation of pigment dependent on environing sources of light). Light is absorbed and assimilated by sensitive tissues and this action brings with it a correlative development of the organs affected. Such a process undoubtedly presupposes an aggregate of mechanisms whose start may be very complex. But, if we adhere to a global description—that of behavior and consequently of psychology—the things seen constitute nourishment essential to the eye since it is they which impose the continuous use to which the organs owe their development. The eye needs light images just as the whole body needs chemical nourishment, energy, etc. Among the aggregate of external realities assimilated by the organism there are some which are incorporated into the parts of the physicological-chemical mechanisms, while others simply serve as functional and general nourishment. In the first case, there is physiological assimilation, whereas the second may be called psychological assimilation. But the phenomenon is the same in both cases: the universe is embodied in the activity of the subject.

In the second place, assimilation reveals the primitive fact generally conceded to be the most elementary one of psychic life: repetition. How can we explain why the individual, on however high a level of behavior, tries to reproduce every experience he has lived? The thing is only comprehensible if the behavior which is repeated presents a functional meaning, that is to say, assumes a value for the subject himself. But whence comes this value? From functioning as such. Here again, functional assimilation is manifest as the basic fact.

In the third place, the concept of assimilation from the very first embodies in the mechanism of repetition the essential element which distinguishes activity from passive habit: the coordination of the new with the old which foretells the process of judgment. In effect, the reproduction characteristic of the act of assimilation always implies the incorporation of an actual fact into a given schema, this schema being constituted by the repetition itself. In this way assimilation is the greatest of all intellectual mechanisms and once more constitutes, in relation to them, the truly basic fact.

But could not this description be simplified by eliminating a concept which is so fraught with meaning that it might seem equivocal? In his remarkable essays on functional psychology Claparède[6] chooses without adding anything as a point of departure of all mental activity the very fact of need. How can it be explained that certain behavior patterns give rise to spontaneous repetition? How does it happen that useful acts reproduce themselves? Because, says Claparède, they answer a need. Needs thus mark the transition between organic life, from which they emanate, and psychic life, of which they constitute the motive power.

The great advantage of this phraseology is that it is much simpler than that of assimilation. Besides, on the basis of what Claparède maintains, it is very difficult not to agree with him. Since need is the concrete expression of what we have called the process of assimilation, we could not raise doubts concerning the ground for this conception to which we personally owe much. But the question is to know whether, precisely because of its simplicity, it does not bring up initial problems which the concept of assimilation permits us to refer to biological study. There seems to us to be two difficulties.

In the first place, if need as such is the motive power for all activity, how does it direct the movements necessary to its satisfaction? With admirable analytical acuteness, Claparède himself has raised the question. Not only, he says, does one not understand why the pursuit of a goal coordinates useful actions, but furthermore, one does not see how, when one means fails, others are attempted. It transpires, in effect, especially when acquired associations are superimposed on the reflex, that an identical need releases a succession of different behavior patterns, but always directed toward the same end. What is the instrument of this selection and of this coordination of advantageous reactions?

It is self-evident that it would be useless to try to resolve these fundamental problems now. But does not the question arise because one begins by dissociating the need from the act in its totality? The basic needs do not exist, in effect, prior to the motivating cycles which permit them to be gratified. They appear during functioning. One could not say,

[6]See *l'Education fonctionnelle,* Delachaux and Niestlé 1931.

therefore, that they precede repetition: they result from it as well, in an endless circle. For example empty sucking or any similar practice constitutes training which augments need as well as the reverse. From the psychological point of view, need must not be conceived as being independent of global functioning of which it is only an indication. From the physiological point of view, moreover, need presupposes an organization in "mobile balance" of which it simply indicates a transitory imbalance. In both kinds of terminology, need is thus the expression of a totality momentarily incomplete and tending toward reconstituting itself, that is to say, precisely what we call a cycle or a schema of assimilation: Need manifests the necessity of the organism or an organ to use an external datum in connection with its functioning. The basic fact is therefore not need, but the schemata of assimilation of which it is the subjective aspect. Henceforth it is perhaps a pseudo question to ask how need directs useful movements. It is because these movements are already directed that need sets them in motion. In other words, organized movements, ready for repetition, and need itself consitute only one whole. True, this conception, very clear with regard to the reflex or any innate organization, ceases to seem so with respect to acquired associations. But perhaps the difficulty comes from taking literally the term "associations," whereas the fact of assimilation makes it possible to explain how every new schema results from a differentiation and a complication of earlier schemata and not of an association between elements given in an isolated state. This hypothesis even leads to an understanding of how a sole need can set in motion a series of successive efforts. On the one hand, all assimilation is generalizing and, on the other hand, the schemata are capable of intercoordination through reciprocal assimilation as well as being able to function alone (see stages IV–VI concerning this).

A second difficulty seems to us to appear when one considers need as the basic fact of psychic life. Needs are supposed, in such a case, to insure the transition between organism and psyche; they constitute in some way the physiological motive power for mental activity. But if certain corporeal needs play this role in a large number of lower behavior patterns (such as the search for food in animal psychology), in the young child the principal needs are of a functional category. The functioning of the organs engenders, through its very existence, a psychic need *sui generis,* or rather a series of vicarious needs whose complexity transcends, from the very beginning, simple organic satisfaction. Furthermore, the more the intelligence develops and strengthens, the more the assimilation of reality to functioning itself is transformed into real comprehension, the principal motive power of intellectual activity thus becoming the need to incorporate things into the subject's schemata. This vicariousness of needs, which unceasingly transcend themselves to go beyond the purely organic plane, seems to show us anew that the basic fact is not need as such but rather the act of assimilation, which embodies in one whole functional need, repetition and that coordination between subject and object which foretells discrepancy and judgment.

To be sure, invoking the concept of assimilation does not constitute an explanation of assimilation itself. Psychology can only begin with the description of a basic fact without being able to explain it. The ideal of absolute deduction could only lead to verbal explanation. To renounce this temptation is to choose as a principle an elementary fact amenable to biological treatment simultaneously with psychological anlysis. Assimilation answers this. Explanation of this fact is in the realm of biology. The existence of an organized totality which is preserved while assimilating the external world raises, in effect, the whole problem of life itself. But, as the higher cannot be reduced to the lower without adding something, biology will not succeed in clarifying the question of assimilation without taking into account its psychological aspect. At a certain level life organization and mental organization only constitute, in effect, one and the same thing.

IV

THE PLACE OF THE PERSON'S COGNITIVE STRUCTURES IN DETERMINING THE NATURE OF EVENTS

1
OVERVIEW

One of the central issues in psychological theory relates to the question of "determinism." Is the response determined by forces and variables outside the organism, or is the organism somehow able to determine the form of the response? The issue relates to the social concern of "moral behavior" and responsibility. Within the discipline of psychology, this issue, in a variety of forms, underlies some of the most serious theoretical arguments.

Rychlak (1968) offers an extensive analysis of the problems that relate to this issue of determinism and to the ancillary question of control over the organism. He traces the core argument in the issue to the forms by which veracity is achieved in argumentation. The Socratic mode calls for the use of "dialectic reasoning" as contrasted to the use of "demonstrative reasoning" in the Aristotelian mode of argument. In the demonstrative mode one proceeds to argue from "demonstrated" premises, whereas in the dialectic mode one proceeds from an "agreed upon" premise. The demonstrative reasoner applies *the* rules of logic to his premises, constantly excluding the "untrue" premises. The dialectician does not attempt to begin with a "given"; he may choose any side in an argument, whereupon he proceeds to analyze the positions by examining basic assumptions, biases, contradictions, and so on.

To Rychlak, this basic dichotomy underlies many of the important arguments in psychological thought. When considering the question of determinism, the demonstrative reasoner tends to see the external variables as those which "control" the responder. The dialectician tends to view his subject as one who has a choice in a stimulus situation. In the tradition of Locke and British associationism, the response emanates from a set of circumstances that fortuitously present the organism with a contiguous arrangement of stimuli. As long as the stimuli are presented in a particular way, a particular response should be predicted. This approach to the subject of psychology, the behavior of the organism, satisfied two goals: First, this approach placed the psychologist firmly into the mold of the physical scientist, who, following the successful scientific method of Bacon and Newton, saw scientific explanation as a matter of defining the cause that brings about the state of affairs. The proper contiguous arrangements of stimuli would bring about the response; the ability to make this kind of statement reflected good scientific form. Secondly, that psychology tried to say something about the form of the subject's epistemology, it made good sense to impart to the subject a kind of functioning that was amenable to explanation in terms of efficient causes. It would not do to postulate a behaving organism that could "make a choice" when it was presented with a stimulus configuration. If this were to be the case, the neatness of efficient cause explanation would dissipate. It was far more convenient, scientifically, to regard the organism as operating in a way that could be amenable to explanation through the demonstrative form of reasoning. The organism that was itself a demonstrative reasoner, that responded to external stimuli as efficient causes, provided a neat subject for scientific study.

The tradition of the "controlled organism" was further strengthened by a conception of an "empty organism." The position of the "empty organism" became an absolute matter with the early behaviorists, who rejected the theoretical use of any concept that implied an internal mechanism not open to observation. Experiments were designed in terms that strictly definied the input and the output—which, in terms of hypotheses, became the independent and dependent variables, respectively. The classic models for the study of the origins of behavior became the learning studies of Ebbinghaus (1948) or the conditioning model of Pavlov (1960). The organism "learned" a response when the bond between the stimulus and the response was sufficiently assured.

There were, of course, theorists who saw the organism as a "dialectical reasoner." If an organism were exposed to a stimulus it could "propose" at least two different responses to that stimulus. Responses did not spring anew from the stimulus, like Athena from the head of Zeus. Responses derived from an organism's pre-existing construction system and several constructions could be "tried on." In Werner's (1948) language, the response was "differentiated" out of the organism's preceding diffuse organizations. For Piaget (1952), the organism "accommodated" previously organized schema to novel stimuli. The organism could, then, apply the newly accommodated, or differentiated, schema to the stimulus; or it could, at least, revert to applying the schema as it was previously organized. In Section VI, we will return to a discussion of the dichotomous nature of a construct in an effort to elaborate the organism's capacity "to engage in a dialectic"—that is, to propose new and varied responses.

Bruner, Goodnow, and Austin (1956) and Postman (1953), have proposed, and elaborated on, the function of the human organism as a "hypothesis maker." They see the person as striving to categorize a stimulus. They, as well as other researchers who use a cognitive model (Hebb, 1949; Bartlett, 1932; Sherif and Cantril, 1947), have tried to show that each individual imposes his own personally developed constructions on incoming stimuli. At times this effort produces what another observer might call a "distortion." Within the cognitive personality theory which we are working to develop, however, we hold that both "the distorter" and the observer who sees him as a "distorter" are engaging in the same psychological process. They are both striving to maintain useful integrations of the sensory input. To do so, they will engage in a process of hypothesis testing, attempting to apply categories developed in previous situations and which are tentatively aroused by the current stimulus pattern. Upon deriving an existing category that can be accommodated to the current situation, the organism will again return to an optimal level of arousal.

Sir Frederic Bartlett (1932) is an outstanding example of a theorist who persisted in attempting to locate and to quantify the individual's imposition of a cognitive structure on incoming stimuli. In his series of studies he showed how a person's past experiences would be reflected in the subject's "memory" of a stimulus event. This work, which unfortunately followed the form of postdiction rather than prediction, showed that the memories a subject reported would be a reflection of the background of experiences he had brought to a task. Thus, an Englishman recalling a story about Indians of the American Northwest might interpose his own construction of the story converting "typically Indian" themes into "typically English" themes.

The current trend toward integrating into behavioristic theorizing those concepts that take into account the ways in which a subject's internal structures "control" stimuli is to be seen in the use of notions such as *mediated generalization* or *partial anticipatory goal responses*. Behavioristic theorists who use these concepts try to take account of the individualized "meaning" the subject injects into the learning task (Osgood, Suci, Tannenbaum, 1957). This trend within the traditional behaviorist model is also appearing in studies of verbal learning, where one finds the experimenter giving more and more attention to the variable of meaningfulness or associativity (Underwood, 1951) and its effects on learning efficiency. Russell and Storms (1955), for example, have shown that if the subject brings useful internal organizations—that is, if there is an "implicit" chain of associations between the verbal response to be given and the stimulus that is presented—he learns far more efficiently than if he cannot produce these associations.

The position that is being developed in this text seeks to bring the subject's internal organizations into the center of the psychologist's focal field. By the focus we are setting, the personality theorist would concentrate on the cognitive organizations of each individual and would define his psychological principles in terms of how these organizations develop, alter, and interrelate. The position here is that the external stimuli are ineffective in an individual's behavior system until they have been "filtered through" that person's cognitive structures. The effect that a stimulus has on the organism's behavior is limited by the individual's construct system. From this position, then, the organism, complete with his cognitive structures, "determines" the stimulus, rather than the stimulus "determining" the organism's response.

The observer of the behavior can easily "see" that many organisms react similarly to similar stimuli. After observing such a series, one can be led to predict that other organisms will react in the same way, and, from that, to conclude that the stimulus determines the organism's responses. Alternatively one could be led to conclude that the series of organisms which were observed brought similar construct systems to the event. The physical and social universe does generate conditions that lead to shared construct systems. In Section X, where we discuss cognitive organization and social interaction, we will explore the social basis for such shared construct systems. In the long run, however, each person's construct system must be regarded as an individual matter. G. Kelly discusses this under his Individuality Corollary: "Persons differ from each other in their construction of events." He states: "No two people can play precisely the same role in the same event, no matter how closely they are associated."

The articles in this section are chosen to illustrate the experimental methods and techniques that have been used to point to individual differences in construct systems. These studies show that there are clear differences in the ways in which individuals categorize the same events. We also see that different individuals have different categories into which events may be placed. In later sections we will see that different relationships among constructs may also be identified and quantified.

REFERENCES

BARTLETT, F. C. *Remembering*. Cambridge: Cambridge University Press, 1932.

BRUNER, J. S., GOODNOW, J. J., & AUSTIN, G. A. *A Study of Thinking*. New York: Wiley, 1956.

EBBINGHAUS, H. Concerning Memory. In W. Dennis (Ed.), *Readings in the History of Psychology*. New York: Appleton-Century-Crofts, 1948. Pp. 304–313.

HEBB, D. O. *The Organization of Behavior*. New York: Wiley, 1949.

OSGOOD, C. E., SUCI, G. J., & TANNENBAUM, P. H. *The Measurement of Meaning*. Urbana, Illinois: University of Illinois Press, 1957.

PAVLOV, I. P. *Conditioned Reflexes.* New York: Dover, 1960.

PIAGET, J. *The Origins of Intelligence in Children.* New York: International Universities Press, 1952.

POSTMAN, L. Perception, Motivation, and Behavior. *Journal of Personality,* 1953, *22,* 17–31.

RUSSELL, W. A. & STORMS, L. H. Implicit Verbal Chaining in Paired-Associate Learning. *Journal of Experimental Psychology,* 1955, *49,* 287–293.

RYCHLAK, J. F. *A Philosophy of Science for Personality Theory.* Boston: Houghton Mifflin, 1968.

SHERIF, M. and CANTRIL, H. *The Psychology of Ego-Involvements.* New York: Wiley, 1947.

UNDERWOOD, B. J. Associative Transfer in Verbal Learning as a Function of Response Similarity and Degree of First-List Learning. *Journal of Experimental Psychology,* 1951, *42,* 44–54.

WERNER, H. *Comparative Psychology of Mental Development.* New York: Science Editions, 1961.

2

A FACTORIAL STUDY
OF PERSONAL CONSTRUCTS[1]
LEON H. LEVY AND ROBERT D. DUGAN

The study Levy reports in this selection relates to a number of issues raised in this text. It is especially appropriate to the issue of hierarchy in personal construct systems. Further, the study is directly concerned with the question of the nature of personal change—that is, the matter of alteration of constructs in the face of disconfirmation of the construction of an event, as well as with the issue of the organism's tendency to instantiate a stimulus in ways that are consistent with its total construct system. The placement of the article in this section is actually guided by a point that is not specified as a major feature of the study. When Levy uses Kelly's Role Construct Repertory Test (RCRT) to extract the constellatory and propositional constructs which the subjects will later use in judging persons in photographs he is making an implicit assumption. He assumes that he would not be able to give his subjects a list of constellatory or propositional constructs, which they would accept as such, and which they would then use to judge the persons in the photographs. The judgments of the persons in the photographs will be made, he is sure, in terms of each individual's personal construct system regarding other humans, and because of this phenomenon he first extracts a definition of the frame of reference which the interpreter will bring to the situation. Levy later elaborated this view that psychological interpretation ". . . consists of bringing an alternate frame of reference, or language system, to bear upon a set of observations or behaviors . . ." (Levy, 1963, p. 7). Even the clinical psychologist, as we also saw in Soskin's article (Section II), must be aware that it is his constructs, his frame of reference, which guides his judgments of others; and that

Reprinted from Journal of Consulting Psychology, *1956, 20, 53–57, by permission of the authors and the American Psychological Association.*
[1]This study draws heavily upon the Personal Construct Theory of George A. Kelly (2), although the authors accept full responsibility for the assumptions and present form of this paper. The data upon which this article is based were collected while the authors were in residence at the Ohio State University.

these constructs are ultimately idiosyncratic matters. There is no doubt that different individuals will use constructs that parallel those of other persons, but the safest assumption when regarding judgments made of other persons is that no two people use the same construct system. This assumption leads Levy to use the RCRT as an instrument to locate each person's constructs before asking them to make judgments of persons in photos. To make a simple check on part of this assumption Levy asked graduate students in psychology to identify those constructs which had been extracted from the subject's RCRT's as constellatory and which had emerged as propositional constructs. The graduate students could not perform this task with greater accuracy than would have been achieved by random guessing.

REFERENCE

LEVY, L. H. *Psychological Interpretation.* New York: Holt, Rinehart, Winston, 1963.

* * *

The purpose of this paper is to present a method for the delineation of an individual's conceptual structure. It has long been an accepted tenet of projective psychology that each individual imposes his own unique structure on the world about him. Accepting this as a basic assumption, one is next required to tease out the dimensions utilized by the individual in this structuration. This is a common goal of the various extant projective techniques. But whereas in these techniques the final delineation rests rather heavily upon an inferential structure which may vary widely from one test analyst to another, it is proposed that the technique to be described below reduces such inferential variability to a minimum.

THE ROLE CONSTRUCT REPERTORY TEST AND UNDERLYING ASSUMPTIONS

The following assumptions are believed to be the minimum necessary for the derivation of the present technique:

a. For each individual there exists a universe of persons which constitutes his social environment.

b. Each individual possesses a repertoire of constructs which is relatively stable over a period of time, and which he utilizes in structuring his social environment.

c. Constructs contained in a given individual's repertoire bear a relationship to each other such that they may be ordered to certain basic dimensions which define the parameters of his construct repertoire.

d. The structure of an individual's social environment may be duplicated by an observer through knowledge of the parameters of his construct repertoire.

An individual's constructs are viewed in much the same fashion as the constructs of the scientist. They are the ways in which order is brought to the unordered, and the bases upon which predictions about outcomes of behavior are made. Defining a construct as *a way in which two or more things are alike and at the same time different from one or more other things,* Kelly (2) has developed the Role Construct Repertory Test (RCRT) as a means of eliciting an individual's construct repertoire.

One form of the RCRT consists of two parts: In the first part there is a list of 15 *role titles* such as: Your mother or the person that played the part of your mother; A person who for some unknown reason disliked you; A teacher for whom you had a great deal of respect; etc. For each of these titles *S* writes down one name and may not use the same name twice. In the second part *S* is presented with 15 combinations of these people taken three at a time and is asked to indicate in a word or phrase how any two in each triad are the same and at the same time different from the third. This constitutes a construct. He is then asked to indicate what he feels to be the opposite of the construct he has just listed. Thus there are elicited 15 constructs and their opposites. Using college students and a slightly different form of the RCRT, Hunt (1) obtained a test-retest agreement of 70 per cent on constructs used, indicating some generality for the constructs elicited.

Having obtained a sample of the individual's construct repertoire the next problem involves ordering these to certain dimensions which may be said to represent the parameters of his construct repertoire. It will be apparent to the reader at this point that this is a similar problem to that found in psychometrics, where one has a large number of scores on various tests and wishes to reduce these to more meaningful dimensions which will explain whatever relationship exists between these scores. The method of choice in psychometrics appears to be factor analysis and this method has been applied to the present study. Thus we propose to present the application of factor analysis to an individual's RCRT protocol as a means of determining the manner in which he structures his social environment.

Although some similarity to Osgood's method of deriving his Semantic Differential (4) will be noted, one important difference is that the dimensions arrived at by the present approach are unique for each individual, whereas the scales contained in the Semantic Differential are nomothetic in nature, having been derived from a large group of *S*s.

While Osgood's procedure permits the specification of the meaning of concepts in a multidimensional space defined by his instrument, we would claim that the factor analysis of an RCRT protocol permits, first, the specification of a multidimensional conceptual space unique for a given individual, and second, the location of persons in this space.

PROCEDURE

The RCRT as described above was administered to each of four Ss.[2] The resulting constructs in each protocol were then designated as five-point rating scales on which S was to rate each of the 15 individuals named in the first part of the test. The low end of the scale meant that the construct was very typical of the person, while the high end meant that the contrasting or opposite construct was very atypical. In order to reduce any halo effect, the S was asked to consider one construct at a time, rating all of the individuals in succession.

One can thus conceive of the constructs as tests on which there are as many scores as there are people rated. It is recognized that the correlations which result from this procedure will be affected by the fact that the individuals rated on a particular construct may have also entered into the formulation of that construct. It was apparent, however, that the correlations were not uniformly affected since they range from high positive to high negative.

The intercorrelations between constructs for each S were factor analyzed using the Thurstone multiple group method. Factors were rotated to orthogonal simple structure. The loadings were then adjusted by the Wherry-iterative procedure (5) so that no residuals in any of the tables exceeded $\pm.15$. Ninety-five per cent of the residuals in each of the tables were between $\pm.10$. Loadings of .30 or greater were considered significant.

RESULTS

Since the purpose of this paper is primarily methodological and heuristic, no data will be presented other than the constructs with their factor loadings and a brief description of the S.

Case I. A 31-year-old, single male graduate student, considered a "capable" person by his associates. He comes from one of the "old families" of the South and has described his home as somewhat puritani-

[2]In order to conserve space only two of the four cases are presented.

TABLE 1 Constructs and orthogonal factor loadings for Case I.

		\multicolumn{5}{c}{Factor loadings}				
\multicolumn{2}{c}{Constructs}					
Construct	Contrasting construct	I	II	III	IV	h^2
1. Unassuming	Pretentious	−19	90	27	−09	93
2. Creative	Uncreative; static	24	27	90	12	95
3. Rigid	Flexible	03	−55	−55	−53	89
4. Original; daring	Unoriginal; conventional	03	−01	40	58	50
5. Sincere; unaffected	Insincere; affected	−19	91	33	07	98
6. Aggressive	Submissive	13	−58	−59	30	79
7. Sexual	Asexual	84	00	03	10	72
8. Intelligent	Stupid	06	29	92	02	93
9. Refined	Crude	00	87	31	19	89
10. Intellectual	Non-intellectual	15	12	89	25	89
11. Non-productive	Productive	05	−02	−62	−25	45
12. Liberal	Conservative	40	−17	62	51	83
13. Ascetic	Sensual	−75	15	04	−52	86
14. Introjected Values	Experience-derived values	−07	−11	−54	−33	42
15. Socially inept	Socially skilled	05	−14	48	−30	34

cal. He is much concerned with problems of creativity and personal freedom.

Table 1 presents his construct repertoire and orthogonal factor loadings. We consider these factors to be an operational definition of this S's mode of structuring his social environment. To attempt to give names to these factors would appear to be of dubious value, while inspecting each factor for those constructs with significant loadings will provide us with some insight into the ways in which the S attempts to make sense out of his world.[3]

Factor I is clearly concerned with sexuality, with the probable identification of sexual expression with liberality and sexual repression with conservatism. One might suspect here that since he describes his family as puritanical, he would perceive them as conservative and hence not condoning sexual expression. The fact that at 31 he is not married may indicate a closer tie to his family than he would be willing to admit. These of course are in the nature of low order hypotheses which such a protocol, taken together with other information, might generate.

Factor II appears to be an affective or attitudinal dimension by means of which people are seen as either unassuming or pretentious with the further implication that persons who are unassuming, submissive, and refined are more to be trusted and relied upon than those for whom the opposite might be true. One would be led to predict here, among other things, that this person might have difficulty relating to persons in certain occupations or social strata where a premium is placed on aggressiveness. Similarly he may be an unduly submissive individual because of the negative implications of aggressiveness. However, he would probably see this more as being flexible than submissive.

Factor III seems to reflect his concern with intellectual freedom and creativity. Interestingly, we also find that the constructs "aggressive-submissive" and "refined-crude" have significant loadings on this factor. Here it appears that creativity and intelligence also carry certain emotional connotations for him and that, perhaps, he is not able or willing to accept a person purely on the basis of his accomplishments in a given area, but also looks for certain nonintellectual components as well.

Factor IV may be the dimension by which he discriminates between people who are like his family and those who are not. If we were interested in transference relationship problems, we might view this factor as mediating the transference. We might expect, if this were true, that having

[3]While no attempt is made in this article to establish the validity status of the RCRT or our method of analysis, it might be mentioned parenthetically that a faculty member in the department in which this S was a student identified the student immediately upon reading this analysis of his protocol, although he had no knowledge that the student had taken part in the study.

TABLE 2 Constructs and orthogonal loadings for Case II.

Constructs		Factor loadings				
Construct	Contrasting construct	I	II	III	IV	h^2
1. Open mind, growing	Closed mind, "set in ways"	91	25	00	30	98
2. Plastic, vital religiously	Distorted, inadequate concepts	50	79	-05	-10	89
3. Understanding	Inward looking, self-seeing only	96	-04	-14	06	95
4. Confused	On firm emotional foundation	-18	12	80	00	69
5. Vital in thinking	Conventional in thinking	84	21	05	42	93
6. Gentle	Severe, critical	88	26	12	-02	86
7. Masculine dominating	Leading, not driving	-93	-10	03	-02	88
8. Likeable	Irritating	69	49	-03	-08	72
9. Devoted to a purpose	Takes life as it comes	32	65	02	00	41
10. Not satisfied with taking other people's thinking	Does no individual thinking	63	23	20	53	77
11. Can talk about philosophical ideas	Not interested in philosophical ideas	73	57	08	26	94
12. Broader outlook	Limited outlook	85	32	00	41	99
13. Stolid	High strung	-23	00	-71	-04	56
14. Resentful	Accepting	-97	03	02	02	94
15. Don't see me as a person	Sympathetic	-91	-03	-07	10	84

placed a nonfamily figure on the same end of this dimension as his family, he would then transfer to them many of the attitudes he holds in regard to his family. Such information would be invaluable to a clinician working with this person.

Case II. By way of contrast we present the factor analysis of the RCRT protocol of a 48-year-old female graduate student, married, and mother of two children. At the time of this study she described herself as confused about the future and considering a fairly radical vocational change. Without going into the protocol in the same detail as the previous one, one is immediately struck by her concern about being accepted, about a *Weltanschauung*, and about emotional stability. If one were working with this woman clinically, he would be particularly interested in the relationship between the construct "masculine dominating—leading, not driving" and the rest of the factor on which it is loaded. Does she indeed see males as dominating, "set in ways," and generally unthinking? If so, how does this enter into her present difficulty? Does she see herself frustrated because this is essentially "a man's world"? These are just a few of the questions and hypotheses which a clinician would raise on the basis of this protocol.

DISCUSSION

We have presented what we believe to be a useful and reliable approach to the "mapping" of the individual cognitive structure. In its present form it would be impractical except for research purposes. However, Kelly (3) is developing a nonparametric equivalent to factor analysis which would permit one to factor a protocol in about one hour's time. We would like in this section to sketch some of the research possibilities which we believe are opened up by this method.

Not losing sight of the fact that the RCRT is a sorting test akin to other concept-formation tests, one immediately wonders what the qualitative relationships might be between the constructs elicited by it and the concepts elicited by these tests. More specifically, since here we obtain a picture of the relationship between constructs, there are certain questions amenable to investigation for the first time. For example: What is the significance of the number of factors derived? Is there a relationship between number of factors derived and complexity of cognitive structure? If so, what are the behavioral correlates of complexity of cognitive structure? Does the number of constructs having significant loadings on a given factor have any significance? One might suspect that the larger the number of constructs significantly loaded on a given factor, the more important that dimension is for the individual. Does factorial structure change along developmental lines?

Aside from the content itself, there are certain implications for clinical research. Since the factors derived are to a good extent the result of functional relationships which the individual himself has imposed upon his constructs, one wonders at the extent to which he is aware of this functional relationship. As a corollary, one might be interested in the correlates of accuracy of awareness of functional relationships between constructs. Such relationships could be studied by having the individual attempt to sort his constructs into as many groups as there were factors, and determining the correspondence between his grouping and the factor grouping. Correspondence could be construed as one form of insight and might be expected to vary with personal adjustment, age, success or failure in psychotherapy, etc. The clinician, interested as he is in problems of interpersonal relationship, could easily investigate such areas as transference, identification, etc., by means of an inverse analysis of the same protocol using the role titles as the variates. Here again it would be interesting to study developmental trends.

Other research opportunities present themselves in the fields of social and industrial psychology where one might be interested in, among other things, the commonality of constructs among members of a given group, the relationship between nature and structure of cognitive structure and leadership ability, etc. The problem of communication could be approached through the study of the personal constructs of the communicators. From the standpoint of communication, this technique provides a means of reproducing each individual's personal coding scheme. One might study such problems as ability to receive and transmit information as a function of the content and structure of individual coding systems.

One last point should be made with respect to the problem of validity. In one sense there is no such thing as an invalid test, since all tests measure something, and it becomes a question of semantics whether the right name has been applied to it; the more important question as we see it is *pertinence*. The responses of an individual on the RCRT constitute a phenomenon; by means of factor analysis we impose a certain structure upon this phenomenon, and now the problem becomes one of the pertinence of this phenomenon and this structure. The entire body of this discussion has been devoted to the description of a program which we believe would yield an answer to this question. To the extent that the information yielded by the RCRT and its factor analysis is found to be functionally related to other psychological phenomena, the technique has pertinence. In this spirit we offer the technique to the psychological public.

SUMMARY

A method is described whereby factor analytic techniques may be applied to the concepts formed by an individual on a sorting test called the Role Construct Repertory Test. Two cases are presented for illustrative purposes and the research implications of this method are discussed.

REFERENCES

1. HUNT, D. Studies in Role Construct Repertory: Conceptual Consistency. Unpublished master's thesis, The Ohio State University, 1951.
2. KELLY, G. A. *The Psychology of Personal Constructs.* New York: Norton, 1955.
3. KELLY, G. A. The Analysis of a Person's Psychological Space. Unpublished manuscript, The Ohio State University, 1952.
4. OSGOOD, C. E. The Nature and Measurement of Meaning. *Psychol. Bull.,* 1952, *49,* 197-237.
5. WHERRY, R. J. A New Iterative Method for Correcting Erroneous Communality Estimates in Factor Analysis. *Psychometrika,* 1949, *14,* 231-241.

3

THE NATURE AND MEASUREMENT
OF MEANING[1]
CHARLES E. OSGOOD

If one is to argue that a person's cognitive structures are to be regarded as the central determiners of the nature of stimuli, he is obligated to produce a measure of the cognitive structures. Further, a good start toward accepting the validity of the proposition would be to demonstrate that the chosen measure does reflect intra-individual variation in cognizing a single event. The semantic differential is the result of Osgood's search for a suitable means of assessing individual "meanings" for various terms. This measuring device provided an excellent means of quantifying elusive internal representations of external stimuli. After Osgood reported this measure, researchers used it in hundreds of studies. The data gathered by the semantic differential are exceptionally appropriate to a number of the issues raised in this text. This paper has been placed in this section in order to highlight our position that a particular stimulus evokes extensively variant cognitive structures. Osgood makes clear his expectation, derived from preliminary research, that such inter-individual variation would be revealed by the semantic differential. Later studies affirmed this expectation. In this article Osgood also indicates, and later work clearly demonstrates (Osgood, Suci, and Tannenbaum, 1957), that there were extensive hierarchical relationships among the scales used to make judgments of stimulus items. As a rule, factor analytic studies show that the two-poled constructs *good-bad, strong-weak,* and *active-passive* largely subsume any other construct that is used in the judgment scales.

Reprinted from Psychological Bulletin, *1952,* 49, *197–235, by permission of the author and the American Psychological Association. The first part of the original article, an extended review of approaches to the measurement of meaning, has been omitted.*
  [1]The research on which in part this report is based is being supported jointly by the University Research Board of the University of Illinois and the Social Science Research Council. Grateful acknowledgment is made to both institutes for their assistance.

REFERENCE

OSGOOD, C. E., SUCI, G. J., and TANNENBAUM, P. H. *The Measurement of Meaning.* Urbana, Illinois: University of Illinois Press, 1957.

*   *   *

SUMMARY ON EXISTING METHODS
OF MEASURING MEANING

The purpose of the preceding review has been to see if there already exist adequate methods of measuring meaning. By "adequate" I mean already meeting most of the criteria of satisfactory measuring instruments. What are these criteria? *(a) Objectivity.* The method should yield quantitative and verifiable (reproducible) data. *(b) Reliability.* It should yield the same values within acceptable margins of error, when the same conditions are duplicated. *(c) Validity.* The data obtained should be demonstrably covariant with those obtained with some other, independent index of meaning. *(d) Sensitivity.* The method should yield differentiations commensurate with the natural units of the material studied, i.e., should be able to reflect as fine distinctions in meaning as are typically made in communicating. *(e) Comparability.* The method should be applicable to a wide range of phenomena in the field making possible comparisons among different individuals and groups, among different concepts, and so on. *(f) Utility.* It should yield information relevant to contemporary theoretical and practical issues in an efficient manner, i.e., it should not be so cumbersome and laborious as to prohibit collection of data at a reasonable rate. While this is not an exhaustive listing of criteria, it is sufficient for our purposes.

1. The *physiological measures* (including action potential, GSR, and salivary records) are of somewhat dubious validity, since there has been no demonstration of the necessity of these peripheral components, and they are not sensitive measures in that we are unable to interpret details of the records in our present ignorance. Their chief drawback, however, is cumbersomeness—the subject has to be "rigged up" in considerable gadgetry to make such measurements. For this reason, even should validity and sensitivity problems be met satisfactorily, it seems likely that physiological indices will be mainly useful as criteria against which to evaluate more practicable techniques.

2. *Learning measures* (including semantic generalizations and transfer/interference methods) are also somewhat cumbersome procedurally, but their main drawback as general measures of meaning is their lack of comparability. Any measure of generalization or interference is made with respect to the original

learning of some standards which necessarily varies from case to case. The chief usefulness of learning measures, therefore, lies in the test of specific hypotheses.

3. The chief drawback with *perception measures* (e.g., what is perceived in ambiguous stimulus forms, the recognition-times for tachistoscopically presented words) is that they are not valid measures of *meaning*. They get at the availability or comparative habit strengths of alternative meanings or ways of perceiving. The fact that a religious person perceives VESPERS with a shorter presentation time than a theoretically oriented person says nothing about *how* the meaning of this term differs for them; the fact that the religious person perceives VESPERS more quickly than THEORY says nothing about the difference in meaning of these two words to this individual. The same statements apply to Skinner's (10) "verbal summator" technique.

4. The selection of responses in *association methods* is partly dependent upon the meaning of the stimulus items (and hence indexes meaning) and partly dependent upon habit strength factors. The chief drawback, as a general measure of meaning, is lack of comparability. The responses of two individuals to the same stimulus, or of the same individual to two stimulus words, are essentially unique as bits of data. Comparability can be obtained with group data, but this limits the method.

5. *Scaling methods* can be viewed as forms of controlled association in which the nature of the association is specified by definition of the scales (favorable-unfavorable, vividness, etc.) but the direction and intensity of association is unspecified. By the very nature of the scaling method, the comparability criterion is usually satisfied (provided the subjects can be shown to agree upon the meaning of the scale and its divisions). As used by Mosier (7), however, the method can have only partial validity. This is because he tapped only one dimension of meaning, the admittedly important evaluative dimension, whereas we know that meanings vary multidimensionally.

THE SEMANTIC DIFFERENTIAL

The method to be proposed here is a combination of associational and scaling procedures. It is an indirect method in the same sense that an intelligence test, while providing objective and useful information, does not directly measure this capacity. However, unlike the intelligence test which treats this ability *as if* it were distributed along a single continuum (e.g., IQ scores vary along a single scale), we accept at the outset that meanings vary in some unknown number of dimensions and frame our methodology accordingly.

Research Origins of the Method. This method had its origins in research on synesthesia, defined by Warren in his *Dictionary of Psychology* (14) as "a phenomenon characterizing the experiences of certain individuals, in which certain sensations belonging to one sense or mode attach to certain sensations of another group and appear regularly whenever a stimulus of the latter type occurs." This implies a sort of "neural short-circuiting" that is present in only a few freak individuals, and it is true that many of the classic case histories in this area gave credence to this view: a subject reported pressure sensations about his teeth and cheeks whenever cold spots on his arms were stimulated (Dallenbach, 2); a girl displayed a rigid system of relations between specific notes on the musical scale and specific color experiences, consistent when tested over a period of seven and one-half years (Langfeld, 6). But here, on the other hand, was a man who imagined the number "1" to be yellow, "2" to be blue, "3" to be red . . . and, of course, "8" to be black (anyone who has played pool will recognize the origin of this system); and here was a little girl who recalled her friends as having pink faces and her enemies as having purple faces. What modalities are crossed in these cases?

A more recent series of investigations by Karwoski, Odbert, and their associates related synesthesia to thinking and language in general (cf.,also Wheeler and Cutsforth, 15). Rather than being a rare phenomenon, Karwoski and Odbert (4) report that as many as 13 per cent of Dartmouth College students regularly indulged in color-music synesthesia, often as a means of enriching their enjoyment of music. These photistic visualizers varied among themselves as to the modes of translation employed and the vividness of their experiences, and their difference from the general population appeared to be one of degree rather than kind. Whereas fast, exciting music might be pictured by the synesthete as sharply etched, bright red forms, his less imaginative brethren would merely agree that terms like "red-hot," "bright," and "fiery," as verbal metaphors, adequately described the music; a slow and melancholic selection might be visualized as heavy, slow-moving "blobs" of sombre hue and described verbally as "heavy," "blue," and "dark." The relation of this phenomenon to ordinary verbal metaphor is evident: a happy man is said to feel "high," a sad man feels "low"; the pianist travels "up" and "down" the scale from treble to bass; souls travel "up" to the good place and "down" to the bad place; hope is "white" and despair is "black." The process of metaphor in language as well as in color-music synesthesia can be described as the parallel alignment of two or more dimensions of experience, defined verbally by pairs of polar opposites, with translations occurring between equivalent portions of the continua (Karwoski, Odbert, and Osgood, 5, pp. 212-221).

Interrelationships among color, mood and musical experiences were studied more analytically by Odbert, Karwoski, and Eckerson (8). Subjects first listened to 10 short excerpts from classical scores and indicated their dominant moods by checking descriptive adjectives arranged in a mood circle (cf., Hevner, 3). Then, on a second hearing, they listed the colors appropriate to each score. Significant relations were shown; the color associations to musical scores followed the moods created. A portion of Delius' *On Hearing the First Cuckoo in Spring* was judged leisurely in mood and preponderantly green in color; a portion of Wagner's *Rienzi Overture* was judged exciting or vigorous in mood and preponderantly red in color. When another group of subjects was merely shown the mood adjectives (with no musical stimulation) and asked to select appropriate colors, even *more* consistent relations appeared, suggesting that the unique characteristics of the musical selections had, if anything, somewhat obscured the purely verbal or metaphorical relations between colors and moods. Almost identical findings have been reported by Ross (9) for relationships between the colors used in stage lighting and reported moods produced in the audience. Data are also available for the effects of color upon mood in mental institutions and in industrial plants.

Responses to complex selections of music such as used in the above studies are themselves too complex for analysis of specific relations between auditory-mood variables and color-form variables. In order to get closer to the mechanisms of translation, Karwoski, Odbert, and Osgood (5) used simple melodic lines recorded by a single instrument (clarinet) as stimuli. In a first experiment the subjects were typical photistic visualizers and they drew their photisms with colored pencils after hearing each selection in a darkened room. The simplest stimulus was a combination of crescendo and diminuendo on a single note—the sound merely grew louder, then softer—and this will serve to illustrate the results. As shown in Figure 2, subject *a* indicates increasing LOUDNESS by making the center of his line *heavier*, subject *b* by increasing *amplitude of vibration*, subjects *e, f,* and *g* by greater *thickness* of a solid form, subject *j* by more *concentrated focusing*, and subject *h* by more *saturated coloring* of the central portion. Subject *i* always created meaningful rather than abstract forms—here, a little car that comes *nearer* and then away again—yet the formal characteristics of his productions were generally like those of abstract synesthetes. These are functionally or meaningfully equivalent responses to the same auditory stimulus dimension—i.e., there are alternate visual continua that can be paralleled with the loud-soft auditory continuum—and the advantage of the method is that its simplicity allows these relationships to show up clearly.

Are these photistic visualizers exercising a "rare" capacity or are they merely expressing overtly modes of translation that are implicit in the language of our culture? A second experiment used subjects who had never even thought of "seeing things" when they heard music (if they reported any such tendencies, they were eliminated). The same simple melodic lines as above were played and the subjects were instructed to

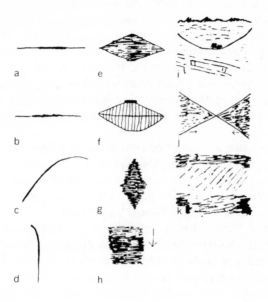

FIG. 2   *Sample of photisms drawn by complex synesthetes to represent a simple tone which grows louder and then softer.*

"force themselves to draw something to represent what they heard." They produce the same types of visual forms and in approximately the same relative frequencies as the experienced visualizers. Finally, a group of 100 unselected students was given a purely verbal *meaning-polarity test,* each item of which appeared in the following form: LARGE–small; SOFT–LOUD, with instructions to circle that word in the second pair which "seems most clearly related to" the capitalized word in the first pair. Here again, essentially the same relations between music-mood variables and color-form variables discovered among sensitive synesthetes were linked meaningfully on the polarity test. *Large* was linked to *loud* by 96 per cent of these subjects, *near* with *fast* by 86 per cent, *bright* with *happy* by 96 per cent, *treble* with *up* by 98 per cent, and so on. It seems clear from these studies that the imagery found in synesthesia is on a continuum with metaphor, and that both represent *semantic* relations.

Are such semantic relations entirely dependent upon culture or is it possible that they reflect more fundamental determinants common to the human species? In an attempt to get at this question, the writer studied anthropological field reports on five quite widely separated primitive cultures—Aztec and Pueblo Indian, Australian Bushman, Siberian Aborigine, Negro (Uganda Protectorate), and Malayan—with the view of obtaining evidence on semantic parallelism. Special emphasis was given to nonmaterial aspects of culture (mythology, religion, arts, medical beliefs, birth, marriage, death complexes, etc.). The numerous pitfalls in the way of such analysis are probably obvious. Particularly, there is the danger of attributing relations to a primitive group when they are actually projections on the part of the observer or borrowings from the dominant Western culture. Therefore the results should be considered merely suggestive.

Nevertheless, the generality of certain relationships was quite striking. For example, *good* gods, places, social positions, etc., were regularly *up* and *light (white)* in relation to *bad* things, which were *down* and *dark (black)*. A prevalent myth tells of how the gods helped the original man to struggle "up" from the "dark," "cold," "wet," "sad" world below the ground to the "light," "warm," "dry," "happy" world on the surface of the earth. Among certain Siberian Aborigines, members of a privileged clan call themselves the "white" bones in contrast to all others who are referred to as "black" bones. And even among the Uganda Negroes we find some evidence for a white god at the apex of the hierarchy, and white cloth is clearly associated with purity, being used to ward off evil spirits and disease. Such data suggest the existence of a pervasive semantic frame of reference. Further study of the problem by more adequately trained investigators could be richly rewarding.

Stagner and Osgood (13) adapted this method and the logic underlying it to the study of social stereotypes. The notion of a continuum between the polar terms was made explicit by using such terms to define the ends of 7-step scales. Rather than studying the relations between continua, as above, a set of scales was used to measure the "meaning" of particular concepts, such as PACIFIST, RUSSIAN, DICTATOR, and NEUTRALITY. Successive samples of subjects were tested between April, 1940, and March, 1942 (including a sample obtained just prior to the Pearl Harbor incident). A single item on the tests appeared as follows:

PACIFIST: Kind___:___:___:___:___:___cruel

with the subject instructed to check that position on the scale which best represented the direction and intensity of his judgment. The concepts and scales related in successive items of the test were randomized to insure as much independence of judgment as possible. The feasibility and efficiency of using this method to record the changing structures of social stereotypes (e.g., the changing meanings of a set of social signs) were demonstrated. That a total shift from an essentially pacifistic to an essentially militaristic frame of reference had been accomplished, even before the Pearl Harbor incident provided the spark to overt expression, was clearly evident in the data.

More important from the point of view of methodology was the following observation: As used by our subjects in making their judgments, the various descriptive scales fell into highly intercorrelated clusters. Fair-unfair, high-low, kind-cruel, valuable-worthless, Christian-anti-Christian, and honest-dishonest were all found to correlate together .90 or better. This cluster represented, we assumed, a single, general factor in social judgments, the evaluative (good-bad) dimension of the frame of reference. Gradients like strong-weak, realistic-unrealistic, and happy-sad were independent of this evaluative group and pointed to the existence of other dimensions within the semantic framework. Enforced shifts in the apparent reference point of the observer (by having subjects judge the same concepts "as a German" or "as an Englishman") produced gross and appropriate changes in the evaluative dimension but did not disrupt the qualitative pattern of each stereotype— e.g., the stereotype GERMANS, when judged by students playing the role of Germans, was still seen as relatively more "strong" and "happy" (remember, this was during 1940-1942) than "noble" or "kind." This illustrates the kind of difficulty experienced when one tries to assume the point of view of another (cf., Stagner and Osgood, 12).

Logic of the proposed method. The researches described above gave rise to the following hypotheses:

1. The process of description or judgment can be conceived as the allocation of a concept to an experiential continuum, definable by a pair of polar terms. An underlying notion in our research is that these "experiential continua" will turn out to be reflections (in language) of the sensory differentiations made possible by the human nervous system. In other words, it is assumed that discriminations in meaning, which is itself a state of awareness, cannot be any finer or involve any more variables than are made possible by the sensory nervous system (cf., Boring, *The Dimensions of Consciousness,* 6). While failure to confirm this notion would not eliminate the proposed method as an index of meaning, its confirmation would greatly enhance the theoretical implications of this work.

2. Many different experiential continua, or ways in which meanings vary, are essentially equivalent and hence may be represented by a single dimension. This functional equivalence of many alternate continua was clearly evident in both the studies on synesthesia and those on the changing structure of social stereotypes. It is this fact about language and thinking that makes the development of a quantitative measuring instrument feasible. If the plethora of descriptive terms we utilize were in truth unique and independent of one another, as most philosophers of meaning seem to have assumed, then measurement would be impossible.

3. A limited number of such continua can be used to define a semantic space within which the meaning of any concept can be specified. From the viewpoint of experimental semantics, this both opens the possibility of measuring meaning-in-general objectively and specifies factor analysis as the basic methodology. If it can be demonstrated that a limited number of dimensions or factors are sufficient to differentiate among the meanings of randomly selected concepts, and if the technique devised satisfies the criteria of measurement stated earlier, then such a "semantic differential" as I have termed it, *is* an objective index of meaning. From the viewpoint of psychological theory, we may look upon the procedures followed in obtaining this measure as an operational definition of meaning, in the same sense that the procedures followed in obtaining the IQ score provide an operational definition of intelligence.

The operations followed in the present instance are explicit. They involve the subject's allocation of a concept within a standard system of descriptive dimensions by means of a series of independent associative judgments. The judgmental situation is designed to be maximally simple. Presented with a pair of descriptive polar terms (e.g., *rough–smooth)* and a concept (e.g., LADY), the subject merely indicates the direction of this association (e.g., LADY-*smooth).* We have developed two different methods for collecting data: In the *graphic method,* a pencil-and-paper technique which has the advantage that data can be collected from groups of subjects and hence very speedily, the subject indicates the intensity of his association by the extremeness of his checking on a 7-step scale. In the *judgment-time method,* which has the advantage that the subject cannot anticipate what concept is to be judged on a particular scale and hence cannot rationalize his reaction, intensity of association is indicated by the latency of the individual subject's choice reaction toward one or the other of the polar terms. In both methods each associative judgment of a particular concept against a particular descriptive scale constitutes one item. In successive items, concepts and dimensions are paired in deliberately rotated orders until every concept has been associated with every scale by every subject.

A factor analysis of meaning. The procedures and results of this factor analysis will be described in detail elsewhere. A total of 50 descriptive scales, selected in terms of their frequency of usage, have been used in the judgment of 20 varied concepts, yielding a 1,000-item test. One hundred college students served as subjects. The graphic method was used.[2] The

---

[2]Apparatus for obtaining latency measurements from individual subjects has been constructed and will be standardized upon the reduced set of descriptive scales we hope to derive from this preliminary factor analysis. While this apparatus has the advantage that materials are projected from a film-strip and responses (directions and latencies) are photographed by a single-frame camera—all automatically—it is still applicable only to a single subject at a time and hence is time-consuming.

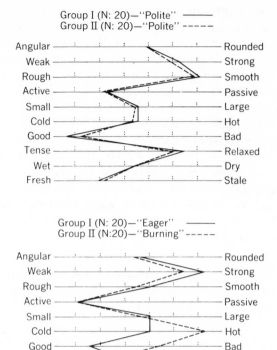

FIG. 3 *Illustration of application of a preliminary form of the semantic differential for measuring the connotative meanings of adjectives: A. Upper profiles, medians for two groups of 20 subjects differentiating "polite"; B. Lower profiles, medians for same two groups of 20 subjects differentiating "eager" and "burning."*

purpose of this factor analysis is to isolate a limited number of general dimensions of meaning having a maximal differentiating power, to try to bring some order out of semantic chaos. The larger the proportion of total variance in meaning accounted for by these factors, the more satisfactory will be the measuring instrument finally set up. A preliminary estimation of factors in the 50×50 matrix (each scale correlated with every other scale) indicates the existence of several roughly independent dimensions. An "evaluative factor" accounts for by far the largest portion of the variance. There is also evidence for a "strength factor," an "activity factor," and several others not clearly defined in this rough approximation. Given such factors, it will be possible to select those specific scales (e.g., good-bad, strong-weak, active-passive, smooth-rough, hot-cold, etc.) which best represent them.

We have done some exploratory work on the use of the semantic differential as a practical measuring device. The two sets of profiles in Figure 3 will serve to illustrate the method. Two groups of only 20 subjects each differentiated the meaning of the adjective "polite"; Group I also differentiated "eager," while Group II also differentiated "burning" (as part of a larger study). Median judgments of the 20 subjects on each scale are plotted. There is high agreement on the differentiation of the same sign, "polite." The different, but somewhat similar signs, "eager" and "burning," show significant points of discrimination: whereas they are equally *strong* and *active,* "burning" is relatively *hot* and *dry* as compared with "eager," and "eager" is relatively *good* and *fresh* as compared with "burning." These differences are obviously what they would have to be if the method has any validity. It must be emphasized that the sample of scales shown here does *not* necessarily represent those to be finally derived from our factor analysis.

Evaluation of the method. Evaluation of this instrument against the criteria of measurement listed earlier will be the subject of future research, but some evidence can be presented now.

1. Objectivity. The semantic differential yields quantitative data which are presumably verifiable, in the sense that other investigators can apply the same sets of scales to equivalent subjects and obtain essentially the same result.

2. Reliability. In the test form from which data for the factor analysis were collected, 40 of the 1,000 items were selected at random and repeated. None of the subjects was aware that this had been done. The reliability coefficient was .85. The minimum variation in profile for the two groups of 20 subjects judging "polite" is another indication of the stability of the method.

3. Validity. All of the data collected so far on several problems display convincing face-validity and several direct experimental checks are planned. These include (a) correlation of attitudes toward various social objects as measured on standard tests with allocation of signs of these social objects within the semantic differential, and (b) the use of experimentally induced changes in meaning of signs (cf., Stagner and Britton). We are not concerned about the problem of "labeling" factors, a point where the precision gained by the factor analytic method is often lost in the obscurities of language. Selection of specific scales to match factors can proceed on a purely objective basis, in terms of the factor loadings for each scale. As a matter of fact, the polar terms which define the scales do not admit much in the way of misinterpretation.

4. The question of *sensitivity* of the method comes down to whether it is able to reflect as fine distinctions in meaning as are ordinarily made. We have incidental evidence that a semantic differential can tease out nuances in meaning which are clearly felt but hard to verbalize deliberately.[3] If there is a real difference in the meaning of two signs, such that they would not be used in precisely the same contexts, and if our measuring instrument includes a sufficient number of dimensions of the semantic space, then a significant difference should appear on at least one of the scales.

5. Comparability. It is here that the most serious questions arise. (a) *Is the method culture-bound?* If the tendency to dichotomize experiential continua is characteristic of Western culture but not necessarily elsewhere, then the method would not have generality. This is an empirical question requiring the skills of anthropologists and linguists for solution. (b) *Is the method limited to the differentiation of nouns against adjective scales?* The structure of our language is such that "adjectives" typically reflect abstracted qualities of experience and "nouns" the concepts and things dealt with. We have found it possible to set up scales like giant–midget, fire–iceberg, god–devil and to judge concepts like INSINUATE and AGITATED against them. This does not seem "natural" to members of our language community, however; it is probably the stem or root meaning of words that our method taps. (c) *Can different concepts be compared?* To the extent that judgments of different concepts involve the same factor structure, any concept may be compared with any other against a single, standardized semantic framework. (d) *Can different individuals be compared?* This also comes down to the generality of the semantic factor structure. It is quite conceivable that different classes of people (scientists, ministers, etc.) have somewhat varied semantic structures, differing in the emphasis upon certain factors and interrelationships among them. In fact, a significant source of individual differences may lie here.

Our method can be criticized on the ground that it only gets at *connotative* meaning, not *denotative* meaning. This is a limitation. Both SIMON LEGREE and WAR might be allocated to approximately the same point in semantic space by our method. This would indicate similar connotative meaning, to be sure, but it would not indicate that these signs refer to the same object. Our differential will draw out the *hard, heavy, cold, ugly, threatening* connotations of the sign HAMMER, but it will not indicate that HAMMER is "an instrument for driving nails, beating metals, and the like, consisting of a head, usually of steel, fixed crosswise to a handle" (Webster's *Collegiate Dictionary*). In part, this limitation stems from our method of selecting descriptive scales in terms of frequency of usage rather than in terms of a logically exhaustive coverage, as given in Roget's *Thesaurus,* for example.

[3] By way of illustration, most English-speaking Americans fell that there is a difference, somehow, between "good" and "nice" but find it difficult to explain. We gave several people these words to differentiate and it turned out that wherever "male" and "female" show a significant divergence, there also were "good" and "nice" differentiated (e.g., "good," like "male," is somewhat stronger, rougher, more angular, and larger than is "nice," which like "female" shifts toward the weak, smooth, rounded, and small directions of the space). Thus "nice man" has a slightly effeminate tone whereas "good woman" (as compared with "nice woman") has a narrowly moral tone.

6. Utility. In any area of science, the development of an adequate method of measuring something (be it the wave length of radiation, blood chemistry, intelligence, or meaning) opens up well-nigh inexhaustible possibilities for application. (a) *Semantic norms.* In much the same way that Thorndike has established his norms for frequency-of-usage of common words in the English language, the semantic differential could be used to compile a functional lexicon of connotative meanings, a quantized thesaurus. Similarly, the gradual drift of changing meanings, both temporally and geographically, could be charted. (b) *Individual differences in meaning.* It is a truism that the meanings of socially significant signs differ for different classes of people. Concepts like CHURCH, LABOR LEADER, STALIN, and TRUMAN have different connotative significance to different people, and the semantic differential can be used to quantify these differences. In this sense, it can be used as a generalized, multidimensional attitude test. For example, 10 people may have identical degrees of favorableness toward NEGRO (evaluative dimension) and yet vary markedly with respect to other dimensions of the meaning-space. (c) *Changes in meaning.* Under the pressure of events, the meanings of social signs change, e.g., the meaning of ITALIANS to Americans during the past half century. Similarly, under the "pressure" of psychotherapy, the meaning or emotional significance of certain critical concepts (e.g., FATHER, THERAPIST, ME, etc.) undergoes change. (d) *Quantification of subjective language data.* We have recently used the semantic differential as a means of scoring TAT reactions; not only is the testing process greatly speeded up, but the data are in easily manipulable form. Preliminary studies indicate that the essential individual differences in meaning of such projective materials, as teased out of complicated verbatim "stories," are sharply etched in the semantic differential data. (e) *Cross-cultural communication problems.* If the structure of the semantic space proves to be sufficiently general that the method can be translated into equivalent differentials in other languages, numerous possibilities are opened up. Are the fundamental factors in meaning and their relationships independent of the language spoken? Can the significant points of deviation in meaning of critical concepts, as between Americans and Russians, for example, be discovered? Can the finer, subtler degrees of acculturation into a new society be traced? And there are other potential applications, to aesthetics, to studying the development of meaning in children, and so on.

SUMMARY

The first portion of this paper describes a behavioral conception of the sign-process as developed from a general mediation theory of learning. The remainder is concerned with the problem of measuring meaning. Various existing approaches to the problem–physiological, learning, perception, association, and scaling methods–have been evaluated against the usual criteria of measurement and have been found inadequate. The development of a semantic differential as a general method of measuring meaning is described. It involves (a) the use of factor analysis to determine the number and nature of factors entering into semantic description and judgment, and (b) the selection of a set of specific scales corresponding to these factors which can be standardized as a measure of meaning. Using this differential, the meaning of a particular concept to a particular individual can be specified quantitatively as a particular point in the multidimensional space defined by the instrument. Some of the possible uses of such a measuring instrument are briefly indicated.

REFERENCES

1. BORING, E. G. *The Physical Dimensions of Consciousness.* New York: Appleton-Century, 1933.
2. DALLENBACH, K. M. Synaesthesis: "Pressury" Cold. *Amer. J. Psychol.,* 1926, *37,* 571–577.
3. HEVNER, KATE. Experimental Studies of the Elements of Expression in Music. *Amer. J. Psychol.,* 1936, *48,* 246–268.
4. KARWOSKI, T. F., & ODBERT, H. S. Color-Music. *Psychol. Monogr.,* 1938, *50,* No. 2 (Whole No. 222).
5. KARWOSKI, T. F., ODBERT, H. S., & OSGOOD, C. E. Studies in Synesthetic Thinking: II. The Roles of Form in Visual Responses to Music. *J. Gen. Psychol.,* 1942, *26,* 199–222.
6. LANGFELD, H. S. Note on a Case of Chromaesthesia. *Psychol. Bull.,* 1914, *11,* 113–114.
7. MOSIER, C. I. A Psychometric Study of Meaning. *J. Soc. Psychol.,* 1941, *13,* 123–140.
8. ODBERT, H. S., KARWOSKI, T. F., & ECKERSON, A. B. Studies in Synesthetic Thinking: I. Musical and Verbal Associations of Color and Mood. *J. Gen. Psychol.,* 1942, *26,* 153–173.
9. ROSS, R. T. Studies in the Psychology of the Theater. *Psychol. Rec.,* 1938, *2,* 127–190.
10. SKINNER, B. F. The Verbal Summator and a Method for the Study of Latent Speech. *J. Psychol.,* 1936, *2,* 71–107.
11. STAGNER, R., & BRITTON, R. H., JR. The Conditioning Technique Applied to a Public Opinion Problem. *J. Soc. Psychol.,* 1949, *29,* 103–111.
12. STAGNER, R., & OSGOOD, C. E. An Experimental Analysis of a Nationalistic Frame of Reference. *J. Soc. Psychol.,* 1941, *14,* 389–401.
13. STAGNER, R., & OSGOOD, C. E. Impact of War on a Nationalistic Frame of Reference: I. Changes in General Approval and Qualitative Patterning of Certain Stereotypes. *J. Soc. Psychol.,* 1946, *24,* 187–215.

4

THE EFFECT OF THE EXPERIENCES OF CONTRASTED GROUPS UPON THE FORMATION OF A NEW SCALE OF JUDGMENT[1]
MARGARET E. TRESSELT

If individuals use different construct systems to order the stimuli of the sensory world, these construct systems should be shown to stabilize as a result of everyday experiences, as well as in the contrived experiences of the laboratory study. In this selection Tresselt argues against the suggestion that the laboratory experience differs from an individual's total life experience as he shapes his internal frames of reference. Weightlifters, who are assumed to have developed an extended range for the construct *light-heavy,* are compared to watch repairmen in their respective judgments of weights. The weights that weightlifters put into the *medium* part of the *light-heavy* range are somewhat heavier than those placed there by the watch repairmen. Tresselt further shows, however, that as more of the specific judgment series is handled, there is an increase in the effect of that specific series, so that *medium* becomes more a function of the experimental series than of the previous life experience.

*　　*　　*

A. INTRODUCTION

One of the problems which have interested social psychologists has been the problem of judgment and particularly the formation of attitudes and opinions. Although it has been classified under the topic of suggestion, one of the most outstanding studies of social judgment was made by Sherif (8,

Reprinted from Journal of Social Psychology, *1948,* 27, *209–216, by permission of the author and Journal Press.*
[1] The author is indebted to Miss Helen Zeeman for collecting part of the data for this experiment.

9) who has shown that when socially interacting individuals are asked to make judgments upon the same stimulus-objects their judgments will tend toward agreement. He tested the subjects individually and then in groups in order to show that a convergence of judgments would take place. His results indicate that a scale of judgment will shift in accordance with the voiced judgments given by other individuals in the group.

It is not necessary however to have socially participating groups in order to shift one's scale of judgment. Tresselt and Volkmann (12) found that when different individuals are asked to make judgments on a series of weights their judgments will approach agreement even though their initial judgments are widely distributed. Their results suggest that uniform opinion upon the same stimuli-objects can be formed under conditions which are essentially non-social.

Since a divergence in judgment has been noted in the beginning of a judgmental period with subjects who had previously built up scales based upon various ranges of stimuli, Tresselt (11) conducted an experiment in which practice was given on a range of weights which consisted of four heavy weights or four light weights before the subjects were given an expanded range of weights. She found that the centers of the scales of judgment, for the expanded range of stimuli, were at first in the direction of the center of the previously existing scale but over a period of time the scales rapidly conformed to the new stimulus-range regardless of whether or not the practice series had contained stimuli at the top or bottom of the expanded scale.

It happens that individuals usually have unequal experience with a series of stimuli before they approach the new situation. In order to show the effect of differing amounts of practice with the pre-existing scale upon the new scale, Tresselt also had five groups of subjects who were given one practice trial, or four, or eight, or 12, or 28 practice trials on each of four weights before being given the entire range. Her results indicated that initially the greater the amount of practice, the more slowly the scale of judgment shifted to its new position. This probably can also be extended to state that the greater the period of practice the slower will be the change of the pre-established scale to conform to the new range of stimuli.

Similarly it is reasonable to expect that continued practice with one range of stimuli in everyday life will affect the judgments on a shifted range of stimuli. Ansbacher (2) has already reported that there is a tendency for familiarity to influence the judgments of number and value of one's own and foreign two-cent and three-cent stamps. He found that the stamps which the subjects considered more valuable also appeared to them to be the more numerous. Bruner (3) recently has reported that children when reproducing the size of a coin are influenced by their familiarity with the coin and the value-judgments they place on the coin, that is, "The tendency or overestimation is significantly more marked among the poor than among rich children" (3, p. 241).

In seeming opposition to the generalization that the findings in psychophysical techniques and everyday judgmental situations are parallel, Johnson (4) points out that in his experiments the subjects would often move a chair or lift a book during their rest pauses without affecting their scales of values which were based on lifting stimulus-weights. He states: "It would be impossible to summate practice effects of a person's experience with a 60 gm. weight if his lifetime or even recent experience were relevant" (4, p. 436). This statement needs clarification.

Does it mean that single experiences have no affect at all upon one's scale of judgment; i.e., that there must be a number of repetitions before there is any resulting influence upon the new scale? Does it mean that we pigeon-hole our scales of judgment in terms of the type of stimuli being experienced at any given time? Or does it mean that we classify and apply our scales on the basis of the degree of similarity to the task of judgment and thereby either include or exclude it from a common scale? The present experiment stems from these questions and so has two purposes: one, to find out whether one can show that everyday past experiences with stimuli which are not physically similar to the stimuli used in the experiment show any effect at all upon the new scale, and secondly to discover if there are degrees of shift corresponding to the similarity of the recent task of the profession and the new task of judgment used in this experiment.

B. PROCEDURE

The stimuli were 12 weighted cylindrical cardboard containers 6.2 cm. in diameter and 3.8 cm. high, whose weight in grams were 11, 60, 110, 160, 210, 260, 310, 360, 410, 460, 510, and 560. The weights were separated by units of 50 grams (except for the first and second weights) in order that a relatively large range of weights be covered by a convenient number of stimuli. The order of presentation for the experiment as a whole was predetermined in such a way that each weight was presented in a different position to each subject. In this way 12 subjects had each of the weights in a different position in the series, that is, the 11 gm. weight would be the first for Subject 1, the second for Subject 2, the third for Subject 3, and so forth.

The subjects were selected from two fields of work in and near New York City: (a) 36 professional weight-lifters or men who had been doing weight-lifting regularly for a duration of at least a year, and (b) 36 professional watch-makers or men who were in their last week of training in the school of watch-making.[2]

Each man was experimented upon individually. The experimenter told the subjects how to grasp the weight, lift it, and then asked them to make absolute judgments in these categories: "You are to tell me whether the weight feels to you heavy, medium, or light." The weights were never lifted by anyone previous to the actual task of judgment. The subject then put on a blind-fold and resting his arm on an arm rest, began lifting.

C. DISCUSSION AND RESULTS

Table 1 presents the data in terms of the mean weight judged *medium*, the frequency of *medium* judgments and the standard deviations of the weight called *medium* as functions of the serial position of presentation for the two groups. The mean weight judged *medium* in the fifth position for the weight-lifters, for example, was 264.2, *n* was 12, with a standard deviation of 129.8.

TABLE 1 Showing the mean weight (in grams) judged *medium (M)*, the frequency of medium judgments *(n)*, and the standard deviation (σ), as a function of the serial position for Watch-makers and Weight-lifters.

Serial position	Watch-makers			Weight-lifters		
	M	n	σ	M	n	σ
1	265.6	9	189.2	295.3	17	178.8
2	243.3	6	84.9	285.0	6	14.9
3	347.5	4	155.6	293.3	3	85.0
4	187.8	9	85.3	210.0	6	122.8
5	214.5	11	115.7	264.2	12	129.8
6	205.0	10	93.4	272.5	12	122.7
7	222.5	8	95.3	297.5	8	147.3
8	278.2	11	98.3	313.8	13	109.0
9	264.2	12	74.9	273.6	11	97.7
10	230.8	12	90.3	264.5	11	111.7
11	220.0	5	48.6	273.6	11	108.9
12	232.7	11	65.2	287.3	11	96.2

[2]The author wishes to express her appreciation for the cooperation of the following in this experimental study: *Watch-makers*—Bulova School of Watch-making. Harmil Watch Co., International Watch Repairing Co., Lewbel, H., Watch-maker, Tudor City Jewelry; *Weight-lifters*—Bothmer's Gymnasium, Broadway Health Club, Inc., Klein's Gymnasium, NYU steamfitters and plumbers, YMCA Weight-lifters Club.

The first question presented for consideration followed from Johnson's statement which implied that our scales of judgment are not disturbed by tasks which are not relevant to the immediate task. Lifting chairs or books, for example, would not in his observation change the scale of judgments. It has already been shown that having a solitary or only a few experiences with a limited portion of a scale will hardly affect the scale even though the practice series included identical stimuli which constituted part of the expanded range (11).

Although a single stimulus does not affect a scale of judgment, everyday past experiences of a similar type of judgmental task, i.e., lifting and judging weights, which have occupied long periods of time may affect the scale formed in the experimental laboratory. In order to show the effect of the specialized training, the Mathisen solution was applied to test whether the mean *medium* judgments of the weight-lifters differed from the mean *medium* judgments of the comparison group, i.e., the 120 subjects used originally by Tresselt and Volkmann[3] (Figure 1). The *P*-value is less than .05, so we may conclude that the two populations are not the same. The past experience or task of these weight-lifters being similar to the experimental task affects the scale of judgment within the limits of the number of judgments called for in this experiment, i.e., there is a slow approach toward uniformity and the center of the new scale lies in the direction of the center of the old scale.

It seems plausible to assume that if the subjects had been asked to make judgments on the experimental stimuli for a longer period of time their judgments may have reached more uniform agreement.

The shifting can also be seen in the standard deviations of the weights called *medium*. In Figure 2 the standard deviations of the watch-makers and weight-lifters are plotted as a function of the serial position as are the standard deviations taken from Tresselt and Volkmann. In the first position both professional groups show a wider variation in their judgments than the students who probably had a scale more appropriate to the stimuli-objects than either of these experimental groups.

After the first initial variation in their judgments both the means and standard deviations of the judgments of the watch-makers are more similar to the students (comparison group) than those of the weight-lifters. In Figure 1 the Means are almost identical from Positions 8 to 12 although they differ in the early part of the curve. In Figure 2 the sigma values are almost identical following about the 4th position. When the Mathisen solution was applied to test the sampling of the watch-makers and the students, the *P*-value was just larger than .05, which means that these two

---

[3]This group (*12*) supplies what is essentially a control group. The subjects were given the same weights with the same instructions and procedures. The chief difference is that the students had an uncontrolled variety of past experiences.

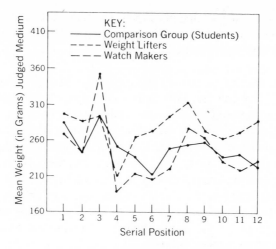

FIG. 1   *The mean weight judged* medium *(in grams) as a function of the serial positions of the weights. The curves comprise the mean weights judged* medium *by the group of weight-lifters and by the group of watch-makers. The results of the group of students were adapted from Tresselt and Volkmann (12).*

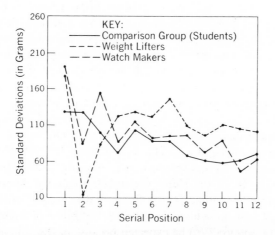

FIG. 2   *The standard deviations of the distribution of the* medium *judgments, in grams, as a function of the serial position of the weights for the two experimental groups, watch-makers and weight-lifters. The solid line represents the findings of Tresselt and Volkmann using students (12).*

samples come from populations which are essentially the same in their scales of judgments. The range of weights that students and watch-makers lift are about the same and neither group judges weight *per se* to any great degree.

The irregularity of pattern in the early part of the curve has already been noted by Tresselt and Volkmann who suggested that there seemed to be two functions present in the curves rather than one. They note a region of discontinuity in the area of the 6th serial position where the first portion may represent the shift of the old scale and the second portion represents the construction of a new scale anchored by the new end-stimuli. It appears here as if an area of change is more apparent in the region of the 4th judgment. Whether this change in the region of shift is the result of the relationship between the distance of the pre-existing scale from the scale used here or the result of different motivation or emotional conditions among these subjects remains for future investigation.

Since the mean *medium* judgment by the weight-lifters is consistently above the mean *medium* value of the students except in the shifting area of the 3rd and 4th position, and the two populations are significantly different; and since the watch-makers are below the mean *medium* judgments of the students in the 3rd and 8th position, with no significant difference, the suggestion might be made that the more similar the task the more displaced the previous scale the more apparent will be the effect of the old scale on the adjustment to a new scale; that is to say, there will be a relatively slower shift in a gradual approach to uniformity with groups which differ significantly from each other and that the center of the shifted scale will reflect the direction of the position of the previous scale in relation to the new scale. Where the scales of stimulus-values are similar, the effect of the old scale will be less marked. Since the tasks of this experiment and the tasks of the watch-makers were dissimilar, the past experience was probably not included or associated to form a common scale.

What can these findings mean for the social psychologist and the future of the psychology of judgment? The data indicate that everyday experiences affect in varying degrees the formation of a new scale of judgment and uniform opinion. Since the shift experiments made by Annis and Meier (1), Knower (5), Rosenthal (7), and Sims (10), among others, involved students whose task in school emphasizes flexibility of mental habits, a marked shift in opinion is to be expected because of the similarity in scales and task. There may be many who do not shift at all or in a negligible manner because of a displacement of the original scale or dissimilarity of the tasks involved. It follows that there is an open field for psychologists to make a study of the functional relationships in judgmental responses with particular emphasis upon quantity or quality of past experience. On the other hand although quantification is desirable, the data show a definite tendency for judgments to change in predictable direction under certain conditions. The persons who are interested in social phenomena should also be interested in the results produced by these experiments involving non-social stimulation since certain basic patterns common to our everyday social behavior are revealed. This methodology could be used as a possible means of investigating the importance of various factors in our attitudes and opinions.

D. SUMMARY AND CONCLUSIONS

The purposes of the present experiment were to discover whether everyday experiences would affect the formation of a new scale of judgment when the new stimuli are not related to previous stimuli, and also to discover if there are degrees of shift corresponding to the similarity in tasks of the pre-existing profession and the present task of judgment.

The subjects were professional weight-lifters whose task in their business world resembled the task of judgment, although their scale should have been established at a range outside of our experimental range, and watchmakers whose task was completely dissimilar to the task required. Both groups however were unacquainted with the experimental stimuli.

Each subject was asked to judge 12 weighted containers presented in a pre-arranged serial order in three categories: heavy, medium, and light. The results indicate:

1. Both groups show a shift of their scales of value to correspond with the new range of stimuli, although in the beginning of the period they differed in their judgments.

2.The center of the new scale lies in the direction of the previously existing scale.

3. The center of the scale of weight-lifters was significantly different from the scale of students or watch-makers throughout the experimental series. The hypothesis is formulated that the more similar the previous task and the more displaced the scale the more apparent will be the effect of the old scale on the adjustment to a new scale. The more dissimilar the tasks and the more similar the range of the scales of values, the less marked will be the effect of the previous experience upon the new scale.

REFERENCES

1. ANNIS, A. D., & MEIER, N. C. The Induction of Opinion through Suggestion by Means of "Planted Content." *J. Soc. Psychol.,* 1934, *5,* 65–81.
2. ANSBACHER, H. Number Judgment of Postage Stamps: A Contribution to the Psychology of Social Norms. *J. of Psychol.,* 1938, *5,* 347–350.

3. BRUNER, J. Social Value and Need as Organizing Factors in Perception. *Amer. Psychol.,* 1946, *1,* 241.

4. JOHNSON, D. M. Generalization of a Scale of Values by the Averaging of Practice Effects. *J. Exper. Psychol.,* 1944, *34,* 425–436.

5. KNOWER, F. H. Experimental Studies of Changes in Attitudes: I. A Study of the Effect of Oral Argument on Changes in Attitude. *J. Soc. Psychol.,* 1935, *6,* 315–347; II. A Study of the Effect of Printed Argument on Changes in Attitude. *J. Abn. and Soc. Psychol.,* 1936, *34,* 522–532; III. Some Incidence of Attitude Changes. *J. Appl. Psychol.,* 1936, *20,* 114–127.

6. MATHISEN, H. C. A Method of Testing the Hypothesis that Two Samples Are from the Same Population. *Ann. Math. Stat.,* 1943, *14,* 188–194.

7. ROSENTHAL, S. P. Change of Socio-Economic Attitudes under Radical Motion Picture Propaganda. *Arch. of Psychol.,* 1934, No. 166.

8. SHERIF, M. & CANTRIL, H. The Psychology of "Attitudes": I. *Psychol. Rev.,* 1945, *56,* 295–319. II. *Psychol. Rev.,* 1946, *53,* 1–24.

9. SHERIF, M. *The Psychology of Social Norms.* New York: Harper, 1936.

10. SIMS, V. M. Factors Influencing Attitude toward the T.V.A. *J. Abn. and Soc. Psychol.,* 1938, *33,* 34–56.

11. TRESSELT, M. E. The Influence of Amount of Practice upon the Formation of a Scale of Judgment. *Amer. Psychol.,* 1946, *1,* 272.

12. TRESSELT, M. E. & VOLKMANN, J. The Production of Uniform Opinion by Non-Social Stimulation. *J. Abn. and Soc. Psychol.,* 1942, *37,* 234–243.

V

THE CONCEPT
OF HIERARCHY
IN COGNITIVE THEORY

1
OVERVIEW

Comprehensive theories of behavior lend themselves to the development of a concept that places responses into a hierarchical arrangement. The student of behavior often regards some types of response as being more salient, more easily evoked, or, in short, more important than other types of responses. Dollard and Miller (1950), in considering why a particular stimulus has an initial tendency to evoke a particular response, propose the notion of heirarchy of response—the arrangement of responses in the order of probability of their appearance. The probability of appearance of the response was determined by the strength of the connection between stimulus and response, which is further related to the amount of reinforcement given to the connection. When a response was elevated in the hierarchy through further reinforcement, the new hierarchial arrangement is the *resultant hierarchy*. Miller and Dollard assume that some of the responses attained a high position in the hierarchy through hereditary factors, and in such cases the hierarchy might be seen as an *innate heirarchy*.

Maslow (1954) views motives as being arranged hierarchically. In his scheme of things, there are "instinctoid" need priorities, and one must fulfill the needs of one level before proceeding to fulfill the needs of the next level. For example, one must satisfy his physiological needs before he can approach the fulfillment of his "safety" and "belongingness" needs. This approach to motivation is not very different from older theories that sought to establish the relative strengths of motivations (Anderson, 1938) through experimenting with an organism's energy expenditure as it attempted to reach various goals. Such work has its roots in efforts to establish a hierarchy of "instinct." Biologically based motivational theories, particularly those related directly to Darwinian evolutionary theory, would be substantially buttressed if it could be demonstrated that living organisms pursue survival goals with more energy than they use in pursuing other goals.

Cognitive theories approach the notion of hierarchy in a slightly different manner. Construction systems are developed so that there are ordinal relationships between the constructs used to structure the incoming stimulation (Kelly's Organization Corollary). The categorization of an event requires the use of sets of interrelated constructs; and several events might be categorized under the same superordinate construct, even though the total constructions of the separate events might be somewhat diverse. For example, several events might be subsumed under the construct "good," but these events might well be differently construed. Within the subject's system, nevertheless, the fact that the two events are subsumed under the concept of "good" will make the two events "similar," for the concept of "good" has been demonstrated in many studies to be a highly prepotent construct. Knowing how the subject construes the event along this central construct allows us to make important predictions about how he will behave toward the stimuli. If it can be demonstrated that events are affecting a construct that is superordinate for an individual, then those events will have a more significant effect than would be achieved were subordinate constructs being affected.

Cognitive theorists stress the importance of superordinate constructions in speaking of a person's *approaches* to solving problems—that is, to categorizing events. The general principle that emerges is that the solution to problems is facilitated markedly by the development of constructs that subsume vast amounts of data, rather than treating the data as separate events which are construed within their own individual construct organization. The validations of this principle are most dramatically illustrated by Piaget. He shows, for example, that a child who has evolved the concept of "conservation of number" (Piaget, 1965a) is far more capable of handling a wide variety of problems of enumeration than is a child who has not developed this construct. When analyzing the child's working in the social world, Piaget shows that a child who has achieved the concept of "reciprocity" in rule-functioning is far more adept at making consistent moral judgments than is a child who is still in the "heteronomous stage," wherein he is required to rely on authority for the definition of each individual case of social conflict (Piaget, 1965b). Harlow (1949) imaginatively demonstrates how "learning sets" in problem solving are achieved as the organism develops superordinate concepts that allow it to see individual problems as exemplars of a larger category.

Staats (1968), attempting to work within the framework of the stimulus-response associationist model, offers an extensive elaboration of Hull's (1934a, 1934b) "habit-family" to work out the idea of superordination in cognitive functioning. He speaks of the development of a concept as the development of anticipatory goal responses (r_g), which is the internal aspect of a response generated by a stimulus. When future stimuli are presented to the organism, they may produce this generalizable internal response, thus imparting "meaning" to the stimuli. Further, if a novel stimulus event is conditioned to a particular habit-family, then that stimulus can come to evoke the previously developed anticipatory goal responses that are available to the organism. Staats supports his theorizing with the extensive work that has been done on "mediated generalization." Direct evidence of this kind of generalization is described by Razran (1961), who shows that after conditioning a response, such as salivating, to a class-descriptive word, the subject will make the same response to a stimulus that has been subsumed under that superordinate term. For example, a subject who has been conditioned to salivate to the word *flower* may also come to salivate to the word *rose*. Another example of mediated generalization is found in transfer studies (Russell and Storms, 1955) that show a positive transfer in learning task *B* if the elements of task *B* are members of a set of elements that were learned as task *A*. For example, learning that the term *rose* is associated with *celog* is facilitated if the subject originally learned that *flower* was associated with *celog*.

Further amplification of the nature of hierarchial construct is found in research that speaks of changing attitudes by making indirect attacks on the attitudinal structure (Peak, 1958; Carlson, 1956). The object of these studies has been to show that one can alter a subject's construction of an event by altering a construct that appears to be tangential, but which is superordinate to the constructions the subject might apply to the event. In Carlson's study, for example, subjects were shown that allowing the integration of Negroes into a white community would lead to the achievement of values that the subjects held to be important. When this was achieved, with subjects who held their position with moderate strength, these subjects changed their position on the total issue of integration.

Within a comprehensive theory of behavior which makes the assumption that external events are represented within an individual, and that these internal representations are the main concern of the psychologist, an assumption of a hierarchial arrangement of constructs has extensive implications. The organism's propensity to use such arrangements will introduce a meaningful economy in its functioning. This economy will be readily observed in memory and problem-solving situations. At the same time, the alteration of a highly superordinating construct will have ramifications throughout the individual's construct system. This will mean that the individual's total economy of functioning will be enhanced if the integrity of superordinate constructs is preserved, while the alteration of a subordinate construct will be a less costly matter. In terms of our motivational assumptions, the organism will be placed into a higher level of arousal with those failures in instantiating that are associated with superordinate constructs than will be the case when subordinate constructs are implicated. The application of this position to the construction of "abnormal behavior" would lead to the proposition that deviant behavior would be more likely to result from failures in the functioning of superordinate constructions; since in these situations the "arousal function" of the stimulus event will take precedence over the "cue function" (Hebb, 1955), and there is little likelihood that the event will be suitably integrated to the subject's cognitive system (Sarbin, 1962). In order to reduce the extensive arousal one might engage in such techniques as taking recourse to chemical anxiety reducers, that is, alcohol, barbituates, and so on; or he could redirect his attention to nonessential stimuli and activity. Further investigation of the utility and validity of an assumption of hierarchical arrangement of constructs will clearly be useful for our general theory.

REFERENCES

ANDERSON, E. E. The Interrelationships of Drives in the Male Albino Rat. *Comparative Psychology Monographs,* 1938, *14*(6), 1–191.

CARLSON, E. R. Attitude Change through Modification of Attitude Structure. *Journal of Abnormal and Social Psychology,* 1956, *52,* 256–261.

DOLLARD, J. & MILLER, N. *Personality and Psychotherapy.* New York: McGraw-Hill, 1950.

HARLOW, H. F. The Formation of Learning Sets. *Psychological Review,* 1949, *56,* 51–65.

HEBB, D. O. Drives and the C.N.S. (Conceptual Nervous System). *Psychological Review,* 1955, *62,* 243–254.

HULL, C. L. The Concept of Habit-Family Hierarchy and Maze Learning. *Psychological Review,* 1934a, *41,* 33–54.

HULL, C. L. The Concept of Habit-Family Hierarchy and Maze Learning: Part II. *Psychological Review,* 1934b, *41,* 134–152.

MASLOW, A. H. *Motivation and Personality.* New York: Harper and Row, 1954.

PEAK, H. Psychological Structure and Psychological Activity. *Psychological Review,* 1958, *65,* 325–361.

PIAGET, JEAN. *The Child's Conception of Number.* New York: Norton, 1965a.

PIAGET, JEAN. *The Moral Judgment of the Child.* New York: Free Press, 1965b.

RAZRAN, G. The Observable Unconscious and the Inferable Conscious in Current Soviet Psychophysiology. *Psychological Review,* 1961, *68,* 99–119.

RUSSELL, W. A. & STORMS, L. H. Implicit Verbal Chaining in Paired-Associate Learning. *Journal of Experimental Psychology,* 1955, *49,* 287–293.

SARBIN, T. R. A New Model of the Behavior Disorders. *Gawein, Tijdschrift voor Psychologie,* 1962, *10,* 324–338.

STAATS, A. W. *Learning, Language, and Cognition.* New York: Holt, Rinehart, Winston, 1968.

2
FORMING IMPRESSIONS
OF PERSONALITY
SOLOMON E. ASCH

This selection from a paper by S. E. Asch represents one of the early solid efforts to clarify the nature of the constructs along which people cognize other people. The study of *person perception* has been highly valuable in elaborating general cognitive theory, and investigators who •
have worked in this area have contributed to establishing useful principles (Tagiuri and Petrullo, 1958). As an extension of this work, Sarbin, Taft, and Bailey (1960) propose that the principles evolved to treat person perception can be extended to a discussion of how clinical "diagnosis" reflects the applications of the diagnostician's cognitive framework.

Asch's pioneering study illustrates several important features of an individual's cognitive functioning. The selection is placed in this section because of its high relevance to the question of hierarchical arrangements of constructs. This is best seen in Experiments I and II, although it is also reflected elsewhere. In Experiments I and II, Asch found that variations in the use of one term—that is, when *warm* is changed to *cold*—significantly influence the resulting description of another person. *Warm-cold* seems to be a superordinate construct that is extensively related to many other constructs. In Experiment IX subjects were willing to make extended judgments of one person simply on the basis of having the other person described as warm or cold. Osgood, Suci, and Tannenbaum (1957) found that *warm-cold* is high in the hierarchy of terms that relate to the even more superordinate construct *active-passive*. Other points that emerge from this study are that even a single term appears to evoke a conglomerate of other terms, and that the

Reprinted from Journal of Abnormal and Social Psychology, *1946*, 41, *258-290, by permission of the author and the American Psychological Association. Several of the experiments described in the original article have been deleted. Tables and intra-text references to tables remain as in the original article.*

The present investigation was begun in 1943 when the writer was a Fellow of the John Simon Guggenheim Memorial Foundation.

same terms will evoke quite different conglomerates in different individuals.

REFERENCES

OSGOOD, C. E., SUCI, G. J., & TANNENBAUM, P. H. *The Measurement of Meaning.* Urbana, Illinois: University of Illinois Press, 1957.

SARBIN, T. R., TAFT, R., & BAILEY, D. E. *Clinical Inference and Cognitive Theory.* New York: Holt, Rinehart, Winston, 1960.

TAGIURI, R. & PETRULLO, L. *Person Perception and Interpersonal Behavior.* Stanford: Stanford University Press, 1958.

*   *   *

We look at a person and immediately a certain impression of his character forms itself in us. A glance, a few spoken words are sufficient to tell us a story about a highly complex matter. We know that such impressions form with remarkable rapidity and with great ease. Subsequent observation may enrich or upset our first view, but we can no more prevent its rapid growth than we can avoid perceiving a given visual object or hearing a melody. We also know that this process, though often imperfect, is also at times extraordinarily sensitive.

This remarkable capacity we possess to understand something of the character of another person, to form a conception of him as a human being, as a center of life and striving, with particular characteristics forming a distinct individuality, is a precondition of social life. In what manner are these impressions established? Are there lawful principles regulating their formation?

One particular problem commands our attention. Each person confronts us with a large number of diverse characteristics. This man is courageous, intelligent, with a ready sense of humor, quick in his movements, but he is also serious, energetic, patient under stress, not to mention his politeness and punctuality. These characteristics and many others enter into the formation of our view. Yet our impression is from the start unified; it is the impression of *one* person. We ask: How do the several characteristics function together to produce an impression of one person? What principles regulate this process?

We have mentioned earlier that the impression of a person grows quickly and easily. Yet our minds falter when we face the far simpler task of mastering a series of disconnected numbers or words. We have apparently no need to commit to memory by repeated drill the various characteristics we observe in a person, nor do some of his traits exert an observable retroactive inhibition upon our grasp of the others. Indeed, they seem to support each other. And it is quite hard to forget our view of a person once it has formed. Similarly, we do not easily confuse the half of one person with the half of another. It should be of interest to the psychologist that the far more complex task of grasping the nature of a person is so much less difficult.

There are a number of theoretical possibliities for describing the process of forming an impression, of which the major ones are the following:

1. A trait is realized in its particular quality. The next trait is similarly realized, etc. Each trait produces its particular impression. The total impression of the person is the sum of the several independent impressions. If a person possesses traits *a, b, c, d, e,* then the impression of him may be expressed as:

I. Impression $= a + b + c + d + e$

Few if any psychologists would at the present time apply this formulation strictly. It would, however, be an error to deny its importance for the present problem. That it controls in considerable degree many of the procedures for arriving at a scientific, objective view of a person (e.g., by means of questionnaires, rating scales) is evident. But more pertinent to our present discussion is the modified form in which Proposition I is applied to the actual forming of an impression. Some psychologists assume, in addition to the factors of Proposition I, the operation of a "general impression." The latter is conceived as an affective force possessing a plus or minus direction which shifts the evaluation of the several traits in its direction. We may represent this process as follows:

Ia. Impression =

$$a + b + c + d + e + G$$

To the sum of the traits there is now added another factor, the general impression.

2. The second view asserts that we form an impression of the entire person. We see a person as consisting not of these and those independent traits (or of the sum of mutually modified traits), but we try to get at the root of the personality. This would involve that the traits are perceived in relation to each other, in their proper place within the given personality. We may express the final impression as

II. Impression =

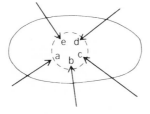

It may appear that psychologists generally hold to some form of the latter formulation. The frequent reference to the unity of the person, or to his "integration," implying that these qualities are also present in the impression, point in this direction. The generality of these expressions is, however, not suitable to exact treatment. Terms such as unity of the person, while pointing to a problem, do not solve it. If we wish to become clear about the unity in persons, or in the impression of persons, we must ask in what sense there is such unity, and in what manner we come to observe it. Secondly, these terms are often applied interchangeably to Propositions II and Ia. It is therefore important to state at this point a distinction between them.

For Proposition II, the general impression is not a factor added to the particular traits, but rather the perception of a particular form of relation between the traits, a conception which is wholly missing in Ia. Further, Proposition Ia conceives the process in terms of an imposed affective shift in the evaluation of separate traits, whereas Proposition II deals in the first instance with processes between the traits each of which has a cognitive content.

Perhaps the central difference between the two propositions becomes clearest when the accuracy of the impression becomes an issue. It is implicit in Proposition II that the process it describes is for the subject a necessary one if he is to focus on a person with maximum clarity. On the other hand, Proposition Ia permits a radically different interpretation. It has been asserted that the general impression "colors" the particular characteristics, the effect being to *blur* the clarity with which the latter are perceived. In consequence the conclusion is drawn that the general impression is a source of error which should be supplanted by the attitude of judging each trait in isolation, as described in Proposition I. This is the doctrine of the "halo effect" (9).

With the latter remarks, which we introduced only for purposes of illustration, we have passed beyond the scope of the present report. It must be made clear that we shall here deal with certain processes involved in the forming of an impression, a problem logically distinct from the actual relation of traits within a person. To be sure, the manner in which an impression is formed contains, as we shall see, definite assumptions concerning the structure of personal traits. The validity of such assumptions must, however, be established in independent investigation.

The issues we shall consider have been largely neglected in investigation. Perhaps the main reason has been a one-sided stress on the subjectivity of personal judgments. The preoccupation with emotional factors and distortions of judgment has had two main consequences for the course investigation has taken. First, it has induced a certain lack of perspective which has diverted interest from the study of those processes which do not involve subjective distortions as the most decisive factor. Secondly, there has been a tendency to neglect the fact that emotions too have a cognitive side, that something must be perceived and discriminated in order that it may be loved or hated. On the other hand, the approach of the more careful studies in this region has centered mainly on questions of validity in the final product of judgment. Neither of the main approaches has dealt explicitly with the process of forming an impression. Yet no argument should be needed to support the statement that our view of the person necessarily involves a certain orientation to, and ordering of, objectively given, observable characteristics. It is this aspect of the problem that we propose to study.

Forming a unified impression: procedure. The plan followed in the experiments to be reported was to read to the subject a number of discrete characteristics, said to belong to a person, with the instruction to describe the impression he formed. The subjects were all college students, most of whom were women.[1] They were mostly beginners in psychology. Though they expressed genuine interest in the tasks, the subjects were not aware of the nature of the problem until it was explained to them. We illustrate our procedure with one concrete instance. The following list of terms was read: *energetic—assured—talkative—cold—ironical—inquisitive—persuasive.* The reading of the list was preceded by the following instructions:

> I shall read to you a number of characteristics that belong to a particular person. Please listen to them carefully and try to form an impression of the kind of person described. You will later be asked to give a brief characterization of the person in just a few sentences. I will read the list slowly and will repeat it once.

The list was read with an interval of approximately five seconds between the terms. When the first reading was completed, the experimenter said, "I will now read the list again," and proceeded to do so. We reproduce below a few typical sketches written by subjects after they heard read the list of terms:

> He seems to be the kind of person who would make a great impression upon others at a first meeting. However as time went by, his acquaintances would easily come to see through the mask. Underneath would be revealed his arrogance and selfishness.
> He is the type of person you meet all too often: sure of himself, talks too

[1]The writer wishes to express his gratitude to the following colleagues for their help in the performance of these experiments in their classes: Drs. B. F. Riess, L. Welch, V. J. McGill, and A. Goldenson of Hunter College; Drs. M. Blum and A. Mintz of the College of the City of New York; Dr. Lois Adams, Mr. Michael Newman, and Mr. Herbert Newman of Brooklyn College.

much, always trying to bring you around to his way of thinking, and with not much feeling for the other fellow.

He impresses people as being more capable than he really is. He is popular and never ill at ease. Easily becomes the center of attraction at any gathering. He is likely to be a jack-of-all-trades. Although his interests are varied, he is not necessarily well-versed in any of them. He possesses a sense of humor. His presence stimulates enthusiasm and very often he does arrive at a position of importance.

Possibly he does not have any deep feelings. He would tend to be an opportunist. Likely to succeed in things he intends to do. He has perhaps married a wife who would help him in his purpose. He tends to be skeptical.

The following preliminary points are to be noted:

1. When a task of this kind is given, a normal adult is capable of responding to the instruction by forming a unified impression. Though he hears a sequence of discrete terms, his resulting impression is not discrete. In some manner he shapes the separate qualities into a single, consistent view. All subjects in the following experiments, of whom there were over 1,000, fulfilled the task in the manner described. No one proceeded by reproducing the given list of terms, as one would in a rote memory experiment; nor did any of the subjects reply merely with synonyms of the given terms.

2. The characteristics seem to reach out beyond the merely given terms of the description. Starting from the bare terms, the final account is completed and rounded. Reference is made to characters and situations which are apparently not directly mentioned in the list, but which are inferred from it.

3. The accounts of the subjects diverge from each other in important respects. This will not be surprising in view of the variable content of the terms employed, which permits a considerable freedom in interpretation and weighting.

In the experiments to be reported the subjects were given a group of traits on the basis of which they formed an impression. In view of the fact that we possess no principles in this region to help in their systematic construction, it was necessary to invent groupings of traits. In this we were guided by an informal sense of what traits were consistent with each other.

The procedure here employed is clearly different from the everyday situation in which we follow the concrete actions of an actual person. We have chosen to work with weak, incipient impressions, based on abbreviated descriptions of personal qualities. Nevertheless, this procedure has some merit for purposes of investigation, especially in observing the change of impressions, and is, we hope to show, relevant to more nautral judgment.

More detailed features of the procedure will be described subsequently in connection with the actual experiments. We shall now inquire into some of the factors that determine the content and alteration of such impressions.

I. CENTRAL AND PERIPHERAL CHARACTERISTICS

A. Variation of a central quality. Observation suggests that not all qualities have the same weight in establishing the view of a person. Some are felt to be basic, others secondary. In the following experiments we sought for a demonstration of this process in the course of the formation of an impression.

Experiment I. Two groups, A and B, heard read a list of character-qualities, identical save for one term. The list follows:
Group A heard the person described as "warm"; Group B, as "cold."

Technique. The instructions were as described above. Following the reading, each subject wrote a brief sketch.

The sketches furnish concrete evidence of the impressions formed. Their exact analysis involves, however, serious technical difficulties. It seemed, therefore, desirable to add a somewhat simpler procedure for the determination of the content of the impression and for the purpose of group comparisons. To this end we constructed a check list consisting of pairs of traits, mostly opposites. From each pair of terms in this list, which the reader will find reproduced in Table 1, the subject was instructed to select

TABLE 1   **Check list I.**

1. Generous—ungenerous	10. Ruthless—humane
2. Shrewd—wise	11. Good-looking—unattractive
3. Unhappy—happy	12. Persistent—unstable
4. Irritable—good-natured	13. Frivolous—serious
5. Humorous—humorless	14. Restrained—talkative
6. Sociable—unsociable	15. Self-centered—altruistic
7. Popular—unpopular	16. Imaginative—hard-headed
8. Unreliable—reliable	17. Strong—weak
9. Important—insignificant	18. Dishonest—honest

the one that was most in accordance with the view he had formed. Terms were included which were quite different from those appearing in the basic list, but which could be related to them. Of necessity we were guided in the selection of terms for the check list (as well as for the experimental lists) by an informal sense of what was fitting or relevant. Some of the terms were taken from written sketches of subjects in preliminary experiments. In the examination of results we shall rely upon the written sketches for evidence of the actual character of the impressions, and we shall supplement these with the quantitative results from the check list.

There were 90 subjects in Group A (comprising four separate classroom groups), 76 subjects in Group B (comprising four separate classroom groups).

Results. Are the impressions of Groups A and B identical, with the exception that one has the added quality of "warm," the other of "cold"? This is one possible outcome. Another possibility is that the differentiating quality imparts a general plus or minus direction to the resulting impression. We shall see that neither of these formulations accurately describes the results.

We note first that the characteristic "warm-cold" produces striking and consistent differences of impression. In general, the A-impressions are far more positive than the B-impressions. We cite a few representative examples:

Series A ("warm"). A person who believes certain things to be right, wants others to see his point, would be sincere in an argument and would like to see his point won.

A scientist performing experiments and persevering after many setbacks. He is driven by the desire to accomplish something that would be of benefit.

Series B ("cold"). A very ambitious and talented person who would not let anyone or anything stand in the way of achieving his goal. Wants his own way, he is determined not to give in, no matter what happens.

A rather snobbish person who feels that his success and intelligence set him apart from the run-of-the-mill individual. Calculating and unsympathetic.

This trend is fully confirmed in the check-list choices. In Table 2 we report the frequency (in terms of percentages) with which each term in the check list was selected. For the sake of brevity of presentation we state the results for the positive term in each pair; the reader may determine the percentage of choices for the other term in each pair by subtracting the given figure from 100. To illustrate, under Condition A of the present experiment, 91 per cent of the subjects chose the designation "generous"; the remaining 9 per cent selected the designation "ungenerous." Occasionally, a subject would not state a choice for a particular pair. Therefore, the number of cases on which the figures are based is not always identical; however, the fluctuations were minor, with the exception of the category "good-looking—unattractive," which a larger proportion of subjects failed to answer.

TABLE 2 Choice of fitting qualities (percentages).

	Experiment I		Experiment II			Experiment III	
	"Warm" N = 90	"Cold" N = 76	"Total" N = 56	"Warm" N = 23	"Cold" N = 33	"Polite" N = 20	"Blunt" N = 26
1. Generous	91	8	55	87	33	56	58
2. Wise	65	25	49	73	33	30	50
3. Happy	90	34	71	91	58	75	65
4. Good-natured	94	17	69	91	55	87	56
5. Humorous	77	13	36	76	12	71	48
6. Sociable	91	38	71	91	55	83	68
7. Popular	84	28	57	83	39	94	56
8. Reliable	94	99	96	96	97	95	100
9. Important	88	99	88	87	88	94	96
10. Humane	86	31	64	91	45	59	77
11. Good-looking	77	69	58	71	53	93	79
12. Persistent	100	97	98	96	100	100	100
13. Serious	100	99	96	91	100	100	100
14. Restrained	77	89	82	67	94	82	77
15. Altruistic	69	18	44	68	27	29	46
16. Imaginative	51	19	24	45	9	33	31
17. Strong	98	95	95	94	96	100	100
18. Honest	98	94	95	100	92	87	100

We find:

1. There are extreme reversals between Groups A and B in the choice of fitting characteristics. Certain qualities are preponderantly assigned to the "warm" person, while the opposing qualities are equally prominent in the "cold" person. This holds for the qualities of (1) generosity, (2) shrewdness, (3) happiness, (4) irritability, (5) humor, (6) sociability, (7) popularity, (10) ruthlessness, (15) self-centeredness, (16) imaginativeness.

2. There is another group of qualities which is *not* affected by the transition from "warm" to "cold," or only slightly affected. These are: (8) reliability, (9) importance, (11) physical attractiveness, (12) persistence, seriousness, (14) restraint, (17) strength, (18) honesty.

These results show that a change in one character-quality has produced a widespread change in the entire impression. Further, the written sketches show that the terms "warm-cold" did not simply add a new quality but to some extent transformed the other characteristics. With this point we shall deal more explicitly in the experiments to follow.

That such transformations take place is also a matter of everyday experience. If a man is intelligent, this has an effect on the way in which we perceive his playfulness, happiness, friendliness. At the same time, this extensive change does not function indiscriminately. The "warm" person is not seen more favorably in all respects. There is a range of qualities, among them a number that are basic, which are not touched by the distinction between "warm" and "cold." Both remain equally honest, strong, serious, reliable, etc.

The latter result is of interest with reference to one possible interpretation of the findings. It might be supposed that the category "warm-cold" aroused a "mental set" or established a halo tending toward a consistently plus or minus evaluation. We observe here that this trend did not work in an indiscriminate manner, but was decisively limited at certain points. If we assume that the process of mutual influence took place in terms of the actual character of the qualities in question, it is not surprising that some will, by virtue of their content, remain unchanged.[2]

The following will show that the subjects generally felt the qualities "warm-cold" to be of primary importance. We asked the subjects in certain of the groups to rank the terms of Lists A and B in order of their importance for determining their impression. Table 3, containing the distribution of rankings of "warm-cold," shows that these qualities ranked comparatively high. At the same time a considerable number of subjects relegated "cold" to the lowest position. That the rankings are not higher is due to the fact that the lists contained other central traits.

___

[2] This by no means excludes the possibility that the nuances of strength, honesty, etc., do change in relation to "warm-cold."

TABLE 3 Rankings of "warm" and "cold": Experiment I.

	"Warm"		"Cold"	
Rank	N	Percentage	N	Percentage
1	6	14	12	27
2	15	35	8	21
3	4	10	1	2
4	4	10	2	5
5	4	10	3	7
6	3	7	2	5
7	6	14	13	33
	42	100	41	100

These data, as well as the ranking of the other traits not here reproduced, point to the following conclusions:

1. The given characteristics do not all have the same weight for the subject. He assigns to some a higher importance than to others.

2. The weight of a given characteristic varies—within limits—from subject to subject.

Certain limitations of the check-list procedure need to be considered: (1) The subject's reactions are forced into an appearance of discreteness which they do not actually possess, as the written sketches show; (2) the check list requires the subject to choose between extreme characteristics, which he might prefer to avoid; (3) the quantitative data describe group trends; they do not represent adequately the form of the individual impression. Generally the individual responses exhibit much stronger trends in a consistently positive or negative direction. For these reasons we employ the check-list results primarily for the purpose of comparing group trends under different conditions. For this purpose the procedure is quite adequate.

Omission of a central quality. That the category "warm-cold" is significant for the total impression may be demonstrated also by omitting it from the series. This we do in the following experiment.

Experiment II. The procedure was identical with that of Experiment I, except that the terms "warm" and "cold" were omitted from the list read to the subject (intelligent—skillful—industrious—determined—practical—cautious). Also the check list was identical with that of Experiment I, save that "warm-cold" was added as the last pair. There were three groups, consisting of a total of 56 subjects.

Under these conditions the selection of fitting characteristics shows a significant change. The distribution of choices for the total group (see Table 2, column labeled "Total") now falls between the "warm" and "cold" variations of Experiment I. It appears that a more neutral impression has formed.

The total group results are, however, largely a statistical artifact. An examination of the check-list choices of the subjects quickly revealed strong and consistent individual differences. They tended to be consistently positive or negative in their evaluations. It will be recalled that the terms "warm-cold" were added to the check list. This permitted us to subdivide the total group according to whether they judged the described person on the check list as "warm" or "cold." Of the entire group, 23 subjects (or 41 per cent) fell into the "warm" category. Our next step was to study the distribution of choices in the two subgroups. The results are clear: the two subgroups diverge consistently in the direction of the "warm" and the "cold" groups, respectively, of Experiment I. (See Table 2.) This is especially the case with the two "warm" series, which are virtually identical.

It is of interest that the omission of a term from the experimental list did not function entirely as an omission. Instead, the subjects inferred the corresponding quality in either the positive or negative direction. While not entirely conclusive, the results suggest that a full impression of a person cannot remain indifferent to a category as fundamental as the one in question, and that a trend is set up to include it in the impression on the

TABLE 4 Rankings of "polite" and "blunt": Experiment III.

Rank	A: "Polite"		B: "Blunt"	
	N	Percentage	N	Percentage
1	0	0	0	0
2	0	0	4	15
3	0	0	3	12
4	2	10	5	19
5	3	16	6	23
6	4	21	1	4
7	10	53	7	27
	19	100	26	100

basis of the given data. In later experiments too we have found a strong trend to reach out toward evaluations which were not contained in the original description.

C. Variation of a peripheral quality. Would a change of *any* character-quality produce an effect as strong as that observed above? "Warm" and "cold" seem to be of special importance for our conception of a person. This was, in fact, the reason for selecting them for study. If there are central qualities, upon which the content of other qualities depends, and dependent qualities which are secondarily determined, it should be possible to distinguish them objectively. On this assumption the addition or omission of peripheral qualities should have smaller effects than those observed in Experiment I. We turn to this question in the following experiment.

Experiment III. The following lists were read, each to a different group:

    A. intelligent—skillful—industrious—*polite*—determined—practical—cautious
    B. intelligent—skillful—industrious—*blunt*—determined—practical—cautious

The A group contained 20, the B group 26 subjects.

The changes introduced into the selection of fitting characteristics in the transition from "polite" to "blunt" were far weaker than those found in Experiment I (see Table 2). There is further evidence that the subjects themselves regarded these characteristics as relatively peripheral, especially the characteristic "polite." If we may take the rankings as an index, then we may conclude that a change in a peripheral trait produces a weaker effect on the total impression than does a change in a central trait. (Though the changes produced are weaker than those of Experiment I, they are nevertheless substantial. Possibly this is a consequence of the thinness of the impression, which responds easily to slight changes.)

D. Transformation from a central to a peripheral quality. The preceding experiments have demonstrated a process of discrimination between central and peripheral qualities. We ask: Are certain qualities constantly central? Or is their functional value, too, dependent on the other characteristics?

Experiment IV. We selected for observation the quality "warm," which was demonstrated to exert a powerful effect on the total impression (Experiments I and II). The effect of the term was studied in the following two series:

    A. obedient—weak—shallow—*warm*—unambitious—vain
    B. vain—shrewd—unscrupulous—*warm*—shallow—envious

Immediately "warm" drops as a significant characteristic in relation to the others, as the distribution of rankings appearing in Table 5 shows. (Compare Table 3 of Experiment I.)

TABLE 5   Rankings of "warm" and "cold": Experiment IV.

| | "Warm" | | | | "Cold" | |
| | Series A | | Series B | | Series C | |
Rank	N	Percentage	N	Percentage	N	Percentage
1	1	4	0	0	1	5
2	0	0	0	0	0	0
3	2	9	1	5	3	15
4	6	27	4	19	2	10
5	7	30	4	19	1	5
6	7	30	12	57	2	10
7	–	–	–	–	11	55
	23	100	21	100	20	100

More enlightening are the subjects' comments. In Series A the quality "warm" is now seen as wholly dependent, dominated by others far more decisive.

I think the warmth within this person is a warmth emanating from a follower to a leader.

The term "warm" strikes one as being a dog-like affection rather than a bright friendliness. It is passive and without strength.

His submissiveness may lead people to think he is kind and warm.

A more extreme transformation is observed in Series B. In most instances the warmth of this person is felt to lack sincerity, as appears in the following protocols:

I assumed the person to appear warm rather than really to be warm.

He was warm only when it worked in with his scheme to get others over to his side. His warmth is not sincere.

A similar change was also observed in the content of "cold" in a further variation. The subject heard List B of Experiment I followed by Series C below, the task being to state whether the term "cold" had the same meaning in both lists.

All subjects reported a difference. The quality "cold" became peripheral for all in Series C. The following are representative comments:

The coldness of 1 (Experiment I) borders on ruthlessness; 2 analyses coldly to differentiate between right and wrong.

1 is cold inwardly and outwardly, while 2 is cold only superficially.

1: cold means lack of sympathy and understanding; 2: cold means somewhat formal in manner.

Coldness was the foremost characteristic of 1. In 2 it seemed not very important, a quality that would disappear after you came to know him.

That "cold" was transformed in the present series into a peripheral quality is also confirmed by the rankings reported in Table 5.

We conclude that a quality, central in one person, may undergo a change of content in another person, and become subsidiary. When central, the quality has a different content and weight than when it is subsidiary.

Here we observe directly a process of grouping in the course of which the content of a trait changes in relation to its surroundings. Secondly, we observe that the functional value of a trait, too—whether, for example, it becomes central or not—is a consequence of its relation to the set of surrounding traits. At the same time we are able to see more clearly the distinction between central and peripheral traits. It is inadequate to say that a central trait is more important, contributes more quantitatively to, or is more highly correlated with, the final impression than a peripheral trait. The latter formulations are true, but they fail to consider the qualitative process of mutual determination between traits, namely, that a central trait determines the content and the functional place of peripheral traits within the entire impression. In Series A, for example, the quality "warm" does not control the meaning of "weak," but is controlled by it.

The evidence may seem to support the conclusion that the same quality which is central in one impression becomes peripheral in another. Such an interpretation would, however, contain an ambiguity. While we may speak of relativity in the functional value of a trait within a person, in a deeper sense we have here the opposite of relativity. For the sense of "warm" (or "cold") of Experiment I has not suffered a change of evaluation under the present conditions. Quite the contrary; the terms in question change precisely because the subject does not see the possibility of finding in this person the same warmth he values so highly when he does meet it (correspondingly for coldness).

Experiment V. The preceding experiments have shown that the characteristics forming the basis of an impression do not contribute each a fixed, independent meaning, but that their content is itself partly a function of the environment of the other characteristics, of their mutual relations. We propose now to investigate more directly the manner in which the content of a given characteristic may undergo change.

Lists A and B were read to two separate groups (including 38 and 41 subjects respectively). The first three terms of the two lists are opposites; the final two terms are identical.

A. kind—wise—honest—*calm—strong*
B. cruel—shrewd—unscrupulous—*calm—strong*

The instructions were to write down synonyms for the given terms. The instructions read: "Suppose you had to describe this person in the same manner, but without using the terms you heard, what other terms would you use?" We are concerned with the synonyms given to the two final terms.

In Table 6 we list those synonyms of "calm" which occurred with different frequencies in the two groups. It will be seen that terms appear in one group which are not at all to be found in the other; further, some terms appear with considerably different frequencies under the two conditions. These do not, however, include the total group of synonyms; many scattered terms occurred equally in both groups.

We may conclude that the quality "calm" did not, at least in some cases, function as an independent, fixed trait, but that its content was determined by its relation to the other terms. As a consequence, the quality "calm" was not the same under the two experimental conditions. In Series A it possessed an aspect of gentleness, while a grimmer side became prominent in Series B.[3]

Essentially the same may be said of the final term, "strong." Again, some synonyms appear exclusively in one or the other groups, and in the expected directions. Among these are:

Series A: fearless—helpful—just—forceful—courageous—reliable
Series B: ruthless—overbearing—overpowering—hard—inflexible—unbending—dominant

The data of Table 6 provide evidence of a tendency in the described direction, but its strength is probably underestimated. We have already mentioned that certain synonyms appeared frequently in both series. But it is not to be concluded that they therefore carried the same meaning. Doubtless the same terms were at times applied in the two groups with different meanings, precisely because the subjects were under the control of the factor being investigated. To mention one example: the term "quiet" often occurred as a synonym of "calm" in both groups, but the subjects may have intended a different meaning in the two cases. For this reason Table 6 may not reveal the full extent of the change introduced by the factor of embedding.

The preceding experiments permit the following conclusions:

1. There is a process of discrimination between central and peripheral traits. All traits do not have the same rank and value in the final impression The change of a central trait may completely alter the

---

[3]In an earlier investigation the writer (2) has dealt with basically the same question though in a very different context. It was there shown that certain phenomena of judgment, which appeared to be due to changes of evaluation, were produced by a shift in the frame of reference.

TABLE 6 Synonyms of "calm": Experiment V.

	"Kind" series	*"Cruel" series*
Serene	18	3
Cold, frigid, icy, cool, calculating, shrewd, nervy, scheming, conscienceless	0	20
Soothing, peaceful, gentle, tolerant, good-natured, mild mannered	11	0
Poised, reserved, restful, unexcitable, unshakable	18	7
Deliberate, silent, unperturbed, masterful, impassive, collected, confident, relaxed, emotionless, steady, impassive, composed	11	26

impression, while the change of a peripheral trait has a far weaker effect (Experiments I, II, and III).

2. Both the cognitive content of a trait and its functional value are determined in relation to its surroundings (Experiment IV).

3. Some traits determine both the content and the function of other traits. The former we call central, the latter peripheral (Experiment IV).

.　.　.

Experiment IX. We select from the series of Experiment I three terms: *intelligent—skillful—warm*—all referring to strong positive characteristics. These form the basis of judgment. The results appear in Table 10.

There develops a one-directed impression, far stronger than any observed in the preceding experiments. The written sketches, too, are unanimously enthusiastic. The impression also develops effortlessly.

Negative characteristics hardly intrude. That this fails to happen raises a problem. Many negative qualities could quite understandably be living together with those given. But the subjects do not as a rule complete them in this direction. This, indeed, they seem to avoid.

Experiment IXa. The next step was to observe an impression based on a single trait. There are two groups; one group is instructed to select from the check list those characteristics which belong to a "warm" person, the second group those belonging to a "cold" person. The results appear in Table 10.

In order to show more clearly the range of qualities affected by the given terms we constructed a second check list (Check List II) to which the subjects were to respond in the manner already described. The results are reported in Table 11.

A remarkably wide range of qualities is embraced in the dimension

TABLE 10 Choice of fitting qualities: Experiment IX (percentages).

	Intelligent-skillful-warm (N = 34)	Warm (N = 22)	Cold (N = 33)		Intelligent-skillful-warm (N = 34)	Warm (N = 22)	Cold (N = 33)
1. Generous	100	100	12	10. Humane	97	100	17
2. Wise	97	95	11	11. Good-looking	72	95	57
3. Happy	100	100	10	12. Persistent	100	78	97
4. Good-natured	100	100	8	13. Serious	100	68	97
5. Humorous	100	100	12	14. Restrained	66	41	97
6. Sociable	100	100	9	15. Altruistic	97	91	3
7. Popular	100	100	6	16. Imaginative	82	95	9
8. Reliable	100	100	87	17. Strong	97	74	87
9. Important	84	68	54	18. Honest	100	100	81

"warm-cold." It has reference to temperamental characteristics (e.g., optimism, humor, happiness), to basic relations to the group (e.g., generosity, sociability, popularity), to strength of character (e.g., persistence, honesty). It even includes a reference to physical characteristics, evident in the virtually unanimous characterizations of the warm person as short, stout, and ruddy, and in the opposed characterizations of the cold person.

TABLE 11 Check list II: choice of fitting qualities: Experiment IXA
(percentages).

	Warm (N = 22)	Cold (N = 33)		Warm (N = 22)	Cold (N = 33)
1. Emotional	100	12	Unemotional	0	88
2. Practical	40	73	Theoretical	60	27
3. Optimistic	95	17	Pessimistic	5	83
4. Informal	95	0	Formal	5	100
5. Cheerful	100	18	Sad	0	82
6. Short	91	8	Tall	9	92
7. Modest	86	9	Proud	14	91
8. Imaginative	95	28	Unimaginative	5	72
9. Thin	15	93	Stout	85	7
10. Intelligent	81	96	Unintelligent	19	4
11. Brave	91	74	Cowardly	9	26
12. Pale	15	97	Ruddy	85	3

The differences between "warm" and "cold" are now even more considerable than those observed in Experiment I. No qualities remain untouched. But even under these extreme conditions the characterizations do not become indiscriminately positive or negative. "Warm" stands for very positive qualities, but it also carries the sense of a certain easy-goingness, of a lack of restraint and persistence, qualities which are eminently present in "cold." A simplified impression is not to be simply identified with a failure to make distinctions or qualifications. Rather, what we find is that in a global view the distinctions are drawn bluntly.

The consistent tendency for the distribution of choices to be less extreme in Experiment I requires the revision of an earlier formulation. We have said that central qualities determine the content and functional values of peripheral qualities. It can now be seen that the central characteristics, while imposing their direction upon the total impression, were themselves affected by the surrounding characteristics.

Upon the conclusion of the experiments, the subjects were asked to state the reason for their choice of one predominant direction in their characterizations. All agreed that they felt such a tendency. Some cannot explain it, saying, in the words of one subject: "I do not know the reason; only that this is the way it 'hit' me at the moment"; or: "I did not consciously mean to choose the positive traits." Most subjects, however, are explicit in stating that the given traits seemed to require completion in one direction. The following statements are representative:

> These qualities initiate other qualities. A man who is warm would be friendly, consequently happy. If he is intelligent, he would be honest.
> The given characteristics, though very general, were good characteristics. Therefore other good characteristics seem to belong. When, for example, I think of a person as warm, I mean that he couldn't be ugly.

This was the tenor of most statements. A few show factors at work of a somewhat different kind, of interest to the student of personality, as:

> I naturally picked the best trait because I *hoped* the person would be that way.
> I went in the positive direction because *I* would like to be all those things.

It is of interest for the theory of our problem that there are terms which simultaneously contain implications for wide regions of the person. Many terms denoting personal characteristics show the same property. They do not observe a strict division of labor, each pointing neatly to one specific characteristic; rather, each sweeps over a wide area and affects it in a definite manner.[4]

Some would say that this is a semantic problem. To do so would be, however, to beg the question by disposing of the psychological process that gives rise to the semantic problem. What requires explanation is how a term, and a highly "subjective" one at that, refers so consistently to so wide a region of personal qualities. It seems similarly unfruitful to call these judgments stereotypes. The meaning of stereotype is itself badly in need of psychological clarification. Indeed, in the light of our observations, a stereotype appears (in a first approximation) to be a central quality belonging to an extremely simplified impression.

[4]On the basis of the last findings an objection might be advanced against our earlier account of the distinction between central and peripheral traits. If, as has just been shown, "warm" refers to such a wide range of qualities, then the force of the demonstration (see Experiment 1) that it exerts a great effect on the final impression seems to be endangered. It is to be wondered at that this quality, which is single only in a linguistic sense, but psychologically plural, should be so effective? And should not the distinction be drawn rather between qualities which contain many other qualities and qualities—such as "politeness"—that are much more specific in range?

The objection presupposes that a quantitatively larger number of qualities will exert a greater effect than a smaller number. But this assumption is precisely what needs to be explained. Why does not the more inclusive term provide a greater number of occasions for being affected by other terms? What the assertion fails to face is that there is a particular direction of forces.

We propose that there is, under the given conditions, a tendency to grasp the characteristics in their most outspoken, most unqualified sense, and on that basis to complete the impression. The subject aims at a clear view; he therefore takes the given terms in their most complete sense. (What is said here with regard to the present experiment seems to apply also to the preceding experiment. In each case the subject's impression is a blunt, definite characterization. It lacks depth but not definiteness. Even when the view is of mediocre character, it is outspokenly so.) The comments of the subjects are in agreement with the present interpretation.

IV. SIMILARITY AND DIFFERENCE OF IMPRESSIONS

The preceding discussion has definite consequences for the perception of identity and difference between the characteristics of different persons. Of these the most significant for theory is the proposition that a given trait in two different persons may not be the same trait, and, contrariwise, that two different traits may be functionally identical in two different persons. We turn now to an investigation of some conditions which determine similarity and difference between personal qualities.

DISCUSSION

I. The investigations here reported have their starting-point in one problem and converge on one basic conclusion. In different ways the observations have demonstrated that forming an impression is an organized process; that characteristics are perceived in their dynamic relations; that central qualities are discovered, leading to the distinction between them and peripheral qualities; that relations of harmony and contradiction are observed. To know a person is to have a grasp of a particular structure.

Before proceeding it may be helpful to note two preliminary points. First: For the sake of convenience of expression we speak in this discussion of forming an impression of a person, though our observations are restricted entirely to impressions based on descriptive materials. We do not intend to imply that observations of actual persons would not involve other processes which we have failed to find under the present conditions; . . . we are certain that they would (see V). But we see no reason to doubt that the basic features we were able to observe are also present in the judgment of actual persons. Secondly: We have not dealt in this investigation with the role of individual differences, of which the most obvious would be the effect of the subject's own personal qualities on the nature of his impression. Though the issue of individual differences is unquestionably important, it seemed desirable to turn first to those processes which hold generally, despite individual differences. A proper study of individual differences can best be pursued when a minimum theoretical clarification has been reached.

Let us briefly reformulate the main points in the procedure of our subjects:

1. There is an attempt to form an impression of the *entire* person. The subject can see the person only as a unit;[5] he cannot form an impression of one-half or of one-quarter of the person. This is the case even when the factual basis is meager; the impression then strives to become complete, reaching out toward other compatible qualities. The subject seeks to reach the core of the person *through* the trait or traits.

2. As soon as two or more traits are understood to belong to one person, they cease to exist as isolated traits, and come into immediate dynamic interaction.[6] The subject perceives not this *and* that quality, but the two entering into a particular relation. There takes place a process of organization in the course of which the traits order themselves into a structure. It may be said that the traits lead an intensely social life, striving to join each other in a closely organized system. The representation in us of the character of another person possesses in a striking sense certain of the qualities of a system.

3. In the course of this process some characteristics are discovered to be central. The whole system of relations determines which will become central. These set the direction for the further view of the person and for the concretization of the dependent traits. As a rule the several traits do not have equal weight. And it is not until we have found the center that we experience the assurance of having come near to an understanding of the person.

4. The single trait possesses the property of a part in the whole. A change in a single trait may alter not that aspect alone, but many others—at times all. As soon as we isolate a trait we not only lose the distinctive organization of the person; the trait itself becomes abstract. The trait develops its full content and weight only when it finds its place within the whole impression.

---

[5]To be sure, we do often react to people in a more narrow manner, as when we have dealings with the ticket-collector or bank teller. It cannot however be said that in such instances we are primarily oriented to the other as a person. The moment our special attitude would give way to a genuine interest in the other, the point stated above would fully apply.

[6]We cannot say on the basis of our observations whether exceptions to this statement occur, e.g., whether some traits may be seen as accidental, having no relation to the rest of the person. It seems more likely that even insignificant traits are seen as part of the person.

5. Each trait is a trait of the entire person. It refers to the characteristic form of action or attitude which belongs to the person as a whole. In this sense we may speak of traits as possessing the properties of Ehrenfels-qualities. Traits are not to be considered as referring to different regions of the personality, on the analogy of geographical regions which border on another.

6. Each trait functions as a *representative* of the person. We do not experience anonymous traits the particular organization of which constitutes the identity of the person. Rather the entire person speaks through each of his qualities, though not with the same clearness.

7. In the process of mutual interaction the concrete character of each trait is developed in accordance with the dynamic requirements set for it by its environment. There is involved an understanding of necessary consequences following from certain given characteristics for others. The envy of a proud man is, for example, seen to have a different basis from the envy of a modest man.

8. On this basis consistencies and contradictions are discovered. Certain qualities are seen to cooperate; others to negate each other. But we are not content simply to note inconsistencies or to let them sit where they are. The contradiction is puzzling, and prompts us to look more deeply. Disturbing factors arouse a trend to maintain the unity of the impression, to search for the most sensible way in which the characteristics could exist together,[7] or to decide that we have not found the key to the person. We feel that proper understanding would eliminate, not the presence of inner tensions and inconsistencies, but of sheer contradiction. (It may be relevant to point out that the very sense of one trait being in contradiction to others would not arise if we were not oriented to the entire person. Without the assumption of a unitary person there would be just different traits.)

9. It follows that the content and functional value of a trait changes with the given context. This statement expresses for our problem a principle formulated in gestalt theory with regard to the identity of parts in different structures (8, 10). A trait central in one person may be seen as secondary in another. Or a quality which is now referred to the person may in another case be referred to outer conditions. (In the extreme case a quality may be neglected, because it does not touch what is important in the person.)

We conclude that the formation and change of impressions consist of specific processes of organization. Further, it seems probable that these

---

[7]Indeed, the perception of such contradiction, or of the failure of a trait to fit to the other, may be of fundamental importance for gaining a proper view. It may point to a critical region in the person, in which things are not as they should be.

processes are not specific to impressions of persons alone. It is a task for future investigation to determine whether processes of this order are at work in other important regions of psychology, such as in forming the view of a group, or of the relations between one person and another.

II. It may be of interest to relate the assumptions underlying the naive procedure of our subjects to certain customary formulations. (1) It should now be clear that the subjects express certain definite assumptions concerning the structure of a personality. The gaining of an impression is for them not a process of fixing each trait in isolation and noting its meaning. If they proceeded in this way the traits would remain abstract, lacking just the content and function which makes them living traits. In effect our subjects are in glaring disagreement with the elementaristic thesis which assumes independent traits (or traits connected only in a statistical sense) of constant content. (2) At the same time the procedure of our subjects departs from another customary formulation. It is equally far from the observed facts to describe the process as the forming of a homogeneous, undifferentiated "general impression." The unity perceived by the observer contains groupings the parts of which are in more intimate connection with each other than they are with parts of other groupings.[8] Discrimination of different aspects of the person and distinctions of a functional order are essential parts of the process. We may even distinguish different degrees of unity in persons. Increasing clearness in understanding another depends on the increased articulation of these distinctions. But in the process these continue to have the properties of parts in a single structure.

If we may for the purpose of discussion assume that the naive procedure is based on a sound conception of the structure of personality, it would by no means follow that it is therefore free from misconceptions and distortions. But in that case the nature of errors in judgment would have to be understood in a particular way. It would be necessary to derive the errors from characteristics of the organizational processes in judgment. The present investigation is not without some hints for this problem. It points to the danger of forcing the subject to judge artificially isolated traits—a procedure almost universally followed in rating studies—and to the necessity of providing optimal conditions for judging the place and weight of a characteristic within the person (unless of course the judgment of isolated traits is required by the particular problem). Under such conditions we might discover an improvement in the quality of judgment and in agreement between judges. At the same time this investigation

[8] If we may assume that the situation in the observed person corresponds to this view, an important conclusion follows for method, namely, that we can study characteristics of persons without an exhaustive knowledge of the entire person.

contains some suggestions for the study of errors in factors such as oversimplification leading to "too good" an impression, viewing a trait outside its context or in an inappropriate context.

III. Returning to the main theoretical conceptions described earlier it is necessary to mention a variant of Proposition I, which we have failed so far to consider and in relation to which we will be able to state more precisely a central feature of Proposition II. It would be a possible hypothesis that in the course of forming an impression each trait interacts with one or more of the others, and that the total impression is the summation of these effects. The impression would accordingly be derived from the separate interaction of the components, which might be represented as follows:

1*b*. Impression =

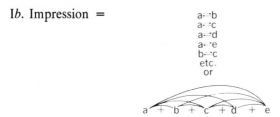

It is important to note that this formulation is in a fundamental regard different from Proposition II. The latter proposition asserts that each trait is seen to stand in a particular relation to the others as part of a complete view. The entire view possesses the formal properties of a structure, the form of which cannot be derived from the summation of the individual relations.[9] In the same manner that the content of each of a pair of traits can be determined fully only by reference to their mutual relation, so the content of each relation can be determined fully only with reference to the structure of relations of which it is a part. This we may illustrate with the example of a geometrical figure such as a pyramid, each part of which (e.g., the vertex) implicitly refers to the entire figure. We would propose that this is the basis for the discovery of central and peripheral traits and for assertions such as that a given person is "integrated," restricted, etc.

On the other hand, the notion of structure is denied in all propositions of the form I, including 1*b*. In the latter, an assumption is made concerning the interaction of qualities, which has the effect of altering the character of the *elements*. Once we have taken account of this change, we have in the final formulation again a sum of (now changed) elements:

1*b*. Impression = $\bar{a} + \bar{b} + \bar{c} + \bar{d} + \bar{e}$

[9]For a basic treatment of the concept of structure the reader is referred to M. Wertheimer (10).

In still another regard there is a difference between Propositions II and I*b*. This has to do with the nature of the interaction between the traits. In terms of Proposition II the character of interaction is determined by the particular qualities that enter into the relation (e.g., "warm-witty" or "cold-witty"). It is doubtful however whether a theory which refuses to admit relational processes in the formation of a whole impression would admit the same relational processes in the interaction of one trait with another.

In view of the fact that Proposition I*b* has not, as far as we know, been explicitly formulated with reference to the present problem, it becomes necessary to do so here, and especially to state the process of interaction in such a manner as to be consistent with it. This we might do best by applying certain current conceptions. We could speak of traits as "conditioned verbal reactions," each of which possesses a particular "strength" and range of generalization. Interaction between traits would accordingly be assimilated to the schema of differential conditioning to single stimuli and to stimuli in combination, perhaps after the manner of the recent treatment of "stimulus configurations" by Hull (4, 5).[10]

How consistent would this interpretation be with the observations we have reported? It seems to us that there are grave difficulties in the way of such an interpretation. In so far as the terms of conditioning are at all intelligible with reference to our problem, the process of interaction can be understood only as a quantitative increase or diminution in a response. This is not, however, the essential characteristic of interaction as we have observed it, which consists in a change of content and function. The gaiety of an intelligent man is not more or less than the gaiety of a stupid man; it is different in quality. Further, the conditioning account seems to contain no principle that would make clear the particular direction interaction takes.

Here we may mention a more general point. We have referred earlier to the comparative ease with which complex situations in another person are perceived. If traits were perceived separately, we would expect to encounter the same difficulties in forming a view of a person that we meet in learning a list of unrelated words. That we are able to encompass the

---

[10]Proceeding in the same manner, it would be possible to restate some of our observations in terms such as the following: (1) the distinction between central and peripheral traits would be referred to a difference between conditioned reactions of greater and lesser strengths; (2) the change from a central to a peripheral trait could be explained by the displacement of a response by other, stronger responses; (3) the factor of direction might be dealt with in terms of changes in the temporal appearance of stimuli; (4) strongly unified impressions could be an expression of highly generalized reactions; etc. Such formulations would, however, fail to deal adequately with the central feature of our findings, namely, changes in the quality of traits and the organized form of the impression.

entire person in one sweep seems to be due to the structured character of the impression.[11] In terms of an interaction theory of component elements, the difficulty in surveying a person should be even greater than in the formulation of Proposition I, since the former must deal with the elements of the latter plus a large number of added factors.

IV. In order to retain a necessary distinction between the process of forming an impression and the actual organization of traits in a person, we have spoken as if nothing were known of the latter. While we cannot deal with the latter problem, one investigation is of particular relevance to the present discussion. We refer to the famous investigation of Hartshorne and May (3), who studied in a variety of situations the tendencies in groups of children to act honestly in such widely varied matters as copying, returning of money, correcting one's school work, etc. The relations between the actions of children in the different situations were studied by means of statistical correlations. These were generally low. On the basis of these results the important conclusion was drawn that qualities such as honesty are not consistent characteristics of the child but specific habits acquired in particular situations, that "neither deceit, nor its opposite, honesty, are unified character traits, but rather specific functions of life situations." Having accepted this conclusion, equally fundamental consequences were drawn for character education of children.

Abstracting from the many things that might be said about this work, we point out only that its conclusion is not proven because of the failure to consider the structural character of personality traits. As G. W. Allport (1, p. 250 ff.) has pointed out, we may not assume that a particular act, say the clandestine change by a pupil of an answer on a school test, has the same psychological meaning in all cases.[12] Once this point is realized, its consequences for the thesis of Hartshorne and May become quite threatening. Let us consider a few of the possibilities in the situation, which would be classified as follows by Hartshorne and May:

Honest

1. The child wants to alter his answer on the test but fears he will be caught.
2. He does not change because he is indifferent to the grade.

Dishonest

1. The child changes his answer because he is devoted to his teacher and anxious not to lose her regard.

[11]It should not, however, be concluded that our views of persons are crystal clear. In fact, they lack the precision with which we grasp a mathematical theorem. We rarely feel that we have exhausted our understanding of another person. This has partly to do with the fact that the person is in constant change.

[12]See also discussion by D. W. MacKinnon (7, p. 26 ff.).

2. He cannot restrain the impulse to change the wrong answer into the answer he now knows to be correct.

Psychologically, none of these acts are correctly classified. Further, two of these are classified in precisely the wrong way. The child who wishes to cheat but is afraid does not belong in the honest category, while the child who cannot bear to leave the wrong answer uncorrected does not necessarily deserve to be called dishonest. We do not intend to say that the psychological significance of the reactions was as a rule misinterpreted; for the sake of illustration we have chosen admittedly extreme examples. But the failure to consider the psychological content introduces a serious doubt concerning the conclusions reached by Hartshorne and May.

V. A far richer field for the observation of the processes here considered would be the impressions formed of actual people. Concrete experience with persons possesses a substantial quality and produces a host of effects which have no room for growth in the ephemeral impressions of this investigation. The fact that we are ourselves changed by living people, that we observe them in movement and growth, introduces factors and forces of a new order. In comparison with these, momentary impressions based on descriptions, or even the full view of the person at a given moment, are only partial aspects of a broader process.

In such investigation some of the problems we have considered would reappear and might gain a larger application. Other problems, which were of necessity excluded from the present investigation, could be clarified in such an approach. We mention one which is of particular importance. It was a constant feature of our procedure to provide the subject with the traits of a person; but in actual observation the discovery of the traits in a person is a vital part of the process of establishing an impression. Since observation gives us only concrete acts and qualities, the application of a trait to a person becomes itself a problem. Is characterization by a trait for example a statistical generalization from a number of instances? Or is it the consequence of discovering a quality within the setting of the entire impression, which may therefore be reached in a single instance? In the latter case, repeated observation would provide not simply additional instances for statistical conclusion, but rather a check on the genuineness of the earlier observation, as well as a clarification of its limiting conditions. Proceeding in this manner, it should be possible to decide whether the discovery of a trait itself involves processes of a structural nature. Only direct investigation based on the observation of persons can furnish answers to these questions.

In still another regard did our investigation limit the range of observation. In the views formed of living persons past experience plays a great role. The impression itself has a history and continuity as it extends over considerable periods of time, while factors of motivation become more important in determining its stability and resistance to change.

Even within the limits of the present study factors of past experience were highly important. When the subject formed a view on the basis of the given description, he as a rule referred to a contemporary, at no time to characters that may have lived in the past; he located the person in this country, never in other countries. Further, experiments we have not here reported showed unmistakably that an identical series of traits produced distinct impressions depending on whether we identified the person as a man or woman, as a child or adult. Distinctions of this order clearly depend on a definite kind of knowledge obtained in the past. Indeed, the very possibility of grasping the meaning of a trait presupposes that it had been observed and understood.

That experience enters in these instances as a necessary factor seems clear, but the statement would be misleading if we did not add that the possibility of such experience itself presupposes a capacity to observe and realize the qualities and dynamic relations here described. The assertion that the properties of the impression depend on past experience can only mean that these were once directly perceived. In this connection we may refer to certain observations of Köhler (6, p. 234 ff.) concerning our understanding of feelings in others which we have not observed in ourselves, or in the absence of relevant previous experiences. In his comprehensive discussion of the question, G. W. Allport (1, p. 533 ff.) has equally stressed the importance of direct perception of a given structure in others, of our capacity for perceiving in others dynamic tendencies.

Nor do we consider it adequate to assert that in the present investigation our subjects were merely reproducing past observations of qualities and of the ways in which they modify each other. When the subject selected a certain trait as central (or when he deposed a once central trait to a minor role within a new context) it is by no means clear that he was guided by specific, acquired rules prescribing which traits will be central in each of a great number of constellations. It seems more in accordance with the evidence to suppose that the system of the traits itself points to a necessary center. And as we have mentioned earlier, the interaction between two traits already presupposes that we have discovered—whether in the past or in the present—the forces that work between them. Given the quality "quick" we cannot unequivocally infer the quality "skillful";[13] but given "quick-skillful" we try to see how one grows out of the other. We then discover a certain constancy in the relation between them, which is not that of a constant habitual connection.

---

[13] That it is at times difficult to infer qualities on the basis of central traits is due to such factors as the liability of the person, the degree to which the actions of a person are directed by a single center, as well as situational forces.

While an appeal to past experience cannot supplant the direct grasping of qualities and processes, the role of past experience is undoubtedly great where impressions of actual people extending over a long period are concerned. Here the important question for theory is whether the factors of past experience involve dynamic processes of the same order that we find at work in the momentary impression, or whether these are predominantly of the nature of associative bonds. It seems to us a useful hypothesis that when we relate a person's past to his present we are again relying essentially on the comprehension of dynamic processes.

REFERENCES

1. ALLPORT, G. W. *Personality: A Psychological Interpretation.* New York: Holt, 1937.
2. ASCH, S. E. Studies in the Principles of Judgments and Attitudes: II. Determination of Judgments by Group and by Ego Standards. *J. Soc. Psychol.,* 1940, *12,* 433–465.
3. HARTSHORNE, H., & MAY, M. A. Vol. I, *Studies in Deceit,* 1928; Vol. II, *Studies in Service and Self-Control,* 1939; Vol. III (with F. K. Shuttleworth), *Studies in the Organization of Character, 1930.*
4. HULL, C. L. *Principles of Behavior.* New York: Appleton-Century, 1943.
5. HULL, C. L. The Discrimination of Stimulus Configurations and the Hypothesis of Afferent Neural Interaction. *Psychol. Rev.,* 1945, *52,* 133–142.
6. KOHLER, W. *Gestalt Psychology.* New York: Liveright, 1929.
7. MACKINNON, D. W. The Structure of Personality. In Hunt, J. McV. (Ed.), *Personality and the Behavior Disorders,* Vol. I. New York: Ronald Press, 1944.
8. TERNUS, J. Experimentelle Untersuchungen über Phanomenale Identität. *Psych. Forsch.,* 1926, *7,* 81–136.
9. THORNDIKE, E. L. A Constant Error in Psychological Rating. *J. Appl. Psychol.,* 1920, *4,* 25–29.
10. WERTHEIMER, M. *Productive Thinking.* New York: Harper, 1946.

3

COGNITIVE
COMPLEXITY-SIMPLICITY
AND PREDICTIVE BEHAVIOR
JAMES BIERI

When Bieri speaks of complex cognitive differentiations rising "from simple ones, and that the presence of the former implies the presence of the latter," he assumes that there is an emergent hierarchy in the development of cognitive constructs. In order to make more adequate differentiations of the behavior of others, a person needs to develop a construct system of greater complexity.

Using Kelly's Role Construct Repertory Test (RCRT), Bieri found that he could isolate a group of subjects whom he calls "cognitively simple" from subjects regarded as "cognitively complex." Cognitively simple persons, rating other people in terms of the constructs they have previously supplied, tend to judge each of the other persons identically on each construct, despite the fact that they used different labels when they supplied the constructs. To use another language: Each person being rated by a cognitively simple person is rated similarly on each supposedly different trait. If one would attempt to use the factor analytic technique used by Levy (Section IV) on the RCRT produced by cognitively simple persons, the result would be that few constellatory constructs would emerge. The constructs that cognitively simple persons use would tend to blend into a single undifferentiated construct.

Although this article is included here as a means of elaborating the nature of the hierarchical relationship between constructs, Bieri was seeking clarification on other issues. The article contributes to an extension of Kelly's general theory, as well as toward understanding how persons of varying levels of cognitive complexity regard the operations of other persons. Cognitively complex persons are in a better position to predict how other persons respond differently from themselves. Having available a variety of constructs applicable to behavior,

Reprinted from Journal of Abnormal and Social Psychology, *1955, 51, 263–268, by permission of the author and the American Psychological Association.*

they apparently can do a better job of gauging the nature of the roles other people seek to occupy. In their perceptions, other people may occupy one of a large number of roles. Cognitively simple people are able to see others filling only a limited range of roles.

$$* \quad * \quad *$$

A common focus of problems in current research has been concerned with what is variously called social perception (9, 16), interpersonal perception (2, 12), understanding others (6), empathy (7), or social sensitivity (1). In these studies, social perceptions often are defined operationally as responses on a questionnaire or rating scale which represent the *predictions* of how the subject (S) felt some other individual responded to the questionnaire or scale. By comparing these predictions with S's own responses and with the other's own responses, certain hypotheses about the accuracy of the perceptions are tested. The multiplicity of findings in this area have been reviewed and discussed elsewhere (4). The purpose of this paper is to present a tentative theoretical framework into which these diverse empirical findings can be placed. From this framework, several predictions will be evolved, and empirical evidence relative to these predictions will be presented.

It is suggested that what is involved in the studies cited above is primarily the *predictive accuracy* of an individual's behavior. That is, one perceives another accurately to the extent his predictions of the other's behavior are accurate. The position taken here is that predictive behavior, and its accuracy or inaccuracy, may be fruitfully viewed as a function of certain behavioral variables within a conception of personality structure. In this sense, predictive behavior is akin to expectancy behavior, as postulated in certain theories of learning and personality (15).

In the present discussion, those aspects of personality functioning which set the necessary conditions for predictive behavior are construed within a general perceptual or cognitive framework. Following the theoretical orientation developed by G. A. Kelly (11), it is assumed that a basic characteristic of human behavior is its movement in the direction of greater predictability of an individual's interpersonal environment. It is further assumed that each individual possesses a system of constructs for perceiving his social world. These constructs are invoked and form the basis for making predictions. The constructs composing the system are the characteristic modes of perceiving persons in the individual's environment. Thus, under the supposition that person X is perceived as "hostile" (construct), an individual may make one kind of prediction about his behavior, while if he were perceived as "friendly," another kind of prediction might be made. The relative success or failure of these predictions are postulated as affecting the constructs upon which they are based. Thus, unsuccessful predictions are presumed to cause greater changes in the construct system than successful predictions. Research results to date have generally substantiated these notions concerning construct change (3, 14).

Assuming these constructs or modes of perceiving persons are fundamental in predictive behavior, the problem arises of determining the predictive efficiency of the individual's system of constructs. A partial answer to this problem should lie in the versatility of the individual's construct system. Inasmuch as constructs represent differential perceptions or discriminations of the environment, it would be expected that the greater the degree of differentiation among the constructs, the greater will be the predictive power of the individual. In other words, there should be a positive relationship between how well an individual's system of constructs differentiates people in the environment and how well the individual can predict the behavior of these people. For our present purposes, we have designated the degree of differentiation of the construct system as reflecting its *cognitive complexity-simplicity*. A system of constructs which differentiates highly among persons is considered to be cognitively complex. A construct system which provides poor differentiation among persons is considered to be cognitively simple in structure.

The first general hypothesis would be: Among a group of *S*s, there should be a significant positive relationship between degree of cognitive complexity and accuracy of predictive behavior.

In analyzing predictive behavior, a comparison may be made between the similarity of the predicter's own responses and his predictions of another individual. This similarity has been referred to as a tendency to perceive others as similar to oneself (2), as projection (1), and as assumed similarity (8). In the attempt to incorporate predictive behavior into the broader realm of personality functioning, it would seem wise to apply more specific terminology to this projective process. Cameron's concept of *assimilative projection* would appear to approximate the type of projection occurring here. That is, the individual assumes others are the same as oneself, often on the basis of insufficient evidence. In reference to persons prone to indulge in assimilative projection, Cameron states (5, p. 167): "The less practiced a person is in the social techniques of sharing the perspectives of others, the less opportunity he will have of finding out how different from himself other ordinary people can be. The less his opportunities for finding out and sharing in such individual differences, the more likely is he to extend assimilative projection farther than the actual conditions warrant." Thus, the individual who has not made finer discriminations among his perceptions of other individuals is posited as having a greater tendency to engage in assimilative projection in reference to his perceptions of other individuals.

This forms the basis for the second general hypothesis: Among a group of *S*s, there should be a significant negative relationship between degree of cognitive complexity and the tendency to engage in assimilative projection in one's predictive behavior.

METHOD

Subjects. The *S*s in this study were a group of 22 female and 12 male university undergraduates. This group was composed of College of Education sophomores and juniors whose vocational interests centered around primary and secondary teaching.

Cognitive complexity. A technique for measuring the degree of cognitive complexity among one's perceptions of others is afforded by the Role Construct Repertory Test (RCRT) developed by Kelly. A detailed description of this test can be found elsewhere (11). Briefly, it consists of a matrix or grid across the top of which *S* lists a certain number of persons in his social environment. The *S* is asked successively to consider three of these persons at a time and to decide in what important personal way two of them are alike and different from the third. In this manner, a series of constructs or modes of perceiving others is formed which is assumed to be relatively characteristic of him as an individual. Each time a construct is formed, check marks are placed in the grid under the names of the persons perceived as similar in some way and the name of the construct is entered next to the grid. After all these sorts have been completed, and a certain number of constructs established, the individual is asked to go through each construct row again and check all the other persons in that row, in addition to the two already checked, whom he considers that particular construct applies to most. No limits are placed upon how many others in each construct row the subject may check. This procedure yields a matrix of check patterns which represent how *S* perceives and differentiates a group of persons relative to his personal constructs. By considering how similar each construct row is to every other construct row in the matrix, in terms of similarity of check patterns, one can objectively ascertain the degree of differentiation the constructs have for the persons in the matrix. That is, if two construct rows have identical check patterns, then these two constructs are presumed to be functionally equivalent, regardless of the verbal labels given the constructs by *S*. Should many of the construct rows have identical or highly similar check patterns, then the person would be said to have low cognitive complexity (i.e., cognitive simplicity) in his perceptions of others. At the opposite extreme, if an individual's construct rows have check patterns which are all quite dissimilar to one another, then he is considered as having high cognitive complexity in his perceptions of others.

The actual scores of cognitive complexity-simplicity in this study were derived in the following way. Each time a construct check pattern was repeated in its identical form in the matrix, it was given a score of −2. Each time a construct check pattern was repeated save for a difference of *one* check mark, it was given a score of −1. The summation of these scores for the entire matrix yielded the individual's cognitive complexity score. The lower the algebraic score, the lower was the cognitive complexity. Although the use of the −2 and −1 scores was somewhat arbitrary, it had its basis in several considerations. First, a 12×12 grid or matrix was employed in the study. That is, there were 12 persons being perceived according to 12 possible constructs. Practical time considerations in the experimental situation were primary in determining the use of this number of constructs. The cognitive complexity scores obtained ranged from 0 (one case) to −22 (one case) and approximated a normal distribution. Determining the reliability of these scores posed certain problems due to the nature of the construct formation task. Thus, it would be tenuous to assume the equivalence of items for either a split-half or odd-even procedure. However, as part of a larger research project (3), retest data on these 34 Ss were available. The time interval between administrations was short, the check pattern data having been collected at the beginning and at the end of the same experimental session. However, as part of the experimental procedure a set was produced in each S for changes to be made on the second matrix which conceivably would lower the reliability. A test-retest reliability coefficient of .78 was obtained under these conditions. Thus, even with a set to change, Ss were highly consistent in their cognitive complexity scores over this short period of time. Further evidence is available indicating a high degree of consistency in constructs formed by Ss over longer periods of time (10).

Predictive instrument. The predictive instrument employed was a Situations Questionnaire consisting of 12 items depicting social situations in which four reasonable behavioral alternatives are presented. A representative item is listed below:
You are working intently to finish a paper in the library when two people sit down across from you and distract you with their continual loud talking. Would you most likely:
a. Move to another seat
b. Let them know how you feel by your facial expression
c. Try to finish up in spite of their talking
d. Ask them to stop talking

Each S completed this questionnaire by selecting one of the four alternative responses and in addition predicted the response of two of his classmates who had previously taken the questionnaire. Thus, a total of 24 predictions were made by each S. These two classmates were also used in the construct sortings on the RCRT. The degree of familiarity with a person would conceivably effect one's predictive ability of his behavior. An attempt was made to control this variable by collecting the data early in the quarter while the students were still developing their class acquaintanceships. Each S was asked to list six classmates and then rank them one through six in terms of how well he felt he knew them.

In every case, two classmates with the intermediate ranks were used in making the predictions (i.e., ranks 3 and 4). Each *S* was encouraged to use his filled-in construct matrix to assist him in making his predictions.

Scores. Three types of data from the questionnaire are used in deriving the scores of predictive behavior. These are: *(a)* the responses which *S* himself gave to the questionnaire, *(b)* the responses the other person being predicted *(O)* gave to the questionnaire, and *(c)* the predictions made by *S* of *O*'s responses on the questionnaire. By considering the relation between these responses, three major scores can be derived, i.e., predictive accuracy, assimilative projection, and actual similarity.

Predictive accuracy scores were obtained by summing the correct number of predictions made by each *S* on both *O*s, the criterion for accuracy being the agreement of *S*'s prediction with the responses given by *O*. *Assimilative projection* scores were obtained by totaling the number of accurate and inaccurate predictions made by an *S* which were identical to the responses given by *S* himself. The scores of predictive accuracy and assimilative projection were used in testing Hypotheses I and II respectively.

Each of these three scores can be broken down into component scores, some of which are shared by the major scores. Analysis of the predictive accuracy score indicates it is composed of two components: *(a)* those accurate predictions representing responses identical to those *S* made himself *(accurate projections)* and *(b)* those accurate predictions which are different from the responses given by *S (accurate perceived differences)*. Similarly, the assimilative projection score contains the accurate projection component plus an *inaccurate projection* component (i.e., *S* and *O* gave different responses but *S* predicted that *O* gave a similar response). If we consider the *actual similarity* between *S*'s own responses and *O*'s responses, we find this score to be composed of the accurate projection component plus those *inaccurate* predictions which are different from the responses given by *S (inaccurate perceived differences)*. In this latter case, *S* and *O* have identical responses but *S* predicts a difference. We may schematize these scores and their components as indicated below:

Predictive accuracy = accurate projection + accurate perceived differences.
Assimilative projection = accurate projection + inaccurate projection.
Actual similarity = accurate projection + inaccurate perceived differences.

For purposes of this study, three component scores were utilized, namely accurate projection, inaccurate projection, and accurate perceived differences. The relationships of these scores to the cognitive complexity measure will be discussed relative to the experimental hypotheses.

RESULTS

Using the Pearson product-moment coefficient, the various scores discussed above relative to predictive behavior were correlated with the cognitive-complexity measure. Inasmuch as directional predictions were made, one-tailed significance tests were employed in assessing results for

Hypotheses I and II. Hypothesis I states that a significant positive relationship exists between cognitive complexity and predictive accuracy. From Table 1, it is observed that the relationship is significant at the .05 level. Considering the two component scores subsumed under predictive accuracy, it is apparent that accurate projection shows no relationship ($r = .02$) to cognitive complexity. However, the correlation between accurate perceived differences and cognitive complexity ($r = .35$) is significant at the .05 level (two-tailed test). Thus, it appears that the cognitive behavior measured here relates more directly to the accurate prediction of *differences* between self and others than to the accurate prediction of similarities between self and others.

Hypothesis II states that a significant negative relationship will exist between degree of cognitive complexity and the tendency to engage in assimilative projection in one's predictions. Reference to Table 1 suggests this is the case. The assimilative projection score correlates negatively ($r = -.32$) with the cognitive complexity score ($p < .05$). It will be noted that the correlations of the two component scores of assimilative projection, namely accurate projection and inaccurate projection, with cognitive discrimination are .02 and $-.40$ respectively. The latter significant negative correlation implies that the tendency for cognitively simple Ss to engage in assimilative projection is largely a function of their tendency to perceive unwarranted or inaccurate similarities between themselves and others.

The correlation between cognitive complexity and actual similarity yields a positive but insignificant correlation ($r = .20$). This suggests there was some tendency for cognitively complex Ss to predict persons who were relatively more similar to themselves in terms of questionnaire responses. However, the accurate projection component of this score contains the only predictive accuracy measure for actual similarity. Since this component correlates only .02 with cognitive complexity, we may infer that actual similarity played no significant role in producing greater predictive accuracy for cognitively complex Ss.

It may reasonably be asked what relationship general intelligence may have to these measures, particularly cognitive complexity. For 28 of the 34 Ss, it was possible to obtain total scores on the Ohio State Psychological Examination (OSPE), which is considered to be primarily a measure of verbal intelligence. The correlations between OSPE scores and the various scores in Table 1, including cognitive complexity were insignificant and low, ranging from .01 to .12.

DISCUSSION

The above results are construed as offering tentative evidence as to the interrelationship of three forms of behavior: *(a)* the degree of complexity in one's perceptions and differentiations of other persons, *(b)* the degree of

TABLE 1   **Correlations of cognitive complexity with measures of predictive behavior (N = 34).**

Predictive behavior	Cognitive complexity
Predictive accuracy	.29
Assimilative projection	−.32
Accurate projection	.02
Accurate perceived differences	.35
Inaccurate projection	−.40
Actual similarity	.20

Note.—One-tailed p values: 1% = .40, 5% = .29.
Two-tailed p values: 1% = .44, 5% = .34.

accuracy with which one can predict the behavior of these other persons and *(c)* the degree to which assimilative projection is invoked in one's predictive behavior. The underlying formulation has been that making adequate differentiations in one's perceptions of others is basic to an optimum predictability of their behavior. Although the relationships posited in the experimental hypotheses are supported at a statistically significant level by the empirical results, the magnitude of the correlations obtained suggests that additional factors must be operating.

Let us consider the relationship between cognitive complexity and predictive accuracy. In this study, our primary concern has been to explain predictive behavior in terms of organismic variables to the partial exclusion of the external behavioral realm to be predicted. Cronbach (6) and others have pointed out that the complexity of the behavioral situation to be predicted may affect accuracy of prediction. Thus, bringing complex differentiations into a simple situation may lead to lower accuracy than would be the case if simple differentiations were invoked. Undoubtedly, there are many situations in which a response based upon a simple yes-no, this-or-that discrimination would be preferable to responses based upon more elaborate cognitive differentiations. We must not infer, however, that the capacity to make complex differentiations in situations is necessarily equivalent to invoking complex behavior in dealing with the situation. Developmentally, we may assume that complex differentiations arise from more simple ones, and that the presence of the former implies the presence of the latter. Thus, the cognitively complex individual has versatility in both simple and complex behavioral realms, so to speak, while the cognitively simple individual is versatile in only one realm. In addition to these situational factors, it is evident that *qualitative* differences are important in terms of the adequacy of interpersonal differentiations. When the paranoid reacts to an insignificant gesture with an elaborate delusional structure, his complex reaction is considered inappropriate to the objectively simple gesture. Something in addition to degree of cognitive complexity is involved in determining the adequacy of this response. In line with these considerations, the effect of differing modes of adjustment upon both the adequacy and degree of cognitive differentiations is currently being studied.

The results of this study cast light upon the importance of assimilative projection in predictive behavior. When we consider the components of assimilative projection, we find no apparent relationship between accurate projection and degree of cognitive complexity. The significant relationship exists between inaccurate projection and cognitive simplicity. These findings reinforce the belief that the condition of cognitive simplicity reflects an incomplete differentiation of the boundaries between self and the external world, leading to unwarranted assumptions of similarity between self and others. Here again, the implicit role of adjustment and developmental factors would appear to warrant further study.

The similarity between the conceptual framework underlying the present study and related research in the area of *meaning* should be noted. Osgood's semantic differential (13) contains certain characteristics of the personal construct. Thus, it is a bipolar dimension ranging from a characteristic to its opposite (e.g., hard to soft) upon which Ss are asked to perceive other individuals. The essential difference between the two approaches rests upon the *source* of the dimensions invoked in perceiving others. Personal constructs represent the individual's own dimensions for differentiating his world, while Osgood, Cronbach, and others use standard, nomothetically derived dimensions. For purposes of conceptual integration into the broader framework of personality functioning, using the person's own perceptions may offer more utility.

SUMMARY

A theoretical approach which conceives predictive behavior to be a function of one's perceptions of others is presented as a means of unifying certain empirical data ordinarily subsumed under the labels of social perception, empathy, or social sensitivity. The viewpoint taken is that all these forms of behavior rest operationally upon the predictive behavior of the individual. Further this predictive behavior is assumed to be dependent upon the interpersonal discriminations or constructs which the individual invokes in making his predictions. The complexity of an individual's cognitive system relative to the degree of differentiation among his perceptions of others should thus affect his predictive behavior. Two major hypotheses were derived: *(a)* There should be a significant positive relationship between degree of cognitive complexity and predictive accuracy, and *(b)* there should be a significant negative relationship between cognitive complexity and assimilative projection. These hypotheses were tested on a sample of 34 *S*s each of whom predicted the behavior of two classmates on a Situations Questionnaire. Both of the hypotheses were supported by the data. By considering the component scores of predictive accuracy and assimilative projection, these relationships were further explored. Thus, cognitive complexity relates especially to the tendency to predict accurately the differences between oneself and others. Similarly, the tendency to engage in inaccurate projections concerning the similarity between self and others relates significantly to cognitive simplicity. It is concluded that the complexity of one's cognitive system for perceiving others is effectively related to one's ability to predict accurately the behavior of others and to one's tendency to engage in assimilative projection in such behavior. Certain suggestions for further investigation are discussed.

REFERENCES

1. BENDER, I. E., & HASTORF, A. H. On Measuring Generalized Empathic Ability (Social Sensitivity). *J. Abnorm. Soc. Psychol.,* 1953, *48,* 503–506.
2. BIERI, J. Changes in Interpersonal Perceptions Following Social Interaction. *J. Abnorm. Soc. Psychol.,* 1953, *48,* 61–66.
3. BIERI, J. A Study of the Generalization of Changes within the Personal Construct System. Unpublished doctor's dissertation, Ohio State University, 1953.
4. BRUNER, J. S., & TAGIURI, R. The Perception of People. In G. Lindzey (Ed.), *Handbook of Social Psychology.* Cambridge, Mass.; Addison-Wesley, 1954. Pp. 634–654.
5. CAMERON, N. *The Psychology of Behavior Disorders.* Boston: Houghton Mifflin, 1947.
6. CRONBACH, L. J. Processes Affecting "Understanding of Others" and "Assumed Similarity." *Tech. Rep. No. 10, Group Effectiveness Research Laboratory* (Contract N6or1-07135). Urbana: University of Illinois, 1954 (Mimeographed).
7. DYMOND, ROSALIND F. A Scale for the Measurement of Empathic Ability. *J. Consult. Psychol.,* 1949, *13,* 127–133.
8. FIEDLER, F. E. Assumed Similarity Measures as Predictors of Team Effectiveness. *J. Abnorm. Soc. Psychol.,* 1954, *49,* 381–388.
9. GAGE, N. L. Accuracy of Social Perception and Effectiveness in Interpersonal Relationships. *J. Pers.,* 1953, *22,* 128–141.
10. HUNT, D. E. Studies in Role Concept Repertory: Conceptual Consistency. Unpublished master's thesis, Ohio State University, 1951.
11. KELLY, G. A. *The Psychology of Personal Constructs.* New York: Norton, 1955. 2 vols.

12. LUNDY, R. M., & BIERI, J. Changes in Interpersonal Perceptions Associated with Group Interaction. *Amer. Psychologist,* 1952, *7,* 306. (Abstract)
13. OSGOOD, C. E. The Nature and Measurement of Meaning. *Psychol. Bull.,* 1952, *49,* 197–237.
14. POCH, SUSANNE M. A Study of Changes in Personal Constructs as Related to Interpersonal Prediction and Its Outcomes. Unpublished doctor's dissertation, Ohio State University, 1952.
15. ROTTER, J. B. *Social Learning and Clinical Psychology.* New York: Prentice-Hall, 1954.
16. SCODEL, A., & MUSSEN, P. Social perceptions of Authoritarians and Nonauthoritarians. *J. Abnorm. Soc. Psychol., 1953, 48,* 181–184.

4
MEMORY MECHANISMS AND THE THEORY OF SCHEMATA[1]
R. C. OLDFIELD

The fascination of Oldfield's theoretical paper is not only that it describes a system of storing "traces," but also that it describes a way of handling codings for extended stimulus sequences. Oldfield's description of a process of compressing large groupings of data into short sequences, which can subsume new data inputs, provides a suitable model for the functioning of a superordinate construct. Oldfield suggests that this type of concept of superordinate coded schemata is a requisite in a storage theory, for other notions of storage involve grossly uneconomical models. This concern with the unwieldy character of an electrical circuit storage system has contributed to the attractiveness of theories that explain memory on the basis of rapidly responsive chemical processes. Oldfield's position, however, attests to the continued viability of the circuitry model.

Oldfield's article follows the tradition of Bartlett. His argument proposes a physical representation of schemata storage. Since Oldfield's basic emphasis is the cognitive processes, his article touches many of the concepts discussed in other selections. He gives a useful summary of Bartlett's famous work on memory. Another point, which Oldfield makes in response to the question of basic foundations of schemata, aligns him with Piaget when Piaget (1952, pp. 23–46) speaks of "reflexes." Like Piaget, Oldfield suggests that the first schema are " 'innate,' simple type-sequences."

REFERENCE

PIAGET, JEAN. The Origins of Intelligence in Children. New York: Int. University Press, 1952.

Reprinted from British Journal of Psychology, *1954, 54, 14–23, by permission of the author and the British Journal of Psychology.*

[1]Read at meetings of the Northern Branch, British Psychological Society, 16 May 1953, and of the Bristol University Psychological Society, 8 May 1953.

I. INTRODUCTION

The conception that, underlying the power of recalling past experiences, there exist *traces* in the mind or brain is not only a very old one, but by its simplicity gained wide acceptance among philosophers and psychologists until quite recently.[2] The idea that, as a necessary condition of reproduction, some *simulacrum* of the past occasion must be preserved carried with it the implication that the alterations in the matter of recall must be quantitative, comparable to the gradual erasure of an inscription on stone, or to the fading of a photograph. Thus many important features of recall were disregarded, though from a theoretical point of view a number of attempts were made to cope with the difficulties of 'fixed, lifeless traces'.[3] Many, however (especially physiologists and neurologists), who had occasion to make use of the conception showed themselves notably blind to the explanatory pitfalls entailed.[4]

The experimental work of Bartlett (1932), following that of Phillippe, disclosed a number of features in the process of recall which ill accorded with the doctrine of fixed, lifeless and independent traces. With some of these difficulties the Gestalt school, especially Koffka (1935), attempted to deal by a relaxation of the original doctrine of traces, in the sense of postulating dynamic interaction between them. Within certain relatively simple and delimited fields this extension of the doctrine may be said to have been heuristically valuable. But intolerable complexities and uncertainties arise when the attempt is made to extend the theory generally, as students of Koffka (1935) will note. Bartlett, seeking a fresh approach based upon the theoretical views of Head (1921),[5] interpreted his experimental findings in terms of a conception which he named the *schema*. This assuredly raises its own problems, but dispenses with the trace as the basic element in the mechanism of remembering.

The trace is a theoretical conception whose concrete exemplar may be any one of those more or less permanent modifications of material substance which, in some more or less direct sense, represent an object or occasion, and which play so large a part in our everyday existence. For all its limitations as a model, it is simple and, as a conception, easily handled in thought. If, however, it must be rejected on account of demonstrated impotence to order empirical findings, it may well be asked what shall

[2] Gomulicki (1953) gives a useful account of the history of trace theories.

[3] For example, the 'apperceptive mass' of Wundt, and the 'dispositions' of Stout.

[4] Cf., for example, Munk (1890).

[5] For reviews of Bartlett's theory and its relation to that of Head, see Oldfield & Zangwill (1942–3), and Northway (1940). Brain (1950) has considered some wider applications of the theory.

replace it. Now it may be noted, that the corresponding method of storing information in terms of permanent traces is equally out of favour with designers of modern computing machines, although for different reasons. In this latter case, a quite novel principle of storage has been evolved. And suggestions have been often made that such a device might form a better model for human memory than does the older one based upon the photograph or gramophone record. Some colour is lent to proposals of this kind by the demonstration of structures in the central nervous system which incorporate inter-connexions similar in kind to those required in the memory-circuits of a modern computing machine. It should be noted, however, that the *known* functions of these structures relate to the temporal prolongation of inhibitory and excitatory effects. No direct connexion with the mechanism of memory as such has been demonstrated. It has been urged, too, that there are grave objections to such a view of the physiological basis of memory (e.g., Eccles, 1953).

The suggestion that the memory-circuit of a computing machine might afford a better analogy for the consideration of remembering has generally been made upon the basis that such a device possesses greater functional flexibility than does the semi-permanent trace. So far as I am aware, however, no effort has ever been made to work out the conception in more detail. In particular, it has not been asked whether a memory founded on this kind of basic element could go any further than does the trace in providing a theoretical formulation agreeable to empirical findings of the kind expounded by Bartlett and his followers. To make this effort is the object of this paper, but discussion will be confined to certain specific points, and no attempt will be made to formulate a general theory of remembering in these terms.

I will first very briefly recapitulate the relevant points of Bartlett's findings; and try to indicate the vital features of his theory. Secondly, the principle of the 'memory-circuit' as used in modern computing machines will be stated, and illustrated by a simple example. We shall then consider whether the latter can be regarded as a suitable element out of which a memory-mechanism could be built, and which would show at least some of the properties required by the known facts.

II. THE CHARACTER OF RECALL

Bartlett, convinced that the experimental constraints employed by Ebbinghaus in the interests of simplicity and quantification in fact prevented the emergence of the salient phenomena of recall, studied the recall of everyday material in the form of pictures and prose. The conditions in which the subject became acquainted with this material approximated to those of ordinary life. His conclusions were, briefly, as follows:

(1) Only in exceptional instances is recall *literal*. In general, changes of various kinds are introduced into the material. One exception, in which recall may be literal, in effect exactly reproducing the original, is that of word-perfect recitation. Another, not mentioned by Bartlett, is that of immediate reproduction of a quantity of material which falls within the immediate memory span of the subject. In all other cases change is the rule.

(2) Such changes include not only omissions but also qualitative alterations, and even importations. Moreover, these changes are not arbitrary, but occur in accordance with the general principle that the material is converted into a form more in keeping with the cognitive conventions, logical and causal, which are current in the social *milieu* to which the individual belongs. There is *conventionalization* and *rationalization*. As Bartlett views it, the function of this kind of change is to render the material more easily handled in recall.

(3) There is a change in the relative emphasis of different parts of the material. Some elements, particularly details such as names, or other features which in the original are outstanding to the individual and attract his interest, possess especial survival-value. They may, indeed, be elaborated or exaggerated. These dominant details may be preserved in the form of a specific image, and they are thought by Bartlett to act, so to speak, as *labels* which identify the original experience, and as *starting-points* around which the rest of it may be rebuilt when the individual is faced with the need to recall.

(4) Recall is thus essentially *reconstructive*, not *reproductive*. Most of our experience is not retained as such, in explicit or concrete form, but is assimilated into the *schemata*, contributing its quota to the remoulding of their structure and adaptive capacity. Some fragments of experience, on the other hand, survive in a relatively unchanged and explicit form. Recall consists in reconstruction, based upon these latter, by the operation of the schemata, which themselves incorporate general laws and principles expressing the uniformities of experience.

Such a view, it is clear, suggests many special problems. But it is at once evident that, if we seek to interpret it in accordance with a mechanical analogy (and the trace-theory itself is a form of mechanical analogy), one important question will arise. How can information be stored in some general or abstracted form, and still allow some explicit, if incomplete, reconstruction of the original? It is sometimes suggested that *no* form of mechanical device could achieve this. But before this can be accepted more detailed consideration of the question is desirable. Accordingly, we shall state and illustrate the general principle according to which the memory-circuit of a modern computing machine operates. We shall then consider the extent to which a system built of such elements could be expected to store information in a generalized form, and subsequently reconstruct the original messages fed into it. It should perhaps be emphasized that such an attempt, though made in specific terms, can do no more than elucidate the basic requirements of the problem. It can, in itself, offer no direct suggestions as to the actual mechanisms, physiological or otherwise, which are involved in memory.

III. CIRCUITAL STORAGE DEVICES

The general principle of the storage devices used in modern computing machines is most simply stated by describing an actual instance. The first requirement is that the information to be stored should be suitably coded. We may, without loss of generality,[6] suppose that all messages consist of sequences of the scale-of-two digits 0 and 1. In this form the message can be propagated in an electrical circuit as a sequence of impulses. So, for instance, the message 101100011011 will appear as the wave shown in Fig. 1.

Now consider Fig. 2. AB is a tube filled with mercury. At the end A is a transducer element which converts electrical into mechanical changes. These are propagated down the mercury and reach B. Here is situated a receptor element which converts them back into electrical changes. The electrical message-sequence from B can now pass along either or both of two routes. In the first it passes to, and may be used in, other parts of the apparatus. In the second it passes back to A, to be retransmitted down the tube. Deterioration in the form of the impulses, occasioned by the transmission and conversions, is corrected in the unit X, which also makes good incidental energy losses in the system. If, now, we pass into the system a given message, it will circulate indefinitely, and is effectively stored. If the electrical circuit BXA is broken for a period corresponding to the time taken for the message to pass down the tube, the system is completely 'cleared', and can be used again to store another message. If the information contained in the message is to be made use of elsewhere in the apparatus, it can be passed out along BC, and can be used any number of times in this way. The length of the message which can thus be

---

[6]It can be shown that anything that is 'information', in the sense that it can be explicitly formulated and represented in symbolic terms, can always be re-coded completely in this form.

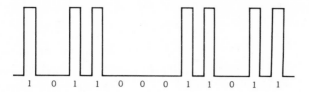

1   0   1   1   0   0   0   1   1   0   1   1

FIG. 1   *Pulse-coded version of message 101100011011.*

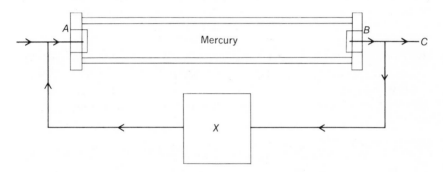

FIG. 2   *Mercury circuital storage element.*

stored is approximately equal to the number of digits in a sequence which occupies the time taken for one impulse to pass down the tube. The time of transmission in the electrical parts of the circuit may be regarded as negligible.

The general principle of storage is thus a novel one and possesses several outstanding features. Among these are (1) the ease with which the message can be constantly repaired, so that it can be preserved unchanged over long periods of time; (2) the ease with which it can be annulled and wholly disposed of when it is no longer required; and (3) the ease with which it can be made available to other parts of the apparatus when required without affecting its continued storage. The particular device just described is but one of the many possible ones operating upon the same circuital principle. It happens to be a relatively poor version so far as storage capacity is concerned, and although others have been developed which are much more favourable in this respect, economy in such devices is of basic importance, and is not irrelevant to our further discussion.

IV. MEMORY SYSTEMS BASED UPON CIRCUITAL STORAGE ELEMENTS

So far our discussion offers nothing novel as an analogue for the mechanism of recall. For if we merely postulate a number of independent circuital storage-elements, we have only returned to another, if perhaps more entertaining and recondite, form of the hypothesis of fixed lifeless traces. The question to be discussed is whether such storage elements could be imagined as built into a system in which there would be some economy of storage without loss of the power to reconstitute the original messages. It does not seem impossible to see, broadly, how this might be done. Consideration of this question raises a number of further points, admittedly speculative, which are of some interest in wider connexions.

We have a 'black box' capable of taking in messages in the form of sequences of 0's and 1's, and storing them. At some future time, on receipt of an appropriate stimulus, the box is to redeliver the original message. For a start we shall suppose that it is to redeliver it in exactly the original form—though we shall later consider relaxation of this condition. The question of what is meant by an 'appropriate' stimulus, and of how it operates to pick out the correct message stored in the box, is, of course, one of great interest and importance. But we shall not, in the first instance, try to answer it. All we wish to do at this stage is to demonstrate the possibilities of economical storage and of reconstruction.

It seems fairly clear that unless the various messages received by the box incorporate *some* detectable elements of common pattern, there is no possibility of economy in their storage. If, however, *any* common patterns run through them, there arises the possibility of re-coding them in briefer form, and so of storing more messages in a given storage space. *One* simple way in which community of pattern might manifest itself, which we may take as an example, is the following. Suppose that all messages handled by the box consist of thirty-six digits, and that the following is one of these:

$$100100011011100011100100011100100011.$$

On inspection, it can be seen that if broken up into sub-sequences of three digits each, all of them are of two kinds only, namely 100 and 011:

$$100.100.011.011.100.011.100.100.011.100.100.011.$$

If we make 1 stand for 100, and 0 stand for 011, we can re-code the message completely as follows:

$$100101101 10.$$

In fact, in this particular case, further re-coding is possible in sequences of three, the only pattern in this case being 110 and 010, and the second re-coded version, if 110 = 1 and 010 = 0 is

$$1011.$$

Neglecting, however, for the moment, this possibility of a second re-coding, we may consider how the first re-coding can introduce economy of storage. Suppose that we store the sub-sequences 100 and 011 in two storage elements, and the re-coded version in a third. The original message can now be reproduced by causing this latter element to draw out the sub-sequence in appropriate order as given by the sequence of digits in the re-coded version. Thus, when the output from the third tube is 1, the sequence 100 is fed out of the box, and when the output of the third tube is 0,011. The original message can, in principle, therefore, be reconstituted. Now the re-coded message is only a third as long as the original, and requires only a third of the storage space. If, therefore, one storage element was just able to store one *original* message, we can store three re-coded versions in the same space. For nine messages, all susceptible of re-coding on the same basis, only five storage elements are required—three for the re-coded versions, and two for the subsequences, in place of nine. It is clear that the advantage will be the greater, the greater the amount of common pattern manifested, and the larger the number of messages possessing this community.

Before we proceed any further a few subsidiary points should be cleared up. The digits 0 and 1 only allow for the re-coding of two types of sub-sequence. If there are more than two, scale-of-two numbers containing more than one digit will have to be used. Thus if the sub-sequences 1001, 0101, and 0010 are found to constitute all messages, code numbers of two digits will have to be used for each, for instance 10, 11 and 01. Hence twice as much storage space will be required for the re-coded version as in the case where only two types are present. Secondly, if a number of re-coded versions are to be stored in a single tube, some indication must be provided to serve as a full stop at the end of each message. This can be any sequence not used as a code for any of the sub-sequences. This circumstance, again, makes some slight extra demand on storage space.

On assumptions such as these it is possible to derive an expression for the economy of storage. This would, however, only be valid for the rather special type of pattern assumed in the incoming messages, and its actual form would be of less interest than is the general principle that economy can be effected without impairing accuracy of reproduction. A number of further questions now require consideration.

V. FIVE QUESTIONS ARISING

(1) As we have already remarked, re-coding with consequent economy is only possible if there are some recurrences, uniformities or common patterns in the incoming messages. This is the case in the information from the environment received by the human organism. On the other hand, it is not, of course, suggested that the type of pattern is that very simple one suggested above. By comparison with this latter, the patterns of human experience are complex and subtle. They may only reveal themselves when some amount of abstraction and elimination of irrelevant detail has been carried out, which would correspond with a re-coding process in our analogy. Thus, for instance, the messages 100111011101100110011101 and 110001001110110001 do not present any obvious similarity of pattern until both have been suitably re-coded, by putting $1001 = 1$ and $1101 = 0$ in the first message, and $110 = 1$ and $001 = 0$ in the second, when the same re-coded version, 100110, is obtained.

(2) How would the performance of such a mechanism as we have considered compare with the use of Bartlett's schemata in recall? Suppose that the box has had considerable 'experience' of incoming messages, and has acquired a store of type sub-sequences. These represent common elements in the events in its 'environment'. Treated as a total organized system, which they form in virtue of the various connexions between them which could be generated by re-codings of higher orders, they might be said to form its 'schemata'. For it is upon the basis of them that reconstruction of particular past messages is possible. Furthermore, we may suppose that, once acquired, the system is used to filter fresh incoming messages in accordance with the hierarchial organization which it possesses. Thereby each new message could be re-coded in such a way that only a certain minimum of storage space is occupied. This minimum is that needed to represent the individual features of the message which cannot be subsumed in more general terms derived from the past experience of the box. Some messages will be banal, in the sense that they incorporate little that cannot be subsumed under the schemata. These will demand little storage space, and will induce little reorganization of the schemata. Viewed in terms of the schemata they may be said to be highly probable, and to contain but little information. Other messages, on the other hand, will present novelty, be improbable, and contain much information. These will only to a small degree be capable of reduction and subsumption by the prevailing schemata. They will demand relatively large storage space. On the other hand, they may induce the operation of fresh coding principles, and thus lead to reorganization of the schemata. In this sense it might be said that the box's schemata form an active organization of past experiences. The demands of novel messages of high

information-content might be supposed to maintain within the schemata persistently active searching for fresh ways of reorganizing the existing system by exploration of the various alternative possibilities of re-coding. In this way complex, clumsy ways of storing information might, sometimes suddenly, be replaced by much simpler and more economical modes of coding and handling the same information. Perhaps in somewhat similar fashion 'insight' may bring about widespread reorganization of a human individual's response-tendencies.

(3) We have spoken, in this last paragraph, of two supposed processes which require some further comment. These are first the 'filtering' of fresh incoming messages through storage elements which contain type-subsequences, and secondly, a spontaneous activity of searching for fresh methods of re-coding material already stored, whether type-sequences or abbreviated, i.e., re-coded, versions of messages.

The filtering process is, in principle, not difficult to conceive, since type-sequences already stored are available for comparison with fresh material, without jeopardizing their continued storage. To take a very simple instance, suppose that the box contains only two stored type-sequences, 010 and 110, and that a fresh message,

$$010010110010110110,$$

is received and stored temporarily as it stands. The output from this storage element is fed to two discriminator units, to one of which is also fed 010, and to the other 110. When the two messages fed to a discriminator unit are identical it responds by sending out a characteristic signal, say 1 for the 010 unit, and 0 for the 110 unit. If the messages are not identical, then the unit does not respond. A sequence of digits is therefore formed by the combined output signals of the two discriminators, in this case 110100, is stored in a further storage element and constitutes the re-coded version. Once the re-coding is complete, the units used for the temporary storage of the original message are cleared and made available for use again.

As to the spontaneous activity of searching for fresh methods of re-coding material already stored, this might be conceived in the following terms. Given a sufficient number of spare storage units for holding temporarily the results of its operation, there is no particular difficulty in supposing the mechanism to explore all the possibilities of re-coding, since this is a type of operation familiar in computing machines. But the mechanism must be controlled in such activities by some general principle, and it must have some criterion according to which it accepts or rejects the results of operations, and continues or ceases its searching activities. Such a general principle might be that of tending to reduce the total amount of storage space occupied by the material stored to date. If this were reduced by any set of re-coding operations, the results would be accepted and stored; and older, now redundant, material annulled. Further activity along these lines would continue until no further economy of storage was produced.

(4) We have suggested that re-coding activities are dependent upon the possession of stored type-sequences, and it might well be asked how, since these must themselves be derived from messages received by the machine, the latter 'gets a start', so to speak, in laying down its 'schemata'. It may, perhaps, be as well not to broach the discussion of this problem, which bears a considerable resemblance to a more famous, but equally troublesome, psychological puzzle. We may remark, however, that if the memory-mechanism we are considering forms part of a more complex machine which interacts with its environment, it may be reasonably supposed that it is endowed with certain 'innate' simple type-sequences.

(5) So far we have been concerned principally to indicate that memory-mechanisms incorporating circuital storage elements could, in theory, effect economy in the storage of incoming information, and that such economy would take the form of storing general patterns common to a number of messages separately from the special features peculiar to each message. A somewhat similar principle would seem, to judge by the experimental findings of Bartlett and his followers, to operate in the mechanisms of human memory, but in this case a further notable feature is the imperfection of the process, as judged against the standard of literal recall. Reproduction, as we have seen, is rarely literal, and we should consider to what this feature would correspond in the model memory-mechanism we have outlined.

The 'defects' in the products of human memory consist in omissions, alterations, and importations. These changes take place in accordance with the principles of conventionalization and rationalization. The stage in the whole process at which these changes occur has been the subject of some dispute. Bartlett, it would seem (and also the Gestalt school), thought of them as being brought about chiefly as a result of reorganization of material during the period between the original presentation and the act of reproduction. That the act of reproduction itself introduces changes cannot be denied, but these have often been regarded as taking an accidental form, rather than as representing the activities of the schemata. The possibility that an important and characteristic part of the change occurs at the time of presentation, and during the immediate process of storage, has been closely considered by Gomulicki (1952) in a number of pertinent investigations. His conclusion is that a very considerable amount of 'editing' takes place at this stage, so that what is stored has the character of a précis of the original material.

Now consider the situation of the mechanism in the face of a message which does not entirely conform to the patterns already incorporated in the machine's 'schemata'. We might suppose it to act in one of three ways. In the first place, it might simply not store the offending material at all. Secondly, it might condone small departures from pre-existing patterns. Thirdly, it might store those parts of the message which do not conform 'in clear', while re-coding those parts which do. The first alternative is not of interest to us. The second would involve the possession of a criterion by the sequence-discriminators, according to which they would treat as an instance of a type-sequence any sequence which did not depart from type by more than a certain number of digits. So, for instance, if the criterion was 'not more than one digit wrong', and the existing type-sequences were 11001 and 00010, the message

$$1100101010000101101111100\mathrm{\ddot{.}}00010$$

will be re-coded 100110, the offending sequences, namely 01010 and 11011, differing from the types by only one digit each, and being coded and stored as the types themselves. If reproduction of this message is called for, it will, of course, appear in a form different from the original, and the alterations could reasonably be said to be ones of 'conventionalization' inasmuch as the material is brought into a form which conforms to the machine's 'past experience' in general.

The third alternative way of handling non-conformatory parts of the material was, it was suggested, by storing such parts in their original form, in much the same way as users of some codes must sometimes leave 'in clear' unusual words not provided for in the code-book. It would be necessary in this case to enclose the sequence in question in a pair of (coded) parentheses to indicate that this material is in clear, so that in the reproductive process such sequences are run straight off without being decoded. If sequences which cannot be assimilated are treated in this way, some points of interest arise. In the first place, the material in question is preserved unchanged and is not subject to processes of 'conventionalization' which may occur in the processes of coding and decoding. Secondly, such outstanding features could act as 'labels', by which such messages might be identified in the course of the further transactions of the system. It seems possible, for instance, that such a label might be operative in the appropriate selection of the message when there is a demand for reproduction. In these respects it might be said that sequences which cannot be assimilated into the schemata resemble the dominant details and images which, in Bartlett's formulation are carried along relatively unchanged, and seem to afford the starting-point for reconstruction.

VI. SUMMARY

An attempt is made to decide whether the memory-model suggested by circuital storage devices in modern computing machines[7] is better adapted to meet the empirical data on recall brought to light by Bartlett and others, than is the type of model which postulates storage in the form of *simulacra,* or traces impressed upon a medium. It is pointed out that unless the circuital storage-elements are functionally organized in such a way as to allow a re-coding of the stored messages, they offer in themselves no advance upon the ordinary trace hypothesis. However, the flexibility of the circuital device might be used to achieve systematic recoding upon the basis of common patterns in the incoming messages. These common patterns would then be stored separately from the particular arrangements of them which constitute different messages. Not only could there be economy of storage space, but the original messages could be reproduced in their original forms. Furthermore, when we consider how such a mechanism might handle messages which contain patterns not already held stored, possible analogies to the processes of rationalization and conventionalization, and to the part played by 'dominant detail', emerge. It is suggested that such a system would have some of the properties of schemata as postulated by Bartlett.

Although such a model is not immediately applicable to laboratory experimentation upon memory processes, it might prove useful in re-orientating our conception of memory-mechanisms over a wide field, including problems of recognition and 'set', of perceptual equivalence, of retroactive inhibition and immediate memory span, and of amnesias and paramnesias.

[7]It has been pointed out to me, and it should be emphasized, that the considerations of this paper are by no means dependent upon the *sequential* aspect of processes of storing information encountered in modern computing machines. A type of machine which stored incoming messages on punched cards, automatically searched through these and punched re-coded versions on fresh cards, rejecting the original cards into a waste-paper basket, would do as well in principle as an exemplar. In fact, this paper might, instead of having its present title, have been called 'Sketch-design for an automatic filing system incorporating a principle of storage-space minimization.' The mechanical details of such a model would, of course, be more difficult to imagine, and for this reason the electrical sequential processes we have considered afford a more helpful picture.

REFERENCES

BARTLETT, F. C. (1932). *Remembering.* Cambridge University Press.

BRAIN, W. R. (1950). The Concept of the Schema in Neurology and Psychiatry. In *Perspectives in Neuropsychiatry,* ed. Richter. London.

ECCLES, J. C. (1953). *The Neurophysiological Basis of Mind.* Oxford University Press.

GOMULICKI, B. (1952). Recall as an Abstractive Process. Thesis submitted for the degree of D. Phil., Oxford.

GOMULICKI, B. (1953). The Development and Present Status of the Trace Theory of Memory. *Brit. J. Psychol. (Monogr. Suppl.),* no. 29.

HEAD, H. (1921). *Studies in Neurology,* II. Oxford University Press.

KOFFKA, K. (1935). *Principles of Gestalt Psychology.* London.

MÜNK, H. (1890). *Über die Functionen der Grosshirnrinde.* 2 Aufl. Berlin.

NORTHWAY, M. L. (1940). The Concept of the 'Schema'. *Brit. J. Psychol.* XXX, 316-25, XXXI, 22-36.

OLDFIELD, R. C. & ZANGWILL, O. L. (1942-3). Head's Concept of the Schema and Its Application in Contemporary British Psychology. *Brit. J. Psychol.* XXXII, 267-86, XXXIII, 58-64, 113-29, 143-9.

VI
THE DICHOTOMOUS
QUALITY
OF COGNITIVE
CONSTRUCTS

1
OVERVIEW

In the Overview to Section IV there was some discussion of the "dialectic" nature of man's psychological functioning. It was suggested that while learning a response to a particular stimulus a person evolved the response from his existing construct system. A theorist with this view would see his learner as having a wide variety of responses that could be applied to construe the stimulus event. This view sees the subject as having some "choice," within the construct system he has available, in dealing with novel stimulus events. It was stated that the stimulus could be construed in one of at least two ways, since all constructs are dichotomous—that is, any construct has the characteristic of having contrasting ends. This being the case, a stimulus probably could be placed in at least one of two points—at either end of the dichotomous construct.

The dichotomous character of human psychological functioning has constantly provided an intriguing area of investigation. Rychlak (1968), in his review of the history of the dialectical principle in man's epistemological functioning, cites several efforts to explain the origins of oppositional thinking in cognitive processes. He recounts one interesting position, advocated by Freud and others, that man's earliest language was constructed of terms that combined opposites. Modern discussions of stimulus generalization (Spence, 1937) and concept development (Kendler, 1960) suggest that oppositional dichotomies existing in nature are available for discrimination learning by organisms. Such propositions do little to clarify the nature of dichotomous constructs, but they do highlight the importance of the issue in theories of behavior.

Ogden's (1967) treatment of "opposition" highlights the ubiquitous nature of the use of opposition concepts in man's thinking. "Our first impression of the universe, after noting its repetitions and monotonies, is that of opposition in everything" (Ogden, 1962, p. 34). Ogden reviews some of the history of concern with opposition, and points out that though the topic has attracted logicians and philosophers, it has received little systematic, analytic treatment. Possibly man learns nothing outside a context of opposition. No stimulus can be incorporated into a person's response repertoire unless that stimulus is somehow contrasted to another stimulus. Professor Kelly (Section I) recognized the centrality of the notion of opposition when he formed his Dichotomy Corollary, which states: "A person's construction system is composed of a finite number of dichotomous constructs."

Let us return to our suggestion that opposition might be so central to psychological function that we take it for granted to the point of overlooking it. We have already pointed out how the issue is implicitly incorporated in discussions of generalization. When one speaks, for example, of generalization on a continuum from "light-to-dark" or "high-to-low" (Hovland, 1937), there is a kind of faith that organisms have "built-in" light-to-dark or high-to-low dimensions. There is, in these studies, an implicit assumption that an absolute novice in our physical world would generalize a salivation response if he were conditioned to a stimulus within one of the above continua. The assumption of opposition is also built into attitude measurement, particularly in attitude scales of the Likert type. The assumption can lead to some interesting problems in "meaning." When a subject responds that he "strongly agrees" to the statement "A student should openly challenge a professor with whom he disagrees," how does his response contrast to the subject who marks the statement "strongly disagree"? Does the subject who disagrees mean that one *should not* openly challenge the disagreeing professor? Is he objecting to some segment of the statement? In attitude scaling it is usually assumed that his disagreement means that he belives that one *should not* make open challenge, and this is probably a valid assumption. But, what features of human functioning bring about this state of affairs? The assumption of bipolarity is very much a part of the theory that underlies factor analytic procedures. Cattell (1957), in his monumental effort to extract the essences of personality functioning through factor analysis, synthesizes all possible behaviors into sixteen bipolar factors. How does a person come to engage in the behaviors that place him along one or the other end of these bipolar dimensions? From what do the dimensions derive? Do they exist "out there" waiting to be practiced? Does society develop bipolar constructs, through its members, and then teach individuals their proper roles by aiding them to locate their personal selves on the dimensions?

As we speak of bipolarity and oppositeness, we are also making an implicit assumption. What is opposition? The discussion has proceeded as if everyone agrees on its nature. Ogden (1967) neatly lays aside any hope that opposition will be neatly defined: "Why is 'not-white' so unsatisfactory to deal with, while 'not-visible' or 'invisible' readily recommends itself as the opposite of 'visible'?" (Ogden, 1967, p. 54). Does *A* and non-*A* constitute a construct? Kelly (1955, p. 59 ff.) manages to become deeply involved in this problem. He apparently found it difficult to state that non-*A* could represent one end of a construct with *A* at its other end. His argument does not leave us convinced. Green and Godfried (1965) systematically investigated the issue. They were concerned that there was a fallacy in Osgood, Suci, and Tannenbaum's (1957) assumption that meanings of concepts could be described by using bipolar terms. They found that many terms did not appear in contrast to other terms when they carried out a thorough factor-analytic technique, and concluded that the assumption of bipolarity was unwarranted. This suggests that many terms have a nebulous "nonentity" as their other pole, and that not every construct is of an *A-B* quality. Ogden's (1967) treatise is, again, of considerable value for its seminal discussion of the possible ways in which bipolarity can be represented. His analysis is purely from a linguistic standpoint, and it would be of great value to have some systematic research to explore how his analysis might be reflected in personal psychological usage.

The subtleties of this issue can be seen by taking a look at how it relates to one of the fundamental philosophical arguments in psychology. In Aristotelian demonstrative reasoning, which is reflected in associationistic learning theories, the opposing pole of *A* is consistently regarded as *not-A*. Everything that is not an exemplar of the concept is irrelevant. This is the kind of model that is offered by Staats (1968) in his discussion of concept development. Concepts are "conditioned on to" stimuli, and are originated in the first place by conditioning an assemblage of anticipatory goal responses. This view evokes images of a straight-line additive process of concept development. This view is also implicit in the work of the Kendlers (Kendler and Kendler, 1959; Kendler, 1960) as they explore the nature of "reversal" and "nonreversal shifts." When they speak of reversal shifting they refer to experiments in which a subject is required to respond to a black stimulus in the same way that he has already learned to respond to a white stimulus. If one treats *black* and *white* as separated stimuli to which a particular response must be cumulatively reinforced, it becomes difficult to derive a suitable explanation of why an older person makes a reversal shift with little difficulty, whereas a child acts as if it were learning a new task. That is, an adult, having learned that black is the "correct" target, will easily transfer the response to white if that becomes the "correct" target. A young child, on the other hand, will need a great deal more practice to learn that the white target has become "correct."

If one is willing to think in terms of an organism using dichotomous constructs and to assume that the older person has thoroughly developed the "black-white" dichotomous construct, then the shift to white is seen as a shift within the same construct. The child, it is assumed, has not developed this construct and must undergo the total process of differentiating the white stimulus along some meaningful dimension before beginning to respond to that color as the "correct" response. This process of differentiating proves to be more difficult than would be the case had the child already developed a construct that related black to white. At this point he might simply use the "white-non-white" formulation. He must make use of this less efficient construction to solve problems. Later, when black becomes polar to white, he easily succeeds with this kind of problem.

This argument, then, suggests that it is much more useful to think of learning in terms of the organism functioning with two-poled constructs. Learning is regarded as a matter of instantiating a novel stimulus event within a construct, which itself must often emerge in novel form from other constructs. To use Piaget's terms, a stimulus must be assimilated to a schemata, and to do so will often demand the accommodation of an existing schemata. When the learning process is viewed in this way, much of what we see can be neatly ordered if we regard constructs as being two-poled. Though it may be obvious, we need to specifically point out that we would deny an assumption that the poles are in any way "given" to the organism. "Up" and "down," for example, are explained as spatial constructs that come from the organism's efforts to relate to the spatial world. Piaget's analysis of the intercoordination of movement and visual stimuli to form spatial schemata (Piaget, 1952, pp. 83–121), along with his further study of the development of geometric concepts (Piaget, Inhelder and Szeminska, 1964) offer a striking explanation of the development of constructs which have, historically, been temptingly viewed as genetic "givens." Because the position we are developing does not allow the assumption that any kind of construct is a given, we want to be quite cautious about using the concept of *generalization*. A generalization that has its basis in stimulus similarity is possible only after an organism has developed constructs along which stimuli may be placed. Our view is that generalization can take place along a two-poled construct, such as black-white, only after the construct has been developed.

At this point the cognitively based theory we are attempting to develop would accept the assumption that constructs are double-ended. There is no doubt about the utility of this notion. Questions about the nature of the data that are taken into account to develop the double-poled concept are yet to be resolved. The research presented here points to the central character of the issue of dichotomization. The writers offer strong evidence that an individual's total "knowing process" is related to the question of similarity and contrast.

REFERENCES

CATTELL, R. B. *Personality: A Systematic, Theoretical, and Factual Study.* New York: McGraw-Hill, 1955.

GREEN, R. F. & GODFRIED, M. R. On the Bi-Polarity of Semantic Space. *Psychological Monographs,* 1965, *79,* whole No. 599.

HOVLAND, C. I. The Generalization of Conditioned Responses: I. The Sensory Generalization of Conditioned Responses with Varying Frequencies of Tone. *Journal of General Psychology,* 1937, *17,* 125–148.

KELLY, G. A. *The Psychology of Personal Constructs.* New York: W. W. Norton, 1955.

KENDLER, T. S. & KENDLER, H. H. Reversal and Nonreversal Shifts in Human Concept Formation Behavior. *Journal of Experimental Psychology,* 1959, *58,* 56–60.

KENDLER, T. S. Learning, Development and Thinking. *Annals of the New York Academy of Science,* 1960, *91*(1), 52–65.

OGDEN, C. K. *Opposition: A Linguistic and Psychological Analysis.* Bloomington, Indiana: Indiana University Press, 1967.

OSGOOD, C. E., SUCI, G. J., & TANNENBAUM, P. H. *The Measurement of Meaning.* Urbana, Illinois: University of Illinois Press, 1957.

PIAGET, J. *The Origins of Intelligence in Children.* New York: Int. University Press, 1952.

PIAGET, J., INHELDER, B., & SZEMINSKA, A. *The Child's Conception of Geometry.* New York: Harper and Row, 1964.

RYCHLAK, J. F. *A Philosophy of Science for Personality Theory.* Boston: Houghton Mifflin, 1968.

SPENCE, K. W. The Differential Response in Animals to Stimuli Varying within a Single Dimension. *Psychological Review,* 1937, *64,* 430–444.

STAATS, A. W. *Learning, Language, and Cognition.* New York: Holt, Rinehart, and Winston, 1968.

2

TO PERCEIVE IS TO KNOW[1]
W. R. GARNER

The assumption that learning is more effective if a person can place a stimulus event along a well-developed, two-poled construct is often implied in studies of learning, particularly if the learning requires discrimination. Garner directs his attention to this issue. He argues that to place a stimulus into a two-poled category is the essence of knowing that stimulus. These two-poled categories derive from ordering sets of stimuli. He shows that they are personal preferences for using particular constructs, a point that add substance to the position (Section IV) that the individual's construct system is the "determiner" of the nature of the stimulus. The same stimulus will be classified differently by different people, though Garner finds that these different people are able to effectively use the same classification. Garner's report elucidates the issue of the dichotomous quality of constructs by pointing out that learning can be facilitated by presenting stimuli in a way that prompts the development of a dichotomous classification along which stimuli may be ranged. Garner also states that subjects employ sets—that is, constructs—whether or not we assume that our learning subjects are doing so. The experimenter who assumes that the subject treats a stimulus as an isolated event, simply because it is presented in isolation, needs to reconsider his assumption. Garner concludes by reporting a study that shows that auditory stimuli are also more readily learned when they can be easily ordered along a dichotomous construct.

*   *   *

This paper is a progress report of research on perception in the broad

Reprinted from American Psychologist, *1966,* 21, *11-19, by permission of the author and the American Psychological Association.*

[1]The research reported here has been supported by the Veterans Administration, the Office of Naval Research, and the National Institutes of Health. The preparation of this paper was supported by Grant No. MH11062 from the National Institute of Mental Health.

sense. The experiments reported are chosen with the expectation that they will illustrate three aspects of perception. These three aspects are:

First, and most general, *to perceive is to know.* Perceiving is a cognitive process involving knowing, understanding, comprehending, organizing, even cognizing. Most of our current research on the topic would suggest that perceiving is responding, naming, discriminating, and analyzing. These psychological processes all exist, and it does not matter that they are *also* called perception. What does matter is that we study perception as a cognitive process. As such, perception is much more closely related to classification, conceptualization, and free-recall learning than to sensory or discriminatory processes.

Second, *the factors known in perception are properties of sets of stimuli,* not properties of individual stimuli (to say nothing of the elements which make up these individual stimuli). Gestalt psychologists have emphasized that perception is concerned with organized wholes, not analyzed parts, but they were talking about single stimulus. Yet a single stimulus can have no real meaning without reference to a set of stimuli, because the attributes which define it cannot be specified without knowing what the alternatives are.

It is convenient to think of three levels of stimulus set. There is the *single stimulus* itself, and often we do want to talk about it. But that stimulus has attributes whose combinations define a *total set,* and the real or assumed properties of this total are also the properties of the single stimulus. In addition, there is usually a *subset* of the total set, a subset which does not include all stimuli from the total set, but which does include the particular stimulus we are concerned about. This subset is redundant in some fashion, since it is smaller than the total set; and it has properties of its own which are not identical to those of the total set.

Now the important point is simply this: How the single stimulus is perceived is a function not so much of what it is, but is rather a function of what the total set and the particular subset are. The properties of the total set and the subset are also the perceived properties of the single stimulus, so we cannot understand the knowing of the single stimulus without understanding the properties of the sets within which it is contained.

Third, *to perceive is an active process,* one in which the perceiver participates fully. The perceiver does not passively *re*ceive information about his environment; rather, he actively *per*ceives his environment. Nor does he simply impose his organization on an otherwise unstructured world—the world is structured. But he does select the structure to which he will attend and react, and he even provides the missing structure on occasion. In particular, as we shall see, the perceiver provides his own total set and subset when these do not physically exist.

FREE VERSUS CONSTRAINED CLASSIFICATION

The first experiment I want to discuss was done in collaboration with Shiro Imai (Imai and Garner, 1965), and it is concerned with perceptual classification of sets of stimuli defined by different numbers and kinds of attributes. More specifically, we compared two types of classification task: a constrained classification, in which the experimenter specifies the attribute by which the subject is to classify; and a free classification, in which the subject chooses his own mode of classification.

The stimuli we used in this experiment are shown in Figure 1. Each stimulus consisted of a small card on which were placed two dots. The locations of these dots could be varied so as to produce three perceived attributes: *Position,* in that the pair of dots could be to the left or right of center; *Distance* between the dots, large or small; and *Orientation,* with rotation to the right or left of vertical. The two levels of each of the three attributes provide the eight possible stimuli in a set. In some cases the sets involved the various combinations of just pairs of these attributes, and such sets contain four different stimuli. And in one situation the stimuli varied on just a single attribute.

Each attribute varied also in discriminability, which we changed by using larger or smaller differences in the two levels of the attribute. We used four degrees of discriminability for each attribute, as equally matched between attributes as we could make them, and we used the degrees of discriminability in all possible combinations to determine the effect of discriminability of attribute on classification.

Constrained classification. In the constrained-classification task the subject was required to sort a deck of 32 cards into two piles as fast as he could, and the attribute by which he was required to sort was specified by the experimenter. With this task the experimental result is the time required to sort the deck of cards.

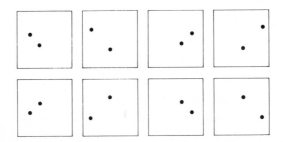

FIG. 1 *Types of stimuli used in free and constrained classification (after Imai & Garner, 1965).*

The major result of this part of the experiment is shown in Figure 2. In this figure, a corrected sorting time is shown as a function of the relative discriminability (on the abscissa) of the attribute by which the subject was sorting. The drop in this function makes it quite clear that sorting is much faster with higher discriminability. So we do know that discriminability of attribute affects how well subjects can do in this constrained task.

The results for all three attributes have been combined in this figure because there were no differences between the attributes. So we also know that the discriminabilities of different attributes can at least be adjusted so that they are quite equivalent with regard to sorting speed.

But there are two functions shown here. One is the function obtained when the stimuli differed on just one attribute. The other function is for all conditions in which there were one or two competing attributes with different degrees of discriminability. All these other conditions have been combined because once again there were no differential effects: Neither the number nor the discriminability of the competing attributes had any effect on sorting speed.

Thus our conclusion is that only the discriminability of the differentiating or classifying attribute affects the nature of the perceived organization.

Free classification. In free classification, the task was somewhat different. A set of either four or eight stimuli (depending on whether two or three attributes were used) was placed in front of the subject, and he was simply required to arrange the stimuli into two groups. With this task

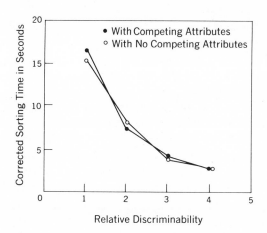

FIG. 2 *Sorting times for decks of 32 cards as a function of relative discriminability of the criterion attribute, with and without the existence of competing attributes (from Imai & Garner, 1965).*

we do not measure how well the subject can do what he is told to do, but rather we measure what in fact he does—that is, what attribute he classifies by.

Some of the results with free classification are shown in Table 1. On the

TABLE 1   Percentage choice of attribute by three types of subjects in free classification.

	Attribute chosen			
Subject type	Distance	Orientation	Position	Other
D preferring (12)	69.0	22.3	5.3	3.4
O preferring (8)	22.8	61.9	12.2	3.1
DO preferring (4)	39.5	40.0	19.0	1.5
All subjects (24)	48.7	38.4	9.9	3.0

Note.—From Imai and Garner (1965).

bottom row is shown the percentage of times that subjects used each of the attributes in making the classification. Distance between dots was used nearly 50% of the time, Orientation was used nearly 40% of the time, and Position was used less than 10% of the time. Since all combinations of discriminabilities had been used in producing the stimulus sets, these results are due entirely to an overall preference of subjects to classify by some attributes rather than by others.

These preferences for attributes are not the same for all subjects, as is shown on the other three rows of data. On the top row, 12 of the subjects preferred Distance, using it 69% of the time. On the second row, 8 of the subjects preferred orientation, using it nearly 62% of the time. And on the third row, 4 subjects preferred both Distance and Orientation equally, using each of them about 40% of the time. No subject preferred Position as the classifying attribute.

So not only are there overall preferences for attributes, but there are also strong individual differences in these preferences. And I hasten to add that these individual differences are not correlated with equivalent differences in speed of sorting with the various attributes.

Still further results are shown in Figure 3. This graph shows data for all the cases where there were just four stimuli in a set; that is, there were just two attributes the subject could use to classify. For each set of stimuli we knew which attribute was preferred over the other on the average, and the discriminability of this attribute is shown on the abscissa. The discriminability of the nonpreferred attribute is shown separately for each of the curves; and the ordinate shows the percentage of times that the preferred attribute was actually chosen. Notice, on the right, that when the preferred

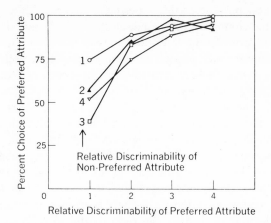

FIG. 3 *Percentage choice of a preferred attribute in free classification as a function of its discriminability and the discriminability of a competing nonpreferred attribute (from Imai & Garner, 1965).*

attribute has high discriminability, it is chosen regardless of the discriminability of the nonpreferred attribute. However, on the left, where the preferred attribute has low discriminability, the discriminability of the nonpreferred attribute affects the choice, even to the extent that it will be chosen more often than the preferred attribute.

So this experiment has shown us that what the subject can do is one thing, but that what he does do is quite another. What he can do is to ignore all attributes of the stimulus which define a larger set except the differentiating one, and he shows no performance advantage of one attribute over another. What he does do is to have definite and personal preferences for attributes, and his perceptual organization is affected by all attributes defining the set of stimuli, To perceive is to know—all properties of the stimulus set, not just those immediately relevant to discrimination.

CLASSIFICATION LEARNING

The next experiment I shall discuss was done in collaboration with James Whitman (Whitman and Garner, 1963), and it concerns the learning of classifications. This type of task is, in a sense, another form of constrained classification since the experimenter sets the rules (that is, he defines the subsets or classes of stimuli to be learned) and the subject is required to perform according to these rules, even having to discover them.

The particular purpose of this experiment can most easily be seen with reference to the stimuli actually used, as shown in Figure 4. This total set of 16 stimuli is formed from four dichotomous attributes: circle or triangle; one vertical line or two; gap on the right or the left; and dot above or below. These 16 stimuli were formed into two classes of 8 in two different ways, as indicated in the figure.

First, notice the two classes formed by a vertical separation. Each of these classes has an equal number of each level of each attribute. For example, the class of stimuli labeled "A" has four triangles and four circles, and so does the remaining set of stimuli, those labeled "B." The same is true for location of gap, number of lines, and location of dot. In addition, within each of these two classes one pair of attributes is perfectly correlated. Specifically, in the eight Class A stimuli, the gap is always on the left of the triangle and on the right of the circle. This same pair of attributes is also correlated in the Class B stimuli, except now the gap is on the right of the triangle and on the left of the circle. The structure of these two classes is called simple because we know from a previous experiment (Whitman and Garner, 1962) that subsets with these simple contingencies or correlations are easy to learn.

Now notice the classes formed with a horizontal separation. Once again, each of the classes has an equal number of each level of each attribute. So there is no difference between the two methods of classification in this regard. However, these classes with complex structure have no pair correlations. To illustrate, in the J class, half the time the gap is on the right of the circle and half the time on the left, and the same is true for the triangles. Nor is any other pair of attributes correlated.

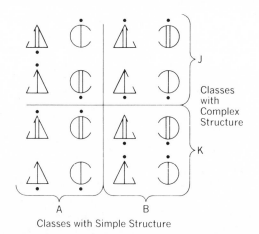

FIG. 4   *Stimuli used in classification learning (after Whitman & Garner, 1963).*

Now our specific experimental question was whether the nature of the classification system affected the ease of classification learning. But more importantly, we wanted to know whether the difference in difficulty of learning (which we really knew to exist in some cases at least) depended on how the stimuli were presented to the subject. In particular, we wanted to know whether presenting classes with simple structure as intact groups, rather than as single stimuli, facilitated learning.

Both classes presented mixed. In the more-or-less traditional method used in concept or classification learning, stimuli from both classes are presented singly and in a mixed order, and this is one of the methods we used. On each trial all 16 stimuli were presented, with the stimuli randomly arranged in order, and with each stimulus labeled. The subject read out the label—the A or B, the J or K—on each stimulus card. At the end of each trial, a shuffled deck of all 16 cards was handed to the subject, who was then required to sort them into the two separate classes.

The learning curves obtained with this method are shown in Figure 5. The percentage of correct responses is shown on the ordinate as a function of trials. These two curves cross and recross, and there is no significant difference between them. The conclusion with this method is that the nature of the structure in the subset does not affect the ease of learning.

One class presented alone. With the other method, we presented just one class of stimuli to the subject—either the A stimuli or the J stimuli, depending on which classification was being learned. Once again the subject read aloud the label on each stimulus, but the label that he read was always the same. The other stimuli were never shown to the subject on

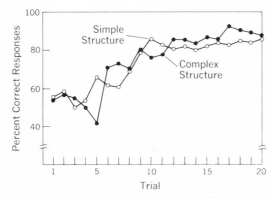

FIG. 5 *Learning curves for simple and complex classifications when both classes are presented mixed (after Whitman & Garner, 1963).*

the presentation trials. After each trial, the subject was again given the full set of stimuli and required to sort them into the two classes.

The results with this method are shown in Fig. 6. Here there is a very clear separation between the two curves, showing that the classification with simple structure is much easier to learn than the classification with complex structure. Incidentally, the bottom curve here is not significantly different from the two curves obtained with mixed stimulus presentation, so this method facilitates learning of the classification with simple structure, rather than making it more difficult with complex structure.

This last point is of some importance, because if we just look at learning of sets with simple structure and compare learning with the two methods of stimulus presentation, we see that learning improves when we show the subject only half the stimuli. This result does not seem reasonable unless we realize that the subjects are in fact learning sets of stimuli, not individual stimuli.

The conclusion is clear: People do perceive properties of sets of stimuli, and these properties affect ease of learning. But the stimuli must be presented so that it is clear to the subject what constitutes a single class or group or subset. If the stimuli are presented so that the subject must learn them as individual stimuli, he can do so, but then he cannot take advantage of some facilitating properties of sets.

VISUAL PATTERN PERCEPTION

The next problem area I want to discuss involves two experiments, in which David Clement and Stephen Handel were my collaborators (Garner and Clement, 1963; Handel and Garner, 1966). The problem is to determine the nature of pattern goodness with visual patterns.

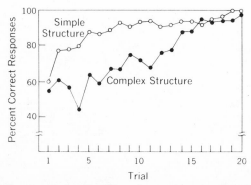

FIG. 6   *Learning curves for simple and complex classifications when one class is presented alone (after Whitman & Garner, 1963).*

In my *Uncertainty and Structure* book (Garner, 1962) I discussed the relation between pattern goodness and the concept of redundancy, or its inverse uncertainty. Goodness is a concept appropriate to a particular pattern, not a subset of patterns. Nevertheless, I had suggested that the goodness of the single pattern is itself related to the size of a subset of patterns in which the particular pattern exists. This subset, however, is not defined objectively, or even by the experimenter, but rather is inferred by the subject. I had stated the specific hypothesis that good patterns come from small inferred subsets, and poor patterns come from large ones. These experiments are concerned with this hypothesis.

The kinds of stimuli used in these two experiments are shown in Figure 7. These stimulus patterns are produced by placing five dots in the cells of a 3×3 imaginary matrix. Although there are 126 patterns which can be formed in this manner, in our first experiment we used just 90 of them, eliminating those patterns in which a row or column had no dot in it. These 90 patterns form several subsets of patterns by the objective rule that all patterns which can produce each other by rotation or reflection are to be considered as a single subset. In this figure, one pattern from each of the 17 such subsets is shown, and our data will be given for these 17 prototypical patterns.

In this first experiment, subjects did two things with these 90 patterns. One group of subjects rated each of the 90 patterns for goodness on the 7-point scale, and we obtained a mean rating for each of the patterns. Another group of subjects was required to sort the 90 patterns into approximately eight groups, keeping similar patterns in the same group. These subjects were not, however, required to have all groups be of the same size, and in fact the measure we used for each pattern was the size of the group in which it had been placed. We used a mean size of group as the summary statistic for this second task.

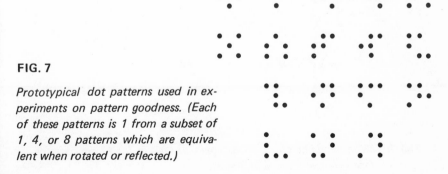

FIG. 7

Prototypical dot patterns used in experiments on pattern goodness. (Each of these patterns is 1 from a subset of 1, 4, or 8 patterns which are equivalent when rotated or reflected.)

Now we have for each of the 90 patterns a mean goodness rating and a mean size group, and the hypothesis states that these two measures should be correlated. The relation between these measures for the 17 prototypical patterns is shown in Figure 8. Here the mean goodness rating (with a small numerical rating meaning a good pattern) is shown on the abscissa, and the mean size group is on the ordinate. The correlation between these two measures is .84, which is quite high enough for us to conclude that the basic hypothesis is essentially correct: Good patterns come from small inferred subsets, and poor patterns come from large inferred subsets.

Nested or partitioned sets? Our basic conception of the different sizes of inferred subsets was as shown in Figure 9. Here the outer bound represents the total set of stimulus patterns, and the smaller regions inside represent the inferred subsets, whose sizes we obtained experimentally. Notice that these subsets differ in size, and are also mutually exclusive; that is, the subsets do not overlap each other. Subset A is, to illustrate, a small subset of good patterns, and Subset I is a large subset of different, poor patterns. This method of obtaining subsets from a total set is called partitioning, and it corresponds exactly to what we required our subjects to do, since they had to form different groups using all of the stimuli, and no stimulus was allowed to be in more than one group.

After this experiment had been completed, it occurred to us that there is at least one other highly possible way in which subjects can infer subsets

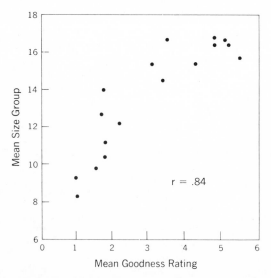

FIG. 8 *Mean goodness rating versus mean size group for 17 dot patterns (after Garner & Clement, 1963).*

of different sizes, and that is with the use of nested sets. A diagram of such a system of subsets is shown in Figure 10. In this conception, Set A includes Subset B and Subset C, and in fact all of the stimuli. Subset B includes Subset C and Subset D, and in fact all of the stimuli except those in Set A which do not overlap with Subset B; and likewise for Set C. In other words, these sets form a kind of inclusive ordering with respect to size of set, since the most inclusive set will contain all stimuli, the next most will contain all but a few of those in the largest set, until finally the smallest set may well contain only a single stimulus.

This conception would have satisfied the requirements of the original hypothesis perfectly well, since all the hypothesis required is that inferred subsets have different sizes. In fact, if the nesting conception of the perceptual process is correct, our obtaining of such a high correlation between goodness and inferred subset size might have been a little

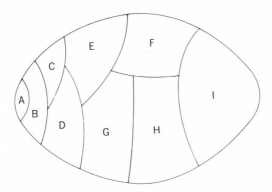

FIG. 9   *A conception of subsets of unequal size produced by partitioning. (All subsets are mutually exclusive.)*

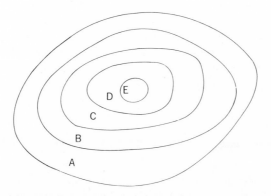

FIG. 10   *A conception of subsets of unequal size produced by nesting. (Each subset includes all smaller ones.)*

fortunate, since in our experimental procedure we forced the subjects to partition, and the partitions formed from nonoverlapping parts need not vary in size.

A very plausible assumption allowed us to get at this problem with a quite different experimental technique. The technique was to obtain pattern "associates" by presenting one pattern to a subject as a stimulus and then asking him to produce one as an associate which was suggested by it, but not identical to it. We carried out this pattern-associates experiment with all of the 126 dot patterns which can be generated with five dots in the nine-cell matrix.

The assumption which makes this experimental procedure interpretable to the nesting conception is simply this: A pattern will be used as an associate to another stimulus pattern only if it lies in the smallest subset in which the stimulus pattern exists. To illustrate, suppose Stimulus x exists in Set A but not in B or any smaller set—that is, it exists in the outer ring. Its smallest subset is the total set, so any pattern in the total set can be used as an associate to it. Now suppose that Stimulus y exists in Subset B but not in that part of A which does not overlap B. Such a stimulus exists in both A and in B, but since B is the smaller subset, any associate must come from Subset B.

The consequence of this assumption is that the associates are unidirectional—they can go toward a smaller subset, but cannot go backward to a larger subset. If we are right that these smaller subsets contain the better patterns, then this assumption means that pattern associates will move toward good patterns. And the actual experimental result will be that some patterns (the poor ones) will have many other patterns as associates, while other patterns (the good ones) will have very few different associates.

The results we obtained with this association experiment are illustrated in Figure 11. In this figure each column stands for a pattern used as a stimulus and each equivalent row for the same pattern used as a response. If our nesting idea is correct, it should be possible to arrange the order of the patterns so that practically all of the associates are above the diagonal line, that is, go toward better patterns, and the ordering shown here is the best that can be obtained with this criterion. (Again, incidentally, we are showing data for prototypical patterns rather than for each individual pattern.)

These actual results strongly confirm our hypothesis (with its working assumption). The small circles represent cells whose frequencies are greater than the expected value (assuming all associates equally likely) and the large circles represent cells where the expected frequency has been exceeded by a factor of 2. The vast majority of the associates are clearly unidirectional. Only with the lower numbered patterns—those presumably nested well within the total set—do we get apparent bidirectionality of

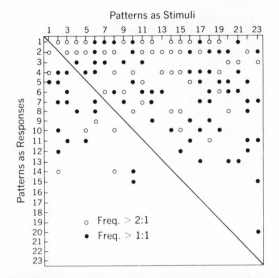

FIG. 11   *The distribution of patterns used as associates to different patterns used as stimuli. (The filled circles indicate a greater than expected ratio of occurrences—after Handel & Garner, 1966).*

associates. We must remember, however, that our technique is limited since subjects were required to produce an associate different from the stimulus. So these bidirectional associates may be an artifact of our method.

The ordering of these stimulus patterns in this figure is based entirely on the association data. We also did obtain goodness ratings of the patterns, and the correlation between the orderings based on associations and those based on goodness ratings is .85. Thus, not only can we feel that the nesting conception is fundamentally correct, but we also know that it is related to pattern goodness.

Furthermore, both of these experiments show that sets and subsets of stimuli do exist for subjects even though we, as experimenters, present a single stimulus and want to act as though the single stimulus exists in isolation. The subject actively participates in the perceptual process by forming sets and subsets of stimuli and his perception of the individual stimulus is really preception of the properties of these sets.

AUDITORY PATTERN PERCEPTION

The last experiment I shall describe concerns auditory pattern perception, and was done in collaboration with Fred Royer (Royer and Garner, 1966). In changing from visual pattern perception to auditory pattern perception, it is inevitable that we change from thinking of patterns as existing in space (which is the primary way in which visual patterns are perceived) to thinking of patterns as existing in time (which is the primary way in which auditory patterns are perceived).

The questions we undertook to investigate were: first, whether the concept of pattern complexity or goodness is appropriate to auditory temporal pattern perception; second, whether such pattern goodness is related to the size of an inferred subset of stimuli; and third, whether the difficulty of perceiving a perceptual organization or pattern is related to the complexity and the size of the inferred subset.

The stimuli we used consisted of dichotomous, qualitatively different elements (two different door buzzers worked quite well for us), presented in a rigidly fixed time schedule of two per second, and at the same intensity and duration. We worked with a basic sequence of eight elements, and actually used all of the 256 sequences which can be generated with dichotomous elements in sequences of eight. However, once a particular sequence was started, it continued indefinitely with no break at the end of the eight elements.

Three of the sequences used, and some results obtained with them, are shown in Table 2. The three actual patterns are shown on the left, with the

TABLE 2   Response uncertainty, delay, and errors for three auditory temporal patterns (after Royer & Garner, 1966).

Pattern	Uncertainty of point of response (bits)	Average response delay	Average no. errors
G 11111000	1.45	20.5	0.34
K 11110010	2.02	33.4	1.59
T 11011010	2.73	48.8	3.34

0's and 1's standing for the two dichotomous elements or buzzers. These 256 different sequences, when repeated, reduce to a much smaller number, because on repetition many of the patterns become the same. To illustrate, Pattern G is shown here as 11111000. Another actual sequence is 11100011, but this sequence, when repeated, becomes exactly the same as pattern G, and can be considered the same as Pattern G except that it is started at the third position of the pattern. Most of the 256 patterns are one of a subset of eight, all of which are the same with continued repetition, and the three patterns illustrated here are all of this type.

Our experimental procedure was moderately straightforward. We started a particular pattern and the subject was required simply to listen to it. As soon as he thought he could, he was to produce the pattern by pushing two telegraph keys in synchrony with the auditory pattern, which continued until the subject had been correct for two complete cycles.

We measured three things: Two of them are measures which reflect the difficulty of a pattern to a subject—first, the delay after the stimulus sequence had begun and before the subject attempted to respond, shown as the average response delay in the middle column; and second, the number of errors made after responding began, shown on the far right as an average per subject per sequence.

The third measure requires a slight explanation. Each pattern was started at each of its eight possible starting points, but there was no requirement that the subject begin responding at that particular point—he was free to begin responding at any point in the sequence. We noted the exact point in the sequence at which the subject started to respond. Not all subjects started at the same point, nor did the same subject start at the same point each time he heard a particular pattern but with a different stimulus starting point. So we have a distribution of beginning response points for each pattern, and the variability of this distribution was measured in bits of uncertainty. It is the measure shown in the first column of numbers.

This number tells us one of two things we want to know. There are not in fact 256 perceived temporal patterns, but considerably fewer, because all alternative modes of organization are not acceptable to subjects. But more important, it makes clear that the number of alternative modes of organization does vary from pattern to pattern, and by a substantial amount. These three patterns have uncertainties which are the equivalent of less than three alternative organizations for Pattern G, to about four for Pattern K, to almost seven for Pattern T.

So there is a difference in size of an inferred, or subjective, subset of patterns which is quite analogous to what we find with visual patterns. Furthermore, this size is obviously related to pattern complexity or goodness—so much so that we did not think it necessary to obtain direct goodness ratings of the various patterns. Good or simple auditory patterns have few alternative modes of organization; poor patterns have many alternative modes.

Now to return to our measures of perceptual difficulty. The average response delay does vary with complexity and uncertainty, being just over 20 elements for Pattern G and almost 49 elements for Pattern T. In like manner, the number of errors made after starting to respond varies from about one error for every three sequences with Pattern G to over three per sequence with Pattern T. So both delay and errors are highly correlated with each other, and either or both of them are highly correlated with the uncertainty of the point at which responding begins.

To summarize, there are simple and complex auditory temporal patterns. Simple patterns (good, in the Gestalt sense) are stable, have few alternative modes of perceptual organization, and are quickly organized with little error. Complex patterns are unstable, have many alternative modes of perceptual organization, are organized only after considerable time, and even after that are organized imperfectly. And again it is clear that the perceiver actively participates in the organizing process.

CONCLUSION

In conclusion, I hope that these experiments have illustrated for you that to perceive is to know. It is to know and comprehend the nature of a stimulus; it is to know the nature of the alternatives to a stimulus; and it is to know the structure and organization of sets of stimuli. Furthermore, the perception of stimuli as existing in sets and subsets is an active process for the perceiver, one in which he will define and organize sets of stimuli which he may never have experienced, if the nature of the stimulus clearly requires such an inference in order for it to be known.

REFERENCES

GARNER, W. R. *Uncertainty and Structure as Psychological Concepts.* New York: Wiley, 1962.

GARNER, W. R., & CLEMENT, D. E. Goodness of Pattern and Pattern Uncertainty. *Journal of Verbal Learning and Verbal Behavior,* 1963, *2,* 446–452.

HANDEL, S., & GARNER, W. R. The Structure of Visual Pattern Associates and Pattern Goodness. *Journal of Perception and Psychophysics,* 1966, in press.

IMAI, S., & GARNER, W. R. Discriminability and Preference for Attributes in Free and Constrained Classification. *Journal of Experimental Psychology,* 1965, *69,* 596–608.

ROYER, F. L., & GARNER, W. R. Response Uncertainty and Perceptual Difficulty of Auditory Temporal Patterns. *Journal of Perception and Psychophysics,* 1966, in press.

WHITMAN, J. R., & GARNER, W. R. Free Recall Learning of Visual Figures as a Function of Form of Internal Structure. *Journal of Experimental Psychology,* 1962, *64,* 558–564.

WHITMAN, J. R., & GARNER, W. R. Concept Learning as a Function of Form of Internal Structure. *Journal of Verbal Learning and Verbal Behavior,* 1963, *2,* 195–202.

3

RATING EXTREMITY:
PATHOLOGY OR MEANINGFULNESS
DENIS O'DONOVAN

One of the arguments offered by psychologists who have used two-poled rating scales centers around the propensity of some subjects to use the extremes of the scale to make judgments of events. As O'Donovan points out, there are writers who propose that the use of extremes is a reflection of "pathology." O'Donovan contrasts this view with a position that the use of extremities in a rating scale might reflect the fact that the construct described by the scale is more "meaningful" to the rater. Or, in terms that are used in his article, when the constructs along which the scaling is being done are clearly a part of the rater's personal system, he will be more likely to place objects at the extremes of the dichotomy. The hypothesis that a construct that is more clearly defined will lead to a subject's use of the extremes, as he tries to construe events, relates to other work (Sherif, Sherif, and Nebergill, 1965) which shows that if a subject personally holds an extreme point of view on an issue he will be more likely to reject moderate views held by others. In a sense, if he has made the issue meaningful to his own self-definition, he will tend to polarize other possible conceptions of the events under consideration. Following O'Donovan's arguments and the evidence he presents, one can comfortably reach a conclusion that learning, which leads to the ability to attribute greater meaning to events, is reflected in marked polarization of the dichotomous constructs that are used in one's personal system.

REFERENCE

SHERIF, C. W., SHERIF, M., and NEBERGILL, R. E. *Attitude and Attitude Change.* Philadelphia: Saunders, 1965.

*　　*　　*

Reprinted from Psychological Review, *1965, 72, 358-372, by permission of the author and the American Psychological Association.*

This article attempts a reconciliation of two constrasting sets of hypotheses about the tendency to use the extremes of rating scales. This tendency is reliable (Peabody, 1962; Rundquist, 1950; Zuckerman, Norton, and Sprague, 1958) and easy to measure, and data have been published in support of each set of hypotheses.

The first set links the use of extreme ratings with pathology. With varying amounts of empirical support, extreme rating style has been suggested as a measure or correlate of neurosis (Johnson, 1946), primitive id impulses (Brenner, 1955), mental-patient status (Borgatta and Glass, 1961), deviance (Berg, 1957), maladjustment (Berg and Collier, 1953; Zax, Gardiner, and Lowy, 1964), anxiety (Lewis and Taylor, 1955), intolerance of ambiguity (Frenkel-Brunswik, 1949; Soueif, 1958), inflexibility (Schutz and Foster, 1963), desire for certainty (Brim and Hoff, 1957), ethnocentrism, authoritarianism, and rigidity (Adorno, Frenkel-Brunswik, Levinson, and Sanford, 1950; Mogar, 1960), and dogmatism (Rokeach, 1960). For instance, Wertheimer and McKinney (1952) report, ". . . neurotics exceed the controls in overreaction in using more often the extremes on a rating device [p. 59]."

In contrast, the second set of hypotheses links the use of extreme ratings with meaningful commitment and constructive behavior. Extremeness of ratings has been used or suggested as an operational definition of decisiveness (Cromwell and Caldwell, 1962), saturation of meaning (Mitsos, 1961), commiting oneself versus evasiveness (Broen and Wirt, 1958), stimulus importance (Blum, 1964), intensity of meaning (Kanungo and Lambert, 1964), involvement (Saper, 1964), emotional investment (Morris, Eiduson, and O'Donovan, 1960), commitment (O'Donovan, 1960, 1962), and meaningfulness (Isaacson, 1962). These studies have been stimulated by the earlier writings of Morris (1938, 1946, 1956) and Kelly (1955, 1958).

The most emotionally neutral term used for extremity of rating is degree of polarization (Osgood, Suci, and Tannenbaum, 1957), defined operationally as the distance from the point of origin (neutral point) on a rating scale. For convenience, polarization will be used in this article to denote a tendency to rate more extremely; depolarization to denote a tendency to rate closer to the neutral point. While the rating scales used in the studies referred to above differ in various details, in each case the average deviation from the neutral point of the ratings of each subject (or group of subjects) was used to test some hypothesis. In other words, degree of polarization was used as an operational definition of some tendency which was also given a conceptual definition.

Polarization is a fourth and relatively neglected aspect of response style. In his review of response style as a personality variable, McGee (1962) states:

This work has been confined almost exclusively to only three types of response tendency: the *social desirability* set, characterized by the consistent endorsement of desirable traits and the denial of undesirable ones; the *deviation* of a pattern of scores from the typical pattern produced by a given population of responders; and the *acquiescence set,* which consists of tendencies to choose the "true," "agree," or "like" option rather than their respective negative alternatives [p. 284].

The role of polarization in the general study of response set in personality assessment (Berg, 1965; Jackson and Messick, 1962) and its relationships to social desirability (Crowne and Marlowe, 1960; Edwards, 1957), deviation (Berg, 1961), and acquiescence (Couch and Keniston, 1960; Martin, 1964) are not clear at this time.

There is one obvious reason for the neglect of polarization. With the exception of Berg's (1961) four-choice Perceptual Reaction Test (PRT), most of the instruments used in response-style studies have been true-false or dichotomous forced choice in form. Under these limited circumstances, deviation, acquiescence, and social desirability all seem more appropriate for study than polarization. However, the definition of depolarization could be considered to cover the use of a permissible-evasive response to a true-false item or even the omission of any response. The tendency to avoid committing oneself is well documented as a stable personality characteristic (Cronbach, 1950; Guilford, 1954; Lorge, 1937). Rubin-Rabson (1954) found a negative correlation between this tendency and self-sufficiency. Edwards and Walsh (1964) found this tendency to be unrelated to acquiescence and social desirability. The difficulty with this use of the concept of depolarization is that the instruments provide no opportunity to measure the full range of the polarization-depolarization continuum.

Six studies suggest that polarization (in its more usual definition) is readily distinguishable from acquiescence, as variously defined.

Couch and Keniston (1960) found that response categories *agree* and *disagree* were more highly correlated with overall agreement score (acquiescence) than were *strongly agree* and *strongly disagree*. Schutz and Foster (1963) found one factor for acquiescence and another for polarization. They suggest that the tendency to choose *strongly agree* probably has a different meaning from the tendency to choose *moderately agree*. In a factor analysis of responses to neutral questions, Broen and Wirt (1958) found two nearly orthogonal factors, one of the tendency to agree and the other of the tendency to disagree, rather than one acquiescence factor. Polarization was positively loaded on the first factor. The tendency to be undecided was negatively loaded on both factors.

Zuckerman, Oppenheimer, and Gershowitz (1965) found that actors differed from teachers in polarization but not in acquiescence. Forehand

(1962) found polarization measures related to each other, acquiescence measures not related to each other, and polarization not related to acquiescence. Zuckerman et al. (1958) found acquiescence positively related to authoritarian parental attitudes, and polarization negatively related to these attitudes.

The relationship between polarization and deviation appears clear at first glance: If the typical pattern is polarized, polarization is not deviant, otherwise it is. However, there are a number of complications. Sechrest and Jackson (1962, 1963) point out some, including the problem of the deviantly nondeviant. Johnston (1964) found a group of psychologists who followed the typical cultural value pattern to a greater extent than the typical American, that is, they rated the accepted values higher and the rejected values lower than the norm group. Whether their polarization defined them as deviant, nondeviant, or deviantly nondeviant is not clear.

When social desirability is added, the picture becomes even more clouded. For instance, Zax, Cowen, and Peter (1963) found that novice nuns *deviated* from college females in showing greater *polarization* on ratings of *social desirability*.

While the present discussion is primarily limited to the one "response style" of polarization, its emphasis on meaningfulness places it in fundamental agreement with the recent reemphasis on item content (McGee, 1965; Peabody, 1964, 1965; Rorer, 1965; Rorer and Goldberg, in press; Samelson, 1964). The present evidence suggests that response style becomes more important than item content as a result of confusion. This confusion could be a result of the pathology or rigidity of the respondent, the ambiguity or meaninglessness of the item (Cronbach, 1950; Gulliksen, 1950), or even the failure of the experimenter to consider relevant stimulus and subject variables. For instance, Zuckerman et al. (1965) found greater polarization for actors than for teachers on the PRT. They suggested two interpretations; "a general behavioral deviancy which expresses itself in an inability to modulate their attitudinal reactions" or "heightened emotionality or drive [p. 170]." The hypothesis that the abstract design of the test might be more meaningful to the actors was not considered. This is consistent with their statement: "The PRT is the most standarized of the non-content tests [p. 169]." While Berg's (1959) statement of the unimportance of test-item content did not go as far as Zuckerman's just-quoted statement, Berg does reveal that the PRT was designed to be relatively meaningless by Berg, W. A. Hunt, and E. H. Barnes, all of whom are teachers and none of whom are actors.

Meaningfulness is a function of the subject and the stimulus. Pathology in the subject may be expressed in response to any stimulus.

This article will attempt to explore the conditions under which degree of polarization is more predictable from the stereotypic and perhaps pathological response style of the subject, and those conditions under which degree of polarization is more predictable from degree of meaningfulness of the rating task.

POLARIZATION AS PATHOLOGY

Several of the studies previously mentioned found a positive relationship between polarization and such social pathologies as authoritarianism and dogmatism, while Barker (1958), Paine (1964), Peak, Muney, and Clay (1960), and Zuckerman et al. (1958) failed to find such a relationship. The present article deals primarily with individual pathology, that is, the contrast between effective behavior and neurotic or schizoid behavior. However, one statement about the measurement of social attitudes seems appropriate. When a bigoted person responds to stimuli related to the subject of his bias, both the pathology hypothesis and the meaningfulness hypothesis would predict polarization. Any test of the two hypotheses would necessarily involve unrelated stimuli. An example of the interactions involved is the study by Mogar (1960). He found that polarization increased with more controversial (here translated meaningful) stimuli and with more authoritarian subjects.

Neuringer (1961) hypothesized that a type of thought disorder called the tendency to think in terms of absolute-value dichotomies leads to a higher probability of suicide. Neuringer's operational definition of this tendency was polarization, as defined above. He used the semantic differential (Osgood et al., 1957) with concepts "pregnant with personal meanings" and dimensions heavily weighted on the evaluative factor. He found that suicidal neurotics and psychosomatic patients exceeded general medical and surgical patients (without obvious neurotic disorders) in polarization. Suicidal and psychosomatic patients did not differ from each other. From these results he concluded that: "Dichotomous Evaluative Thinking seems to be a common characteristic of emotionally disturbed persons [p. 449]."

Certain assumptions explicit or implicit in Neuringer's (1961) study can be questioned. He explicitly assumed that the normal hospitalized subjects were under the least stress and did not follow up on the possibility that stress or disinterest might have resulted in constriction of their ratings. He seems to have assumed that the experimental task was equally meaningful for each group of subjects, though no subjects were consulted on this question. Most important, the statement of the conclusion quoted above seems to include schizophrenics, though no known schizophrenics were included in the study. Zax, Loiselle, and Karras (1960) report no significant differences in extreme ratings between schizophrenics and controls, but greater use by schizophrenics of neutral ratings. It should be added, however, that Zax et al. (1964) found greater use of extremes by schizophrenics.

A more comprehensive reformulation of Neuringer's (1961) conclusion might be that the tendency to respond with similar behavior in dissimilar situations is a common characteristic of disturbed persons. Dichotomous evaluative thinking or polarization, when inappropriate, is simply a special case of this general tendency shown by *some* disturbed persons, notably those with certain cognitive organizations often labeled neurotic.

Long before the current flurry of response-style research, Fenichel (1945) said: "Patients, instead of reacting vividly to actual stimuli, according to their specific nature, react repeatedly with rigid patterns [p. 542]." The three key words in this interpretation are: vividly, suggesting that an intense response is sometimes appropriate; repeatedly, suggesting that more than one sample of behavior is needed to assess rigidity; and patterns, suggesting that no one pattern is *the* rigid pattern.

One example of effective organization is the statement of a scientist quoted by Eiduson (1962): "If you never chase sidelines, you never find anything new; if you chase all the sidelines, you never find anything because you are running down too many blind alleys [p. 126]." This suggests to the writer than an effective person polarized toward meaningfulness: already existing meaning in the adjusted person, potential meaning in the creative person. He neither dissipates his energy in intense responses to every trivial stimulus nor misses chances for appropriate polarization.

In contrast, the ineffective person's behavior is more predictable from his customary response style, even when the situation calls for quite different responses. The general case has been called stereotype, rigidity, perseveration, lack of discrimination, etc. Two special cases are polarization and depolarization.

DEPOLARIZATION AS PATHOLOGY

A large number of studies have been conducted on the predictability or stereotypy of behavior in monkeys (Harlow and Zimmerman, 1959; Mason and Green, 1962), chimpanzees (Davenport and Menzel, 1963; Menzel, Davenport and Rogers, 1963), mental defectives (Berkson and Davenport, 1962), institutionalized infants (Ribble, 1943), schizophrenics (Adams, 1960; Armitage, Brown, and Denny, 1964; Hunter, Schooler, and Spohn, 1962; Luchins, 1959; Painting, 1961; Rodnick and Garmezy, 1957), and process versus reactive schizophrenics (Reisman, 1960; Zlotowski and Bakan, 1963). All of the subjects displaying more stereotypic behavior had been deprived of normal maternal care, by inference in the human subjects, by experiment in the infrahuman subjects. All displayed what is commonly called flattened affect. The evidence of depolarization in these subjects must be considered an analogy. However, anyone observing a mother-raised and a cubicle-raised monkey would probably find it plausible to rate the former as more of a polarizer than the latter.

More direct evidence of depolarization in schizopherenics is found in Bopp (1955), O'Donovan, Morris, and Eiduson (1959), and Morris et al. (1960). Evidence of depolarization in less-effective guidance counselors and in schizophrenics is found in O'Donovan (1960).

POLARIZATION AS MEANINGFULNESS

Three studies using the same measure of polarization as Neuringer (1961) illustrate the second set of hypotheses. Mitsos (1961) had subjects choose the 9 (of 21) semantic-differential scales most personally meaningful. Polarization was greater on these scales than on others. Cromwell and Caldwell (1962) found greater polarization on subjects' own dimensions, taken from their Role Construct Repertory Tests (Kelly, 1955), than on dimensions taken from the RCRTs of others. Saper (1964) found greater polarization on a specially designed "involvement" questionnaire for subjects who discussed a case history with each other than for subjects who merely read the case history. Subjects also reported that the group discussion was a meaningful experience.

As can be seen from these examples, the concept of meaningfulness has been given various operational definitions. This fact calls for much further careful work but is no bar to continued progress. We can expect that meaningfulness, being a stimulus characteristic, will continue to have more operational definitions than will polarization, a response characteristic. It is very easy to make any stimulus more meaningful; this is done every time an organism is conditioned. The most ambitious attempt at a rigorous hypothetico-deductive system in psychology (Hull, 1943, 1952) limits itself to four basic response measurements while allowing for an infinite variety of stimulus measurements.

Various operations, many of which are discussed by Underwood and Schulz (1960) and Osgood et al. (1957), have been used to define cultural or consensual meaningfulness.

Most studies using personal or idiographic meaningfulness as an independent variable have followed the reasoning of Allport (1953, 1961) or of Kelly (1955). Allport advises the experimenter to ask the subject.

Using this technique, O'Donovan (1964) found greater polarization for value statements checked as meaningful than for those not so checked. Kelly asserts that a person's own dimensions (constructs) are more meaningful to him than are those constructed by other persons. Isaacson (1962) found greater polarization for subject's own constructs than for those derived from Butler and Haigh (1954) or Osgood et al. (1957).

Informal evidence indicates that subjects differ greatly in what they consider meaningful. They even differ greatly in what they mean by the word "meaningful." Yet they respond readily when asked to rate meaningfulness and proceed as if they know what they are doing. That is, this task seems meaningful, or makes sense, to them.

The foregoing is not meant to predict that the various operational definitions of meaningfulness will be found to refer to the same underlying mechanisms in the individual subject, but to predict that all operational definitions of meaningfulness used in the studies mentioned will be found to correlate positively with polarization.

It is possible to argue that a person becomes the victim of pathological thinking as evidenced by dichotomous evaluation when concepts or scales meaningful to him are used. But it seems equally plausible to speak of meaningfulness leading to strong commitment. A pattern of intense yeasaying and naysaying may be most appropriate in the most meaningful situations. Mild affect and tolerance for ambiguity may be out of place when being pursued by a bear or pursuing the girl one loves.

POLARIZATION IN THE LABORATORY

The laboratory situation is here considered a special case of the meaningful situation. This assertion will not be defended here. Several recent discussions (Farber, 1963; O'Donovan, 1963; Orne, 1962; Riecken, 1962) suggest that the subject may find meaning even when none is intended by the experimenter. If it is agreed that the laboratory experience is meaningful and is more meaningful when meaningful stimuli and/or scales are used, then the following relationships between polarization and measures of retention and reliablilty fit into the general rubric of meaningfulness.

Heretofore neglected in the literature on extreme-response tendencies is evidence relating what looks like polarization to effective learning, psychophysical, and psychometric behavior. A thorough review of these studies would cover virtually the history of psychology, at least from Yerkes and Dodson (1908). Rapaport (1942) summarizes many studies relating intensity of emotional response to retention. Koch (1930) reports a curvilinear relationship between related pleasantness of examination grades and later recall of these grades, with grades rated "indifferent" being most likely forgotten. Postman and Murphy (1943) found that word pairs either strongly compatible or strongly incompatible with subjects' attitudes were retained better than word pairs only mildly compatible or incompatible.

Pertinent studies focus on meaningfulness and learning. Thorndike (1935) reported superior retention of "cherished" over "worthless" material. Underwood and Schulz (1960) have thoroughly reviewed relationships between extremity of rating and meaningfulness (particularly pp. 19–25) and between meaningfulness and learning. Noble (1958) deals directly with emotionality or affectivity ratings and meaningfulness. Osgood et al. (1957, pp. 155–159) report a relationship between polarization and speed of response. Earlier, Postman and Zimmerman (1945) had linked intensity of attitude to speed of response. A line of studies dating at least to Henmon (1911) reports similar findings. Slamecka (1963) relates speed of response to stimulus meaningfulness. In short, there is evidence linking stimulus meaningfulness, speed of response, and polarization.

It may be that polarization, far from being considered pathological, is now taken for granted in the learning laboratory. For instance, Mechanic (1962) writes: "It may also be assumed that the high-meaningful items will evoke strong differential responses at the outset, while the low-meaningful items will not readily evoke such responses [p. 594]."

What is meaningful when the subject enters the laboratory is related to his prior commitments. Three studies using the Allport-Vernon (1931) or Allport-Vernon-Lindzey (1951) *Study of Values* illustrate this point and its effect on response measures. Havron and Cofer (1957) found easier paired-associate learning for religious subjects when the response word is a religious one than when it is one with politico-economic meaning, and the reverse finding for subjects with strong politico-economic values. Vaughan and Mangan (1963) found greater resistance to group pressure for religious subjects when religious questions are discussed, and for subjects with strong economic values, when economic questions are discussed. Postman, Bruner, and McGinnies (1948) found that subjects more quickly recognized words related to their stronger values.

Some studies in social psychophysics or person perception, such as those of Sherif and Hovland (1961), directly relate polarization with meaningfulness. Polarization increases with greater involvement of the subject (Hovland and Sherif, 1952; Manis, 1960; Pettigrew, Allport, and Barnett, 1958), with the introduction of rewards or valued stimuli to an ordinary psychophysical-judgment task (Tajfel, 1959; Tajfel and Cawasjee, 1959), and with personal relevance of rating categories (Hastorf, Richardson, and Dornbusch, 1958).

Tajfel and Wilkes (1964) maintain that "knowing what is important to the rater may enable us to predict how and when he will tend to use his more extreme judgments [p. 48]." Their conclusion was:

Attributes which appear early and which are repeated frequently in free descriptions of other people tend to be assigned more extreme ratings than attributes which have low frequency and priority and tend to be judged as more important in a person than low ranking attributes [p. 47].

It has long been observed that rating scales and stimuli which do not encourage polarization have poorer reliability. Block (1957, p. 359), studying the phenomenology of emotions, notes that subjects tended to emphasize middle intervals in rating certain affects, such as nostalgia, in contrast to more meaningful or vivid affects, such as love, thus bringing about lower reliabilities. Luria (in Osgood et al., 1957, p. 250) found a correlation of .81 between polarization and test-retest reliability. A direct empirical tie-in of meaningfulness, polarization, and reliability was attempted by Smith and Kendall (1963). In a technique somewhat similar to that of Kelly (1955), nurses were evaluated in the nurses' own terminology. In contrast to the usual findings with supervisors' ratings, the extremes of these scales were used by raters. Smith and Kendall (1963) conclude that "dimensions meaningful to the raters" were the chief factor in obtaining evaluative rating-scale reliabilities above .97.

COMPARISON OF DIFFERENT STUDIES

There are certain obvious differences between those studies apparently linking polarization with pathology and those apparently linking polarization with meaningfulness. The pathology-polarization hypotheses are supported by studies in which rating dimensions are imposed upon the subject. He has no choice as to which dimensions he uses or which stimuli he rates. We assume that the stimuli and dimensions vary in personal meaningfulness, since when we do ask the subjects, they say that they do. We further assume that motivation for responses of varying polarization is provided, to use Hull-Spence terms, by a mixture of relevant and irrelevant drives and the increase in generalized drive level concomitant with anxiety and neuroticism (Hull, 1952; Janet T. Spence, 1963; K. W. Spence, 1960; Taylor and Spence, 1952).

On the other hand, the meaningfulness-polarization hypotheses are supported by studies in which the subject has an opportunity to provide his own personally meaningful dimensions (Cromwell and Caldwell, 1962; Isaacson, 1962), choose which dimensions or stimuli are more meaningful

(Mitsos, 1961; O'Donovan, 1964), or take part in what he or others believe to be a more meaningful experience (Saper, 1964; also laboratory references).

This brings us back to the central question of this discussion: Under what conditions is degree of polarization more predictable from stereotypic and perhaps pathological response style, and under what conditions is degree of polarization more predictable from meaningfulness of the stimuli being rated and/or the rating scales being used?

Most of the studies cited have measured or categorized only the meaningfulness of the stimuli or the personality classification (e.g., normal versus disturbed) of the subjects. What is needed is a set of propositions leading to predictions of the interaction of stimulus meaningfulness and personality-classification. The following propositions are suggested.

BASIC PROPOSITIONS

1. Inappropriate or pathological rigidity in an organism is best studied by measuring lack of differentiation between responses in two or more functionally dissimilar situations, to use Dollard and Miller's (1950) term. In this discussion situations differing in meaningfulness have been stressed. However, this proposition does not depend on any of the other propositions. Even should the present propositions concerning meaningfulness and polarization not prove useful, the reader should still be wary of using one set of responses to functionally similar stimuli as an operational definition of pathological rigidity.

2. The extremeness of an organism's response will depend to some extent on the meaningfulness of the stimuli. If we arbitrarily dichotomize the variable of meaningfulness, this proposition leads to the prediction that response to meaningful stimuli will tend toward the extreme (polarize), while response to meaningless stimuli will tend toward the indifferent (depolarize).

3. The extent to which degree of polarization depends upon the meaningfulness of stimuli is related to other personality characteristics.

4. Effective behavior and lack of emotional disturbance are associated with selective use of extreme responses. The more effective and/or less disturbed the individual, the more probable that Proposition 2 will predict his actual behavior.

5. Ineffective behavior and emotional disturbance are associated with less discriminate use of extreme responses, with less differentiation between meaningful and meaningless stimuli. In the event of total collapse

of effective behavior patterns, the predictive power of Proposition 2 will also collapse.

6. As Proposition 2 loses predictive power, propositions based on the individual's usual response style gain predictive power.

7. Predictions can also be based on personality classifications. Two examples follow.

SPECIFIC PROPOSITIONS FOR GROUPS DEFINED BY PATHOLOGY

8. Neurotics and psychosomatic patients polarize both meaningful and meaningless stimuli.

9. Schizophrenics and schizoid persons depolarize both meaningful and meaningless stimuli.

An example of results postdicted by these propositions is found in Lindeman and Adams (1963). Normals rated simple light flashes in a different style than they rated abstract designs, while schizophrenics did not. Their interpretation was that "the smaller number of response differences found in the schizophrenic group would seem to indicate some basic factor common to the schizophrenic process. While the data are not conclusive it is possible that the small number of significantly different responses is the result of poor discrimination or lack of attention frequency found in schizophrenic patients [p. 77]."

Two studies dealing with meaningfulness and retention, but not explicitly with polarization, showed results consistent with these propositions. Sherman (1957) discovered that normal prison subjects retained meaningful material—but not nonsense syllables—better than did neurotic subjects. Nidorf (1964) used the serial-anticipation method to test learning of nonsense-syllable lists differing in meaningfulness. Increased meaningfulness facilitated the learning of both normals and schizophrenics, but facilitated the learning of normals significantly more than it did the learning of schizophrenics. Neither of these studies suggested the mechanism responsible for these differences. If we follow the reasoning of the propositions and suggest that Mechanic's (1962) assumption "that the high-meaningful items will evoke strong differential responses at the outset [p. 594]" is at least a parallel of polarization, both of these findings would be expected.

These propositions are also consistent with the results both of studies cited in support of the pathology hypothesis and of those cited in support of the meaningfulness hypothesis. Where meaningfulness is not evaluated, these propositions predict that neurotics will polarize (Neuringer, 1961;

Wertheimer and McKinney, 1952), and schizophrenics depolarize (Bopp, 1955; Morris et al., 1960; O'Donovan, 1960). Where meaningfulness is evaluated, meaningful stimuli and/or rating scales lead to polarization (Cromwell and Caldwell, 1962; Isaacson, 1962; Mitsos, 1961; O'Donovan, 1964; Saper, 1964).

For the effective individual (or for the normal, if that is the best approximation available), these propositions predict a response whose vigor correlates with the meaningfulness of the stimuli. For the disturbed or less effective individual, predictions made from knowledge of the person's usual response style or his personality classification will be more powerful than predictions made from knowledge of the meaningfulness of the stimulus.

IMPLICATIONS FOR FURTHER RESEARCH

More sophisticated techniques of measuring stimulus meaningfulness (Jenkins, Russell, and Suci, 1958; Staats and Staats, 1959), polarization (Blum, 1964; Peabody, 1962), and their relationships (Jenkins, 1960; Koen, 1962; Wimer, 1963) are currently available. For instance, Amster (1964) reports significant effects of contextual pleasantness on polarization and recall. Ziller, Shear, and De Cencio (1964) present evidence of the effect on polarization of the interaction between the status of the rater and the instructions given him. These new techniques and, in general, the findings and more solidly developed methods of the verbal learning and verbal behavior field need to be applied to rating extremity studies. It is clear that whether polarization is considered "sick" or "healthy" has generally depended on whether the particular study focused on stimulus characteristics or subject characteristics. Focusing on the interaction between stimulus and subject characteristics may provide considerable clarity and even a reconcilation of the studies mentioned.

Some important questions in this area may only be answered by studies extending over time. The most certain test of whether a person's cognitive system is rigid or allows change is the *ex post facto* measurement of change. Such studies are now being conducted at the University of Missouri Mental Hygiene Clinic (Landfield, Nawas, and O'Donovan, 1962). Results to date (Ourth, 1963) conflict with the hypothesis that polarization is a reliable measure of pathology and suggest that polarizers may be more capable of improvement in psychotherapy than depolarizers. The rating scales used in these studies were derived from the dimensions of personality description used by the individual clients themselves before entering psychotherapy and by their assigned psychotherapists. Following the logic of the propositions, we would expect that those who find their own dimensions and those of their therapists meaningful will polarize, and will later find their psychotherapy more meaningful and hence more successful.

Landfield (1964) had clients in psychotherapy rank in order of "felt usefulness in describing others" the dimensions which they themselves and their therapists had used to describe significant persons. Clients then rated themselves on these dimensions. It was discovered that *(a)* self-ratings on clients' own dimensions were more polarized, and *(b)* ratings of dimensions ranked as more useful were more polarized.

Further research based on these propositions might investigate whether successful therapy or other positive experience leads to increased differentiation in degree of polarization to meaningful and meaningless stimuli. As an individual becomes more autonomous or self-actualizing, his responses may more consistently follow Proposition 2. He may also have a clearer, more conscious notion of what is meaningful to him. The ability to state to oneself and to others what is meaningful and to respond accordingly (as predicted by Proposition 2) may emerge as a psychological model of human freedom.

REFERENCES

ADAMS, H. E. Statistical Rigidity in Schizophrenic and Normal Groups Measured with Auditory and Visual Stimuli. *Psychological Reports,* 1960, *7,* 119–122.

ADORNO, T. W., FRENKEL-BRUNSWIK, ELSE, LEVINSON, D. J., & SANFORD, R. N. *The Authoritarian Personality. New York: Harper, 1950.*

ALLPORT, G. W. The Trend in Motivational Theory. *American Journal of Orthopsychiatry,* 1953, *23,* 107–119.

ALLPORT, G. W. *Pattern and Growth in Personality,* New York: Holt, Rinehart, & Winston, 1961.

ALLPORT, G. W., & VERNON, P. E. *A Study of Values.* Boston: Houghton, 1931.

ALLPORT, G. W., VERNON, P. E., & LINDZEY, G. *A Study of Values.* (Rev. ed.) Boston: Houghton-Mifflin, 1951.

AMSTER, HARRIET. Evaluative Judgment and Recall in Incidental Learning. *Journal of Verbal Learning and Verbal Behavior,* 1964, *3,* 466–473.

ARMITAGE, S. G., BROWN, C. R., & DENNY, M. R. Stereotypy of Response in Schizophrenics. *Journal of Clinical Psychology,* 1964, *20,* 225–230.

BARKER, E. N. *Authoritarianism of the Political Right, Center, and Left.* (Doctoral dissertation, Teacher's College, Columbia University) Ann Arbor, Mich.: University Microfilms, 1958, No. 58-2525.

BERG, I. A. Deviant Responses and Deviant People: The Formulation of the Deviation Hypothesis. *Journal of Counseling Psychology,* 1957, *4,* 154–161.

BERG, I. A. The Unimportance of Test Item Content. In B. M. Bass and I. A. Berg (Eds.), *Objective Approaches to Personality Assessment.* New York: Van Nostrand, 1959. Pp. 83–99.

BERG, I. A. Measuring Deviant Behavior by Means of Deviant Response Sets. In I.

A. Berg & B. M. Bass (Eds.), *Conformity and Deviation.* New York: Harper, 1961. Pp. 328–379.

BERG, I. A. (Chm.) Response Set in Personality Assessment. Symposium presented at Louisiana State University, 1965.

BERG, I. A., & COLLIER, J. S. Personality and Group Differences in Extreme Response Sets. *Educational and Psychological Measurement,* 1953, *13,* 164–169.

BERKSON, G., & DAVENPORT, R. K., JR. Stereotyped Movements of Mental Defectives: I. Initial Survey. *American Journal of Mental Deficiency,* 1962, *66,* 849–852.

BLOCK, J. Studies in the Phenomenology of Emotions. *Journal of Abnormal and Social Psychology,* 1957, *54,* 358–363.

BLUM, J. M. *A Moving Rating Scale and the Multiple Component Analysis of Evaluation.* (Doctoral dissertation, University of Florida) Ann Arbor, Mich.: University Microfilms, 1964, No. 65-2414.

BOPP, JOAN. *A Quantitative Semantic Analysis of Word Association in Schizophrenia.* (Doctoral dissertation, University of Illinois) Ann Arbor, Mich.: University Microfilms, 1955, No. 13,458.

BORGATTA, E. F., & GLASS, D. C. Personality Concomitants of Extreme Response Sets (ERS). *Journal of Abnormal and Social Psychology,* 1961, *55,* 213–221.

BRENNER, C. *An Elementary Textbook of Psychoanalysis.* New York: Doubleday, 1955.

BRIM, O. G., JR., & HOFF, D. B. Individual and Situational Differences in Desire for Certainty. *Journal of Abnormal and Social Psychology,* 1957, *54,* 225–229.

BROEN, W. E., JR., & WIRT, R. D. Varieties of Response Sets. *Journal of Consulting Psychology,* 1958, *22,* 237–240.

BUTLER, J. M., & HAIGH, G. V. Changes in the Relation Between Self-Concepts and Ideal-Concepts. In C. R. Rogers & Rosalind F. Dymond (Eds.), *Psychotherapy and Personality Change.* Chicago: University of Chicago Press, 1954. Pp. 55–75.

COUCH, A., & KENISTON, K. Yeasayers and Naysayers: Agreeing Response Set as a Personality Variable. *Journal of Abnormal and Social Psychology,* 1960, *60,* 151–174.

CROMWELL, R. L., & CALDWELL, D. F. A Comparison of Ratings Based on Personal Constructs of Self and Others. *Journal of Clinical Psychology,* 1962, *18,* 43–46.

CRONBACH, L. J. Further Evidence on Response Sets and Test Designs. *Educational and Psychological Measurement,* 1950, *10,* 3–31.

CROWNE, D. P., & MARLOWE, D. A New Scale of Social Desirability Independent of Psychopathology. *Journal of Consulting Psychology,* 1960, *24,* 349–354.

DAVENPORT, R. K., JR., & MENZEL, E. W., JR. Stereotyped Behavior of the Infant Chimpanzee. *Archives of General Psychiatry,* 1963, *8,* 99–104.

DOLLARD, J., & MILLER, N. E. *Personality and Psychotherapy.* New York: McGraw-Hill, 1950.

EDWARDS, A. L. *The Social Desirability Variable in Personality Assessment and Research.* New York: Dryden, 1957.

EDWARDS, A. L., & WALSH, J. A. A Factor Analysis of ? Scores. *Journal of Abnormal and Social Psychology,* 1964, *69,* 559–563.

EIDUSON, BERNICE. *Scientists: Their Psychological World.* New York: Basic Books, 1962.

FARBER, I. E. The Things People Say to Themselves. *American Psychologist,* 1963, *18,* 185–197.

FENICHEL, O. *The Psychoanalytic Theory of Neurosis.* New York: Norton, 1945.

FOREHAND, G. A. Relationships Among Response Sets and Cognitive Behaviors. *Educational and Psychological Measurement,* 1962, *22,* 287–302.

FRENKEL-BRUNSWIK, ELSE. Intolerance Toward Ambiguity as an Emotional and Perceptual Personality Variable. *Journal of Personality,* 1949, *18,* 108–143.

GUILFORD, J. P. The Validation of an "Indecision" Score for Predicting Proficiency of Foremen. *Journal of Applied Psychology,* 1954, *38,* 224–226.

GULLIKSEN, H. *Theory of Mental Tests.* New York: Wiley, 1950.

HARLOW, H. F., & ZIMMERMAN, R. R. Affectional Responses in the Infant Monkey. *Science,* 1959, *130,* 421–231.

HASTORF, A. H., RICHARDSON, S. A., & DORNBUSCH, S. M. The Problem of Relevance in the Study of Person Perception. In R. Tagiuri & L. Petrullo (Eds.), *Person Perception and Interpersonal Behavior.* Palo Alto: Stanford University Press, 1958. Pp. 54–62.

HAVRON, M. D., & COFER, C. N. On the Learning of Material Congruent and Incongruent with Attitudes. *Journal of Social Psychology,* 1957, *46,* 91–98.

HENMON, V. A. The Relation of the Time of a Judgment to its Accuracy. *Psychological Review,* 1911, *18,* 186–201.

HOVLAND, C. I., & SHERIF, M. Judgmental Phenomena and Scales of Attitude Measurement: Item Displacement in Thurstone Scales. *Journal of Abnormal and Social Psychology,* 1952, *47,* 822–832.

HULL, C. L. *Principles of Behavior.* New York: Appleton-Century-Crofts, 1943.

HULL, C. L. *A Behavior System.* New Haven: Yale University Press, 1952.

HUNTER, M., SCHOOLER, C., & SPOHN, H. E. The Measurement of Characteristic Patterns of Ward Behavior in Chronic Schizophrenics. *Journal of Consulting Psychology,* 1962, *26,* 69–73.

ISAACSON, G. A Comparative Study of the Meaningfulness of Personal and Cultural Constructs. Unpublished master's thesis, University of Missouri, 1962.

JACKSON, D. N., & MESSICK, S. Response Styles and the Assessment of Psychopathology. In S. Messick & J. Ross (Eds.), *Measurement in Personality and Cognition.* New York: Wiley, 1962. Pp. 129–155.

JENKINS, J. J. Degree of Polarization and Scores on the Principal Factors for Concepts in the Semantic Atlas. *American Journal of Psychology,* 1960, *73,* 274–279.

JENKINS, J. J., RUSSELL, W. A., & SUCI, G. J. Studies in the Role of Language in Behavior. Technical Report No. 20, 1958, University of Minnesota.

JOHNSON, W. *People in Quandaries.* New York: Harper, 1946.

JOHNSTON, H. T. *An Empirical Study of the Value Orientations of Psychologists.* (Doctoral dissertation, University of Missouri) Ann Arbor, Mich.: University Microfilms, 1964, No. 64–13,293.

KANUNGO, R., & LAMBERT, W. E. Effects of Variations in Amount of Verbal Repetition on Meaning and Paired-Associate Learning. *Journal of Verbal Learning and Verbal Behavior,* 1964, *3,* 358–361.

KELLY, G. A. *The Psychology of Personal Constructs.* New York: Norton, 1955.

KELLY, G. A. Man's Construction of His Alternatives. In G. Lindzey (Ed.), *Assessment of Human Motives*. New York: Rinehart, 1958. Pp. 33–64.

KOCH, HELEN L. The Influence of Some Affective Factors Upon Recall. *Journal of General Psychology*, 1930, *4*, 171–189.

KOEN, F. Polarization, *m*, and Emotionality in Words. *Journal of Verbal Learning and Verbal Behavior*, 1962, *1*, 183–187.

LANDFIELD, A. W. Self Conception and Meaningfulness as Related to own Versus Therapists's Personal Construct Dimensions. Unpublished manuscript, University of Missouri, 1964.

LANDFIELD, A. W., NAWAS, M. M., & O'DONOVAN, D. Improvement Ratings by External Judges and Psychotherapists. *Psychological Reports*, 1962, *11*, 747–748.

LEWIS, N. A., & TAYLOR, JANET A. Anxiety and Extreme Response Preferences. *Educational and Psychological Measurement*, 1955, *15*, 111–116.

LINDEMAN, H. H., & ADAMS, H. E. Deviant Responses to Ambiguous Visual Stimulus Patterns. *Psychological Record*, 1963, *13*, 73–77.

LORGE, I. Gen-like: Halo or Reality? *Psychological Bulletin*, 1937, *34*, 545–546. (Abstract)

LUCHINS, A. S. *Rigidity of Behavior*. Eugene: University of Oregon Press, 1959.

MANIS, M. The Interpretation of Opinion Statements as a Function of Recipient Attitude. *Journal of Abnormal and Social Psychology*, 1960, *60*, 340–344.

MARTIN, J. Acquiescence—Measurement and Theory. *The British Journal of Social and Clinical Psychology*, 1964, *3*, 216–225.

MASON, W. A., & GREEN, P. C. The Effects of Social Restriction on the Behavior of Rhesus Monkeys: IV. Responses to a Novel Environment and to an Alien Species. *Journal of Comparative and Physiological Psychology*, 1962, *55*, 363–368.

MᶜGEE, R. K. Response Style as a Personality Variable: By What Criterion? *Psychological Bulletin*, 1962, *59*, 284–295.

MᶜGEE, R. K. Response Set in Relation to Personality: An Orientation. Contribution to I. A. Berg (Chm.), Response Set in Personality Assessment. Symposium presented at Louisiana State University, 1965.

MECHANIC, A. The Distribution of Recalled Items in Simultaneous Intentional and Incidental Learning. *Journal of Experimental Psychology*, 1962, *63*, 593–600.

MENZEL, E. W., JR., DAVENPORT, R. K., JR., & ROGERS, C. M. Effects of Environmental Restriction Upon the Chimpanzee's Responsiveness in Novel Situations. *Journal of Comparative and Physiological Psychology*, 1963, *56*, 329–334.

MITSOS, S. B. Personal Constructs and the Semantic Differential. *Journal of Abnormal and Social Psychology*, 1961, *62*, 433–434.

MOGAR, R. E. Three Versions of the F Scale and Performance on the Semantic Differential. *Journal of Abnormal and Social Psychology*, 1960, *60*, 262–265.

MORRIS, C. W. Foundations of the Theory of Signs. *International Encyclopedia of Unified Science, 1(2)*. Chicago: *University of Chicago Press, 1938*.

MORRIS, C. W. *Signs, Language, and Behavior*. New York: Prentice-Hall, 1946.

MORRIS, C. W. *Varieties of Human Value*. Chicago: University of Chicago Press, 1956.

MORRIS, C., EIDUSON, BERNICE, & O'DONOVAN, D. Values in Psychiatric Patients. *Behavioral Science,* 1960, *5,* 297–312.

NEURINGER, C. Dichotomous Evaluations in Suicidal Individuals. *Journal of Consulting Psychology,* 1961, *25,* 445–449.

NIDORF, L. J. The Role of Meaningfulness in the Serial Learning of Schizophrenics. *Journal of Clinical Psychology,* 1964, *20* 92.

NOBLE, C. E. Emotionality (*e*) and Meaningfulness (*m*). *Psychological Reports,* 1958, *4,* 16.

O'DONOVAN, D. The Value of Valuing. In F. McKinney (Chm.), Teaching Values. Symposium presented at American Psychological Association, Chicago, September 1960.

O'DONOVAN, D. Commitment with Openness. In S. Cook (Ed.), *Research Plans in the Fields of Religion, Morality, and Values.* New York: Religious Education Association, 1962. Pp. 67–72.

O'DONOVAN, D. Questions That Can Be Answered. In H. D. Kimmel (Chm.), Awareness as a Factor in Verbal Operant Conditioning. Symposium presented at Southeastern Psychological Association, Miami Beach, April 1963.

O'DONOVAN, D. Polarization and Meaningfulness in 6300 Value Judgments. Unpublished manuscript, University of Missouri, 1964.

O'DONOVAN, D., MORRIS, C., & EIDUSON, BERNICE. One Way of Life in Relation to Psychological Health. *American Psychologist,* 1959, *14,* 365. (Abstract)

ORNE, M. T. On the Social Psychology of the Psychological Experiment: With Particular Reference to Demand Characteristics and Their Implications. *American Psychologist,* 1962, *17,* 776–783.

OSGOOD, C. E., SUCI, G. J., & TANNENBAUM, P. H. *The Measurement of Meaning.* Urbana: University of Illinois Press, 1957.

OURTH, L. L. *The Relationship of Similarity in Therapist-Client Pairs to Client's Stay and Improvement in Psychotherapy.* (Doctoral dissertation, University of Missouri) Ann Arbor, Mich.: University Microfilms, 1963, No. 64–1719.

PAINE, C. B. A Tentative Model of Creativity. Unpublished Master's Thesis, University of Missouri, 1964.

PAINTING, D. H. The Performance of Psychopathic Individuals Under Conditions of Positive and Negative Partial Reinforcement. *Journal of Abnormal and Social Psychology.* 1961, *62,* 352–355.

PEABODY, D. Two Components in Bipolar Scales: Direction and Extremeness. *Psychological Review,* 1962, *69,* 65–73.

PEABODY, D. Models for Estimating Content and Set Components in Attitude and Personality Scales. *Educational and Psychological Measurement,* 1964, *24,* 255–269.

PEABODY, D. Authoritarianism Scales and Response Set. Unpublished manuscript, Swarthmore College, 1965.

PEAK, HELEN, MUNEY, BARBARA, & CLAY, MARGARET. Opposites Structures, Defenses, and Attitudes. *Psychological Monographs,* 1960, *74* (8, Whole No. 495).

PETTIGREW, T. F., ALLPORT, G. W., & BARNETT, E. O. Binocular Resolution and Perception of Race in South Africa. *British Journal of Psychology,* 1958, *49,* 265–278.

POSTMAN, L., BRUNER, J. S., & MCGINNIES, E. Personal Values as Selective Factors in Perception. *Journal of Abnormal and Social Psychology,* 1948, *43,* 142–154.

POSTMAN, L., & MURPHY, G. The Factor of Attitude in Associative Memory. *Journal of Experimental Psychology,* 1943, *33,* 228-238.

POSTMAN, L., & ZIMMERMAN, C. Intensity of Attitude as a Determinant of Decision Time. *American Journal of Psychology,* 1945, *58,* 510-518.

RAPAPORT, D. *Emotions and Memory.* Baltimore: Williams & Wilkins, 1942.

REISMAN, J. M. Motivational Differences Between Process and Reactive Schizophrenics. *Journal of Personality,* 1960, *28,* 12-25.

RIBBLE, MARGARET A. *The Rights of Infants.* New York: Columbia University Press, 1943.

RIECKEN, H. W. A Program for Research on Experiments in Social Psychology. In N. F. Washburne (Ed.), *Decisions, Values and Groups.* Vol. 2. New York: Pergamon Press, 1962, Pp. 25-41.

RODNICK, E., & GARMEZY, N. An Experimental Approach to the Study of Motivation in Schizophrenia. In M. B. Jones (Ed.), *Nebraska Symposium on Motivation: 1957.* Lincoln: University of Nebraska Press, 1957. Pp. 109-184.

ROKEACH, M. *The Open and Closed Mind.* New York: Basic Books, 1960.

RORER, L. G. The Great Response-Style Myth. *Psychological Bulletin,* 1965, *63,* 129-156.

RORER, L. G., & GOLDBERG, L. R. Acquiescence in the MMPI? *Educational and Psychological Measurement,* in press.

RUBIN-RABSON, G. Correlates of the Non-Committal Test-Item Response. *Journal of Clinical Psychology,* 1954, *10,* 93-95.

RUNDQUIST, E. A. Response Sets: A Note on Consistency in Taking Extreme Positions. *Educational and Psychological Measurement,* 1950, *10,* 97-99.

SAMELSON, F. Agreement Set and Anticontent Attitudes in the F Scale. *Journal of Abnormal and Social Psychology,* 1964, *68,* 338-342.

SAPER, M. B. Involvement in Reading a Case History. Unpublished master's thesis, University of Missouri, 1964.

SCHUTZ, R. E., & FOSTER, R. J. A Factor Analytic Study of Acquiescent and Extreme Response Set. *Educational and Psychological Measurement,* 1963, *23,* 435-447.

SECHREST, L., & JACKSON, D. N. The Generality of Deviant Response Tendencies. *Journal of Consulting Psychology,* 1962, *26,* 395-401.

SECHREST, L., & JACKSON, D. N. Deviant Response Tendencies: Their Measurement and Interpretation. *Educational and Psychological Measurement,* 1963, *23,* 33-53.

SHERIF, M., & HOVLAND, C. I. *Social Judgment: Assimilation and Contrast Effects in Communication and Attitude Change.* New Haven: Yale University Press, 1961.

SHERMAN, L. J. Retention in Psychopathic, Neurotic and Normal Subjects. *Journal of Personality,* 1957, *25,* 721-729.

SLAMECKA, N. J. Choice Reaction-Time as a Function of Meaningful Similarity. *American Journal of Psychology,* 1963, *76,* 274-280.

SMITH, PATRICIA, & KENDALL, L. M. Retranslation of Expectations: An Approach to the Construction of Unambiguous Anchors for Rating Scales. *Journal of Applied Psychology,* 1963, *47,* 149-155.

SOUEIF, M. I. Extreme Response Sets as a Measure of Intolerance of Ambiguity. *British Journal of Psychology.* 1958, *49,* 329-334.

SPENCE, JANET T. Learning Theory and Personality. In J. M. Wepman & R. W. Heine (Eds.), *Concepts of Personality.* Chicago: Aldine, 1963, Pp. 3-30.

SPENCE, K. W. *Behavior Theory and Learning.* Englewood Cliffs, N. J.: Prentice-Hall, 1960.

STAATS, A. W., & STAATS, CAROLYN K. Meaning and *m:* Correlated but Separate. *Psychological Review,* 1959, *66,* 136–144.

TAJFEL, H. The Anchoring Effects of Value in a Scale of Judgments. *British Journal of Psychology,* 1959, *50,* 294–304.

TAJFEL, H., & CAWASJEE, S. D. Value and the Accentuation of Judged Differences: A Confirmation. *Journal of Abnormal and Social Psychology,* 1959, *59,* 436–39.

TAJFEL, H., & WILKES, A. L. Salience of Attributes and Commitment to Extreme Judgments in the Perception of People. *British Journal of Social and Clinical Psychology,* 1964, *3,* 40–49.

TAYLOR, JANET A., & SPENCE, K. W. The Relationship of Anxiety Level to Performance in Serial Learning. *Journal of Experimental Psychology,* 1952, *44,* 61–64.

THORNDIKE, E. L. *The Psychology of Wants, Interests, and Attitudes.* New York: Appleton-Century, 1935.

UNDERWOOD, B. J., & SCHULZ, R. W. *Meaningfulness and Verbal Learning.* New York: Lippincott, 1960.

VAUGHAN, G. M., & MANGAN, G. L. Conformity to Group Pressure in Relation to the Value of the Task Material. *Journal of Abnormal and Social Psychology,* 1963, *66,* 179–183.

WERTHEIMER, RITA, & MCKINNEY, F. A Case History Blank as a Projective Technique. *Journal of Consulting Psychology,* 1952, *16,* 49–60.

WIMER, CYNTHIA. An Analysis of Semantic Stimulus Factors in Paired-Associate Learning. *Journal of Verbal Learning and Verbal Behavior,* 1963, *1,* 397–407.

YERKES, R. M., & DODSON, J. D. The Relation of Strength of Stimulus to Rapidity of Habit-Formation. *Journal of Comparative Neurology,* 1908, *18,* 459–482.

ZAX, M., COWEN, E. L., & PETER, MARY. A Comparative Study of Novice Nuns and College Females Using the Response Set Approach. *Journal of Abnormal and Social Psychology,* 1963, *66,* 369–375.

ZAX, M., GARDINER, D. H., & LOWY, D. G. Extreme Response Tendency as a Function of Emotional Adjustment. *Journal of Abnormal and Social Psychology,* 1964, *69,* 654–657.

ZAX, M., LOISELLE, R. H., & KARRAS, A. Stimulus Characteristics of Rorschach Ink Blots as Perceived by a Schizophrenic Sample. *Journal of Projective Techniques,* 1960, *24,* 439–443.

ZILLER, R. C., SHEAR, H. J., & DECENCIO, D. A. A Professional Response Set—Dogmatism. *Journal of Clinical Psychology,* 1964, *20,* 229–303.

ZLOTOWSKI, M., & BAKAN, P. Behavioral Variability of Process and Reactive Schizophrenics in a Binary Guessing Task. *Journal of Abnormal and Social Psychology,* 1963, *66,* 185–187.

ZUCKERMAN, M., NORTON, J., & SPRAGUE, D. S. Acquiescence and Extreme Sets and Their Role in Tests of Authoritarianism and Parental Attitudes. *Psychiatric Research Reports,* 1958, No. 10, 28–45.

ZUCKERMAN, M., OPPENHEIMER, CYNTHIA, & GERSHOWITZ, D. Acquiescence and Extreme Response Sets of Actors and Teachers. *Psychological Reports,* 1965, *16,* 168–170.

4

ON PSYCHOLOGICAL SIMILARITY[1]
MICHAEL A. WALLACH

Wallach presents a stimulating discussion of the question of how "similarity" is determined. His pursuit of the issues gives us some sharp insights into the assumptions about, and the character of, several familiar concepts in psychology. As Wallach speaks of similarity, the notions of transfer and of stimulus generalization are given incisive analysis. He leads us to consider the value of a position that psychological similarity is the product of an organism bisecting a domain of events into a set that exemplifies a certain property and a set that does not. After this dichotomization has taken place, behavior will be transferred to other events that are representative of one end of the dichotomy.

Wallach does not approach the more radical position suggested in the Overview—that is, that all learning must take place within the context of dichotomous constructs; but his discussion of relevant research indicates the utility of this approach. In any case, the view that psychological functioning constantly involves dichotomous constructs is attractive.

* * *

When Hume spoke of composite ideas, such as *table* or *chair,* as being compounded from simple ideas, such as *brown* or *hard,* he found himself facing the question of how one simple idea could resemble a second one more than a third one. He could handle the question of similarity between

Reprinted from Psychological Review, *1958, 65, 103-116, by permission of the author and the American Psychological Association.*

[1] The writer is greatly indebted to Jerome S. Bruner for invaluable encouragement and aid in the preparation of this paper. Thanks are also due Albert J. Caron and George Mandler for critical readings of the manuscript. Preliminary research for this paper was done while the writer held a Westengard Travelling Fellowship from Harvard University to the Department of Psychology, University of Cambridge, England.

composite ideas easily enough; the degree of similarity of two composite ideas depended on the number of simple ideas they had in common. But what about similarity between simple ideas themselves? What does it mean to say blue is more similar to green than to red? Hume could not answer this beyond suggesting that similarity between simple ideas is somehow given to us directly—a capitulation that could never satisfy a British empiricist (1; 11, pp. 585–689).

Let us take Hume's predicament as our starting point. Whence does his problem arise? Its origin lies in two omissions: a failure to note the full range of attributes in terms of which objects and events can be grouped and a failure to separate the question of *potential* similarity from that of *psychological* similarity. Consider the first matter. What are the attributes in terms of which objects and events can be grouped or separated? Hume limited himself here—for a reason noted below—to considering simple sensory attributes displayed by the object itself—for example, the brownness or hardness of a table. But a table can be defined in terms of many more attributes than these. To mention but a few possiblities, it can be defined in terms of use (the things done upon it), of location (the places where it is found), or of construction (how it is built). Such attributes as these are no less reducible to a sensory basis than the ones mentioned by Hume, and they suggest a possible answer to Hume's question. We may say green seems more similar to blue than to red because there indeed *are* more attribute-values that green and blue but not red have in common, while there are fewer that green and red but not blue have in common. Hume may, that is to say, be able to retain his common attribute view of similarity by accepting a wider definition of the term "attribute." Thus, for instance, green and blue—but not red—have in common the attribute-value of being colors of grass in the country, colors of water and hence cool colors, summer landscape colors, and so on.

But we have not fully answered the question yet. Some people may *not* say that green and blue are more similar than green and red. The attributive basis for judgment of similarity may be present and yet the judgment not be made; and, on the other hand, an attributive basis for such a judgment may be lacking and yet the items may be judged similar. There would seem to be a difference, then, between potential similarity and psychological similarity. Part of Hume's difficulty seems to arise from equating the two. This leads him to fill the perceiver's head with similacral (i.e., photographic) representations of environmental attribute-values, and hence to ignore the possibility that the observer may perform a selecting and ignoring function with regard to attribute-values which are environmentally available. Indeed, it is this view that leads him to the first omission we noted—his failure to specify the full range of environmental attributes. For insofar as one assumes the organism to register in similacral fashion what the environment offers, one must conceive of that environment as relatively meager in its offerings, or else the organism would be swamped with information. If, however, one conceives of the organism as selecting some attributes by which to compare items and ignoring other attributes, then it becomes reasonable to suggest a difference between potential and psychological similarity. Potential similarity may well be most usefully measured in terms of the number of common environmental features that two objects or events are found to display—using the broad definition of attribute noted above, and determining the commonalities by reliable means.[2]

This definition has its basis in the old view of similarity as common stimulus elements, to be sure—but is is very different from that view, since the common-stimulus-elements approach used the narrow definition of attribute for which we criticized Hume, and that view was thought to apply to psychological similarity, which we shall see is often not the case. Establishment of the degree of potential similarity between two things provides us with an important baseline: It lets us validate or contravalidate individual reports of similarity. A person may, for instance, report that two problems are similar in the sense that the same solution is thought to be applicable to both; to ask whether this feeling of similarity is valid is to ask whether the same solution is in fact applicable to both problems; are they potentially similar in the sense of having this property in common? Or a person may report that two objects are similar in the sense that both are thought usable for driving a nail into a board. To validate or contravalidate this impression of similarity, we determine whether both objects can in fact be used in this way.

Broadening the definition of "attribute" and recognizing that potential and psychological similarity are distinct but related issues, suggest that the question of psychological similarity may lie at the basis of diverse kinds of psychological research on cognition that have hitherto usually been considered apart from each other—ranging from studies on stimulus generalization to studies on learning and thinking. We submit it may be fruitful to inquire how some of this research bears on the issues we have raised, and this for two reasons. First of all, we have not yet examined the possible ways in which psychological similarity might be defined, although we have suggested what seems to us a tenable definition for potential similarity. Insofar as this research really bears on psychological similarity, it may help us weigh alternative definitions of the term. Secondly, such

[2]The problem of just what means to use and how, has been treated at length by Brunswik (3) in his discussion of ecological validity. The means are, basically, responses of a sample of judges—and they may be responses as varied as reading a light meter or judging a painting's colors to be warm or cool. The validation, then, is consensual in nature.

exploration of definitions may well have experimental implications for further research in these diverse areas.

SOME DEFINITIONS OF PSYCHOLOGICAL SIMILARITY

One may suggest at least four ways of defining psychological similarity. The first derives from Hume's approach. Hume, in equating potential and psychological similarity, supposes that if common properties are present in the environment, they will be perceived by the person. Hence, impressions of similarity can be directly controlled by varying the environment's potential similarity in the sense of the common values of attributes it displays. The selecting and ignoring capacities of the organism are neglected, and psychological similarity is defined in terms of *common environmental properties*. An alternative approach is to recognize the organism's selective functions, and suggest that recognition of common environmental properties depends upon making a common response to instances that share this attribute-value. The attribute-value may be environmentally present in two items and yet the person may not offer a common response to them; or the attribute-value may be absent and yet a common response be made. There is not necessarily a direct relation between psychological and potential similarity. Psychological similarity here, then, is defined in terms of *common responses*. Yet another possible approach is to suggest there are neural traces laid down along various dimensions when a stimulus impinges, and psychological similarity depends on how far a new stimulus is from the old stimulus on such a dimension—the view of *primary stimulation gradients*.

A fourth view may also be proposed. It is related, to be sure, to the view of common responses, but seeks to separate the process of recognizing similarity from making a common response. Yet this fourth approach is not that of stimulation gradients, for it does not assume that there is necessarily an inverse relationship between degree of recognized similarity and distance of new from old stimuli along some dimension. The position may be put somewhat as follows. Although a common response may be forthcoming to signal the recognition of similarity when two events occur, this response is itself a rather trivial matter (it may be made with the big toe as well as with the vocal cords, and need not be of fixed character), and its being made depends on the prior learning of a rule for categorizing events as equivalent. This rule specifies what property (attribute-value) or properties must be conjointly found in order to assign events to the same class, and also tells us the nature of the contrast being made—the relevant alternative class whose members are to be judged non-exemplars of the class of interest.[3] We construct this contrast class in such ways as the

[3]See Bruner, Goodnow, and Austin (2), p. 38; and Kelly (13), pp. 303-305.

following. *(a)* By implication, from the degree of complexity of the class of interest; since the more complex that class is, the more likely we are to consider small deviations from it as the only relevant alternative class or classes, and to totally neglect large deviations.[4] Thus for instance, we are likely to contrast cocker spaniels with setters or poodles and not with all other animals, whereas "all other animals" would be a relevant contrast class if we were interested in dogs rather than cocker spaniels. *(b)* By experience with all the instances, positive and negative, to which we are exposed, for these establish the domain of material relevant to us. Construction of a contrast class in turn suggests which properties we may best use for discriminating positive from relevant negative instances. For example, while the attribute of size will not let us discriminate dogs from all other animals, it does suffice to separate setters from cocker spaniels.

The classification rule that we learn, then, has two aspects: it tells us on what basis we are to group two events in one class and also tells us the range of other events with which we are contrasting positive instances of the class of interest—it tells us what negative instances are relevant. The rule serves to delimit a particular domain of events, and to draw a *contrast* between two subsets within that domain: positive and negative instances of the class in question. This rule stipulates that certain properties must be found compresent, i.e., together, in order to place an instance in a given class. Such a rule for class-inclusion becomes harder to attain, the greater the number of properties which the rule requires to be compresent before inclusion in the given class is warranted. This is the case because the larger the number of properties whose compresence is required in this way for class-inclusion, the greater is the number of properties which are found compresent in at least some of the relevant negative instances as well as in all positive instances of the class in question, thus making it more difficult to locate the difference between positive and negative instances.

In brief, then, this fourth proposal suggests that recognition of similarity depends on applying a rule which leads one to *assign items to a common category*. There is much more to similarity than the response of making this assignment. For prior to that, one must learn the rule which guides the response.[5]

---

[4]The "implication" in question here is not one of logical necessity, but rather a strategy that people tend to use—and indeed a valuable one—for determining the level of classifi-category discriminations to make in particular situations.

[5]If one prefers to argue that such a rule is simply a complex response, it is incumbent upon one to specify the responses constituting that rule. The suggestion often made at this juncture is that the rule is no more than the verbal responses which express it. But in animal learning studies discussed later—where one cannot, therefore, say the rule is nothing more than verbal responses—we shall note that the common responses which are present do not in fact constitute the basis of the rule that is learned.

Each of these ways of defining psychological similarity has much to be said in its favor, but no one of them seems able to account for all the evidence. Our aim in the following pages is to suggest some possible limitations which various of these views face, and to sketch the possible fruitfulness of exploring more fully the one of these approaches that defines psychological similarity in terms of assigning events to a common category.

If, as we have suggested, diverse areas of psychological research all concern psychological similarity, one is led to ask whether these areas may be using the same kind of procedure, since a common concern sometimes intimates a common procedure of inquiry. This seems indeed to be the case here, and the procedure in question is that of transfer—the influence of experience in one situation on the handling of a subsequent situation. Insofar as something learned in a first situation will aid performance in a second one, then the subject will show positive transfer if he recognizes the two situations to be similar; while insofar as something learned in that first situation will hinder performance in the second, then he will show negative transfer if he recognizes the two situations as similar. Transferability of learning thus provides a set of operations for determining whether recognition of similarity occurred. As we turn to various experiments now, in further considering the definitions of psychological similarity that we have reviewed, we shall find that all of them in effect use this transferability procedure.

COMMON ENVIRONMENTAL PROPERTIES

Since this is, perhaps, the most familiar and earliest view as to the nature of psychological similarity, we need not dwell on the many kinds of evidence from which it arose—for instance, motor learning studies, of which the work by Lewis, McAllister, and Adams (20, 21) provides a recent example. Commonality of the environmental properties is established by the identity of measurement readings of the centimeter-grams-seconds variety in the two situations being compared (call them Original Learning, OL, and Transfer Learning, TL). The evidence indicates that frequently, to be sure, transferability of learning, and hence psychological similarity, is related to presence of common environmental properties in these two situations. But there are, on the other hand, cases where presentation of common properties in OL and TL does not result in psychological similarity of the two and hence in greater transfer.

Consider, for instance, a study by Schwarz (27). In the OL task, the subject learned to attach a certain response to a certain stimulus. In the TL task, he had to learn to link a different response to that old stimulus. If transfer here depends on common environmental properties, one would expect associative interference—that is, the old stimulus should tend to elicit the old response; it should be transferred to the TL task despite its inappropriateness there. Actually, such associative interference occurred only if the subject was forced to pay attention to something other than this particular task; if allowed to attend to this task, the old response was not transferred despite identity of stimulus. When the subject was "paying attention" he was grouping environmental events differently than when he was "not paying attention." When not paying attention, stimulus identity was allowed to become the attributive basis for classification; but when paying attention, the temporal difference between "stimulus in the OL task" and "stimulus in the TL task" was effective in directing the subject to assign the OL and TL stimuli to different classes based on this temporal distinction, even though they were physically identical. Assigning them to different classes meant that negative transfer was avoided.

Or consider a study by Ellis (4) in which college students learned finger mazes. Three different mazes were used in all, Maze 3 consisting of Mazes 1 and 2 linked together. One group learned Mazes 1 and 3, another learned Mazes 2 and 3, and a third learned Maze 3 alone. Whereas an indentical-stimulus-elements approach would predict marked positive transfer for the first two groups in their learning of Maze 3, in actuality those two groups were not significantly better in their learning of Maze 3 than the group learning that maze *de novo*. Objectively identical stimulus elements did not *per se* lead to recognition of similarity.

Common environmental attributes, then, do not seem to be an infallible indicator of psychological similarity. Such similarity may, under these conditions, be present for the person—but then again it may not.

COMMON RESPONSES

It was perhaps the Kantian revolution in philosophy that first called into question Hume's conception of the organism as a mirror of environmental stimulation, and suggested instead that the organism is a filterer and arranger of environmental events. The "mentalism" of Kant's approach banned it from having direct repercussions in American psychology until it was realized that considering the organism an active mediator does not require descent into its depths, but rather can be achieved by noting how the organism responds to its environment. One need not go beyond the relation between environmental stimuli and a person's responses. If, according to this view, a person was found to respond the same way to two objectively different situations, then those two situations were psychologically similar for him. And if, on the other hand, a person responded differently despite repetition of the same situation (common environmental properties), then no such psychological similarity obtained. Such an approach constituted a tremendous advance. The Humian assumption of man as capable merely of similacral representations of his environment was overcome, and in its place the capacities of the organism to select, ignore, and emphasize environmental attributes were recognized. The exciting effects of this idea can be seen, for example, in the early work by Shipley (28, 29). In one experiment, linking an eyewink response to both light and shock, where shock elicited finger withdrawal, resulted in light becoming adequate to elicit finger withdrawal too. The common response of winking made to both light and shock indicated their psychological similarity for the subject. Whereas we would say this response was a signal of this similarity, proponents of the common response view would hold that this response itself constitutes that similarity. The implications of this kind of approach are ably developed by Osgood (25), among others, and its applicability to many questions of psychological similarity is clear.

The common-response view leaves us, however, with some uneasiness. For one thing, those who maintain it sometimes seem to rely on the magical efficacy of the term *response* to provide an aura of explanation where none really exists. The premise of the approach is that transfer will occur, and hence two events will seem similar, to the extent to which the organism makes the same response to both. But from here on the going becomes less simple. Paradoxically enough, the insufficiency of this premise seems to be tacitly recognized, for the full view consists of an attempt to defend the premise's lacks. Since the hypothesized common response that supposedly mediates the transfer sometimes cannot be located even though transfer is found, one meets the rationalization that sometimes the common response linked to disparate stimuli is not observable, but in all such cases these unobservable responses are supposed to have developed as fractional anticipations of observable ones. This is an empty-organism theory with a new twist. The organism gets filled eventually, but only with fractions of things that were overt responses once.

It seems relevant to remember that much of the impetus behind this view derives not from considerations of scientific adequacy as such, but rather from the cultural milieu of an earlier behaviorism in which the model of the organism as capable of transforming representations of its environment was still held in disrepute, as "mentalistic." The common response theory hence sought to make this model acceptable to the scientific community by framing it in the language of responses. This end has been accomplished long since, however, so it would perhaps be advisable now to restrict more carefully use of the term "response" to its usual meaning: muscular and glandular reactions. We would note that the restraints imposed by the nature of muscles and glands imply that behavior must be more limited and have fewer dimensions about it than what goes on inside the organism.[6] Why, then, limit on *a priori* grounds one's conception of what goes on in the organism to fractions of behavior? It does not make constructs more scientific to frame them in the same terms as observables. Rather, the reason we postulate constructs is that the relations among observables are extremely complex, and it often proves necessary to invest our constructs with properties different from those of behavior in order the better to predict that very behavior. The interests of explanation are not served simply by filling the organism with analogues of behavior. Hospers (9) and other philosophers have well pointed out that such reduction to the familiar is not what we really mean by scientific explanation.

But were our uneasiness over the common-response approach to stem only from general considerations such as these, it might well be dismissed. Dismissal becomes more difficult, however, when one notes the gradual accumulation of experimental evidence that questions the sufficiency of response identity for mediating transfer of learning. Consider, for instance, a recent study by Bruner, Mandler, O'Dowd, and Wallach.[7] Rats were overtrained to run left-right-left-right at successive choice points of a linear maze, and then were faced with the task of learning to run right-left-right-left in the same maze. The object was to find whether there was positive transfer from learning the first turn sequence to learning its mirror-image reversal.

According to the response-mediation approach, transfer is said to depend on identity of response, and the greatest identity of response between OL and TL here is the single-alternation weaving motion whereby the rat alternates from one side to the other at successive choice points. The faster a rat runs from start box to goal box, the more of a weaving motion he learns. Insofar, then, as transfer depends on the identity of a weaving-alternation response in OL and TL, rats running faster should show more positive transfer than rats running more slowly. The results do not support this prediction. There was no correlation between speed of running during OL and degree of positive transfer on TL, within any of the groups run. Furthermore, considering differences in running speed between groups—differences that were created by varying

[6]One way to indicate this difference between behavior and what goes on inside the organism, is in combinatorial terms: there are more elements that can be combined, and hence a greater variety of possible outcomes, at the neuron level, than at the level of muscle and glands.

[7]Bruner, J. S., Mandler, Jean M., O'Dowd, D., & Wallach, M. A. "The role of overlearning and drive level in reversal learning." To be published.

hunger conditions—groups whose drive conditions resulted in their running slowly during either OL or TL or both showed positive transfer, while the group whose drive conditions resulted in its running fast during both OL and TL showed no transfer. Apparently, therefore, something other than a common response of weaving single alternation causes the transfer in the present experiment.

Or take North's finding (23, 24) that the performance of rats on discrimination reversals was no better when the rat was made to correct overtly his mistakes than when mistakes were left uncorrected. It was expected that reversal learning would be better in the former condition, since it permitted a correct response to occur after a wrong choice, and this correct response was supposed to become associated to the present maze stimuli, and hence be evoked by these stimuli on the next trial, thereby mediating a full-fledged overt correct response. Identity of response thus was expected to mediate reversal learning. Much positive transfer in the learning of successive reversals occurred, but it was not due to response mediation. It occurred, rather, only when there was a sufficient amount of overtraining on each reversal—a result also obtained in the study on single alternation cited above. Apparently, for the animal to classify initial and later situations in terms of the more abstract property which they in fact have in common, he must be given enough practice on the former situation so that its more concrete properties no longer require all his attention. The abstract property in question was single alternation in the case of the first study noted; reversal of position reponse on encountering an error, in the case of the second study. The concrete properties involved were particular sorts of muscular kinesthesis that occur in relation to particular olfactory and visual cues from various parts of the maze.

To be sure, insofar as one broadens the definition of "response" to include anything going on inside the organism, as some theorists such as Osgood (25) and Mandler (22) advise, evidence of the above sorts does not run counter to the common-response view. But broadening the definition in this way would seem more to cloud than to clarify the issues. There are grounds, then, for suggesting that presence or absence of common responses is not an infallible indication of presence or absence of psychological similarity, although there are certainly cases where such responses do serve in this manner.

PRIMARY STIMULATION GRADIENTS

Many studies have been done in support of a view of psychological similarity which may be stated somewhat as follows. When a stimulus impinges on a receptor and becomes associated to a response, a neural gradient is laid down such that other stimuli will also elicit this response but to lesser degree, response elicitability decreasing with increasing distance of the new stimulus from the training stimulus along some dimension of stimulus differences—for instance, intensity or pitch of tones. The dimension of primary stimulus generalization need not be innate, as was assumed by those proponents of this approach who were most directly in the Pavlovian tradition, like Hull (10); but rather may be the product of learned differentiation (i.e., discrimination training)—a coming into closer contact with stimulus differences—as in the manner suggested by Gibson and Gibson (5). But however the dimensions are thought to arise, the position in question assumes the shape of the gradient laid down upon them to fall off on either side of the point of stimulation along these dimensions; and, if training and test stimuli are presented at discriminably separate points along a dimension which the individual has learned to discriminate, or can innately discriminate, then generalization is expected to occur along that dimension.

These ideas of a normal distribution of intensity of excitation about a point of stimulation, and the automatic fashion in which generalization is expected to occur between discriminable points on any discriminable dimension when these points are stimulated in succession, were derived from an earlier era of physiological research in which spatial representations of sensory qualities in the cortex were a prime concern—we may see it in such apparently opposed currents of thought as Pavlov (26) on the one hand, and Köhler (19) on the other. And some work, to be sure, does seem best interpretable in terms of such ideas (e.g., Guttman and Kalish, 8). But there appear to be other studies which, although ostensibly dealing with the same processes, may perhaps be better interpreted in different terms. In a number of experiments on "stimulus generalization" in humans, psychological similarity may be mediated not by that process but rather by the class to which the subject assigns various inputs. The magnitude of the subject's response to a test stimulus can depend, one may suggest, on whether or not he places both training and test stimuli in a common class. There may well be individual differences as to whether these two stimuli are placed in the same category or not; and in addition, experimental conditions may be set up in such a manner as to induce or discourage the placement of those two stimuli in the same class without varying these stimulus presentations themselves. If such diffuse factors as these were to cause differences in magnitude of response to the test stimulus—despite the facts that the dimension along which the training and test stimuli fall and the differences along that dimension are easily discriminable by the subject, and the training and test stimuli presented are the same for all these subjects—then the sufficiency of a stimulus-generalization explanation for such data would be called into question.

And, in fact, there do seem to be cases where differences of these kinds occur.

We may note, for example, a study by Wickens, Schroder, and Snide (32), using the GSR. Adult subjects in one group received shock-reinforced presentations of a particular tone, and then were given extinction trials with one of three tones at varying frequency distances from the training tone. Subjects in another group underwent the same regimen, except they heard a nonreinforced click interspersed among the reinforced tone presentations during training. The group not hearing clicks—qua group—yielded a gradient of decreasing GSR magnitude as distance between training and test stimuli increased; but the height and shape of the gradient differed on different extinction trials, and only by averaging the results of large numbers of subjects (24 in each extinction subgroup) could one tease out even these not very great consistencies. The group hearing clicks showed no clear gradients at all, even as a group.

Why the different results from these two conditions? Recall what we noted earlier concerning the two aspects of rules for classing events as equivalent: that they specify the range of negative instances we are seeking to discriminate, as well as the nature of positive exemplars of the class of interest. We would suggest that presence versus absence of clicks during training resulted in the learning of different rules for the classification of test stimuli during extinction. The group hearing clicks used the property "tones" as definitive for class-inclusion, and excluded clicks. All test tones were assigned to one class. Because of what they experienced during the training series, the domain of instances for this group consisted of "tones" and "clicks." The group not hearing clicks, on the other hand, used the properties "tones, and within such-and-such range of pitch" as definitive for class-inclusion, and excluded tones of other pitch—these latter being the relevant negative exemplars for them. Only some test tones met the specifications for this class. Because, then, this group experienced only the repeated tone during training—i.e., heard no clicks—this group's domain of instances consisted of "tones of various pitches." Hence, we would expect the GSR to the test tones far from the training tone to be much less than that to the test tone closest to the training tone for the group not hearing clicks—and this was in fact the case. These subjects assigned only the nearest test tones to the same class as the training tone, further-away test tones being excluded. But we would expect no clear trends of differences in GSR among the test tones for the group hearing clicks—and this also was the case. These subjects assigned all test tones to the same class as the training tone, clicks being the items which were excluded from the class. The difference between the click and no-click conditions, then, seems to be that the subject was induced to classify the tones differently in each case.

It may be that many other "generalization" experiments also involve a categorization process like that we postulate for the "no-click" group in the above study: Test stimuli close to the training stimulus are placed in one class with the latter, those further from the training stimulus being excluded. The widths of the class in question vary across individuals, and hence one finds a smooth normal-curve type of gradient only when one averages all subjects together. But there are further individual differences in classification, and, what is more, classifications may change as a test series proceeds. Hence one finds, for instance, nonconsistent results over extinction trials taking groups of subjects as wholes—as in a study by Grant and Schiller (7). That these effects are due to categorization differences seems a reasonable hypothesis when one considers work like that by Wickens et al., where on our interpretation, the probabilities of alternative rules for classification were varied, and this was found to cause differences in magnitude of response to a test stimulus.

Although primary stimulation gradients seem able to account for some cases of psychological similarity, then, there are others in which a different process may well be at work.

ASSIGNMENT TO A COMMON CATEGORY

Each of the three definitions of psychological similarity noted above has been found to have only limited applicability. Such is also the case with this fourth definition. Since, however, it is younger than the others, its implications have not yet been thoroughly explored; and since it seems relevant in many cases where the other definitions cannot easily be applied, it seems advisable to examine it further with regard to its range of utility.

According to this fourth definition, when we have attained a rule which bisects a domain of events into a set that exemplifies a certain property or conjunction of properties and a particular contrasting set that does not, then we will transfer behavior from one to another of two events that fall into the former set, but will tend not to transfer behavior from either of them to an event in the latter set. Again, then, the relation has two aspects: It tells us the range of negative instances which are relevant to our purposes of discrimination, as well as the basis on which we are to declare events positive exemplars of the class of interest. In short, recognition of the similarity of two events depends on their being classed as equivalents—as exemplifying the property or conjunction of properties in question, and as standing in contrast to a particular range of nonexemplars.[8] We learn to take one or more particular properties as criterial for sorting a domain of events.

[8]This view is related to those of Goodman (6) and Kelly (13), and was first approached in Klüver's early work (14).

There would seem to be two main determinants of the kinds of classification rules we attain: the nature of the instances presented (i.e., the environmental properties to which we have been exposed); and our predilections for some bases of classification and prejudices against others. Varying either the nature of the instances or our classification preferences hence should influence psychological similarity in predictable ways.[9] Let us see if this approach seems to contribute anything in considering two psychological issues: the first, transposition—a matter around which much empirical study has centered; and the second, distinctive similarity—Köhler's demonstration of the importance of similarity in guiding attempts at more complex human problem-solving.

Transposition. Some years ago, Köhler (17, pp. 217–227) and Koffka (15) argued that discriminating in terms of such relations as "brighter than" or "larger than" is more primitive, more basic, than discriminating in terms of absolute sensory qualities such as brightnesses and sizes. Spence (30) argued just as insistently, however, that responding on the basis of absolute stimulus qualities such as brightness or size is more primitive, and relational responding is a result of the algebraic summation of response tendencies to absolute stimuli. But one may suggest a third alternative. Perhaps higher organisms (and certainly humans) can learn to respond either in terms of relations between stimuli or in terms of absolute stimulus qualities, and which selection they will make depends largely on the conditions instituted concerning classification preferences and the nature of the instances.

Consider, for example, the nature of the instances. We would predict a greater tendency for subjects to respond relationally on a transfer test, when trained on couplets of one large and one small form apiece, and when the particular forms used vary in size (but not shape) across couplets, than if the same amount of training were given on one repeated couplet of a large and small form; in both cases response to the larger form is always rewarded during training. In the former condition, the nature of the instances is such as to permit the subject to rule out the possibility of classifying the data in terms of the absolute stimulus quality of size, and the only class into which all data fit is one defined by the relational property of "larger than"; whereas in the latter condition, the kinds of instances presented permit classification on the basis of absolute size or relative size. We could just as well, of course, arrange our instances so as

[9]Since the present paper's aim is to compare this fourth approach to psychological similarity with the other three and to provide initial indications of that approach's empirical utility, we cannot discuss this approach in greater detail than is provided in the present paragraphs and in the earlier section where this view was introduced. More detailed discussion of this view in particular will be provided in a subsequent paper.

to rule out the possibility of classifying on the basis of relative size, simply by always rewarding choice of the same particular stimulus form, and having it appear sometimes paired with a larger form, sometimes with a smaller form. In a like manner, whether the subject will classify on an absolute, relational, or even some other basis depends on his biases for or against particular bases of classification, as induced by instructions or other means. Given variation in the nature of the instances and in such biases, it would seem one can create conditions that will induce the subject to classify the training instances, and hence to transfer, on any basis we desire.

Thus, work with children by Jackson and Jerome (12), for instance, indicates that how the child categorized the training instances depends on whether he is asked to decide which stimulus is correct after the presentation of both, or rather is required to indicate, after each stimulus is presented, whether it is the correct or incorrect stimulus. As we would expect from the differing emphases on relational versus absolute classifying implied by these different conditions of instance presentation, relational choices were preponderant when the child gave one over-all response after simultaneous or successive presentation of both stimuli, whereas absolute choices were in the majority when the child had to respond to one stimulus before the second was presented. Requiring the subject to make a separate response to each stimulus favors classifying on an absolute basis, whereas requiring the subject to make a single response to both stimuli as a pair favors classifying on a relational basis.

Stevenson, Iscoe, and McConnell (31) found that college students varied in the basis they used for responding on the first transposition test trial; many, to be sure, responded on a relational basis, but some responded on an absolute basis. Apparently, different subjects received different impressions about what was required of them, and hence classified the data presented to them in different ways. What seem needed in this area, then, are studies analyzing the conditions of instance presentation and biases concerning particular attributes that influence the basis the subject chooses for classifying the training stimuli—conditions which therefore influence the kind of transposition shown.

Distinctive Similarity. Köhler (16) uses the term "distinctive similarity" for denoting that particular items resemble each other more than they resemble the rest of the situation. The nature of this greater or lesser resemblance is itself, however, left unanalyzed, although an earlier experiment by Köhler and von Restorff (18) had explored the effects of such similarity on complex human problem-solving. Two groups were taught a principle for solving an arithmetic problem, and transfer was measured later to the solution of a new arithmetic problem on which that principle—an arithmetic shortcut—could also be used. Between these two occurrences, one group was given arithmetic problems to which however, this principle was not applicable, whereas the other group was given entirely different tasks to do—the solution of matchstick puzzles. The latter group showed greater transfer of the principle to the new problem than did the former group. Thus similarity of the first to the last problem, in particular, was greater for the latter group than for the former group; in one case it was "distinctive," in the other case it was not. But of what does this psychological similarity consist?

One may suggest that analysis of the classification tasks facing the subjects in Köhler and von Restorff's groups casts light on something which these authors really left shrouded in mystery—the nature of distinctive similarity. After being shown the application of the principle to the initial arithmetic problem, the task of the subject became, essentially, that of attaining the rule specifying what property or properties must be conjointly found in order to assign problems to the class to which this principle is applicable, and specifying the relevant range of negative instances with which the subject must concern himself. The group performing better on the transfer test learned but a simple rule for classification: only one obvious property made an item a positive exemplar of the class of items to which the shortcut principle was applicable— namely, that the item be an arithmetic problem; and the degree of overlap of positive and relevant negative instances in terms of compresence of properties was minimal—no more than that they were all "problems." The group performing less well on the transfer test was given the task of learning a more complex rule for classification; a conjunction of properties was required to make an item a positive exemplar of the class in question: the item had to be an arithmetic problem *and also* had to exhibit certain additional features. For this group there are more properties compresent for positive and relevant negative instances (e.g., that the task be not only a problem but also an *arithmetic* problem is compresent for both) than for the other group. In the first case, the domain of relevant events is "arithmetic and matchstick problems," and the contrast is between these two types. In the second case, the domain is "arithmetic problems," and the contrast is between arithmetic problems with certain features and arithmetic problems with other features. Again, the nature of the instances presented to the subject determines the kind of classification attempted. In short, "distinctive similarity" of two events means that the rule for assigning them to the same class provides for a minimum number of properties to be found compresent in at least some of the relevant negative instances, as well as all the positive instances of that class. The difference between positive and relevant negative exemplars is easier to locate.

Could the rule for the group that does poorly be rendered easier by a change in biases of the subjects toward particular attributes? Let us consider the following variation on the Köhler and von Restorff experiment. Suppose we give another group all mathematics problems and in the same order as the original group, but tell them, after the shortcut has been explained, that not all the subsequent problems are amenable to the shortcut, but that some will be. We have thereby set these subjects to remain vigilant throughout the series for the features of later problems that are the same as those in the initial one—the features that hence permit the principle to be applied—and would expect them to apply the shortcut to the last problem more often than did the group not given this set. Without changing the problems, then, we would expect the percentage of shortcut solutions to increase because of this change in set; these subjects have been more sharply tuned to try to find what features of artihmetic problems permit application of the shortcut. They have been encouraged to try to take a particular conjunction of properties as criterial for sorting events.

If one wishes to study distinctive similarity in the transfer of principles for problem-solving, then, the recommendation would seem to be this. Let us determine the conditions of instance presentation and attribute biases that aid or hinder the arrival of the subjects at rules for classifying tasks in terms of properties which they potentially have in common—conditions which aid or hinder, in other words, a match between psychological similarity and potential similarity.

CONCLUSION

The aim of this discussion has been twofold. First, after pointing out the ubiquitousness of the issue of psychological similarity in various areas of research on cognition, to note the way in which a common procedure, that of the transfer experiment, tends to unite them, and to urge that they be conceptualized in an integrated manner. Second, to consider the values and difficulties of four conceptions of psychological similarity, defined in terms of common environmental properties, common responses, primary stimulation gradients, and assignment to a common category. All four definitions are, to be sure, of limited applicability—but the last of them appears to apply in many instances where the first three do not. Several experimental implications of defining psychological similarity in terms of assignment to a common category were explored, and were taken to indicate that further work with this approach may well prove fruitful.

REFERENCES

1. AARON, R. I. *The Theory of Universals.* Oxford: Clarendon Press, 1952.
2. BRUNER, J. S., GOODNOW, JACQUELINE J., & AUSTIN, G. A. *A Study of Thinking.* New York: Wiley, 1956.
3. BRUNSWIK, E. *Perception and the Representative Design of Psychological Experiments.* Berkeley: University of California Press, 1956.
4. ELLIS, W. D. Memory for Physically Identical Elements in Human Maze Learning: A Transfer Problem. *Psychol. Bull.,* 1939, *36,* 545–546.
5. GIBSON, J. J., & GIBSON, ELEANOR J. Perceptual Learning: Differentiation or Enrichment. *Psychol. Rev.,* 1955, *62,* 32–41.
6. GOODMAN, N. *Fact, Fiction & Forecast.* Cambridge: Harvard University Press, 1955.
7. GRANT, D. A., & SCHILLER, J. J. Generalization of the Conditioned Galvanic Skin Response to Visual Stimuli, *J. Exp. Psychol.,* 1953, *46,* 309–313.
8. GUTTMAN, N., & KALISH, H. I. Discriminability and Stimulus Generalization. *J. Exp. Psychol.,* 1956, *51,* 79–88.
9. HOSPERS, J. On Explanation. *J. Phil.,* 1946, *43,* 337–356.
10. HULL, C. L. The Problem of Stimulus Equivalence in Behavior Theory. *Psychol. Rev.,* 1939, *46,* 9–30.
11. HUME, D. An Enquiry Concerning Human Understanding. In E. A. Burtt (Ed), *The English Philosophers From Bacon to Mill.* New York: Modern Library, 1939. Pp. 585–689.
12. JACKSON, T. A., & JEROME, E. A. Studies in the Transposition of Learning by Children. VI. Simultaneous vs. Successive Presentation of the Stimuli to Bright and Dull Children. *J. Exp. Psychol.,* 1943, *33,* 431–439.
13. KELLY, G. A. *The Psychology of Personal Constructs.* Vol. 1. *A Theory of Personality.* New York: Norton, 1955.
14. KLUVER, H. *Behavior Mechanisms in Monkeys.* Chicago: University of Chicago Press, 1933.
15. KOFFKA, K. *The Growth of the Mind.* New York: Harcourt, Brace, 1928.
16. KOHLER, W. *Dynamics in Psychology.* New York: Liveright, 1940.
17. KOHLER, W. Simple Structural Functions in the Chimpanzee and in the Chicken. In W. D. Ellis (Ed.), *A Source Book of Gestalt Psychology.* New York: Humanities Press, 1950. Pp. 217–227.
18. KOHLER, W., & VON RESTORFF, HEDWIG. Analyse von Vorgangen im Spurenfeld. II. Zur Theorie der Reproduktion. *Psychol. Forsch.,* 1935, *21,* 56–112.
19. KOHLER, W., & WALLACH, H. Figural After-Effects: An Investigation of Visual Processes. *Proc. Amer. Phil. Soc.,* 1944, *88,* 269–357.
20. LEWIS, D., MCALLISTER, DOROTHY E., & ADAMS, J. A. Facilitation and Interference in Performance on the Modified Mashburn Apparatus: I. The Effects of Varying the Amount of Original Learning. *J. Exp. Psychol.,* 1951, *41,* 247–268.
21. MCALLISTER, DOROTHY E., & LEWIS, D. Facilitation and interference in performance on the Modified Mashburn apparatus: II. The Effects of Varying the Amount of Interpolated Learning. *J. Exp. Psychol.,* 1951, *41,* 356–363.

22. MANDLER, G. Response Factors in Human Learning. *Psychol. Revl,* 1954, *61,* 235–244.

23. NORTH, A. J. Improvement in Successive Discrimination Reversals. *J. Comp. Physiol. Psychol.,* 1950, *43,* 442–460.

24. NORTH, A. J. Performance During an Extended Series of Discrimination Reversals. *J. Comp. Physiol. Psychol.,* 1950, *43,* 461–470.

25. OSGOOD, C. E. *Method and Theory in Experimental Psychology.* New York: Oxford University Press, 1953.

26. PAVLOV, I. P. *Conditioned Reflexes.* London: Oxford University Press, 1927.

27. SCHWARZ, G. Uber Rückfalligkeit bei Umgewöhnung. *Psychol. Forsch.,* 1927, *9* 86–158.

28. SHIPLEY, W. C. An Apparent Transfer of Conditioning. *J. Gen. Psychol.,* 1933, *8,* 382–390.

29. SHIPLEY, W. C. Indirect Conditioning. *J. Gen. Psychol.,* 1935, *10,* 337–357.

30. SPENCE, K. W. The Differential Response in Animals to Stimuli Varying Within a Single Dimension. *Psychol. Rev.,* 1937, *44,* 430–444.

31. STEVENSON, H. W., ISCOE, I., & MCCONNELL, CLAUDIA. A Developmental Study of Transposition. *J. Exp. Psychol.,* 1955, *49,* 278–280.

32. WICKENS, D. D., SCHRODER, H. M., & SNIDE, J. D. Primary Stimulus Generalization of the GSR Under Two Conditions. *J. Exp. Psychol.,* 1954, *47,* 52–56.

VII

CONSISTENCY
IN THE
PERSON'S
COGNITIVE ORGANIZATION

1
OVERVIEW

If an organism has been motivated to develop constructs, has developed dichotomous constructs, and has been presented with stimuli that are now to be construed, does the organism's choice of constructs follow definable principles? Is there any order to the selection of the particular constructs that are applicable to specific stimuli, and to the positioning of the stimulus at a particular point along the construct which is to be used? It becomes almost impossible to conceive of a theory of behavior that would ascribe the instantiation of individual stimuli to a random probability function. The probabilities of a stimulus being construed along particular dimensions, and the theorist's capacity to predict the way the subject will locate the stimulus in his construction system, become core demands in a comprehensive theory of behavior. The inability to meet these demands would shatter a theoretical effort.

The meeting of these demands is necessary to the basic assumptive structure of our cognitively based theory. In Section II, where we discussed the central motivational principles of our system, we pointed out that the organism constantly seeks to avoid the arousal which is a direct function of the inability to locate a stimulus within its cognitive organizations. In Section V we established the validity of the principle that an individual's construct system is hierarchically arranged so that each construct is related to larger segments of one's construction system. The principle we now propose, which guides the immediate instantiation of a stimulus situation, derives from our position on the basic issues of general motivation and the hierarchical organization of construct systems.

Borrowing liberally from G. A. Kelly's statement of his Choice Corollary (Section I), we propose that a person will instantiate a stimulus in a way that will allow for the greatest extension and elaboration of his existing construct system. The stimulus event is placed along a dimension that does least violation to the total construct system; and, further, its placement contributes to extending the system as well as to defining it. In laying out this principle we are relying on a point that has had a central place in cognitive theorizing since William James made his efforts to formulate a thorough personology. The person can be seen to be working toward maintaing a *self-consistency* in his approach to stimuli. In James' (1958) theorizing, the person sought, for example, to evolve a religious position that would give a complete and consistent view of the universe, so that the most insignificant as well as the most magnificent events in that universe could be "explained." A religious "explanation" was, and can still be, an acceptable way to "predict and understand" the mysteries that surround a person's life. And religious explanation can be immensely flexible as well as socially validatable.

The same kinds of principles that can explain the use of a religious position to attain a consistent world-view are also available to explain the use of any other system. Theories of cognitive consistency are now attracting extensive attention. Here we will try only to illustrate the utility of the position. A current sourcebook (Abelson, et al., 1968) devotes about 900 pages to the topic, reporting the work of dozens of researchers who explore the assumption that a person's behavior is a reflection of his effort to maintain psychological consistency.

The most useful way of showing that a person construes a stimulus consistently within his total construct system is to show how it is possible to predict the way in which he will behave in the presence of a new stimulus. Sarbin, in a series of articles on the use of metaphor in discussions of mental health, excellently captures the nature of an individual's future construing of a stimulus in ways that are consistent with past construction (Sarbin, 1964, 1967, 1968). He speaks of such metaphors as "mental illness" and "anxiety," but the principles remain the same as those that would explain the construing of any stimulus. Historically, students of behavior spoke about people who engage in "unusual" behaviors in terms of their behaving *as if* they were "ill." The metaphoric use of "ill," however, allowed a person to transpose his available constructs for the term "illness" to those events in the environmental ecology (in Sarbin's sense) which might better be labeled "unusual behavior." Following this transposition, the student of "unusual" behavior could then consistently attempt to "diagnose," to "treat" and to "cure" the "mental illness" which was reflected in "unusual" behavior. The metaphoric quality of the term *mental illness* has disappeared, and there is a consistency in the total use of the "illness" model.

This process, Sarbin (1968) aptly suggests, is related to the principle reflected in the classic study by Carmichael, Hogan, and Walter (1932). In that study, subjects had been shown figures that could be described by two labels. Two connected circles, for example, were presented, and one set of subjects was led to believe that they.*looked like* a pair of eyeglasses. Another set of subjects was told that the same figure *looked like* a dumbbell. When the subjects were later asked to reproduce the figure, they reflected the use of their total construct system by drawing eyeglasses or dumbbells, depending on which label was used in presenting the original figure.

The Hovland and Sherif (1952) study (Section II) illustrated the utility of the idea of internal structures as a central concept for psychological study, and demonstrated the propensity of persons to judge objects in ways that extend and define the subject's existing construct system. The study shows that the position a person holds on a general issue will significantly influence his judgment of individual stimulus items. People who held strong positions on the general issue of race relations tended to see "neutral" statements as being more prejudicial than other subjects did who held a less committed position. We might say that a strongly committed person will project his commitment into the stimuli he receives. If he assumes the world is made up of persons who share his commitments, he finds support for holding strongly to his position. If we accept the Hovland and Sherif findings, we would assume that a person who holds an extreme position would have a greater readiness to see people as being "for" or "against" him than would others who have "mild" positions. Thus, one who holds an extreme position on the issue of race relations would feel that the issue demands constant attention and effort toward a resolution of the issue.

Another rich field of investigation, relating to a person's effort to define and elaborate his existing construct system, is frequently discussed under the topic of "defensive" operations. Defensive operations, according to traditional psychoanalytic theory, reflect the organism's efforts to bring impulse function into line with "reality." As the Overview to Section IV suggests, the distinctions between "reality" and "unreality" in psychoanalytic theorizing are less than satisfactory, and the need to maintain these distinctions can be eliminated by adopting other theoretical positions. In essence, by placing the individual's construct system at the core of our theory, and by ascribing the total "meaning" of a stimulus to the personal constructions placed upon the stimulus, the theorist can eliminate the need to distinguish "reality" from "unreality." Within this position there is no need to speak of conflict between "pleasure principles" and "reality principles"; instead, one would speak of "internally produced stimuli" rather than "impulses" and of external efforts to instruct the person about how these stimuli are to be construed rather than of "reality principles." Instead of speaking of impulse conflicts, and efforts to resolve these conflicts, one can speak of a person's inability to place internal stimuli (much of which derives from his deviation from optimal levels of arousal) along construct dimensions in ways that would further define and extend his existing system. This formulation, then, would treat internal stimulation within the same set of principles used to treat external stimulation.

Should our theory call for propositions that state that a person will "successfully" construe stimuli by ignoring them; or by violently removing them under pressure of the high arousal state defined as aggression; or by reducing the arousal that accompanies unassimilable stimuli by using "artificial" chemical arousal-reducers; then these propositions will apply in discussions of both internally produced and externally produced stimuli. If a theory would speak of "defense mechanisms" in one case—that is, when speaking of internally produced stimuli—it must also make the same statements about the defensive operations of withdrawal, aggression, drug use, etc., when the organism is working to construe personally complex, externally-produced stimuli.

There is another concept that has the same negative social loading as does the concept of defense mechanism. Sometimes a person achieves an instantiation of a stimulus situation that successfully defines and extends his personal construct system; but, to an outside observer who would apply another set of constructs, the person is regarded as "crazy" or "primitive." Some of the modern novelists (Heller, 1961) have adopted the technique of deliberately instantiating stimuli into "wild, crazy" patterns. To the theorist who concerns himself with "reality," a novelist who uses the forms that Heller uses could be regarded as writing about "defensive operations." Perhaps Heller's hero in *Catch-22* might even earn the superordinate classificatory label of "manic." Following the case study practice of traditional psychoanalysis, one could show that Heller's protagonist is warding off a massive depression. The protagonist, Yossarian, could be seen as being in a high state of anxiety resulting from the threat that oral impulses will completely overrun him. Infantile orality might be revived by the spectre of death which accompanies the bombing missions to which he is assigned. His "wild" decision to desert his duty and to try to join his friend, whom Yossarian believes to have paddled in a raft from the Mediterranean to Sweden, could be seen as a manic effort to avoid the "reality" of doing his "duty." One might also conclude that his decision was as "rational" as that which was reached by his comrades-in-arms who decided that they should stay with the bombing group in order to add more oak leaves to their unit citations. Yossarian's decision, though it earns the opprobrium of standard society, represented a personally successful way of construing his existing world.

Within the position that we are seeking to construct in this text, there are conditions under which it might be useful to speak of a concept of "defense mechanisms." One might speak of defensive operations when the subject is observed to avoid instantiating a stimulus so that it is integrated to his total existing construction system. This kind of functioning would be expected to take place when the stimulus is of such a nature that its instantiation would require a radical revision of the person's existing cognitive organizations. Using Hebb's (1955) terms, one would say that the "arousal function" has superceded the "cue function." Under these circumstances the existing cognitive organizations are maintained by avoiding an incorporation of the troublesome stimulus into the subject's existing construction system. An illustration of this kind of functioning is found in a study reported by Mills and Jellison (1968). The subjects in their study were asked to select one of many attractive products as a gift. After they had made the choice, they were asked to evaluate the quality of advertisements of the products from which they had selected their gifts. Half of the subjects were asked to compare two advertisements, one of which was an advertisement for the product they had chosen. The other half of the subjects were given two advertisements both of which were irrelevant to the product they had chosen. The subjects who had been given a set of irrelevant advertisements read them much more critically than did the other subjects who compared advertisements relevant to the product they had chosen. Mills and Jellison point out that subjects, having made their choice, had already resolved uncertainty. In our terms, they had already made a satisfactory instantiation of the stimuli that had been presented to them. The reading of advertisements, particularly of products other than the one they had chosen, would serve to upset the certainty which they had achieved. To avoid arousal, therefore, the subjects resorted to giving only cursory attention to the advertisements that contrasted the chosen to the unchosen products. In this way they would be spared the possibility that they might need to alter the instantiation they had already made. In essence, the subjects who hastily reviewed the advertisements were "defending" against exposing themselves to the arousal that would accompany a restructuring of their cognitions. If this simple study can neatly illustrate the operation of "arousal function," we can expect to see clearer signs of this functioning in situations that expose a subject to the possibile need to restructure large segments of his construct system, including highly central constructs. Defense mechanisms would represent behaviors that are designed to avoid an integration of a stimulus, and to thus preserve intact a person's construct system.

There is, then, a wide variety of empirical and theoretical support for the principle that a person seeks to instantiate current stimuli into his existing construct system in ways that allow for extension and definition of that system. The readings in this section provide direct demonstrations of how the person's existing construct system will influence his reactions to a stimulus. These readings do not, however, include an exploration of the means by which a person defends his system by avoiding the instantiation of stimulus patterns, despite our awareness that this part of a person's functioning is related to the issue of defining and extending one's construct system. Our readings illustrate the principle that a person's construction system will "guide" the instantiation of stimuli, so that his judgment of the stimulus will reflect an effort to maintain and extend his system rather than to show the use of an "objective" set of judgmental criteria. These studies show that the individuals who are being observed have already developed a construct system that inexorably leads them to view the produced stimulus event in a particular way. Had they developed a different construct system, their reactions would have been quite different. Where the reactions of one group are contrasted to the reactions of another, we see that the group members were selected on the basis of their existing construct systems; and in the end, it was the subjects' initial construct systems that determined their final reactions.

REFERENCES

ABELSON, R., ET AL., (Eds.). *Theories of Cognitive Consistency.* Skokie, Illinois: Rand-McNally, 1968.

CARMICHAEL, L., HOGAN, H. P., & WALTER, A. A. An Experimental Study of the Effect of Language on the Reproduction of Visually Perceived Form. *Journal of Experimental Psychology,* 1932, *15,* 73–86.

HEBB, D. O. Drives and the C. N. S. (Conceptual Nervous System). *Psychological Review,* 1955, *62,* 243–254.

HELLER, J. *Catch-22.* New York: Dell Publishing, 1961.

HOVLAND, C. I. & SHERIF, M. Judgmental Phenomena and Scales of Attitude Measurement. *Journal of Abnormal and Social Psychology,* 1952, *47,* 822–833.

JAMES, W. *The Varieties of Religious Experience.* New York: New American Library, 1958.

MILLS, J. & JELLISON, J. Avoidance of Discrepant Information Prior to Commitment. *Journal of Personality and Social Psychology,* 1968, *8,* 59–62.

SARBIN, T. R. Anxiety: The Reification of a Metaphor. *Archives of General Psychiatry,* 1964, *10,* 630–638.

SARBIN, T. R. On the Futility of the Proposition that Some People Be Labeled Mentally Ill. *Journal of Consulting Psychology,* 1967, *31,* 447–453.

SARBIN, T. R. Ontology Recapitulates Philology: The Mythic Nature of Anxiety. *American Psychologist,* 1968, *23,* 411–418.

2

THE ACHIEVEMENT MOTIVE
AND RECALL OF INTERRUPTED
AND COMPLETED TASKS[1]
JOHN W. ATKINSON

It is possible to speak of achievement motivation as a matter of an individual having construed himself at the *achiever* end of a two-poled construct labeled *achiever-laggard*. Having first placed himself at a point on that continuum, he will then be able to "predict himself" in a variety of events. If he characteristically locates himself at the *achiever* end of the construct, and is then placed in a situation that raises the possibility that he would be placed at the *laggard* end, he is being exposed to a stimulus situation that would be disconfirming to his existing construction system. We would expect, then, that he would try to avoid this kind of inner conflict. He would seek to act in ways that are consistent with his total construct system—that is, to obtain confirmation of himself as an achiever.

Atkinson's study indicates that subjects high in achievement motivation—that is, subjects who have clearly differentiated an *achievement versus nonachievement* construct, and who tend to regard themselves at the achievement end—will be greatly disturbed by not arriving at complete achievement. Subjects high in achievement motivation tend to recall the tasks that they did not complete. Subjects low on achievement motivation do not show this tendency. In our view, it is the greater activation of high achievement-motivation subjects that increases their

Reprinted from Journal of Experimental Psychology, *1953, 46, 381–390, by permission of the author and the American Psychological Association.*

[1]This paper is based on a portion of a doctoral dissertation presented to the faculty of the University of Michigan (3). The author is appreciative of the helpful interest and criticism of his committee: Drs. D. G. Marquis (chairman), E. L. Walker, D. R. Miller, T. M. Newcomb, and A. F. Zander. The investigation is part of a larger program of research on achievement motivation supported by the Office of Naval Research. A report of this study was given at the APA meeting, 1951.

recall of incomplete achievement. Such a situation disturbs their view of themselves as high achievers. Their motivational activity would indeed move them toward successful completion of tasks—that is, toward high achievement. And in nonexperimental conditions we would expect that heightened activation and continued attention would result in the achievement-motivated subject's eventually attaining a conception of the event that would be consistent with his self-view.

* * *

One important obstacle to satisfactory integration of the studies of motivation that have utilized the interruption-of-tasks method has been the lack of an adequate measure of individual differences in strength of motivation. The present investigation was an attempt to determine the effect of strength of achievement motivation on recall of interrupted and completed tasks and to determine whether the measure of the achievement motive developed by McClelland and his co-workers (14, 16) fills the need for a measure of strength of motivation.

Several recent reviews (20), particularly Glixman's (7), Alper's (2), and Rosenzweig's (18), treat the literature in a comprehensive manner. The present experiment attempts specifically to resolve the conflicting results of studies in which either presumed individual differences or experimentally induced changes in achievement-related motivation have been related to differences in recall of incompleted and completed tasks. The results of Zeigarnik (22) and Marrow (12,13), for example, imply that the greater the motivation to achieve, the greater the tendency to recall more incompleted than completed tasks. The results of Rosenzweig (17, 19), Lewis and Franklin (9), and Glixman (8), however, seem to imply just the opposite relationship.[2]

In the present experiment, differences in recall of interrupted and completed tasks are studied in relation to individual differences in strength of the achievement motive (n Achievement) with different experimental instructions comparable to those of the earlier conflicting studies. Different groups of Ss were exposed to three different instructions prior to performance on 20 paper-and-pencil tasks, half of which were interrupted before completion. The different instructions were designed to vary the probability that Ss would perceive completion of tasks as evidence of personal accomplishment (or success) and incompletion as evidence of personal failure. The method used to obtain an n-Achievement score for each S has been experimentally validated and elaborated elsewhere (14, 16).

---

[2]See also Alper's (1) earlier demonstration that these opposite trends in selective recall can be related to a number of differences in personality.

PROCEDURE

Experimental conditions. In a *Task Orientation* condition, *E* made no deliberate attempt to create any kind of experimental atmosphere. He simply passed out the task folders after being introduced as Mr. _____ and read an instruction for performance of the tasks adapted from Marrow (12). Tasks were timed without calling attention to the fact. He interrupted by saying, "All right, we'll go on to the next one now." After the twentieth task he immediately read instructions for the "test of creative imagination" (measure of n Achievement) and followed the standard procedure in administering this measure (14, 16). After the final story, recall was asked for in the following manner: "Now on the back of your story sheet, you are asked to recall as many of the tasks as you can that you did before the story test. Just jot them down in the order they come to mind, not necessarily in the order they were given. Be descriptive enough so that I will know which one you mean. When you can't think of any more, I'll take your paper." The *S*s took from 2 min. to a 5-min. maximum in recall. Names and sex were not asked for until *S*s brought their folders to *E*.

A *Relaxed* and an *Achievement Orientation* condition represent alterations of the basic procedure of the Task Orientation condition, on the one hand in the direction of minimizing the importance of the tasks, and on the other of increasing their importance by making them seem to be measures of highly valued attributes.

In the *Relaxed Orientation* condition, *E* lounged on the desk, joked with students, and in general attempted to create a relaxed atmosphere before being introduced as a graduate student who wanted to try out some tasks. This attitude was maintained in making the following remarks before the task instruction: "I have worked out a series of paper-and-pencil tests that I plan to use with college students in some research later. Right now I am simply trying them out to find out which ones are suitable for my purposes. You don't have to sign your names or anything since I'm not interested in your individual scores. However, I will appreciate your serious cooperation so that we can learn something about the suitability of the tests." From this point on the procedure was the same as Task Orientation.

In the *Achievement Orientation* condition, *E* conducted himself in a serious manner in passing out the folders and giving instructions. He was introduced as Mr. _____ who had some tests to give the class. The following preliminary statement was made: "During the war years, psychologists were called on to develop many different kinds of tests in order to select people with high executive capacity, intellectual alertness, the capacity for making quick decisions, and leadership. Now I am going to give you a series of tests in order to compare your scores with those of other college students. Without opening the folder, will you write your name and sex on the outside of the folder. If you know your IQ you might write that under your name and your grade point average for the first semester." After completing the same instruction for the tests used in Task Orientation, he added, "Your work will be interpreted as representing the full extent of your ability, so do your best." The procedure already outlined was followed with these changes: *(a)* E made it clear to Ss that they were being timed; *(b)* while Ss worked on the tasks, E walked about the room as if noticing how well or poorly they were performing; *(c)* after the seventh task he said, "Change tests quickly, you need the time"; *(d)* after the tenth task he said, "Some of you are taking a lot of time on these."

Measurement of n Achievement. The four pictures projected on a screen before the group to elicit imaginative stories for the measurement of n Achievement with their usual code designations were: *(B)* two men working in a shop; *(H)* a boy seated at a desk holding his head; *(A)* the heads of two men (TAT 7BM); and *(G)* boy in foreground with surgical mural behind (TAT 8BM).

Stories were scored according to a modification (B) of the original method (A) which correlated .95 with the original method (16). An S's n-Achievement score represents the frequency of imaginative responses (Need, Instrumental Acts, Anticipatory Goal States, etc.) indicating concern over excellence of performance in his stories. Rescore reliability of the n-Achievement scores for the 83 Ss was .93. Scores obtained from Picture H were eliminated when another study run concurrently (3) indicated certain inadequacies of the scoring procedures when applied to this picture. The scores of Ss on the three remaining pictures, B, A, G, having an estimated equivalent-form reliability of .56 (3) were used in the analysis of results.

The distribution of n-Achievement scores within each experimental condition was divided as near to the median as possible to provide comparable high and low n-Achievement groups within each condition. The mean n-Achievement score of each high group fell between 9 and 10 and of each low group between 2 and 3.

Tasks. Folders containing one set of 20 paper-and-pencil tasks modeled after Marrow (12) and MacKinnon (11) in a prearranged order and story blanks for the measurement of n Achievement were distributed at the start of regularly scheduled class periods. Two versions of each task had been constructed. One could normally be completed in 75 sec., the time allotted for each task; the other was rarely completed in that time.

Two sequences of the 20 tasks were randomly determined. Location of 10 short and 10 long versions was also randomly determined. Given two forms (XA and ZA) alike in location of short and long versions but different in sequence of tasks, two other forms (XB and ZB) were constructed reversing the location of short and long versions.

Test folders were distributed in such a manner that Ss in adjacent seats would be working on different tasks at the same time and every S would have the experience of being interrupted when others near him had finished. Some Ss in each section received folders containing only short versions of tasks for another purpose not reported here.

The intended four-way classification of Ss according to form of the test was precluded by an unequal distribution of the four forms among Ss having high and low n-Achievement scores. Therefore Ss were classified only in terms of the location of short and long tasks in the series. Forms XA and ZA were combined and will now be referred to as Form A, and their combined counterparts as Form B. The two forms differ in the distribution of short tasks (easy to finish) in the four quarters of the sequence of 20 tasks. On Form A, the distribution of short tasks was 3, 3, 3, and 1; on Form B, 2, 2, 2, and 4. A fortuitous result of the random placement of short and long tasks is a greater number of short tasks in the early (1–5) and late (16–20) serial positions usually favored in recall on Form B, and long tasks in those locations on Form A.

Subjects. The Ss were 83 male students in ten introductory psychology sections at the University of Michigan in the spring of 1949, distributed among experimental conditions as follows: Relaxed Orientation, 27; Task Orientation, 32; Achievement Orientation, 24. To eliminate any effect on recall resulting from great disparities between the number of tasks completed and interrupted, 17 other Ss who completed fewer than 8 or more than 12 tasks were excluded as were 9 others who failed to understand directions, confused the order of tasks, or complained of illness.

Treatment of recall data. The Ss were classified according to strength of motivation, experimental condition, and form of the task-test to allow systematic control of the three variables which might influence recall in analysis of variance. Since the number of tasks completed varied between 8 and 12, the percentage of tasks of each type recalled is the appropriate measure of recall. In order to apply analysis of variance, each S's percentage recall was converted to angles by the *arc sin* $\sqrt{percentage}$ transformation (21, p. 447). Subclass N's resulting from the triple classification of Ss were not seriously disproportionate. Analysis of variance by the method of proportional subclass numbers was accomplished following an adjustment for expected N's (21, p. 295; 10).

RESULTS

The mean n-Achievement scores of the Relaxed (4.93), Task (5.63), and Achievement Orientation conditions (5.17) were not significantly different *(F* = .22, *df* = 2 and 80). Evidently the experimental procedures did not differ sufficiently to produce over-all differences in intensity of motivation of the magnitude previously reported when stimulating conditions were more extreme (14).

However, the three experimental orientations did produce differences in recall, which are evident when high and low n-Achievement groups within conditions are separated (Table 1). The *Zeigarnik effect* is represented here as the difference between recall of incompletions and completions (IR–CR). Table 1 shows that both of the conflicting trends of earlier studies occur when Ss are grouped according to the strength of their motivation to achieve. The Ss high in n Achievement show an increasing

TABLE 1 Mean recall of incompleted tasks (IR), completed tasks (CR), and difference in recall of incompleted and completed tasks (IR-CR).*

Orientation	Form	High n Achievement					Low n Achievement				
		N					N				
		Ob-served	Ex-pected**	IR	CR	IR-CR	Ob-served	Ex-pected**	IR	CR	IR-CR
Relaxed	A	5	5.8	43.2	41.5	1.7	7	7.9	54.0	43.3	10.7
	B	6	5.6	43.8	43.0	.8	9	7.7	48.1	41.8	6.3
	A + B	11	11.4	43.5	42.3	1.3	16	15.6	51.1	42.5	8.5
Task	A	9	6.8	49.6	40.2	9.4	8	9.4	49.4	43.3	6.1
	B	5	6.7	45.9	46.6	-.7	10	9.1	45.4	45.1	.3
	A + B	14	13.5	47.8	43.4	4.4	18	18.5	47.4	44.2	3.2
Achievement	A	5	5.1	64.7	44.1	17.6	8	7.0	48.4	46.1	2.3
	B	5	5.0	50.4	48.8	1.6	6	6.9	40.8	46.2	-5.4
	A + B	10	10.1	57.7	46.5	11.2	14	13.9	44.6	46.1	-1.5

* Percentage recall of each S was converted to angles by the *arc sin* $\sqrt{percentage}$ transformation (22).
** Adjusted subclass N's for analysis of variance by the method of proportional subclass numbers (10, 22).

tendency to recall more incompleted tasks as experimental instructions increase the probability that completion and incompletion will be perceived as success and failure. Just the opposite is true of Ss low in n Achievement; the tendency to recall more incompletions decreases. The difference between high and low n-Achievement groups in showing the Zeigarnik effect is due to diametrically opposite trends in recall of incompletions between Relaxed and Achievement Orientation. While both groups increase in recall of completions, the high n-Achievement group shows an even greater increase in recall of incompletions and the low n-Achievement group an almost equally great decrease.

Tables 2 and 3 provide a basis for evaluating the significance of these differences. Table 2 is a summary of separate analyses of variance for the IR–CR difference, IR, and CR. Table 3 contains tests of the significance of particular differences.

The Zeigarnik effect (IR–CR). Differences in Zeigarnik effect attributable to the interaction of Motivation with Orientation and to Form were both significant at the 5% level of confidence (Table 2). Since neither first-order interaction involving Form was significant, their sums of squares were combined with that of the triple interaction term to provide a combined estimate of error having 5 df.

The interaction of Motivation with Orientation is elaborated in Table 3. The Zeigarnik effect of Ss low in n Achievement is significantly greater under Relaxed Orientation than Achievement Orientation, while Ss high in n Achievement show a near significantly greater Zeigarnik effect under Achievement Orientation than Relaxed Orientation. The only significant difference between high and low n-Achievement groups occurs in the Achievement Orientation condition where the high n-Achievement group shows the greater Zeigarnik effect.

As expected, Form A in which interrupted tasks were located in serial positions favoring recall produced the larger over-all Zeigarnik effect; the over-all mean IR (not shown in Table 1) was 51.1 and the CR was 43.1. On Form B, the IR was 45.6 and the CR was 45.1.

Recall of incompleted tasks (IR). Table 2 shows that Form and the interaction of Motivation with Orientation also contribute significantly to the variance in recall of incompleted tasks. The first-order interactions involving Form were again combined with the triple interaction as an error estimate. Table 3 shows that under Achievement Orientation, the high n-Achievement group recalls significantly more incompleted tasks than the low n-Achievement group. The high n-Achievement group's recall of incompletions is significantly greater under Achievement Orientation than under Relaxed or Task Orientation. Under Relaxed Orientation,

TABLE 2 Analyses of variance of difference in recall of incompleted and completed tasks (IR-CR), recall of incompleted tasks (IR), and recall of completed tasks (CR).

Source	df	IR-CR Mean Square	F	IR Mean Square	F	CR Mean Square	F
1. Orientation	2	25.72		50.64		95.81	8.89*
2. Motivation	1	64.18		43.31		1.82	
3. Form	1	1161.99	10.91*	638.86	9.36*	77.43	
4. M x O	2	620.34	5.83*	662.98	9.72*	2.21	
5. M x F	1	71.66		.68		85.98	67.13**
6. F x O	2	146.05		103.35		28.84	22.52**
7. M x F x O	2	84.34		66.90		1.28	
Combined error							
(5, 6, 7)	5	106.49		68.24		—	
(4, 6, 7)	6	—		—		10.78	

* $p < .05$ using the combined error term.
** $p < .05$ using the triple interaction term.

TABLE 3 Significance of particular differences shown in Table 1.

Comparison	Mean difference	$\sigma_{diff.}$	t	p
IR–CR				
Relaxed to achievement orient.				
High n achievement	9.96	4.46*	2.23	.10
Low n achievement	−10.02	3.81	2.63	.05
High vs. low n achievement under achievement orient.	12.71	4.27	2.98	.05
IR				
Relaxed to achievement orient.				
High n achievement	14.16	3.57	3.97	.02
Low n achievement	−6.41	3.05	2.10	.10
Task to achievement orient.				
High n achievement	9.85	3.44	2.87	.05
High vs. low n achievement under achievement orient.	13.02	3.41	3.81	.02
under relaxed orient.	−7.55	3.22	2.35	.10
CR				
Relaxed to achievement orient.				
High n achievement	4.20	1.42	2.96	.05
Low n achievement	3.60	1.21	2.98	.05

*The $\sigma_{diff.}$ and df are derived from the error term of the appropriate analysis of variance.

the low n-Achievement group recalls near significantly more incompleted tasks than comparable *S*s under Achievement Orientation and near significantly more incompletions than the high n-Achievement group under the same relaxed instructions.

Recall of completed tasks (CR). Differences in recall of completed tasks attributable to the experimental orientations are signicant at the 5% level of confidence[3] and there is no interaction of Motivation with Orientation in this case (Table 2). Table 3 shows that both high and low n-Achievement groups increase significantly in recall of completed tasks from Relaxed to Achievement Orientation. And Table 1 shows that there is not even a suggestion of a difference between the two motivation groups under any experimental condition.

The meaning of the significant interaction of Motivation with Form may be quickly summarized. Even though the short, completable tasks were located in relatively unfavorable serial positions for recall on Form A, *S*s low in n Achievement recalled as many completions (across orientations) on Form A, 44.1, as on Form B, 44.3. The high n-Achievement group, however, showed the expected difference between forms; their CR on Form A was 41.8 and on Form B, 46.1. The Form with Orientation interaction was the result of a greater increase in CR between Relaxed and Achievement Orientation on Form B (5.0) than on Form A (2.8).

DISCUSSION

A study of the relationship of n Achievement to thresholds for recognition of success and failure words by McClelland and Liberman (15) first suggested that while high n-Achievement scores indicated a positive disposition to excel, lower n-Achievement scores may imply something more than indifference or lack of *positive* motivation to achieve. Their data allow the inference that persons high in n Achievement are predominantly success-oriented and have as their goal the feeling of satisfaction accompanying personal accomplishment while persons lower in n Achievement are more concerned with avoiding feelings of failure. This inference provides a basis for interpreting the distinctly opposite trends in recall of *S*s classified high and low in n Achievement.

[3]Actually, differences due to Orientation are not significant when tested against the Form with Orientation interaction term alone. With only 2 *df* in the error term, differences due to Form with Orientation are sufficiently large to preclude the possibility of revealing over-all differences due to Orientation. However, when all interactions involving Orientation are combined providing an error term having 6 *df*, the differences between orientations are found to be significant at the 5% level of confidence.

The most clear-cut differences in recall between high and low n-A-chievement groups occur in the Achievement Orientation condition, where the probability that completion would be perceived as evidence of personal accomplishment (or success) and incompletion as failure was maximized. The greater recall of incompletions and greater Zeigarnik effect by the high n-Achievement group are consistent with the theoretical expectations and empirical findings of both Zeigarnik (22) and Marrow (12, 13); the greater the motivation to complete the tasks, the greater the relative recall of incompleted tasks.

The recall trends of the high n-Achievement group from Relaxed to Task to Achievement Orientation are also consistent with the findings of Zeigarnik and Marrow. When the situation is deliberately designed to *decrease* perception of performance on the tasks as instrumental to the goal of personal accomplishment (Relaxed Orientation), Ss high in n Achievement recall only slightly more incompletions than completions, and relatively few of either compared to their significantly greater recall when success and failure are at stake (Achievement Orientation). This resembles the behavior of Zeigarnik's "disinterested" Ss who failed to show any preference in recall. We may take this to mean that motivation to achieve was not engaged by the "relaxed" instructions and that other possible motives, e.g., a feeling of obligation to E, intrinsic interest in the tasks themselves, etc. (22, p. 303), were insufficient to produce persistent striving towards completion. However, as the perception of completion as success and incompletion as failure is favored by task- and achievement-orienting instructions, the achievement motive is apparently increasingly engaged. Both the recall of incompletions and completions and the Zeigarnik effect increase from Relaxed to Task to Achievement Orientation for the high n-Achievement Ss—essentially Marrow's finding.

The Ss low in n Achievement show just the opposite trend in selective recall, the so-called defensive or anxiety-reducing trend. As instructions increase the probability that completion will be perceived as success, and what is apparently more important to them, that incompletion will be perceived as failure, there is an increase in recall of completions, the predominant trend appearing in Rosenzweig's group data (17); and a decrease in recall of incompletions, a trend accentuated in Glixman's group data (8). Both trends were reported by Lewis and Franklin (9). The decreasing tendency of Ss low in n Achievement to recall incompletions suggests that they are increasingly motivated by an *unmeasured* fear of failure.

Thus when recall of incompleted tasks is viewed as *instrumental behavior,* the traditional interpretation of the Zeigarnik effect, the differences in recall trends reported for high and low n-Achievement groups support the hypothesis that in achievement situations their goals differ.

When the goal is to experience feelings of success and personal accomplishment, then persistence of the interrupted activity in recall and subsequent resumption of it are instrumental to attainment of that goal. When, however, the goal is to avoid feelings of failure, non-recall of past failures and presumably non-resumption of previously failed activities are instrumental to the avoidance of renewed feelings of failure.

Interaction of perception and motivation. This interpretation leans heavily on an assumption that the achievement motive measured in imaginative behavior becomes a determinant of overt striving only to the extent that a particular performance is perceived as instrumental to the goal of personal accomplishment. The achievement motive is viewed as a latent characteristic of personality which is manifested in behavior only when engaged or supported by appropriate environmental cues. This is the assumption commonly made by learning theorists: environmental cues signify the *occasion* for the performance of previously learned instrumental acts (6, p. 32). A hungry man is more likely to reach for, pick up, and chew an object on a table at which he is sitting if the object happens to be a sandwich than if it happens to be an ashtray.

If instructions that the tasks measure an attribute of personal competence engage achievement motivation to a greater degree than instructions designed to deny the importance of the tasks, then there should be evidence that Ss worked harder in response to the former. An independent estimate of how hard Ss were working on the tasks is the number of tasks completed.

The expected increase in mean number of completions between the Relaxed and Achievement Orientation conditions occurred for both high and low n-Achievement groups. The smallest mean number of tasks completed (8.91) was that of the high n-Achievement group under Relaxed Orientation, supporting the hypothesis based on the absence of Zeigarnik effect in their recall, that they were relatively disinterested. The mean number of completions increased to 10.00 under Task and further to 10.60 under Achievement Orientation in a manner consistent with the assumption that achievement motivation was increasingly engaged by these instructions.

The mean number of completions of the low n-Achievement group increased from 9.56 under Relaxed Orientation to 9.61 under Task Orientation to 10.14 under Achievement Orientation. Under Task and Achievement Orientation, when the achievement motive had been engaged, the number of completions was greater for the high n-Achievement group, reflecting their stronger motivation. In general, the hypothesized interaction of perception and motivation in the determination of instrumental striving is supported by analysis of performance data.

But an important question remains: why did the low n-Achievement group complete more tasks, recall more incompletions, and show a greater Zeigarnik effect than the high n-Achievement group under Relaxed Orientation? The facts imply that the low n-Achievement group was more motivated to complete the tasks than the high n-Achievement group in this condition and furthermore, that they were apparently unconcerned about failure. The assumption that the relaxed instructions minimized the probability of completion and incompletion being perceived as success and failure does not rule out the possibility that the relaxed instructions might have engaged some other motive more characteristic of persons in the low than the high n-Achievement group. There is a reason for thinking that this might have been the case. Zeigarnik observed that, in addition to personal ambition, *a feeling of obligation to E* and intrinsic interest in the tasks were often motives to complete the tasks. A recent study by R. Brown (4) has shown that persons in the middle and low thirds of the n-Achievement score distribution obtain higher scores on the F Scale measure of authoritarian personality than persons in the upper third on n Achievement. While the relaxed instruction de-emphasized personal achievement, it did urge cooperation and suggested that E *would be pleased if Ss complied with his instructions.* There is, in other words, some basis for thinking that the instruction which produced indifference in the high n-Achievement group might have engaged more motivation to comply in the low n-Achievement group.

Reconciliation of conflicting results. Can we account for the comparability of the trends of Ss high in n Achievement with the group results reported by Marrow (12, 13) and the diametrically opposite trends of Ss low in n Achievement with the group results of Rosenzweig (17), Lewis and Franklin (9), and Glixman (8)? Were there no evidence that Marrow's Ss as a group were more highly motivated to achieve than those of the other three studies, the present finding would be little more than suggestive. But in light of the implications of high and low n-Achievement scores discussed earlier, there is evidence to support the argument. Marrow's Ss were all volunteers; Ss in the other studies were not. Marrow makes a point of mentioning that "no pressure was exerted to compel attendance . . . to insure a cooperative attitude towards the work" (12, p. 16). Glixman's Ss, on the other hand, were all "draftees"; his Ss, members of an introductory course, "were told by the instructor that they were expected to devote a two-hour period to departmental research." In addition, the instructor called off the names of Ss who were to participate each day "to lend prestige to the calling of Ss" and discourage "bias of sampling which is possible when Ss volunteer" (8, p. 228). Subjects in Rosenzweig's "informal group" were employed while those in his "formal group" were "enlisted from the freshman student advisees responsible to the director of the clinic and were personally invited by him" (17, p. 65). Lewis and Franklin's (9) Ss were apparently unaware that they were taking part in an experiment, having been asked individually merely to help out with some work that had to be done.

If persons low in n Achievement are concerned with avoiding failure, it is unlikely that they would voluntarily place themselves in a test situation in which they might fail. On the other hand, an appeal for volunteers to take part in some kind of testing could be viewed as a challenge by the person highly motivated to achieve. For him, volunteering is a goal-directed instrumental act. So the suggestion for reconciling the gross contradiction between the trend in selective recall reported by Marrow and those of the other studies considered becomes a hypothesis subject to experimental verification: Ss who volunteer are characteristically more highly motivated to achieve than a group of randomly selected or drafted Ss.

Since both increases and decreases in recall of interrupted tasks occur with changes in experimental instructions when Ss are classified according to strength of motivation to achieve, there can be little hope of reconciling many of the other inconsistencies in experiments with no basis for estimating the motivation of particular Ss. However, the promise of the measure of n Achievement for extended theoretical integration of studies utilizing the interruption-of-tasks method is indicated when the results of Cartwright's study (5) of the effect of interruption, success, and failure on attractiveness of activities are considered in light of present findings. His experimental condition was comparable to the Achievement Orientation of the present investigation. Spontaneous remarks following interruption and interviews after the experiment revealed that Ss who raised their attract-iveness ratings of tasks following interruption and failure anticipated success at the time of interruption or viewed failure as a temporary obstacle to be overcome by subsequent success on the same activity. Cartwright suggests that for these Ss "it is possible that one could speak of a 'need for success' " (5, p. 12). Those who reported anticipating failure at the time of interruption or viewed interruption "as an escape from certain failure" (5, p. 5) more often decreased attractiveness ratings following interruption or failure.

A simple experiment run by the author confirms the expectation that the differences noted by Cartwright could be attributed to differences in n Achievement. Nineteen Ss performed the same tasks used in the present experiment under achievement-orienting instructions and were interrupted on half of them. They were then asked to look through a test booklet similar to the one they had worked on and choose the five tasks they liked the best. Only one of ten Ss low in n Achievement chose more incompletions than completions; five of nine Ss high in n Achievement chose more incompletions than completions. The predicted difference between the groups is significant at the 5% level of confidence.

SUMMARY

The interruption-of-tasks experiment was performed with male college students under three different experimental instructions presumed to vary the probability that Ss would perceive completion as evidence of personal accomplishment (or success) and incompletion as failure. The Ss in each experimental condition were classified high or low in motivation to achieve on the basis of a thematic apperception measure of n Achievement.

When instructions clearly signified that completion meant success and incompletion meant failure, Ss high in n Achievement recalled more incompleted tasks and showed a greater Zeigarnik effect than Ss low in n Achievement. Recall of incompletions and the tendency to show the Zeigarnik effect increased for Ss high in n Achievement as instructions increased the probability that completion and incompletion would be perceived as success and failure. Just the opposite trend occurred for Ss low in n Achievement.

Results are consistent with a hypothesis advanced by McClelland and Liberman that n Achievement is essentially positive motivation to experience feelings of accomplishment and success and that lower n-Achievement scores imply relatively greater anxiety about failure. In addition, results were interpreted to mean that the n-Achievement score obtained from thematic apperception stories is an estimate of the strength of latent achievement motivation which is manifested in overt striving to the extent that it is engaged by appropriate environmental cues.

A basis is proposed for reconciling the apparently contradictory implications among several earlier studies concerning the relation of Zeigarnik effect to strength of motivation to achieve, and a subsidiary experiment on attractiveness of interrupted tasks is reported to show the value of an independent measure of individual differences in n Achievement for theoretical integration of experiments using the interruption procedure.

REFERENCES

1. ALPER, T. G. Memory for Completed and Incompleted Tasks as a Function of Personality: Correlation Between Experimental and Personality Data. *J. Pers.*, 1948, *17*, 104–137.
2. ALPER, T. G. The Interrupted Task Method in Studies of Selective Recall: A Re-evaluation of Some Recent Experiments. *Psychol. Rev.*, 1952, *59*, 71–88.

3. ATKINSON, J. W. Studies in Projective Measurement of Achievement Motivation. Unpublished doctor's dissertation, University of Michigan, 1950.

4. BROWN, R. W. A Determinant of the Relationship Between Rigidity and Authoritarianism. *J. Abnorm. Soc. Psychol.*, 1953, *48*, 469–476.

5. CARTWRIGHT, D. The Effect of Interruption, Completion, and Failure Upon the Attractiveness of Activities. *J. Exp. Psychol.*, 1942, *31*, 1–16.

6. DOLLARD, J., & MILLER, N. E. *Personality and Psychotherapy.* New York: McGraw-Hill, 1950.

7. GLIXMAN, A. F. An Analysis of the Use of the Interruption-Technique in Experimental Studies of "Repression." *Psychol. Bull.*, 1948, *45*, 491–506.

8. GLIXMAN, A. F. Recall of Completed and Incompleted Activities under Varying Degrees of Stress. *J. Exp. Psychol.*, 1949, *39*, 281–295.

9. LEWIS, H. B., & FRANKLIN, M. An Experimental Study of the Role of the Ego in Work: II. The Significance of Task-Orientation in Work. *J. Exp. Psychol.*, 1944, *34*, 195–215.

10. LINDQUIST, E. F. *Statistical Analysis in Educational Research.* Boston: Houghton Mifflin, 1940.

11. MACKINNON, D. W. *Experimental Studies in Psychodynamics. A Laboratory Manual.* Cambridge: Harvard University Press, 1948.

12. MARROW, A. J. Goal Tensions and Recall: I. *J. Gen. Psychol.*, 1938, *19*, 3–35.

13. MARROW, A. J. Goal Tensions and Recall: II. *J. Gen. Psychol.*, 1938, *19*, 37–64.

14. MCCLELLAND, D. C., CLARK, R. A., ROBY, T. B., & ATKINSON, J. W. The Projective Expression of Needs. IV. The Effect of the Need for Achievement on Thematic Apperception. *J. Exp. Psychol.*, 1949, *39*, 242–255.

15. MCCLELLAND, D. C., & LIBERMAN, A. M. The Effect of Need for Achievement on Recognition of Need-Related Words. *J. Pers.*, 1949, *18*, 236–251.

16. MCCLELLAND, D. C., ATKINSON, J. W., CLARK, R. A., & LOWELL, E. L. *The Achievement Motive.* New York: Appleton-Century-Crofts, 1953, in press.

17. ROSENZWEIG, S. An Experimental Study of "Repression" with Special Reference to Need-Persistive and Ego-Defensive Reactions to Frustration. *J. Exp. Psychol.*, 1943, *32*, 64–74.

18. ROSENZWEIG, S. The Investigation of Repression as an Instance of Experimental Idio-dynamics. *Psychol. Rev.*, 1952, *59*, 339–345.

19. ROSENZWEIG, S., & MASON, G. An Experimental Study of Memory in Relation to the Theory of Repression. *Brit. J. Psychol.*, 1934, *24*, 247–265.

20. SEARS, R. R. Personality. In C. P. Stone (Ed.), *Annual Review of Psychology.* Vol. 1. Stanford: Annual Reviews, 1950. Pp. 105–118.

21. SNEDECOR, G. W. *Statistical Methods.* Ames: Iowa State College Press, 1946.

22. ZEIGARNIK, B. On Finished and Unfinished Tasks. In W. D. Ellis (Ed.), *A Source Book of Gestalt Psychology.* New York: Harcourt Brace, 1938. Pp. 300–314.

3

EXPECTATION AND THE
PERCEPTION OF COLOR
JEROME S. BRUNER, LEO POSTMAN, and JOHN RODRIGUES

When Bruner, Postman, and Rodrigues speak of a subject becoming "tuned" toward a class of stimuli, or of his having "made a hypothesis," one could reasonably speak of his having tentatively "construed" or "instantiated" that class of stimuli. They observe the organism as it seeks to derive a hypothesis that will be solidly confirmed. They carry out a series of studies to define the nature of the organism's functioning under conditions in which the stimulus situation does not provide a wealth of information to confirm or deny the subject's initial hypothesis. They demonstrate that when that hypothesis is generated, but the stimulus situation provides little information regarding the hypothesis, that hypothesis will retain major status in the judgment of the nature of the event. Specifically, if a subject construes a stimulus as a "tomato," he will judge it to be redder than another stimulus that has been construed as an "orange," despite there being no measurable difference between the light wave lengths reflected from both stimuli. Sherif and Cantril (1947, p. 62) develop a proposition that corresponds to the one demonstrated in this article. The greater the ambiguity of a stimulus situation, the greater the possibility that judgments will reflect the application of each individual's idiosyncratic, personal frames of reference. In short, judgments of stimuli are made in a way that maintains the consistency and stability of an individual's existing construct system. Tomatoes simply cannot be yellow!

REFERENCE

SHERIF, M. & CANTRIL, H. *The Psychology of Ego-Involvements.* New York: Wiley, 1947.

*   *   *

Reprinted from American Journal of Psychology, *1951*, 64, *216–227, by permission of Jerome S. Bruner and the University of Illinois Press.*

The present experiment tests a proposition derived from a general theory of perception. Although the general theory has been stated in tentative terms elsewhere, a brief outline of it is necessary here as an introduction to our theme.[1]

We shall assume that perceiving can be analyzed as a three-step process. First, the organism gets set or prepared in a certain way, selectively 'tuned' toward some class of stimuli or events in the environment. When the organism is thus set or tuned, it is said to have an *hypothesis*. The second step consists of the *input of stimulus information*. By using the term 'stimulus-information,' or simply 'information,' we seek to indicate that we are dealing with the cue characteristics of the stimulus rather than with the energy characteristics of stimulation.[2] In the third step of the cycle the hypothesis is *confirmed* or *infirmed*. Given a certain quantity and kind of information, an hypothesis will be confirmed and lead to a stable perception. If the critical quantity of 'cue' information is not present, the hypothesis will be infirmed partially or fully. Under these circumstances, an unstable perceptual field will result and an alteration in hypothesis will follow, that will, in turn, be 'tested' against incoming information. The cycle of checking altered hypotheses against incoming information will continue until there is a stabilized perception. The range of information or of 'cues' which is known by independent test to be potentially confirming or infirming of an hypothesis, we shall call *appropriate* or *relevant* to that hypothesis. Thus, for example, an hypothesis about the size of an object can be confirmed by a variety of cues to magnitude, distance, and so on. The appropriateness of these cues can be determined independently by traditional cue-reduction experiments familiar in the study of the constancies. Note particularly that appropriate information is necessary either to confirm *or* infirm an hypothesis.

The hypothesis with which an organism faces a situation at the moment of initial stimulus-input we shall refer to as the *initial hypothesis*. The hypotheses which develop when an initial hypothesis is not confirmed we shall refer to as *consequent hypotheses*. The difference is an heuristic one and does not connote a qualitative distinction in the operation of initial and consequent hypotheses.

[1] J. S. Bruner, Personality and the Process of Perceiving, in *Perception: An Approach to Personality*, edited by R. R. Blake and G. V. Ramsey, 1951 (in press); Leo Postman, Toward a General Theory of Cognition, in *Social Psychology at the Crossroads*, edited by J. H. Rohrer and M. Sherif, 1951 (in press). In our development of the concept of hypothesis we have, of course, leaned on the work of E. C. Tolman and I. Krechevsky, Means-and-Readiness and hypothesis—a contribution to comparative psychology, *Psychol. Rev.*, 40, 1933, 60–70.

[2] R. S. Harper and E. G. Boring, Cues, this Journal, 61, 1948, 119–123.

An hypothesis may vary in strength. *The greater the strength of an hypothesis, the less the amount of appropriate information necessary to confirm it.* One may vary the amount of appropriate information given to the organism in numerous ways: by changing the amount of time a stimulus is available, by altering the illumination of the stimulus-field, by changing the extent to which a stimulus-field is in focus, and the like. The strength of an hypothesis (and, therefore, the amount of appropriate information necessary to confirm it) varies as a function of its past use, past success, the degree to which it competes with other hypotheses and many other conditions which need not concern us here.

In the present experiment, we shall not be concerned with varying the strength of hypotheses. We shall assume it to be constant. Our concern is rather with the role of *appropriateness of information* as it affects the confirming of initial hypotheses of equal strength. The specific proposition which we seek to test is the following; the smaller the quantity of appropriate information, the greater the probability of an established initial hypothesis being confirmed, even if environmental events fail to agree with such hypotheses. An inverse way of restating this proposition is to say that the greater the quantity of appropriate information present, the greater the opportunity for infirming an initial hypothesis where necessary and developing 'fitting' consequent hypotheses.

THE EXPERIMENT

The basic task of all *S*s was to make a color match between a stimulus-patch and a variable color-mixer. Conditions of judgment and the color and shape of the stimulus-patch varied systematically in the four experimental conditions to be described.

Stimuli. The stimuli used consisted of eight patches cut from paper to represent the following objects:

Ovaloid objects: shaped to represent (and designated as)
    Tomato (5.0 cm. horizontal axis, 3.0 cm. vertical axis)
    Tangerine (5.1 cm. horizontal, 3.0 cm. vertical)
    Lemon (5.1 cm. horizontal, 2.9 cm. vertical)
    Neutral oval (5.1 cm. horizontal, 3.0 cm vertical)

Elongated ellipsoid objects:
    Boiled lobster claw (7.6 cm. horizontal, 2.4 cm. vertical)
    Carrot (7.7 cm. horizontal, 2.2 cm. vertical)
    Banana (7.7 cm. horizontal, 2.0 cm. vertical)
    Neutral elongated ellipse (7.6 cm. horizontal, 2.3 cm. vertical)

The matching task. It was the task of *S* to match these patches, shaped and designated as specified, to a variable color-wheel (20 cm. in diameter) made up of yellow and red segments. The color-mixer could be shifted in hue from a well saturated red through the oranges to a well saturated yellow without stopping the wheel. A modified method of adjustment was used, *E* altering the color-wheel at the instruction of *S*. In all four conditions to be discussed, a group of 8 *S*s being allocated to each condition, the color-wheel was at a distance of 150 cm. from *S*, at approximate eye-level.

Order of presentation of the eight stimulus-patches was controlled in the same way throughout. Every object-patch appeared in each of the eight positions and, therefore, every serial position contained all of the eight objects for each of the four groups. Upon the presentation of an object-patch, *S* made two successive matches, one with the initial positon of the color-wheel at red, the other with the initial position at yellow. Whether initial yellow or initial red came first for a given match was randomly determined.

The four experimental conditions. The four groups of eight *S*s were treated as follows.

Group I. Induced color group (uninformed). A stimulus-patch was placed on a table before *S*, illuminated by a 150-w. GE Reflector Spot sealed-beam in a shielded alcove 60 cm. above the table, shining directly on the patch. Each patch (tomato, tangerine, etc.) was cut from neutral gray paper (Stoelting #19), and placed on a blue-green sheet of paper (Stoelting #10) of the dimensions 15 × 15 cm. Gray figure and blue-green background were covered by a finely ground glass, also 15 × 15 cm. All these operations were performed behind a cardboard screen which had been dropped between *S* and the field. When the screen was lifted, *S* saw before him on the brown table a poorly saturated blue-green square on which could be seen a brownish orange figure. The color-wheel and the rest of the field were illuminated by four 40-w. fluorescent lamps overhead.

S was instructed that his task was to match the color-wheel to the object before him on the table. Between the stimulus-patch and the color-wheel there was approximately 80° of visual arc so that the comparison was perforce successive rather than simultaneous. As each object-patch was presented for matching, *S* was told what it was, e.g. "This is a tangerine. Make the color-wheel the same color as it." As already indicated, two matches were made for each object-patch, one from the yellow and one from the red initial positions of the color-wheel. *S*s experienced some difficulty in making the match since the induced color was not sufficiently pronounced in hue to provide a good basis for judging. It was also impossible to reproduce a color on the wheel which was alike in surface and saturation to the stimulus-patch. Finally, the hue-match was only approximate, since no combination of the yellow and red sectors would yield a hue identical to the induced orange brown.

After making two matches to each of the eight stimulus-patches, *S* was given a 5-min. rest-period. Following this, he repeated the identical procedure. Then came a rest-period of 10 min., following which *S* was asked to make *from memory* settings on the color-wheel for each of the eight patches already seen. Again, two settings were made for each patch. In all, the first procedure required about an hour of *S*'s time.

Group II. Induced color group (informed). This group received the same treatment as the preceding group, with one exception. At the end of the first judging-period and during the 5-min. rest, *S* was given a brief lecture on induced color and shown how the color was produced in the stimulus-patches judged. In short, their second series of judgments and their memory-matches were made with knowledge of the 'illusory' quality of the colors before them. A judging session required about an hour.

The second condition was designed, of course, to provide additional information to our *S*s about the hue of the stimulus-patches which they were being asked to judge. The third and fourth groups, as we shall see, were provided with still more information.

Group III. Stable color group. The judging procedure for this group was exactly the same as for Group I, save that in place of induced color, a 'real' color was used for the stimulus-patches. This was a well saturated orange-color which matched very closely the middle region of the red-yellow mixture on the color-wheel both with respect to hue and to saturation. The stimulus-patches were pasted on glossy white cardboard plaques, again 15 × 15 cm. in dimension. As in the first two conditions, the cards bearing the stimuli were so placed before *S* on the table that about 80° of visual arc intervened between the stimulus and the color-wheel, thus necessitating successive comparison. The color-wheel and the stimulus-patch were illuminated by 150 w. sealed-beams of the type previously described at a distance of 60 cm. Judgments required about an hour.

Group IV. Optimal matching group. An effort was made in designing the procedure for this group to provide *S*s with a maximum of appropriate information for making their matches with a minimum of irrelevant information in the situation. Put in communications-engineering terms, we sought to establish a judging condition in which the signal-to-noise ratio was at a maximum. A box was constructed, 150 cm. in length, 61 cm. in width, and 50 cm. in height. At one end of the box an eyepiece was inserted, approximately 3.5 × 11 cm. in size. At the far end of the box, the wheel of the color-mixer and the stimulus-patch appeared side by side. The inside floor, ceiling and the walls of the box were painted a homogeneous medium gray (matching Hering gray #15). Set in concealed alcoves on either side of the box were two spotlights (150 w., GE sealed-beams) which were trained from a distance of 60 cm. on the color-wheel and on the stimulus-patch. The appearance of the field, viewed from the eyepiece, was of a homogeneous, gray, well-lighted, closed tunnel, at the far end of which were the wheel of the color-mixer and a stimulus-patch in the same frontal parallel plane. Stimulus-patches were cut of orange paper of identical hue and saturation with those used in the immediately preceding condition and mounted on cardboard. The cardboard, 17.5 × 30.5 cm. in dimension, was inserted into the box through a slide opening. When the cardboard was thus inserted, there was a distance of 10 cm. from the edge of the stimulus-patch to the edge of the color-wheel. Such a separation of patch and wheel at a distance of 150 cm. from the eye made the task of simultaneous comparison quite easy. Group IV, then, was the only one which could make matches by simultaneous comparison. It should be remarked, finally, that Group IV had the very minimum of extraneous stimulus-input, competing cues from the room and general background of the room being eliminated by the use of the 'reduction' tunnel. Because of the easier judging conditions, Ss required but three-quarters of an hour to complete this procedure.

RESULTS

Recall the proposition advanced for testing. The smaller the quantity of appropriate information, the greater the probability of an initial hypothesis being confirmed even if environmental events fail to agree with such hypotheses. In proportion to the deficiency of stimulus-information, established initial hypotheses will determine the color match. The results, generally, confirm this prediction.

Table 1 contains a summary of the judgments made by the four groups

TABLE 1   Average settings of color-wheel for various objects during first series of matches.

Settings are expressed as deviations in degrees of yellow from the average of settings made for all objects by a given group. Positive sign denotes more yellow; negative sign, less yellow.

Stimulus-objects	Group I (Induced color, Ss uninformed)	Group II (Induced color, Ss informed)	Group III (Stable color)	Group IV (Stable color, optimal cond.)
Red	$-14.2°$	$-12.1°$	$-3.6°$	$+2.9°$
Orange	$-0.6°$	$-0.2°$	$+3.4°$	$-4.5°$
Yellow	$+19.2°$	$+10.6°$	$-0.8°$	$+4.5°$
Neutral	$-5.6°$	$+1.7°$	$+1.2°$	$-2.4°$
Mean (yellow)	$121.4°$	$118.5°$	$141.1°$	$191.6°$
SD	$39.9°$	$37.0°$	$23.4°$	$15.6°$

during the first matching series. In order to estimate the effect of initial hypotheses in the matches, we computed first a grand mean in degrees of yellow on the wheel of all the matches made by a group in this series, regardless of the patch which was being matched. We then computed the difference between this grand mean and the mean match made for each kind of stimulus patch: 'red' objects, 'orange' objects, 'yellow' objects, and neutral objects. The final row of Table 1 also contains the standard deviation of all the judgments of a group. The latter may be taken as a rough approximation of sensitivity to hue differences under the particular judging conditions imposed upon each group.

Consider first the matches made for 'red', 'yellow', and 'orange' objects. In both Groups I and II (the groups which worked with contrast-induced colors), normally red objects were judged considerably redder, normally yellow objects, considerably yellower than the average level. In both groups, moreover, the 'orange' objects were matched to a color almost exactly at the average level. It is interesting to remark in passing that Ss in these groups preferred the information that they believed all their matches to be the same. Nevertheless there is between the setting made for 'red' objects and those made for 'yellow' objects for Group I an average difference of 33.4° of yellow segment on the wheel. The difference for Group II is 22.7° (Fig. 5). Both of these color-differences are grossly supraliminal, the difference between a yellowish orange and a reddish orange.

With improvement of judging conditions as provided in the procedures applied to Groups III and IV, the effect is first reduced and finally washed out. Sufficiently stable stimulus-information is provided to alter the initial hypothesis established by such instructions as "This is a lemon," or "This is a carrot." Note too in these groups a striking reduction in the standard deviation of all judgments which results from the increase in appropriate stimulus-information. Both 'orange' and neutral objects yield matches which fluctuate closely about the grand mean.

Table 2 contains a summary of matching in the second series—a second

TABLE 2   Average settings of color-wheel for various objects during second series of matches.

Settings are expressed as deviations in degrees of yellow from the average of settings made for all objects by a given group. Positive sign denotes more yellow; negative sign, less yellow.

Stimulus-objects	Group I (Induced color, Ss uninformed)	Group II (Induced color, Ss informed)	Group III (Stable color)	Group IV (Stable color, optimal cond.)
Red	−9.9°	−15.9°	−5.4°	+3.6°
Orange	+3.7°	+0.5°	−0.2°	−2.8°
Yellow	+13.9°	+12.8°	+5.8°	−0.3°
Neutral	+2.2°	+2.5°	+0.4°	−0.3°
Mean (yellow)	113.3°	113.1°	142.1°	184.7°
SD	41.0°	35.5°	23.4°	15.9°

series of judgments of the eight patches after a 5-min. rest. Save in Group II, this second series may be regarded simply as a replication of the first series. Recall that Group II received a brief lecture on, and demonstration of, color contrast before embarking on these judgments. The results were substantially the same as before. Note that the lecture and demonstration seemed to have no effect on Group II. Where before the color-distance between 'yellow' and 'red' object matches was slightly less than 23° of yellow segment, now it is somewhat more than 28° In this second series, Group III seems to succumb more to the effect of the labeling or meaning of the objects judged than in the first series. Note again that for Groups I, II, and III, 'orange' and neutral objects fall close to the grand mean.

Group IV, working with simultaneous comparison under optimal conditions of illumination and surround, shows no systematic effect at all and continues to exhibit a strikingly high sensitivity as one may infer from the size of the standard deviation of their judging distribution.

When we come to the third series of matches—matches made from memory—a striking effect is obtained. These results are summarized in Table 3. Differences for the first three groups are of great magnitude.

TABLE 3 **Average settings of color-wheel for various objects during memory matches.**

Settings are expressed as deviations in degrees of yellow from the average of settings made for all objects by a given group. Positive sign denotes more yellow; negative sign, less yellow.

Stimulus-objects	Group I (Induced color, Ss uninformed)	Group II (Induced color, Ss informed)	Group III (Stable color)	Group IV (Stable color, optimal cond.)
Red	−25.9°	−13.0°	−13.4°	−1.9°
Orange	+4.5°	+3.9°	+0.4°	−1.9°
Yellow	+22.3°	+11.5°	+11.3°	+5.5°
Neutral	−0.4°	−2.5°	+1.6°	−1.1°
Mean (yellow)	109.3°	103.0°	141.2°	187.3°
SD	44.7°	27.2°	20.2°	21.7°

Between the 'yellow' and 'red' matches of Group I, there is a separation of 48.2° of yellow segment; for Group II it is 24.5°; and for Group III, 24.7° (Fig. 5). Under memory-matching conditions, Group IV begins to exhibit a systematic judging tendency, although it is not great; a separation of 7.4° of yellow segment between 'red' and 'yellow' object matches, the meaning of which is rendered somewhat dubious by the lack of distinction between matches for 'red' and 'orange' objects.

The results reviewed above are presented in somewhat different arrangement in Figs 1–4. In these figures, all scores are again expressed as deviations in degrees of yellow from grand means for each series of judgments. The rearrangement of the data emphasizes the change in matches made by a group from series to series. Fig. 5 gives an overall view of the changing color-distance between matches made to designated red and yellow objects.

To test the significance of results, the matching data of each of the four groups were subjected to an analysis of variance. The contribution of the following sources of variance was tested.

Series (first, second, and memory matches)
Shape of objects (whether ovaloid or ellipsoid)
Designation of objects (whether normally red, orange, yellow, neutral)
Initial wheel position (whether judgment started from yellow or red position of color wheel)
Variance of individual Ss

The analysis was performed on untransformed data, entries comprising the number of degrees of yellow in each setting.

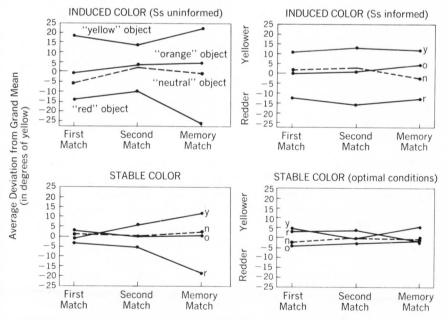

FIGS. 1-4   *Average Settings of Color-Wheels for Various Objects During Two Matches with Objects Present and Memory Matches*
Settings are expressed as deviations in degrees of yellow from grand mean of settings made for all objects by a given group.

The analysis of Group I yielded highly significant F-scores, all the sources of variance, save one which was significant at less than the 0.1% level of confidence. That was stimulus-shape, which was far short of significance.[3] Group II showed a pattern much like the first group. All sources, save stimulus-shape, contributed significantly at levels beyond 0.1%. Shape was not significant. Two sources contribute at the 0.1% level: Ss and the designated color of the stimulus-objects. The variance due to initial color-wheel position is significant at a level between 5% and 1%. The contribution of the three matching series is insignificant as, again, is stimulus-shape.

Group IV presents a problem in the analysis of variance. All individual sources of variance contribute significantly, although designated color of objects is significant only at the 5% level, while in all previous groups designated color contributed at the 1% level or better. It is important to remember that although a significant F-score was obtained for designated color, *no intelligible trend can be found in the means of this group*. 'Red' objects, for example, were sometimes judged yellower than 'yellow' objects. In general, the rank order of the settings approaches randomness. The remaining sources of variance for this group yielded F-scores significant at the 0.1% level, variance of S being at the 0.1% level of confidence. As to the question why judging series and the shape of the objects become significant sources without any discernible trend in means, we must simply say that the variability of judgments in Group IV, operating under optimal conditions of judgment, was so very small that *anything* (including the degree of incredulity in the Ss' view of our proceedings) was likely to prove significant.

INTERPRETATION

We have reported an experiment which is at once as old as Hering's conception of memory-color[4] and at the same time is presented as supporting evidence for a contemporary theory of perception. Perhaps we should first come to terms with history. Hering, of course, introduced the conception of memory-color to account for certain phenomena of color-constancy.

[3] The interested reader who may wish to examine in more detail the results of the statistical analysis of our data may obtain a fuller summary by writing directly to the authors at the Laboratory of Social Relations, Harvard University. Limitations of space permit the barest summary here.

[4] E. Hering, *Grundzüge der Lehre vom Lichtsinn*, 1905, 1–80. See also G. K. Adams, An Experimental Study of Memory Color and Related Phenomenon, this Journal, 34, 1923, 359–407.

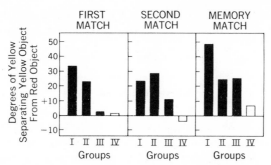

FIG. 5 *Separation Between Settings for Color-Linked Objects Differences between 'yellow' objects and 'red' objects are expressed in degrees of yellow.*

Duncker showed that a notion such as memory-color or trace-color could be used in the interpretation of the mode of appearance of meaningful objects under constancy conditions using hidden illumination.[5] Duncker demonstrated, for example, that a leaf cut from green felt and bathed in a hidden red illumination was judged greener by his *S*s than a donkey cut from identical material in identical illumination. Indeed, it is patent that the role of 'memory' as a determinant of attributive judgment has long been recognized as important in the field of perception.

A more recent and more systematic attempt to describe the effects of past experience with colors upon present judgments of them has been undertaken by Helson in a provocative paper on adaptation-level.[6] In very brief summary, adaptation-level theory would hold that, within limits, the judgment of an attribute will depend upon the relation of the stimulus judged at any one moment to the weighted geometric mean of the series of stimuli presented previously in the judging situation. It is difficult to apply Helson's conception to our own data for one quite obvious reason. Each of our judging groups judged only one color. The difference in the stimuli was not in their photometric colors, but in their designation as objects implying certain normal colors. The effect of the designation, however, may be referred not to the situational adaptation-level but to the adaptation-levels for various types of objects built up in the course of past commerce with tomatoes, tangerines, lemons, and other like objects. However clarifying such a statement may be, we should like to go beyond it to a consideration of the cognitive processes involved in the type of our own judging situations.

We turn accordingly to the theoretical framework presented in general

[5]K. Duncker, The Influence of Past Experience Upon Perceptual Properties, this Journal, 52, 1939, 255–265.

[6]H. Helson, Adaptation-Level as a Basis for a Quantitative Theory of Frames of Reference, *Psychol. Rev.,* 55, 1948, 297–313.

terms in our introductory paragraphs. Let us interpret the behavior of our *S*s in terms of the three-cycle conception of 'hypothesis-information-confirmation.' Assume the following sequence of events to be occurring, for example, in Group I. *S* is given the initial hypothesis by instruction that the poorly saturated patch before him represents a tomato, an hypothesis readily confirmed by shape-cues from the stimulus-patch. The hypothesis 'tomato' is not, however, fully confirmed by the color cues provided. Because of the poorness or instability of the color-information, the initial hypothesis is not, however, completely infirmed. That this initial hypothesis plays a large part in determining the final color match, in short is not fully replaced by a consequent 'corrected' hypothesis, is indicated by the systematic tendency of *S*s to make a redder match to objects designated as tomatoes and boiled lobster claws than to objects not normally red (see Fig. 1). Given an input of inadequate information, the initial hypothesis plays a proportionally greater role by virtue of not having been infirmed.

Nor are initial hypotheses infirmed appreciably by providing Group II with added verbal information about the nature of the contrast-color which is used in the stimulus-patch. From the first to the second matching situation, there is no discernible change (see Fig. 2). As in the case of verbal efforts to dispel such classical illusions as the Muller-Lyer, here too our instructions seemed to provide no effective perceptual information. Perhaps verbal instruction does not basically alter the *stimulus* information given *S*.

The only difference between Groups I and II appears to be in the tendency of the second group to show a decreasing variability of judgment with more experience in the judging situation (Tables 1–2). We do not know why this occurred.

In Group III, stimulus-information is better, serves more adequately to infirm the initial hypothesis which links the various stimulus-patches with certain 'normal' object-colors. In consequence, the matches made by this group show less of a tendency to redden objects designated as 'normally red' and to yellow objects designated as 'normally yellow.' Yet the information, somewhat contaminated as it is by extraneous information in the perceptual field is not sufficiently appropriate to infirm the initial hypothesis altogether. In this group, moreover, as in the preceding groups, judgments are made under conditions of successive comparison. What does this imply? Essentially, it means that there is a moment intervening between looking at the stimulus-patch—the relevant stimulus-information—and making an adjustment on the color-wheel to match the patch. Granted, the intervals consumed in turning successively through the 80° separating patch and color are not great in duration, yet separation may serve to reinforce the systematic judging tendency by introducing reliance on memory-information. We shall return to this point shortly in discussing the results of the memory series.

Group IV, making its judgments under optimal conditions with a minimum of competing information in the situation and with opportuniity for simultaneous comparison shows no systematic effect at all. Stimulus-information is sufficiently stable and adequate to infirm the initial hypothesis, and the matches which are made reflect not the color of objects designated by the E but rather the photometric color of the patches themselves.

We turn finally to the results of the memory series. Note that under all conditions represented by our four groups, some systematic effects were found; e.g., in memory, orange-colored tomatoes are redder than orange-colored lemons. The greatest effect was exhibited by the naïve groups operating with induced contrast-color (Group I). For them, there were 48.2° of yellow separating their matches for red and yellow designated objects (Fig. 5). Note the marked difference, however, between Groups I and II. The only distinction between the two groups was that the second was given information about color-contrast. Whether for this, or for some other reason, the memory effect of object-color designation was markedly reduced in spite of an equality of the effect in the second perceptual matching situation.

How may we account for the heightened effect of the initial hypothesis on memory matches? We should like to propose the following approach, one which recommends itself for the continuity it suggests between phenomena usually called perceptual and phenomena conventionally designated as memory. In any given situation, the individual may depend upon input stimulus-information for the confirmation of hypotheses or, lacking such perceptual input, upon memory-information as represented by traces. We suggest, furthermore, that trace-information is less stable, or less appropriate information, or both, for confirming or infirming initial hypotheses of the kind built into our Ss. This being the case, initial hypotheses should have a determinative effect upon memory-matches in much the same way that the initial hypotheses of Groups I and II had a determinative effect upon the perceptual matches because of poor stimulus-information provided.

CONCLUSION

Given less than optimal stimulus-conditions, certain factors of past experience may play a determinative part in perceptual organization. For past experience is normally among the determinants of initial hypotheses.

Insofar as we may adopt the above as a general conclusion, it is also possible to draw a methodological lesson from our results. When an experiment demonstrates under certain conditions an effect of needs or past experience on perception, that experiment is not necessarily invalidated by another done under other conditions and showing that the alleged effect has not appeared. The basic question is under what conditions of stimulus-information does the effect occur and by what improvement in stimulus-information can it be destroyed.

4

EFFECTS OF INTERACTION
OF MOTIVATION AND FEEDBACK
ON TASK PERFORMANCE[1]
ELIZABETH G. FRENCH

Studies of reinforcement have shown that rewards which are chosen by the subject are more effective in promoting learning (Brackbill and Jack, 1958). This study by French offers support for a concept of reinforcement as confirmation of the validity of the subject's construction of events. French's study deals with the phenomena of achievement motivation, as did Atkinson's study. Essentially, she chose one group of persons who construed themselves as *achievers* and another group who construed themselves as *affiliators,* and then provided each group with varied confirmation of their self-view as they worked on a task. When achievement-motivated persons were told that their behavior was congruent with achievement orientation, they functioned more efficiently than when they were told that they were behaving in an affiliative manner. Affiliation-motivated persons performed more adequately if their self-view was confirmed by the experimenter's report of her observations of their behavior.

An observation of increased efficiency in problem solving can be regarded as validation of the assumption that motivational factors are functioning so that an individual has been placed in an optimal level of activation. If the same formula is acceptable in considering French's study, we would say that her subjects were more adequately motivated when they were presented with data that was congruent with their self-concept. When they were led to view themselves acting in ways that were consistent with their total self system, they were motivated in a

Reprinted from J. W. Atkinson (Ed.), Motives in Fantasy, Action and Society, *copyright 1952, by D. Van Nostrand, and used with the permission of the author and the publisher.*
[1]This study was carried out as part of the United States Air Force Personnel and Training Research and Development Program. The opinions expressed, however, are those of the author and are not to be construed as reflecting the views or endorsement of the Department of the Air Force.

way that promoted more effective problem-solution. In the Overview to this section we point out that maintenance of self-consistency could be regarded as a basic motivational construct. Having arranged the conditions of the study as she did, French gives us an opportunity to interpret her data as evidence that people function more efficiently—that is, they are more adequately motivated—when they believe that they are acting in ways that are congruent with their previously developed self-constructions.

REFERENCE

BRACKBILL, Y. & JACK, D. Discrimination Learning in Children as a Function of Reinforcement Value. *Child Development,* 1958, *29,* 185–190.

*   *   *

Recent work of Gibb and his associates (Lott, Schopler and Gibb, 1955)[2] has led them to conclude that feeling-oriented feedback, that is, feedback dealing with the personal interaction of the group members, produces higher task efficiency than feedback directly related to the accomplishment of the group task. The feeling-oriented feedback, they hypothesize, reduces defensiveness and permits effective action. Earlier studies by the present author, while not directly comparable, suggest circumstances in which Gibb's finding might not hold. In one experiment (French, 1956) the situation was so structured that the *S* was required to choose as a work partner either a friend who had demonstrated lack of competence on the task to be performed or a man he didn't especially like who had demonstrated competence. When the kinds of choices made were tabulated according to previously obtained motivation scores of the choosers, it was found that *S*s high in achievement and low in affiliation motivation tended to choose for competence rather than friendship. On the other hand, *S*s high in affiliation and low in achievement motivation chose their friends. The experiment was not set up to permit ratings of effectiveness of the friendly and nonfriendly pairs, but the high achievement-motivated *S*s indicated by their choices that they didn't expect to be disturbed by a certain amount of lack of friendliness in the work situation—at least not to the extent of giving up the best chances to succeed. The affiliation-motivated *S*s were not willing to expose themselves to possible unfriendliness even at the risk of task failure.

In another experiment (French, 1955) it was shown that when *S*s could satisfy achievement goals when working on tasks in which success was primarily dependent on the effort *S* was willing to expend, task scores were

---

[2]See also Gibb, Smith, & Roberts, 1952, and Roberts, 1955.

related to achievement motivation. When the task was presented in such a way that working on it could satisfy affiliation goals, then performance was related to affiliation motivation and not to achievement.

These findings lead to the prediction that the two kinds of feedback would affect achievement-motivated and affiliation-motivated Ss differently. Affiliation-motivated Ss should react as did Gibb's Ss since there is evidence that they are the ones who show concern for friendly relations even in a working group. In addition, feeling feedback could conceivably serve the function of making good group relations at least a subsidiary task goal since the task is discussed in group relations terms. Then, to the extent that success on the task depends on the Ss' efforts, affiliation-motivated Ss should do better. Achievement-motivated Ss would be expected to do better with task feedback. Since they are less concerned over interpersonal relations, they would be indifferent to efforts to reduce tension. Also they would be expected to respond with lessened effort toward a primarily affiliation goal and heightened effort to an achievement one. And finally, they would attend more to the task feedback and so profit from it.

The specific hypothesis to be tested is that Ss high in achievement and low in affiliation motivation will perform better on a task when given task relevant feedback than when given feeling feedback. Ss with the opposite motivation pattern will perform better when given feeling rather than task feedback.

Also tested was the hypothesis that achievement-motivated Ss would get higher scores if the problem appeared to them to be more of an individual than a group task and that the reverse would be true for affiliation-motivated Ss. The reasoning behind this hypothesis is that the possibility of a feeling of individual accomplishment would provide the achievement oriented with additional incentive plus freedom from frustration and from the feeling of being dependent on others. The sense of belonging to the group is more important to the affiliation motivated, on the other hand, and minimizing the group aspects of the task might be expected to be disturbing to them and reduce their efficiency.

These two hypotheses were tested experimentally by subjecting groups of Ss of known motivation patterns to both kinds of feedback under both kinds of task orientation.

METHOD

Groups of four Ss worked together on a story assembly problem. The subjects in any given group all had the same motivation pattern: either they were all high in achievement and low in affiliation or all the reverse.

While giving the initial instructions to the Ss, the E established the task as either group or partly individual, as appropriate. The groups worked for a specified amount of time, during which the E interrupted twice to record scores and give the appropriate feedback, either task or feeling. A final task score, taken at the expiration of the time limit, provided the performance measure. The interim solutions were taken merely to provide an easy opening for the feedback discussions.

Formation of motivation groups. Before their scheduled reporting for the experimental session, flights of basic airmen at Lackland Air Force Base were given the Test of Insight (French, 1955) as a measure of achievement and affiliation motivations. A total of 128 men with achievement motivation scores above the median score of 6 and affiliation scores below the median score of 5 were selected as the high-achievement-motivation Ss. A like number of men with affiliation scores above 5 and achievement below 6 were selected for the high-affiliation-motivation Ss. In both cases the additional criterion that the two scores for a particular man must be three points apart or more was used. Ss with similar motivation patterns were assembled in groups of four. Inevitably there were variations in the average motivation scores for the groups. Care was taken to assign groups to conditions in such a way that the distribution of group scores was the same for all conditions. Likewise the Armed Forces Qualifications Test (AFQT) scores, which indicate intelligence level, varied from group to group. Again care was taken to assure similar distributions of AFQT scores in all conditions. With these restrictions in mind eight High-Achievement and eight High-Affiliation groups were assigned to each of the following experimental conditions: Task Feedback–Group Orientation and Task Feedback–Individual Orientation, Feeling Feedback–Group Orientation and Feeling Feedback–Individual Orientation. F tests demonstrated that the equating of motivation and intelligence across experimental conditions was adequate.

The task. The suggestion for the task also came from Gibb *et al.* (1955), though the actual problem was constructed by the author. It consisted of 20 phrases or short sentences which made up a little story when put together correctly. Each S was given five cards with one phrase on each card. The Ss' task was to reconstruct the story, with the restriction that it must be done at the verbal level. No S could show another his cards and no one was permitted to write anything down. In scoring, one point was given for each phrase used, and an additional point if it followed its correct predecessor. In addition, five extra points were given if the complete and correct sequence was given before the time limit expired. This procedure provides a possible range of scores of zero to 45.

Instructions to the group. The Ss' perception of the group or individual nature of the task was created at the same time that the general instructions were given. The main part of the instructions was the same for all groups and read:

"The problem today is to fit together the parts of a story. I have here four packs of five cards each. There is a sentence or a part of a sentence written on each card. When they are all fitted together in the proper order, they will tell a sensible story. All the cards fit in and there is only one right way to do it. Each one of you will get a packet. The task is to decide in what order the cards should be read to tell the story. No one person will have cards which he can put together; each man has to fit his in with all the others. *But* you must do this without showing the cards to each other. It must all be done by conversation. You may read aloud and discuss all you like, but each man keeps his own cards and shows them to no one. You work out the proper order by discussion.

"You will work for 10 minutes, and I will stop you and ask for your solution as far as you've gone; then we'll talk about how you are getting along. After that you'll work 10 minutes longer, stop again to read your solution and discuss progress; and finally you'll work a third 10 minute period. At the end of that period I'll ask you for your final solution. You may, of course, make changes from one solution to the next as well as additions."

For the Group problem orientation the Ss were then told:

"I'll give you two minutes warning before the final time limit, so you will be prepared to give the best single solution you can."

The Individual orientation was provided by the instruction:

"I'll give you two minutes warning before I call for your final solution. I should say here that either on the final solution or on either of the other two, it is not necessary that you all agree. One or more of you may submit different versions, if you like."

The feedback periods. During the working periods the groups were observed and desirable task behavior or interpersonal behavior, according to the condition to which the group was assigned, was checked against a prepared list as it occurred. Only positive feedback was used since positive and negative feedback have been found to have different effects (Gibb, Smith, and Roberts, 1955) and it seemed best not to include an additional variable. At the end of 10 minutes the E interrupted the group, asked that the Ss read whatever parts they had put together, and recorded the phrases read. Then, for the Task Feedback groups the two-minute discussion was introduced by, "This group is working very efficiently." Following that, five of the specific behaviors previously noted by the E were mentioned. These included such points as: reading off all cards immediately, trying to rough out possible plots, making use of grammatical cues, identifying characters in the story, etc.

For the Feeling Feedback groups the introductory phrase was, "This group works very well together." The specific behaviors mentioned included: praising each other for making good suggestions, giving everyone a chance to contribute, not becoming impatient with poor suggestions, failing to argue or keeping arguments friendly, etc.

After two minutes the Ss returned to the task and worked 10 minutes longer, at the end of which the recording of the phrases and the feedback discussion were repeated. Essentially the same points were made, but the wording was sufficiently different to avoid a feeling of repetition.

Ss then worked for a final 10 minutes and read off the final solution. This concluded the experiment except for the reading of the correct solution by E, which was invariably demanded by the Ss.

RESULTS

Although several of the Ss in the individual condition took advantage of the opportunity to give separate solutions the first and second times, none of them did in giving the final solution. This fact greatly simplified the handling of the data even though it did suggest that the second hypothesis might not be completely tenable. The performance score means, standard deviations and ranges for the eight experimental groups are given in Table 1 and the analysis of variance of the interactions in Table 2. The test of the

TABLE 1   Task-score means, standard deviations, and ranges for the eight experimental conditions.

		Achievement		Affiliation	
		Grp.	Ind.	Grp.	Ind.
	Mean	40.50	39.38	29.12	25.12
Task	SD	3.68	4.48	5.14	3.44
	Range	36-45	33-45	24-36	20-32
	Mean	29.25	30.87	38.38	31.50
Feeling	SD	3.86	3.34	4.45	8.43
	Range	25-37	27-36	30-45	19-45

main hypothesis is, of course, the interaction between kind of motivation and kind of feedback. This is significant at well beyond the .001 level. The

TABLE 2   Analysis of variance of task scores.

Source	df	MS	F	P
Motivation	1	252.02	12.25	
Feedback	1	17.02	—	
Orientation	1	107.64	5.23	
M × F	1	1251.38	60.83	.001
M × O	1	129.39	6.29	.05
F × O	1	.02	—	
M × F × O	1	31.64	1.54	
Within	56	20.57		

second hypothesis was tested by the interaction between kind of motivation and kind of orientation to the problem. This F ratio was significant at
the .05 level. In interpreting these F ratios attention should perhaps be
called to the very small ratio which would be obtained for the interaction
between feedback and orientation. A ratio as small as this would occur by
chance only about 4 times in 100, which circumstance suggests the
possibility that some unspecified variable is affecting the results. No ready
idea of what it might be comes to mind, and as the other Fs present no
unusual problems, the results are discussed as if this small ratio is actually
one of the four in 100 that would occur by chance. The other possibility
should not be completely ignored, however. When the means are examined, it appears that three-Achievement-Task-Group, Achievement-
Task-Individual, and Affiliation-Feeling-Group—form a cluster at the upper
end of the range and that the Affiliation-Task-Individual group is
considerably lower than the others. Tukey's gap test defines a significant
gap in the first instance and identifies the low group as a straggler. These
results give clear support to the first hypothesis that performance is more
favorably influenced by feedback which is relevant to the S's primary
motivation than by feedback not so relevant. The second hypothesis was
partially substantiated. The significant interaction appears to be due
entirely to the effect of the Group versus Individual orientation on the
high-affiliation Ss. The Achievement-Motivation groups failed to perform
better under the Individual condition and, as pointed out earlier, failed to
submit individual solutions in the final period. The Affiliation-motivated
groups, on the other hand, did perform more poorly under the Individual
orientation. The Affiliation-Feeling-Individual mean was significantly
lower, as indicated by the gap, than the Affiliation-Feeling-Group mean.
The lowest mean of all was that for the Affiliation-Task-Individual
condition.

DISCUSSION

The results concerned with the first hypothesis are in complete accord with the prediction and require little discussion. The achievement-motivated Ss did respond with better performance to the heightened achievement cues provided by task feedback than to the introduction of affiliation cues by feeling feedback. The affiliation-motivated Ss apparently did find the atmosphere created by the feeling feedback easier to work in. While the study provided no systematic measure of lessening tension, observations of the behavior of the affiliation Ss when good group relations were pointed out to them supported the tension-reduction notion. The achievement Ss tended to show lack of interest or even impatience with the feeling feedback, though they listened carefully to discussions of their task performance.

The second hypothesis was substantiated only as it related to affiliation-motivated Ss. There was no difference in the Achievement groups associated with the Ss' perception of the task as group or individual. That those in the Individual groups remembered that part of the instructions is attested to by the fact that some individual interim solutions were given. Possibly the instructions weren't enough to overcome the essentially cooperative nature of the task. Or perhaps this dimension cuts both ways, with the more capable Ss seeing a group product as a disadvantage and the less capable as an advantage. At any rate, the prediction that achievement-motivated Ss would profit by being permitted to give individual products was not upheld. The affiliation Ss, however, did markedly less well under the Individual condition, especially, of course, with task feedback. Since their primary motivation is by definition social, taking away the sense of belonging may be assumed to reduce their interest and effort as well as cause discomfort.

At this point the variance in the Affiliation-Feeling-Individual condition should be pointed out (Table 1). Although the chi-square yielded by Bartlett's test for homogeneity of variance did not reach the customary .05 level of significance, it did approach the .10 level. The possibility that the large standard deviation for the aforementioned condition may represent a true difference should not be overlooked. The actual scores for that series were 45, 39, 38, 35, 27, 24, and 19. There seem to be two sets of scores separated by a gap about as wide as the range for either set. These Ss of course, were given conflicting information. On the one hand they were told they could—and maybe some interpreted this to mean they should—give individual answers. But the feedback was all in terms of their behavior as a group. One may speculate that some groups resolved the seeming incompatibility by ignoring the implication of the instructions and some by ignoring the implications of the feedback. This is given some support by the observation that the Ss in the group making the score of 38 agreed explicitly that they would work together and give a single solution. Possibly the other high-scoring groups in this condition reacted in the same way without verbalizing their reaction.

In conclusion, some behavioral observations of considerable interest might be mentioned. The E went to the experimental sessions without knowledge of the motivational characteristics of the groups in order to keep any bias from influencing treatment of the groups. However, it soon became apparent that in most cases the behavior of the Ss in the situation was quite different for groups with different motivation. Achievement groups were eager to get on with the task, timed themselves, argued violently (with one coming to physical contretemps), etc. The Affiliation groups failed to show these forms of behavior, were quieter and less intense about the task, and in some cases definitely quite interested in being friendly with each other and E. When differences began to appear, E kept a record of her predictions of the motivational composition of the group. Twenty-nine of the 32 Achievement groups were correctly identified. Thirteen of the Affiliation groups were correctly identified because they showed affiliative behavior, and eight more because they failed to show the behavior typical of the Achievement groups: eight were not predicted, and three were misclassified. Apparently, especially among the Achievement groups, a real and observable variable is operating. Had the groups been brought together for social purposes, identification of Affiliation groups might have been more positive and that of the Achievement groups less so.

One further finding which, if it holds up under systematic study, is of real importance, is the relation between intelligence, motivation, and group score. The AFQT level was equated across conditions on the assumption that intelligence would be related to performance. Out of curiosity, a rough estimate of the extent of this relationship was made by putting all 64 performance scores into a single distribution and correlating them with three sets of AFQT scores: average of the four group members, highest of the four, and lowest of the four. All coefficients were essentially zero. A fourth correlation, between performance scores and the AFQT score of the man with the highest achievement motivation (Achievement groups only) had a value of .35, significant at the .05 level. Admittedly, these obtained figures are distorted representations of the actual relationships since the differences in performance due to the experimental conditions are ignored. They do suggest as an hypothesis for systematic testing that group performance tends to be keyed to the ability level of the group's highly motivated member.

SUMMARY

This experiment tested the hypothesis that task-relevant feedback for achievement-motivated subjects and "feeling" feedback for affiliation-motivated subjects would produce higher performance scores than the reverse. In addition to the motivational and feedback variables, the extent to which the task was presented as a group or as an individual problem was varied. The results included a highly significant interaction between kind of motivation and kind of feedback in the predicted direction and a significant interaction between kind of motivation and perceived nature of the task with subjects with high affiliation motivation doing less well under the individual orientation. Findings also suggested that group performance may be keyed to the intellectual level of the S with the highest achievement motivation.

REFERENCES

FRENCH, ELIZABETH G. Some Characteristics of Achievement Motivation. *J. Exp. Psychol.*, 1955, 50, 232–236.

FRENCH, ELIZABETH G. Motivation as a Variable in Work-Partner Selection. *J. Abnorm. Soc. Psychol.*, 1956, 53, 96–99.

LOTT, A. J., SCHOPLER, J. H., & GIBB, J. R. Effects of Feeling-Oriented and Task-Oriented Feedback Upon Defensive Behavior in Small Problem-Solving Groups. *Amer. Psychologist,* 1955, 10, 335.

GIBB, J. R., SMITH, E. E., & ROBERTS, A. H. Effects of Positive and Negative Feedback Upon Defensive Behavior in Small Problem-Solving Groups. *Amer. Psychologist,* 1955, 10, 335.

ROBERTS, A. H., ET AL. Effects of Feeling-Oriented Classroom Teachings Upon Reactions to Feedback. *Amer. Psychologist,* 1955, 10, 420.

VIII

LIMITS OF THE APPLICABILITY OF A COGNITIVE ORGANIZATION

1

OVERVIEW

The foregoing discussion of the nature of constucts should make it clear that certain personal constructs are applicable only to a limited set of environmental events. Kelly makes the unequivocal statement, in presenting his Range Corollary, that "a construct is convenient for the anticipation of a finite range of events only" (Section I). For every individual, then, each of his constructs will subsume a definable segment of his world. Furthermore, following the proposition that people differ in their construction of the same events, we would expect that people who would have similar constructs will differ in terms of the extensiveness of the applicability of these constructs.

Not every construct is applicable to every event in the life of a person. Some constructs are, indeed, very extensive and will subsume a tremendous variety of stimuli. For example, a participant in modern cultures will apply the construct *good-bad* to an enormous set of events, often encompassing stimulus items that can be included only by applying highly remote associations. To the person who uses his good-bad construct in this way, however, the salience of the construct is in no way reduced by an outsider's pronouncements that the construct is barely applicable. On the other hand, people also develop constructs that apply only to a narrow range of stimulus events. Though useful for the events it subsumes, the construct *herbivorous-carnivorous* has little general use in the modern urban world. In some cases it is necessary to develop broad constructs in order to be able to anticipate events. In other cases there are few instances of events, and then there is a call for the development of narrower constructs. People who reside in temperate climates do not achieve any particular predictive advantage by being able to perceive *snow* in terms of a series of narrow constructs. An Eskimo will find that his anticipating power is enhanced by developing narrow categories into which varieties of snow can be construed. A temperate-zone dweller who has become enamored with the sport of skiing might, nevertheless, develop several narrow categories, rather than one broad category, for treating snow.

There is great variation in the range of applicability of different people's constructs. In the mass culture of the United States, for example, a variety of events can be subsumed under the construct *masculine-feminine*. At a highly masculine, all-male college, the wearing of overshoes or overcoats becomes subsumed, under the *masculine-feminine* construct, at the feminine end. We can also observe wide variation in applying a construct like *stealing-earned gain*. Some people would regard it as *stealing* if one were to surreptitiously remove canned goods from the shelves of a supermarket. But accepting five dollars in excess change at the cash register would be construed in other terms, perhaps under the *careless-careful* construct. To other people the construct *stealing-earned gain* applies to both events.

The work of those researchers who are studying the concept of "risk-taking" is relevant to the range of applicability of one's constructs. The study of risk-taking is generally conducted in relation to the broad topic of "decision-making," which we relate to our notion of "instantiation" or placing events into a construction system. In their early work, Bruner, Goodnow, and Austin (1956) suggest that a person can be induced to make judgments that include greater risk if he can be led to believe that greater pay-off is contingent on more rapid decision. Since that early lead was offered, several of Bruner's co-workers (Kogan and Wallach, 1964; Tajfel, Richardson, and Everstine, 1964) and numerous other researchers have extensively explored the variables that expand or reduce a person's willingness to place a stimulus event into a particular construct. In a recent review of research on risk-taking, Kogan and Wallach (1967) compile the results of studies on the relationships between individual variation in setting boundaries to categories and individual variation in risk-taking. Among other things, they found that ". . . particularly among the maximally defensive females, the persons who set wide category boundaries not only were conservative on explicit indicators of risk-taking tendencies, but also were low in the general confidence with which they made judgments. They were the more uncertain as well as the more conservative people. Maximizing a category's boundary thus seems to be a cognitive maneuver serving to reduce uncertainty by assigning category membership to as many events as possible" (Kogan and Wallach, 1967, p. 221). Their view, then, is that the use of *broad* categories is the most efficient way of avoiding the arousal attendant to an inability to make a decision; for by using broad categories, one "minimizes the number of events relegated to the limbo of not belonging to the category in question" (Kogan and Wallach, 1967, p. 221). They believe that the broad categorizer is the more conservative—that is, he is less prone to risk-taking.

In their 1967 review, Kogan and Wallach give a large part of their attention to the issue of "the role of personal characteristics in risk-taking." They explore the utility of a generalized propensity toward a particular level of risk-taking and try to assess the probability that such a propensity is related to other behavioral characteristics. A similar effort is found in studies of individual variation in the use of broad or narrow categories. This kind of research usually points out that the user of narrow constructs is handicapped in relating to his environment (Frenkel-Brunswik, 1949; Rokeach, 1951). Such studies are usually related to Freudian psychoanalytic theory, wherein the semiperjorative term *compulsive* is used to label a person who reflects the effects of a difficult bout of toilet-training. "Compulsive" persons are identified by their tendency to impose rigid order on the world. Theoretically they do this in order to avoid the possibility that they will need to face "messy" situations. Continuing the development of this theory-by-analogy, the compulsive person is then expected to strive to impose rigid constructions on his universe so that he can neatly sort out his environment, thus allowing him to avoid situations that cannot be comfortably categorized. More fortunate persons, those who are not compulsive, can use "looser" constructs and are not impelled to shove all manner of stimuli into their own narrow, tight-fitting construct.

Whatever the utility of this particular theory, the reported research seems to support the notion that people can be identified on the basis of whether they use broad or narrow categories (Pettigrew, 1958; Gardner, 1953; Bruner and Tajfel, 1961). Though this trend does appear in research findings, we would exercise caution in applying this generalization. First, there is interesting evidence that the range of applicability of a concept is related to the nature of the person's placement of himself on that construct (Sherif and Hovland, 1953). If a person places himself at the extremes of a construction he will use a much narrower range as he construes other persons on that same judgmental dimension than will the person who places himself in the middle ranges of that particular construction. Further, when Pettigrew (1958) identifies broad and narrow categorizers by using his scale, he does so by having his subjects react to a series of items that are to be judged in numerical terms. The persons whom he identifies as broad or narrow categorizers might well be people who use broad or narrow categories only when judging items in terms of number characteristics. It would be useful to ascertain that these same people are also broad or narrow categorizers, respectively, when they are using other types of constructs.

Our second reason for advising caution in speaking of broad or narrow categorizers is that there is good evidence that intra-individual variation in the range of applicability of a construct depends on the nature of the array of stimuli that are to be construed (Berko and Brown, 1960, pp. 532 ff.). It appears that if the adoption of a broad category for a particular array allows for a more systematic predictability, a person will tend to adopt a broad category. If it is more useful to break an array into smaller categories, then subjects will develop the categories that permit more efficient groupings. The object of category formation and use, we propose, is always motivated by avoidance of excessive cognitive strain or dissonance. Though it is conceivable that people can learn to develop a propensity toward narrow or broad categories, as a means of maintaining optimum arousal, it makes theoretical sense to propose that the range of a construct will ultimately be determined by how well the construct works in avoiding dissonance.

The investigation of the issue of broad or narrow categorization as a "cognitive style" has served purposes other than settling the central matter. This kind of study has shown that there is indeed variation in how different individuals will extend the range of a category. In addition, the researchers have shown us something about the differences in functioning of people as they use different types of constructs. And finally, these studies give suggestions about the variables that bring about a broadening or a narrowing of the range of applicability of a particular construct. The studies in this section illustrate the research methods and findings that are used to clarify the issue of the range of applicability of a cognitive structure.

REFERENCES

BERKO, J. & BROWN, R. Psycholinguistic Research and Methods. In P. H. Mussen (Ed.), *Handbook of Research Methods in Child Development*. New York: Wiley, 1960, pp. 517–557.

BRUNER, J. S., GOODNOW, J. J., and AUSTIN, G. A. *A Study of Thinking*. New York: Wiley, 1956.

BRUNER, J. S. & TAJFEL, H. Cognitive Risk and Environmental Change. *Journal of Abnormal and Social Psychology*, 1961, *62*, 231–241.

FRENKEL-BRUNSWIK, E. Intolerance of Ambiguity as an Emotional and Perceptual Personality Variable. *Journal of Personality*, 1949, *18*, 108–143.

GARDNER, R. Cognitive Styles in Categorizing Behavior. *Journal of Personality*, 1953, *22*, 214–233.

KOGAN, N. & WALLACH, M. A. *Risk-taking: A Study in Cognition and Personality.* New York: Holt, Rinehart and Winston, 1964.

KOGAN, N. & WALLACH, M. A. Risk-taking as a Function of the Situation, the Person, and the Group, In *New Directions in Psychology III*. New York: Holt, Rinehart and Winston, 1967.

PETTIGREW, T. F. The Measurement of Category Width as a Cognitive Variable. *Journal of Personality*, 1958, *26*, 532–544.

ROKEACH, M. "Narrow-Mindedness" and Personality. *Journal of Personality*, 1951, *20*, 234–251.

SHERIF, M. & HOVLAND, C. I. Judgmental Phenomena and Scales of Attitude Measurement: Placement of Items with Individual Choice of Number of Categories. *Journal of Abnormal and Social Psychology,* 1953, *48,* 135–141.

TAJFEL, H. A., RICHARDSON, A., & EVERSTINE, L. Individual Judgment Consistencies in Conditions of Risk-Taking. *Journal of Personality,* 1964, *32,* 550–565.

2

COGNITIVE RISK AND
ENVIRONMENTAL CHANGE[1]
JEROME S. BRUNER AND HENRI TAJFEL

Bruner and Tajfel execute a highly competent study of differences in
"categorizing behavior." First, they clearly show that individuals differ
in the range of variability allowed within a single dimension. While
some subjects were willing to include about 90 per cent of the stimulus
series in the *20* category, others included only 30 per cent of the stimuli
in that category. Second, the study shows that subjects who use
identifiably different ranges for a particular construct will show a course
of construct change, as the stimuli set changes, that is identifiably
different from the course of change shown by subjects using other
ranges for that construct. The authors urge that we learn more about
the cognitive process of categorizing before seeking to derive generalizations about the relationships of range preferences to other "personality variables," such as "ethnocentrism," "compulsivity," and so on. In
another language, we must be cautious about treating range preference
as another "trait," which is then fed into computerized correlational
matrices. Range preference needs to be treated as a conception unto
itself; and its functioning as a cognitively based concept, needs to be
better understood if it is to have value. The nature of the process of
changes in construct range, in persons of varying range preference, is,
then, a factor that should contribute to the greater understanding of
cognitive function. This reading is included in this section because it is
addressed directly to the question of individual variation in range
preference.

*   *   *

Reprinted from Journal of Abnormal and Social Psychology, *1961, 62, 231-241, by*
permission of Jerome S. Bruner and the American Psychological Association.

[1]This research was done as part of a research project in cognition, supported in part
by USPHS Grant M-1324.

It is the objective of the present paper to examine wherein breadth of categorizing reflects the manner in which people deal with the risk of errors of judgment—specifically, the risk of saying that things are similar when they might be different, or that they are different when they might be similar.

Breadth of category—or, as it has sometimes been called, equivalence range—refers to the range of stimuli that are placed in the same class or category and share a common label. The criteria for placing objects in a common category may be many or few, explicit or implicit. In psychophysical experiments using unidimensional continua, such as length, breadth of category defines the limits beyond which stimuli are no longer classified as X, or "long," but either as non-X, "not long," or as Y, "short." In more complex arrays of stimuli, there is no such unidimensional simplicity, and the criteria for classification are often combined relationally or disjunctively in the process of deciding whether something does or does not belong in a class—as, for example, in classifying men as "competent" or "eligible to vote."

In recent years, individual differences in categorizing, particularly in breadth of categorizing, have been thought to reflect important general differences in cognitive functioning. Four trends of research on this problem can be distinguished: the investigation of changes in breadth of category as a function of changes in categorizing conditions, the study of individual consistencies in breadth of categorizing in different judging situations, the search for relationships between various emotional and personality factors and the individual's general preference for broad or narrow classifications, and the exploration of relationships between breadth of categorizing and various forms of abnormal mental functioning.

A word about each of these trends as they relate to the present study. It is apparent that when one alters the conditions of decision breadth of category changes. Thus, a sentry, deciding whether approaching figures in the twilight are friends or foes will have a broader inclusion category of "foes" than will an inspector judging machine parts as defective or not. For the consequences obviously vary in the two instances and one can control the severity of these consequences by altering breadth of category (See Bruner, Goodnow, and Austin, 1956). In general, it can be said that when the perceived consequences of overinclusion are more severe than the consequences of overexclusion, inclusion categories narrow. When overexclusion leads to more severe consequences, inclusion categories broaden.

We mention this line of research for two reasons. In the first place, it underlines the risk-regulating character of categorizing. But beyond that, it points to the possible meaning of consistencies in categorizing breadth that appear to be associated with different personality characteristics—the subject matter of the last three of the four lines of inquiry mentioned above. Thus, Gardner (1953), Hamilton (1957), Klein (e.g., 1958), and others remark that obsessive, anxious doubters tend to prefer narrow inclusion categories in their sensory judgments. Perhaps they have a tendency to minimize risk of error by the naysaying route, preferring the consequences of error that come from avoiding contact with threatening objects. It has been shown, too, that the ambivalent, ethnocentric personalities studied by Frenkel-Brunswik (1949) and Rokeach (1951) show a tendency to narrow categorizing. Yet, on the other hand, Arnhoff (1956) has noted among ethnocentrics a tendency to overgeneralization—which is indeed what ethnocentrism implies. Interestingly enough, Arnhoff (1957) obtained completely negative results in an attempt to replicate his study. This negative replication, while one must be cautious in interpreting it, may be revealing in the sense that there may be two opposing tendencies operative in the ethnocentric personality: a tendency toward overgeneralization under certain conditions, and toward narrow categorizing under others. Zaslow (1950) suggests, and perhaps his suggestion is relevant in this connection, that normal subjects, in contrast to schizophrenics, tend to use middling wide categories, whereas schizophrenics veer either toward overnarrowness or overgeneralization.

In any case, it seems patent that experiments seeking to relate categorizing breadth either to conditions of judgment or to personality cannot get very far unless and until we understand much more about the intimate texture of the act of categorizing itself. This is not to say that we do not recognize the degree to which categorizing is affected by these two sets of determinants. Rather, we feel that an examination of the underlying judgmental processes involved in categorizing is necessary for a fuller understanding of the role played by motivational and personality variables.

We turn now to the series of experiments with which the present paper is concerned. Our central interest is in the specific behavior of broad and narrow categorizers in a highly simplified judging task. Two questions concern us. The first has to do with consistency of preference for broad and narrow categorizing in a stable stimulus situation. But consistency is not as simple as it might at first appear. There is an equally important question concerning reactions to a changing stimulus environment. Is there some consistent manner in which broad and narrow categorizers alter their judgments in the face of changes in the stimulus situations with which they must cope?

With respect to the second question, some predictions can be made. If we assume that a narrow categorizer is one who is compelled to attend to differences in stimuli, whereas a broad categorizer tends to overlook differences, then it should follow that narrow categorizers will be more likely to *alter the breadth of their categorizing* to conform to changes in the stimulus world. Thus, narrow categorizers should show more susceptibility to anchoring effects in psychophysical judgment than do broad categorizers by virtue of being more sensitive or reactive to change and contrast. Indeed, we would say, it is precisely this sensitivity to change that constitutes the hedge against risk that characterizes the narrow categorizer. For to the narrow categorizer, differences and change are highly relevant, and, as Tajfel shows (1959), these relevant differences tend to be accentuated. And if this is the case, not only should the narrow categorizer alter his breadth of category more readily in response to stimulus changes, but he should also adapt more quickly when the change persists and becomes a new steady state of stimulation.

There is another way of stating our prediction, one taken from the language of anchoring experiments. When a subject has been judging a range of stimuli in terms of categories of absolute magnitude, the introduction of new stimuli larger than the range has either a "contrast" or an "assimilation" effect. A contrast effect is responding strongly to the newly-introduced stimulus—say a stimulus larger than any previously encountered—by judging previous stimuli as contrastingly smaller. Assimilation, both in common sense terms and technically, is "not heeding" the new anchoring stimulus, i.e., judging it as no larger than the stimuli previously encountered. We might well predict that narrow subjects, sensitive to differences, will be subject to contrast effects. Broad subjects, on the other hand, should by virtue of their less acute reactiveness to change, show less of the contrast effect and may indeed assimilate the stimuli of the extended range to the psychophysical scale established with the smaller range of stimuli.

With these predictions in mind, we may turn now to the experiments proper.

EXPERIMENT I

Subjects and Procedure. Forty-eight fifth grade school children served as subjects in this experiment. They were tested individually.

Stimuli consisted of projected slides containing clusters of dots, cast on a beaded screen at an exposure time of .5 second per cluster. The subject, facing the screen 12 feet away, was seated next to the table on which the 35 millimeter Bell and Howell projector was placed. At the beginning of the session, each subject was told that his task would be to decide whether each of the clusters to be flashed on the screen contained 20 dots or did not contain 20 dots. If he thought that there were 20 dots in the cluster he was to say "yes"; if he thought that the cluster did not contain 20 dots, he was to say "no." The subject was then told that 20 would be the smallest number of dots in any of the clusters that he would see, and was shown two sample clusters of 20 dots each, as demonstrations.

The presentation of the experimental series followed immediately. In order to avoid the possibility that the decision about the number of dots might be determined by the recognition of the shape of a cluster once seen, four clusters with different dispositions of dots in them were used for each number of dots, and, in addition, each of these slides was shown in different positions at its successive presentations.

The experimental presentations were divided into two parts. First, a series of clusters containing from 20–26 dots was presented eight times successively—a total of 56 presentations. The presentations were randomized in such a way that each cluster of the series appeared once before the whole series was repeated in a different random order. Following this, in the second part of a session, four series of clusters containing from 20–30 dots were presented in varying random orders—a total of 44 presentations.

The session was interrupted by two periods of rest of approximately 2 minutes, the first after three presentations of the series; the next, three presentations later.

The scoring was based on the percentage of yes responses, representing for each subject the proportion of the stimuli which for him fell into the category "20." These percentages were taken for each subject for three separate phases of the presentations of stimuli: for the initial range of 20–26 dots in its eight consecutive presentations (Phase I), for the stimuli 20–26 of the extended range in its first two presentations (Phase II), for the stimuli 20–26 of the extended range in its last two presentations (Phase III). Breadth of category was defined as the proportion of stimuli assigned by a subject to the inclusion category 20 in Phases I, II, and III, and a comparison of these phases provides us with comparative data for testing our hypotheses.

Results. Before the results are reported and discussed, the hypothesis stated in general terms earlier should be stated specifically in the context of the procedure just described. It was assumed that during the initial eight presentations of the stimuli in the original range, each subject would settle to his characteristic pattern of assigning a certain proportion of stimuli to the inclusion category of 20. The subjects could, thus, be divided, by means of ranking, into three groups: a group of broad categorizers with the largest proportions of number of calls of 20; a middle group, and a group of narrow categorizers with the smallest number of calls of 20.

Extending the series of stimuli from clusters ranging from 20–26 dots to clusters ranging from 20–30 dots was conceived as a form of anchoring, introducing a larger difference between the two extremes of the range. According to the argument outlined previously, this change should have been more salient and effective for the narrow than for the broad categorizers. In other words, after the introduction of the additional larger stimuli, the narrow categorizers should, in their responses to this part of the new range which constituted the original range (clusters from 20–26 dots), increase the proportion of clusters called 20 more than the broad categorizers. The narrow categorizers should, moreover, adapt back to their old narrow pattern with the continued experience of the new range provided by Phase III.

1. Initial breadth of category. The range in breadth of category for the original series of stimuli was wide: from 89.5%–30.3%, with the median proportion of calls of 20 being about 55%, with six subjects calling 40% or fewer 20, and eight calling more than 70% of the stimuli 20.

The division of subjects into three groups was made at "cut-off" points nearest to 27% of the distribution (Kelly, 1939) for the upper and lower ends of the distribution. This resulted in 12 subjects with the largest percentages of yes responses being assigned to the broad group, (with breadths ranging from 64.3%–89.5%), and 13 subjects with the lowest percentages of yes responses being assigned to the narrow group (with breadths ranging from 30.3%–44.6%). The difference between the number of subjects in the groups is due to a run of ties at the upper end of the distribution. Assigning all the remaining 23 subjects to the middle group seemed the least arbitrary procedure.

2. Change in breadth of category as a function of extending the range. As a first test of the general hypothesis, a rank correlation was run between breadth of category in Phase I and the shift from Phase I to Phase II in the percentage of calls of 20. This correlation was of the order of rho $= -.433$; with 46 df this is significant at $p < .005$. Thus, the larger the number of stimuli initially assigned to the category 20 by a subject, the less did he tend to increase this number for stimuli of 20–26 dots in the first two presentations of the extended range.

As Hamilton (1957) rightly points out, however, "there are few forms of behavior, especially in the cognitive sphere, which cannot be shown to vary with intelligence. In fact, it might be thought that intelligence is maximally involved in any process requiring perceptual judgments" (p. 203). In pursuit of this point, a rank correlation between IQ and breadth of category in Phase I was obtained. It was of the order of $-.53$. The initial breadth of category appears then to be determined, in part at least by the subjects' intelligence—more intelligent subjects tended to use narrower categories. The mean IQ of the broad group was 107.4; of the middle group, 113.6; and of the narrow group, 122.7. The difference between the broad and narrow groups is significant at $p < .002$.

The testing of predictions outlined above depended, however, on the relationships found between the breadth of category shown by the subjects in Phase I and the amount of shift from Phase I to Phase II. A rank correlation between the amount of shift and IQ was obtained, and found to be .27, reflecting the fact that narrow subjects shifted more. However, a partial correlation between IQ and shift, holding breadth of category constant, reduced this figure to .05. A complementary finding is that the partial correlation between breadth of category and amount of shift, this time holding IQ constant, remained as high as −.35. Thus, it would seem that, though breadth of category is consistently related to intelligence, the amount of judgmental shift that occurs when the environment changes is related not to intelligence but to breadth of category.

The Wilcoxon matched-pairs signed-ranks test (Siegel, 1956) was applied to assess the significance of the increase in the percentage of yes responses to stimuli 20–26 after the extension of the range for each of the groups. The results for the broad group were not significant. Out of 12 subjects in this group, 6 actually shifted in the direction of *decreasing* the proportion of their yes responses after the extension of the range. In the middle group the shift was significant at $p < .005$ (19 out of 23 subjects increased the proportion of their yes responses). In the narrow group, all 13 subjects increased their proportion of yes responses. The mean increase in percentages of yes responses from Phase I to II for broad categorizers was +.45, the range being from −21.4–+21.4. The comparable increase for the narrow categorizers was +20.1, with a range from +3.6–+37.5. The middle categorizers were in between: mean increase in percentage of yes responses being 12.3 with a range from −12.5–+30.4. Mann-Whitney U tests were then applied to compare the amount of shift found in the different groups. All of them were found to be significantly different from each other (broad vs. narrow, $p < .01$; broad vs. middle, $p < .02$; narrow vs. middle, $p = .05$).

It might also be said parenthetically that the broad and narrow groups behaved consistently in their placement of dot clusters ranging in number from 27–30 in Phase II. Some 40.6% of these were called 20 by the broad categorizers in contrast to 20.2% called 20 by the narrow categorizers, a difference significant at $p < .025$ by the U test.

3. Changes in breadth of category as a function of adaptation to the extended range of stimuli. Let us now compare the change from Phase II to Phase III—the subjects now having had experience with two presentations of the extended range and confronting the two additional series. In the narrow group, out of 12 subjects (data for this shift for one of the subjects were not available), 8 subjects shifted back towards fewer yes responses for the 20–26 part of the range, 1 did not shift, and 3 shifted towards more yes responses. The comparable figures for the broad group are interesting. Only 2 subjects in this group showed a decrease in yes responses in Phase III in comparison with Phase II; 7 subjects increased their yes responses and the remaining 3 subjects showed no shift at all. A comparison of means tells the same story. On the average, subjects in the broad group *increased* their yes responses by 7.0% between Phase II and III. Narrow categorizers *decreased* theirs 9.7%. The difference between the two groups tested by the Mann-Whitney U test is significant at a $p < .025$.

Here again there is a correlation of .37 between the initial breadth of category and the amount of shift from Phase II to Phase III, indicating that broad categorizers tend to broaden their range more as they get more exposure to the changed stimulus situation, the narrow categorizers having done most of their changing when the stimulus situation was first altered. A correlation of $-.29$ was found to hold between IQ and the amount of shift, an obvious consequence of the fact that the more intelligent subjects had already done their shifting in Phase II. A partial correlation was computed between IQ and the amount of shift, from II to III, holding breadth of category constant. It was found to be $-.12$. But a partial correlation between breadth of category and amount of shift, holding IQ constant this time, is .27. It can be argued then, that the amount of shift from Phase II to Phase III, reflecting adaptation to the new range, is related to the initial breadth of category but not to intelligence, though intelligence and the initial breadth of category are related to each other.

The data for all subjects in the three phases of experiment are summarized in Table 1 in the form of percentage of yes responses given.

Figure 1 summarizes the findings. The main feature of the results is the relative stability of performance in the broad group and the sharp changes from phase to phase in the narrow group. This is congruent with the general conception of broad and narrow categorizers as outlined in this paper and in others (e.g., Gardner, 1953). The broad categorizers do not react to change markedly or rapidly; the small and insignificant amount of shift that they show after the extension of the range maintains a slow and steady increase as the new range continues to be presented. Narrow categorizers react to change strongly, but then they seem to revert rapidly to their preferred mode of response as soon as there is habituation to the new situation.

Our main hypothesis—that the narrow categorizers are more sensitive to change than broad ones—is confirmed.

There is one other point to be made in connection with cognitive risk. One can conceive of risk regulation in terms of a cost-for-gain reckoning. That is to say, for a gain in accuracy or security or some other "good," one pays a cost. In the case of the broad categorizers in Experiment I, we see that they do in fact call more of the stimuli containing 20 dots correctly. The cost of this is calling many more of the other dot clusters incorrectly.

TABLE 1   Percentage of yes responses given by the subjects in the three phases of Experiment I and in Experiment II.

Group	Phase I (20-26)	Phase II (20-26)	Phase III (20-26)	Phase II (27-30)	Phase III (27-30)	Experiment III
Broad						
1	89.5	71.4	78.6	62.5	62.5	58.9
2	85.7	100.0	100.0	37.5	75.0	64.3
3	83.9	78.6	100.0	0	37.5	69.5
4	80.3	64.3	85.7	37.5	50.0	71.4
5	80.3	92.8	100.0	100.0	100.0	100.0
6	75.0	71.4	85.7	25.0	37.5	75.0
7	71.4	50.0	78.6	62.5	50.0	94.6
8	71.4	78.6	50.0	62.5	75.0	58.9
9[a]	69.6					64.3
10	67.8	85.7	70.1	37.5	37.5	83.9
11	67.8	50.0	78.6	25.0	75.0	58.9
12[a]	64.3					62.5
13[a]	64.3					62.5
14	64.3	78.6	78.6	25.0	25.0	58.9
15	64.3	85.7	85.7	12.5	50.0	58.9
M[b]	75.1	75.6	82.6	40.6	56.2	
M[d]	73.3					69.5
Middle						
1	62.5	64.3	71.4	25.0	0	55.4
2	62.5	64.3	85.7	62.5	25.0	57.1
3	62.5	50.0	64.3	37.5	0	58.9
4	60.7	78.6	85.7	25.0	25.0	53.6
5	58.9	78.6	57.1	12.5	25.0	51.8
6	57.1	85.7	78.6	25.0	25.0	41.1
7	57.1	71.4	57.1	12.5	50.0	50.0
8	57.1	64.3	57.1	37.5	25.0	92.9
9	57.1	85.7	71.4	12.5	12.5	44.6
10	57.1	71.4	78.6	62.5	50.0	66.1
11	57.1	85.7	78.6	50.0	25.0	60.7
12	55.3	42.8	35.7	37.5	50.0	55.4
13	53.6	71.4	50.0	37.5	12.5	73.2
14[c]	53.6	78.6	71.4	37.5	12.5	
15[a]	51.8					57.1
16	51.8	50.0	50.0	37.5	12.5	48.3
17	51.8	64.3	85.7	25.0	62.5	41.1
18	51.8	71.4	64.3	0	12.5	57.1
19	50.0	64.3	78.6	37.5	12.5	50.0
20[a]	50.0					50.0
21	48.2	50.0	57.1	12.5	25.0	39.3

TABLE 1   *Concluded.*

Group	Phase I (20-26)	Phase II (20-26)	Phase III (20-26)	Phase II (27-30)	Phase III (27-30)	Experiment III
			Experiment I			
22	48.2	78.6	64.3	0	0	55.4
23[e]	46.4	57.1	35.7	0	37.5	57.1
24[c]	46.4	42.9	50.0	25.0	12.5	
25[e]	46.4	64.3	57.1	62.5	50.0	44.6
M[b]	54.5	66.8	64.6	29.4	24.5	
M[d]	55.3					55.2
Narrow						
1	44.6	78.6		12.5		51.8
2	42.8	57.1	71.4	0	12.5	48.3
3	41.1	71.4	50.0	12.5	25.0	51.8
4	41.1	50.0	42.9	25.0	12.5	64.3
5	41.1	64.3	50.0	0	0	60.7
6[c]	41.1	78.6	78.6	87.5	87.5	
7	41.1	57.1	21.4	0	0	62.5
8	39.3	64.3	78.6	25.0	25.0	39.3
9[c]	39.3	42.9	35.7	0	0	
10	35.7	50.0	14.3	87.5	87.5	64.3
11	33.9	57.1	64.3	0	25.0	46.4
12	32.1	57.1	35.7	12.5	0	35.7
13	30.3	35.7	28.5	0	0	46.4
M[b]	38.7	58.8	47.6	20.2	22.9	
M[d]	39.7					51.8

[a]Subjects not included in the analysis of Experiment I, and added subsequently for comparison of their performance in Experiments I and III.

[b]Means for Experiment I, not including subjects marked a.

[c]Subjects taking part in Experiment I, and not available for Experiment III.

[d]Means for comparison of performance in Experiments I and III, not including subjects marked c.

[e]Subjects falling in the lower part of the distribution (narrow group) for comparison between Experiments I and III, and included in means for narrow group (d).

The narrow categorizers show a considerably sharper slope in their discrimination function. The price they pay for *not* being wrong about the excluded items is missing some of those that should be included among the 20s. Broad subjects, in short, pay their price for being right; narrow subjects seem to pay theirs for not being wrong.

But before these, or any other conclusions are finally drawn from the

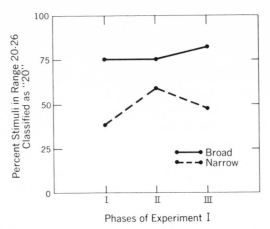

FIG. 1   *Mean percentage of stimuli in range 20-26 classified as 20 (yes responses) by broad and narrow categorizers in the three phases of Experiment I.*

results, some very obvious artifactual possibilities must be dealt with. The results may have been due not to the narrow group's more abrupt reaction to change, but to the fact that by definition the narrow categorizers have more room to expand their proportion of yes responses. A broad categorizer who started out with 80% of yes responses cannot, of course, achieve an increase of 25%. This "ceiling effect" may account for the broad group showing less increase in yes responses than the narrow group. Yet, the reversal of trends in shift from Phase II to Phase III argues in some measure against this artifactual explanation; so does the fact that half of the broad subjects *decreased* their proportion of yes responses from Phase I to Phase II, some of them quite considerably. The results, at least the shift from Phase I to Phase II it might also be argued, could have been due to regression effects. Experiment II was conducted to test further the validity of interpretation given to the results of Experiment I, particularly with respect to ceiling effects and regression effects.

Another artifact, possibly lurking in the results, is that the narrow group is "narrow" not because of its preferred mode of taking cognitive risks, but simply because, for one reason or another (such as, for example, interest in the task), the capacity of narrow subjects to discriminate was better than that of the broad group. The relationship between intelligence and breadth of category, previously reported increases the likelihood of some such interpretation. Under the conditions of Experiment I and with the small number of yes responses that we obtained, the narrow group could by definition get closer to the actual leptokurtic distribution of the "correct" stimuli than the broad group. Thus, in Phase I, the proportion of clusters containing 20 dots was 14.3%, and decreased to 9.1% in Phases II and III. But note, however, that 7 out of 13 subjects in the narrow group *increased* their proportion of yes responses to the new range presented to them in Phase II, while only 3 out of 12 subjects in the broad group did so, a difference that is significant at the .02 level as estimated by a U test. There remains the possibility, however, that there is some intrinsic relationship between intelligence test scores and narrow categorizing based on the possible bias of intelligence tests in favor of the precise or narrow categorizers. Yet this is not borne out by the indifferent partial correlation between IQ and shift from Phase II to Phase III. But such indirect evidence is not sufficient. Consequently, Experiment III was conducted in order to explore further the question of accuracy.

EXPERIMENT II

In Experiment I, change was introduced by extending the series beyond its initial range. Using the same series of stimuli, it should be possible to shift judgments in the opposite direction by biasing the distribution of stimuli through *cutting off* a part of the range. The order of presentation used in Experiment I was reversed in Experiment II: The subjects were first confronted with the range of 20–30 dots, then the larger end of the series was eliminated and only the 20–26 range presented. If it is true that change has a greater effect on narrow than on broad categorizers, then in Experiment II the narrow categorizers should *decrease* their proportion of yes responses in the 20–26 range from the original to the reduced series more than the broad categorizers.

Twenty-four new subjects were used in this experiment, this time drawn from the fifth grade. The initial series of 20–30 dot clusters was run through randomly eight times, (a total of 88 presentations), and then followed by four presentations of the reduced range of 20–26 dots for a total of 28 presentations. Apart from this difference, the procedure was the same as in Experiment I. The subjects were ranked in the order of their percentage of yes responses to the 20–30 initial range to establish broad, middle, and narrow groups.

Results. The range in breadth of category for Phase I (now 20–30 dots) was from 95.4% to 21.6%. The 27% cut-off point resulted in six subjects being assigned to each of the two extreme groups: the broad and the narrow. The range in breadth of category for the broad group was 95.4%–59%; for the narrow group, 36.4%–21.6%.

This time, as one shifts from Phase I to Phase II, one finds the narrow subjects *decreasing* their calls of 20 in response to the narrowing of the range—all of them doing so with a mean shift in percentage of yes

TABLE 2   Percentage of yes responses given by subjects in the three phases of Experiment II.

Group	Phase I (20-30)	Phase I (27-30)	Phase I (20-26)	Phase II (20-26)	Phase III (20-26)
Broad					
1	95.4	90.6	98.2	100.0	100.0
2	80.7	53.1	96.4	85.7	64.3
3	67.0	40.6	82.1	78.6	71.4
4	62.5	31.2	80.4	64.3	57.1
5	62.5	71.9	57.1	57.1	85.7
6	59.0	34.4	73.2	92.9	71.4
M	71.2	53.6	81.2	79.8	75.0
Middle					
1	56.8	37.5	67.9	57.1	50.0
2	55.6	37.5	66.1	78.6	85.7
3	54.4	34.4	66.1	71.4	42.9
4	52.3	28.1	66.1	42.9	42.9
5	50.0	25.0	64.3	42.9	57.1
6	50.0	37.5	57.1	78.6	57.1
7	47.7	12.5	67.9	64.3	42.9
8	46.6	15.6	64.3	57.1	57.1
9	46.6	50.0	44.6	35.7	57.1
10	42.0	28.1	50.0	42.9	57.1
11	40.9	40.6	41.1	57.1	57.1
12	37.5	9.4	53.6	57.1	57.1
M	48.4	29.7	59.1	57.1	55.3
Narrow					
1	36.4	12.5	50.0	28.6	50.0
2	35.2	3.1	53.6	42.9	21.4
3	32.9	34.4	32.1	21.4	21.4
4	32.9	9.4	46.4	42.9	42.9
5	31.8	34.4	30.4	14.3	14.3
6	21.6	12.5	26.8	7.1	14.3
M	31.8	17.7	39.9	26.2	27.4

responses of -13.7 (Table 2). The broad group again hardly reacts to change: three of the subjects decrease their proportion of yes responses, one does not change, and two increase the number of yes responses. The mean percentage decrease of yes responses for the broad group is -1.4. The difference, as measured by a U test, is significant at the .03 level.

The shift from Phase I to II goes counter to what would be expected by virtue of "ceiling" and "floor" effects, or, indeed, according to the effect of regression. Those who have been calling few of the clusters 20 decrease the number of their calls much more markedly than those who have been calling many clusters 20. While these results provide an effective answer to the query raised in the last section about the possible contribution of artifacts to the results of Experiment I, they also raise some interesting questions of interpretation.

Take first the narrow categorizers. When the range of stimuli to which they are exposed broadens, their categorizing broadens. It is, if you will, now safer to take positive fliers on doubtful stimuli, and more dot clusters are labeled as 20. When the universe of stimuli narrows in range, narrow categorizers show a response of caution, and the bounds of their inclusion class are narrowed. Interestingly enough, both reactions go counter to the "reality" situation. That is to say, in Experiment I the proportion of actual clusters of 20 dots decreases from Phase I to Phase II—yet the yes responses of narrow subjects increases. In Experiment II it is the reverse: the proportion of clusters of 20 dots increases from Phase I to Phase II, but the calls of 20 decrease for narrow subjects. It seems plain then, that while these subjects are responding to change in the environment, they are doing so in terms of *internal* requirements, not *external* ones. What is also interesting is that whereas in Experiment I narrow subjects reverted to narrow categorizing after they had habituated to the extended range, in Experiment II they do *not* change in Phase III after they have narrowed their categorizing in response to a narrowed range of stimuli. There is no change in the percentage of yes responses from Phase II to Phase III (Table 2). In short, a change in categorizing in the preferred direction sticks, a change in the nonpreferred direction (toward greater breadth) habituates out.

Now consider the broad categorizers. In Experiment I we show that they did not respond on the average to an extension of the range of stimuli to which they were exposed in shifting from Phase I to Phase II. But in Phase III, habituation to the extended series, or possibly an insignificant and delayed reaction to the change of stimulation, led to a moderate increase in the breadth of their 20 category. They, too, respond to increased diversity in environmental stimulation, but more slowly and more modestly. In Experiment II, the picture is very similar: as before, and in contrast to narrow categorizers, their response to change is slow and insignificant.

One last check on possible artifacts in Experiment I is provided by the design of Experiment II—a check on regression effects. In Experiment I, the transition from the initial to the extended range occurred after 8 successive presentations of the 7 stimuli of the initial range—a total of 56 presentations. This was followed by Phase II which consisted of a series of 11 stimuli repeated twice—22 presentations. As Phase I in Experiment II consisted of 11 stimuli repeated 8 times, it was possible to ascertain whether any regression effect (which would consist of an increase in the proportion of yes responses for the narrow group and of a decrease for the broad group) had occurred at the point of presentations nearest to the transition point between Phases I and II in Experiment I. This was done by comparing the percentages of yes responses for the first 5 presentations of the series (a total of 55) with the same percentages for the 2 following presentations (a total of 22). There was no evidence of any trend towards increase for the narrow categorizers, or towards decrease for the broad ones.

EXPERIMENT III

This experiment was conducted in order to ascertain whether the results of Experiment I were due to consistent differences between the broad and the narrow categorizers in their preferred mode of dealing with an uncertain cognitive situation, rather than to a tendency of the narrow group to be more accurate, presumably under any conditions. A subject who is in the group of narrow categorizers in Experiment I because he might be intent to perform as accurately as possible should become a broad categorizer in a situation where the distribution of stimuli is such that most stimuli fall into the inclusion or target category. The converse is, of course, not necessarily true: if a broad categorizer performed as he did because he was bored and was paying very little attention to the task, he might still perform in a similar manner when confronted with any distribution of stimuli—assuming that yes responses are easier for maintaining an attitude of nondiscriminating boredom.

Though we have spoken of "accuracy," there is one general question concerning it that is difficult to answer in these experiments. In most cognitive situations flexibility and avoidance of extreme response tendencies probably lead in the end to most "adaptive" responses—that is, to responses which keep in closest touch with the normally distributed and continuously changing environment. There may be situations, however, in which either a very narrow or a very broad type of response is most useful. This, as Bruner, Goodnow, and Austin (1956) have shown, is a function of the "payoff matrix" in the situation, of the respective consequences that errors of overinclusion or of overexclusion may have. It is, therefore, impossible to state *a priori* which of the two extreme forms of categorizing is the "better" or the most useful save in a restricted way applying to specific situations.

The arrangement of stimuli in Experiment I favored the narrow categorizer in the sense that few stimuli were in fact 20s. We decided, therefore, to run another experiment in which a broad style of categorizing would lead to performance corresponding more closely to the actual distribution of stimuli. This time, the great majority of stimuli would belong in the inclusion class and the preferred response distribution of broad categorizers would conform to the distribution of "correct" or inclusion stimuli.

Subjects and Procedure. Experiment III was conducted with 45 subjects who took part in Experiment I plus 4 subjects who were added subsequently. The latter were first subjected to the procedure of Experiment I, and then, a few days later, took part in Experiment III. Stimuli consisted of straight lines drawn on rectangles of white cardboard, 11″ × 14″ in size. The inclinations and positions of lines on the rectangles were varied randomly. There were 56 rectangles: on 48 of them (6 out of 7) lines 5″ long were drawn, one to a rectangle. The remaining 8 rectangles contained lines varying in length from 5¼″ to 5¾″. The subjects, tested indivually, were seated at one end of a table, the experimenter at the other, separated by a distance of 3 feet. The lines were shown one by one, the order of presentation so arranged that one line longer than 5″ appeared in each successive series of six 5″ lines, the serial position of the longer line varying at random. Subjects were told to decide whether a line was 5″ long or not. If they thought that it was, they should say "yes"; if they thought not, "no." They were duly informed that some of the lines would be 5″ long, some slightly longer. Two 5″ lines were shown first, and the subjects told what they were. The presentation of the experimental series followed immediately. Time of exposure was not limited, the cardboard rectangle being held up until the subject made his decision.

Scores again consist of the percentages of yes responses given to the total of 56 stimuli presented—a number equal to the number of clusters of dots presented in Phase I of Experiment I. The prediction, of course, is that if the subjects' performance in Experiment I reflected their preferred mode of categorizing, they should perform in a similar manner in Experiment III, despite the radical change in the frequency of stimuli belonging to the inclusion class— that is, broad categorizers should respond more broadly in both experiments.

Results. The range of percentage of yes responses was from 100% to 35.7% with a median of 57.1%. Table 1 sets out the distribution of the subjects according to the percentage of their yes responses.

1. *Comparison of breadth of category in Experiment I and Experiment III.* The subjects were ranked according to their breadth of category in both experiments. A rank correlation was run between their performances in the two experiments. This was found to be of the order of rho = .572, significant at $p < .0005$.

A further assessment of the similarity of performance in the two tasks was made by selecting the subjects who in Experiment I belonged to the broad and narrow groups, and comparing the difference in the performance of these two groups in Experiment III. The cut-off point for the groups in Experiment I was slightly different from the one used in the previous analysis of results for this experiment, as some subjects dropped out and some were added. Taking ties into account, the nearest point to 27% now included 15 subjects in the broad group, the narrow group consisting as previously of 13 subjects. The difference, as assessed by a *U* test, is highly significant, the confidence level being less than .001. The mean percentage of yes responses in the previously defined broad group is 69.5. The percentage of yes responses in Experiment III of the previously defined narrow group is 51.8.

2. *Comparison of accuracy of performance in Experiment I and Experiment III.* The group of narrow categorizers performed more accurately in Phase I of Experiment I than the group of broad categorizers. Accuracy of performance was assessed by assigning to each subject a score that consisted of the proportion of his number of yes responses assigned by him to clusters containing 20 and 21 dots. The percentage of accurate calls for the narrow group was 45.9, as compared with 33.4 for the broad group, a difference significant at the .001 level.

The same measure of accuracy could not be applied in Experiment III, as almost all subjects gave all correct no responses to the eight lines that were longer than 5″. Therefore, the assessment of accuracy here was made by summating *all* incorrect responses made by a subject: no responses given to 5″ lines, and yes responses given to the longer lines. Of the 25 subjects belonging to the broad and narrow groups in Experiment I whose accuracy of performance in that experiment had been originally compared, 23 were still available in Experiment III. Their accuracy of performance in the new task was compared and the broad subjects were found to have 81.5% of their calls accurate, in contrast to 71.4% for the narrow subjects—a difference significant at the .01 level.

To sum up Experiment III, then, subjects maintain their relative positions with respect to breadth of categorizing when they shift from a situation where few stimuli fit the specifications of an inclusion class to one where many stimuli fit that specification: ones who are narrow in the first situation tend to be narrow in the second, and so, too, for those who are at the broad end of the distribution. One finds, moreover, that whereas in a situation where few stimuli fit the specifications for inclusion in the target class, narrow categorizers are more accurate, whereas when many stimuli fit, the broad categorizer turns out more accurate. Accuracy, in brief, seems more a function of a happy fit between response preference and stimulus properties than of discrimination capacity, much as in an experiment of Tagiuri, Bruner, and Blake (1958), where accuracy of social perception was a systematic resultant of two response patterns that had nothing to do with discriminative finesse. It would seem, then, that *not* only does discriminative capacity not determine categorizing breadth, but that, in a paradoxical way, it is the other way round.

CONCLUSIONS

Several things appear quite plain. To begin with, there appear to be consistencies in breadth of categorizing. We find, moreover, that narrow categorizers tend to be more sensitive to changes in the stimulus environment. They show more alteration in their categorizing breadth in response to change and show it more swiftly—though in a way that is not necessarily "rational." That is to say, when the range of stimuli to which they must respond *broadens,* they broaden their equivalence range for stimuli of a target class, although the specifications of the target class have not changed, and although their response may lead to more errors. It is as if they were "exploring" the new and wider range. Broad categorizers, on the other hand, do not change as much in response to an increase in the range of stimuli to which they must respond. They appear to be "holding on" to old methods in the face of a new situation. When the changed stimulus situation persists and becomes a steady state, the narrow categorizer reverts to his more precise and narrow mode of categorizing and reduces error. The broad categorizer, slower to react in the first place, begins to respond to change only when the change becomes more permanent.

An analogous picture holds when the stimulus world to which broad and narrow categorizers are exposed is constricted and becomes less varied. The narrow categorizer "follows" the change more swiftly by narrowing his categorizing range for the target class. Again even though logically it may lead to more error, for the specification of the target class has not changed. This time his response seems to be in the direction of closer analysis of a narrower range. The broad categorizer responds with no discernible change, as if he were riding out the narrowing of the stimulus world that runs counter to his preference for breadth rather than changing with it.

It should not be surprising then—although we were taken unawares—that breadth of category is associated with intelligence, the narrow categorizers having a higher average IQ than the broad ones. Interestingly enough, though, shift in categorizing in the face of stimulus change is found to be related to breadth of categorizing but not to intelligence. Regardless of intelligence, the narrow categorizer handles change by shifting, by reacting to contrast; the broad categorizer shifts much less and later. In sum, reaction to change appears to be a strategy of dealing with the consequences of error. The narrow categorizer appears to prefer the risk of *reacting* and possibly being wrong. The broad categorizer prefers the risk of *not reacting* to change and possibly being wrong. Now we are in a position to ask about personality. What personality characteristics produce such preferences?

REFERENCES

ARNHOFF, F. N. Ethocentrism and Stimulus Generalization. *J. Abnorm. Soc. Psychol.*, 1956, *53*, 138–139.

ARNHOFF, F. N. Ethnocentrism and Stimulus Generalization: A Replication and Further Study. *J. Abnorm. Soc. Psychol.*, 1957, *55*, 393–394.

BRUNER, J. S., GOODNOW, JACQUELINE J., & AUSTIN, G. A. *A Study of Thinking.* New York: Wiley, 1956.

FRENKEL-BRUNSWIK, ELSE. Intolerance of Ambiguity as an Emotional and Perceptual Personality Variable. *J. Pers.*, 1949, *18*, 108–143.

GARDNER, R. W. Cognitive Styles in Categorizing Behavior. *J. Pers.*, 1953, *22*, 214–233.

HAMILTON, V. Perceptual and Personality Dynamics in Reactions to Ambiguity. *Brit. J. Psychol.*, 1957, *48*, 200–215.

KELLY, T. L. The Selection of Upper and Lower Groups for the Validation of Test Items. *J. Educ. Psychol.*, 1939, *30*, 17–24.

KLEIN, G. S. Cognitive Control and Motivation. In G. Lindzey (Ed.), *Assessment of Human Motives.* New York: Rinehart, 1958. Pp. 87–115.

ROKEACH, M. "Narrow-Mindedness" and Personality. *J. Pers.*, 1951, *20*, 234–251.

SIEGEL, S. *Nonparametric Statistics for the Behavioral Sciences.* New York: McGraw-Hill, 1956.

TAGIURI, R., BRUNER, J. S., & BLAKE, R. R. On the Relation Between Feelings and Perception of Feelings Among Members of Small Groups. In Eleanor E. Maccoby, T. Newcomb, & E. Hartley (Eds.), *Readings in Social Psychology.* New York: Henry Holt, 1958, Pp. 110–116.

TAJFEL, H. The Anchoring Effects of Value in a Scale of Judgments. *Brit. J. Psychol.*, 1959, *50*, 294–304.

ZASLOW, R. W. A New Approach to the Problem of Conceptual Thinking in Schizophrenia. *J. Consult. Psychol.*, 1950, *14*, 335–339.

3

COGNITIVE STYLES
IN CATEGORIZING BEHAVIOR[1]
RILEY W. GARDNER

Gardner's paper, one of the pioneering studies of equivalence range, reports an investigation of the relationship between equivalence range—that is, the range over which a construct is applicable—and other aspects of judgmental phenomena. Specifically, Gardner produces data that relate equivalence range to judgments of constancy in visual-spatial perceptions. Gardner's experimental procedure reverses the most frequently used method in constancy judging. In most constancy studies the subject is asked to gauge the "actual" nature of a distant or "distorted" object and to make a match of that object to another standard. Gardner asked his subjects to judge when the distant or "distorted" object was a *sensorial* match of the standard figure. In other words, the subject was asked to indicate when retinal images were matched, rather than to produce a judgment that the two stimuli were "actually" identical. In life situations our judgments are ordinarily directed toward predicting the "actual" nature of the event. Gardner's experimental procedure prompts us to take an extended liberty in reinterpreting his results. Translating his material into the language of this text, Gardner investigated the proposition that a subject who uses a narrow equivalence range is better able to disregard his tendency to judge within his existing construct system. For example if the experimenter asked that a subject look out on the world at a distant, retinally

Reprinted from Journal of Personality, *1953, 22, 214–233, by permission of the author and* Duke University Press.

[1]Based on a dissertation submitted to the Department of Psychology of the University of Kansas in partial fulfillment of the requirements for the degree of Doctor of Philosophy. The investigation is one of a series supported by grants to the Perception Laboratory of the Menninger Foundation by the National Institutes of Health.

small object, he will be able to "suspend" his usual practiced construction of that object. He will be able to judge its equivalence to other objects in terms of its retinal size, without interference of his habituated frame of reference which tells him that the distant stimulus is "actually" larger. Conversely, this study shows that a person with a wide equivalence range does not suspend his learned tendency to judge the distant object as being larger. If we pursue this reinterpretation of Gardner's study, we could use its findings to support a view that narrowness of range tends to occur in subjects who are unable to yield the "egocentric mode," in Piaget's sense. People who avoid the use of complex, inclusive categories, tend to be unable to regard their perceptions as perceptions and, instead, treat them as the "reality" of the external world. They persist, for example, in seeing a retinally small, distant object as "large" when they are asked to class it with an object of similar size, but which is "actually" smaller.

This reinterpretation of Gardner's findings is ventured in order to illustrate Bruner and Tajfel's (see above) point that we still need to be cautious before concluding that equivalence range functioning is an identifiable personal characteristic. We are not yet ready to conclude that an individual can be classified as a broad or narrow categorizer. These studies do strongly suggest, however, that individuals will differ in terms of the range of stimuli they will include in the same category.

*   *   *

INTRODUCTION

The experiments reported here have their roots in an approach to personality theory which expresses itself through studies of individual differences in adaptive modes of organizing and experiencing the stimulus world. The emphasis in these studies has been upon personal organization (12). The perceptual apparatus has been selected as the "window" into the person because of the unique opportunities it offers for observing in action the individual's style of adaptation to the world about him. Studies of individual differences in respect to certain perceptual properties have suggested several meaningful dimensions along which such differences can be arranged, e.g., leveling-sharpening and tolerance *vs.* intolerance for instability (5, 9, 10, 13, 14). The extremes of these dimensions have been said to reflect contrasting cognitive attitudes or "*Anschauungen*" (8). The present study is an attempt to establish another such meaningful dimension. The phenomena we are concerned with can best be subsumed under the general heading of individual differences in equivalence range.

THE NATURE OF THE PROBLEM

It is an everyday clinical observation that persons vary widely in the "span" or "realm" (cf. 18) of objects, qualities, and so on, which they are willing to subsume under one conceptual rubric as being "the same" in the sense of being "not different." For example, in clinical sorting tests some persons seem perfectly comfortable in designating a wide variety of objects as "tools" or a wide range of colors as "red." Others become noticeably uncomfortable when confronted with such groupings and seem impelled to subdivide the ralms into more categories, with fewer objects or a narrower range of qualities included in each. Thus, some persons seem constantly and spontaneously to be "honeycombing" stimuli into small compartments, as if this were for them an especially important mode of coming to terms with the world about them. Others seem most comfortable with more inclusive categorizations. Clinical observation thus suggests that a *preferential* mode is at work in such behavior—a factor which is not tied solely either to intelligence or to capacity as these are usually understood.

It should be stated here that the present study is not concerned *solely* with the kinds of equivalence-range phenomena which appear in such highly conceptual activities as object-sorting tests. It is assumed that the person's response to a sorting task is but one expression of certain centrally determined modes of organization of stimuli, and that these modes will be demonstrable also in tasks which involve much less of conscious conceptualizing.

Klüver (16) has suggested that variations of the method of equivalent stimuli may be useful in the study of personality. He also has pointed out that the classical constancy situations involve one kind of equivalence judgment. The ways in which equivalence judgments in sorting tasks and in constancy situations are related, however, are not easily discernible. Most constancy studies have been aimed at general factors operative in all individuals. Only a very few studies (e.g., 22, 23, 26) have hinted at the possibility that personal styles of experiencing may in part account for the wide individual differences in constancy judgments. Thouless's (23) data, for example, indicate large variations between persons, extending in apparent size judgments from the choice of comparison figures approximating the real object to figures producing almost the same retinal image as the standard stimulus. He suggested tentatively that there may be a relationship between such a dimension as introversion-extroversion and the degree to which a subject's judgment reflects "regression toward the real object." But he did not explore his own suggestion further. Thus, although wide individual differences have been observed in constancy judgments, the meaning of these differences for the persons involved remains obscure.

In view of the somewhat different approach made to equivalence-range phenomena in the present study, the voluminous literature on concept-formation tasks and constancy judgments is not immediately relevant to the problem at hand. It should be noted, however, that other experimenters, e.g., Sheehan (20), have found low correlations between various kinds of constancy judgments. Also, in her study, variations in the stimulus materials seemed to produce marked changes in the subjects' responses. Sheehan concluded that there is no central organizing principle which controls any one person's functioning in all constancy situations. Agreed. But there are other ways to think about the organization of a subject's behavior in constancy situations.

In Sheehan's study, as in many others in the area of constancy phenomena, subjects were given relatively brief instruction and were allowed relatively little time in which to make their judgments. A section has been included below on the ways in which subjects in the present experiment were treated and instructed in order to facilitate their making the best or most preferential judgments possible.

As an extension of the thinking about equivalence-range phenomena in categorizing and constancy tasks, the writer included one additional kind of judgment in the experiment: a judgment of the point at which two patches of light are exactly the same brightness. The writer was stimulated to include this task in the battery by certain suggestions of Klein (6) concerning the possible meaningfulness of individual variations in differential thresholds.

SAMPLING THE SUBJECT

The writer believes that the results of this experiment can be understood, and the experiment itself made reproduceable, only if particular care is taken to describe the emotional atmosphere provided for the subjects, the way in which he attempted to relate himself to the subjects, and the nature of the judgments the subjects were encouraged to make. This precaution seems especially pertinent since, on superficial examination, the results of this experiment may seem to be at variance with those of some previous studies. Also, close review of the procedures of many constancy studies reveals that subjects were sometimes provided with minimal instructions and were given relatively little time to make their judgments. It was the writer's experience during pilot experimentation that he obtained one kind of response from a subject if he gave brief instructions, hurried the subject through the judgments, or suppressed questions about the experiment, but obtained another kind of response if he acted otherwise.

Some subjects seemed to approach the task with the anticipation that there was an "answer" which they should try to discern. With these persons particular care was taken to emphasize that "there is no correct answer to this," and that "everyone does it his own way." In the constancy situations it was discovered that even very bright subjects may have considerable difficulty in "getting the feel" of the experience of apparent size or shape. In no case was a subject allowed to make experimental judgments until the writer had demonstrated the phenomenon and until the subject could report convincingly that in an exaggerated example he could make a judgment of apparent qualities. Thus, the time spent with individual subjects preliminary to the judgments varied.

During the actual testing, subjects were repeatedly encouraged to take their time with the judgments. It was the impression of the writer that to allow all subjects identical, brief periods in which to make judgments would have been to obtain from one of them a fairly accurate picture of how he preferred to organize the stimuli; from another, an incomplete stage of approximation in making the judgment; from still another, a guess.

These comments on the approach to the subjects represent the belief that the investigation of preferential modes of organizing experience is a unique kind of experimental endeavor calling for special consideration of the experimenter's relationship with the subject. It was a repeated observation in pilot and prepilot studies, for example, that a person who is treated as "someone to make a judgment" does not achieve the kind of ease, comfort, and freedom to express himself which allows his uniqueness to display itself to best advantage. It was the writer's impression that when subjects were treated in this way the consistency of individual differences across tests tended to decrease. Although the specific relationships hypothesized in the next section might have appeared without such special considerations, it is felt that their significance was enhanced by allowing each of the test situations *to be* an adaptive task and by eliciting from the subject the kind of sample of his behavior most likely to reflect his unique attributes.

There is some evidence in the literature on ego-involvement which gives support to this impression. Allport points to several studies, including one by Klein and Schoenfeld (15), as demonstrating the principle (1, p. 461): "When there is ego-involvement there are general traits; when there is no ego-involvement there are no general traits." Although ego-involvement was not achieved in the usual ways in the present experiment, the difference in results under varied approaches to the subjects makes it appear that something very similar to what Klein and Schoenfeld reported occurred with the subjects of our pilot studies.

HYPOTHESES

The general hypothesis is that individuals are characterized by differences in equivalence range which can be demonstrated in a variety of adaptive tasks.

The more specific hypotheses can be stated as follows: The smaller a subject's conceptual realms in the object-sorting test, i.e., the smaller his categories, the more he will be able (*1*) in a constancy situation, to "analyze out" the retinal impression from his knowledge or awareness of the real object; (*2*) in a brightness judgment, to make an objectively accurate estimate of equivalence. That is, in constancy situations calling for judgments of apparent size and shape, we expect subjects with smaller conceptual realms in the sorting test to make *sensory* judgments more accurately than subjects given to broader categorizations. On the other hand, when object judgments are requested, we expect the same persons to be better able to "analyze out" the true object size in the face of interfering conditions, such as different distances to the standard and comparison stimuli. In a task requiring subjects to equate the brightness of two patches of light, we again expect these subjects to make more accurate judgments.

EXPERIMENTAL PROCEDURES

The subjects for this study were 30 women and 20 men, ranging in age from 18 to 30, with a mean age of 23.02. Of this group 19 were university students, 27 were employees of the Menninger Foundation (secretaries, adjunctive therapy workers and students, office workers), three were housewives, and one was a kindergarten teacher. A rough check of intelligence level is supplied by the fact that 44 of the subjects attended or were graduated from a college or university. Most of those who had not attended college were employed at tasks usually requiring a college degree. All subjects were judged to be of at least normal intelligence, with most of them in the bright normal to superior range.

Subjects were seen individually for the following tests: *(1)* object-sorting test; *(2)* size-constancy (object) judgments; *(3)* size-constancy (sensory) judgments; *(4)* shape-constancy (sensory) judgments; *(5)* brightness judgments.

All constancy judgments in the experiment were made in a section of the laboratory enclosed by walls of black cloth. Lighting for these situations consisted of ordinary room illumination from two overhead fixtures.

Object-sorting test. Materials for this test were 73 objects, most of them familiar to the subjects from everyday experience.[2] The items were selected with an eye to variations in materials, colors, shapes, sizes, and combinations of these. They were presented to the subjects in random order. Subjects were first asked to examine the objects and to inquire about any they were not familiar with. They were instructed as follows:

> First of all, I want you to know that there is no answer to this test. Everyone does it in his own way. I want you to do it in the way that seems most natural, most logical, and most comfortable to you. The instructions are simply to put together into groups the objects which seem to you to belong together. You may have as many or as few objects in a group as you like, so long as the objects in each group belong together for one particular reason. If, after you have thought about all the objects, a few do not seem to belong with any of the others, you may put those objects into groups by themselves. Please sort all the objects.

During the sorting, the experimenter made notes on qualitative features of the subject's performance, such as comments, regroupings, questions, and the like. Following the grouping of all objects, he asked for and recorded the subject's reason for including the objects in each group. Thus, moving from group to group, he asked: "Why do these objects belong together?" and recorded verbatim the subject's response.

The score used was the number of groups each subject made. In those rare instances in which a subject obviously had one large group with very definite subdivisions (e.g., a hierarchical arrangement), each definite subgroup was considered a separate group.

Size-constancy (object) judgments. Apparatus for this test was similar to one described by Thurstone (25). The standard was a black cardboard triangle, nine inches on each side, mounted on a 15-by-16-inch white cardboard field. This triangle was placed six feet from the subject's eyes. The comparison stimulus was a black cardboard triangle whose size could be varied by pulling it through a horizontal slit in a sheet of white cardboard 28 by 34 inches. It was supported by a fine white cord running over a pulley and was counterbalanced by a weight. The maximum size of this triangle was 18 inches on each side. This comparison stimulus was placed 12 feet from the subject's eyes.

The test consisted of one ascending and one descending trial. The instructions were:

[2]A complete description of the items of this test and of the other procedures of this study appear in the dissertation, which is on file at the University of Kansas library.

This is the only judgment of its kind in this experiment. It is a judgment of *actual* size. This figure will remain the same (examiner points to the standard). You will see that here (examiner points to the comparison stimulus) I have an apparatus with which I can vary the size of this second figure (demonstrates). First, I will slowly increase the size of this figure until you tell me the two figures are exactly the same size. If you wish to stop and check at any point, just tell me. And if you overshoot the first time, feel free to direct me so that the two triangles are exactly the same actual size.

After the subject had made his first judgment, he was asked to look away for a few seconds and then check his judgment, "to make sure that it is the best judgment you can make." Subjects were encouraged to take their time and to check as many times as they wished. Following the ascending trial, these instructions were given:

Now I will begin with this figure at its largest size and slowly decrease its size until you tell me again that the two figures are exactly the same actual size.

As in the ascending trial, subjects were asked to look away and to check their judgments.

The score used was the average error of the two trials. This error was measured in centimeters by means of a scale attached to the back of the comparison stimulus. The height of the standard triangle was approximately 20 cm.

Size-constancy (sensory) judgments. This situation was modeled after one of Thouless's techniques (23). The standard figure was a circle of white cardboard, 39.7 cm. in diameter. It was placed at right angles to the subject's line of vision (monocular) at a distance of 230 cm. The subject viewed all figures through a reduction screen having a 2 by ¾ inch aperture 48.5 cm. above the table. A series of 23 circles varying in diameter from 29.7 cm. to 39.7 cm. was presented to the subject at right angles to his line of vision at a distance of 172 cm. and to the left of the standard. The diameter of the comparison circles varied by 1¼ per cent of the diameter of the standard. The sizes of retinal images for the apparent size and shape situations were estimated by means of methods suggested by Graham (4). The comparison figure making an equivalent retinal image at 172 cm. to that of the standard at 230 cm. would be approximately 29.7 cm. in diameter. The test proper consisted of an ascending and a descending trial.

Prior to actual testing, there was a demonstration period in which the writer assured himself that each subject understood the nature of the judgment. This demonstration period took the following form:

Before we actually do this part of the experiment, I want to make sure it is clear to you just what kind of a judgment is called for. First of all, I would like to have you *imagine* that you are looking at a house which is a mile away. You will realize that at that distance it will *look* very, very small. If you put your thumb up in front of your eye (examiner demonstrates), your thumb might "cover" the house. That is, your thumb might *look* larger than the house, although you know perfectly well that the house is actually many times larger. That is what we mean by *apparent* size or *seeming* size. And that is the kind of judgment we are going to make here. We are not interested in how large the objects actually are, but in how large they appear or seem to be.

Following this, the experimenter instructed the subject to close one eye and to observe the smallest figure (29.7 cm.) as he brought it closer and closer to the subject's eye. When the subject reported that it seemed to grow larger as it was brought closer, he was asked to compare its apparent size at approximately six inches from his eye to that of the standard at 230 cm. When the subject reported with confidence that the nearer circle *seemed* larger, the reduction screen was placed on the table and he was given the instructions proper:

Now I am going to present a series of figures, gradually increasing in size, here (examiner points to black wooden stand). After I place each figure here, I want you to compare it with the one at the end of the table and tell me if the apparent size of the one I place here is larger or smaller than the one at the end of the table. If a figure looks exactly the same, you may say "same." You will look through the slit in the cardboard here (examiner points). Take your time and rest your eye any time you wish. You may look back and forth between the two figures as many times as you need to in order to decide whether the one I place here is larger than, smaller than, or the same in *apparent* size as the figure at the end of the table.

Following the ascending series, the subject was instructed as follows:

Now we are going to do the same thing exactly, except that I will begin with the largest of the figures and gradually decrease the size of these circles. Tell me each time whether the figure I place here is larger than, smaller than, or the same in apparent size as the figure at the end of the table.

It should be noted that for a few subjects several of the figures appeared to be "the same" apparent size as the standard stimulus. When this occurred, the subject usually commented upon it in surprise. In each such case, he was encouraged to make his judgment for each figure separately, "since it sometimes happens that several look just the same." In these cases, the largest figure called "the same" in the ascending trial and the smallest in the descending trial were used in the scoring.

The score for this test was the average size of the comparison figure judged "the same." There were no instances in which subjects did not say "the same" for one of the figures.

Shape-constancy (sensory) judgment. The shape constancy technique was a modification of a situation described by Thurstone (25). The standard stimulus, viewed through a 5-inch by ¾-inch slit in the black cardboard, one foot above the table surface, was a square of white cardboard four inches on a side. This was presented flat on the table at a distance of seven feet (213.36 cm.) from the subject's eye. Twenty-two comparison figures drawn in India ink on a white cardboard field 28 by 34 inches were presented at right angles to the subject's line of vision at a distance of 119.25 cm. The horizontal axis of each comparison figure was 5¾ inches (equal to that of the standard). Vertical axes varied from 5¾ inches to ½ inch, in steps of ¼ inch. The comparison figure producing an equivalent retinal image at this distance would have a vertical axis of approximately ½ inch. Instructions for this test were:

> I want you to look through this slit in the cardboard, keeping one eye closed at all times. You see that this figure is a square (examiner picks up standard and shows to subject at a distance of about three feet from the subject's eyes). If I turn the figure this way (examiner rotates figure 45 degrees clockwise), it looks like a diamond. Now you will notice (examiner rotates the top of the figure away from the subject slowly) that if I rotate this figure it will seem to change its shape. For example, if I hold it this way (parallel to the subject's line of vision) it may even look like a straight line. (Examiner varies position of the figure until the subject indicates that he understands these instructions.) Now I will lay the figure on the table, here.

> I want you to look at it carefully. After you feel that you see clearly what its apparent shape is in *this* position, I want you to look at this board (comparison figures) and tell me which figure on the board is most like the *apparent* shape of the figure you see in front of you. Take your time. Your may look back and forth as many times as you wish, but always keep the same eye closed. When you have selected the figure on the board which is most like the apparent shape of the figure in front of you, please point to it.

One judgment was made. The score was the ratio of the vertical to the horizontal axis in the figure chosen.

Brightness judgments. Apparatus for this test consisted of two identical light boxes, each containing a 100-watt bulb and a polaroid lens attachment which could be adjusted by the experimenter through an aperture at the back of the box. Each light patch was a square one inch on a side. Judgments were made with the boxes in three positions: adjacent (distance between the centers of the patches of light, 21 inches); 90 degrees, and 180 degrees apart on an imaginary circle five feet in radius. Judgments were made in a dark room. The light patch on the right was the standard in each of the three judgments (one for each position). It was set at 110 footlamberts in each case, although the experimenter appeared to reset it each time and the subject was not told whether the standard was changed or not. The left-hand patch was variable from 180 footlamberts above the brightness of the standard to 90 footlamberts below it. In each position, the experimenter gradually decreased the brightness of the comparison stimulus until the subject reported the two patches "exactly the same" in brightness. Instructions for this test were:

> This next situation calls for a *brightness* judgment. It has nothing to do with the size, shape, color, etc., of the two lights. This light on your right is the standard. I will set it each time. After that it will not change. You will see that I can change the brightness of the light on your left from very bright to very dim (examiner demonstrates very slowly). Do you have any questions about this? (If there were none, examiner proceeded with the remainder of the instructions.) Now I am going to begin with the light on your left at very bright. I will gradually decrease its brightness. I want you to tell me when the two lights are exactly the same brightness. Take your time, so as to make your best possible judgment. If you wish to stop to check or to rest your eyes at any point, just tell me. If you overshoot the mark, feel free to direct me to change the brightness of this light until it seems to you exactly the same as that of the standard.

After the first judgment the subject was asked to look away or to close his eyes before checking. All subjects took advantage of this suggestion to rest their eyes and to make more careful decisions. When the judgment in the first position was completed, the writer moved the boxes 90 degrees apart and "reset" the standard. Instructions then were:

> This time we are going to make exactly the same kind of judgment, except that the lights will be farther apart. Direct me as you did before, until you are as sure as you can be that the two lights are exactly the same in brightness.

Following this judgment, the writer placed the boxes in the 180-degree position. Instructions were:

> We are going to make one more judgment of exactly the same kind. This time the boxes will be directly opposite each other. Direct me as before, until you can say that the lights are exactly the same in brightness.

The score for this test was the average error (footlamberts) for the three judgments.

RESULTS

Qualitative observations. It was the writer's impression that there were several "routes" by which different subjects could attain the same number of groups in the object-sorting test. Some of the subjects with many groups seemed to be doubt-ridden and obsessive in their approach to the task.

They tended to sort and resort. It seemed that some could not reach a point at which they were thoroughly satisfied with their groupings. It was the writer's observation, clouded perhaps by the fact that this was one of his speculative expectations, that as a class the subjects with many groups were somewhat more intent, determined, and less comfortable in the test situations than those with few groups. Not all the subjects with many groups displayed doubtfulness and indecision, however. Some organized the objects in this way rapidly and spontaneously, as if for them there were no other possibility.

Among the subjects who verbalized aloud their thoughts while sorting, differences in sensitivity to subtle differences in the objects appeared to vary widely. This was true both among the subjects with few groups and among those with many. Thus, some subjects seemed to have many groups partly because they were unable to discern similarities. Others put the emphasis directly and squarely upon subtle differences. And some of those with very few groups offered a running stream of comments indicating a notable sensitivity to differences and excellent vocabularies for capturing, say, slight variations in color or material. In spite of these differences in the "routes" by which either few or many groups could be achieved, one crucial factor seemed to separate the two parts of the population: the subjects with many groups seemed *impelled to act* upon their awareness of differences, however vaguely they could conceptualize or verbalize this awareness. The subjects with fewer groups seemed to adopt a more "easygoing" approach to their categorizations, whether or not they gave evidence of being highly aware of differences.

Quantitative findings. In all the statistical analyses, subjects were arranged according to the number of groups they produced in the object-sorting test. Thus, Subject 1 had three groups; Subject 50, 30 groups. T-scaling was required to make scores on the five tests directly comparable for some of the statistical analyses. The formula $T = 50 - \dfrac{(X - M)}{\sigma}$ was used. In the process of tabulating the data, the distribution of scores for each test was arranged in the direction implied by the hypothesis for that test. This was necessary since subjects with the fewest groups in the object-sorting test were expected to have the largest values on the other four tests. Chi-square tests were done for each of the five experimental situations with subjects divided into two groups according to: *(1)* age, *(2)* sex, and *(3)* student versus nonstudent status. None of these values approached significance.

The first step in the statistical analysis was to correlate the scores of the three constancy situations and the brightness-judgment situations with the number of groups produced in the object-sorting test. Pearson r's were: with the size-constancy (sensory) scores (average size of comparison figure selected), .66; with the size-constancy (object) scores (mean error in centimeters), .29; with the shape-constancy (sensory) scores (ratio of vertical to horizontal axis in comparison figure chosen), .21; with the brightness-judgment scores (mean error in footlamberts), .35. The .05 level of confidence was .28; the .01 level, .36; and the .001 level, .44. The differences in the correlations between number of groups produced in the object-sorting test and the scores for the three constancy situations can perhaps not be explained fully at this point. Closer inspection of the data suggests, however, that the size-constancy (sensory) situation is perhaps the most difficult one in that it produced the greatest spread of scores from the 50 subjects. This, in turn, may have improved the correlation somewhat. Thus, the size-constancy (sensory) situation might be termed, in this experiment, the most effective of the three constancy situations in bringing out the hypothesized tendencies towards broad or narrow categorizing. It is noteworthy that judgments in the size-constancy (sensory) situation ranged from choices of a comparison figure equivalent in actual size to the standard (39.7 cm.) to a comparison figure approximately equivalent in retinal image to the standard (29.7 cm.).

Multiple correlations were done with scores for the three constancy situations and scores for the three constancy situations plus those for the brightness judgments in relation to the number of groups produced in the object-scoring test. The first of these R's was .69; the second, .72. Both are significant at better than the .001 level of confidence. Also, the latter R is significantly different from the former (at the .05 level of confidence), suggesting that the brightness-judgment scores add something tangible to the predictive power of the three constancy situations in relation to the results of the object-sorting test.

Table 1 demonstrates that in general the subjects tend to be consistent

TABLE 1 Variance table for data on five tests

Source	df	Variance estimate	F	P
Subjects	49	210.552	Subjects/Residual = 2.81	.001
Tests	4	1.468		
Residual	196	74.899		
Total	249			

with themselves in the various tests; this is in accordance with the hypothesis. In spite of the fact that some subjects are more consistent than others in the five tests, the general trend is toward preservation by individual subjects of unique modes of response which differentiate them from each other. Closer inspection of the data indicates that many subjects deviate on one or more tests from the general arrangement of scores hypothesized. This appears to be true for both those with few and those with many groups. (It is obvious that in the process of T-scaling, which equates the means for the five tests, the possibility of investigating the variance attributable to tests was necessarily sacrificed.)

As a further test of these findings, a pattern analysis (Table 2) was done

TABLE 2 Pattern analysis for data on four tests: variance table.

Source	df	Variance estimate	F	P
Variables	3	1.927	Groups/Individuals = 44.04	.001
Groups	1	3755.844		
Individuals	48	85.282		
V by G				
Interaction	3	179.541		
Residual	144	80.653		
Total	199			

for the two groups of subjects according to a method suggested by Block, Levine, and McNemar (2). One way of understanding this pattern anlysis is to say that it tests the degree of interaction between the means of the two groups of subjects on four tests. The object-sorting test results were excluded, since the subjects were arranged in accordance with this "criterion" measure. The F value which results when the group's variance is tested by the individual's variance indicates that the over-all means of the four tests are significantly different for the two groups of subjects.

Table 3 brings out quite sharply the fact that when subjects are divided into two groups on the basis of their performance in the object-sorting test their mean scores are significantly different for each of the other tests.

On the brightness judgments, the mean-error values for the 25 subjects with fewest and the 25 with most groups in the object-sorting test were: *(1)* adjacent: 25.45 and 17.07; *(2)* 90 degrees: 30.96 and 19.13; *(3)* 180 degrees: 24.67 and 19.27; *(4)* grand means: 27.02 and 18.45. The t-test values were 2.1323, 2.4094, 1.3953, and 2.7120, respectively. All except that for the 180 degrees position are significant at better than the .02 confidence level (one-tail test). The one nonsignificant difference is in the direction hypothesized. It is difficult to understand the drop in average error when the light boxes are 180 degrees apart. It was originally hypothesized that this would be the most difficult of the three positions and that the two groups of subjects would diverge most widely on this judgment. It is perhaps possible that the subjects were more challenged by

TABLE 3 Significance of differences between 25 subjects with fewer groups and 25 subjects with more groups in the object-scoring test.

Test	Mean of subjects with fewer groups (N = 25)	Mean of subjects with more groups (N = 25)	Difference	t	P
Size-constancy (object). Mean error (cm.)	2.040	1.360	.680	2.786	.01
Size-constancy (sensory). Mean diameter of com parison figure (cm.)	36.27	31.47	4.80	7.001	.001
Shape-constancy (sensory). Vertical/horizontal axis of comparison figure	.347	.282	.065	2.038	.02
Brightness. Mean error (footlamberts)	27.02	18.45	8.57	2.712	.01

this judgment and exerted greater effort in making it. Qualitative observations offer little to support or deny this possibility.

Obviously, the difference in the degree of conscious conceptual activity involved in the object-sorting test and the brightness judgments is great. And, whereas the former task involves a kind of equivalence-range judgment closely akin to those of everyday experience, none of the subjects reported having done a laboratory-brightness judgment previously.

To summarize the quantitative findings, it can be said that results of all the statistical analyses suggest that—in spite of the obvious differences between the various tasks and their demands upon the subject, and in spite of the many other factors which must be involved in each of the tasks, and which cannot be investigated here—common adaptive modes are being tapped in the five measures.

DISCUSSION

The results of this study support the hypothesis that persons are characterized by consistent differences in what they will accept as similar or identical in a variety of adaptive tasks. It is notable that the hypothesized differences appear in spite of the fact that the subjects were drawn from a relatively homogeneous level of intellectual capacity. Subjects who were working at similar jobs at comparable levels of efficiency (e.g., the adjunctive therapy workers) varied widely in their positions on the scales. Differences in age (within our 18- to 30-year range), sex, and student versus nonstudent status seemed to contribute negligibly to the results.

It is especially interesting that the individual differences also appear in predictable fashion in the brightness judgments. This task involves a less complex kind of conceptualizing than does the object-sorting test. In one sense, these judgments supply a rough estimate of the person's differential limen for brightness under these conditions. The results suggest the need for further research in the area of DL differences, including other tasks and other modalities than those investigated here.

Qualitative observations of performances in the object-sorting test suggest that subjects can "solve the problem" by placing the items in very few groups in spite of the fact that they may be cognizant of the subtle differences. It would seem that the subjects with few groups may choose not to *act* upon their awareness of difference. It is thus not a matter of unawareness of, but of "tolerating" differences by virtue of a rather relaxed attitude towards them.

It might be hypothesized that difference-identity continua as such have very different meanings for persons falling at the extremes of the distributions. It seems possible that such continua, as aspects of the perceptual field, have much greater importance for some of the subjects with narrow equivalence ranges. This is supported by the observation that a number of these persons seemed impelled to act upon their awareness of differences, and that this impulsion took the form of further subdivision of potentially broad categories. Other observations point to the possibility that these subjects somehow attach a greater importance to distinguishing between the "objectively" accurate and the more apparent qualities of stimuli (whichever is demanded at the moment). It would appear that the extreme subjects may differ markedly in their preferred ways of *knowing* the world about them. It seems especially important for some of the subjects with narrow equivalence ranges to know the world in terms of its reducible, classifiable features. It may be that for persons given to broad equivalence ranges knowledge of the exact nature of the outer world is relatively less important as a mode of reality-testing because they can utilize their feelings more effectively in the process of reality-testing.

Affect-control may not be as pressing a problem for the persons with broad equivalence ranges, who seem to adopt a more relaxed approach in tune with "adaptive economy" rather than objective verity. This is not to assume that the persons with narrow equivalence ranges would *express* less affect-laden material in the testing situations. Their expressions might be of an order which would reveal their dissatisfaction with "open" situations and their tendency to search for the objectively verifiable by virtue of focusing upon the task and increasing their psychological distance from the experimenter. Their affect-laden expressions thus might be more negative, more critical, and less conducive to a warm relationship than those of persons with broad equivalence ranges.

These are some of the possibilities which arise from an examination of both the quantitative and the qualitative results. It is obvious that these questions can be answered only by further investigations.

Relations to other studies of perceptual attitudes. From the point of view of theory construction, and as an economical method of checking hypotheses about our subjects, it will be important to compare their performances in the present experiment with their modes of approach to tasks developed in the same laboratory and from the same general matrix of thinking about perceptual phenomena and personality theory. It was noted in the size-constancy (sensory) situation, for example, that several of the subjects with broad equivalence ranges seemed to experience from two to as many as four or five circles in the series of comparison figures as "apparently the same" as the standard. Although the present study was not designed to take full advantage of such observations, they suggest that some of the subjects with few groups may be similar in schematizing behavior to what has been called the "leveler" (5, 9, 10) on the basis of performance in tasks especially designed to elicit schematizing preferences. Other studies from this laboratory which may have interesting relations to our findings include explorations of individual differences in susceptibility to interference (19); in characteristic response to an experimentally induced need; and, as was suggested above, in response to situations tapping tolerance *vs.* intolerance for instability (13, 14).

SUMMARY AND CONCLUSIONS

Fifty subjects between the ages of 18 and 30 were tested in five tasks— an object-sorting test and a series of constancy and brightness judgments— in the expectation that their performances would reflect consistent individual differences in equivalence ranges. All the experimental results seemed to support the hypothesis that persons are characterized by unique equivalence-range preferences in a variety of adaptive tasks.

Both the quantitative and qualitative results suggested that certain central aspects of an individual's orientation towards the outer world (aspects which can, as yet, only be speculated upon) find expression in tasks demanding widely different degrees of conscious conceptualizing.

An attempt was made to utilize the qualitative observations of the subjects as aids in the formulation of hypotheses about the meaning for the person of a particular kind of equivalence-range preference. It was speculated, for example, that persons at the extremes of the distributions may relate themselves to the world about them in quite different ways in their preferred modes of reality-testing, in their ways of "knowing" the external world, and in their modes of affective response to persons and things.

REFERENCES

1. ALLPORT, G. W. The Ego in Contemporary Psychology. *Psychol. Rev.*, 1943, *50*, 451–478.
2. BLOCK, J., LEVINE, L., & MCNEMAR, Q. Testing for the Existence of Psychometric Patterns. *J. Abnorm. Soc. Psychol.*, 1951, *46*, 356–359.
3. BRUNSWIK, E. Distal Focussing of Perception: Size-Constancy in a Representative Sample of Situations. *Psychol. Monogr.*, 1944, *56*, No. 254.
4. GRAHAM, C. H. Visual Perception. In S. S. Stevens (Ed.), *A Handbook of Experimental Psychology*. New York: John Wiley, 1951. Pp. 868–920.
5. HOLZMAN, P. S. Cognitive Attitudes of Leveling and Sharpening in Time-Error Assimilation Tendencies. *J. Pers.*, 1953, *22*.
6. KLEIN, G. S. Adaptive Properties of Sensory Functioning: Some Postulates and Hypotheses. *Bull. Menninger Clin,.* 1949, *13*, 16–23.
7. _____ A Clinical Perspective for Personality Research. *J. Abnorm. Soc. Psychol.*, 1949, *44*, 42–49.
8. _____ The Personal World Through Perception. Chapter XII in R. R. Blake and G. Ramsey (Eds.), *Perception: An Approach to Personality*. New York: The Ronald Press Co., 1951.
9. _____ & HOLZMAN, P. S. The "Schematizing" Process: Perceptual Attitudes and Personality Qualities in Sensitivity to Change. *Amer. Psychol.*, 1950, *5*, 312 (Abstract).
10. _____, _____. Perceptual Attitudes of Leveling and Sharpening: I. Sensitivity to Change and to Embedded Stimuli (In preparation).
11. _____ & KRECH, D. The Problem of Personality and Its Theory. *J. Pers.*, 1952, *20*, 2–23.
12. _____ & SCHLESINGER, H. J. Where Is the Perceiver in Perceptual Theory? *J. Pers.*, 1949, *18*, 32–47.
13. _____, _____. Perceptual Attitudes Toward Instability: I. Prediction of Apparent Movement Experiences from Rorschach Responses. *J. Pers.*, 1951, *19*, 289–302.
14. _____, _____, & GARDNER, R. W. Perceptual Attitudes Toward Instability. II. Prediction From Apparent Movement Responses to Other Tasks Involving Resolution of Unstable Fields (In preparation).
15. _____, & SCHOENFELD, H. The Influence of Ego-Involvement on Confidence. *J. Abnorm. Soc. Psychol.*, 1941, *36*, 249–258.
16. KLUVER, H. The Study of Personality and the Method of Equivalent and Non-Equivalent Stimuli. *Char. & Pers.*, 1936, *5*, 91–112.

17. MᶜNEMAR, Q. *Psychological Statistics.* New York: John Wiley, 1949.
18. RAPAPORT, D., GILL, M., & SCHAFER, R. *Diagnostic Psychological Testing.* Chicago: The Year Book Publishers, Inc., 1946, Vols. I and II.
19. SCHLESINGER, H. J. Cognitive Attitudes in Relation to Susceptibility to Interference. *J. Pers.,* 1954, *22,* No. 3.
20. SHEEHAN, M. R. A Study of Individual Consistency in Phenomenal Constancy. *Arch. Psychol.,* 1938, *31,* No. 222.
21. THOULESS, R. H. Phenomenal Regression to the "Real" Object. *Brit. J. Psychol.,* 1931, *21,* 339–359.
22. _____. Phenomenal Regression to the "Real" Object. II. *Brit. J. Psychol.,* 1932, *22,* 1–30.
23. _____. Individual Differences in Phenomenal Regression. *Brit. J. Psychol.,* 1932, *22,* 216–241.
24. _____. The General Principle Underlying Effects Attributed to the So-Called Phenomenal Constancy Tendency. *Psychol. Forsch.,* 1934, *19,* 300–310.
25. THURSTONE, L. L. A Factorial Study of Perception. *Psychometr. Monogr.,* 1944, No. 4.
26. WEBER, C. O. The Relation of Personality Trends to Degrees of Visual Constancy Correction for Size and Form. *J. Appl. Psychol.,* 1939, *23,* 703–708.

4

ASSIMILATION
AND CONTRAST EFFECTS
OF ANCHORING STIMULI
ON JUDGMENTS[1]
MUZAFER SHERIF, DANIEL TAUB, CARL I. HOVLAND

Piaget speaks of *assimilation* as the process of incorporating a stimulus into an already available schema. When the stimulus situation is somewhat incongruent with the existing schema, the existing schema, the schema may be *accommodated*—that is, altered—to incorporate the stimulus. Sherif and his associates have also used the term *assimilation* with similar connotations. In this study Sherif, Taub, and Hovland investigate the issue of the extent of "tolerable" diversity within a construct range. The study suggests[1] that only a certain amount of accommodation can be induced, and that when the limits are reached the person will not only reject the inclusion of the "anchor," or divergent, stimulus within the range being used for the judgment, but will also compress the range of the applicable construct in the direction away from the anchor.

In other studies Sherif and his coworkers have shown that this principle also emerges when individuals make judgments within the framework of social attitudes (Section IV). An individual who holds a solid, extreme view on an issue—that is, who maintains a nonassimilable anchor position—will more strongly reject moderate positions. In other words, he will narrow the judgmental range in the direction opposite from his own.

Aside from making a clear-cut empirical statement of the assimilation-contrast effect, we would like to obtain the cohesiveness that would derive from saying how this empirical finding relates to the issues of the

Reprinted from Journal of Experimental Psychology, *1958, 55, 150–155, by permission of Muzafer Sherif and the American Psychological Association.*
[1] This study was conducted as part of the Yale Communication and Attitude Program which is supported by a grant to Carl I. Hovland from the Rockefeller Foundation. The Foundation's support is gratefully acknowledged.

dichotomous character and the range of applicability of constructs. This is difficult. To the person who holds a moderate view it appears as if a legitimately large range is narrowed and is made more clearly dichotomous by a person who holds an extreme view. This effect is a reflection of the point made by O'Donovan (Section IV) that use of extremes can be conceptualized as a matter of "meaningfulness." The narrowing of the construct range under the influence of sharp contrast might also be reflected in the kind of phenomena explored by Kogan and Wallach (Overview above), wherein narrow categorizers are conservative in risk-taking. A conservative risk-taker could well be a person who strives to be assured that stimuli are clearly assimilable to the construct, and he will sharply define the limits of a construct in order to be sure that stimuli are "correctly" located. Whatever future speculative conceptions emerge, and whatever the research efforts that they produce, Sherif, Taub, and Hovland supply clear evidence that ranges of construct applicability are subject to manipulations that cause them to expand and contract.

*   *   *

In complex social communication the introduction of reference points may produce two opposing effects. Under some conditions the introduction of a reference point or stand beyond S's current position tends to move him toward the new position. Thus, telling him that experts think it will be at least 10 years before peaceful use of atomic power is feasible, may cause an individual to increase his own estimate from one of 5 years to one of 6 or 7 years. Under other conditions the introduction of communication results in a rejection of the new proposal and a stronger entrenchment in his original position. Here one has the frequently mentioned "boomerang effect" (2, 3, 7, 9). To some extent at least, these phenomena may be the result of judgmental processes and may be conceptually closely akin to the phenomena of assimilation and contrast in the judgment of simple stimulus material. Before proceeding to a study of the complex factors involved in communication it was thought desirable to start with an analysis of these judgmental effects with simple stimulus materials in a manner applicable to the social area.

The research of Rogers (11) suggested the feasibility of doing such a study with weight-lifting. Accordingly, the procedures closely paralleled his. Judgments were first obtained as to the categorization of stimuli from 55 to 141 gm. in weight along a 6-point scale, using the method of single stimuli. In the second and subsequent sessions the weights were presented in pairs with the first ("anchor") weight described as being in the topmost category. The anchoring stimuli ranged from 141 to 347 gm. While the procedure was essentially a replication of Rogers' experiment, his formulation was not in the present terms and unfortunately he does not present his data in a form permitting the type of analysis required for the present hypotheses.

The general hypothesis of the study is that whether one obtains an "assimilation effect" or a "contrast effect" depends on the position within or distance from the original series of the introduced anchors (standards). When an anchor is introduced at the end or slightly removed from the end of the series, there will be a displacement of the scale of judgment toward the anchor and assimilation of the new reference point in the series. When, however, the reference point is too remote there will be displacement in the opposite direction (i.e., away from the anchor), with a constriction of the scale to a narrower range.

More formally, two hypotheses are presented for testing:

1. In judgments of graded stimuli ranging from low to high in some dimension, the introduction of anchors at the end points of the series or immediately above or below the series will cause displacement in the distribution of judgments of series stimuli in the direction of the anchor (assimilation effect).

2. As the anchors are placed at increasing distances from the upper or lower ends of the series, the distribution of judgments will be displaced in the direction away from the anchor and the whole judgmental scale will be constricted (contrast effect).

One or the other of these effects has been suggested by a number of previous experiments (1, 4, 5, 10, 11, 13) but the factor of distance has not been systematically varied to investigate both phenomena in a single study.

PROCEDURE

The basic procedure consisted of obtaining judgments of weight by the method of single stimuli with and without anchoring stimuli. Judgments were made in terms of a 6-point scale, "1" being the lightest, "6" the heaviest. The anchoring stimuli in the main experiment were all equal to or greater than the top stimulus value in the original stimulus series and each was described as a stimulus within the topmost category.

The apparatus consisted of a frame designed to offer sturdy support for the mechanical lifting of a set of weights. The lifting system consisted of light cordage, heavily waxed, placed horizontally over two plastic slide wheels. A horizontal pull upon a handle attached to the cordage provided for an upward motion of the weight attached. Since weight containers were of equal height and the cordage was knotted, pull was of uniform length for the different weights.

The weights were concealed from Ss by a masonite board pierced appropriately to permit passage of the cordage. This procedure of weighing provided few cutaneous cues to S and proved to be a satisfactory procedure for the study.

Pretests established that most Ss could comfortably place the stimuli in the series (without introduced anchors) correctly in at least 50% of the trials.

The stimulus series consisted of weights of 55, 75, 93, 109, 125 and 141 gm. and is referred to here as the "original stimulus series." The anchoring stimuli were weights of 141, 168, 193, 219, 244, 267, 288, 312 and 347 gm. It will be noted that the 141-gm. anchor is the same as the topmost weight in the original series.

In the first session, the operation of the mechanism was demonstrated by E. Then the following instructions were given: "The stimuli you are to judge will be a series of weights. You are to lift these by pulling up the handle as demonstrated. Following the lifting of a weight you are to judge its location on a scale of 1 to 6 inclusive. Make a judgment after each lifting even though at first you may not have adequate basis for judgment."

The weights were presented in haphazard order, one by one in sections of 50 presentations with a rest period of 5-10 min. between sections.

Only those Ss who correctly discriminated the original stimulus series in at least 50% of the trials were used in subsequent sessions in which anchors were introduced. Two Ss were not used because they failed to meet this criterion.

In anchor sessions the following instructions were read: "The stimuli will now be presented in pairs instead of singly. The first member of each pair will tell you what you are to call 6, the second you are to judge, as before, on a scale of 1 to 6. Tell me of your judgment after the second member of each pair even though at first you may not have an adequate basis for judgment."

These instructions were read to S at the beginning of each of the nine anchor sessions. The order in which anchors were introduced in successive sessions was haphazard. Only one anchor weight was used in any one session. No S took part in more than one session on any one day.

Subjects. The Ss in the main experiment were six male students from the University of Oklahoma. They were naive Ss who did not know the purpose of the experiment and had not previously served as Ss in a psychological experiment. Each S gave 300 judgments per session and each served in 10 experimental sessions (one with only the original stimulus series and one with each of the nine anchors). Thus, 3000 judgments were obtained from each S.

In addition to the above, extensive pretesting was carried out. In this pretesting phase the anchor beyond the scale was removed far beyond the highest anchor (viz., 347 gm.) reported in this paper.

RESULTS

The principal results of the experiment are shown in Fig. 1, where the distribution of judgments of weights is given for the original stimulus series (without anchor) and for the same stimuli when judged with anchors at, or varying distances above, the top stimulus in the series. It will be

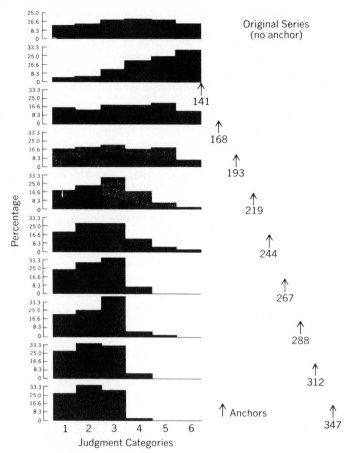

FIG. 1 *Distribution of judgments for original series of weights without anchor (top) and with anchors at increasing distances above original series (heaviest anchor at bottom).*

observed that the distribution of judgments in the original series without anchor is rectangular and does not deviate too greatly from the flat distribution represented by equal frequencies in each category. When an anchor, whose weight in grams corresponds to the top stimulus value in the original stimulus series is used, the result is a displacement of the distribution in the direction of the anchor. Anchors more distant from the top stimulus value in the series tend to produce the opposite effect, causing a displacement of judgments to the lower end of the scale. The effects shown in Fig. 2 hold for each S with only minor variation. These effects can be represented more clearly by plotting the median judgment given to the stimulus series without anchor and with anchors varying distances from the original stimulus series, as in Fig. 2. The median judgment

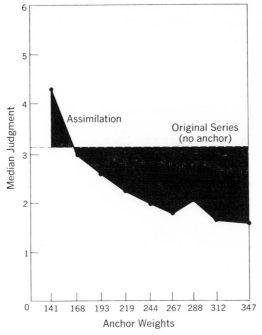

FIG. 2   *Median judgments with anchors at increasing distances from the series (abcissa) plotted against the median judgment without anchor.*

during the original series without anchor is used as the baseline from which to evaluate change.

SUPPLEMENTARY EXPERIMENTS

The preceding results indicate the operation of the predicted assimilation and contrast when the anchor is above the series. It seemed desirable to replicate the experiment to determine whether the effects obtained in the main experiment are also found when anchors are introduced at the lower end of the original stimulus series and at increasing distances from it. This was demonstrated in a supplementary experiment which was carried out in two separate series.

SERIES I[2]

Procedure. The stimulus series used in the main experiment had to be modified because the remaining range to zero point below the lower end of the original series made the introduction of only a few anchors possible. Accordingly

[2]Series I was conducted by B. Jack White, University of Oklahoma.

the lightest weight (55 gm.) was eliminated and the series of five remaining weights was used (75, 93, 109, 125 and 141 gm.). Anchors of 75, 71, 67 and 43 and 35 gm. were employed. It will be noted that the first three anchors were close to the series and actually within the original stimulus series used in the main experiment. They were chosen to be maximally sensitive to assimilation effects. The lighter anchors were selected as conducive to contrast with a gap in the region between 67 and 43 gm.

Instructions to *S*s were substantially the same as those in the main experiment. The principal procedural difference involved the use of direct lifting of weights in cylindrical containers 9.6 cm. high and 5.5 cm. in diameter.

Each *S* served for six sessions (one original series session without anchor and five anchor sessions) with from 12 hr. to 3 days between sessions. Only one anchor was used during a session. Four different orders of anchors were used for the 4 *S*s.

Results. The distributions without anchor and with anchors at varying distances from the series are shown in Fig. 3A. It will be noted that both the 75-gm. anchor and the 71-gm. anchor, which was slightly below the end stimulus, produced shifts in the distribution toward the anchor ("assimilation"). Anchors further removed from the end produced a contrast effect similar to that shown in Fig. 1 although the effects are less pronounced.

SERIES II[3]

Procedure. Use of the original stimulus series in the main experiment and introduction of anchors below the series, even as used in the modified procedure in Series I above, posed procedural problems, since too few possible anchors remained below the series and since sensitivity and judgment are atypical in this range (14). So a new series of five weights was prepared of 97, 118, 137, 153, and 169 gm. The anchors selected were 97, 89, 81, 49 and 41 gm.

In pretests, it was found that *S*s could correctly place the five test stimuli without anchors at least 50% of the trials. Special note should be made that the highest anchor is identical in value to the lowest stimulus in the original series. Intervals between the three highest anchors were less than half the distance between series stimuli. There was a gap between these three and the two anchors further removed from the series.

Instructions to *S*s were substantially the same as those in the preceding experiments. The principal difference in procedure involved the direct lifting of weights, which were in cylindrical containers 8.3 cm. high and 8.5 cm. in diameter.

Each *S* served for six sessions (one for the original series and one for each anchor) with from 12 hr. to 2 days between sessions. Only one anchor was used during a session. Three different orders of anchors were used for the 3 *S*s.

---

[3]Series II was conducted by William R. Hood, University of Oklahoma.

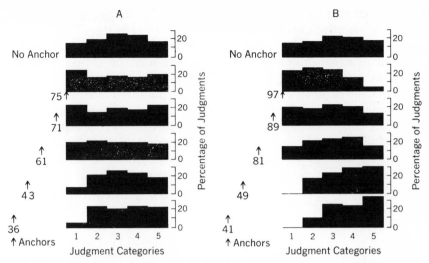

FIG. 3 *Distribution of judgments for two different stimulus series without anchor and with anchors at distances below each series (indicated by arrows).*

Results. In Fig. 3B the distributions of judgments for the five test weights without anchor and with anchors varying distances removed are presented. It appears quite likely that an assimilation effect occurs in the lower range with the first anchor and the anchor just removed from the series. Anchors further removed resulted in contrast effects much like those obtained in the main experiment. All three Ss show the assimilation and contrast effects indicated for the average.

DISCUSSION

The foregoing results support our hypothesis in showing a range immediately above or below the stimulus series in which assimilation occurs *(assimilation range)* and another range beyond this where contrast occurs *(contrast range)*. In the present experiment the assimilation range is rather narrow. We would expect that the range of assimilation would be wider with a greater range of stimuli. On the basis of judgmental relativity we would expect that the range of assimilation would be influenced not only by the absolute distance of the anchor from the extreme stimuli but also by the range of the stimulus series itself. Thus a series from 500–700 gm. would undoubtedly have different assimilation and contrast ranges than a series with the same midpoint (600 gm.) but ranging from 400–800 gm. Thus the effects of scales and anchors are not independent but are reciprocal in their effects.

The present demonstration helps to clarify some of the relationships which obtain in social judgments. Here we find that an individual places a verbal statement on an issue both in terms of the item's relative proximity to his own position and the latitude which is acceptable to him around that focal point of acceptance (8). This result is not easily explained in terms of "indifference points" or "neutrality regions" (5, 6). Similarly, in an earlier study (12) we found that a person's position on a social issue serves as the major anchor when he places opinion statements concerning the issue into what he considers the most appropriate number of different categories. The Ss with extreme stands on the issue tended to use very few categories and to utilize some categories with disproportionate frequency, while Ss with middle-of-the-road positions distributed their judgments into a larger number of categories. Here again the displacement of judgments was related to S's position on the issue, which served as a major anchor.

SUMMARY

The hypothesis was tested that introduction of anchoring stimuli immediately adjacent to the stimuli being judged will cause displacement of judgments in the direction of the anchor. This would constitute an "assimilation effect." Anchors considerably beyond the stimulus range were also employed to replicate previous findings that this will produce a displacement of judgments away from the anchor ("contrast effect").

In the first experiment weights of 55, 75, 93, 109, 125 and 141 gm. were judged. The anchoring stimuli were weights of 141, 168, 193, 219, 244, 267, 288, 312 and 347 gm. In the first session judgments were made without anchors. In subsequent sessions anchors were introduced before each stimulus being judged. Six male college students gave 300 judgments per session. Clear evidence for the hypothesis was obtained, with pronounced displacement of judgments *toward* the anchor when it was introduced at the top of the series and displacement *away* with more distant anchors.

In two further experiments, anchors were introduced at and below the lightest weights in the series. Again anchors at or slightly removed from the stimulus series resulted in displacement of judgments toward the anchor, while anchors more distant from the series produced the familiar displacement away from the anchor.

The relationship of these results to allied phenomena with social judgments is discussed.

REFERENCES

1. BEEBE-CENTER, J. G. *Pleasantness and Unpleasantness.* New York: Van Nostrand, 1932.
2. COOPER, E., & JAHODA, M. The Evasion of Propaganda: How Prejudiced People Respond to Anti-Prejudice Propaganda. *J. Psychol.,* 1947, *23,* 15–25.
3. FLOWERMAN, S. H. The Use of Propaganda to Reduce Prejudice: A Refutation. *Internat. J. Opinion & Attit. Res.,* 1949, *3,* 99–108.
4. HEINTZ, R. K. The Effect of Remote Anchoring points Upon the Judgment of Lifted Weights. *J. Exp. Psychol.,* 1950, *40,* 584–591.
5. HELSON, H. Adaptation-Level as Frame of Reference for Prediction of Psychophysical data. *Amer. J. Psychol.,* 1947, *60,* 1–29.
6. HELSON, H. Adaptation-Level as a Basis for a Quantitative Theory of Frames of Reference. *Psychol. Rev.,* 1948, *55,* 297–313.
7. HOVLAND, C. I., JANIS, I. L., & KELLEY, H. H. *Communication and Persuasion.* New Haven: Yale University Press, 1953.
8. HOVLAND, C. I., & SHERIF, M. Assimilation and Contrast Effects in Reactions to Communication and Attitude Change. *J. Abnorm. Soc. Psychol.,* 1957, *55,* 244–252.
9. LAZARSFELD, P. F. Communication Research and the Social Psychologist. In W. Dennis, (Ed.), *Current Trends in Social Psychology.* Pittsburgh: University of Pittsburgh Press, 1948, 218–273.
10. LONG, L. A Study of the Effect of Preceding Stimuli Upon the Judgment of Auditory Intensities. *Arch. Psychol.,* 1937, No. 209.
11. ROGERS, S. The Anchoring of Absolute Judgments. *Arch. Psychol.,* 1941, No. 261.
12. SHERIF, M., & HOVLAND, C. I. Judgmental Phenomena and Scales of Attitude Measurement: Placement of Items with Individual Choice of Number of Categories. *J. Abnorm. Soc. Psychol.,* 1953, *48,* 135–141.
13. VOLKMANN, J. The Anchoring of Absolute Scales. *Psychol. Bull.,* 1936, *33,* 742–743. (Abstract)
14. WOODWORTH, R. S. *Experimental Psychology.* New York: Holt, 1938.

IX

THE DEFINITION
OF PERSONAL CHANGE

1
OVERVIEW

In the preceding sections we have emphasized the organism's propensity to maintain optimum arousal by preserving the integrity of its cognitive organizations. At several points we tried to highlight the point that the maintenance of optimum arousal was not dependent on precise maintenance of one's cognitive structure. Optimality, in fact, seems to be related to slight variation in the personal complexity of the stimulus acting on the organism. Our motivation principles, then, would not posit that an organism finds its most satisfying state to be one in which all incoming stimuli are immediately integratable to existing cognitive structures. Rather, the organism seeks out stimuli that are of "interest," to use Piaget's notion. And "interesting" stimuli are those that demand some accomodation, to again use a Piagetian concept, of the organism's schema. From another perspective our position might be that the organism seeks to be "competent," in White's (1959) sense. Again, however, we hasten to forestall a possible misreading of our position. We would not speak of the organism being "pulled" toward competence. Our view is that the organism is seen to seek "competence" because its inability to instantiate a stimulus has produced arousal which the organism seeks to reduce. In sum, our organism's hedonism does not drive it toward immobility. Constructs and the constructions of events are retained as long as they predict events, but the studies of exploratory behavior and curiosity show us that the organism does not long remain in a situation that allows perfect predictability; and when the organism goes exploring it will need to alter its constructs in order to integrate the novel stimuli it will encounter. At any rate, even if it does not go exploring, the active organism would have a difficult time avoiding novel stimuli which demand construct change.

When we speak of personal change within the kind of cognitive theory we are developing, we need to speak of two aspects of change. On the one hand the theory would address itself to change in the person's constructs. On the other hand, one would need to consider changes in the particular construction that is placed on an event. For example, the average person in our culture will construe the numerical world in terms of the decimal system that is most commonly taught. With training he can change his constructs and can then regard numbering within the system of binary enumeration that is used in computerization. Imaginative researchers have given us more systematic views of the nature of construct change. For example, Piaget's original work (1965) has shown the changes that are to be seen in the child's number constructs. The average pre-four-year-old child, when asked to carry out tasks of enumeration, cannot be assumed to have developed the concept that number remains constant unless there is addition or subtraction of units. Some of these children can go through the process of counting out items, and can report the number of items that are available. However, an alteration of a feature, such as the density of the clustering of the items, that is irrelevant to the number of items in the array, will induce a pre-conservation child to change his judgment of the quantity of items in the set. Given two equal-numbered sets, one of which is spread over a large area whereas the other is in a small area, he might persist in reporting the scattered set as having more items even after counting both sets. At a later age the child is aware that the construct of number needs to include the feature of conservability, and will not alter his initial judgment of the number included in the set despite the nature of nonrelevant changes.

Life situations also provide examples of the second kind of construct alteration—that is, alterations in the constructions that are placed on events. In *King Lear*, Shakespeare's masterful portrayal of a person undergoing massive disconfirmation of his constructs, Lear progresses from a noble king who sees his daughters as worthy of sharing his kingdom, into a raging father who would address them as "you unnatural hags." In this literary piece one could argue that the change did actually take place in the daughters, rather than in the constructs of the king.

If, instead of looking to literary efforts for examples of altering the construction of an event, we look at careful studies of perceptual judgment, such as those of Boring (1946) and Rock and Kaufman (1962), we have strict assurances that the identity of the stimulus event is maintained. A disc of light placed in a distant field, which contains few cues about the distance of the disc from the retina, is judged to be smaller than a disc of the same objective size that is located in a field that offers cues that suggest distance. In Rock and Kaufman's study (1962) of the moon illusion they showed that the moon is judged to be "very large" when it is at the horizon, for the horizon is judged to be very distant. An object located at the "distant" horizon which occupies the retinal space occupied by the moon's disc "must be huge." The same-sized disc at the zenith, which somehow "seems" closer than the horizon, is judged to be smaller than the moon disc at the horizon. The placement of the moon along the *small-large* construct is altered by the construction system of the observer. The moon's "objective" size has not changed, nor has there been a change in its retinal size, but the observer's instantiation of it has changed. This objectively identical event can be construed differently as a result of its position in the total construct system hierarchy that the individual uses.

As we have said, to produce change in one's construct system a person must be placed into a situation where his efforts to construe a stimulus meet disconfirmation. It should also be clear that the person will not alter those constructs directly related to a specific stimulus if he finds a means of withdrawing from the situation. Our discussion of defensive operations, in Section VII, prepares us to recognize that a person can evade excessive arousal by eliminating the source of stimulation. At the same time, and we again refer to our discussion in Section VII relating to a person's use of "unusual" constructs, we cannot predetermine which construction a person will evolve from his experiences. This formulation puts us on constant guard against deciding that a person is not "learning" when he does not evolve the particular construction that we would apply. A marriage counselor who sets out to have his client construe marriages as creations of heavenly forces is simply asking to have his own chosen conceptions disconfirmed. In the course of the time covered by the marriage counseling, the client can come to construe his marriage as having been the creation of demoniacal forces. He did learn something, nonetheless, for he has altered his construct system. In some situations one person might obtain control over another person, and thereby arrange contingencies in a way that leads the controlled person to construe a situation as one in which his adoption of the controlling person's constructs allows for greater predictability in a situation. For example, Sarbin (1968) convincingly aruges that a "schizophrenic" has achieved an adequate cognitive organization of the confusing world that presses in on him by accepting the psychiatrist's construction of himself as a "schizophrenic." By adopting the role of "schizophrenic" that is defined by power-laden psychiatric workers, the patient can derive a meaningful organization of the world that surrounds him. Another kind of coercion to have a subject adopt a controlling person's construction occurs when an authority appeals to a somewhat tangential construction, like physical violence, in order to prevent a child from stealing. This procedure might convince the child to desist from stealing in instances where he feels he might be caught; but that authority cannot allow himself to believe that the child has "learned" the society's accepted constructions of the matter of property rights. The fact that the child's external behaviors seem to correspond with his having altered his constructs in the pre-ordained direction does not demonstrate such an alteration, and in this sense the child has not "learned" anything about property rights.

One other important line of research that bears on the issue of the modifiability of constructs is raised when we speak of developing "constructs about constructs." In recent years a large amount of this work has been related to Piaget's seminal work on the development of "operations" (Inhelder and Piaget, 1958). Alterations in cognitions are guided by the operations in which a person can engage as he seeks to develop applicable schema. If, for example, he can use only "egocentric modes," he cannot treat his schema as phenomena separate from an external event. Under these conditions he will be unable to "reverse" a schema and cannot, for example, successfully deal with elements A and A' as subclasses of B; he cannot recognize that after having separated A out of B he can reverse the procedure to reassemble B as the sum of A and A'. The subject's ability to develop constructs, then, is dependent on the operations he has available to work on the material to be construed.

Another phenomenon that reflects the alteration, or development, of "constructs about constructs" is treated in efforts to define "set." Once having developed a construction of an event, how does an organism construe the maintenance of that construct? The same trends which we observe in the thinking on the issue of "broad" or "narrow" categorization are seen to appear in the thinking on the issue of set. Much effort has gone into attempting to define "set" or "rigidity" as a "personality variable" complete unto itself. The rationale has had the same tone as that which appears in the study of broad and narrow categorization. A person who is assumed to have been trained to perceive danger in the possibility of incorrectly construing elements of his world avidly would seek to preserve those constructs that served to enhance prediction in past events. If we trace the history of the concept of set or rigidity we inevitably come across the work of Duncker (1945), who defined the notion of "functional fixedness." Duncker's studies show that once a set of events has been categorized in a particular way, the person who has done the categorizing would find it difficult to derive an alternate way of construing the situation. Specifically, once having construed a set of boxes as "containers" for candles, matches, and tacks, a subject could not easily construe them as "platforms" that could be tacked to the wall to be used as shelves on which to put lighted candles. In current stimulus-response associationistic language, we would find these phenomena explored under discussions of the concepts of *proactive inhibition* and *transfer* (Osgood, 1949).

Much of the recent work on the issue of modifiability of constructs emanates from the line of research originated by Luchins (1942), who gave this topic a rare, simple objectivity by showing the possibility of measuring the establishment of *einstellung* by the use of his water jar problems. Subjects were induced to develop a standard solution to problems that required them to produce a desired amount of water by using measuring jars of various sizes. If the varied-sized jars were labeled *A, B,* and *C,* the set solution to the problems would be: Fill *B,* subtract *A* from *B,* then subtract *2C* from the remainder. In each case this approach would leave the requested amount of water. For example, the problem is to obtain 100 quarts of water from three jars holding 21 quarts, 127 quarts, and 3 quarts, respectively, and labeled *A, B,* and *C.* After filling the 127-quart jar *(B),* the subject can subtract 21 quarts *(A)* and 3 quarts twice *(C)* to obtain the required 100 quarts. After solving six problems in this way, the subject was presented with a problem that could be solved with this same formula, but could also be solved by the more direct route of subtracting *C* from *A.* (One could obtain 20 quarts of water using a 23-quart jar [*A*], a 49-quart jar [*B*] and a 3-quart jar [*C*] by either formula: *B* minus *A,* minus *2C,* or simply *A* minus *C.)* Few subjects used the direct means of reaching the solution. After this beginning, Luchins (1959) went on to give extensive consideration of the situational variables that will maximize or minimize a person's tendency to continue to apply a previously useful, but no longer efficient, construction. After Luchins' original work, a large amount of effort was given to studies of the feasibility of treating *einstellung* as a variable which might be related to other features of a person's behavioral repertoire (Cowen and Thompson, 1951; Rokeach, 1948). *Einstellung,* in other words, was tried for the possibility that it could be designated as a continuous personality *trait.*

In our view, the effort to treat set as a personality trait has proven to be an unsatisfactory venture. Luchins' (1959) attempt to treat the issue within the broad problems of thinking and cognition seems to be the most profitable course of action, for this approach considers the situational variables that produce the kinds of cognitive disruption that will arouse the subject to alter his construction of the events that must be successfully subsumed. The study of situational variables that effect the maintenance of "set" shifts attention to what we regard as the central variable to be studied—that is, the utility or nonutility of the construct that the subject has devised to integrate the stimulus at hand. The phenomena of *einstellung* are regarded as matters related to the issue of the circumstances in which construct change is retarded or promoted.

In our first paragraph above, we noted that studies of exploratory behavior and curiosity indicate that the organism does not long remain in a situation that allows perfect predictability. If one is placed in a "monotonous" environment (Dember, 1956; Butler, 1957), he will engage in activity that will reduce the monotony. In terms of the structure we are advancing, when an organism is put into a situation wherein it can integrate all the available stimuli, it will find the under-arousal that is associated with monotony to be as intolerable as it will find a situation in which it is exposed to continuous unassimilable stimuli. It follows that a person who has been placed in a monotonous environment, and then seeks to produce stimulus variation, must, in the course of producing varied stimuli, concurrently place himself into situations that will bring about change in his construct systems. If he explores new aspects of his environment he will necessarily find himself in situations that will require a certain degree of cognitive restructuring.

To summarize our chain of ideas: It is argued that it is most useful to speak of personal behavioral change in terms of personal construct change. Pursuing the principles of motivation that were outlined in previous sections, it is assumed that construct change will occur when novel stimuli—that is, stimuli which are not assimilated to previously developed constructs—are introduced. In other words, as the *einstellung* studies show, construct change is difficult to induce if an old construction of events can be applied. The motivational proposition that has been suggested, however, allows us to expect that an organism will seek out novel stimuli, stimuli that will instigate construct change; for optimal arousal is not a matter of absence of arousal. G. Kelly asserts his view that construct change is the nature of personal change when he proposes his Experience Corollary: "A person's construction system varies as he successively construes the replication of events" (Section I).

The choice of reading for this section was difficult because of the abundance of discussion available to help clarify the issues that surround the matter of construct change. In choosing a selection, however, we made sure to include a deliberate demonstration that the treatment the subject received was designed to force him to evolve an altered construction of the stimulus situation. In each of these studies the subject begins the process with one mode of response and then is exposed to situations that bring about a new mode of response. We also believe that the studies presented here allow us to infer that the subjects did evolve a different internal representation of the external event.

REFERENCES

BORING, E. G. The Perception of Objects. *American Journal of Physics*, 1946, *14*, 99–107.

BUTLER, R. A. The Effect of Deprivation of Visual Incentives on Visual Exploration Motivation in Monkeys. *Journal of Comparative and Physiological Psychology*, 1957, *50*, 177–179.

COWEN, E. L. & THOMPSON, G. G. Problem Solving Rigidity and Personality Structure. *Journal of Abnormal and Social Psychology*, 1951, *49*, 165–176.

DEMBER, W. N. Response by the Rat to Environmental Change. *Journal of Comparative and Physiological Psychology*, 1956, *49*, 93–95.

DUNCKER, K. On Problem Solving. *Psychological Monographs*, 1945, *58*, Whole No. 270.

INHELDER, B. & PIAGET, J. *The Growth of Logical Thinking from Childhood to Adolescence.* New York: Basic Books, 1958.

LUCHINS, A. S. Mechanization in Problem Solving: The Effect of *Einstellung. Psychological Monographs,* 1942, *54,* Whole No. 248.

LUCHINS, A. S. *Rigidity of Behavior.* Eugene, Oregon: University of Oregon Press, 1959.

OSGOOD, C. E. The Similarity Paradox in Human Learning: A Resolution. *Psychological Review,* 1949, *56,* 132–143.

PIAGET, J. *The Child's Conception of Number.* New York: Norton, 1965.

ROCK, I. & KAUFMAN, L. The Moon Illusion, II. *Science,* 1962, *136,* 1023–1031.

ROKEACH, M. Generalized Mental Rigidity as a Factor in Ethnocentrism. *Journal of Abnormal and Social Psychology,* 1948, *43,* 259–278.

SARBIN, T. R. Schizophrenic Thinking: A Role Theoretical Analysis. Duplicated paper (submitted for publication), 1968.

WHITE, R. Motivation Reconsidered: The Concept of Competence. *Psychological Review,* 1959, *66,* 297–333.

2

COMPARISON OF THE
EFFECTIVENESS OF
IMPROVISED VS. NONIMPROVISED
ROLE-PLAYING IN PRODUCING
OPINION CHANGES[1]
BERT T. KING AND IRVING L. JANIS

A change of constructs is the hallmark of personal change. It becomes important, then, to demonstrate that producing effective change in one's constructs is a means of producing permanent change. This issue is related to a perplexing problem that is associated with all learning studies. When a person "learns" a word list, has he produced a change in his behavior? Obviously, at the time of learning the list, his behavior has changed. Can a word list learning study be considered as an analogue to the kind of learning we have in mind when we speak of "formal school learning"? Naive psychological theory recognizes that people "learn for the examinations," which implies that there are learning situations wherein the person does not "learn" in order to produce a permanent change in his behavior.

An explanation of this naive observation can be neatly achieved by proposing that a change in internal cognitive organizations is the hallmark of personal change. Short-term memory is different from permanent change of cognitive organizations. The use of this formulation, however, will depend on further demonstration of a difference between short-term memory and the kind of memory that will result from schema alteration or the incorporation of an event into a schema. A number of researchers are now producing evidence that short-term

Reprinted from Human Relations, *1956, 9, 177–186, by permission of Bert T. King and* Plenum Publishing Corporation.

[1]This study was conducted at Yale University as part of a program of research on factors influencing changes in attitude and opinion. The research program is supported by a grant from the Rockefeller Foundation and is under the general direction of Professor Carl I. Hovland, to whom the authors wish to express appreciation for helpful suggestions and criticisms.

memory and long-term memory are different matters (McGaugh, 1966; and Neisser, 1967, pp. 219 ff). Obviously, there is still room for greater clarification of this latter issue. At this point, we will adopt the position that long-term memory—that is, relatively permanent behavior change—is a matter of cognitive reorganization.

King and Janis, though they do not specifically address their study to this issue, supply us with tangential evidence that the "exercise" and successful use of one's personal constructs produce personal change more effectively than does an extrinsic supply of "satisfaction." Subjects were asked to adopt a role in which they were to apply a set of cognitive organizations—in Sherif's terms, "attitudes" or "frames of reference"—which were divergent from those they previously used. One group was asked to devise its own verification by demonstrating a consistency for the adopted role. The other group was provided with a neatly arranged consistency. Clearly, both groups, as they presented arguments that were divergent from their previous position, had changed their behavior. Does this behavior change signify learning? The findings show that the improvisation group achieved a greater change from their own initial position toward the position of the role. It appears justifiable to conclude (1) that the more active the involvement of one's own construct system, the greater the change to be expected in the system, and (2) that the change is more likely to be a permanent change.

REFERENCES

MCGAUGH, J. L. Time-Dependent Processes in Memory Storage. *Science,* 1966, *153,* 1351–1358.
NEISSER, U. *Cognitive Psychology.* New York: Appleton-Century-Crofts, 1967.

*   *   *

The judgments, opinions, and attitudes that one overtly expresses to friends and associates frequently come from norm-setting communications to which all persons who have a given status position within the community are expected to conform. In order to live up to social role expectations, a person will often repeat a message to others as if it were his own position, even though it may not be in accord with his private convictions. Experimental evidence, reported by the authors in an earlier paper (3), indicates that role-playing activity can exert a marked influence on the individual's private opinions. Further evidence bearing on the way in which outer conformity affects inner conformity will be presented in the present report, which describes an experiment designed to test two explanatory hypotheses suggested by the earlier findings.

In the earlier experiment we obtained measures of the effectiveness of three persuasive communications, each of which was presented under conditions of active role-playing and passive exposure. A greater amount of opinion change was observed when subjects were induced to play the role of a communicator who is attempting to convince others of the arguments and conclusions, than when they were allowed to remain passive members of an audience who merely read and listened to the material. Thus, the evidence indicates that overt verbalization induced through role-playing tends to augment the effectiveness of a persuasive communication. This outcome seems to bear out the notion that "saying is believing."

The psychological processes activated when a person is participating in the role of a communicator may involve many different factors that could affect his degree of attention, comprehension, and motivation to accept the content of the persuasive message. From among the numerous factors that theoretically could contribute to the superiority of active participation over passive exposure, we have singled out two for systematic investigation— "improvisation" and "satisfaction." In our earlier experiment, there were some supplementary observations and suggestive correlational data that led us to formulate an "improvisation" hypothesis and a "satisfaction" hypothesis as alternative explanatory concepts to help account for the observed gain from role-playing.

The "improvisation" hypothesis asserts that people tend to be especially impressed by their own persuasive efforts when they are stimulated to think up new arguments and appeals in order to do a good job of convincing others. According to this hypothesis, a person will end up by convincing himself of the validity of the point of view he is required to defend, provided that he has been induced to improvise new supporting ideas.

The "satisfaction" hypothesis postulates that the individual's sense of achievement or satisfaction with his performance in a social role provides a special source of reward that is capable of reinforcing the opinions he overtly verbalizes in that role. According to this hypothesis, role-playing will have a positive effect with respect to changing private opinions in circumstances in which the individual feels satisfied with his overt performance.

In order to investigate the relative importance of the "improvisation" and the "satisfaction" factors, the present experiment was set up to compare the effects of role-playing under laboratory conditions such that each of the two factors would be varied through direct experimental manipulation.

METHODS AND PROCEDURES

The subjects (male undergraduate students) were assigned at random to various experimental groups, each of which was exposed to the same persuasive communication. Written in the style of ordinary mass-media magazine articles, the communication presented arguments in support of two main conclusions: *(a)* that over 90 per cent of college students will be drafted within one year of their graduation, and *(b)* that the majority of college students will be required to serve at least three years in the armed forces (i.e. one year longer than the present requirement). Since all subjects were eligible for military service, it was assumed that this topic, unlike the relatively impersonal ones used in the earlier experiment, would be of considerable personal concern to them.

Opinion changes were observed by obtaining each subject's opinion responses (on a series of five questions) immediately after the communication. These answers were compared with the answers the subject had given to the same question in an opinion survey that had been conducted several months earlier.

The role-playing instructions were similar to those used in our earlier experiment (3). The procedure was modelled after those described by Lippitt (5), Maier (6), Moreno (7), and other investigators who have employed psychodramatic situations requiring the subject to enact a role in which he expresses beliefs, judgments, and attitudes that are not necessarily compatible with his own private convictions. In the present experiment, the subjects were requested to play the role of a sincere advocate of the point of view expressed in the communication on military service, which they read silently beforehand. Each active participant was told that the purpose of this role-playing activity was to help us develop a new oral speaking-test and that his talk would be tape-recorded for later presentation to a group of judges. Each passive control subject, on the other hand, merely read the script silently.[2]

In order to assess the effects of the improvisation and satisfaction factors, two different groups of active participants were used: Group A was given a relatively difficult task that required a high degree of improvisation. The subjects in this group were required to play the role of an impromptu speaker, presenting the talk without the written script, immedi-

[2]The level of attention and related factors that might be a function of the "set" to deliver an oral presentation were controlled for both groups through the supplementary use of an irrelevant communication. Each of the active and passive subjects was asked to read to himself two different scripts, and was told that when finished he would be required to give a talk based on one or the other of the two communications. After this standard preparation, the active participants were requested to give a full-length talk based on the communication that discussed the prospects of military service, while the passive controls were asked to deliver a brief talk based on the other (irrelevant) communication. Thus the procedure was designed to elicit a comparable set from the passive controls and the active participants during the primary exposure to the main communication. Moreover, a test covering the essential information content of the communication was included along with various opinion measures in the post-communication questionnaire, so as to determine whether the additional rehearsal involved in giving the talk (cf. 2, pp. 263–5) had any observable effect on learning.

ately after having read it silently. Group B was assigned a much easier role, which could be expected to heighten the degree of satisfaction—that of a speaker who reads aloud from the completely prepared script without being required to do any improvising. In effect, comparison of the two groups pits the improvisation factor (represented by Group A) against the satisfaction factor (represented by Group B).

RESULTS

In order to determine whether the experimental treatments succeeded in eliciting different degrees of satisfaction, every subject in Groups A and B was asked to rate four different aspects of his own oral speaking-performance immediately after he had given the talk. The results presented in Table 1 indicate that on each of the four items the percentage giving favorable self-ratings was significantly higher in Group B than in Group A. This evidence verifies our assumption that the more difficult task of improvising assigned to Group A would make for more self-criticism and dissatisfaction with respect to the individual's oral speaking-performance. Hence, the prediction from the "satisfaction" hypothesis is that Group B should show significantly more opinion change than Group A.

The "improvisation" hypothesis makes the opposite prediction. Among the subjects in Group A, all of whom were required to formulate the communication in their own words, a substantial percentage introduced new arguments or original elaborations of the prepared script into their talks, whereas the nature of the task assigned to Group B precluded such improvisation. If the improvisation factor is a critical one in mediating the effects of role-playing, Group A should be found to show significantly more opinion change than Group B.

The opinion change data for the two groups of active participants and for the group of passive controls are presented in Table 2. The results, based on the five key questions included in the pre- and post-communication questionnaires, show that Group A was more influenced by the communication than was Group B. This trend is apparent on all five opinion items. The superiority of Group A is reliable at the .01 confidence level on the combined index of change, which shows the percentage of those in each group who changed on three or more items in the direction of the conclusions advocated by the communication. Moreover, Group A showed more opinion change than Group C (the passive control group) on four of the five items and differed reliably from Group C on the combined index. Thus, the results support the 'improvisation" hypothesis, since they

TABLE 1 Percentage of the improvisation and non-improvisation groups giving favorable self-ratings on oral speaking-performance.

Self-rating	Group A (Improvisation) (N = 32) %	Group B (Non-improvisation) (N = 23) %	% Diff. (B − A)	p-value
1. Participant felt his performance was at least "satisfactory"	63	96	33	<.01
2. Participant felt he did *not* distort any arguments	53	96	43	<.01
3. Participant felt his voice was *not* monotonous	65	91	26	.01
4. Participant felt he gave impression of being "sincere"	47	70	23	.04

indicate that there is a significant gain from active participation when the individual is required to engage in improvised role-playing.

Predictions from the "satisfaction" hypothesis, on the other hand, are not confirmed. First of all, Group B failed to show as much opinion change as Group A, despite the fact that the subjects in the former group expressed a markedly higher degree of satisfaction. Secondly, Group B did not differ significantly from the passive control group on any of the five items; on the combined index there is a non-significant difference in the reverse direction ($p > .30$). Thus, there was no observable gain in opinion change from the relatively satisfying form of active participation in which Group B engaged.

A third set of pertinent data was obtained from a supplementary procedure that had been introduced into the experiment to provide an independent measure of the effects of the "satisfaction" variable. Within the improvisation group, different degrees of satisfaction were elicited by means of performance ratings that were given by the experimenter at the end of each subject's talk. On a random basis, Group A was divided into three sub-groups, one receiving favorable ratings, another unfavorable ratings, and the third no ratings. In effect, the experimenter differentially administered social rewards and punishments for the purpose of varying the satisfaction variable under conditions in which improvisation was held constant.

As expected, self-ratings were found to be significantly affected by the experimenter's ratings. But on the five key opinion items the subjects who received favorable ratings (and expressed the highest degree of subjective satisfaction) showed approximately the same amount of opinion change as those who received unfavorable ratings or no ratings. These supplementary findings together with the data in Table 2 indicate that there was no observable gain in opinion change when feelings of satisfaction were experimentally induced by two different methods.

DISCUSSION

The results from this experiment substantiate the observations on the importance of improvisation noted in our earlier experiment, but fail to confirm the findings on the relationship between degree of satisfaction and amount of opinion change. Since in the present study the experimental conditions were actually manipulated so as to induce variations in the degree of satisfaction, more confidence may be placed in these results than in the correlational evidence from the first experiment. The weight of the

TABLE 2 Opinion changes produced under improvised and non-improvised role-playing conditions.

| Opinion Items[1] | Net opinion change: percentage changing in the direction advocated by the communication minus percentage changing in opposite direction. | | |
	Group A (Improvisation) (N = 32) %	Group B (Non-improvisation) (N = 23) %	Group C (Passive exposure) (N = 20) %
1. Estimates of required length of service for draftees	41	27	5
2. Estimates of college students' chances of being deferred	44	26	25
3. Estimates of college students' chances of becoming officers	70	47	45
4. Expectations concerning the length of one's own military service if drafted	59	46	50
5. Expectations concerning the length of one's own deferment before being drafted	50	26	55
Combined index: percentage influenced on three or more of the five opinion items	87½	54½	65

p-value = .01

p-value = .03

[1]Copies of the questionnaire (showing the exact wording of each of the five key questions) are available upon request from the Institute of Human Relations, Yale University.

evidence now available clearly favors the improvisation variable as being a more important determinant of role-playing effects. Mere repetition of a persuasive communication, even under very favorable circumstances, apparently has little or no effect as compared with improvised restatement of the message.

This tentative conclusion still leaves open the theoretical question as to how and in what particular way improvisation heightens the acceptance of new ideas. One possibility is that when a person engages in improvised role-playing his learning efficiency is improved because of increased attention. Data bearing on the effects of variations in the level of attention, discussed in our earlier report (3), suggest that this variable probably is not a crucial factor that could account for the augmented opinion change produced by experimentally induced role-playing. In the present experiment, additional findings pertinent to the attention variable were obtained from the recall test, which had been given to all our subjects shortly after they had been exposed to the main communication. If level of attention is a determining factor, the active participants, and particularly the improvisers, should have benefited from heightened learning efficiency and therefore should have obtained higher recall scores than the passive controls. But the results show that the improvisation group, as well as the oral reading group, did *not* obtain higher recall scores than the group that was passively exposed to the communication. Hence, it seems unlikely that attention factors—or any related factors that operate through raising the level of learning efficiency—could account for the observed gain in opinion change produced by improvised role-playing.

Another type of explanation is suggested by the fact that improvisation requires the participant to reformulate the communication in his own words. The mere act of translating the message into one's own more familiar vocabulary might make the communication more meaningful, perhaps by ensuring that the implications of the content will be better understood and more easily assimilated into one's pre-existing framework of beliefs, attitudes, and values. But, to the extent that the reformulation factor is assumed to operate by facilitating the audience's comprehension of the communication, it does not seem to offer a plausible explanation of the outcome of our two role-playing experiments. The communications used in the first experiment and in the present one generally relied on relatively simple and familiar arguments that presumably could be easily understood by the college students who served as subjects. In the earlier experiments, one of the three communications contained a number of complicated arguments that made use of technical scientific concepts; but this communication proved to be the one with respect to which active participation had the least effect.

Since neither the attention hypothesis nor the reformulation hypothesis appears to be a satisfactory explanation, we must seek for some other characteristic of improvisation that may provide a more promising lead. For the present, it seems likely that the critical variable has to do with the *inventive* aspect of improvising. Here we are referring to one of the most salient features of an improvised performance: the spontaneous additions and elaborations of the arguments contained in the communication. This characteristic was found to be associated with the amount of opinion change in both of our role-playing experiments and in Kelman's experiment on the effects of a persuasive communication on school children who were induced to write essays in conformity with the communicator's position (4).

It seems plausible that there is a lowering of psychological resistance whenever a person regards the persuasive arguments emanating from others as his "own" ideas. This assumption might help to explain the effects of improvised role-playing. Hollingworth (1) contends that the effectiveness of a suggestion depends in part on the extent to which it appears to be of personal origin: resentment and negativistic reactions may interfere with acceptance of a *direct* suggestion from others, whereas the individual's belief that he is making a decision on his own initiative may increase the influence of an *indirect* suggestion. The notion that a direct approach tends to stimulate internal resistance seems to be a major assumption in theoretical discussions of the rationale for nondirective psychotherapy (8).

In the present experiment, improvised role-playing might have been successful in helping to overcome resistance by reducing the intensity of those internal responses which normally interfere with the acceptance of persuasive messages. Among the major types of interfering response that one might expect to find in everyday communication situations would be doubts about the communicator's trustworthiness, thoughts about opposing arguments, and conflicting anticipations concerning the consequences of adopting the communicator's position. Any device that successfully decreases the occurrence of such interfering responses could be expected to heighten acceptance of a persuasive communication. Perhaps it is in this way that improvised role-playing facilitates opinion change.

When passively exposed to a persuasive communication, many persons may fail to be convinced because, although capable of fully comprehending the meaning of the arguments, they fail to have the sort of thoughts or anticipations that would motivate them to change their minds. Consider, for example, the communication on the prospects of military service for college students used in the present experiment. One of the main arguments was that college students are urgently needed in the military service because of a critical shortage of skilled personnel. When someone merely reads this argument he may think of it in purely abstract terms, wonder whether it is really true, and remain unconvinced. But if the same person is required to play a role in which he must "put this idea across" to others, he may be less likely to think of criticisms or objections and more likely to experience the convincing thought-sequences and vivid anticipations that will incline him to accept a new position on the issue.

Improvised role-playing might be viewed as a technique that induces the recipient to contribute to making the communication as effective as possible; he is stimulated to think up new arguments, cogent illustrations, and impressive appeals that will help to "sell" the conclusion. In effect, the customer is not simply asked to examine the ready-made material in the original communication but is given scissors, needle, and thread to hand-tailor the material to suit himself.

SUMMARY AND CONCLUSIONS

This report deals with an experimental investigation of the conditions under which inner beliefs or opinions are affected when one is induced to become an active participant with respect to communicating a persuasive message. The hypotheses tested were derived from an earlier experiment (3), which showed that subjects who were required to play a role in which they verbalized a communication aloud to others tended to be more influenced than those who were passively exposed to the same communication. The present experiment was designed to assess the importance of two factors that could mediate this role-playing effect: (a) improvisation of one's own arguments in support of the assigned conclusion; and (b) satisfaction with one's own speaking-performance.

Three equivalent groups of college students were given the same persuasive communication, which took the position that they would soon be drafted into the armed forces and would be required to serve a year longer than current draftees. The passive controls merely read the communication silently to themselves. One group of active participants read the script aloud, and a second group was required to give an improvised talk after having silently read the script. The oral reading-task, which involved no improvision, evoked a markedly higher degree of satisfaction than the more difficult improvisation task, as indicated by the students' self-ratings. Additional variations in degree of satisfaction were introduced by subdividing the improvisation group so that some received favorable ratings from the experimenter on their speaking-performance while others received unfavorable ratings or no ratings.

The improvisation condition was found to be the only experimental variation that produced a significant increase in personal acceptance of the persuasive communication. The results consistently indicate that the amount of opinion change produced through active participation is dependent upon the amount of improvisation, but is not related to amount of satisfaction. Various psychological mechanisms were discussed that might help to explain the importance of improvisation in transforming outer conformity into inner conformity.

REFERENCES

1. HOLLINGWORTH, H. L. *The Psychology of the Audience.* New York: American Book Co., 1935.
2. HOVLAND, C. I., LUMSDAINE, A. A., & SHEFFIELD, F. D. *Experiments on Mass Communication.* Princeton: Princeton University Press, 1949.
3. JANIS, I. L., & KING, B. T. "The Influence of Role-Playing on Opinion-Change," *J. Abnorm. Soc. Psychol.,* 1954, Vol. 49, pp. 211–18.
4. KELMAN, H. C. "Attitude Change as a Function of Response Restriction." *Hum. Relat.,* 1953, Vol. 6, pp. 185–214.
5. LIPPITT, R. "The Psychodrama in Leadership Training." *Sociometry,* 1943, Vol. 6, pp. 286–92.
6. MAIER, N. R. F. *Principles of Human Relations.* New York: Wiley, 1952.
7. MORENO, J. L. *Psychodrama.* Vol. 1. New York: Beacon House, 1946.
8. ROGERS, C. R. *Counseling and Psychotherapy.* New York: Houghton Mifflin, 1942.

3

HABITUATION OF THE
AROUSAL REACTION
SETH SHARPLESS AND HERBERT JASPER

In Section III we made the point that a psychological theorist is constantly obliged to return to the work of the physiologist to ascertain that he is not taking his behavior theory into flights of fancy from which he cannot return to sound physical ground. In this section we are attempting to clarify the nature of personal change, and we have taken the position that personal change is a matter of changing constructs and constructions of events. Sharpless and Jasper give us a superb demonstration of a part of the physiology that is related to a change in the construction of an event. They show that habituation, which we interpret as the accomplished construction of an event, is accompanied by extinction of the activation of the central nervous system. This is particularly the case for the long-lasting, tonic reactions which appear to be mediated by the ascending reticular system. These findings, of course, refer back to the questions of basic motivational states which were raised in Section III. In addition to providing specific evidence that the psychological event, habituation, is related to the physiological event, reduction of electrical activity in the central nervous system, this article points to the broader conception that the organism is physiologically activated at those times when it is presented with a stimulus that it cannot immediately integrate to its existing cognitive organizations. It was proposed in Section III that this state is one that the organism seeks to avoid. Sharpless and Jasper convincingly expound a set of concepts about arousal, and its relation to the achievement of a cognitive integration of a stimulus, which we believe to be the essence of personal change.

*   *   *

If a drop of water falls on the surface of the sea just over the flower-like

Reprinted from Brain, *1956, 79, 655–680, by permission of Seth Sharpless and the editors of* Brain.

disc of a sea anemone, the whole animal contracts vigorously. If, then, a second drop falls within a few minutes of the first, there is less contraction, and finally, on the third or fourth drop, the response disappears altogether (Jennings, 1906). Here, in this marine polyp with the primitive nerve net is clearly exhibited one of the most pervasive phenomena of the animal kingdom—decrement of response with repeated stimulation. Almost every species studied, from amoeba to man, exhibits some form of response decrement when the stimulus is frequently repeated or constantly applied (Harris, 1943). The ubiquity of the phenomenon plus its obvious survival value suggests that this kind of plasticity must be one of the most fundamental properties of animal behaviour.

It is hardly likely that the same mechanisms subserve response decrement in animals so morphologically distinct as the amoeba, the sea anemone, and the higher vertebrates. Indeed, in animals possessing a synaptic nervous system, it is usually possible to distinguish several kinds of response decrement—sensory adaptation, nerve accommodation, effector fatigue, and what may be called "association fatigue" (Piéron, 1913), "internal inhibition" (Pavlov, 1927), "habituation" or "negative adaptation" (Humphrey, 1933; Hilgard and Marquis, 1940). Habituation (which appears to be a more neutral term than the others) like learning is clearly referable to some form of plasticity in the central nervous system, and, like learning, it has yet to be explained by any known neurophysiological principles. Habituation differs from both sensory adaptation and nerve accommodation in its temporal characteristics; it develops even when many minutes intervene between successive presentations of the stimulus and may persist for hours or even days. It does not depend on effector fatigue, since a response which has become habituated to a specific stimulus may still be elicited by an appropriate novel stimulus, whereas a fatigued effector will fail to respond, not only to the repeated stimulus, but to all other stimuli of the same relative intensity.

Such practically important phenomena as decrease of alertness during human watch-keeping, work decrement in monotonous tasks and boredom are demonstrably not due to effector fatigue or sensory adaptation, but rather to some form of habituation referable to the central nervous system (Mackworth, 1950; Bartley and Chute, 1947). Similarly, such obscure psychological phenomena as curiosity, the capacity of novel stimuli to capture attention and compel behaviour (Berlyne, 1951; Montgomery, 1953), insomnia produced by an unfamiliar environment, etc., seem to point to an initial sensitivity of the central nervous system to novel stimuli and a subsequent loss in sensitivity as the stimulus becomes familiar. Yet, despite the ubiquity of the phenomenon and its practical importance in human affairs, it has rarely been studied intensively from a neurophysiological point of view.

In studying habituation, we have given particular attention to the arousal reaction for several reasons: In the first place, it is reflected in readily recorded changes in the electrical activity of the brain—the "activation pattern" of Rheinberger and Jasper (1937). The large, slow rhythmic potential changes passing over the cortex during sleep are abruptly displaced by a rapid, low voltage discharge which may persist for many minutes after the termination of the arousal stimulus. Secondly, the neural mechanisms of arousal and wakefulness have been thoroughly investigated in recent years, work which has culminated in the present view of the brain-stem reticular system as essential to wakefulness and consciousness (cf. Adrian, Bremer and Jasper *Mechanisms and Consciousness,* 1954). A study of habituation of the arousal reaction should be interesting not only for its own sake but because of the light it may throw on the principles governing the sensitivity of the reticular system to afferent stimulation. Thirdly, the arousal reaction is known to habituate rapidly. Thus, Ectors (1936), Rheinberger and Jasper (1937), Clark and Ward (1945) and others, recording directly from the cortex of unanaesthetized animals, have observed that a clap or a whistle which is sufficiently intense to produce cortical activation and behavioural arousal loses this capacity when it has been repeated several times. Similarly, there is a decrement in the human alpha-blocking response to repeated stimuli (Knott and Henry, 1941), and Popov (1953) has reported that habituation of the alpha-blocking response may persist from one day to the next. Finally, the practical significance of habituation of the arousal reaction is evident in connexion with decrease of alertness during human watch-keeping, work decrement and similar phenomena.

Our experiments were designed to elucidate; firstly, the general properties of habituation—the duration of the state of habituation, its selectivity for specific stimuli, the interaction of stimuli to which the animal had become habituated with other, novel stimuli, etc.; secondly, the site and nature of the changes underlying habituation of the arousal reaction; and thirdly, the principles governing the organization and sensitivity of the brain-stem arousal mechanism.

MATERIAL AND METHODS

Thirty-five cats were used. Multilead cortical plate and subcortical needle electrodes of the type devised by Delgado (1952) were permanently implanted with the usual aseptic precautions. The plate electrodes consisted of 3–5 stainless steel discs less than 0.5 mm. in diameter separated by distances of 4 mm. and embedded in a polyethylene plate. Plate electrodes were introduced through a small trephined hole over the posterior suprasylvian gyrus. The dura was slit and the polyethylene plate was slid rostrally under the dura until it lay over sensorimotor and frontal cortex. In some experiments, electrodes were also placed over auditory cortex, location of the electrodes being controlled by the cortical response to clicks as observed on a cathode-ray oscilloscope during the operation. Subcortical needle electrodes were oriented by means of a stereotaxic instrument, according to the atlas prepared by Jasper and Ajmone-Marsan (1955), and fixed to the skull by dental cement. Outside the cranium, wires from both plate and needle electrodes were encased in polyethylene tubing and tied to the skull by stainless steel wire. The tubing issued through a skin incision just over the occipital protuberance and terminated in a tiny polyethylene socket to which leads could be attached during recording sessions.

Cortical lesions were produced by aspiration, no effort being made to spare the white matter underlying the area to be destroyed. Subcortical lesions were produced by passing high-frequency current (500 kc) generated by a Wyss coagulator through electrodes oriented by means of the stereotaxic instrument.

Records were taken on an Offner six-channel dynograph at night when the laboratory was quiet and usually with the animal housed in its home cage in a sound-insulated room. Unless otherwise indicated, all the data reported below were obtained from bipolar recording techniques. Occasionally, when responses of auditory cortex were to be recorded, a cathode-ray oscilloscope was used and the tracings were recorded photographically. Each recording session lasted from four to ten hours, occurring from two days to six weeks following the implantation of electrodes, as many as ten sessions being devoted to a single cat.

Usually sounds were used as arousal stimuli. These were produced by a four-inch loud-speaker placed one to three feet from the animal and driven through a transformer by the output of a Grass (model S 4) stimulator. The absolute intensity of the signal was not measured, but the output voltage of the stimulator provided a rough measure of intensity within the frequency range used. A 500 cycle tone at 50 volts had a loudness of about 64 db based upon a human threshold of about 0.03 volt for this sound. In most experiments, sounds of at least this intensity were used. In some experiments, tape-recorded signals were used to avoid variation introduced by manual operation of the stimulator—particularly when "modulated tones" were to be presented, i.e. sounds which varied continuously in frequency, say, from 500 to 1,000 c/sec. in a period of four seconds. Experiments were designed to take account of possible differences in the intensity or "subjective loudness" of different stimuli.

The position of cortical electrodes was determined by inspection at autopsy. The position of subcortical electrodes and the site and extent of lesions were determined by examination of stained serial sections of the brain.

RESULTS

In order to observe and compare the activation patterns produced by successive stimuli, it was necessary to establish a relatively persistent and stable synchrony in the electrical activity of the brain. This proved to be the greatest single technical problem confronted during this series of experiments. The use of sedatives and hypnotics proved impracticable, since it was impossible to maintain the delicate adjustment required over a sufficiently long period of time to compare the effects of successive stimuli. Consequently, all the data reported here were obtained during natural sleep without the aid of anaesthesia, sedation or restraint. After feeding the cat with warm milk, and seeing that it was comfortably housed in its home cage in the sound-insulated room, the experimenter simply waited until an appropriate degree of sleep was indicated by the electrocorticogram (Hess, Koella and Akert, 1953) before stimulating. This proved to be a workable procedure, although it was tedious and inflexible. The results of many recording sessions had to be discarded because of a failure to obtain the appropriate level of sleep.

The typical pattern of habituation obtained using this method is indicated by the following abstract of a protocol obtained from a normal cat two days after the electrodes had been implanted (see Fig. 1).

After being fed with warm milk, the cat with leads attached was placed in the experimental room. Recording began about 8 p.m. During the first hour, the cat was restless, moved frequently, washed, etc., and, during this period, all channels showed very rapid activity with many movement artifacts. By 9:30 the cat had settled down, and occasional slow waves and spindles appeared in the electrocorticogram. A consistent sleep pattern lasting for many minutes did not appear until about 10:30.

The first stimulus, an intense (50 volts) 500 c/sec. tone of about 3 seconds' duration, was presented at 10:45. This aroused the animal, producing runs of activation in all channels which lasted slightly over 3 minutes (Fig. 1, 1st tracing). Atypically, the first stimulus failed to produce overt movements. As soon as sleep patterns had returned to the electrocorticogram, the 500 c/sec. tone was repeated, and so on for many trials. The duration of activation patterns progressively decreased, rapidly during the first 10 trials and slowly and irregularly thereafter (Table 1).

During the period from 10:45 to 12:00, the stimulus was repeated 35

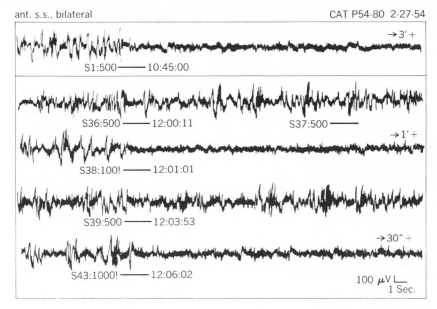

FIG. 1 *Cortical electrograms from the suprasylvian gyrus of a normal cat showing typical habituation of the arousal reaction to a 500 cycle tone after about 30 trials. In the first tracing the response to the first presentation of the 500 cycle tone is shown (S1:500). The solid bar shows the duration of the stimulus followed by the time in hours, minutes, and seconds (10:45:00). In the second tracing is shown the 36th and 37th trials (S36 and S37). Then a novel tone (!) of 100 cycles is presented in the 38th trial (S38: 100!) followed by a repetition of the habituated tone (S39:500) and then another novel tone (S43:1,000!). The figures at the right above the E.E.G. traces indicate the duration of the activation in each trial.*

times. By the 30th trial, the animal had become more or less completely habituated to the 500 c/sec. tone, and subsequent presentations of this tone produced little or no alteration in the electrocorticogram (2nd tracing). After several repetitions of the 500 c/sec. tone failed to produce activation, a new tone (100 c/sec.) was presented. The animal was immediately aroused and remained awake for over a minute (3rd tracing). When sleep patterns had returned to the electrocorticogram, the familiar 500 c/sec. tone was repeated several times and consistently failed to produce arousal (4th tracing). On the 43rd trial, another novel stimulus—a 1,000 c/sec. tone—was presented. This too aroused the animal, producing runs of activation which lasted well over 30 seconds (5th tracing). Several

TABLE 1   Duration of activation patterns pro-
                           duced by the first ten stimuli during
                           a typical recording session. Time in
                           seconds.

Duration of activation	Time since last stimulus
192	0
100	220
210	337
30	262
15	112
19	90
5	69
75	115
12	182
7	32

subsequent presentations of the familiar 500 c/sec. tone failed to produce activation, and the recording session ended.

Changes in the activation pattern during habituation. The habituation process seldom proceeded in a perfectly regular and consistent manner. Nevertheless, certain general changes in the activation patterns elicited by successive stimuli were commonly seen during these experiments: (i) The most striking and reliable change was a progressive decrease in the duration of activation. In all preparations, the period of activation decreased rapidly at first and then more slowly. After the first 5 or 10 presentations of an intense tone, the period of activation rarely lasted longer than 10 or 15 seconds. This remaining brief activation reaction, however, proved very resistant to habituation, as many as 20 or 30 trials being required before it disappeared entirely. (ii) As the stimulus was repeated, the time elapsing between the onset of the stimulus and the beginning of the activation action increased. Unlike the change in duration of activation, the increase in latency tended to occur slowly at first (perhaps 0.2 second in the first 10 trials). Later, after habituation had been partly established, the latency of activation varied greatly, and, occasionally, activation patterns might appear on the cortex as long as 10 or 20 seconds after the termination of the stimulus. Such enormous latencies were difficult to interpret, but the frequency with which they occurred in various experiments even when the record exhibited stable sleep patterns for many minutes preceding the onset of the stimulus convinced us that they were not due to coincidental associations between spontaneous arousal and the arousal stimulus. (iii) With the development of habituation, slow, large-amplitude waves and spindles tended to encroach on the activation pattern, so that the apparent flattening of the electrocorticogram became less marked with successive stimuli. Often, these slow waves occurred in such a way as to break the activation pattern into two phases.

Depth of sleep and speed of habituation. It seemed quite clear that habituation required fewer trials during deep sleep. Moreover, there was a tendency for the animal to fall more and more deeply asleep as the experiment progressed. This being the case, it was necessary to institute controls to make sure that the loss of responsiveness was due to an actual habituation process resulting from repetition of the stimulus and not simply to a spontaneous increase in the depth of sleep. When possible, the following controls were used: (i) Arousal stimuli were presented only when the electrocorticogram indicated fairly deep sleep (Hess, Koella and Akert, 1953). (ii) Stimuli were commonly used which were sufficiently intense to arouse the animal on their first occurrence regardless of the depth of sleep. The use of intense stimuli retarded habituation considerably, but if such a stimulus subsequently failed to produce arousal, one could be sure that the loss of responsiveness was due to repetition of the stimulus. (iii) Finally, if a novel stimulus of equal or less intensity aroused the animal after it had ceased to respond to a familiar stimulus, the effect could not be ascribed to an increased depth of sleep.

The inflexibility of our method, requiring as it did that the animal fall into a natural, spontaneous sleep before each stimulus was presented, prevented us from carrying out reliable, quantitative studies of the speed of habituation. However, the range of magnitudes encountered with the normal cat varied from 6 trials (click) to 60 (modulated tone—changing continuously in pitch from 500 to 1,000 c/sec. in a period of 3 seconds). In all preparations, modulated tones were more effective in producing arousal initially and more resistant to habituation than constant tones of the same or greater intensity.

It should be pointed out that the speed of habituation probably depends on the inter-trial interval as much as anything else. In our experiments, this interval varied from about 20 minutes to 20 seconds, dependent on the speed with which the animal returned to sleep after each arousal stimulus. The inter-trial interval usually became shorter as the experiment progressed.

Brain-stem activity during habituation. In five cats, records were taken simultaneously from cortical and subcortical structures. In general, potentials led from mesial thalamus, posterior hypothalamus and midbrain reticular formation were not strikingly different from those recorded for the surface of the cortex. In the alert waking state, both cortical and subcortical regions exhibited rapid, low-voltage activity, and during sleep the same regions displayed trains of slow, large-amplitude waves. Spindle bursts were less frequent in posterior hypothalamus and mid-brain reticular formation than in mesial thalamus and sensorimotor cortex, and the contrast between sleep and waking activity was not always as marked in the reticular formation as in the sensorimotor areas of the cortex. Occasionally, cortical activation patterns outlasted activation patterns recorded from deep structures by several seconds.

The results obtained during habituation may be summed up as follows: Wherever arousal was accompanied by flattening in the electrical activity of the brain, whether in cortex, diencephalon or mesencephalon, this flattening diminished and finally disappeared entirely as the animal became accustomed to the stimulus (Fig. 5). During habituation, changes in activation patterns recorded from subcortical structures exactly paralleled changes in activation patterns recorded from the cortical surface.

Specificity of the habituation process. If either the intensity or duration of a stimulus to which the animal had become completely habituated was increased, it became capable of arousing the animal. More interesting, however, was the specificity of the habituation process to the quality of the repeated stimulus. Thus, if the animal had become completely habituated to a repeated tone, it could still be aroused by a light touch, a change in illumination, or by a tone of a different frequency. In the protocol abstracted above, the animal had become habituated to a 500 c/sec. tone; yet a novel 100 or 1,000 c/sec. tone retained the capacity to produce cortical activation. Habituation in all normal animals exhibited at least this degree of specificity. There was, however, some generalization along the pitch continuum. If habituation to a 500 c/sec. tone had been established, a 600 c/sec. tone would usually be ineffective in producing arousal, and even a 1,000 c/sec. tone would have lost some of its initial effectiveness.

Habituation was occasionally specific not only to the pitch of a sound, but also to the arrangement of tonal elements within the sound—its pattern. This was demonstrated in the following way: A tape-recorded modulated tone (falling in pitch from 5,000 to 200 c/sec. in a period of 4 seconds) was repeatedly presented until the animal had become completely habituated (Fig. 2). Then, by presenting the same sound in the reversed order (so that it rose in pitch instead of falling), the animal was exposed to a novel arrangement of the same tonal elements. This change in the pattern of the stimulus was sometimes sufficient to produce cortical activation even though the original stimulus, identical in frequency range, produced little or no alteration in the electrocorticogram. However, a

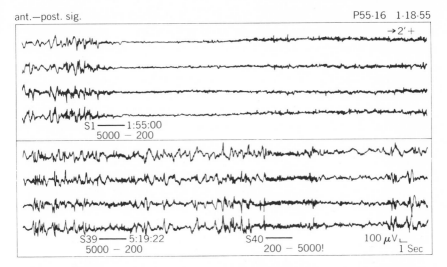

FIG. 2 *Habituation to a sound pattern consisting of a uniform "sliding" frequency change from 5,000 to 200 cycles shown in cortical electrograms from left and right anterior and posterior sigmoid areas. The first trial is shown in the first four tracings, habituation in the 39th trial below, followed by the same tonal sequence presented in the reverse order (S40, 200-5,000!) which acts as a relatively novel stimulus.*

change in the pattern of a stimulus after habituation was much less effective in producing arousal than a change in pitch. Pattern-specific habituation was not observed in all intact animals, and it was never observed in animals in which the auditory system had been damaged in any way.

Duration of habituation. In discussing the duration of states of habituation it will be useful to distinguish between "phasic" activation patterns—those which barely outlast the stimulus—and "tonic" activation patterns, which may persist for many seconds or minutes. After an animal had become completely habituated to a repeated tone, the lapse of a few minutes during which the tone was not presented would be sufficient to restore a phasic activation reaction. However, a quarter of an hour or more might be required before the stimulus regained its capacity to elicit a sustained, tonic reaction, dependent upon the number of times the stimulus had been presented during the experimental procedure.

We were struck by the fact that the animals seemed less responsive generally and became habituated more rapidly to experimental stimuli on the second and third days of recording than on the first. This seemed to indicate, at the very least, that a state of habituation to the experimental situation had developed which persisted from one day to the next. The effect was so marked in some cases that it was necessary to interpose several days' rest between successive recording sessions. Given such a rest, the animal's normal responsiveness was usually restored.

In another experiment, a 500 c/sec. tone was sounded every quarter of an hour for about ten days. Then two days were allowed to elapse during which the cat was not exposed to the stimulus. The first occurrence of the familiar 500 c/sec. tone produced a rather poorly differentiated phasic reaction lasting not longer than 15 seconds (1st tracing). The first occurrence of a novel 100 c/sec. tone, on the other hand, awakened the animal completely, producing a tonic activation pattern lasting over 15 minutes (2nd tracing). Normally, a 500 c/sec. tone is slightly more effective in producing arousal than a 100 c/sec. tone—certainly not less so. With repetition, the 100 c/sec. tone rapidly lost its initial advantage and this

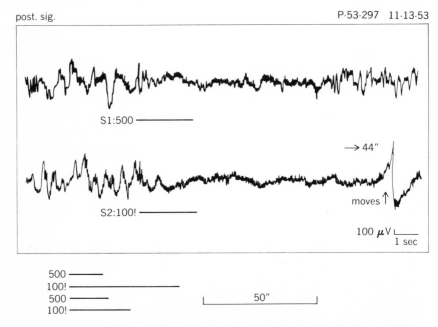

post. sig.   P-53-297   11-13-53

S1:500 ————

→ 44″

S2:100! ————

moves ↑

100 μV ⌐——
          1 sec

500 ————
100! ————————
500 ————
100! ————

⌐————50″————⌐

FIG. 3   *Illustration of degree of persistence of frequency-specific habituation in animal with bilateral ablation of auditory cortex (P53-297, fig. 6). In the first trace is shown the brief response to a previously habituated 500 cycle tone following a two-day rest period. The second trace shows the much longer response to a novel 100 cycle tone. Graphic representation of the duration of response to the first four stimuli following the two-day rest period is shown below.*

advantage was never recovered even after a rest period. The long-lasting state of habituation generalized very rapidly to include the 100 c/sec. tone and remained general throughout the experiment (which was continued for several days). In Fig. 3 is shown a similar long-lasting habituation in an animal with bilateral dilation of auditory cortex.

Inhibition and disinhibition. In the classical studies of conditioning, it was observed that the frequent repetition of a conditioned stimulus without reinforcement often led to drowsiness and sleep. Pavlov attributed this effect to an inhibitory process—the repeated stimulus acquiring the capacity to inhibit the activity of the hemispheres (Pavlov, 1927). The possibility that the Pavlovian hypothesis of internal inhibition applies to the habituation of the arousal reaction was tested in the following way: After the animal had become thoroughly habituated to a loud 500 c/sec. tone, this tone was presented simultaneously with a puff of air delivered through a glass tube taped to the animal's back. If the familiar tone caused a generalized inhibition to be exerted on the arousal mechanism or the cerebral hemispheres, the activation pattern produced by the novel but weak tactile stimulus should have been suppressed. However, as Fig. 4 shows, if there was any interaction, it was one of summation rather than inhibition. Similar results were obtained when two tactile stimuli were used.

Pavlov also observed that the sudden introduction of an unfamiliar stimulus into the experimental situation might restore temporarily an extinguished response. In accordance with his belief that extinction depended on an inhibitory process, he referred to the momentary revival of an extinguished reflex by an irrelevant, novel stimulus as "disinhibition." Disinhibition (or "dehabituation" as it has sometimes been called) is frequently seen after the habituation of unconditioned reflexex in vertebrates. It has been reported after habituation of the withdrawal reflex in turtles (Humphrey, 1933), after habituation of the startle reflex in rats (Prosser and Hunter, 1936) and after habituation of the eyelid reflex in man (Oldfield, 1937).

It seems likely that the "disinhibition" of extinguished reflexes by novel, irrelevant stimuli depends on the potent non-specific activating effects of these stimuli, not on the blocking of some internal inhibition as the term implies. This interpretation is supported by the fact that disinhibition was seldom observed in the present experiments if the arousal effects of the novel stimulus were allowed to wear off completely before the familiar stimulus was repeated. Thus, in the protocols abstracted above, after the animal had become completely habituated to a 500 c/sec. tone, a novel 100 c/sec. tone was presented which produced a brief run of activation. When the animal had returned to sleep, the familiar 500 c/sec. tone was

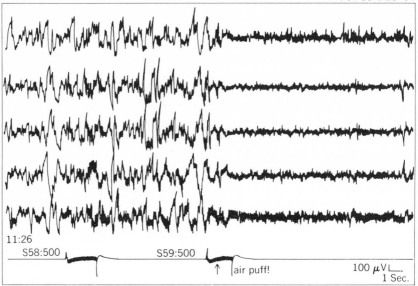

FIG. 4 *Generalized activation of the cortical electrogram from sigmoid
and suprasylvian areas bilaterally is produced by a novel tactile
stimulus (air puff!) when presented simultaneously with a tone to
which the animal had been thoroughly habituated in 58 trials
(S58:500). This illustrates lack of general inhibition in the habituation process.*

still incapable of eliciting arousal. The process of habituation to a 500
c/sec. tone was not reversed by the introduction of a novel stimulus. Many
times, however, we observed that a familiar stimulus which was by itself
incapable of producing arousal might intensify the level of activation it it
were presented while the animal was still partly aroused by the effects of a
novel stimulus.

The activity of auditory cortex during habituation. In investigating the
site of the change on which habituation of the arousal reaction depends,
we naturally considered first the primary sensory pathways. Recently,
Hernandez-Peon and Scherrer (1955) and Galambos, Sheatz and Vernier
(1956) have shown that when click stimuli are presented continually at
intervals of 1–3 seconds over a period of hours or days, evoked potentials
recorded from the cochlear nucleus and auditory cortex diminish in size. It
is possible, therefore, that habituation of the arousal reaction depends on a
change in the primary sensory pathways, that signals entering these

pathways are damped or inhibited before they reach either the arousal mechanism or higher auditory centres.

This possibility was investigated by recording primary responses from auditory cortex during habituation of the arousal reaction. A series of 12 clicks, 2/sec., was used as the arousal stimulus. Thus, a single arousal stimulus consisted of a train of 12 clicks lasting altogether about 6 seconds. Following the usual method, this stimulus was repeatedly presented at varying intervals until it no longer produced activation patterns. If habituation of the arousal reaction depended on the establishment of a block in the primary sensory pathways, we should expect to find evoked potentials recorded from sensory cortex diminishing in size or increasing in latency or both as the stimulus lost its power to produce generalized activation. However, this was not the case. There was no change in latency (about 8 msec.). The size of the potentials did change, but not in the predicted direction. Rather than diminishing as habituation of the arousal reaction developed, the size of evoked potentials increased. The results from one such experiment are shown in Fig. 5. In this experiment, the potentials increased from a mean size of 98μ before habituation to 108μ after habituation. The probability that this increase was due to chance variation was computed and found to be quite small (p < .02 using the standard t-technique for testing the significance of differences between means).

Thus, we cannot attribute habituation of the arousal reaction to the establishment of a block in the primary sensory pathways. That such a block may be established by prolonged, continual stimulation at short inter-trial intervals has been shown by the experiments cited. But it cannot play a necessary role in habituation of the arousal reaction. The latter occurs even when many minutes intervene between successive presentations of the stimulus, it may persist for hours or days in the absence of stimulation, and it is accompanied by an increase rather than a decrease in the size of the primary response.

Why the primary cortical responses increase in size during habituation of the arousal reaction is an interesting question. It is unlikely that the habituation procedure itself produces the increment. After habituation, the stimuli fail to arouse the animal so that the primary responses are recorded against a background of sleep activity, and evoked potentials tend generally to be somewhat larger during sleep and anaesthesia. Direct stimulation of the brain stem reticular formation, producing the electrical changes associated with alert wakefulness, is known to result in a diminution of the amplitude of potentials recorded from afferent tracts in the cord and from other afferent structures including the cochlear nucleus (Kerr and Hagbarth, 1954; Hernandez-Peon and Scherrer, 1955; Galambos, 1956). In our experiments, if clicks at 2/sec. were presented continu-

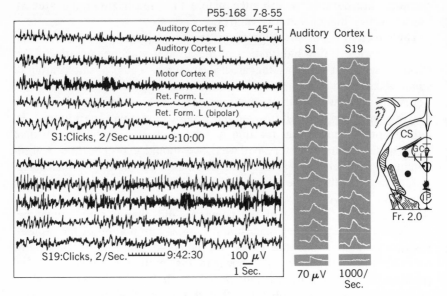

FIG. 5 *Cortical electrograms together with electrograms from the mid-brain reticular formation (see diagram at right) showing general activation response to auditory clicks at 2/sec. together with oscilloscope records of evoked potentials from auditory cortex (S1). After habituation (S19) of the activation response, evoked potentials are slightly increased.*

ally *to the waking animal,* the evoked potentials recorded from auditory cortex disappeared occasionally for 2 or 3 seconds at a time. This tended to occur at moments when the animal was quite active. We considered and rejected as unlikely the possibility that the momentary disappearance of evoked potentials was an artifact produced by movement. It seemed rather that the phenomenon was of genuine physiological significance, tending to occur at moments of extreme activation. However, it must be distinguished from habituation of the arousal reaction and probably also from the attenuation of evoked auditory potentials resulting from prolonged, continual stimulation.

There seem, then, to be three distinct phenomena whose relations to one another are quite obscure: (i) habituation of the arousal reaction; (ii) a diminution of evoked auditory potentials resulting from prolonged, continual stimulation (Hernandez-Peon and Scherrer, 1955; Galambos, Sheatz and Vernier, 1956), and (iii) a diminution of evoked auditory potentials resulting from extreme activation.

Habituation after destruction of auditory cortex. Auditory cortex continues to respond to stimuli which, through repetition, have lost their power to elicit generalized activation. This does not rule out the possibility that primary sensory cortex plays an essential role in habituation of the arousal reaction, perhaps by modulating the activity of the arousal mechanism through corticifugal pathways. We were interested, therefore, in the effects of destruction of auditory cortex on habituation to sound.

Four animals were prepared with bilateral cortical lesions. In one cat (Fig. 6, 296) the lesion was restricted to auditory I and II and the posterior ectosylvian gyrus, with some extension inferiorly in the pseudosylvian region. In the second (Fig. 6, 297) the lesion was extended to include most of the suprasylvian gyrus. In the third and fourth cats, the lesion was extended still further to include somatic II and all of the neocortex except gyrus proreus and a strip of cortex along the sagittal fissure (Fig. 6, 131 and 147).[1]

The animals were tested at various intervals (up to four months in one case) following the cortical ablation. It should be borne in mind that our method permitted considerable variation in depth of sleep and inter-trial interval, thus making it impossible to detect small quantitative individual differences in the parameters of habituation. However, so far as could be determined within the limitations imposed by the method and the small number of subjects, the cats with extensive cortical lesions did not differ in any systematic way from normal animals in their capacity to become habituated to sounds of a specific frequency. The remarkable specificity of the habituation phenomenon even in animals with the most extensive cortical lesions is indicated in Fig. 7. This cat, with bilateral lesions including auditory I and II, somatic II, suprasylvian and posterior marginal gyrii, after having become completely habituated to a 700 c/sec. tone could still be aroused by either a 200 or a 1,200 c/sec. tone.

One cat with auditory I and II and suprasylvian gyrus destroyed (Fig. 6) was also tested for the day-to-day persistence of habituation. The procedure was essentially the same as that described above (under "duration of habituation.") About ten weeks after the cortical ablation, a loud speaker was attached to the home cage, and the cat was exposed to a 500 c/sec. tone every quarter of an hour. Ten days later, electrodes were implanted, and two days were allowed to elapse during which the cat was not exposed to the stimulus. After the two-day rest period, a novel 100 c/sec. tone was more effective in producing cortical activation than the familiar 500 c/sec. tone. As in the case of the normal cat, however, the 100 c/sec. tone lost its initial advantage in a few trials.

Efforts to obtain habituation selective for the *pattern* of a given sound in animals lacking auditory cortex were generally unsuccessful. At present, it

[1]Retrograde degeneration in the thalamus of these animals is being studied at present.

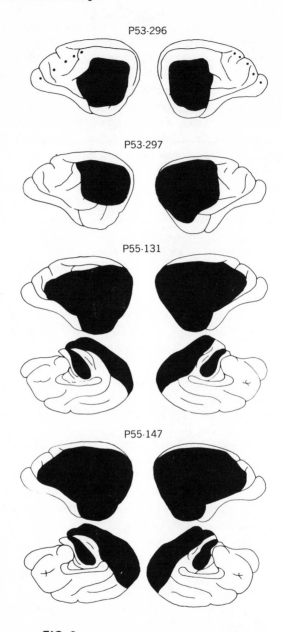

FIG. 6

Diagrammatic representation of cortical excisions as reconstructed from serial histological sections of the cat's brain.

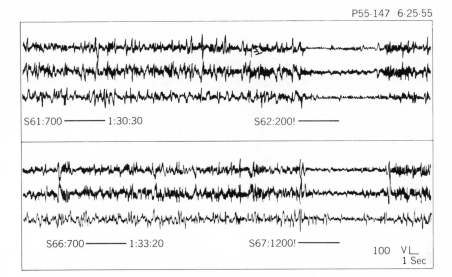

FIG. 7 *Frequency specific habituation to a 700 cycle tone in cat following large neocortical excision as shown fig. 6 (P55-147).*

is not possible to say whether this indicates a genuine impairment of function due to the operation, or whether it was the result of chance variation, since we were not always successful in obtaining pattern-specific habituation even in intact animals.

Thus, so far as could be determined with the present method, the parameters of habituation are unchanged after extensive bilateral damage to the cortical areas subserving audition, except, possibly, the capacity of the habituation process to be selective for the pattern of a repeated sound. It is interesting to compare these results with the results of a previous studies which have used the conditioned reflex method. Diamond and Neff (1953) have reported that complete ablation of electrically excitable auditory cortex does not prevent animals from acquiring conditioned differential responses to tones, although it does prevent conditioned pattern discrimination. On the other hand, according to Meyer and Woolsey (1952), if somatic II is bilaterally destroyed in addition to auditory I and II, pitch discrimination is permanently lost. In the present experiment, however, we were unable to detect any differences between animals in which only auditory I and II had been destroyed and animals in which the lesion included also somatic II.

It would appear that the relatively primitive kind of pitch discrimination observed in our experiments does not require auditory cortex even when the latter is given the most broad interpretation.

Habituation after interruption of the brain-stem auditory pathways. In the experiments of Lindsley, Schreiner, Knowles and Magoun (1950), cats in which the auditory pathways had been severed at the level of the superior colliculi could still be aroused by intense sounds, presumably through the mediation of collateral pathways entering the reticular activating system below the collicular level. It occurred to us that considerable light might be shed on the habituation phenomenon by the study of preparations in which the primary sensory tracts had been interrupted leaving intact only the collateral pathways to the reticular system through which auditory signals could be communicated to the hemispheres.

In four animals, an attempt was made to destroy the lateral lemniscus bilaterally below the level of the inferior colliculus by passing high-frequency current through electrodes which had been introduced through the posterior fossa and oriented along the horizontal plane (H-2) of the stereotaxic instrument. In no case were the lemnisci completely severed. Even in the best preparation, it was possible to pick up some evoked potentials from one hemisphere during a terminal experiment. This animal was not somnolent, but the threshold of the arousal reaction was greatly elevated. The animals could be aroused by intense tones, however, and it became habituated to these stimuli rapidly. The habituation was specific to the frequency of the repeated sound, but it was apparently not pattern-specific.

In later experiments, we attempted to sever the somewhat more accessible brachia of the inferior colliculi. During the operation, the responses of auditory cortex to clicks were monitored on an oscilloscope, and the coagulated area was enlarged until the primary cortical responses disappeared. An example of one of these lesions is shown in Fig. 8. In one of the three cats prepared in this way, some evoked potentials were subsequently obtained from the auditory area of one hemisphere.

None of the three cats was somnolent after the first few days following the operation, but the threshold of the arousal reaction to sound was greatly elevated. Tonic activation patterns could be produced fairly reliably by the use of unusually intense tones. Frequently, these activation patterns had extremely long latencies—many seconds intervening between the termination of the stimulus and the onset of cortical activation. In this connexion, we may mention the apparent *summation* over a series of arousal stimuli which often occurred in these preparations. If an ineffective arousal stimulus were repeated several times at intervals of 30 seconds or so, even though it failed completely on its first occurrence to produce any detectable alteration in the electrocorticogram, it might on its third or fourth repetition produce a full-fledged run of EEG activation.

Studies of habituation gave similar results for the three preparations.

The animals became habituated very rapidly to intense tones, usually in three or four trials. The selectivity of the habituation for the frequency of the repeated stimulus was greatly impaired. In spite of many attempts, we were able to obtain evidence in only one instance of frequency-specific habituation in animals in which the brachia of the inferior colliculi had been severely damaged. In that instance, a cat which had become habituated to a 1,000 c/sec. tone could be aroused momentarily by a novel 100 c/sec. tone. Usually, once the animal had become habituated to a repeated tone, it failed to respond to all tones of the same intensity. The habituation was modality-specific, however, since it was possible to arouse the animals by near-threshold tactile stimuli after they had become completely habituated to an auditory stimulus.

The failure to observe a similar loss of specificity of the habituation phenomenon in animals with lesions below the level of the inferior colliculus was probably due to incomplete severance of the lemnisci.

DISCUSSION

In discussing our results, we shall propose several hypotheses concerning the organization of the arousal system, and the site and nature of the changes underlying habituation. These hypotheses must be regarded as tentative, suggested but not finally proven by the available evidence.

In interpreting the present results, it is helpful to distinguish between two kinds of activation reactions. One, the "phasic" reaction, rarely outlasts the stimulus by more than 10 or 15 seconds, it has a short latency, it is very resistant to habituation, and once habituated, it recovers within a few minutes. The other, the "tonic" reaction, varies in duration from a few seconds to many minutes, it may have a remarkably long latent period (up to 30 seconds), it is labile, subject to rapid habituation, and it tends to recover slowly, over periods of hours or days.[2]

In normal animals, the two occur together and cannot be distinguished except in special circumstances—e.g., after partial habituation, when only the phasic type of reaction is elicited. However, the two types of reactions may be dissociated by brain-stem lesions. Thus, animals in which the primary sensory pathways have been severed at the collicular level so that the thalamus is deprived of direct auditory innervation are apt to exhibit long latency, tonic activation patterns which habituate extremely rapidly.

[2]In a paper delivered at the XIV International Congress of Psychology on "Higher Nervous Activity and the Problem of Perception," E. N. Sokolov of Moscow University makes a similar distinction two forms of the "orienting reflex."

On the other hand, animals in which the mesencephalic reticular system has been damaged leaving the sensory pathways to the thalamus intact exhibit only brief arousal patterns which barely outlast the stimulus (Lindsley *et al.,* 1950). Unfortunately habituation has not yet been studied in preparations of the latter type.

It will be helpful, perhaps, to distinguish between the upper and lower components of the activating system. In the present experiments, interruption of the auditory pathways (and perhaps also some adjacent portions of the brain-stem) at the collicular level seemed to prevent signals from reaching the mechanism responsible for the phasic, habituation-resistant type of reaction. Yet, bilateral destruction of auditory cortex including auditory I and II, somatic II and suprasylvian gyrus had no such effect. This suggests that direct stimulation of the upper component of the activating system from adjacent sensory structures produces the phasic type of reaction, whereas stimulation of the reticular system through collaterals in the lower brain-stem is responsible for the tonic type of reaction. Thus, the medial geniculate bodies and closely associated structures may serve a very important function in controlling the rapid but brief alerting reactions mediated by the upper, diencephalic component of the activating system.

Another difference in the two components of the activating system appears if we consider the selectivity of the habituation process for the repeated stimulus. There is marked loss of specificity of habituation to the frequency of the repeated sound after the primary sensory tracts have been interrupted at the collicular level. Thus, habituation of the tonic reaction mediated by the reticular system is apt to be much less specific than habituation of the phasic reaction originating in the diencephalon. This is consistent with the considerable degree of convergence of afferent signals in the reticular formation (French, Verzeano and Magoun, 1953). It may also explain the tendency of long-lasting states of habituation to generalize rapidly over a wide range of stimuli, especially if the tonic reactions originating in the reticular formation recover only slowly after habituation as compared with the phasic reactions originating in the diencephalic portion of the activating system.

It is evident that if the activating system is to play an important role in the *waking* animal—alerting the central nervous system and compelling attention in the presence of novel and biologically important stimuli, it must be sensitive to slight changes in the quality of stimuli impinging on the organism's receptors. Moreover, it must be capable of producing rapid but brief shifts in the reactivity of the central nervous system. Our evidence indicates that only the diencephalic component of the activating system has these properties. The more caudally situated reticular system is capable only of crude differentiation between stimuli and produces long-lasting, persistent changes in the level of reactivity. The properties of the brain stem reticular system, therefore, are well-suited to the maintenance of wakefulness over long periods of time, but ill-adapted to the sudden and brief changes in reactivity that must occur in response to highly specific stimuli if the animal is to meet the demands of its waking environment.

What is the anatomical substrate of the important diencephalic component of the activating system? On this point, we have only presumptive evidence. According to the present conception of the organization of the activating system, it is supposed that activity initiated in the reticular formation of the mesencephalon is communicated to the cortex through both thalamic and extra-thalamic pathways (Starzl, Taylor and Magoun, 1951). The thalamic pathway has been provisionally identified with the unspecific projection system of the thalamus, first studied in the classical experiments of Morison and Dempsey (1942). There is abundant evidence that this system has physiological properties distinct from those of the lower reticular activity system. As one example, we may mention the fact that slow, repetitive stimulation of the unspecific thalamic projection system is apt to produce recruitment, whereas slow, repetitive stimulation of the mesencephalic reticular formation produces a marked attenuation in the size of evoked potentials (Jasper, 1949; French, Verzeano and Magoun, 1953). On the other hand, rapid, repetitive stimulation of either system elicits widespread cortical activation (Morruzi and Magoun, 1949). It is possible, therefore, that the phasic reaction observed in the present experiments depended on stimulation of this unspecific thalamic projection system from the medial geniculate bodies and associated sensory structures. One of us has previously suggested that the unspecific thalamic system is strategically situated for subserving attentive processes in the conscious animal—a proposal which is consistent with the present evidence (Jasper, 1949; Adrian, Bremer and Jasper, 1954, p. 374).

What can be said about the site of the neural changes underlying habituation of the arousal reaction? In the first place, it is clear that this kind of habituation does not depend on changes occurring in the primary sensory pathways—i.e., the pathways responsible for conveying impulses to the cortical projection areas, since primary cortical responses could still be obtained from the projection areas, and indeed were somewhat larger, after the stimulus lost its power to elicit generalized activation. Nor can the change upon which habituation of the arousal reaction depends be restricted to sensory cortex, since complete removal of auditory cortex did not prevent animals from showing habituation highly selective for specific tones. This leaves the multisynaptic, extralemniscal systems—the unspecific thalamic projection system and the lower reticular activating system with their associated "collateral" pathways—as the probable site of the changes on which habituation of the arousal reaction depends.

The remarkably long latent periods occasionally observed in these experiments, especially in animals in which the primary sensory pathways had been severed at the collicular level, deserve some comment. One might suppose that an activation reaction could be initiated in the mesencephalic reticular system and could spread slowly—over many seconds—to the cortical mantle, but electrodes placed in the reticular formation in the present experiments failed to reveal any characteristic sign of activation during the latent period preceding the onset of cortical activation. This does not preclude the possibility that some form of functional activity not distinguished by an easily observable electrical sign occurs in this area during the latent period. In this connexion, it has been shown that cortical activation may be produced by adrenaline acting directly on structures in the region of the mesencephalic reticular formation (Bonvallet, Dell, and Hiebel, 1954; Dell, Bonvallet and Hugelin, 1955; Rothballer, 1955), and since adrenaline and noradrenaline are normally present in this area in significant quantities, it has been suggested that an adrenaline-like neurohumor may act as a transmitter substance in the mesencephalic reticular system (Vogt, 1954; Dell, Bonvallet and Hugelin, 1955; Rothballer, 1955). The gradual accumulation of such a relatively stable neurohumor may account for the long-latency, tonic reactions that we have described. In an unpublished experiment, Sharpless and Rothballer (1955) were able to produce long-latency (about 30 seconds) reactions quite reliably by presenting a weak tactile stimulus to a cat in which the lateral sensory pathways in the brain stem had been severely damaged. Since the same effect could be produced with equal reliability after bilateral adrenalectomy, it was concluded that the long-latency, tonic reactions did not depend on the participation of the adrenal glands.

The present experiments shed little light on the ultimate nature of the habituation process. The longest known after-effect of stimulation in peripheral nerve is a slight lengthening of the refractory period following prolonged repetitive stimulation (von Brucke, Early and Forbes, 1941). Such effects may be more marked in the central nervous system. We know that different neural tissue is differentially susceptible to habituation. The mesencephalic reticular system with its collateral pathways must be particularly susceptible, whereas the unspecific thalamic projection system and the pathways through which it is connected with the sensory apparatus of the thalamus seem to be less susceptible. The primary sensory tracts themselves show response decrement only if the stimulus is repeated at relatively short intervals over long periods of time. It is known from studies of animal behaviour that different reflex arcs differ in their susceptibility to habituation. Monosynaptic reflexes and some polysynaptic reflexes (e.g. the pupillary reflex) show very little habituation, and, of course, responses to painful stimuli tend to be resistant to habituation (Prosser and Hunter, 1936; Lehner, 1941).

In connexion with the differential susceptibility to habituation of different neural tissue, it is significant that Vogt (1954) found that drugs which stimulate the medial portion of the brain stem caused a depletion of the adrenaline and noradrenaline commonly found in this area. Prolonged electrical stimulation of preganglionic nerves produces no parallel fall in the sympathin content of the stimulated ganglia. She points out the possibility that the processes of resynthesis in the brain are less efficient in keeping up with utilization than in the periphery. Further evidence along this line may help us to understand the ultimate nature of the changes in neural functioning produced by experience.

SUMMARY AND CONCLUSIONS

Habituation of the arousal reaction, as indicated by a characteristic activation pattern in the electrical activity of the cortex, has been studied in cats. Repetition of a specific tone, which initially produces long-lasting arousal of a sleeping cat, fails to do so after 20 or 30 trials. A study of the effect of variations of the stimulus, and the effect of cortical and subcortical lesions upon this habituation phenomenon has led to the following conclusions.

(1) Habituation of the arousal reaction is specific to the quality, modality or pattern of a given stimulus.

(2) There are two types of arousal reaction, one of short latency and brief duration, another of longer latency and greater persistence after the end of stimulation. These have been called the phasic and tonic form of reaction respectively.

(3) The long-lasting tonic reaction was most susceptible to habituation; the rapid phasic reaction was much more resistant to habituation.

(4) The electrical "activation pattern" (low voltage rapid activity) was similar in thalamus, medial brain-stem and cortex, and disappeared from all these areas with repetition of the stimulus.

(5) Habituation of the arousal reaction does not depend on changes occurring in the specific auditory system, as judged by the persistence (and even enhancement) of cortical auditory potentials with repeated stimuli which produced complete habituation of the arousal reaction.

(6) The specificity of habituation to the frequency of the repeated sound is unaffected by complete ablation of all cortical auditory receiving areas and adjacent cortical structures. Discrimination between tonal patterns, however, may be impaired by such cortical destruction.

(7) Complete section of the brachium of the inferior colliculus bilaterally raises the arousal threshold, abolishes the rapid phasic response, increases

the speed of habituation and greatly impairs the tonal specificity of habituation.

(8) The tonic slow and persistent arousal response is probably mediated by the lower portions of the ascending reticular system which is capable of habituation selective for a given modality of sensory stimulation (auditory vs. somatic) but not for more highly differentiated qualities of the stimulus.

(9) The more rapid and more highly differentiated arousal response is probably mediated by the upper portions of the activating system, particularly the unspecific thalamic projection system and adjacent sensory structures.

ACKNOWLEDGMENTS

We should like to express our gratitude to our many colleagues in the Montreal Neurological Institute and the Department of Psychology of McGill University for their suggestions and aid. In particular we should like to thank Dr. Jerzy Olszewski for help in histological studies and operations, Dr. Peter Milner for valuable suggestions and for participation in several experiments, and Dr. David Ingvar for operative and procedural help during the early phases of the study.

REFERENCES

ADRIAN, E. D., BREMER, F., & JASPER, H. H. (1954) Brain Mechanisms and Consciousness, Oxford.

BARTLEY, S. H., & CHUTE, E. (1947) "Fatigue and Impairment in Man." New York.

BERLYNE, D. E. (1951) *Brit. J. Psychol., 42,* 269.

BONVALLET, M., DELL, P., & HIEBEL, G. (1954) *Electroenceph. Clin. Neurophysiol., 6,* 119.

CLARK, S. L., & WARD, J. W. (1945) *J. Neurophysiol., 8,* 99.

DELGADO, J. M. R. (1952) *Yale J. Biol. Med., 24,* 351.

DELL, P., BONVALLET, M., & HUGELIN, A. (1954) *Electroenceph. Clin. Neurophysiol., 6,* 599.

DIAMOND, I. T., & NEFF, W. D. (1953) *Fed. Proc., 12,* 33.

ECTORS, L. (1936) *Arch. Int. Physiol., 43,* 267.

FRENCH, J. D., VERZEANO, M., & MAGOUN, H. W. (1953) *Arch. Neuro. Psychiat., Chicago, 69,* 505.

GALAMBOS, R. (1955) *Fed. Proc., 14,* 53.

———. (1956) *J. Neurophysiol., 19,* 424.

———, SHEATZ, G., & VERNIER, V. G. (1956) *Science* (in press).

HAGBARTH, K. E., & KERR, D. I. B. (1954) *J. Neurophysiol., 17,* 295.

HARRIS, J. D. (1943) *Psychiat. Bull., 40,* 385.

HERNANDEZ-PEON, R., & SCHERRER, H. (1955) *Fed. Proc., 14,* 71.

HESS, R., JR., KOELLA, W. P., & AKERT, K. (1953) *Electroenceph. Clin. Neurophysiol., 5,* 75.

HILGARD, E. R., & MARQUIS, D. G. (1940) "Conditioning and Learning." New York.

HUMPHREY, G. (1933) "The Nature of Learning in its Relation to the Living System." New York.

JASPER, H. (1949) *Electroenceph. Clin. Neurophysiol., 1,* 405.

———, & AJMONE-MARSAN, C. (1955) "A Stereotaxic Atlas of the Diencephalon of the Cat." National Research Council, Ottawa, Canada.

JENNINGS, H. S. (1906) "Behavior of the Lower Organisms." New York.

KNOTT, J. R., & HENRY, C. E. (1941) *J. Exp. Psychol., 28,* 134.

LEHNER, G. F. J. (1941) *J. Exp. Psychol., 29,* 435.

LINDSLEY, D. B., SCHREINER, L. H., KNOWLES, W. B., & MAGOUN, H. W. (1950) *Electroenceph. Clin. Neurophysiol., 2,* 483.

MACKWORTH, N. H. (1950) *Med. Res. Council, Spec. Rep. Ser.,* No. 268, London.

MEYER, D. R., & WOOLSEY, C. N. (1952) *J. Neurophysiol., 15,* 149.

MONTGOMERY, K. C. (1953) *J. Comp. Physiol. Psychol., 46,* 129.

MORISON, R. S., & DEMPSEY, E. W. (1942) *Amer. J. Physiol., 135,* 281.

MORUZZI, G., & MAGOUN, H. W. (1949) *Electroenceph. Clin. Neurophysiol., 1,* 455.

OLDFIELD, R. C. (1937) *Brit. J. Psychol., 28,* 28.

PAVLOV, I. P. (1927) "Conditioned Reflexes." London.

PIÉRON, H. (1913) *Annêe Psychol., 19* 19.

POPOV, N. A. (1953) *Annêe Psychol., 53,* 415.

PROSSER, C. L., & HUNTER, W. S. (1936) *Amer. J. Physiol., 117,* 609.

RHEINBERGER, M. B., & JASPER, H. H. (1937) *Amer. J. Physiol., 119,* 186.

ROTHBALLER, A. B., "Studies on the Adrenalin-Sensitive Component of the Reticular Activating System." Thesis, McGill University, 1955.

SHARPLESS, S., & ROTHBALLER, A. B. (1955) *Unpublished experiments.*

SOKOLOV, E. N. (1955) Proc. XIX International Congress of Psychol., Montreal.

STARZL, T. E., TAYLOR, C. W., & MAGOUN, H. W. (1951) *J. Neurophysiol., 14,* 461.

———, ———, ———. (1951) *J. Neurophysiol., 14,* 479.

VOGT, M. (1954) *J. Physiol., 123,* 451.

VON BRÜCKE, E. TH., EARLY, M., & FORBES, A. (1941) *J. Neurophysiol., 4,* 80.

4

RIGIDITY
AS LEARNED BEHAVIOR
HAROLD M. SCHRODER AND JULIAN B. ROTTER

In the Overview we raised the matter of the development of constructs about the nature of constructs. This matter is treated under a variety of terms. Harlow (1949) neatly demonstrated his conception of "learning sets" when he arranged for his monkeys to develop highly efficient ways to develop constructions about individual discrimination problems. A series of writers (Newell, Shaw and Simon, 1958; Miller, Galanter and Pribram, 1960; Reitman, 1965), using computer model and information theory concepts, have highlighted the utility of invoking notions of personal constructs about constructs when speaking of cognitive functioning.

In the following article Schroder and Rotter raise the question of whether or not "flexibility" can be reinforced. Flexibility would be an information-processing approach which would prepare the organism to expect alternative means of construing a situation. It is worth noting Schroder and Rotter's statement of the implicit assumption that "rigidity," the effort to preserve a previously satisfactory construction of an event, is the organism's primary method of choice in cognitive functioning. This assumption is generally in agreement with our assumptions about motivation to change constructions. We are sympathetic to Schroder and Rotter's approach, whereby they seek to show that it is the tendency to shift constructs that is learned.

These researchers show that the tendency to shift solutions can be induced in a singular situation. They point out that this particular approach to cognitive structuring can be altered through experience, but their study does not make a definitive statement about whether flexibility can be established as a generalized personality factor. It is doubtful that Schroder and Rotter would have obtained their results with young children, who, following Piaget's formulations, are egocen-

Reprinted from Journal of Experimental Psychology, *1952, 44, 141–150, by permission of* Harold M. *Schroder and the American Psychological Association.*

trically bound to an epistemology of perceptual isomorphism. If a child treats his perceptions as a representation of reality, we would wonder if there would be any value in trying to train him to seek "alternative solutions." Piaget shows, for example, that it is characteristic of a child to regard his last construction as the one that he has always had; it simply is not conceived as a new alternative (Piaget, 1928, pp. 165 ff.). Further, as we have indicated in the Overview, we find no evidence of profit in pursuing rigidity or flexibility as though they were traits. There is much to be gained from continuing to investigate the situational variables that induce an individual to persist in using a particular construction of an event.

REFERENCES

HARLOW, H. F. The Formulation of Learning Sets. *Psychological Review,* 1949, *56,* 51–65.

MILLER, G. A., GALANTER, E., & PRIBRAM, K. H. *Plans and the Structure of Behavior.* New York: Holt, Rinehart and Winston, 1960.

NEWELL, A., SHAW, J. C., & SIMON, H. A. Elements of a Theory of Human Problem Solving. *Psychological Review,* 1958, *65,* 151–166.

PIAGET, J. *Judgment and Reasoning in the Child.* New York: Harcourt, Brace, and World, 1928.

REITMAN, W. R. *Cognition and Thought.* New York: Wiley, 1965.

*　　*　　*

Although psychologists have been concerned for some time with inflexible or fixated behavior, systematic study of the concept of rigidity has been relatively recent. Freud with his concept of fixation and Adler with his concept of style of life have described behavior which appears to be consistently inappropriate to a present set of cues or at least is responsive only to a very limited set of cues in a variety of situations. These clinical approaches, however, fail to clearly describe the conditions under which this behavior will occur except, perhaps, at a high level of generality.

For Lewin (4), rigidity was a central construct. It was defined as "the state of the boundaries between psychological regions." Kounin (3) has applied Lewin's rigidity construct to the feebleminded. Goldstein (1) has approached the problem from the point of view of mental set, and Luchins (5) has placed emphasis on the field conditions rather than on the individual.

In general these approaches fail to describe the specific learning or training conditions which will account for individual differences in "rigid" behavior. Nor do they provide theories broad enough to account for the similarity of behavior seen in so-called feebleminded, neurotic, brain-injured, and some normal individuals who appear to have in common a lack of flexibility, a resistance to change or shift, or a repetitiveness of the same behavior in what appear to be a variety of situations.

The present study tests some hypotheses drawn from a social-learning theory of behavior developed by Rotter (9) and his students. From this point of view we would ask the question: What sequence of learning experiences would make for greater or lesser potentiality to try out alternative solutions in a problem situation rather than a repeated use of the same behavior? Restated, we might ask under what conditions does an individual enter a problem situation with an expectancy that a single behavior will lead to reinforcement and under what conditions will he expect that there may be more than one way of reaching the goal, the best solution varying from situation to situation. We would hypothesize that the looking for alternative solutions or pathways to goals is itself a higher-level behavior which is reinforceable and may have differential strengths following varied training sequences. It might be called nonrigid behavior— its absence, rigid behavior. Interestingly enough, in this formulation it is the nonrigid behavior which is acquired, and rigidity as a specific trait or entity which is itself modifiable is nonexistent. That is, "rigidity" is a failure to learn something rather than an inherent or original trait. Although not working with the concept of rigidity as such, Harlow (2) has been particularly successful in demonstrating the existence of higher-level learning skills in monkeys which make for flexibility and adaptability.

If the hypothesis stated above were to be correct it would be necessary to develop its implications before constructing a test. In order to develop this behavior of looking for alternatives it would be necessary to provide a learning sequence in which apparently similar problems would lead to solution or reinforcement in different ways and S would be forced to adopt different solutions. The more times in the series the correct solutions (which could easily be arrived at) shifted, the more S would approach each new problem by asking which solution is right and the sooner he would perceive that his previous solution was incorrect. The S without such training would take longer to make shifts to changes in the situation but once such shifts would occur, he would then use his new solution more consistently than the S who has more reinforcement for trying out alternatives. Since the design called for a task in which generalization effects from previous experience and from one solution to another were at a minimum, it was felt necessary to develop a new task, rather than use the technique developed by Luchins (5). The method described below was designed to test these various aspects of the main hypothesis.

EXPERIMENTAL DESIGN

Materials. Sixty-six cards were constructed, 3.5 in. square and consisting of thick cardboard. Each card contained *(a)* color (blue, gold, or silver), *(b)* an outside form, and *(c)* an inside form. These figures were drawn on the cards with thick lines using black India ink and are shown in Fig. 1 and 2.

The task consisted of grouping. Each trial consisted of S grouping six cards into three pairs on the basis of color, inside form, or outside form. Generally the cards were constructed so that grouping was only possible on one of the above bases. The experimental design is shown in Table 1. The table is read in terms of the following considerations: *(a)* Each letter (e.g., x_1) refers to a trial, i.e., when S is handed six cards which have to be grouped into three pairs on the basis of form or color. *(b)* x = grouping possible on outside form only; y = grouping possible on color only; z = grouping possible on inside form only; z' = grouping possible on inside and outside form. *(c)* No single grouping is difficult once the relevant principle is selected. *(d)* From x_1 to x_7 there is a progression from grouping on outside forms which are exactly alike to grouping on outside forms not so objectively similar. That is, the difficulty increases if difficulty is defined as greater objective dissimilarity of the forms which must be grouped together. *(e)* x_5 was given last in each training sequence, so that comparisons between the groups were possible. *(f)* z_1, z_2 and z_3 contained inside form as the basis of grouping into pairs. In each instance the forms to be paired were alike. *(g)* In z_4 the inside forms were the only basis for grouping, but were not objectively similar. *(h)* From z'_8 there is a progression in that (1)

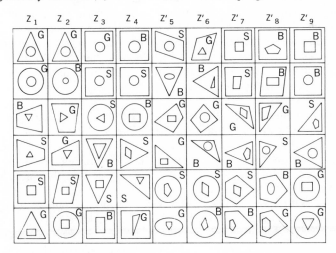

FIG. 1 *Cards Used in Training Trials*
Letters indicate the color of each card. Gold is represented by the letter G, silver by the letter S, and blue by the letter B.

$$X_1 \quad X_2 \quad X_3 \quad X_4 \quad X_5 \quad X_6 \quad X_7 \quad Y_1 \quad Y_2$$

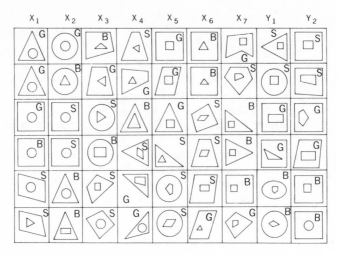

FIG. 2 *Cards Used in Testing Trials*
Letters indicate the color of each card. Gold is represented by the letter G, silver by the letter S, and blue by the letter B.

inside figures as a basis for grouping become more dissimilar, and (2) outside figures as a basis for grouping become more similar.

For Groups 1 and 2 the training sequences consist of training in grouping the cards on outside form for all trials. In Groups 3 and 4 the grouping was made on outside form and color. The experimental sequence, which is constant for each group, demands a new behavior or solution for all sequences on z_1 (inside form). This solution must be repeated four times, experimentally controlled so as to allow progressive predictions for each group. After this, S can change his basis of grouping back to outside form (x) on any trial. In this series $(z'_5-z'_8)$ grouping on inside form becomes progressively more difficult and on outside form progressively less difficult.

The four training sequences are deductions from the hypothesis, Sequence 1 being the most rigid and Sequence 4 the most nonrigid in terms of expectancy for change to occur. In Sequence 2, S learns, apart from solving a problem by outside form, which all groups learn, to solve *all* problems by outside form. According to the hypothesis he is learning to expect a reinforcement by using the same behavior. In Sequence 3, S learns to expect a reinforcement from two behaviors and to expect a reinforcement by changing his solution on two trials. In Sequence 4, S learns the same behaviors as in Sequence 3, but reinforcement occurs after a change or shift in correct solution on four trials. Therefore, expectancy for a reinforcement to occur by changing solutions should be highest in Group 4.

Sequence 1 was included for two reasons: *(a)* The longer the training in building up an expectancy for reinforcement to follow a single behavior, the lower the expectancy that a change will be reinforced. *(b)* It provides a necessary

TABLE 1 Experimental design.

Group	Training trials							Experimental trials								
	1	2	3	4	5	6	7	1	2	3	4	5	6	7	8	9
1	x_1	x_2	x_3	x_4	x_6	x_7	x_5									
2	x_1	x_2	x_3	x_4	x_5			z_1	z_3	z_3	z_4	z'_5	z'_6	z'_7	z'_8	x_9
3	x_1	y_1	y_2	x_2	x_3	x_4	x_5									
4	x_1	y_1	x_2	y_2	x_3	x_4	x_5									

control in that Sequences 3 and 4 have seven trials and it cannot be assumed that a longer training period, or sheer time in looking at the cards, has no effect on the results. Sequence 1 is expected to take an equivalent training time and Sequence 2, the lowest, having five trials.

The following quantitative measures may be made: *(a)* The time of grouping, in seconds, for each trial; *(b)* the trial in the z series $(z'_5–x'_9)$ where S changes his basis of grouping from z to x; *(c)* the number of times S changes from grouping on x to grouping on z, or vice versa, in the experimental series.

Predictions. Four specific hypotheses or predictions were made regarding differences among the four groups.

Hypothesis A. There will be a progressive decrease in time taken to group on z_1 from Groups 1 to 4. This would be expected since this would be the reverse of the order in which the groups would stop trying to solve the task by an outside form *(x)* solution and would begin looking for alternative solutions.

Hypothesis B. There will be a progressive decrease in the difference scores between time taken to solve z_1 and z_2 from Groups 1 to 4. In Groups 3 and 4 the learning of z or inside form continues to increase the expectancy of change and the behavior of looking for alternatives. In Groups 1 and 2, although such an expectancy may arise, it is still relatively weak and these Ss are likely to expect z or inside figures to be the correct solution now and to apply it immediately.

Hypothesis C. From Groups 1 to 4 the change back to grouping on x (outside form) in the z series will occur progressively earlier. In spite of the fact that Group 1 had the most x trials, Group 4 which has the highest potential for seeing alternative solutions should be the first to discover that it is possible to group on outside form in the z series.

Hypothesis D. There will be progressively more changes or alternations in z and x solutions moving from Groups 1 to 4. This hypothesis is an obvious corollary of the one above.

Subjects. The Ss consisted of 104 beginning psychology students who were randomly selected. The group contained about an equal number of males and females and they were fairly homogeneous in respect to age and intelligence. The Ss were given the instructions without E knowing in advance to which group each S was assigned. This was decided immediately before giving the test by drawing a number from a pool so constructed that 26 Ss would be assigned to each group.

Instructions. When S entered the testing room, the cards were spread out on a table, face downward. The following instructions were read to each S:

"For the next 20 min. or so, I want you to do a series of simple tasks for me. As you can see I have a number of cards here, and at the moment they are turned face downward. On each trial, and there will be a number of trials, I will hand you six cards. Each card has a number of characteristics on it.

"Your task is to group these six cards into three pairs. It may become clear to you if I give you an example. Suppose I hand you six insects and ask you to group them into pairs. Insects have a great number of characteristics, e.g., wings, legs, feelers, etc.: the cards here are much simpler. However, you may try to group them on the number of legs they have, but since they all have six legs, no differentiation is possible. You may find three large and three small insects, but this is not a grouping in pairs. Eventually you may see that two have large wings, two medium-sized wings, wings, and two have very small wings. This would be a legitimate grouping for our purposes because *(a)* all insects have wings—the characteristic chosen for grouping and *(b)* you only used one basis for grouping on that trial. For example, you would not mix the bases of grouping by putting two insects together because they had similar wings, two others because they had similar feelers, and two others together for some other reason.

"When six cards are grouped into pairs they must all have the characteristic chosen as the basis of grouping. Further, each pair must be alike in terms of this characteristic, and the three pairs must be differentiated in terms of the same characteristic.

"So the two cards you put together each time must be alike in some way. They need not be exactly alike, as long as they are near enough to be differentiated from the other pairs.

"Your task is to find the basis of grouping or the characteristic on the cards which will permit a grouping into three pairs, on each trial. You can group on *anything* you like, as long as you use a single basis which does separate them into three pairs. There is no right or wrong grouping, and no particular grouping is any better than another from my point of view. Just group them as quickly as you can each time I hand you six cards, but do not rush it. You will find the task fairly simple. Any questions?"

Few Ss asked questions. If they did, E reread and elaborated the instructions, using the insect example. Every attempt was made to insure that each S had a clear notion of what was required and to stress that it was a free situation, in that he could use whatever bases he pleased. For S the only aim was to arrive at some kind of grouping.

The S was then instructed to: *(a)* sit with his back to the cards so that E could select each set of six cards without S's knowledge and without disturbing him;

(b) to start grouping immediately when E spread the cards out face up on the table in front of him; *(c)* when finished, the cards should be in three groups of two, separated for inspection and face upward; and *(d)* as soon as this was done he should notify E. This was stressed because it was pointed out that E had no other indication and could not check the time until he was notified.

The time of grouping was taken from the time E had the cards face up on the table in front of S to the time when S notified E he was finished. Apart from the time taken for each trial, E noted the basis of grouping on each trial in the z series.

RESULTS

The important results relating to the training *(x)* series are given in Table 2. Time in the x series for Group 2, which had only five trials, was significantly less than the other groups but there are no differences approaching significance among Groups 1, 3, and 4. The reader may be struck by the disparity between Group 2 and the results obtained for all other groups over the training sequence. The differences seem larger than could be expected on the basis of two extra trials. However, Groups 3 and 4 each have two groupings on color after establishing the form solution, while Group 1 contains two extra and more difficult outside form solutions to master. The difficulty of these form solutions was purposely increased to bring Group 1 up to a similar total training time as Groups 3 and 4. If Group 1, therefore, differs from Groups 3 and 4 on any of our experimental measures it cannot be related to differences in training time.

It can be noted that there is an increasing progression in time of completing the last *(x_5)* task of the series for Groups 1 to 4. This suggests that differences in the groups due to more trying out of alternative pathways are already appearing in the last of the training series. Differences between any two groups, however, are not significant below the 10% level.

Trial by trial results for the experimental *(z)* series for all groups are shown in Table 2 and Fig. 3.

Bartlett's test for homogeneity of variance was applied to all measures relating to the four hypotheses. In all cases the assumption of homogeneity was supported. The F ratios failed to reach the accepted criterion of significance on all individual test trials with the exception of Trial 1. Table 3 presents the means and standard deviations for *(a)* the mean trial at which each group changed from Solution z (inside form) back to Solution x (outside form) and *(b)* the mean number of alternations in the method of solution for each group in the testing series.

TABLE 2 Mean time (seconds) for total training trials, X_5 and all testing trials.

Trials	Group 1		Group 2		Group 3		Group 4	
	Mean	SD	Mean	SD	Mean	SD	Mean	SD
Training								
All	211.3	85.2	69.0	27.1	196.2	62.0	209.8	106.0
x_5	16.7	14.6	16.3	12.0	21.2	11.0	23.5	17.8
Testing								
z_1	24.00	11.80	19.77	10.42	15.42	8.77	11.59	4.42
z_2	12.19	6.50	12.50	4.11	13.19	6.12	14.88	7.74
z_3	12.80	8.08	13.80	9.14	13.54	8.60	16.14	6.72
z_4	17.80	14.00	14.15	4.14	26.53	23.60	20.73	15.76
z'_5	16.46	15.30	25.80	30.80	34.30	40.60	19.07	16.16
z'_6	14.04	8.40	13.96	7.21	15.50	6.80	14.19	7.30
z'_7	11.00	4.40	13.46	7.56	17.46	8.43	13.80	4.12
z'_8	12.85	7.80	15.46	10.04	17.69	10.70	16.53	9.24
x_9	13.81	6.10	18.34	14.50	14.76	7.18	16.34	10.40

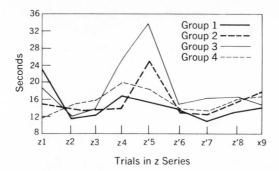

FIG. 3 *Mean times of grouping on each trial in testing series for all age groups.*

TABLE 3 **Mean trial on which each group changed from z to x solutions and the number of alternations in solution.**

Group	Change from z to x		Number of changes	
	Mean	SD	Mean	SD
1	7.423	1.590	.6153	.4800
2	7.230	1.440	.8070	.5500
3	6.5000	1.360	1.0000	.4800
4	6.030	1.220	1.5760	.6200

Hypothesis A. An over-all analysis of variance for the four groups and time in solving the first experimental task (z_1) resulted in an F of 7.66, significant at the 1% level. Individual probability levels are given in Table 4. It can be seen most clearly in Fig. 3, however, that a clear progression exists from Group 1 to Group 4 in the predicted direction.

TABLE 4 p **levels between groups for trial z_1.**

Groups	2	3	4
1	.15	.01	.01
2		.11	.01
3			.06

Hypothesis B. An analysis of variance of the differences between time for z_1 and z_2 was made to test Hypothesis B. Again the analysis showed significant differences between groups. An F ratio of 11.75 was obtained, significant at the 1% level. Probability levels between groups are indicated in Table 5.

TABLE 5 p levels for differences between time of grouping z_1 and z_2.

Groups	2	3	4
1	.01	.01	.01
2		.05	.01
3			.02

Inspection of Fig. 3 reveals a progression from Group 1 to Group 4 in the predicted direction. While the first two groups reduced their solution time considerably, Group 3 reduced only slightly and Group 4 took longer on z_2 than z_1. This tendency, particularly in relation to Group 4, is hard to account for on the basis of any hypothesis other than that the successful solution of z_1 strengthened or reinforced a behavior of looking for new or different solutions to the point that it seriously competed with a tendency to resolve z_2 with the same kind of behavior as z_1.

Hypothesis C. To test Hypothesis C the mean trial in which the groups switched back to their first x solution in the ambiguous trials z'_5 to z'_8 was calculated (Table 3). On these trials solution either by an x hypothesis (outside form) or a z hypothesis (inside from) is possible but is progressively more difficult for z (inside from). Analysis of variance results in an F ratio of 5.07, significant at the 1% level. Differences between groups are given in Table 6, while Fig. 4 shows a clear progression from Groups 1 to 4 in the predicted direction.

TABLE 6 p levels between groups for change from Z to x solutions.

Groups	2	3	4
1	.65	.05	.01
2		.05	.01
3			.22

Hypothesis D. Hypothesis D was tested by comparing the mean number of times that the groups changed solutions (or switched back and forth between inside form and outside form) in the ambiguous trials z'_5 through z'_8. Analysis of variance yielded an F ratio of 14.66, significant at the 1% level. The progression along predicted lines for Groups 1 to 4 is shown in Fig. 5. Probability levels between groups are given in Table 7.

TABLE 7 *p* levels for number of alternations in solution.

Groups	2	3	4
1	.20	.01	.01
2		.20	.01
3			.01

FIG. 4

Mean trial at which each group changed back to grouping on x (outside form).

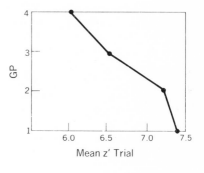

FIG. 5

Mean number of alternations in solution for each group in testing series.

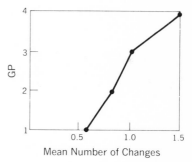

DISCUSSION

All four specific hypotheses appear to be unequivocally supported by the results. In all the tests made, Groups 1, 2, 3, and 4 followed the same progressive order—Group 1 behaving in the most "rigid" manner and Group 4 in the least rigid manner.

Rigid behavior as here described is characterized as the approaching of a given situation with restricted attention to a given set of cues and an expectancy that there is a single pathway to reinforcement or solution that does not change. Such behavior makes for speed of performance and efficiency once the solution is learned, if the solution does not change. Nonrigid behavior, on the other hand, is characterized as the learning to attend to many cues and to expect that more than one pathway to reinforcement is present in a situation, or that the best or correct solution may be expected to be different or change in repeated trials. Such behavior makes for speed in grasping new principles or new solutions, for more alternation of behavior when more than one solution is possible, and for slightly less efficient performance when the situation remains the same and S presumably attends to cues not necessary for solution.

Conditions in this experiment leading to rigid behavior consist of repetition of the same or similar situations with reinforcement always following the same type of solution (outside form): The more trials the greater the rigidity. Nonrigid behavior was learned by introducing trials where an alternative solution was possible and sufficiently easy that it could be readily grasped when S discovered that the previously correct method would not work. The more times S is forced to adopt another solution the greater is the potential that he will expect and look for change in the situation.

By including Groups 2 and 3 as controls it was possible to demonstrate that the differences between Groups 1 and 4 are not merely a function of the number of trials in which outside form is the correct solution since Groups 3 and 4 were consistently less rigid than Group 2 as well as less rigid than 1. The inclusion of Group 3 made it possible to demonstrate that the results cannot be accounted for merely on the basis of the number of times color was the correct basis for grouping or on the basis of any positive transfer or generalization from color to inside form as a means of solution, since Group 4 with the same number of color solutions but more shifts or changes in the situation than Group 3 was consistently less rigid on all measures.

Reed (7) has obtained somewhat similar results in a study using the white rat. He found that longer training times on an initial problem resulted in slower subsequent learning when the correct solution was reversed. His results are comparable to those obtained with Group 1 which was slow on the first z solution but then improved with great rapidity.

These results are also consistent with the findings of Harlow (2) and his evidence of higher-level skills in the discrimination learning behavior of monkeys.

It seems to the authors that any explanation of the results in terms of more specific habits or skills cannot be logically maintained. Although it might be possible to explain the results of the first test of speed of grouping on the first z trial on the basis of differential strengths of an x solution habit and negative transfer, such an explanation would be unable to account for the fact that the groups which solved z_1 most quickly were also the ones which first returned to an x solution.

In devising this study no predictions were made regarding differences among the groups at Trial z_5, the first trial which was solvable by either z or x solutions. The differences which were obtained there were somewhat of a surprise although it should be pointed out that the two largest differences are only at the 5% and 8% level of significance and an over-all analysis yields an F of only 2.047, significant between the 8% and 10% levels of confidence. The marked slowness of Group 3 is difficult to interpret. Perhaps this group was able to recognize that more than one solution was possible and was disturbed by the conflict of deciding which was correct. This would affect Groups 1 and 2 less since they were less likely to perceive more than one solution as possible, and to disturb Group 4 less since it was more prepared for any kind of change in the situation. Such explanations, however, are obviously *post hoc*.

Although the training series in this experiment differs from the traditional partial reinforcement design, certain similarities exist. For example, Group 1 takes longer to change its solution on Trial z_1, but quickly thereafter accepts a new solution, as indicated by the results on Trial z_2. This suggests that the same phenomena may be involved as in the rapid extinction following 100% reinforcement. In a similar fashion there are analogies between Groups 3 and 4 and the results from less than 100% reinforcement. The evidence for partial reinforcement in terms of the slower extinction in the partially reinforced Groups 3 and 4 is also demonstrated by the fact that these groups return more easily to the original x solution.

It would seem that the occurrence of a reward following a nonreward for a particular solution not only strengthens or weakens a particular habit, but also increases the expectancy that rewards follow nonrewards. From the point of view taken in this paper, the two situations are similar in that in each, another expectancy is being learned other than the one that leads directly to the reinforcement.

Application to personality study. The description of the behavior of our rigid group fits fairly well the description of rigid behavior in feebleminded subjects given by Kounin (3) as well as other workers. However, we cannot at this time generalize from these findings to clinical groups or to the behavior of maladjusted individuals. We do not know to what extent such behavior is specific to given situations or whether or not the behavior of individuals operating in much more complex social situations can likewise be predicted using the same principles as were used in making predictions for our experimental groups. Nevertheless such principles appear to provide a basis for explaining a similarity of behavior in widely disparate groups such as those considered maladjusted, feebleminded, brain-injured, and institutionalized. In addition these principles have the advantage of going beyond immediate description and defining the conditions which allow for prediction and perhaps therapy. Somewhat oversimplified examples of the application of such principles are given below.

In the case of the feebleminded S he is both limited in learning alternative solutions and has frequent experiences of failure which lead him to seize upon any positively reinforced or correct solution and maintain it. The single solution is maintained in spite of its failure in changing situations because of his low expectancy for positive reinforcement from any other pathway. The brain-injured, likewise, operate under physical handicaps which limit the kinds of solutions they can learn and have frequent experiences of failure and inadequacy. In the case of the so-called neurotic or maladjusted individual whose rigidity consists mainly of maintaining some defense or avoidance behavior in the absence of any "real threat," the avoidance behavior itself may be regarded as a single solution which is regularly reinforced by preventing the reoccurrence of some trauma, thus providing the conditions making for single-solution learning. Individuals who spend much time in institutions where there are relatively inflexible rules, precedents, schedules, etc., to determine behavior are in a situation that may be characterized as single-pathway learning.

Some mention should be made here of an obvious application to the problems of therapy. In the case of persistent maladjustment it would seem important that S does not merely learn another single solution as better but that he learn and have reinforced a behavior of looking for or seeking alternative solutions. Morton (6) in using a very brief therapy technique demonstrated the effectiveness of such techniques in one of the rare psychotherapy studies in which matched controls were used.

For the time being, however, such speculations regarding application of these results must be considered as hypotheses for further experimental investigation.

SUMMARY

Adopting a social-learning framework developed by Rotter and his students, the problem of rigidity was approached in this study not as a trait or entity but as a kind of behavior predictable from specific learning experiences. Briefly, it was hypothesized that nonrigidity or flexibility was a kind of higher-level behavior which consists of expecting change and looking for alternative pathways. Rigid behavior is typified by the absence of such learning, or by the expectancy of a single correct solution which remains the same. Four groups, each of 26 Ss, were tested using a problem-sorting task. The procedure for each group was varied to control all relevant conditions other than differences in training for an expectancy of change and alternative solution. Four different tests of the major hypotheses were supported at significant levels. The groups showed consistent progressive differences in predicted directions. Some possible applications of these results to other similar experimental and social-learning situations were considered.

REFERENCES

1. GOLDSTEIN, K. Concerning Rigidity. *Character & Pers.,* 1943, *11,* 209–226.
2. HARLOW, H. F. The Formation of Learning Sets. *Psychol. Rev.,* 1949, *56,* 51–65.
3. KOUNIN, J. J. Experimental Studies of Rigidity: I. The Measurement of Rigidity in Normal and Feebleminded Persons. II. The Explanatory Power of the Concept of Rigidity as Applied to Feeblemindedness. *Character & Pers.,* 1941, *9,* 251–282.

4. LEWIN, K. *A Dynamic Theory of Personality.* New York: McGraw-Hill, 1933.
5. LUCHINS, A. S. Rigidity and Ethnocentrism: A Critique. *J. Pers.,* 1949, *17,* 449–466.
6. MORTON, R. B. A Controlled Experiment in Psychotherapy Based on Rotter's Social Learning Theory of Personality. Unpublished Ph.D. dissertation, Ohio State University, 1949.
7. REED, S. Development of Non-Continuity Learning from Continuity Learning in the Albino Rat. Unpublished Ph.D. dissertation, Ohio State University, 1949.
8. ROKEACH, M. Generalized Mental Rigidity as a Factor in Ethnocentrism. *J. Abnorm. Soc. Psychol.,* 1948, *43,* 259–278.
9. ROTTER, J. B. Tentative Formulation of Basic Principles for a Social Learning Theory of Personality. Mimeo., Ohio State University, 1948.
10. ROTTER, J. B. Tentative Formulation of Some Social Learning Constructs. Mimeo. 1–7, Ohio State University, Jan. 1950–June, 1951.

X
COGNITIVE ORGANIZATION
AND
SOCIAL INTERACTION

1

OVERVIEW

During the past half-century, as personality theorists wandered in the mazes of trait definitions and medical diagnosis, many social psychologists tried defining the cognitive functioning of the individual (Sherif and Cantril, 1947; Krech and Crutchfield, 1948; Festinger, 1957). A fascinating task awaits the historian of psychology who attempts to explain this state of affairs. Why did the personality theorists focus on "dynamic" matters that centered around the conflicts between basic needs and social restrictions on need gratification, while many social psychologists found it more attractive to formulate principles of behavior revolving around cognitive organization and social influence on cognitive structure. Though we cannot yet advance a definitive hypothesis, we suggest that the social psychologists were influenced by the great sociologists who stressed the central importance of society as a definer of reality. When Durkheim (1951), Thomas and Znaniecki (1918), and Mead (1934) focused on this issue they forced a theoretical line that centered on the individual's interpretation of the world, rather than on his helpless struggle with his urges and drives.

In the terminology of this text, society provides individuals with construct systems. In his efforts to define a predictably useful frame of reference, a person can be well served by the constructions that society can offer him. In the course of his life, a person makes constant use of the social group as a definer of reality. Despite the general acceptance of the point that the society does define reality for the individual, one does not find general agreement on the means by which a person develops the propensity to accept the reality of society.

In casting about for explanations of the development of social imitation one is certain to come across the simple theory that humans are innately gregarious. They copy because they are destined to become like other humans. Another line of thought, which is best exemplified by the writing of Homons (1961), states that people adopt the views of the group because the group is in the position to dispense status. Status is a secondary reinforcer, deriving its basic reinforcing properties from previous association with primary need reduction. A strict Freudian psychoanalytic explanation of the person's copying behavior sees the roots of that behavior in the Oedipus triangle. A child begins to "identify" with its like-sexed parent in order to develop the behavior that will allow it to become attractive to the opposite-sexed parent. Sherif and Sherif (1964) describe an individual's acceptance of group norms and values in terms of the security attained through using the group to anchor one's self-definitions. If the concept of reinforcement were to be introduced into Sherif and Sherif's position, one could say that the reference group provides reinforcement through its constant affirmation of the validity of the predictions that are made through using the constructs that the group provides.

It is Sherif and Sherif's formulation that comes closest to the position that would best fit society into the cognitive theory of personality being developed in this text. Since society surrounds the person, directing him to apply the concepts that have been worked out by his forebears and peers, and then arranging circumstances that demonstrate the predictive value of these constructs, the person will find that he can best avoid an inability to predict by adopting the concepts that are used by others around him. And furthermore, he finds that he is most comfortable when he is surrounded by others who use his constructions; for if others would apply constructions that vary from his, they will, in essence, disconfirm the validity of his own "reality." And if this process is not enough to establish the "tyranny of the majority," we find some societies that promote the construction that the society's constructions reflect the most insightful wisdom that can be created. In its excesses, these societies might develop a massive army of professional psychiatrists, psychologists, and guidance counselors to ferret out and to clearly label those who develop deviate conceptions. By exercising constant threats to disconfirm the perceptions of its member, and to thereby put him in a state of high arousal, a society can capitalize on each individual's effort to avoid cognitive strain and can work toward the Utopian conflict-free world of 1984.

Several of our other propositions, however, allow us to predict that the Utopian 1984 is not to be easily grasped. We will turn to Piaget for explication of another effect of the social world. In discussing the dichotomous nature of constructs, we suggested the possibility that the learning of an organism *must* take place in a way that establishes a bipolar construct; that the organism does not learn something unless it can learn it through contrasting one probability with another. This point is most applicable as we talk about society providing the individual with confirmation of his constructs. The person cannot develop the positive value of conceptual confirmation without simultaneously learning the negative value of nonconfirmation. One of Piaget's many great contributions to psychological theory is his clarification of how the child yields his egocentric behavior as a result of receiving societal disconfirmation of schema. In his discussion of the progress of the child's development in making moral judgments (Piaget, 1965), for example, he points out that as the child becomes aware of his disagreement with the concepts of his peers, he is forced to recognize that there is not a synonymity between his personal schema and reality. His implicit belief that his schema are a duplication of the reality of the external world, a world-view which Piaget labels with the term *egocentrism,* is most effectively destroyed by his exposure to communications that inform him that others do not employ the same schema as he does. If others do not perceive the world in the same terms as he does—that is, if each person's constructs are personal affairs—then it becomes imperative to establish a construction of events that will allow a mutual interchange. In this way the social interaction, which first forced the yielding of egocentrism, is now altered to facilitate taking the other person's perceptions into account. This transaction, Piaget maintains, has far-reaching effect on the child's language behavior (1926) and on his views of the nature of social regulation (1965). A study of the form of a child's language shows that he at first sees no need to ascertain that his speech is creating a particular desired perception in the listener. Later he speaks in a way that shows that he learns that not everyone views the world as he does. In his social interaction he comes to recognize that rules are a social necessity, but that they can be altered and revised to meet the changes in the perceptions that are evoked during the social interchange. His development has led him to the point where he perceives that the world of rules can no longer be arranged heteronomously by the powerful adult authority.

As the child approaches adolescence, he ordinarily develops a level of cognitive functioning in which his perceptions can be "operated" on as though they have been "loosened" from the immediate concrete world. Now he can be liberated from the "tyranny of the majority," for he begins to recognize that a wide variety of constructions can be placed on the same event. And, in addition to his own inexorable psychological evolution, there is a part of current society that will happily provide confirmation of the position that the broad society does not have control of the market of truth. The existential philosophers and the phenomenologically oriented cognitive psychologists provide a reference group for the adolescent rebel who would challenge the established authorities to demonstrate that their own reality has the greater validity. If the adult world is currently reluctant to recognize that social reality and the cognizable universe are not necessarily synonymous, there are sizable bands of youth who will willingly instruct them in this interpretation of man's relationship to reality. Meanwhile, psychology needs to accelerate the development of concepts that will explain the interaction among society, reality, and the individual who is working to devise his personal constructions of the world around him.

Another facet of the interaction between two or more people holding their own personal constructs is that of the "attractiveness" of these interacting persons toward each other. In the common sense we are aware that people who are "like" one another happen to "like" one another. In explicating and developing his intriguing view of "naive" psychological theory, Heider (1958) proposed the theory of "psychological balance." In a situation involving two people and a third person, or event, there is balance if persons *A* and *B* construe person or event *C* in a similar manner. In Heider's terms, if *A* and *B* both like, or both dislike, *C,* there is balance in the system. On the other hand, if *A* likes *C* and *B* dislikes *C,* while *A* and *B* like each other, there is imbalance in the system. Balance may be restored by a variety of techniques. *A,* or *B,* could decide that he no longer likes the other person. *A,* or *B,* could decide that the other person is correct in his evaluation of *C.* Or, *A* or *B* may avoid recognizing the other person's judgment.

Another way of stating the points made by Heider is that two people who hold the same construct system, as they interact with each other, will probably not create arousal in the other person by disagreeing with him. As one of these two similar people reacts to a third event, the other stands by, in that he holds the same constructions of the event, to confirm the initial actor's construct system. A minimum of arousal is created by this interaction, and the two people will like each other. Newcomb's article (1956), reproduced in this section, shows the utility of this kind of conception in explaining the nature of personal attraction.

Two dissimilar people can, however, interact without excessive personal arousal. If one or more of the participants in the interaction is able to construe the construction system of the other person, the situation can be manipulated so that excess arousal is avoided. Good teaching can be viewed within this framework. A successful teacher is one who understands the construct system of his student in a way that allows him to present stimuli that produce an optimum level of arousal. It is during this optimal state of arousal that the most effective construct change can take place. Ausabel's (1960) study of the effectiveness of the use of "advance organizers" demonstrates this point. If, by building them in before other material is presented, a teacher ascertains that a student will have available the advance organizers—that is, the basic constructs that will facilitate the integration of the material—then the student will show greater gain from his study of the data. Good leadership is also a reflection of the leader's ability to construe the construction system of his follower. By knowing where his follower is, conceptually, he can appeal to the follower by grading communications so that the follower is successively led to the conclusion that the leader seeks. Demagoguery reflects the epitome of this skill, for its use implies that the leader is aware that he is manipulating social reality; and, though he does not personally accept his follower's constructs, he allows the presumption that he believes as does his follower in order to achieve personal gain. Perhaps the modern advertiser is the best example of the use of great skill in manipulation of socially shared constructs.

The studies in this section are explorations of the interactions of social and personal constructs. The material that is available to clarify this interaction is already vast. The papers included here are only a sample of what is available; they are intended to illustrate that (1) there are shared construct systems, and (2) sharing construct systems produces comfort in individuals who interact socially.

REFERENCES

AUSABEL, D. P. The Use of Advance Organizers in the Learning and Retention of Meaningful Verbal Material. *Journal of Educational Psychology,* 1960, *51,* 267–272.

DURKHEIM, E. *Suicide.* New York: Free Press, 1951.

FESTINGER, L. *A Theory of Cognitive Dissonance.* Stanford, Calif.: Stanford University Press, 1957.

HEIDER, F. *The Psychology of Interpersonal Relations.* New York: Wiley, 1958.

HOMONS, G. C. *Social Behavior: Its Elementary Forms.* New York: Harcourt, Brace, and World, 1961.

KRECH, D. & CRUTCHFIELD, R. S. *Theory and Problems of Social Psychology.* New York: McGraw Hill, 1948.

MEAD, G. H. *Mind, Self, and Society.* Chicago: Chicago University Press, 1934.

NEWCOMB, T. M. The Prediction of Interpersonal Attraction. *American Psychologist,* 1956, *11,* 575–586.

PIAGET, J. *The Language and Thought of the Child.* New York: Harcourt, Brace, and World, 1926.

PIAGET, J. *The Moral Judgment of the Child.* New York: Free Press, 1965.

SHERIF, M. & CANTRIL, H. *The Psychology of Ego-Involvements.* New York: Wiley, 1947.

SHERIF, M. & SHERIF, C. W. *Reference Groups.* New York: Harper and Row, 1964.

THOMAS, W. I. & ZNANIECKI, F. *The Polish Peasant in Europe and America.* Boston: Badger, 1918.

2

LATITUDE OF ACCEPTANCE
AND ATTITUDE CHANGE:
EMPIRICAL EVIDENCE
FOR A REFORMULATION[1]
ALVIN L. ATKINS, KAY K. DEAUX, AND JAMES BIERI

A large number of studies are now available to demonstrate, in fascinating variety, the principle that individuals will accept consensual validation as a means of confirming the reality of a particular construction of an event. If, however, this lone principle were be be the determinant of the instantiation of events, an individual would be constantly altering his constructions to match those used by the numerous divergent persons who construe the same events as he does. We must assume, in social situations, that there is a continued functioning of the principle that an individual will construe events so that he can better define and extend his existing system. Thus, the nature of an individual's existing system must be taken into account if one seeks to predict the effects of social influence.

Atkins and his associates discuss the effects of social validation on college students who impose differing constructions on a salient event: fraternity life. They relate their study to the investigations of M. Sherif and C. Hovland, and their coworkers. In summary, this study shows that a communication from an authoritative source will have a greater effect on a person's construction of an event, if that communication is within the person's existing "latitude of acceptance." Relating this finding to our general motivational principle, if a communication diverges from one's construction system to a point that creates a high arousal level, that communication will have little effect on the person's existing construct system. The communication will have greater effect—that is, will produce learning—when it creates optimum arousal. Social influ-

Reprinted from Journal of Personality and Social Psychology, *1967, 6, 47–54, by permission of Alvin L. Atkins and the American Psychological Association.*

[1]This research was supported under Grant GS-842 from the National Science Foundation.

ence, then, is effective under the same motivational conditions that produce alterations of constructs in any other situation. One cannot assume that a person whose view is invalidated by another individual with whom he is interacting will be primarily motivated to adapt his position to that of the disconfirming individual.

*   *   *

With the study of attitude-change processes becoming a major concern in social psychological research, there has been growing recognition of the importance of developing improved techniques for the assessment of attitudes. The concept of latitude of acceptance and latitude of rejection, a device for establishing an individual's stand toward a social issue, was conceived as a technique which permitted dimensional analysis of responses to various positions toward a social object (Sherif and Hovland, 1961; Sherif, Sherif, and Nebergall, 1965). The need for such an approach stemmed from the realization that to consider a single scalar position as indicating the attitude of an individual does not adequately reflect the multifaceted nature of his reactions to the social issue in question.

Analysis of the individual's latitude of acceptance provides an opportunity to examine both the range of statements which comprise his attitude as well as the susceptibility to attitude change implied by such a range of acceptable statements. Latitude of acceptance has value, then, not only as a technique for assessment of own attitude, but also as a predictive tool in attitude change. Although not attempting a direct empirical test of degree of attitude change in relation to size of latitude of acceptance and rejection, Hovland, Harvey, and Sherif (1957) proposed that attitude change will occur only under the condition in which the communication advocating change falls *within* one's latitude of acceptance. In operationalizing the concepts of latitude of acceptance and rejection, they asked their subjects to indicate the positions on an issue that were *most* acceptable and *most* objectionable as well as those other positions that were also acceptable or objectionable. As a result, they were able to investigate item placement in relation to one's own position. It was found that, in comparison to moderate subjects, extreme subjects accepted fewer statements and rejected more statements. Hovland et al. observed that subjects with extreme positions had raised thresholds of acceptance and lowered thresholds of rejection in placing items, which resulted in their having smaller latitudes of acceptance and greater latitudes of rejection than subjects with moderate positions. Since more subjects with moderate positions changed in the direction of the position advocated in the communication, it was inferred that wide latitudes of acceptance facilitated attitude change.

An alternative approach to the prediction of attitude change derives from Festinger's (1957) dissonance theory. Using this theoretical framework, Zimbardo (1960) reasoned that opinion conformity will be greatest when a communication is widely discrepant from one's own position, presumably creating maximum dissonance. Under these conditions, change should be greatest when a communication falls within one's latitude of rejection. In his experimental design, Zimbardo provided subjects with a friend's rating of a case study which was either slightly discrepant or widely discrepant for each subject. In the latitude of acceptance condition, the statement selected as the friend's "most acceptable" statement was one scale position removed from the subject's own most acceptable rating, while the latitude of rejection condition was three scale units removed. Consistent with his predictions, Zimbardo found that significantly more change was produced by widely discrepant communications falling within subjects' latitudes of rejection than by slightly discrepant communications falling within subjects' latitudes of acceptance.

Considering that the predictions of Hovland et al. and of Zimbardo derive logically from their respective theoretical assumptions, these conflicting results are difficult to reconcile. Despite the findings reported by Zimbardo, the expectation that attitude change should be greater when the communication falls within one's latitude of acceptance is a reasonable one which requires further empirical investigation. However, if the concept of latitude of acceptance and rejection is to have predictive utility in attitude change, we must specify a number of additional considerations.

1. In proposing a measure of latitude of acceptance, Hovland et al. (1957) actually used a frequency criterion. That is, the *number* of statements a subject considered acceptable defined his latitude of acceptance. Since a subject who held an extreme position tended to accept fewer statements and reject more statements than a subject with a more moderate position, Hovland et al. proceeded to formulate a theoretical model of latitude of acceptance which made the size of the latitude of acceptance a function of the scale position of the subject's stand on the issue. For example, an individual at the most extreme position was expected to accept the item adjacent to his own position, to be neutral toward the next statement, and to reject all those statements beyond that point. This procedure, based solely on scale position, gives no recognition to individual differences among those subjects falling at the same scale point. Rather, it assumes that a particular position necessitates a particular range of acceptance.

2. Assuming that two individuals do, in fact, endorse the same number of items, can we infer that these items actually represent equivalent scalar distances for these individuals? We need to specify not only the number of items endorsed, but also the position on the scale where each subject placed these items.

3. Both Hovland et al. (1957) as well as Zimbardo (1960) provided subjects with communications at predetermined distances from their own positions. Such a procedure fails to take into account differences among the subjects in the way in which this communication is evaluated and judged. If we are to make predictions based upon latitudes of acceptance, it is important that we allow each subject not only to specify his own range of acceptable statements, but also to indicate where this communication falls on the same scale. If the communication is differentially perceived, then we are justified in assuming that it will be associated with differential effects in the stability or change of attitudes.

In the present study we have reconceptualized latitude of acceptance by defining it in terms of a *range* criterion consisting of the scalar distance covered by the items indicated as acceptable by each subject. Furthermore, we have analyzed the validity of such an approach for predicting attitude change.

Two basic hypotheses were advanced:

Hypothesis 1: Regardless of the actual scalar position represented by the communication, attitude change in the direction of a persuasive communication will occur when the communication is perceived to lie *within* one's latitude of acceptance.

Hypothesis 2: Drawing upon the investigations of own position as an anchor (Bieri, Atkins, Briar, Leaman, Miller, and Tripodi, 1966; Sherif and Hovland, 1961), it was hypothesized that the evaluation of a persuasive communication will be subject to judgmental distortion. In order to facilitate the acceptance of a position at some distance from one's own, it is to be expected that the communication will be judged as "really not too far from one's own," making a shift in own position a plausible outcome. Such judgmental distortion is to be found in the phenomenon of assimilation. Thus, it was hypothesized that attitude change would be associated with tendencies toward assimilative distortion of the persuasive communication.

METHOD

Subjects. As part of a larger study, male college undergraduates were given a student activities questionnaire designed to yield information on students' attitudes toward extracurricular activities. Students rated statements on a number of topics, including the degree to which they felt that fraternities were desirable on the college campus. A 15-point graphic rating scale was used in which 1 indicated very undesirable, and 15 indicated very desirable. From the responses obtained in this questionnaire, 54 subjects, divided approximately equally among pro, neutral, and anti own-attitude positions, were selected at random to participate in this study. The mean scale position for these three groups were 13.67 (pro), 8.18 (neutral) and 2.42 (anti).

Procedure. Latitude of acceptance. Thirty-three statements, compiled originally by Segall (1959) to cover the range from extremely profraternity items to extremely antifraternity items, comprised the item pool. Initially, each subject was asked to judge each statement on a 15-point graphic scale in terms of the degree of favorableness of the attitude represented in each statement. Each subject was permitted to use any number of scale positions he wished, with any frequency.

At a second session, in conjunction with other tasks, each subject was given the same series of statements and asked to do the following: *(a)* indicate the one statement closest to his own point of view on the topic, *(b)* indicate any other acceptable statement or statements, *(c)* indicate the one most objectionable statement, and *(d)* indicate any other objectionable statement or statements.

Persuasive communication. Following this, a communication advocating one of three possible positions (moderately pro, moderately anti, and extremely anti) was presented to each subject. Within each group of pro and anti subjects, approximately half received a moderately pro communication, while the other half received a moderately anti communication. Among the neutral subjects, approximately half received a moderately anti communication while the other half received an extremely anti communication. A moderately pro communication is presented below as a sample:

A statement made recently by the Committee
on Undergraduate Affairs
at a Major Eastern University

In evaluating the role of fraternities on a college campus, it is obvious that a number of factors must be taken into account. Certainly some students can function quite independently of organized groups and do not require the reassurance that others receive from feeling that they have been accepted by their peers. For those who have developed enough of a sense of security and an ability to make friends easily, fraternities may not add very much. However, statistics indicate that most undergraduates actually do depend upon the guidance and advice of others, both in intellectual and social matters. In this regard, fraternities can provide a cushion against the new environment, especially for boys coming to the impersonal campus of a large university. While many opportunities exist for the newcomer to adjust to a college setting, the fraternity system offers a quick means of gaining the fellowship of other undergraduates who are facing similar probjems at the same crucial period in their lives.

In order to determine the approximate scale position of each of these communications, a group of 20 judges drawn from the same student population, but with neutral positions toward fraternities, served as a control group for providing mean judged scale positions. The mean values for the communications were 11.3 (moderately pro), 5.0 (moderately anti), and 1.9 (extremely anti).

After reading his communication, each subject was asked to consider the position advocated in the communication and to indicate which scale position on the 15-point rating scale he had previously used best represented the stand taken in the communication. Following this, each subject again indicated how desirable he felt it was to have fraternities on the college campus, in a manner identical to that used to assess his position initially.

RESULTS

The results will be presented under two major headings—the reformulation of the latitude of acceptance, and the application of this approach to the prediction of attitude change.

TABLE 1 Mean number of statements accepted, rejected, and neutral.

S's own position	N	No. accepted[a]	No. rejected[a]	No. neutral[a]
Pro	18	7.61	9.39	16.00
Neutral	17	6.53	10.18	16.29
Anti	19	6.21	9.42	17.37

[a]None of the comparisons between own-position groups for number of statements accepted, rejected, or neutral was significant.

Reformulation of latitude of acceptance. Before considering a range criterion for the analysis of latitude of acceptance, the data were examined in terms of a frequency criterion, that is, by the number of statements accepted and rejected, as well as those presumably neutral items not checked which Sherif et al. (1965) characterize as the latitude of noncommitment. In contrast to the results reported by Hovland et al. (1957), who found that extreme subjects rejected significantly more items than did more moderate subjects, the differences found in this study are in the opposite direction, although not statistically significant. In Table 1 it can also be observed that there is no tendency for neutral subjects to accept more items than do extreme subjects, as is suggested by the Sherif-Hovland model.

In applying a range criterion, the following approach was used. If a subject accepted two statements, we considered where he placed these statements on the 15-point scale provided. If he had judged one of these statements to be represented by Point 7 and the other by Point 10, then his latitude of acceptance was the range of scalar distance between these two points, that is, 3 units. If a subject accepted three statements, one represented by Point 6, another by Point 7, and the third by Point 8, then his latitude of acceptance consisted of 2 scale units and was smaller than the former. In this manner we determined individually for each subject a latitude of acceptance based on the statements which he found acceptable and the range of the scale covered by these statements.

TABLE 2   **Mean range of statements accepted in relation to own position.**

Own position	N	Mean range[a]	SD
Pro	18	5.83	2.69
Neutral	17	5.71	3.83
Anti	19	6.00	2.81

[a]Differences between groups are not significant.

That it is necessary to consider the latitude of acceptance for each subject individually can be seen in Table 2, where the mean range of statements accepted for all subjects grouped according to their own-attitude positions is reported. As can be observed, these means do not differ significantly from each other. Thus, it appears that although subjects do vary considerably in the range of statements they are willing to accept, this variation reflects individual differences which are not consistently related to own-attitude positions.

Application of latitude of acceptance to prediction of attitude change: Hypotheses 1. The initial hypothesis proposed that regardless of the actual distance between the communication and one's own position, those subjects who perceive the communication as lying within their latitude of acceptable statements will be more susceptible to its influence. By considering each subject's judgment of the scale position represented by the persuasive communication, it was possible to determine if the subject perceived this communication as lying within the range of statements which he endorsed. Table 3 presents the results obtained when the mean change in own position for the group of subjects for whom the communication fell *inside* their latitude of acceptance is compared with the group for whom the communication fell *outside* their latitude of acceptance. For those subjects who judged the persuasive communication as falling inside their latitude of acceptance, the average change was 2.74 units in the direction of the communication, while the average change was .25 unit in the opposite direction for the comparison group. This difference is significant at the .01 level.

TABLE 3 **Mean change of own attitude in relation to judgment of communication.**

	Pro	Neutral	Anti	Overall (pro, neutral, & anti combined)
Communication judged inside latitude of acceptance ($N = 27$)				
Mean change[a]	+ .89	+4.33	+3.33	+2.74
SD	2.57	2.16	2.96	2.93
	($N = 9$)	($N = 6$)	($N = 12$)	
Communication judged outside latitude of acceptance ($N = 27$)				
Mean change	.00	−1.82	+1.86	−0.25
SD	.87	1.78	1.57	2.07
	($N = 9$)	($N = 11$)	($N = 7$)	

Note.—Overall mean change: $t = 4.15, p < .01$.
[a]In all cases, + = a change in the direction of the communication; − = a change in the direction away from the communication.

Inspection of the separate own-attitude group scores in Table 3 reveals that the overall change scores cannot be attributed to the shifts for one group alone. Within the inside latitude of acceptance condition, for example, both the neutral and anti groups demonstrated considerable positive change. It should also be pointed out that within these own-attitude groups some subjects showed a shift in attitude that at times exceeded the position advocated in the communication. An analysis of variance of the change scores for the own-attitude groups in relation to latitude of acceptance indicates that a significant difference between own-attitude groups was obtained ($F = 4.99, p < .05$), as well as a significant interaction between own attitude and latitude of acceptance ($F = 3.57, p < .05$).

On the other hand, we could attempt to predict attitude change on the

TABLE 4   Mean attitude change in relation to distance of communication from own-attitude position.

Own position	Moderate distance[a]	Far distance
Pro	+ .78 (N = 9)[b]	+ .11 (N = 9)[c]
Neutral	− .62 (N = 8)[c]	− .33 (N = 9)[d]
Anti	+3.33 (N = 9)[c]	+2.90 (N = 10)[b]
Mean change	+1.23	+ .96

Note.—Moderate versus far distance: $t = .329$, ns.
[a]In all cases, + = a change in the direction of the communication.
− = a change in the direction away from the communication.
[b]Moderately pro communication.
[c]Moderately anti communication.
[d]Extremely anti communication.

basis of the *distance* between the subject's own attitude and the location of
the persuasive communication, as determined by preestablished control-
group ratings. Such an analysis derives from the assumption that communications which are at relatively short distances from the subjects' own
positions would probably fall within their latitudes of acceptance and
would, therefore, probably gain greater acceptance (e.g., pro subjects
receiving a moderately pro communication as compared with pro subjects
receiving a moderately anti communication). Such an assumption would
accord with the Sherif and Hovland theoretical interpretation. However, as
reported in Table 4, no evidence was found that subjects who received a
communication closer to their own position showed any significantly
greater susceptibility to change than did subjects at a greater distance
from the communication. Furthermore, there is no evidence to suggest that
greater distance between the subject's own position and the persuasive
communication results in change of attitude as a mode of dissonance
reduction, as argued by Zimbardo (1960). It seems that distance as
established by predetermined scale location of the communication does
not in and of itself represent the crucial factor for consideration in
susceptibility to change. Rather, the subject's own perception and judgment of the location of this communication, which reflect his interpretation of the content of the communication, appear to constitute an
important variable in the prediction of change.

Hypothesis 2. The second hypothesis posits that own position will
operate *differentially* as an anchor to distort judgment of the communication depending upon whether the communication is within or without the
latitude of acceptance. That such distortions can operate in a systematic
fashion so as to exaggerate or minimize perceived differences between

one's own position and that advocated in the communication has been demonstrated (Bieri et al., 1966; Sherif and Hovland, 1961). However, it is possible to argue that a dual process of change is operating here, facilitated by the distortion of the message represented in the communication. Subjects who perceive the communication as falling inside their latitude of acceptance not only change in the direction of the communication but may, at the same time, judge the communication to be closer to their own position than it actually is (assimilation). Change, then, comes about by changing own position toward the location of the communication while simultaneously changing the location of the communication in the direction of one's own position. By comparing each subject's judgment of the scale position of the communication in relation to the average judgment given to this communication by the control group, we can see the extent to which the communication is distorted in the direction of one's own position. Table 5 indicates that inside latitude of acceptance subjects did show significantly greater "assimilative" distortion of the communication toward their own position than did outside latitude of acceptance subjects. Similarly, rejection of the persuasive communication by outside latitude of acceptance subjects appears to be facilitated by a "contrast" distortion.

TABLE 5 Distortion of communication in relation to latitude of acceptance.

	Mean distortion[a]
Communication judged inside latitude of acceptance ($N = 27$)	+0.84
Communication judged outside latitude of acceptance ($N = 27$)	−0.56

Note.—Overall mean distortion: $t = 2.59, p < .05.$

[a]In this case, + = a distortion of the communication toward one's own position; − = a distortion of the communication away from one's own position.

DISCUSSION

The results of this study provide further support for the theoretical significance of latitude of acceptance and for its predictive value when assessment of the latitude of acceptance is based upon a measure reflecting individual differences in the range of items accepted. The fact that no differences were found when comparisons were made between the attitude change obtained under conditions of relatively small as opposed to relatively large discrepancies between the position of the subjects and that advocated in the communication argues even more strongly for the value of the latitude of acceptance variable.

One may speculate at this point concerning a number of factors which may possibly mediate the influence of latitude of acceptance on attitude change. For example, it is conceivable that judging the communication as lying within the range of acceptable items simply reflects an inability on the part of such subjects to discriminate among different scale positions. If so, change may be a function of poor discriminability rather than latitude of acceptance. Based on several informational measures of ability to discriminate among statements representing different attitudinal positions toward fraternities (Bieri et al., 1966), comparisons between inside latitude of acceptance subjects and outside latitude of acceptance subjects were made. None of these comparisons was significant. Similarly, comparisons on attitude change between inside and outside latitude of acceptance subjects who differed on the Pettigrew Category Width Scale failed to yield any significant results.

Perhaps subjects who change are merely demonstrating a tendency to respond in a consistently positive manner toward all statements and communications provided for judgment. In this way, acceptance of the argument presented in the communication may reflect an acquiescent personality characteristic which may underlie the latitude of acceptance variable. Again, a comparison between inside latitude of acceptance subjects and outside latitude of acceptance subjects on the basis of scores derived from an acceptance of authority scale revealed no significant differences on this dimension.

Since we cannot attribute these latitude of acceptance findings to such underlying factors of personality or cognitive functioning, it is important to explore those unique components which this variable may possess. In his paper on communication and discrepancy, Zimbardo (1960) reports that those subjects who conformed accepted a wider range of statements initially than did nonconformers; that is, they had large latitudes of acceptance. This threshold of acceptance was thought to provide a useful potential indicator of susceptibility to persuasive communications. If we compare the mean range of inside latitude of acceptance subjects (7.52 units) with that of outside latitude of acceptance subjects (4.18 units), we also find that the former group has a significantly wider latitude of acceptance ($t = 4.54, p < .01$). This finding may support the interpretation that a wider latitude of acceptance results in a flexibility in attitudinal position which makes possible the restructuring of one's own stand in the face of a persuasive communication. One mechanism which may facilitate such a restructuring may be the tendency to perceive the persuasive communication as somewhat closer to one's own position than is actually the case. Through a process of assimilative distortion, subjects who changed apparently were able to perceive the persuasive communication as sufficiently close enough to their own position to accept some of its content. That such assimilative distortion was not solely responsible for change, however, can be inferred from additional findings concerning distortion and amount of attitude change. Subjects who showed the greatest degree of change did not differ significantly in degree of assimilation of the persuasive communication from those who changed the least.

To gain a clearer picture of the relevance of these findings to the broader context of attitude-change research, let us consider the features of this study which are either similar or dissimilar to previous research in this field.

1. The topic under study was both salient to the subjects and related to the natural college setting in which they lived. It has been noted (Sherif et al., 1965) that attitude-change research often deals with unfamiliar topics, highly technical material (scientific, medical detail), or issues unrelated to the everyday, ongoing experiences of the subjects. In the present research the issue of fraternities was highly salient on the campus and constituted an issue which drew strong response from the student body.

Similarly, it has been proposed (Sherif and Hovland, 1961; Sherif et al., 1965) that a number of previous findings of attitude change refer to situations where ego involvement was minimal. The present research suggests that attitude change in response to a persuasive communication is not limited to noninvolving issues. While no direct measure of involvement independent of extremity was obtained, it can reasonably be argued that the issue was ego involving for the subjects. Since the question of the desirability of fraternities on the college campus was a hotly debated topic on the campus at the time, it can be assumed that for many students this topic was an emotionally charged one. Because the subjects were randomly selected from the questionnaire responses (with no refusals), it can be assumed, further, that the sentiments prevailing on the campus generally were reflected in the sample used for the study.

2. The perusasive communication was attributed to a "Committee on Undergraduate Affairs at a Major Eastern University" in an attempt to give the source of the message high credibility. Consistent with previous research (Sherif and Hovland, 1961), it was to be expected that a highly credible source was an important variable in producing effective communication results. In this respect, then, this research is similar to earlier attitude-change designs.

3. Since three different messages were used, representing moderate and

more extreme discrepancies between own position and that of the communication, we have demonstrated that discrepancy cannot be considered the sole or major determinant of attitude change. Further, since change was observed under two discrepancy conditions, it is clear that if distance is to be considered an important variable at all, it must be viewed in terms of its interaction with other subject and situational variables.

Strikingly, subjects who are extreme in own-attitude position demonstrated change as well as did the moderate ones. Based on earlier findings (Sherif and Hovland, 1961), it is to be expected that when change occurs, it is to be found among the moderate, less-committed subjects. In this research, we have found that both extreme antifraternity subjects as well as subjects moderate in attitude toward fraternities had shifts in own position in the direction of the communication. It would seem that future attitude-change research must consider parameters other than merely extremity and involvement of own attitude in predicting shifts in position.

5. Recent investigations (Sherif et al., 1965) have suggested that the latitudes of rejection and noncommitment be studied independently of the latitude of acceptance. In concentrating the present research upon a refinement of the latitude of acceptance variable, we have demonstrated that the latitude of acceptance is predictive of own-position change. Certainly studies are needed to indicate whether the latitudes of acceptance, rejection, and noncommitment are simply complementary variables or whether they differ in their predictive utility for attitude change.

6. Finally, it is to be noted again that in contrast to previous studies in which no assessment of each judge's perception of the communication was obtained, the subjects here were allowed to specify the location of the persuasive communication according to their own judgments. In this way, individual differences in evaluation and judgment have been utilized in an attempt to make the latitude of acceptance sensitive to the variety of interpretations and perceptions to be found even within a relatively homogeneous sample.

REFERENCES

BIERI, J., ATKINS, A. L., BRIAR, S., LEAMAN, R. L., MILLER, H., & TRIPODI, T. *Clinical and Social Judgment.* New York: Wiley, 1966.

FESTINGER, L. *A Theory of Cognitive Dissonance.* Evanston, Ill.: Row, Peterson, 1957.

HOVLAND, C., HARVEY, O. J., & SHERIF, M. Assimilation and Contrast Effects in Reactions to Communication and Attitude Change. *Journal of Abnormal and Social Psychology,* 1957, *55,* 244–252.

SEGALL, M. The Effects of Attitude and Experience on Judgments of Controversial Statements. *Journal of Abnormal and Social Psychology,* 1959, *58,* 61–68.

SHERIF, M., & HOVLAND, C. *Social Judgment.* New Haven: Yale University Press, 1961.

SHERIF, C., SHERIF, M., & NEBERGALL, R. *Attitude and Attitude Change.* Philadelphia: Saunders, 1965.

ZIMBARDO, P. G. Involvement and Communication Discrepancy as Determinants of Opinion Change. *Journal of Abnormal and Social Psychology,* 1960, *60,* 86–94.

3

INTERPERSONAL ATTRACTION
AS A FUNCTION
OF AFFILIATION NEED AND
ATTITUDE SIMILARITY[1]
DONN BYRNE[2]

Byrne's study clearly shows how interpersonal attraction is related to shared attitudes. However, two tangential matters are also raised in his discussion. It is our view that affiliation motivation could best be pursued as a variable that has an inverse correspondence to achievement motivation. Whereas achievement motivation appears to be a matter of having developed a tolerance of arousal in nonconfirmed or novel situations, affiliative motivation appears to be a matter of high reliance on others as a source of confirmation of the constructions that one imposes on situations. Affiliation-motivated persons would be comparable to Reisman's "other-directed" persons, who constantly send out radar signals to bounce them off the concepts of others in order to establish congruency (Reisman, Glazer, Denney, 1950). Byrne considers whether affiliation motivation acts as a variable that increases positive attraction toward persons who hold similar attitudinal positions. His data suggest that higher affiliation motivation does not produce higher attraction toward others of similar attitude.

Another point made by Byrne is that a person is more likely to attribute a whole series of other characteristics to other persons who are judged to hold a particular attitude on an issue. Byrne's analysis leads to the conclusion that when a subject perceives another person to hold attitudes that are similar to his own, the subject will rate the agreeing

Reprinted from Human Relations, *1961, 14, 283–289, by permission of the author and* Plenum Publishing Corporation.

[1]This investigation was supported in part by research grants (EF-140, EF-143) from the University of Texas Research Institute.

[2]The author would like to express his appreciation to Mr. John Sheffield, who served as a research assistant, and to Miss Elane Abbott, who scored the affiliation need protocols.

person in more positive terms. The willingness to attribute other characteristics to the judged person corresponds to the findings reported by Asch (Section V), and again illustrates the workings of a person's total construct system. One needs, however, to question why the attributed characteristics are positive. Why does a person who agrees with a subject tend to become a "good" person? Could it be that one's own position on any issue is invariably linked to the superordinate construct *good*? It would then follow that other persons holding the same position must be placed at the *good*-related end of every other construct.

REFERENCE

REISMAN, D., GLAZER, J., & DENNEY, R. *The Lonely Crowd.* New York: Doubleday, 1950.

*   *   *

In a previous paper (Byrne, 1961) the author hypothesized that interpersonal attraction is a function of propinquity, affiliation need, response to the overt stimulus properties of each individual, and the number of reciprocal rewards and punishments which are present in the interaction. Attitude similarity was proposed as a special case of the latter variable and was found to exert a significant influence on interpersonal attraction.

In the present study, need for affiliation is considered. It seems reasonable to propose that a measure which indicates concern over establishing, maintaining, or restoring a positive affective relationship with others should be useful in predicting individual differences in responding with feelings of attraction or repulsion toward another person. Previous studies lend support to this proposition. It has been found that affiliation need is positively related to approval-seeking behavior as rated by peers (Atkinson, Heyns, and Veroff, 1954), self-ratings of popularity (French and Chadwick, 1956) and the frequency with which an individual makes local telephone calls and writes letters (Lansing and Heyns, 1959).

Generally, Ss high in *n* Affiliation would be expected to respond more positively to other people than would Ss low in *n* Affiliation. In this study, affiliation need will be investigated in conjunction with another independent variable: attitude similarity.

It has been proposed (Byrne, in press) that the expression of dissimilar attitudes by another individual constitutes a punishing and threatening element in the interaction. Dollard and Miller (1950) point out that people receive a great deal of social training which establishes learned drives to be logical and to make a correct report of the environment. The major criterion for assessing the degree to which we or anyone else is logical or correct in interpreting the world is through consensual validation. We are constantly checking our percepts and concepts against those of others. Such checking is most important with respect to what Festinger (1952) has called social reality, in contrast to physical reality. As Newcomb (1953) suggests, individuals rely on social confirmation in inverse proportion to the possibility of testing their assumptions by observing the physical consequences of them. It is proposed that disagreement acts to frustrate our learned need to be logical and to remain in contact with reality in that the possibility is raised that we are lacking in this respect. An alternative, and usually more acceptable, perception of the situation is that it is the other person who is perceiving incorrectly. In any event, the threat posed by disagreement tends to decrease interpersonal attraction.

The same relationships are described in a similar way by Heider (1958) and Newcomb (1953). Heider proposed that a state of harmony or balance exists if entities which belong together are all positive or if they are all negative. States of imbalance such as disagreement between two friends about some impersonal entity will bring about a stress to change; e.g., an alteration in sentiment toward either the friend or the object. Newcomb's A-B-X model deals with a need for cognitive symmetry with respect to the attitude of two individuals toward one another and toward the object of communication. A strain toward symmetry operates, and equilibrium is advantageous because it (i) makes the other person's behavior more predictable and (ii) increases one's confidence in his own cognitive and evaluative orientations.

The effect of affiliation need and similar attitudes should summate so that Ss with strong affiliative needs would respond more positively to an agreeing stranger than Ss with relatively weak n Affiliation. Response to a stranger with dissimilar attitudes is more difficult to predict. It could be argued that Ss high in affiliation need are so concerned over establishing interpersonal relationships that they will minimize the attitude discrepancy and respond positively to the other person. Burdick and Burnes (1958) reported that Ss high in n Affiliation tended to change their opinions to conform with those of a liked E. Another possibility is that interpersonal relationships are so important to high n Affiliation Ss that the threat posed by a disagreeing stranger (and hence negative feelings toward him) is even greater than for those low in need for affiliation. In an experimental situation in which there was no external pressure toward uniformity of opinions, only high n Affiliation Ss responded negatively toward an individual whose opinions were unlike their own (Berkowitz and Howard, 1959).

Assuming that each of the reported results represents a stable finding, the conflict between the positive influence of affiliation need and the negative influence of attitude dissimilarity on interpersonal attraction can apparently be resolved in either direction. Still a third possibility is that these opposing influences could cancel one another out. The outcome of such a conflict is probably a function of the strength of n Affiliation, the degree of attitude dissimilarity, amount and type of contact with the other person prior to disagreement, and a host of unknown parameters.

Therefore, it is hypothesized that (a) a stranger who is known to have attitudes similar to those of the S is better liked by Ss high in affiliation need than by Ss low in affiliation need and (b) a stranger who is known to have attitudes dissimilar to those of the S is liked differentially by Ss high and low in affiliation need. (Because there is no basis on which to predict the direction of the resolution of this conflict, direction cannot be specified.) In addition, this study contains a replication of the previous one in which a stranger known to have attitudes similar to those of the S was found to be better liked and to be judged as more intelligent, better informed, more moral, and better adjusted than a stranger with dissimilar attitudes.

METHOD

Procedure. The previously reported attitude scale[3] consisting of 26 issues was administered to 84 students (44 males, 40 females) enrolled in introductory psychology courses at the University of Texas. About two weeks later they were asked to report to the Laboratory for Personality Research in groups of five to ten as part of the course requirement to serve several hours as research Ss. At this time they were falsely informed that the attitude scale formed part of a study in interpersonal prediction. They were told that other students had been given the same scale, pairs of students matched on the basis of sex, and that each member of a pair would be given the attitude scale of the other (anonymously) in order to determine the accuracy of judgments based on limited information.[4]

Actually, each S was given a fake attitude scale filled out by the E. Half of the Ss received scales with attitudes similar to their own indicated, and half received scales which expressed views opposite to their own.

Interpersonal attraction. The Interpersonal Judgement Scale consists of six seven-point rating scales. Two of these constitute the operations

---

[3]The attitude measure and the rating scales for interpersonal attraction and evaluation have been deposited with the American Documentation Institute. See Byrne (in press) for information about ordering microfilm or photo copies.

[4]In addition, half of the Ss were given instructions which were intended to serve as anxiety cues. This experimental manipulation was unsuccessful; therefore both groups are combined in the discussion.

defining interpersonal attraction. On one, Ss indicate the extent to which they feel that they would like or dislike the stranger. On the other, they indicate the degree to which they would dislike or enjoy working with the other person as a partner in an experiment. The other four scales, important here only in the replication, deal with evaluations of the other person's intelligence, knowledge of current events, morality, and adjustment. No relationship between affiliation need and these latter variables was postulated.

Affiliation need. One week later, using a different experimental room, another E administered four thematic apperception slides in a standard manner (Atkinson, 1958, pp. 836-7).[5] The slides consisted of pictures 28, 83, 102, and 103 in the list presented by Atkinson (1958, pp. 832-4). The protocols were scored by our research assistant according to the Heyns, Veroff, and Atkinson (1958) manual. A subsample of 29 protocols was scored independently by an experienced scorer at the University of Michigan. High interjudge reliability is indicated by a correlation of .95 between the two sets of scores. For the 84 Ss, the mean n Affiliation score was 2.67 with a standard deviation of 2.54. Ss were divided approximately at the median into low ($N = 38$, scores of 0-2) and high ($N = 46$, scores of 3-10) groups.

RESULTS

Hypotheses. In order to test the effect of the two independent variables, a two-way analysis of variance was run for each dependent variable, correcting for disproportionality among cases in the four cells (Wert, Neidt, and Ahmann, 1954). An examination of the data reported in Tables 1 and 2 indicates little support for the first hypotheses. The fact that one of

[5]In this study n Aff is conceptualized as an independent variable. That is, an individual's characteristic affiliation concern is found to influence interpersonal attraction. Because these response measures were obtained in reverse order, it would be possible to interpret the results to mean that need affiliation scores vary as a result of the nature of attraction ratings given to a stranger. Only a study in which the order is reversed could give a definite answer to this question. Antoher possibility is that exposure to the attitude scale of a disagreeing stranger elevates n Aff scores. With affiliation need considered as a dependent variable, the subject breakdown in Table 1 almost reaches significance at the .05 level ($x^2 = 3.81$, df $= 1$, p between .10 and . 05).

However, the fact that the two portions of the experiment were given in different rooms on different floors of the building by different Es with a time interval of one week between sessions would lend support to the idea that affiliation need affected attraction rather than the possibility that some lingering effect of the rating session influenced response to the thematic apperception slides.

TABLE 1 Effect of attitude similarity and affiliation need on interpersonal attraction.

| | Personal feelings | | | | | |
| | Similar attitudes | | | Dissimilar attitudes | | |
	N	M	S.D.	N	M	S.D.
Low *n* Aff	23	5.83	.82	15	3.53	1.31
High *n* Aff	18	5.78	.98	28	2.71	1.10
	Desirability as a work partner					
	Similar attitudes			Dissimilar attitudes		
	N	M	S.D.	N	M	S.D.
Low *n* Aff	23	5.04	1.52	15	4.20	1.28
High *n* Aff	18	5.56	1.01	28	3.04	1.57

TABLE 2 Summary of analysis of variance of effect of attitude similarity and affiliation need on interpersonal attraction.

| | Personal Feelings | | | | |
Source	Sum of squares	df	Mean square	F	P
Attitude similarity	147.60*	1	147.60	128.54	$<.001$
Affiliation need	3.63*	1	3.63	3.16	N.S.
Interaction	2.95*	1	2.95	2.57	N.S.
Within (error)	91.86	80	1.15		
	Desirability as a work partner				
Source	Sum of squares	df	Mean square	F	P
Attitude similarity	61.58*	1	61.58	29.90	$<.001$
Affiliation need	1.44*	1	1.44	.70	N.S.
Interaction	14.45*	1	14.54	7.02	$<.01$
Within (error)	164.77	80	2.06		

*Adjusted

the interactions is significant at the .01 level while the other approaches significance at the .05 level warrants the use of the *t* test to compare the high and low *n* Affiliation groups. In responding to a stranger with similar attitudes, affiliation need influences neither Personal Feelings ($t = .17$, df $= 39, p > .10$) nor Desirability as a Work Partner ($t = 1.22$, df $= 39, p > .10$).

With respect to both dependent variables, the second hypothesis was confirmed. In responding to a stranger with different attitudes, Ss with low n Affiliation rate the stranger higher in terms of Personal Feelings ($t =$ 2.13, df $= 41, p < .05$) and Desirability as a Work Partner ($t = 2.40$, df $= 41, p < .05$).

Replication. The reported effect of attitude similarity on all six variables contained in the Interpersonal Judgement Scale was confirmed. Table 2 indicates that a stranger with similar attitudes is rated more positively than one with dissimilar attitudes on both interpersonal attraction scales. The differences in each case are significant at beyond the .001 level.

For the other four scales, the replication is equally confirmatory. A stranger with similar attitudes is rated higher with respect to Intelligence ($t = 4.79$, df $= 82, p < .001$), Knowledge of Current Events ($t = 3.69$, df $= 82, p < .001$), Morality ($t = 6.13$, df $= 82, p < .001$), and Adjustment ($t = 0.43$, df $= 82, p < .001$) than a stranger with dissimilar attitudes.

DISCUSSION

Within the limits imposed by this experimental design, it appears that affiliation need assumes importance only in the prediction of interpersonal attraction toward an individual with a deviant set of opinions. In terms of the rating scales, individuals with low n Affiliation react to a disagreeing stranger with indifference. Those with high affiliation needs respond to such a stranger with dislike. Regardless of one's status on the affiliation variable, a disagreeing stranger is seen as relatively unintelligent, uninformed, immoral, and maladjusted.

Why was the n Affiliation variable important with respect to attraction to a disagreeing stranger and not to an agreeing one? Individuals who obtain high scores on this personality dimension are those who respond to relatively unstructured pictorial stimuli with imagery containing references to establishing, maintaining, or restoring positive affective relationships. In addition to this concern on the verbal level, there is some evidence that such individuals tend behaviorally to seek positive affective responses from others (Atkinson, Heyns, and Veroff, 1954; French and Chadwick, 1956; Lansing and Heyns, 1959). Therefore, in a relatively neutral interpersonal setting, it seems likely that those high in affiliation need would respond positively to other people as potential sources of gratification.

When another person is found to have a *few* negative characteristics such as a dissimilar opinion about a moderately important topic, those high in n Affiliation will perhaps attempt to resolve the conflict in such a way as to maintain the positive relationship. In the Burdick and Burnes (1958) experiment, the resolution was accomplished through the Ss altering their own opinions. However, as the negative characteristics of the other person increase (as in the present study), such a resolution becomes increasingly difficult. In this instance, the other person is an unpleasant stimulus and not valued positively by anyone (including low n Affiliation Ss). To those high in affiliation need, he is even more unpleasant because he not only offers consensual invalidation by disagreeing, but fails to gratify strong friendship motives as well. Thus, an additive function is proposed to account for the negative reactions to a stranger with dissimilar attitudes in both the present study and the one by Berkowitz and Howard (1959).

The failure of the first hypothesis can perhaps be explained on the basis of the strength of attitude similarity as a variable. That is, an agreeing stranger evokes a positive response regardless of affiliation need. If the similarity of the stranger's attitudes had been somewhat less than perfect, it is hypothesized that affiliation need would be positively related to interpersonal attraction.

Summing up, the findings and the speculations growing out of them suggest that when a stranger's attitudes are identical, the response is a positive one, regardless of affiliation need; when there is a moderate degree of attitude dissimilarity, affiliation need is positively related to attraction; and when the attitudes are consistently dissimilar, affiliation need and attraction are inversely related.

SUMMARY

The effect of affiliation need and attitude similarity on interpersonal attraction was investigated. A group of 84 students was given an attitude scale which deals with 26 issues. Two weeks later they were given the same scale which was supposed to have been filled out by another student. Actually, the scale had been filled out by E. They were asked to rate this 'stranger' on scales dealing with interpersonal attraction and to evaluate him with respect to intelligence, knowledge of current events, morality, and adjustment. At another testing session, they responded to four thematic apperception cards, and their protocols were scored for affiliation need.

It was found that (a) a stranger with attitudes similar to those of S was rated equally positively by individuals high and low in affiliation need, (b) a stranger with attitudes dissimilar to those of S was rated significantly more negatively on both measures of interpersonal attraction by individuals high in *n* Affiliation than by those low in *n* Affiliation, and (c) a previous finding was replicated in that a stranger with attitudes similar to those of *S* was rated as significantly better liked, more desirable as a work partner, more intelligent, better informed about current events, more moral, and better adjusted than a stranger with dissimilar attitudes.

REFERENCES

ATKINSON, J. W. (Ed.) (1958). *Motives in Fantasy, Action, and Society.* Princeton, New Jersey: D. Van Nostrand.

ATKINSON, J. W., HEYNS, R. W. & VEROFF, J. (1954). The Effect of Experimental Arousal of the Affiliation Motive on Thematic Apperception. *J. Abnorm. Soc. Psychol., 49,* 405–10.

BERKOWITZ, L. & HOWARD, R. C. (1959). Reactions to Opinion Deviates as Affected by Affiliation Need (n) and Group Membership Interdependence. *Sociometry, 22,* 81–91.

BYRNE, D. (1961). Interpersonal Attraction and Attitude Similarity. *J. Abnorm. Soc. Psychol., 62,* 713–715.

BURDICK, H. A. & BURNES, A. J. (1958). A Test of 'Strain Toward Symmetry' Theories. *J. Abnorm. Soc. Psychol., 57,* 367–70.

DOLLARD, J. & MILLER, N. E. (1950). *Personality and Psychotherapy.* New York: McGraw-Hill.

FESTINGER, L. (1952). Informal Social Communication. In L. Festinger, K. Back, S. Schachter, H. H. Kelley, & J. Thibaut, *Theory and Experiment in Social Communication.* Ann Arbor, Michigan: Edward Brothers. Pp. 3–17.

FRENCH, ELIZABETH G. & CHADWICK, IRENE (1956). Some Characteristics of Affiliation Motivation. *J. Abnorm. Soc. Psychol., 52,* 296–300.

HEIDER, F. (1958). *The Psychology of Interpersonal Relations.* New York: Wiley.

HEYNS, R. W., VEROFF, J. & ATKINSON, J. W. (1958). A Scoring Manual for the Affiliation Motive. In J. W. Atkinson (Ed.), *Motives in Fantasy, Action, and Society.* Princeton, New Jersey: D. Van Nostrand. Pp. 205–18.

LANSING, J. B. & HEYNS, R. W. (1959). Need Affiliation and Frequency of Four Types of Communication. *J. Abnorm. Soc. Psychol., 58,* 365–72.

NEWCOMB, T. M. (1953). An Approach to the Study of Communicative Acts. *Psychol. Rev., 60,* 393–404.

WERT, J. W., NEIDT, C. O. & AHMANN, J. S. (1954). *Statistical Methods in Educational and Psychological Research.* New York: Appleton-Century-Crofts.

4

CULTURAL PATTERNS
IN NARRATIVE
BENJAMIN N. COLBY

It has been stated that a culture creates and disseminates its own unique constructs. Colby presents a technique of quantifying and then isolating some of the constructions that make up the cognitive systems of specific cultures. Social scientists have frequently referred to folk stories as having a place in the transmission of particular cultures. Colby opens his study with the assumption that folk stories are culture carriers, and finds that the stories of different cultures do, indeed, reflect isolable thematic material. Furthermore, the thematic material concerns phenomena that are salient to the culture producing the stories. The culture, then, appears to produce stories that transmit constructs and constructions to its members, and the schemas it produces in its members are further reflected as new stories are composed.

Colby points out that effective cultures would be expected to provide large numbers of cognitive organizations that encapsulate socially salient behavior styles. Adding the general conclusion that there is personal attraction between persons holding similar attitudes, we suggest that high cohesion will be achieved by cultures that clearly define salient constructs in their mythos. An unsystematic glance at history suggests that this has been the case.

*   *   *

There has been a revival of interest in the anthropology of folk literature and valuable studies are beginning to appear. The main hurdle has been the difficulty of developing operational procedures and of

Reprinted from Science, *1966,* 151, *793–798, by permission of the author and the American Association for the Advancement of Science. Copyright 1966 by the American Association for the Advancement of Sciences.*

validating results through links to other aspects of culture. Only very recently has it become possible, through the use of computers, to process large numbers of narrative texts having many variables in order to discover statistically significant patterns which are culturally distinctive and amenable to testing in the field. We now have the means to test the theories of the Russian folklorist Vladimir Propp, who analyzed folk tales structurally, and those of the French anthropologist Claude Lévi-Strauss, who views myths as vehicles for the expression of opposing dualities and their mediating elements [as in the opposition between sky and earth, with mist as the mediator (1)]. Both these scholars have maintained, despite contrary beliefs and indifference on the part of most traditional folklorists, that folk tales and myths are patterned.

Anthropologists often speak of culture patterns, but only in a few sectors of culture have they found clear evidence for patterned relationships. Language is one such sector. What kind of cognitive apparatus permits a child to understand sentences of his language that he has never before heard, or to produce understandable sentences which he himself has never before spoken? In order to study how novel sentences are created, linguists postulate the existence of some sort of cognitive structure (the organization of information in the brain), and they search for phonemic relationships, rules of grammar, and other linguistic patterns which evidence this structure. But there is much that remains unfathomed, for we have little understanding of the mental structure that undoubtedly lies behind these patterns.

Kinship and social organization are other areas in which patterns have traditionally been discerned by anthropologists. Now, advances are being made toward greater understanding of the distinctive semantic components of systems of kinship terminology. These components, though they vary with different systems, characteristically concern such matters as the generation and sex of the relative or connecting relative (2), the sex of the speaker, and the lineality. The kinship terms can be diagrammed in matrices that demonstrate how these semantic components combine to define the kin terms (3).

More ambitiously, anthropologists speak of broad configurations which characterize total cultures. By "broad configurations" anthropologists usually mean unstated premises, values, and goals, which are intuitively arrived at. The most widely known discussion of overall culture patterning is Ruth Benedict's *Patterns of Culture* (4), which presented the view that cultural configurations pervade all behavior. Benedict described two types of cultures—cultures of the Apollonian pueblos of the Southwest and those of the Dionysian Indians of the Great Plains. Apollonian cultures emphasize tradition, even-tempered restraint, moderation, harmony, and distrust of individualism. Dionysian cultures emphasize danger, power, violence, self-reliance, and lack of inhibition. Benedict described a number of other societies that seemed to fit her more masculine Dionysian type to an extent which, in the case of the Dobu of Melanesia and the Kwakiutl of Vancouver Sound, reached paranoid proportions. In these characterizations, her own preference was clear.

Other anthropologists who have known the cultures described by Benedict dispute her interpretation. Where she felt that pueblo people were highly integrated by a pervading set of harmonious values, others considered them to be divisive, tense, and suspicious. Where Benedict felt that pueblo individuals had relative freedom of action, others felt that they were authoritarian and suppressive (5). As a result of these and other disagreements involving radically different views of the same culture, anthropologists have begun to reappraise their methods.

NEW DIRECTIONS IN ETHNOLOGY

While still espousing a faith in underlying structures or logical systems in cultures, many anthropologists have turned away from any attempt at total "characterization" and have concentrated on those less disputable aspects of culture where the data can be subjected to formal procedures of validation and analysis. Some have studied the folk sciences of a culture in search of logical systems underlying native beliefs about plants or animals (6). Related to this first interest are studies of native terminologies for kinship (7), diseases (8), plants (9), and color (10). Other anthropologists have used logical and statistical techniques to focus on sectors of culture long neglected in anthropology: oaths and ordeals (11), omens (12), and divination (13). Some have turned to mathematics and logic for analyzing data of continuing interest (14). Others have concentrated on interviewing individuals in the native language in such a way as to insure that the questions asked are culturally meaningful to the native (15). All this work is still based on the assumption that there are cultural patterns and structures. But, as in linguistics, the patterns and structures are usually not directly observable. The search for them must thus be rigorously controlled to avoid subjective and disputable interpretations.

The emphasis on control has, unfortunately, imposed a bias in the selection of ethnographic subject matter toward the more explicit aspects of culture, where there is high consensus among culture members, as in semantics. The more abstract aspects—art, religion, and folk literature—have usually been neglected.

STUDY OF NARRATIVE PATTERNS WITH COMPUTERS

During the last few years I have sought ways to investigate the more abstract aspects of culture with methods less subjective than those customarily used. For example, I have made a study of folk narratives—primarily folk tales and myths—through word counts. Counts of words belonging to different conceptual domains—domains such as affection, assistance, cognition, competition, perception, space, and time—have suggested interpretations of folk tales which can be tested in various ways. More importantly, I have found conceptual patterns in narratives—patterns of words belonging to a given conceptual domain whose frequencies in the various sections (1 to 9) of the narrative or narratives differ for different cultures (16).

Underlying this study is the assumption that the patterns found are indications, however imperfect, of a more basic cultural system of mental "templates" or pattern components which are used in telling folk tales. Each folk tale reflects the influence of such a template system, but because the pattern measurements are only approximations and the patterns are interwoven and superimposed in complex ways, gross patterns emerge only when we examine a very large number of folk tales.

Narrative—at least narrative as we usually define it—has certain requirements which seem to be universal. These include a setting in time and space. The listener must be able to orient himself before the events of the narrative begin. Examples are the familiar "Once upon a time" or "Long, long ago" of the folk stories we know best. In general, one expects to find a high frequency of time words at the beginning of folk stories. In Eskimo and Japanese folk tales [which I have been studying recently, in translation (17)], this seems to be the case. When one divides the text of each folk tale studied into nine sections of equal length, one finds that the combined first ninths of all the folk tales in the study contain more time words than any of the other ninths.

Similarly, in both the Eskimo and Japanese folk tales, words for places and areas are most frequent at the beginning of the folk tales. The occurrence, by text section, of words for natural place and general place in the Japanese tales is shown in Fig. 1 (patterns 9J and 4J).

It is probable that a high occurrence of time words at the beginning of the narrative is characteristic of folk tales in all cultures, but a graph of the Japanese pattern for time words (Fig. 2, left) suggests that the secondary peak or modal point is culturally distinctive. An examination of the text sections which correspond with the secondary modal points reveals that many of the tales tend to emphasize time as part of the plot movement toward the middle of the story. The frequencies (by text section) of all sentences mentioning the time when something is expected to happen or does happen were tallied with the frequencies for all sentences in which the time for a task is stipulated or in which there is mention of limitations on a time period. When these frequencies were graphed (Fig. 2, right) it was clear that the primary modal point now corresponded with text section 6, while the height of the peak for section 1 was greatly diminished. In this way two different patterns of time words can be identified and isolated from one another.

As one analyzes the beginning sections of folk tales in more detail he notices differences which probably reflect differences in culture. The earlier parts of the Eskimo narratives have a higher frequency of "search" words than the later parts. The frequencies of these words decrease linearly as the tale proceeds. This decrease is due to the fact that Eskimo tales deal with a search for people or game. The observation of landmarks, terrain, tracks, and footprints is important to this search, but search words are needed less as the stories progress and the people sought or the animals hunted are found. (As one would expect, this pattern parallels the patterns for words describing spatial orientation.)

In Japanese folk tales no such pattern exists for search and observation words, which are used for other purposes—for example, to show or reveal objects, secrets, or special places to the protagonist. In the Japanese tales the frequencies of these words increase as the tale proceeds. This pattern demonstrates the interest in strategies of deception and secrecy characteristic of more complex societies, which contrasts with the great interest in physical skill and hunting ability in the less complex Eskimo culture (18).

In almost all folk tales or myths the characters in the story are confronted by a problem. In Eskimo and Japanese stories, concern over the problem builds up to a high point at about the middle of the story; this buildup requires the use of many words indicating communication and conversation—words such as *tell* and *say* (Fig. 3). In the stories people communicate with each other more freely when they are attempting to solve the problem. In Japanese folk tales this greater intensity of communication is accompanied by frequent use of the second person (Fig. 1, pattern 1J).

Heightened preoccupation with a problem is not accompanied by an increase in words denoting routine activities such as hunting and fishing, or in words describing custom, manner, or direction (Fig. 1, pattern 9E). Such words occur most frequently in the first few sections of Japanese and Eskimo stories, because the activities they describe are interrupted when the plot begins to develop (19).

As may be seen in Fig. 1, there are many conceptual categories for which very significant patterns are obtainable for one culture but not for

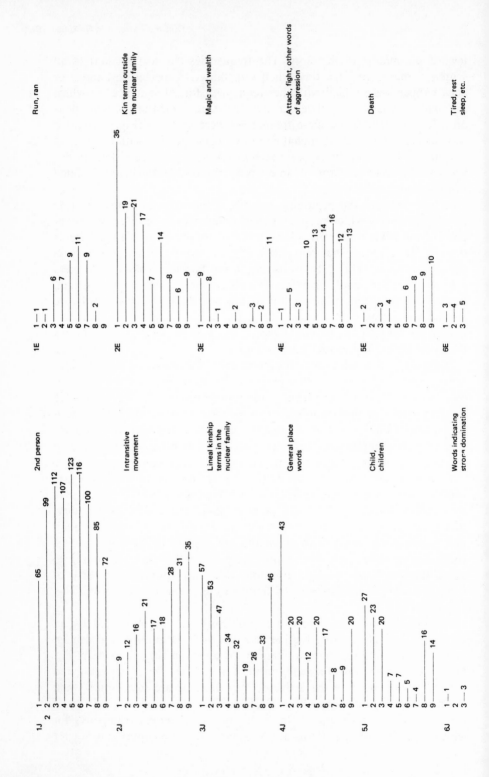

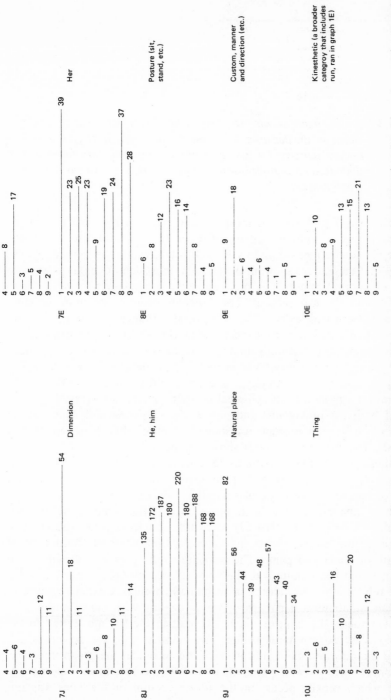

FIG. 1 *Graphs of the ten most significant patterns of word-group frequencies, from the beginning (section 1) to the end (section 9) of the Japanese folk tales (graphs at left) and Eskimo folk tales (graphs at right). The lengths of the horizontal lines indicate relative frequencies of occurrence of words belonging to the conceptual domain indicated ("2nd person," "run, ran," and so on). Numerals to left of lines refer to text sections; numerals to right of lines, to number of occurrences.*

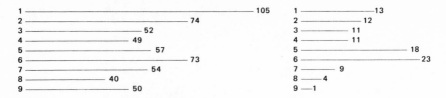

FIG. 2   (Left) Graph showing the frequency of occurrences of time-unit words in the Japanese folk tales, by text section. (Right) A secondary pattern- for words or phrases denoting anticipated and limited time periods-isolated from the data on which the left graph is based.

the other. In Fig. 1 the ten most definite patterns for each culture, as determined by a combined ranking of the most significant results obtained by the chi-square method and by Kendall's tau test, are presented. On the theory that these areas showing the clearest, most definite patterns are also areas of cultural importance, one can make a number of general statements about the two cultures. The Japanese seem to be more oriented toward concern with external, usually social, situations, while the Eskimo are more oriented toward concern with the abilities and capabilities (mainly physical) of the individual. The Japanese folk tales show a pattern in the conceptual category "dimension" (Fig. 1, pattern 7J), which applies to objects and people external to the protagonist, while the Eskimo folk tales reveal a pattern in the physical position or "posture" (Fig. 1, pattern 8E) of both the protagonist and others. The Japanese folk tales have a pattern in the use of concepts translated as "thing" (Fig. 1, pattern 10J) in English. The Eskimo folk tales show a pattern for concepts of physical, kinesthetic action (Fig. 1, patterns 1E and 10E). In Eskimo stories, words in the category "tired" (Fig. 1, pattern 6E) are used in connection with sleep or rest to restore physical strength.

In the Japanese stories the limitations on action tend to be external domination (Fig. 1, pattern 6J) or instruction from other individuals, whereas in the Eskimo stories the limitations on action are limitations of strength or scarcity of game. The response to the presence of game or to human threat has a pattern in the "attack" category (Fig. 1, pattern 4E), which relates either to hunting or to human conflict. Another response to problem situations is a pattern of words dealing with magic and wealth (Fig. 1, pattern 3E), both of which are goals in the Eskimo stories. In the Eskimo tales, supernatural beings give humans magical powers which enable them to find game, restore life, and so on. In the graph, however, the concern with wealth predominated, and the receipt of supernatural power which usually occurs in the fourth section of the tales was not indicated by this word group. In the Japanese stories there is a strong

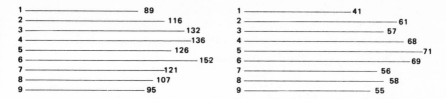

FIG. 3   *(Left) Japanese and (right) Eskimo patterns for words concerned with communication in the folk tales, by text section.*

pattern of words (Fig. 1, pattern 2J) indicating belief in an impersonal divine justice; in these stories, for example, an object simply falls off a ledge and strikes the evil character dead. This, again, is emphasis on the external situation rather than on inner personal power—an emphasis which seems to distinguish the Japanese from the Eskimo culture.

The pattern of the concept of death in the Eskimo tales (Fig. 1, pattern 5E) reflects the continual preoccupation with life and death of people in a difficult environment. It illustrates the Eskimo's inevitable concern with such basic matters as food, hunting, maintaining physical strength, and staying alive. The Japanese, on the other hand, are more concerned with subtle social situations and strategies than with human survival.

The pattern, in the Japanese tales, of words for members of the nuclear family (Fig. 1, pattern 3J: *father, mother, son, daughter*) and of the word *child* (Fig. 1, pattern 5J) shows an interest in family origins and in the establishing of a new family. It shows the dependency of children and of aged parents in the Japanese culture, and a great pride and love for children, even for children who are not normal or are physically incapable of helping their parents. In one story a boy is only 1 inch tall. In another he is a snail. The Eskimo people, on the other hand, are vitally concerned about the economic burden that children constitute. In extremely difficult times they have sometimes practiced infanticide.

The Eskimo pattern of words for blood relations outside the nuclear family (Fig. 1, pattern 2E: *uncle, grandmother,* and so on) reflects a movement from a broader dependency of kinship toward greater self-sufficiency, and an ability to provide for several wives rather than a desire to establish a line of descendants. Often the word *her* (Fig. 1, pattern 7E) is used to denote the possession of affinal kin, as in "her husband."

The pattern for *he* and *him* in the Japanese tales (Fig. 1, pattern 8J) probably reflects the dominance of males in the culture. The women in the folk tales have a limited number of roles—wife, mother, daughter, and grandmother (exceptions are priestess, queen, and supernatural beings), as opposed to the many different roles of Japanese men. Animals also are usually referred to, in the English translations, as "he" or "him."

This is a brief summary of the most salient of the many patterns which were shown, by means of the chi-square test, to be statistically significant. Of 74 basic conceptual categories and 195 subcategories, 58 (or 22 percent) were statistically significant at the .01 level for the Japanese folk tales and 70 (or 26 percent) for the Eskimo tales (20).

CULTURAL TEMPLATES AND CULTURAL MODELS

Man is a pattern-seeking animal. At the subliminal level he continually seeks patterns or regularities in his environment and unconsciously organizes such regularities in a mental structure. I propose the hypothesis that, in hearing the narratives of others, one derives patterns from them and constructs cognitive templates for future use in telling his own stories. These templates must be stored in some organized way, to be called forth by schemata (rules, formulas, programs) or by some other means, at a higher level of mental organization according to different behavioral situations.

Why use the word *template* rather than *pattern* for this kind of mental organization? *Pattern* implies a total arrangement of elements in a fixed relationship to each other. This suggests a cognitive rigidity which is difficult to reconcile with the infinite number of behavioral variations that are possible in human action. *Template,* on the other hand, suggests pattern parts, rather than wholes, and allows for flexibility and dynamic relationships. Thus, the word *template* is used here, in the sense of a cognitive element for producing folk tales and controlling behavior in general. The word *pattern* seems more appropriate when one is discussing patterned regularities that can be found in the folk tale, or behavior that results from activation of various template combinations.

It is reasonable to expect that an individual, if he is to function efficiently in new behavioral situations, must construct templates and mentally store them even when their immediate use is unlikely. For example, a child unconsciously learns the parental role while he is growing up but does not assume it until he himself is a parent.

The subliminal search for regularities in one's surroundings cannot include everything at once. There must be a focus on things and activities which are meaningful to the individual or to the people with whom he is interacting, or which might be useful in situations that he has not yet directly experienced. Here the theory of cultural models put forward by John M. Roberts and Brian Sutton-Smith is important. According to Roberts, Sutton-Smith, and their colleagues (21), every culture has an array of models. Folk tales and myths constitute only one of many model types: others are graphic art, sculpture, drama, literature, toys, maps, plans, and games. Roberts views these models as devices, external to the individual, for storing information (22). Through personal involvement with them one can learn useful behavior. Individuals who become addicted to certain models (for example, poker-playing or listening to music) become so because of psychological conflict created by unsatisfactory earlier experiences in the behavior-area modeled. Involvement with the model assuages the conflict. These models, therefore, provide ready strategies and behavior plans which permit the learning of culturally useful behavior, particularly in the case of children who become absorbed in activities that model behavior normally inaccessible to them until adulthood.

The theory of cultural models fits with what we are beginning to understand about the learning process in young children. There were adumbrations of this theory in the work of Maria Montessori when she made didactic models that held the interest of small children sometimes for hours. The theory also fits well with what ethologists have learned about imprinting periods or critical stages—stages when animals are best able to learn certain types of behavior if the environment offers the necessary learning stimulus (23). Such periods undoubtedly occur for humans ("sensitive periods" Montessori called them in her work with children), but in humans they are more diffused. Also, if the sensitive period is passed without receipt of the necessary stimulation from models or from the patterned behavior of others, the consequences are less drastic or irreversible for humans than for animals. Man's ability to learn a second language is the most obvious example.

Model addiction, as described by Roberts and Sutton-Smith, suggests that in some people a blocking process in pattern learning has occurred, so that these people need many repetitions of the learning cycle, whereas others need relatively few repetitions. If the theory of cultural models is valid, one would expect that the frequency with which a folk tale is repeated, the frequency with which its elements are repeated within the tale, and the degree of patterning of these elements indicate the importance of the topics treated in the folk tale to the people of the culture. One would also expect an effective culture to provide a large number of models that encapsulate culturally important behavior styles. It may even be possible to speak of the vitality or richness of a culture in terms of the number and quality of its models.

THE MODEL-TEMPLATE CYCLE

While work on the theory of cultural models has so far dealt primarily with the psychological effects of deep involvement in the model, with the extent to which models are used in different cultures, and with the antecedent variables making for high model addiction, the theory has wider implications for the production of models and the formation of cognitive templates as well. One might assume that the hypothesized templates are formed through the individual's involvement with a model in much the same way that, in children, linguistic patterns are unconsciously learned from speech. The process could be as follows. Subliminal patterns are derived from observed behavior, or models. Templates and schemata are formed from these patterns. The schemata select the combination of templates necessary in a given context for guiding behavior in a meaningful way. The behavior, in turn, may then lead to the further production or perpetuation of models (Fig. 4).

The construction of cognitive templates is based both on subliminal perceptions of human life and on experience with the array of cultural models available. But the cultural models themselves, being patterned and "ready-made" in a coded, condensed form, are more likely to yield information on the nature of these templates than observations of actual behavior are, since behavior, being less highly structured, can be rearranged and interpreted more in line with personal inclination. The anthropologist's own cultural inclinations would thus be less likely to bias his description of a patterned model produced by another society than to bias his description of behavior in that society. It appears, therefore, that more valid results, with less interference from the anthropologist's own culture, are attainable from a study of cultural models than from a study of simple behavior sequences. If this proves to be the case, there can be far-reaching consequences for ethnographic investigations in the field, particularly those concerned with the collection of narratives and other native texts.

CONCLUSION

When we tell a story, is the way we tell it culturally determined? Is freedom only an illusion? A linguistic analogy suggests an answer: We are free to say anything we like, but if we wish to be understood, we have to follow the rules of our language when we say it. Artists, too, whether operating in a formalist tradition or at the very edge of new trends, are expressing their freedom and creativity within certain bounds, some of them culturally determined. These bounds are in no sense unconscious Freudian restraints, which should, if possible, be brought to the level of consciousness. They are entirely different. Edward Sapir was speaking of non-Freudian, culturally patterned constraints when he said (24), "It would seem that we act all the more securely for our unawareness of the patterns that control us."

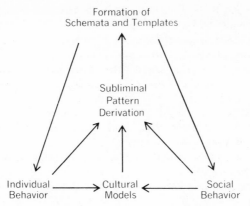

FIG. 4 *Schematic representation of the model-template cycle in which behavior and involvement with cultural models leads to derivation of a subliminal pattern. The subliminal pattern, in turn, leads to the formation of schemata and templates which are used in future behavior, and to the production and perpetuation of cultural models.*

While most structural studies in anthropology—usually of kin groupings and social organization—have been described in static terms, the structural study of narrative promises something more dynamic. Like language patterns, narrative patterns are concerned with sequences of behavior. Due to limitations in the capacity of the human brain, these sequences must necessarily be mentally encapsulated and organized, in ways we are far from understanding. Through study of the resulting patterns in cultural productions and models, such as folk tales, we hope to move in the direction of greater understanding.

REFERENCES

1. V. PROPP, "Morphology of the Folktale," L. Scott, Transl., *Indiana Univ. Res. Center in Anthropol., Folklore, and Linguistics, Bloomington, Publ. 10* (1958); C. Lévi-Strauss, in *Myth: A Symposium,* T. A. Sebeok, Ed. (Indiana University Press, Bloomington, 1956), pp. 428–444.
2. A connecting relative is the person through whom a relationship exists—for example, one's mother or father for a grandparent.
3. A. F. C. WALLACE, *Science, 135,* 351 (1962).
4. R. BENEDICT, *Patterns of Culture* (Houghton Mifflin, New York, 1934).
5. J. W. BENNETT, *Southwestern J. Anthropol., 2,* 361 (1946).
6. B. N. COLBY, *El Palacio, 70,* No. 4, 5, (1963).
7. W. H. GOODENOUGH, *Language, 32,* 195 (1956); F. G. Lounsbury, *ibid.,* p. 158; A. K. Romney and R. G. D'Andrade, in *Transcultural Studies in Cognition,* A.

K. Romney and R. G. D'Andrade, Eds. (American Anthropological Association, Washington, D. C., 1964), pp. 146-170.

8. C. O. FRAKE, *Amer. Anthropologist, 63,* 11 (1961).

9. H. C. CONKLIN, *Intern. J. Amer. Linguistics, 28,* 119 (1962).

10. E. H. LENENBERG & J. M. ROBERTS, "The Language of Experience: A Study in Methodology," *Intern. J. Amer. Linguistics Mem., 13,* (1956).

11. J. M. ROBERTS, *Amer. Anthropologist,* in press.

12. T. A. SEBEOK & F. J. INGEMANN, *Studies in Cheremis: The Supernatural* (Wenner-Gren Foundation, New York, 1956); B. N. Colby, *Akten Intern. Amerikanisten Kong., 34, wien* (1960), p. 670.

13. E. Z. VOGT & R. HYMAN, *Water Witching, U. S. A.* (University of Chicago Press, Chicago, 1959).

14. H. HOFFMANN, *Behavioral Sci., 4,* 288 (1959); P. Kay, *Amer. Anthropologist, 65,* 1027 (1963).

15. D. METZGER & G. E. WILLIAMS, *Amer. Anthropoligist, 65,* 1076 (1963).

16. This technique was first worked out in a study of Thematic Apperception Test protocols for the Navajo and Zuni cultures (B. N. Colby, *Amer. Anthropologist,* in press). Because the technique requires a special keypunching of the original data and samples consisting of at least 30,000 words, the work on which the results reported here are based was limited to two cultures—Eskimo and Japanese. Brief inspection of other folk tales, however, supports the assumption that patterns occur in the folk tales of other cultures as well.

17. R. F. SPENCER, "*The North Alaskan Eskimo, A Study in Ecology and Society,*" *Smithsonian Inst. Bur. Amer. Ethnol. Bull. 171* (1959), pp. 383-439; K. Seki, Ed., *Folktales of Japan,* R. J. Adams, Transl. (University of Chicago Press, Chicago, 1963). For those who are concerned about problems of translation in studies such as those reported here, see B. N. Colby, *Amer. Anthropologist,* in press.

18. J. M. ROBERTS, B. SUTTON-SMITH, & A. KENDON, *J. Social Psychol., 61,* 185 (1963).

19. In the Eskimo tales a secondary pattern of sentences dealing with direction in terms of line of sight, pointing, or travel route has the same shape as pattern 9E of Fig. 1.

20. More detailed analyses and discussion of the results will be found in forthcoming publications: B. N. Colby, "*Studying Eskimo Folktales by Computer*" (Museum of New Mexico Press, Sante Fe, in press); _____, "*World View and Values in Japanese Folktakes,*" in preparation; _____, and Chien-Pai Han, "*The Content Analysis of Anthropological Texts,*" in preparation.

21. J. M. ROBERTS & B. SUTTON-SMITH, *Ethnology 1.* 166 (1962); _____, and A. Kendon, *J. Social Psychol. 61,* 195 (1963); B. Sutton-Smith, J. M. Roberts, R. M. Kozelka, *ibid., 60,* 15 (1963).

22. J. M. ROBERTS, in *Explorations in Cultural Anthropology,* W. H. Goodenough, Ed. (McGraw-Hill, New York, 1964), pp. 433-454.

23. E. H. HESS, *Science 146,* 1128 (1964.)

24. E. J. SAPIR, in *Selected Writings of Edward Sapir,* D. G. Mendelbaum, Ed. (University of California Press, Berkely, 1951), p. 549.

25. The research reported here was supported in part by NIH research grant MH 08854–01. It was made possible by the General Inquirer System of content analysis (see P. J. Stone et al., "The General Inquirer." M.I.T. Press, in press). I especially thank Phillip J. Stone of the Harvard Laboratory of Social Relations, who programmed my dictionary of conceptual categories (the "Santa Fe Dictionary") for the General Inquirer System and whose interest and time spent on seeing the data through the computer in the initial runs made all the difference between success and failure in the research. I also thank Marshall Smith for his helpful statistical advice and for the use of his statistical programs. Chien-Pai Han for making the statistical analysis, and Donald Eid and James Toler of the Albuquerque Public School Data Processing Center for allowing me to use their 1401 computer.

5

THE PREDICTION
OF INTERPERSONAL
ATTRACTION[1]
THEODORE M. NEWCOMB

One of the points we have made about social interaction and
cognitive organization is that people who are alike in their constructs
will be attractive to one another. This principle, in the light of our
previously developed motivational position, can be considered a case of
two persons inducing in each other an optimal amount of arousal as a
result of providing reciprocal, continuous confirmation of each other's
construct system. There are other theoretical descriptions of the
motivation for personal attraction. One could argue, for example, that
people like each other because they supply each other with a maximum
gratification of each other's "primary biological needs." Newcomb
analyzes various ways to approach the issue of how interpersonal
attraction is engendered, and states that "insofar as communication
results in the perception of increased similarity of attitude toward
important and relevant objects, it will also be followed by an increase in
positive attraction."

*   *   *

During the past 30 years, according to my estimate, 9,426 articles and
books, plus or minus 2,712, have been published in English on the topic of
"attitudes." A large proportion of them deal with attitudes toward people—
most commonly toward family members, toward categories like ethnic,
religious, or occupational groups, or toward prominent individuals like
Franklin D. Roosevelt or Adolf Hitler. At the level of psychological

Reprinted from American Psychologist, *1956, 11, 575–586, by permission of the author and*
the American Psychological Association.
[1]Address of the President at the Sixty-Fourth Annual Convention of the American
Psychological Association, Chicago, Illinois, September 2, 1956.

generalization, such studies have probably taught us more about the organization of individual personality, and about group influences upon individual motivation and cognition, than about the nature of person-to-person relationships. At any rate, it seems appropriate to pose the question whether persons, as objects of attitudes, have properties that distinguish them from other classes of objects. If so, it is possible that the determinants of attitudes toward persons are in some respects different from those of other attitudes. Since it is convenient to have a distinctive label for something that one wishes to keep distinct, I shall use the term "attraction" to refer to attitudes toward persons as a class of objects.

Today I shall be primarily (though not exclusively) concerned with the motivational-affective aspects of attraction. Though I shall be referring mostly to its simpler manifestations—like choosing to spend time with a person, or expressing a generally favorable attitude toward him—I want to note, in passing, that there are several dimensions of attraction which are operationally distinctive and (to me, at any rate) conceptually necessary. Though I shall not stop to label these dimensions, what they all have in common is degree and direction on an approach-avoidance continuum, together with associated cognitive content.

I think it not much of an exaggeration to say that there exists no very adequate theory of interpersonal attraction. It has often seemed to me that even we psychologists, who like to pride ourselves in recognizing that nothing occurs apart from its necessary and sufficient conditions, have come very close to treating the phenomena of personal attraction as an exception to the general rule. It is almost as if we, like our lay contemporaries, assumed that in this special area the psychological wind bloweth where it listeth, and that the matter is altogether too ineffable, and almost passeth even psychological understanding.

I hope you will regard this last comment as being in part, but not *in toto,* a rhetorical exaggeration. The fact is, of course, that both theoretical and empirical efforts have been devoted to the problem. To some of these I now turn.

Perhaps the simplest—and, in many ways, still the most convincing—of the notions concerning determinants of positive attraction is that of *propinquity*. In its baldest form, the proposition of propinquity reads as follows: other things equal, people are most likely to be attracted toward those in close contact with them. Everyday illustrations readily leap to mind. Adults generally have strongest attraction toward those children, and children toward those adults, with whom they are in most immediate contact—which is to say, their own children and their own parents. And this commonly occurs, let me remind you, in spite of the fact that neither parents nor children choose each other. Or, if we are willing to accept the fact of selection of marriage partners as an index of positive attraction, then the available data are strongly in support of a theory of propinquity. If we use an adequate range of distance—miles, or city blocks rather than yards, or within-block distances—there is a neat, monotonic relationship between residential propinquity and probability of marriage, other criteria of eligibility being held constant (e.g., 1, 2, 3).

It is, of course, a truism that distance per se will have no consequences for attraction; what we are concerned with is something that is made possible, or more likely, with decreasing distance. I think we may also consider it a truism that that something is behavior. Further, it is behavior on the part of one person that is observed and responded to by another: it is interaction. So widespread and so compelling is the evidence for the relationship between frequency of interaction and positive attraction that Homans (9) has ventured to hypothesize that "If the frequency of interaction between two or more persons increases, the degree of their liking for one another will increase." Actuarially speaking, the evidence is altogether overwhelming that, *ignoring other variables,* the proposition is correct in a wide range of situations.

Why should this be so? Accepting the proposition only in an actuarial sense, and ignoring for the moment the other variables obviously involved, what theoretical considerations will enable us to make psychological sense out of it? The principle which comes first to mind is that of *reward and reinforcement.* Two simple assumptions will enable us to make direct use of this principle: first, that when persons interact, the reward-punishment ratio is more often such as to be reinforcing than extinguishing; and second, that the on-the-whole rewarding effects of interaction are most apt to be obtained from those with whom one interacts frequently. These assumptions, together with the principles of reward and reinforcement and canalization, would account for the general association of frequency of interaction with positive attraction; they would not, of course, account for the many observed exceptions to my generalization.

To return to my earlier illustrations, this set of assumptions and principles would not apply in exactly the same way to the facts of attraction between parents and children and to the facts of marital selection. One difference, of course, is that selection is possible in the latter but not in the former case. As applied to the facts of parent-child attraction, the principle of propinquity asserts, in effect, that we are attracted to those whom "fate" has made rewarding. As applied to the facts of marital selection, the principle of propinquity says little more, in addition to this, than that the likelihood of being rewarded by interaction varies with opportunity for interaction. The problem of selection, among those with whom opportunity for interaction is the same, still remains.

The principle of *generalization* has often been called upon to account for selective attraction among those with whom opportunities for interaction are the same. Many Freudians, in particular, have assumed that in adolescence or adulthood attractions are largely determined by personal qualities resembling those of parents or siblings, initially determined by the Oedipus configuration—as illustrated by the old refrain, "I want a girl just like the girl that married dear old Dad." This principle, together with its variants, obviously cannot be omitted from a complete theory of interpersonal attraction, but neither can it be considered as a major contribution to it, since, in itself, it says nothing about the initial basis of attraction but only about extensions from one already attractive person to another, similar one. Perhaps the chief contribution of the principle of generalization lies in the enhanced probability that thresholds for interaction with persons resembling those toward whom one is already attracted are lower than for other persons; if so, then the likelihood of the rewards of interaction with such persons is greater than for other persons.

There is an interesting consequence of the proposition that attraction toward others varies with the frequency of being rewarded by them. Opportunities for being rewarded by others vary not only with propinquity, as determined by irrelevant considerations like birth and residence, but also with the motivations of the potentially rewarding persons. This suggests that the likelihood of being continually rewarded by a given person varies with the frequency with which that person is in turn rewarded, and thus we have a proposition of *reciprocal reward:* the likelihood of receiving rewards from a given person, over time, varies with the frequency of rewarding him. This proposition is significant for my problem in various ways, especially because it forces further consideration of the conditions under which continued interaction between the same persons is most likely, and under which, therefore, the possibilities of continued reciprocal reward are greatest.

The first of these may be most simply described as the possession by two or more persons of common interests, apart from themselves, that require interdependent behavior. If you like to play piano duets, or tennis, you are apt to be rewarded by those who make it possible for you to do so, and at the same time you are apt to reward your partner. Insofar as both partners are rewarded, another evening of duets or another set of tennis is likely to ensue, together with still further opportunities for reciprocal reward. Thus attraction breeds attraction.

The second condition favorable to continued reciprocal rewards has to do with complementary interests (rather than with similar ones) that require interdependent behavior. These are symbiotic relationships, like that in which cow and cowbird become attracted to each other: the cow provides sustenance for the bird in the form of parasitic insects, the removal of which is rewarding to both. Or, at the human level, consider the exchange of gratifications between a pair of lovers. Here, too, under conditions of complementary rather than of similar motivations, the general rule is that attraction breeds attraction.

There have also been interesting attempts, of late, to test the proposition that symbiotic personality needs tend to characterize marriage partners—who, it may be presumed, are reciprocally attracted to a greater than average degree. Professor E. L. Kelly's work, some of which was reported on this occasion one year ago (11), has quite consistently revealed the existence of similar rather than complementary traits, both among spouses twenty-odd years married and among engaged couples. It is interesting, however, that his findings since last year suggest a curvilinear relationship between initial homogeneity and marriage durability; the best prognosis is provided by neither too much nor too little similarity. These findings, however, are not conclusive for my present problem—first because there are many determinants of marriage durability other than personal attraction; and second, because comparatively few of the traits that he measured were such as could either confirm or disconfirm the hypothesis of personality symbiosis.

This problem, has, however, been directly attacked by Professor Robert Winch, using measures derived from Murray's list of needs. My own perusal of his research reports (17, 18) suggests no conclusive findings for my problem, but if his personality ratings are free from contamination it seems clear that, within his sample of 25 middle-class couples, traits or needs can be found with regard to which spouses are more likely to be different than alike—in particular a dimension labeled "assertive-receptive." It is not possible, from Winch's data (nor from any other data known to me), to estimate how much of the variance in marital selection can be accounted for in terms of symbiotic personality needs. But it is surely a plausible notion that an individual with strong needs for assertiveness is more likely to find himself rewarded in this area of his life by interaction with a person who is receptive to his assertiveness than with one who is not.

The most detailed of the analyses of sociometric structures, especially those of Jennings (10), reveal analogous kinds of personality symbiosis; the over-chosen need the under-chosen, and vice versa. Many of the phenomena of choosing and accepting "leaders" (cf. 7) are also understandable from this point of view.

There is another common notion about interpersonal attraction, to the effect that it varies with similarity, as such: birds of a feather flock together. It is not a very useful notion, however, because it is indiscriminate. We have neither good reason nor good evidence for believing that persons of similar blood types, for example, or persons whose surnames have the same numbers of letters, are especially attracted to one another. The answer to the question, Similarity with respect to what?, is enormously complex—because similarities of many kinds are associated with sheer contiguity, for one thing. I shall therefore content myself with the guess (for which fairly good evidence exists[2]) that the possession of similar characteristics predisposes individuals to be attracted to each other to the degree that those characteristics are both observable and valued by those who observe them—in short, insofar as they provide a basis for similarity of attitudes.

Up to this point I have noted that we acquire favorable or unfavorable attitudes toward persons as we are rewarded or punished by them, and that the principles of contiguity, of reciprocal reward, and of complementarity have to do with the conditions under which rewards are most probable. From now on I shall be primarily concerned with a special subclass of reciprocal rewards—those associated with communicative behavior.

The interaction processes through which reciprocal reward occurs have to do not with the exchange of energy but with the exchange of information, and are therefore communicative. I prefer the term "communicative behavior" to "social interaction" because it calls attention to certain consequences that are characteristic of information exchange, but not of energy exchange, among symbol-using humans. The use of symbols, needless to say, involves the expenditure of energy, but—even in so obvious an example as that of receiving a slap in the face—it is the consequences of the information exchange rather than the energy exchange which interest us, as psychologists.

I shall note two of these consequences, in the form of very general propositions—though each of them is in fact subject to very specific limitations. The first is this: Communicators tend to become more similar to each other, at least momentarily, in one or more respects, than they were before the communication. At the very least (assuming more or less accurate receipt of a message that has been intentionally sent), both sender and receiver now have the information that the sender wishes to call the attention of the receiver to the object of communication—i.e., that which the symbols symbolize. If we stipulate still further conditions, the proposition will apply to a wider range of similarity. Suppose, for example, that a person has just expressed an opinion about something—say the United Nations; to the degree that he is sincere, and insofar as the receiver trusts his sincerity, the communication (if accurately received) will be followed by increased cognitive similarity, to the effect that the transmitter holds the stated opinion. Now suppose we add a further stipulation—that the receiver not only trusts the sender's sincerity but also respects his knowledgeability; under these conditions the opinions of sender and receiver are likely to be more similar than they were before.

[2]Such evidence will be presented in my forthcoming monograph.

It is this last kind of similarity—i.e., that of attitudes—that has a special importance for the problem of interpersonal attraction. In fact, the proposition, as applied to similarity of attitudes toward objects of communication, has already introduced, as independent variables, certain dimensions of attraction—namely, trust and respect. Change toward similarity in one kind of attitude following communication, I have asserted, varies with another kind of attitude—i.e., attraction.

My second proposition reverses this relationship: Attraction toward a co-communicator (actual or potential) varies with perceived similarity of attitudes toward the object of communication. Before specifying the limited conditions under which this proposition applies, let me briefly present its rationale.

While there are, of course, many exceptions, it is a highly dependable generalization that the life history of every human has made accurate communication rewarding far more often than punishing. Such is our dependence upon one another, from the very beginnings of communicative experience, and such is our indebtedness to culture, which is transmitted via communication, that success in the enterprise of becoming socialized depends upon success in transmitting and receiving messages. Insofar as accurate communication is in fact rewarding, reward value will attach to the co-communicator—which is to say that positive attraction toward him will increase (other things equal) with frequency of accurate communication with him. Please note the qualification: "insofar as accurate communication is in fact rewarding"; there are many messages— e.g., "I hate you"—the accurate receipt of which is not in fact rewarding.

If, as I have maintained, increased similarity in some degree and manner is the regular accompaniment of accurate communication, it would be no surprise to discover that increased similarity becomes a goal of communication, and that its achievement is rewarding. And if, as I have also maintained, the reward value of successful communication attaches to the co-communicator, then it follows that the two kinds of reward effects— perception of increased similarity as rewarding, and perception of the co- communicator as rewarding—should vary together. This, in brief, is the rationale of my second proposition.

It is, however, a very general statement, and its usefulness can be enhanced by a further specification of conditions. I shall mention only two of them. First, the discovery of increased similarity is rewarding to the degree that the object with regard to which there is similarity of attitudes is valued (either negatively or positively). The discovery of agreement between oneself and a new acquaintance regarding some matter of only casual interest will probably be less rewarding than the discovery of agreement concerning one's own pet prejudices. The reward value of increased similarity increases, secondly, with the common relevance of the attitude object to the communicators. The success of a certain presidential candidate, for example, is likely to be seen as having consequences for both, whereas matters regarded as belonging in the area of personal taste—like taking cream in one's coffee—are viewed as devoid of common consequences. The discovery of similarity of the latter kind is not very likely to have much reward value.

The thesis that interpersonal attraction varies with perceived similarity in regard to objects of importance and of common relevance is, from one point of view, opposed to the thesis of complementarity. In my own view, however, they are not in opposition; indeed, I regard the thesis of complementarity as a special case of similarity. Let me illustrate. Suppose, as Winch's data may indicate, that an assertive person is more likely to be attracted toward a receptive than toward another assertive person, as a marriage partner. It is my guess that this would most probably occur if they have similar attitudes to the effect that one of them should be assertive and the other receptive. (Whether or not they use these words—and whether, indeed, they are able to verbalize the matter at all—does not matter.) In short, I am attempting to defend the thesis that interpersonal attraction always and necessarily varies with perceived similarity regarding important and relevant objects (including the persons themselves). While I regard similarity of attitudes as a necessary rather than a sufficient condition, I believe that it accounts for more of the variance in interpersonal attraction than does any other single variable.

As the foregoing implies, and as I have elsewhere suggested (13), attraction and perceived similarity of attitude tend to maintain a constant relationship because each of them is sensitive to changes in the other. If newly received information about another person leads to increased or decreased attraction toward him, appropriate changes in perceived similarity readily ensue—often at the cost of accuracy. And if new information—either about the object or about another person's attitudes toward it—leads to perceptions of increased or decreased similarity with him, then the direction or the degree of attraction toward him easily accommodates itself to the situation as newly perceived. Change in attraction is one, but only one, of the devices by which some sort of tension state, associated with perceived discrepancy about important and relevant objects, is kept at a minimum.

At the outset, I raised the question whether persons, as objects of attitudes have properties that distinguish them from other objects. I ought now to acknowledge that I have already assumed that they do. I have been assuming that persons, as *objects* of attitudes, also *have* attitudes of their own—and, in particular, that they have (or can have) attitudes toward the *same* objects as do persons who are sources of attitudes toward the object-persons. Further, I have been assuming that object-persons have the same capacities for being disturbed by perceived discrepancies as do those who are attracted toward them. In degree, if not *in toto,* these are distinctively human characteristics, as G. H. Mead long ago noted (12), and any theory of interpersonal attraction that is at all distinctive from a general theory of attitudes must, I believe, pay homage to this fact.

The remainder of this paper is devoted to some tests of specific predictions derived from the two propositions already presented, which may be telescoped as follows: Insofar as communication results in the perception of increased similarity of attitude toward important and relevant objects, it will also be followed by an increase in positive attraction. I shall therefore consider perceived similarity of attitude as a predictor of attraction. I shall also, for obvious reasons, be interested in actual, or objective, similarity.

Since the findings which I shall present were obtained in a single research setting, I shall stop briefly to note the nature of that setting. I started with the research objective of observing the changing interrelationships, over time, between attraction and similarity of attitudes. Since it seemed important to start with a base line of zero, as far as attraction was concerned, it was necessary to find a population of persons who were complete strangers to each other. It also seemed desirable to provide a setting in which it would be possible for a high degree of positive attraction to develop, and in which regular and repeated observations could be made. All of these requirements seemed to be met by the following arrangements. A student house was rented; male transfer students, all strangers to the University of Michigan, were offered the opportunity (several weeks before their planned arrival at the University) of receiving free room rent for a full semester; in return they were to spend four or five hours a week in responding to questionnaires and interviews, and in participating in experiments. Among those who submitted applications to live in the house under these conditions, 17 (the capacity of the house) were selected, no two of whom had ever lived in the same city, nor attended the same school. All 17 men arrived within a 24-hour period, and all responded to a questionnaire within a very few hours thereafter. The men were given no voice in the selection of roommates, but (within the limits of University regulations) they were given complete freedom to conduct the house, including the cooking and eating arrangements, as they chose. The entire procedure was repeated, with a different but strictly comparable group, one year later. So far however, the data have not been very fully analyzed, and unless otherwise noted the findings that I shall report are from the second year only.

In this setting, data were obtained by questionnaire and interview, at semi-weekly intervals. A wide range of attitude responses was obtained, as well as rather complete data concerning interpersonal attraction. Measures of the latter were derived both from responses to direct questions about how favorably each house member felt toward each of the others, and from reports by each about informal, freely associating subgroups of two or more. It turned out that there were some important differences between these two measures of attraction. The "General Liking" responses (as we labeled the former) were the more amenable to parametric measurement, and unless otherwise specified those findings that I shall mention here depend upon this measure. But the "clique" measure (as we came to call it) was probably the more valid index of attraction for the purpose of testing many of our hypotheses, since it was based upon the reports of many observers having constant opportunity to notice who spent most time, and therefore had most opportunity for communication, with whom. The General Liking measure was probably the more sensitive toward the negative pole of attraction, since a full sixth of all pairs received zero scores on the other measure; but toward the positive pole it was often a more valid index of "admiration at a distance" than of direct contact and communication.

I turn now to some specific predictions. First, if the basic generalization is correct, it should follow that, regardless of the content of communication, positive attraction will increase with opportunity for communication, other things equal. The only additional assumption involved in this prediction is that the likelihood of being rewarded by a co-communicator increases with opportunity for communication. I might add that there is nothing new about this prediction; it is, in fact, a restatement of our old friend, the principle of propinquity. Previous studies—e.g., by Festinger, Schachter, and Back (5) and by Deutsch and Collins (4)—have provided convincing support for it.

Our own data give partial, but not complete, support for the prediction. Perhaps the best illustration of our findings that I can offer stems from an experimental "failure." During our first project year, roommate assignments had, literally, been drawn from a hat. In planning for the second year, however, we decided to assign roommates by experimental criteria. Half of the roommate combinations were therefore assigned in such manner as to insure (as we thought) that *minimal* attraction between roommates would result, and *maximal* attraction in the other half of the combinations. (Our assignments were based upon data provided by mail, some weeks before the men arrived.) Our predictions received no support whatever; from the very beginning, and during each of the succeeding 15 weeks, the mean level of attraction between roommates—including those for whom we had predicted low attraction—was higher than for all non-roommate pairs. It is also worth reporting that, at the beginning but not at the end of the semester, mean attraction among all pairs living on each of the two floors of the house was higher than for all inter-floor pairs. During the final week, 90 per cent of all inter-roommate choices were in the upper three-eighths of all choices.

These findings, as I have said, were obtained during our second year. Now I must report that, during the first year, the relationship between attraction and room propinquity was nothing like so close. I shall not stop to give you the actual figures, but at the end of the semester inter-roommate attraction was only slightly higher than that between non-roommates. This inconsistency would be frustrating, indeed, if there were no other variables to which the differences could be related; after describing these other variables, I shall show that they account for much of this inconsistency with regard to proximity. Meanwhile, the proposition under consideration is that proximity, alone, cannot account for attraction, but only to the degree that it facilitates the development of perceived similarity of attitude does it contribute to attraction.

The remainder of my predictions, unlike the first, take into account the content of communication. They are of the following general form: If and when increased attraction between pairs of persons does occur with opportunity for communication, it will be associated with increased similarity of attitude toward important and relevant objects.

The first of these predictions is based upon the additional assumption that one's self is a valued object to oneself. If so, then attraction should vary closely with self-other agreement about oneself. More specifically, insofar as a person's presumably ambivalent self-orientations are predominantly positive, his attraction toward others will vary directly with their attraction toward him. In testing this proposition, reciprocal attraction may be treated either as "objective" (i.e., as actually expressed by others toward the individual being considered) or as "perceived" (i.e., as that individual estimates that others will express attraction toward himself). The latter prediction, however—that one's attraction toward others varies with their perceived attraction seems almost untestable except in circular fashion; there are few ways in which it can be demonstrated in a "natural" situation, that attraction toward others is the dependent variable and that perceived attraction toward oneself the independent variable.

Whatever the causal direction, our data show that an individual's distribution of General Liking among his associates is realted to their liking for him. The relationship is almost as close on the fourth day as at the end of the fourth month, and as a general tendency is highly significant, though there are individual exceptions. One can predict an individual's liking for another individual with much better than chance accuracy if one knows the latter's liking for the former, at any time after the fourth day.

The prediction will be a good deal more accurate, however, if it is made from an individual's *estimate* of how well he is liked by the other. At any time from the second week on (when such estimates were first made), about three of every four estimates of another person's liking for oneself were in the same half of the distribution as own liking for that other person. Median rank-order correlations were .86 at the end, and .75 at the beginning, between each man's liking for each other man and his estimate of the reciprocals. As might be expected, this relationship was especially close at the extremes; 5 out of 6 predictions of liking for other persons would be in the correct quarter of the distribution, if based only upon subjects' estimates that they are in the highest or lowest quarter of reciprocated liking. Such findings correspond closely to those previously reported by Tagiuri (16).

Apparently the close relationship between General Liking and its estimated reciprocal is but slightly influenced by communication. At any rate, the relationship does not increase significantly from near-strangership to close acquaintance, nor is the relationship significantly closer for roommates, at the end of the four-month period, than for nonroommates. Neither, as a matter of fact, does accuracy in estimating reciprocal liking increase with further acquaintance, for most subjects. Estimates of others' liking for oneself are so closely correlated with own liking for those same persons (the relationship approaches the self-correlation of either measure, at any given time), that most of the variance of either can be accounted for by the other. Whatever influences either of them influences both in about the same way.

These facts—that perceived reciprocation remains closely tied to own liking without increasing in accuracy over time—do not mean that estimated reciprocation is purely autistic. On the contrary, it tends to be quite accurate, differing from chance distributions at beyond the .001 level. Two of every three estimates, at all times, are in the correct half. What these facts do mean, apparently, is that both attraction toward others and its estimated reciprocal are jointly determined by autistic and by "realistic" factors, in such manner as to remain closely bound together in a relationship that does not change over time. I believe that a clue to the manner of interaction between autistic and "realistic" influences is provided by the following additional fact. Without exception, the men whose liking status rose with time either became more accurate in their estimates of reciprocation or maintained the earlier degree of accuracy, while those whose status declined tended to become less accurate. Our subjects had no difficulty in adapting, realistically, to the fact of rising sociometric status, but acceptance of declining status was only partial. All subjects distributed about the same range of liking scores, but each tended to receive a distinctive distribution. Estimated reciprocals represent a compromise between own liking for the individual in question and *amour propre*.

The proposition that perceived similarity in valuing the self contributes heavily to variance in attraction, together with the assumption that self-valuation tends to remain high at all times, is thus well supported. All persons, at all times, are liked according as they are judged to agree with oneself about oneself. These judgments become more accurate over time to the degree that one's actual changes in status make it possible to judge them accurately and at the same time continue to believe that one's own likings are reciprocated. For those who are discovering that their actual status is relatively low, the conflict—or, more specifically, the strain of perceived discrepancy—thus aroused is reduced at the cost of accuracy.

I have already implied that attraction is hypothetically predictable from cognitive as well as from cathectic similarity regarding objects of importance. I shall present findings concerning cognitive similarity regarding only one kind of object—persons. Each subject was asked to describe himself as well as the other house members by checking adjectives drawn from a list prepared by Professor Harrison Gough (8). Each was also asked to describe his "ideal self," by using the same list, and to describe himself as he thought other house members would describe him. By comparing these responses with self-descriptions, we obtained measures of perceived similarity regarding the self. (This work closely parallels that by Fiedler [6] concerning "assumed similarity.")

Attraction turns out to be closely related to perceived agreement (at considerably less than the .001 level). When the same data are analyzed individually, only two of 17 subjects fail to show the relationship in the predicted direction, and only one of these reverses it. This finding is more impressive than it would be if it resulted from attributing only favorable judgments of oneself to high-liked others, and only unfavorable judgments to low-liked others. Actually, eight of the ten subjects who accepted unfavorable adjectives as describing themselves, and who indicated that one or more others agreed with them, showed more agreement in these unfavorable descriptions with high-liked than with low-liked others. The relationship between attraction and perceived agreement on favorable items is, not surprisingly, a good deal closer. At any rate, the finding that attraction varies with perceived cognitive agreement about the self is not merely an artifactual result of the common-sense assumption that one is attracted toward those who are believed to think well of one. Judging from our data, it is also true—and perhaps contrary to common sense—that we are attracted to those whom we perceive as seeing both our foibles and our virtues as we ourselves see them. Many psychotherapists, I am told,[3] can readily confirm this observation. I believe, by the way, that the patient's perception of converging attitudes toward himself, by himself and thera-

---

[3]Dr. Keith Sward, in particular, has called this to my attention.

pist, has much to do with the phenomena of positive attraction in "transference."[4]

My next prediction deals not with the self as object of attitudes but with other house members. Of all the objects about which we obtained responses, nothing compared in importance or in group relevance with the house members themselves. Very early they became differentiated in attraction status, so that it was easy to measure similarity, on the part of any pair of persons, in attraction toward the remaining members. Correlations were calculated between the attraction scores of each member and those of each other member (there were 136 such pairs, each year) toward all of the other 15 members; this was done for each of the 16 weeks that the group lived together. Thus the proposition could be tested that the greater the similarity between any two members in assigning General Liking scores to the other 15 members, the higher their attraction for each other. A related prediction is that this relationship will increase with communication—that is, with time.

Both propositions receive clear support, according to both criteria of attraction. On the fourth day the relationship between within-pair General Liking and within-pair correlation of General Liking for remaining members is barely significant, and only slightly higher a week later. It increases fairly steadily till, at the end of four months, two-thirds of all within-pair attractions would be correctly placed in the upper or lower half of the distribution, judging only from the fact of being in the upper or the lower half of the distribution of correlations. This finding emerges more clearly by comparing the mean within-pair correlations for various categories of within-pair attraction, as shown in Fig. 1.

Individuals in high agreement with each other about the other 15 house members clearly tend to be attracted to each other. The opposite tendency is much less pronounced; none of the categories involving subjects in the lower eight ranks has a mean correlation much below the average of the total set of pairs. The lowest of all the mean correlations (shown by the "X" in Fig. 1) is that of all pairs of which one member—and only one—is in the lowest quarter of attraction (ranks 13–16). For these 44 pairs the mean correlation is .35—not significantly different from zero. Thus, the correlations predict not only to within-pair attraction but also (particularly at the extremes) to interpersonal mutuality, regardless of level of attraction; the relationship between them, as calculated by X^2, is in fact significant at the .001 level.

Though it has, in general, proven easier to predict to high than to low

---

[4]Cf. Rogers, *15* (pp. 66–96) for empirical evidence to the effect that, in at least one case of successful psychotherapy, the correlation between the patient's self-sort and the therapist's description of the patient, by a sorting of the same items, increased over time. I do not know of other data on this point.

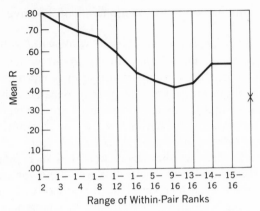

The x-axis label reads "Range of Within-Pair Ranks" with values:

1-2, 1-3, 1-4, 1-8, 1-12, 1-16, 5-16, 9-16, 13-16, 14-16, 15-16

The y-axis label reads "Mean R" with values .00 through .80.

FIG. 1 *Mean within-pair correlations of attraction toward other members.*

attraction, those lowest in our house totem pole deserve a paragraph. The lowest three in our second-year group were truly rejected (according to objective criteria which I cannot stop to specify); they were literally disliked as none others were. (The next lowest two, on the other hand, were near-isolates, who were withdrawn and more or less ignored but not generally disliked.) All six of the attraction responses given and received within this set of three rejects were among the lowest possible three ranks, their average being exactly 15, when 15.5 is the lowest possible average; they were liked by each other even less than others liked them. At the same time, the three intra-pair correlations among these three rejects are slightly above the average for the entire group of subjects, and .7 sigmas above the mean correlation for the same individuals with all others except the rejects themselves (.52 as compared with .39). In short, they disliked each other but tended to agree with each other about the remaining individuals more than they agreed with the remaining individuals. This, of course, is very perverse of them, and it is tempting to conclude that such wilful thwarting of my favorite hypotheses is all of a piece with their personalities, as rejected persons. I shall content myself, however, with suggesting that these three rejects developed a special set of standards: personal inoffensiveness in others was highly valued. If such standards did indeed exist, I believe they were developed by each of the three men in relative independence of the other two. They disliked each other too much to be very much influenced by each other. Some agreement as there was among them concerning the remaining men occurred, we know, without benefit of much communication, and it is well to be reminded that attitudinal similarity can occur on the part of individuals in the same predicament facing the same objective world, quite independently of one another's influence.

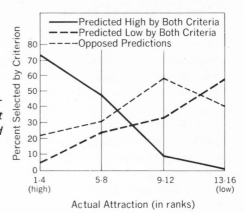

FIG. 2

Per cent of 256 attraction scores selected, at each of four levels, by joint criteria (estimated reciprocals and within-pair correlations).

Since these two predictors (estimated reciprocation and within-pair agreement) are far from perfectly correlated (their relationship is indicated by a contingency coefficient of .60), one may ask about their comparative and their combined predictive power. The statistical breakdowns will eventually be published, and so I shall not present them here. The fact is that if one merely wishes to pin-point the individual instances of high attraction, the estimated reciprocal, alone, is the most successful of all predictors; 97 per cent of the highest quarter of attractions are selected by the criterion of the upper half of the estimated reciprocals. But if one wishes to account for maximum variance, and at both ends of the distribution, the combined criteria are better than either alone. As indicated by a coefficient of contingency of .53 between the combined predictors and actual attraction scores, almost one-third of the variance in attraction is thus accounted for. As shown in Fig. 2, high attraction is particularly well predicted by the joint criteria; virtually none of those predicted as high are in fact in the lower half of attraction scores.

These findings, based upon small numbers, would be subject to much suspicion were they not perfectly consistent. Whether by very loose or by very restrictive criteria, the predicted relationships emerge; the more restrictive the criteria, the greater the excess over chance expectations.

At a theoretical level, I consider it highly significant that these two predictors, the combined effects of which are more successful than either alone, include one subjective index (estimates of reciprocal attraction) and one that is objective, in the sense of describing a relationship between a pair of persons and not referring to either person alone. Theoretically speaking, this is as it should be. Doubtless most forms of social behavior, like attraction, are jointly determined by individual characteristics and by relationships to others—relationships which pertain to the recipient of behavior quite as much as to the behaver himself.

Now let me return, briefly, to our finding that, in one year but not in the other, the mere fact of being a roommate accounted for much of the variance in the development of attraction. I have already implied that propinquity is a facilitator but not a sufficient condition for the development of positive attraction. It should follow, therefore, that attraction between roommates will be relatively high only insofar as their propinquity contributes to the development of one or more of the conditions favorable to high attraction. This is exactly what our data show: roommates scored much higher on both predictor variables during the second year than did non-roommates, but not during the first year.

As shown in Figs. 3 and 4, the year-to-year differences in the relationship between attraction and room proximity are paralleled by comparable differences in the relationship between proximity and one of the predictor variables, namely, within-pair correlation of attraction toward the other members. Roommates differ from all others by one full standard deviation at the end of the second year, but by only one-fifth of a standard deviation at the end of the first year. According to the other predictor variable, perceived reciprocality of liking, the differences are of exactly the same order, and the curves are correspondingly parallel.

It seems likely, therefore, that proximity contributes to attraction only by way of the predictor variables. As to why room proximity facilitated the development of the predictor variables in such a way as to lead to high roommate attraction in one year but not in the other, I can only say that I have some reason to believe that more detailed analysis will provide at least partial answers.

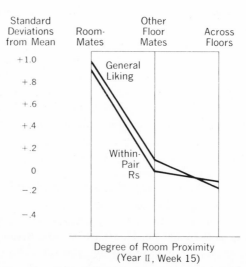

FIG. 3 *Deviation from means of general liking and of within-pair correlations of liking for other members, as related to room proximity.*

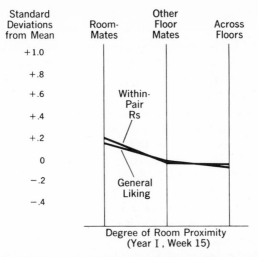

FIG. 4 *Deviation from means of general liking and of within-pair correlations of liking for other members, as related to room proximity.*

You are doubtless wondering about the generality of the proposition that attraction is predictable from similarity of attitude toward important and relevant objects, since the only objects that I have mentioned, so far, are persons. Although our analyses are far from complete, they indicate that the proposition also applies to objects other than persons, though at lower levels of confidence. But is already clear that, in this research setting, there were no objects which compared in relevance, *for all members,* to house members themselves. We sampled a range of attitudes that extended virtually from cabbages to kings; there were several pairs of subjects for whom kings (or at least presidents) were highly relevant, and there may have been some whose within-pair attraction was influenced by attitudes toward cole slaw. There were, however, no *single* non-person objects of sufficient relevance for *all* members to account for very much variance in the attraction level among all pairs.

One way of describing this complication is to note that our subjects knew so much about so many of each other's attitudes that no single one was crucial for all pairs. This predicament is well illustrated by a series of experimental findings. On several occasions, outsiders were brought in to present a point of view on a controversial topic; our subjects' General Liking for these speakers, about whom they knew nothing apart from the one topic, was (as predicted) closely correlated with perceived agreement with them. Perhaps the moral to this story is that, if one wants uncomplicated findings, one should stick to brief, laboratory-like, rather than to long-term, "natural," situations.

There were two ways in which we were able, nevertheless, to show relationships between attraction and similarity in attitude toward non-person objects. The first of these was by regarding highly generalized values as objects. For example, agreement in Allport-Vernon scores was related to attraction, for the total population of 136 pairs; the significance levels ranged from .05 to .01, depending upon the exact measures of each variable. If Osgood's three-dimensional measure of meaning structure (14) may be regarded as a highly generalized attitude, of both cognitive and cathectic nature, toward things-in-general, then the results of using this measure are also relevant. "Semantic harmony," derived from responses to a wide range of stimulus words (e.g., father, politics, sex, money), was significantly related to at least one of our measures of attraction, for all 136 pairs.

Our second approach was to take as an index of attitude similarity the *number* of non-person objects about which there was a given degree of similarity, rather than the *degree* of similarity regarding a single object. This index was related to attraction, for at least one of our two sets of subjects, though not, apparently, at significance levels below .05. This was one of the few measures, by the way, of pre-acquaintance similarity which successfully predicted, among all pairs, to later attraction. If, as appears to be the case, its predictive value tended to increase with time, this finding would be consistent with the assumption that, over time, our subjects tended to sort each other out as they gradually discovered one another's attitudes on a wide range of issues.

I have two brief and final comments concerning the significance of findings such as I have been presenting. First, as to the very limited setting in which they were obtained, there is no reason to believe that the particular students whom we happen to have studied differed very greatly from other groups of young-adult peers, in the kinds of relationships here reported, at comparable stages of acquaintance. Indeed, it is likely that the very fact of their homogeneity in regard to age and sex and student status tended to reduce the variance of many of their attitudes; if so, at least some of the predictors here reported would prove still more satisfactory with more varied groups. I feel, therefore, that I am not grossly over-extending the application of my own findings when I report, with considerable confidence, that the conditions under which attraction develops and changes or remains stable are orderly ones. It is possible, moreover, to formulate statements of these conditions into a consistent body of propositions.

Secondly, as to the common-sense nature of much that I have reported, none of you has been overcome with astonishment on learning, for example, that our subjects tended to like those by whom they thought they were liked, or by those who, they thought, would describe them in most favorable terms. My concern is not so much to point out that some of our findings are *un*expected—e.g., that perceived agreement with others concerning one's own *un*favorable traits is a reasonably good predictor of positive attraction. Nor is it to repeat the ancient truism that no one knows whether what every one knows is true is really true until it has been properly tested. Rather, I want to note that several different propositions (some conforming to common sense and some not), which superficially have nothing to do with one another, are derivable from the same set of assumptions.

The fact seems to be that one can predict to interpersonal attraction, under specified conditions, from frequency of interaction, from the perception of reciprocal attraction, from certain combinations of personality characteristics, and from attitudinal agreement. There is no self-evident reason why such diverse variables, viewed common-sense-wise, should belong together; one might almost suspect that they had been drawn out of a hatful of miscellaneous variables. But predictive propositions about those variables all flow, as I have tried to show, from a very few psychological assumptions. I believe the confluence to be both theoretically required and empirically supported. These considerations seem to me to lend confidence to the point of view that a limited theory about a limited class of objects—namely, persons—can profit by taking account of the significant properties of those objects, and in particular those properties closely related to the fact of human dependence upon communication.

You may remember an old story whose punch line is "Vive la différence"—Thank God for the little difference. If we are inclined to take a favorable view of positive interpersonal attraction, perhaps we should also be grateful for similarities: Vive la similarité!

REFERENCES

1. BOSSARD, J. H. S. Residential Propinquity as a Factor in Marriage Selection. *Amer. J. Sociol.,* 1932, *38,* 219–224.
2. CAMPBEL, W. D. The Importance of Occupation, as Compared with Age and residence, in Marital Selection. Unpublished Master's Thesis, University of Michigan, 1939.
3. DAVIE, M. R., & REEVES, R. J. Propinquity of Residence before Marriage. *Amer. J. Sociol.,* 1939, *44,* 510–517.
4. DEUTSCH, M., & COLLINS, M. E. *Interracial Housing: A Psychological Evaluation of a Social Experiment.* Minneapolis: University of Minnesota Press, 1951.
5. FESTINGER, L., SCHACHTER, S., & BACK, K. *Social Pressures in Informal Groups.* New York: Harper, 1950.
6. FIEDLER, F. Assumed Similarity Measures as Predictors of Team Effectiveness. *J. Abnorm. Soc. Psychol.,* 1954, *49,* 381–388.
7. GIBB, C. A. Leadership. In G. Lindzey (Ed.), *Handbook of Social Psychology.* Cambridge, Mass.: Addison-Wesley, 1954. Vol. II, pp. 877–920.

8. GOUGH, H. *Reference Handbook for the Gough Adjective Checklist.* Berkeley: Institute Personality Assessment and Research, University of California, 1955 (mimeographed).

9. HOMANS, G. C. *The Human Group.* New York: Harcourt Brace, 1950.

10. JENNINGS, HELEN H. *Leadership and Isolation.* (2nd Ed.) New York: Longmans, Green, 1950.

11. KELLY, E. L. Consistency of the adult personality. *Amer. Psychologist,* 1955, *10,* 659–681.

12. MEAD, G. H. *Mind, Self, and Society.* Chicago: University of Chicago Press, 1934.

13. NEWCOMB, T. M. An Approach to the Study of Communicative Acts. *Psychol. Rev.* 1953, *60,* 393–404.

14. OSGOOD, C. E. The Nature and Measurement of Meaning. *Psychol. Bull.,* 1952, *49,* 197–237.

15. ROGERS, C. R. *Studies in Client-Centered Psychotherapy.* III: The Case of Mrs. Oak. Washington: Psychological Service Center Press, 1951.

16. TAGIURI, R. Relational Analysis: An Extension of Sociometric Method with Emphasis upon Social Perception. *Sociometry,* 1952, *15,* 91–104.

17. WINCH, R. F., KTSANES, T., & KTSANES, VIRGINIA. Empirical Elaboration of the Theory of Complementary Needs in Mate-Selection. *J. Abnorm. Soc. Psychol.,* 1955, *51,* 508–513.

18. WINCH, R. F., & MORE, D. M. Quantitative Analysis of Qualitative Data in the Assessment of Motivation: Reliability, Congruence, and Validity. *Amer. J. Sociol.,* 1956, *61,* 445–452.

XI

COGNITIVE THEORY
AND
UNCONSCIOUS FUNCTION

1

OVERVIEW

Freud, in writing one of the first of the papers that established his fame as the originator of psychoanalysis, stated that, "The decidedness of my attitude on the subject of the unconscious is perhaps specially likely to cause offence, for I handle uncounscious ideas, unconscious trains of thought, and uncounscious emotional tendencies as though they were no less valid and unimpeachable psychological data than conscious ones" (Freud, 1950, p. 135). In his treatise on psychopathology in everyday life (Freud, 1951, p. 131), he discusses how he "unconsciously" arrived at what might have appeared to have been a randomly chosen number, the figure 2,467, as he wrote a letter to his friend. In the course of explaining his "unconscious" operations, he speaks of going through addition and subtraction exercises that would be something of a chore even if one had paper and pencil.

In a current text on clinical psychology Holzberg says, "one of the prime characteristics of projective techniques has been their purported sensitivity to motivation of which the subject was unaware and their ability to penetrate to levels of unawareness that had hitherto not been possible with other assessment devices" (Holzberg, 1966, p. 107). We can infer that these passages from Freud and Holzberg refer to *the unconscious,* an "active mind." They speak of "another place," where problems are solved, wishes are wished, and from where motives push the organism toward behavior. It is a subsidiary mind, one that seems to carry out the same kinds of functions that are carried out by the mind we "observe" as we go through our daily function. In this formulation, then, the organism has two "minds."

If nothing else, these statements about the unconscious tell us of the perplexities of trying to fathom some of the most mysterious aspects of human behavior. But then, the mysteries of unconscious functioning are a reflection of the obscuring mists that swirl about to confuse our understanding of any aspect of behavior. If, for example, we are forced to devise arcane concepts about the nature of "thought," then we will emerge with vague concepts about unconscious function. We might even argue that the concept of unconscious as a "place" was derived in order to give us a way of dismissing some of the confusions that surround the issues concerning the nature of thought.

Since the concept of "thought" is closely related to the issue of unconscious, we digress to consider some points that emerge in discussion of thinking and consciousness. In our culture it appears to be very difficult, no matter the level of sophistication of the speaker, to shed the concept that thought is somehow a matter of engaging in an active process of hearing, seeing, feeling, and so on, "inside of one's self." One is thinking when these internal representations are active, and when they are active one is "conscious" of them. We can agree that there are times when we go through whole processes of behavior wherein such internal representations of sound, sights, and pressures, are absent. Yet, the process we carried through was complex; and we are convinced that there must have been sensory input, otherwise the process would not have terminated successfully. In fact, it was necessary to have "made decisions" to carry out the process. How were these decisions made? Enter the concept of unconscious! How convenient it is to speak of the process being guided by "the other mind," the unconscious.

Dollard and Miller (1950) offer another kind of solution. Unconscious function is largely a matter of behavior that is carried through without verbal labels. They are careful not to state that unconscious refers only to nonverbalization, but nonverbalizability is the key feature of unconscious behavior. "According to our hypothesis, drives, cues, and responses that have never been labeled will necessarily be unconscious" (Dollard and Miller, 1950, p. 216). In their formulation of the development of neurosis, a person who is the victim of repression has been conditioned out of verbalizing matters that require attention. In psychotherapy, the "neurotic" must come to use the labels that apply to the troublesome issues. In a chapter whose title reflects their assumptions—*Labeling: Teaching the Patient to Think about New Topics*—Dollard and Miller speak of the necessity of having the neurotic overcome his "stupidity" so that through labeling, he "can represent this response in reasoning" (Dollard and Miller, 1950, p. 281). Once he has labeled his cues, drives, and responses, the person can subject them to the higher mental processes that earn the label of reasoning or thinking.

Dollard and Miller are not alone in this formulation. In psychology classes one can quickly find that most young adults in our culture will conceptualize thinking in terms of verbalization. One needs simply to ask students whether animals "think," and he will find that most students will say that they do not, because they are incapable of verbalizing. Verbalization, which is regarded as a uniquely human activity, also gives man the unique capacity to think.

A different view of "thinking" is suggested by writers who emphasize the individual's cognitive processes (Piaget, 1952; Bruner, Goodnow, and Austin, 1956; and Bartlett, 1958). Thinking in terms of a view derived from these writers is a matter of placing an event into a frame of reference. In short, thinking is a matter of instantiating a stimulus within the construct system that a person has available. Piaget's greatest value as a theorist has been to show that the most complex thought is the final product of an epigenetic process that grows from the infantile thought process of imposing *use* conceptualizations upon objects. Piaget's own words best convey the substance of his position: "On the other hand, the secondary schemata constitute the first outline of what will become 'classes' or concepts in reflective intelligence: perceiving an object as being something 'to shake,' 'to rub,' etc. This is, in effect, the functional equivalent of the operation of classification peculiar to conceptual thought" (Piaget, 1952, p. 183). Bruner, et al., suggest the use of a similar concept of thinking when, in their monograph on the subject, they indicate that they will concern themselves "with the 'attainment of concepts,' the behavior involved in using discriminable attributes of objects and events as a basis of anticipating their significant identity" (Bruner, et al., p. 21). They strive to clarify issues related to the process of developing concepts and placing events within those concepts.

The last representative of this group of theorists, Bartlett, makes the point that thinking can be regarded as a high level skill, analogous to the process of moving an object from one physical location to another (Bartlett, 1958). "In all such cases the operator's performance consists of a series of bodily movements with interspersed halts. For instance, in the simple case of picking up an object and transporting it to another assigned position, the hand stretches out, hovers, picks up, transports, hovers again, and finally sets the object down. The interesting thing is that the hovering, or halting, almost always occurs just when those points are reached at which it becomes necessary to pay attention to environmental characters such as the exact position, the size, shape, probable weight of the object, and in many cases the disposition in space of a number of objects relative one to another. That is to say, the stationary components of what may seem to be continuous skilled movements make their appearance when something that is novel, insofar as the movement is concerned, has to be *perceived,* when, therefore, central neurological processes of a more complex order than those which bring about the movements must come into play" (Bartlett, 1958, p. 17). "Paying attention" or "perceiving" is a part of the physical movement, and thought is a matter of carrying out the action in a smooth, skilled manner. A skilled performance is dependent on making decisions about distances, weights, muscular adjustments, and so on. In other terms, the person needs to fit a myriad of stimulus events into his constructions regarding the nature of space, weight, and muscle movement. His actions are a form of thinking. He "pays attention" at those times that an immediate instantiation of the stimulus event is not available.

Having accepted the assumption that the organism is constantly placing stimuli into frames of reference, we would be willing to say that the organism, no matter what its overt activity, is constantly thinking. If the stimuli can be immediately instantiated into a suitable frame of reference, and if arousal is maintained near an optimal level, we operate "unconsciously." Within this framework, the distinction between "consciousness" and "unconsciousness" is a distinction between a prolonged period of deviation from optimum arousal and the maintenance of optimum arousal. If we navigate our automobile over a familiar route, and if all the stimuli that come in to us are those that we have previously placed into a suitable frame of reference, then we will complete our trip "unconsciously." The presence of an unusual stimulus, one that cannot be slipped into a handy category, will arouse our attention, and we will become conscious of what is taking place. Such unconscious actions happen thousands of times each hour.

When we look across a large room and "unconsciously" calculate that the door at its other end is large enough to allow us to pass through it, we do so on the basis of applying a highly valid construct system. Consider the fact that the door occupies less space on our retina than does our own thumb. We would not assert that we can pass through a space the size of our thumb, but we have secure faith in the construction that we can pass through the door. Suppose that we were being victimized by a clever psychologist, one who arranged the visual field in a way that caused the "door" at the other end of the room to occupy the same retinal space no matter how closely we approach that door. As we advance toward the door, and as we come to doubt our initial instantiation of it as an exit, we will be sure to become conscious of that stimulus situation. In daily practice this artificially produced situation is unlikely to occur, so we develop an automatically applicable set of constructs that allow us to move toward and pass through "retinally small" doors "unconsciously."

This same principle can be applied to other areas of function. In a social situation where one "has confidence in himself," he is deftly able to instantiate his person in relation to the other people around him. His performance will be smooth and anxiety-free. Each response will reflect his smooth and immediate application of adopted roles, those which he is sure are roles that "define" him. The person who "lacks confidence" becomes "conscious" of everything he does. His self-consciousness is revealed as he bumbles through actions that reflect his flitting from one unpracticed role to another. His "self-assurance" will emerge when he can carry out his personal instantiation in an "unconscious" manner. Others will say, "He is being himself," indicating their recognition of his having adopted a satisfactory set of self-definitions which will emerge in continuous contacts. He "is not himself" when he casts about to "consciously" assume roles that he hopes will be viewed as valid roles.

The principle of "unconsciousness" as the immediate and facile application of well-developed construction systems is best demonstrated through visual perception experiments. In such studies we see subjects immediately carrying out instantiations that had previously been determined to be highly reliable. Such instantiations become practiced to the point where the subject can be led to make them even at times when the physical data can be demonstrated, through alternative criteria, to be incongruent with the instantiation that is made. If a situation is arranged in which two sets of well established constructions are placed into conflict with each other, subjects, as they try to resolve the situation, will frequently report considerable anxiety and discomfort. At the same time, they are often unable to verbalize the basis of this discomfort. Under these circumstances we can begin to understand why it is tempting to regard thinking within a context of verbalization. Verbalization does facilitate the manipulation of stimulus events, for, as Inhelder and Piaget (1958) argue, thinking by the manipulation of symbols is considerably more facile than thinking by manipulation of the internal representation of the concrete stimulus. Many of the spatial constructions we use simply do not have verbal representations, and when, for example, we are placed into situations that create spatial illusions, we are hard pressed to translate the illusory effect into verbal terms. The inability to derive a resolution of the incongruous elements can be confusing and arousing enough, as those who have been motion-sick will testify, to induce violent autonomic nervous system reactions.

Our major proposition is that an organism frequently instantiates complex stimuli by automatic processes. Since this happens as a regular occurrence, and since the instantiation is highly probably a "correct" instantiation, we do not experience a distracting level of arousal. We find the best research examples of the process of "unconscious operation" in studies relating to spatial orientations. The selections in this section are, then, basically studies of individuals making judgments of space.

REFERENCES

BARTLETT, F. C. *Thinking: An Experimental and Social Study.* New York: Basic Books, 1958.

BRUNER, J. S., GOODNOW, J. J., and AUSTIN, G. A. *A Study of Thinking.* New York: Wiley, 1956.

DOLLARD, J. & MILLER, N. *Personality and Psychotherapy.* New York: McGraw-Hill, 1950.

FREUD, S. Fragment of an Analysis of a Case of Hysteria. In E. Jones (Ed.), *Freud: Collected Papers.* London: Hogarth Press, 1950, *3,* 11–146.

FREUD, S. *Psychopathology of Everyday Life.* New York: New American Library, 1951.

HOLZBERG, J. D. Projective Techniques. In J. A. Berg and L. A. Pennington (Eds.), *An Introduction to Clinical Psychology.* New York: Ronald Press, 1966, pp. 106–153.

INHELDER, B. & PIAGET, J. *The Growth of Logical Thinking from Childhood to Adolescence.* New York: Basic Books, 1958.

PIAGET, J. *The Origins of Intelligence in Children.* New York: Int. University Press, 1952.

2
VISUAL PERCEPTION
AND THE ROTATING
TRAPEZOIDAL WINDOW
ADELBERT AMES

The work of the "transactionalists" in perception can be placed among the most imaginative in all of psychology. Their primary intent has been to demonstrate that perception represents a "transaction" between the observer's organizations and the stimulus event—that is, that the observer's organizations "determine" the nature of the event. Basically, their demonstrations seek to produce a stimulus event that will evoke a set of organizations which would ordinarily be effective in the interpretation of a daily event, but which are objectively "incorrect" in the contrived situation. For example, these researchers accept the premise that most of us, when viewing a common object that casts a retinally large image, will "assume" that the object is closer to the eye than is a similar object that casts a retinally small image. They then artificially produce a stimulus situation in which the common object casts a large retinal image. This can be done by making the stimulus objectively larger. Under the proper conditions a person can be led to treat the artificially retinally-large object as though it were close, despite the fact that it is a good distance away. This demonstration is one of the simpler manifestations of the subject-object transaction.

For our purposes at this point, we will highlight only one of the important issues that these demonstrations can illuminate. When subjects view the rotating trapezoid and are led to assume that it stops in its clockwise course to then reverse its direction, they are applying their already highly developed constructions about the nature of linear relationships in space. By "seeing" the trapezoid return in its course they are "making sense" of a stimulus configuration with which they have had years of experience. Yet, no subject will verbalize his

Reprinted from Psychological Monographs, *1951, 65 (Whole number 324), pp. 2–21, by permission of Mrs. Adelbert Ames, Jr. and the American Psychological Association. Parts of the article, several footnotes, and references have been omitted.*

conclusion that, "that was the only way to make sense of the situation." Even more dramatically, when subjects "see" the bar that is suspended within the window "dissolve" the mullions, they again "make sense" of the event without any verbalizable effort to do so. We would say that the instantiation of the event has taken place "unconsciously."

As an aside, referring to our general motivational concepts, it is noted that subjects who view the trapezoid with the suspended bar often report a noticeable anxiety at the point where there is a demand for coordinating the impressions of a counterclockwise rotation of the window while the bar continues its clockwise rotation. The "unconscious resolution" of the problem situation is achieved, and the motivating arousal is thereupon diminished.

*   *   *

DESCRIPTION OF APPARATUS

The apparatus used in this demonstration was designed to enable observers experiencing the demonstration to perceive certain characteristic alterations of visual phenomena that result from varying the trapezoidal form of a rotating window.[1]

A photograph of the appratus is shown in Fig. 1. It consists of the rectangular window (see RW) suspended by a vertical shaft S', which is driven by an electric motor M, which is attached to the ceiling. The trapezoidal window TW is suspended on the vertical shaft S^2, which is rigidly fixed to the bottom of the window RW. On this shaft there is a sleeve F with two lock nuts so that the two windows can be set at any desired angle relative to each other. All the altered appearances can be seen irrespective of the relative angles between the two windows, but comparisons of alteration in size are more easily made when they are set in the general relative position to each other shown in Fig. 2. When the motor is going, the rectangular window and the trapezoidal window rotate at the same speed about a common vertical axis. This arrangement enables the observer to compare the appearances of the two windows and note what alterations in his visual phenomena result from variation of the trapezoidal form of the rectangular window.

The speed of the motor M can be controlled by a rheostat. A convenient speed for most observations is around 3 to 6 rpm. It is also desirable to have a switch so that the motion of the windows can be stopped at any desired position

---

[1]The significance of what is disclosed in an empirical investigation primarily depends upon the nature of the factor the experimenter selects to vary. It therefore seems important to explain why it was decided to vary the trapezoidal form of a rectangular configuration and, also, why the particular variation of the trapezoidal form was adopted. As this explanation is of necessity lengthy and would unduly interrupt the description of the demonstration, it seems advisable to add it as an appendix.

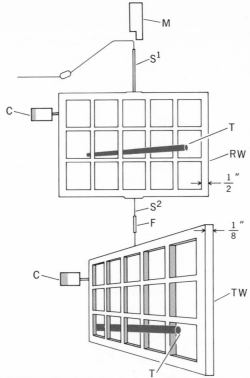

FIG. 1   *Line drawing of apparatus*
The surfaces of the rectangular window and the trapezoidal
window are in the same plane, which is perpendicular to the eye.
The dimensions of the rectangular window are: length, 23½";
height, 16½"; thickness, ¼"; width of mullions, ¼". The outside
dimensions of the trapezoidal window are: length, 19½"; height
of long side, 23 and 5/8"; height of short side, 12½"; thickness,
1/8".

of rotation. The direction of the rotation of the shaft *S* can be reversed by a
device on the motor controlled by a string pull.

Small cubes *C* and *C* are attached to the upper edge of the shorter side of the
trapezoidal window and in a corresponding position on the rectangular window,
and paper tubes *T* and *T* are attached in the middle of both windows so that
they extend out on both sides (see Fig. 1 and Chart I). The role these cubes and
tubes play will become evident later.

The dimensions of the two windows are given in the caption of Fig. 1. The
trapezoidal window is cut out of thin aluminum. Its particular dimensions were
arrived at as shown in Fig. 2. *AB* represents the three-dimensional rectangular
window tipped at an angle of 16½° to the line of sight of an observer at the
distance of 10 feet with the right-hand side farther away; *CD* represents a plane
tipped at an angle of 22° to the line of sight, with the right-hand side nearer

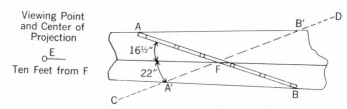

FIG. 2 *Plan showing design of the Trapezoidal Window*
AB represents the Rectangular Window set at an angle of 16½°
to the line of sight EF ten feet from the viewing point E. A'B'
represents the Trapezoidal Window which is a projection from E
of the Rectangular Window and its mullions on a plane CD
tipped 22° to the line of sight EF.

$A'B'$ represents the aluminum cut-out of the projection of the window AB on the plane CD.

The projections of the shadows cast on the actual window by an overhead light are painted on both sides of this trapezoidal cutout. The trapezoidal windows should be equally illuminated on both sides with low illumination in an otherwise dark room.

The alterations in visual phenomena that are related to the variation of the trapezoidal form of a window are empirically demonstrated by the differences between what observers with normal vision see when looking at the rotating rectangular window with its small cube and tube and when looking at the rotating trapezoidal window with its small cube and tube.

DESCRIPTION OF WHAT OBSERVERS EXPERIENCE
WHEN LOOKING AT THE ROTATING TRAPEZOIDAL
WINDOW AND APPENDED CUBE AND TUBE

The reader must realize that the phenomena disclosed by the demonstration can be comprehended only when they are personally experienced and that the following verbal and pictorial description of them can at best be only a second-hand communication. Moreover, the full significance of these phenomena can only be comprehended as they are related to other phenomena disclosed by the other demonstrations. However, described in general terms, all observers with normal vision, when looking at the rectangular window slowly rotating about a vertical axis, see a rectangular window of constant size and form at a constant distance rotating at a constant speed about a vertical axis, and the small cube and tube appear and move with it in an expected manner, and this holds irrespective of the

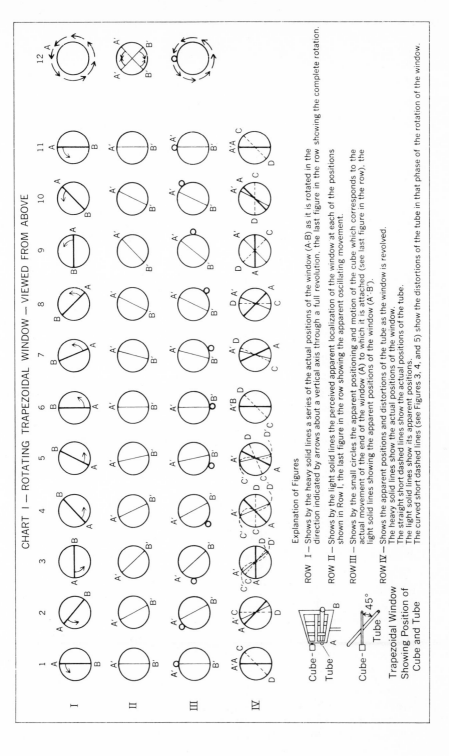

CHART I — ROTATING TRAPEZOIDAL WINDOW — VIEWED FROM ABOVE

Explanation of Figures

ROW I — Shows by the heavy solid lines a series of the actual positions of the window (A-B) as it is rotated in the direction indicated by arrows about a vertical axis through a full revolution, the last figure in the row showing the complete rotation.

ROW II — Shows by the light solid lines the perceived apparent localization of the window at each of the positions shown in Row I, the last figure in the row showing the apparent oscillating movement.

ROW III — Shows by the small circles the apparent positioning and motion of the cube which corresponds to the actual movement of the end of the window (A) to which it is attached (see last figure in the row), the light solid lines showing the apparent positions of the window (A'-B').

ROW IV — Shows the apparent positions and distortions of the tube as the window is revolved.
The heavy solid lines show the actual positions of the window.
The straight short dashed lines show the actual positions of the tube.
The light solid lines show its apparent positions.
The curved short dashed lines (see Figures 3, 4, and 5) show the distortions of the tube in that phase of the rotation of the window.

distance, direction, or elevation from which they look, or whether they use one eye or two.

On the other hand, described in general terms, observers with normal vision, when looking (with both eyes from a distance of around 25 feet, or with one eye from nearer distances) at a trapezoidal window slowly rotating about a vertical axis, see a rectangular window of continually changing size and form oscillating at a continually varying speed through only a sector of a complete circle of revolution. They see the small cube sailing around the trapezoidal window and the tube bending at certain positions of revolution of the window.[2] However, these appearances are altered if the observer varies the distance, the direction, or the elevation from which he looks, and if he uses both eyes instead of one at near distance.

Detailed descriptions of the various appearances of the rotating trapezoidal window will now be taken up.

1. Description of apparent movements both in direction and speed of the rotating trapezoidal window without the cube or tube, observed from a distance of about 10 feet with one eye at the level of the middle of the trapezoidal window. As the trapezoidal window slowly rotates about a vertical axis, instead of appearing to rotate completely around, it appears to oscillate back and forth through an angle of about 100°. An understanding of the nature of this movement may be obtained from a study of Chart I. In the lower left-hand corner of the chart is a drawing in elevation of the trapezoidal window, the shorter side being designated by the letter A and the longer side by the letter B. In the four rows of figures in the chart the letters A and B and the heavy solid lines show a series of the actual positions of the short and long sides of the trapezoidal window AB as it is rotated in the direction indicated by arrows about a vertical axis through a full revolution, the last figure in the row showing the complete rotation. The letters A' and B' and the light solid lines show the apparent position of the short and long sides of the trapezoidal window. The top row of figures shows by the heavy solid lines marked AB, a series of the actual positions of the window (AB). The second row (II) shows by the light solid lines marked $A'B'$ the apparent localization of the window at each of the positions shown in Row I, the last figure in the row showing the apparent oscillating movement.

By comparing the apparent positions shown in Row II with the actual

---

[2]The above appearances are perhaps those most commonly experienced by most observers and for purposes of communication it will be those appearances that will be dwelt upon. However, not only are different appearances reported by different individuals, but the appearances reported by any one individual can be altered by varying either "subjective" or "objective" factors.

positions shown in Row *I,* it can be seen that as the window rotates in a counterclockwise direction, it appears to move in the same direction as it is actually moving, but lags behind, appearing to move more slowly. When the window has rotated 90° (see third figure in Row *I*), it appears to have rotated only about 50° (see *A'B'*, third figure, Row *II*). As the window rotates farther than 90°, it appears very slowly to reverse its direction of rotation (see fourth figures in both Rows *I* and *II*). From then on it appears to rotate in a reverse direction to its actual rotation until the window reaches a position normal to the line of sight (see ninth figures in Rows *I* and *II*). From then on it appears to move in the direction of the actual rotation until it reaches its starting position (compare first and eleventh figures in both Rows *I* and *II*).

The region of the apparent oscillating movement is shown in the last figure, Row *II*. The short side of the trapezoid appears to move from *A,'* to *A'* and the long side from *B'* to *B'*. No part of the window ever appears to enter into the areas included between *A'* and *B'*. The angle of apparent oscillation with the particular trapezoidal form used is about 100°. The point of actual rotation where the apparent rotation starts to reverse is when the window is normal to the line of sight and thus subtends the largest visual angle.

The apparent speed of movement varies greatly from the actual speed. As the window approaches a position normal to the line of sight, it appears to slow up gradually, come to a dead stop, remain stopped for an appreciable length of time, and then slowly to reverse its direction of movement.

2. Description of apparent alterations of shape and size of trapezoidal window when observed with one eye from a distance of about 10 feet, eye at the same level as middle of window. As the trapezoidal window slowly rotates about a vertical axis, it appears as a rectangular window,[3] but it appears to be continually changing in both shape and size. These alterations are made very apparent by comparing them to the shape and size of the rectangular window just above, which remain constant. This comparison can be best made when the trapezoidal window is positioned on its supporting rod so that it is at an angle of about 38° to the rectangular window above it. When the two windows are turned so the observer's line of sight makes an angle of about 16° to the rectangular window (see Fig. 2) with the shorter side of the trapezoidal window *A* toward the observer, the trapezoidal window appears to be in the same

[3]This is more definitely the case when the trapezoidal window is seen alone. When the rectangular window just above it is seen at the same time, although the trapezoidal window is still seen as rectangular, one is bothered by the nonparallelism of the bottom of the rectangular window and the top of the trapezoidal window.

plane and of the same shape and size as the rectangular window, as is shown in Fig. 3.

On the other hand, when the two windows are turned so that the trapezoidal window is positioned to subtend a slightly smaller angle, it appears in the same plane as the rectangular window, but it appears much shorter and gives the impression of being smaller, as is shown in Fig. 4. And when the two windows are turned so that the trapezoidal window is approximately positioned as shown in the second figure of Row *I* of the chart, it again appears in much the same plane as the rectangular window, but in this case it appears much longer than the rectangular window and gives the impression of being larger, as is shown in Fig. 5. In intermediate positions of rotation the trapezoidal window appears of intermediate shapes and sizes.

3. Description of apparent alteration of distance of trapezoidal window when observed with one eye from a distance of about 10 feet, eye at same level as middle of window. As the two windows are observed while they slowly rotate, it is noticeable that when the trapezoidal window appears longer and larger, it also appears nearer. However, this appearance is equivocal and seems to be counteracted by conflicting indications such as those from the supporting rod and the rectangular window.

To test what would be observed free from other possible conflicting indications, the trapezoidal window was set up in a dark room so that its image reflected from a half-silvered mirror could be seen uniocularly directly in front of the observer in a field in which there was a series of posts that were binocularly seen, by which the observer could judge the apparent distance of the uniocularly seen trapezoidal window. The window was first set so that it appeared longer and larger and then set so that it appeared shorter and smaller. Only preliminary observations were made, but for two observers it appeared nearer when it appeared longer and larger, and farther away when it appeared shorter and smaller, than the rectangular window.

4. Description of the apparent movement and changes in shape and size of the trapezoidal window when viewed from a distance of about 10 feet with one eye from levels above or below the middle of the trapezoidal window. Whether viewed from above or below the level of the middle of the trapezoidal window, the window appears to oscillate and change speed and shape and size just as it appears to do when viewed with the eyes at the level of the middle of the window. However, instead of appearing rectangular as it revolves, it appears in trapezium form, the amount of distortion being related to the angular distance of the viewing point above or below. Its vertical axis also appears to oscillate back and

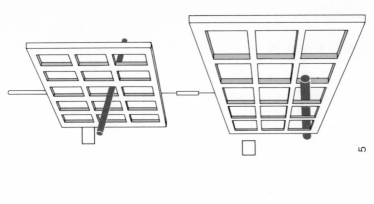

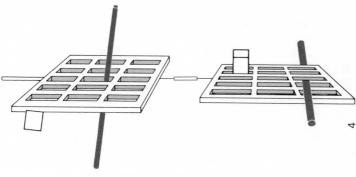

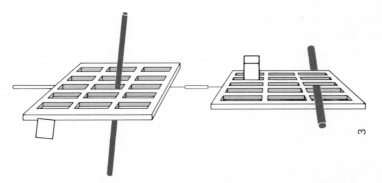

FIGS. 3, 4, and 5. *Line drawings of Rectangular Window (above) and Trapezoidal Window (below), showing the apparent differences of shape and size of trapezoidal window at different positions of its rotation.*

When in position shown in Figure 3, it appears approximately the same shape and size as the rectangular window.

When in position shown in Figure 4, it appears shorter.

When in position shown in Figure 5, it appears longer and larger.

forth. And, further, in certain positions of revolution it appears somewhat curved.

5. Description of the apparent movements and alterations in shape and size of the trapezoidal window when observed with two eyes from a distance of about 10 feet and from greater distances. If at a near distance of around 10 feet both eyes are used, what is perceived is a variable mixture of the above-described appearances and the appearances of an actual trapezoidal window rotating in the same way and at the same rates of speed as the rectangular window above it.[4]

When the observer, using both eyes, moves back from the windows to a distance of around 15 feet (the exact distance varying with the observer), the appearances of the trapezoidal window become less a mixture and more like what is observed monocularly. If the viewing distance is increased to around 20 or 25 feet (varying with the observer), the appearances of the trapezoidal window are almost the same as those experienced when it is viewed with one eye from a near distance.

Everything that has been said above holds true irrespective of the elevation of the observer's eye or eyes, and irrespective of his lateral position relative to the trapezoidal window. However, when his eyes are above or below, other second-order variations also are perceived.

6. Description of apparent movement of small cube attached to the upper part of the short side of the rotating trapezoidal window when observed with one eye from a distance of about 10 feet, eye at same height as middle of window. As the trapezoidal window slowly rotates from its position as shown in Fig. 1, Row I, of Chart I, the cube which is attached by a wire as shown in the drawing in the lower left-hand corner of the chart, appears to leave its point of attachment and float through the air around the front of the window, returning to its original attached position just before the trapezoidal window reaches its position shown in Fig. 11, Row I, Chart I. The apparent position of the cube relative to the apparent position of the rotating trapezoidal window is shown by the figures in Row III of the chart. Throughout its course, in which it appears to rotate once about its own vertical axis, the cube appears of relatively constant size and appears to be going at a relatively constant rate of speed.

7. Description of apparent movement and distortion of the tube which is suspended through the lower middle pane of the trapezoidal window, when observed with one eye from a distance of about 10 feet, eye at

---

[4]One observer who had a markedly dominant eye and very poor stereoscopic vision got the same appearance with two eyes as he did with one from a near viewing point.

same height as the middle of the window. The tube is suspended tipped at an angle of about 45° to the plane of the window, as shown in the drawing in the lower left-hand corner of Chart I. The appearances to be described can be seen with the tube at any inclination to the window, but are possibly more marked when it is at the inclination shown in the drawing.

As the trapezoidal window slowly rotates from its position as shown by the heavy solid line A in Fig. 1, Row IV, of the chart, the tube shown by the dotted line CD appears to swing around with the trapezoidal window until the window starts to reverse its direction of rotation. When this occurs, the tube and the window appear to be rotating in opposite directions, the tube apparently moving clockwise and the window apparently moving counterclockwise. The tube then appears to swing until the left side of the tube comes up against the mullions on the left of the window and the right side of the tube comes up against the mullions on the right of the window. Up to that position the tube appears straight, but from there on it appears to begin to bend (see dotted lines marked $C'D'$ in Fig. 3. Row IV, of chart) and seems to bend more and more (see dotted lines $C'D'$ in Figs. 4 and 5, Row IV, of chart). When the trapezoidal window gets in the position shown in Fig. 6, Row IV (chart), the tube suddenly snaps straight again and for the most observers remains straight during the remaining positions of revolutions shown in Figs. 7, 8, and 9 of Row IV in Chart I.[5] The rate of movement of the tube also appears to change, as does its apparent length.

If the tube is set at right angles to the plane of the window instead of at an angle of 45°, it appears to bend and straighten out through the same sections of its rotation described above, although it starts to bend a little later and does not appear to bend quite so much. If the direction of rotation of the window is reversed, to many observers the tube appears bent in that section of its revolution where it appeared straight when it was revolving in its original direction and straight in that section where it appeared bent.

When both eyes are used at a near distance, variations in the appearances of the cube or tube are observable. These variations are related to variations in the appearances of the window. When both eyes are used at distances of around 12 or 15 feet, this also holds. When both eyes are used at distances of around 20 or 25 feet, about the same appearances are observable as were seen at near distance with one eye.

When the window is looked at with the eye or eyes at a level slightly above or below the middle of the trapezoidal window, appearances similar to those described above are observed, but they become markedly

---

[5]There are a number of variations of these appearances.

different as the distance of observation above and below is greatly increased.

The observer sees all the above-described appearances when he looks at the trapezoidal window with the appended tube and cube. If he looks at the rectangular window with its tube and cube, the appearances are quite different. The rectangular window appears constant in form, size, and movement; its cube appears at a constant relative position; its tube appears at a constant relative position, shape, and size; and none of these aspects changes when two eyes are used or when point of view changes in direction or in level. Of course, the subjective sense of the positioning of the window and its distance alters with its rotation and with the change of the point of view either in distance or direction or level.

8. Description of apparent movements and alterations in shape and size of the trapezoidal window and of the cube and tube when viewed from different distances and different directions. With variation of the distance of observation, the only marked alteration of all of the above-described appearances is in respect to the apparent changes in size of the trapezoidal window. At greater viewing distances the apparent alterations in size of the rotating trapezoidal window are greater.

With variation of the observer's tangential point of view there is no alteration of the above-described appearances. That is, irrespective of the direction from which he looks he will see the same oscillation, changes in shape and size of the trapezoidal window, movement of the small cube, and bending of the tube.

Although a given observer looking at the rotating trapezoidal window from different tangential points of view will perceive certain definite phenomenal happenings (i.e., the oscillating window, the flying cube, and the bending tube), it is important to note that the visual happening he sees from a particular viewpoint at a particular moment he *would not* see at that same moment if he were at another point of view. What he sees can be seen only at one particular moment from one particular point of view.

This also holds if the trapezoidal window is stationary and the observer is looking at it as he walks around it. As he walks around it, he will see all the phenomenal happenings he would see if he stood still and the window rotated. But the visual experiences he sees from one point of view can be seen only from that point of view. No other observer walking around with him can see what he sees at the same moment he sees it. So a number of observers standing around the rotating trapezoidal window at the same distance from its axis will all perceive the same visual happenings occurring, *but no two* of the observers will see the same visual happenings occurring at the same moment.

While it is clear that what each observer sees is determined by his viewpoint both in space and time, there are certain aspects of what each oberver sees that are the same from any point of view at all times and for all other observers at other points of view and at other times. For example, the rectangular appearance of the trapezoidal window and the form and size of its small cube remain constant for all observers from all points of view at all times.

When the rectangular window is viewed from different distances and different directions, quite different phenomena occur. Irrespective of the distance or direction from which the rectangular window is viewed, the visual happenings an observer sees from a particular viewpoint at a particular moment he would see at the same moment if he were at another point of view. In other words, he would see a rectangular window of the same shape and size rotating at a constant rate of speed with the small cube in a constant relation to it and a tube of constant shape and length moving at a constant speed at the same moment, irrespective of his point of view. And a number of observers standing around the rotating rectangular window, irrespective of their distance, would perceive the same visual happenings occurring, *and all* observers would see the same visual happenings occurring at the same moment.

This concludes our attempt to communicate to the reader what he would have visually experienced if he himself had witnessed the demonstration. Next we will attempt to explain why one sees what he sees when looking at the rotating trapezoidal window, and why what he sees is so different from what he sees when he looks at the rotating rectangular window just above it. It is the same type of explanation that was formulated to account for the phenomena disclosed by the earlier, simpler demonstrations of the perception of the static aspects of the environment and of motion, and it seems adequately to account for the more complex phenomena described above. We have no illusion, however, that this account is the final word in the matter, but we present it because it seems to us the most intrinsically reasonable one that we can formulate at this time. Our hope is that its presentation will lead others to formulate still more intrinsically reasonable accounts.

EXPLANATIONS OF VISUAL PHENOMENA[6]

A. Explanation of the variations in appearance of the trapezoidal window. The appearances of the trapezoidal window give rise to many questions, among them the following:

[6]The explanations of the significances of the phenomena can at best be only partial explanations. For a more complete explanation, it is necessary to take account of other phenomena which are not disclosed by the demonstration now being considered, such as action, purpose, value, and emergent value-quality, which are beyond the scope of this paper.

1. Why does the trapezoidal window appear rectangular in shape?

2. Why does the rotating trapezoidal window appear to oscillate instead of rotate? Why does the trapezoidal window never appear to be where it actually is?

3. Why does the trapezoidal window, which is moving at a constant rate, appear to be moving at different rates?

4. Why does the trapezoidal window, which is constant in shape, appear of changing shapes?

5. Why does the trapezoidal window, which is constant in size, appear to be of changing size?

6. Why does the trapezoidal window appear rectangular when the eye or eyes are at the level of the middle of the window, but of trapezium form and sometimes curved when the eye or eyes are at other levels?

7. Why, when viewed with both eyes from a distance of around 24 feet (which is well within the distance at which stereoscopic vision is effective), does the trapezoidal window appear essentially the same as it appears with one eye?

It would seem apparent that there is no possibility of accounting for these appearances in causal terms of interactional effects between the objective phenomena and subjective appearances. The so-called "objective factor" that is varied is the trapezoidal shape of a rectangular window, i.e., making one side of a rectangular window longer and the other shorter. Among the many subjective appearances related to this variation is an alteration of the appearance of length and size. To say that it was caused by change in the trapezoidal form of the "object" in no way helps us to account for the apparent change in length and size. The obscurities that give rise to the above questions can be cleared up only by taking into account more particulars, i.e., other phenomenal processes that play a role in the situation, and understanding the nature of their relationships. This we shall attempt to do.

In what has been said so far, mention has been made of only two aspects of the situation, one, the characteristics of what the observer looks at, i.e., the so-called "objective" revolving trapezoidal window; the other, what the observer visually perceives. It is well known that there are many other phenomenal processes involved in every visual situation, among which is the physiological stimulus pattern that plays the role of relating the "objective" window and its subjective visual awareness.

As an aid in helping the reader understand the role played by the observer's physiological stimulus processes, we will introduce the use of a large artificial eye consisting of a lens corresponding to the dioptric system of the eye and a ground glass marked off in rectangular squares, corresponding to the retina. If this is set up pointing towards the trapezoidal window, the observer can see on the ground glass, stimulus patterns of the same characteristics that exist on his retina when he looks at the trapezoidal window. If this artificial eye is set up at the same level as the middle of the trapezoidal window, he will note as the window revolves that: *(a)* the image on the ground glass goes through a series of varying trapezoidal forms; *(b)* the pattern on the ground glass is never rectangular; *(c)* there is no change in speed or oscillation of the trapezoidal pattern corresponding to the apparent change in speed or oscillation of the trapezoidal window; and *(d)* there is no change in form or size of the trapezoidal pattern corresponding to the apparent change in form and size of the trapezoidal window.

It is apparent that a knowledge of the characteristics of these stimulus patterns in themselves does not help us in understanding why the observer sees what he does when he looks at the rotating trapezoidal window.

Let us, then, try to see if a knowledge of the characteristics of a stimulus pattern will help us in understanding what we see when we look at the rectangular window. Let us point the artificial eye at the rectangular window and note the characteristics of the images formed on the ground-glass retina by the rectangular window. It will be noted that these images have the same general characteristics as the images of the trapezoidal window, although the appearances of the rectangular window are different from those of the trapezoidal window, as has been pointed out. It is evident that a knowledge of the characteristics of our stimulus pattern considered in connection with a knowledge of the object viewed and our perceptual awareness alone do not suffice to provide us with an answer to our questions.

Where shall we turn? Apparently a question we can ask gives us a lead, namely: "Why, when we look at the rectangular window, do we see a rectangular window, when the characteristics of its images formed on our retina are trapezoidal?" This question has extra significance because when we look at the trapezoidal window we see it, also, as rectangular, which means that the perceived rectangular form does not come from either the stimulus pattern or the object. If it does not come from the stimulus pattern or the object, whence does it come? This same question has occurred with all our previous demonstrations. In each case the most profitable and reasonable answer lay in bringing into consideration the past experience of the observer, and that consideration appears to be equally reasonable and profitable in this instance.

In his past experience the observer, in carrying out his purposes, has on innumerable occasions had to take into account and act with respect to rectangular forms, e.g., going through doors, locating windows, etc. On almost all such occasions, except in the rare case when his line of sight was normal to the door or window, the image of the rectangular configuration formed on his retina was trapezoidal. He learned to interpret the particularly characterized retinal images that exist when he looks at doors, windows, etc., as rectangular forms. Moreover, he learned to interpret the particular degree of trapezoidal distortion of his retinal images in terms of the positioning of the rectangular form to his particular viewing point. These interpretations do not occur at the conscious level; rather, they are unconscious and may be characterized as *assumptions* as to the probable significance of indications received from the environment. A person's perception thus provides him with an awareness not only of the form of the "thing" he is looking at, i.e., "what it is," but also "where it is" relative to his viewing point.

Let us now take into account past experience in explaining what the observer sees when he is looking at the revolving rectangular window. Suppose the rectangular window is in an edge-on position when it starts to revolve. When it has turned a little, the image formed by its farther side will be shorter than that formed by its nearer side. The retinal image will be trapezoidal, the particular difference in length of its sides being determined by the length of the window and the observer's distance from it. As the window revolves, the lengths of the two sides will become more and more nearly the same until the window is normal to his line of sight, when they will be equal. Then the side which was the far side will become longer and reach its greatest relative length when at its nearest to the observer, i.e., when the window is in an edge-on position. As the window turns farther, the image of the now nearer side will decrease and the image of the farther side increase until the completion of the revolution. The observer interprets these changes in trapezoidal form as changes of position and interprets the continuing changes of position as a rotation of a rectangular window.

It would seem that the above begins to provide a basis for understanding why an observer sees what he does when he looks at the rotating trapezoidal window. Suppose the trapezoidal window starts rotating from the position shown in Fig. 1, Row *I,* Chart I, when its shorter side *A* is farther away and the longer side *B* nearer. When it has turned a little (see Fig. 2, Row *II,* Chart I), the image formed by the farther side *A* will be shorter than that formed by its nearer side *B*. This difference in length is greater than the difference in length of the images of the far and near sides of the rectangular window above it. As it revolves, the image formed by the far side *A* will increase in length and that of the near side *B* decrease. But their relative change will not be as great as that of the images of a rectangular window at the same inclination. So the trapezoidal window will not appear to rotate so far or fast as the rectangular window above it, which is moving at a constant speed. When the trapezoidal window has rotated to a position normal to the line of sight, with the short side *A* to the left (see Fig. 3, Row *I,* Chart I), the image of its side *A* will still be shorter than the image of its side *B*, so it appears tipped back on the left in the position shown in Fig. 3, Row *II*, Chart I. This is as far forward as the short side ever appears to come. With further rotation the vertical dimension of the image of the side *A* will increase in length and that of the side *B* decrease. But the image of the short side *A* of the trapezoidal window can never become longer than that of the long side *B*, and so it can never be seen as nearer. However, this could not explain why the trapezoidal window appears to reverse its direction.

The explanation of the reversing phenomenon is apparently as follows: As the trapezoidal window starts to rotate from the position shown in Fig. 3, Row *I*, Chart I, to those shown in Figs. 5 and 6, Row *I*, Chart I, the total horizontal angle that the trapezoidal window subtends to the eye decreases. At the beginning of this decrease the trapezoidal window appears tipped back on the left (see Fig. 3, Row *II*, Chart I). It has been learned from past experience with rectangular forms that a decrease of the total horizontal angle of our retinal images of a rectangularly perceived form which appears tipped away from us on the left could only take place if the side on the left went farther away. If it came nearer, the total horizontal angle of our retinal images would have to increase. So we interpret this decrease in the total horizontal dimension of our retinal stimulus pattern as a going-away of the left side of the window. That is, the window appears to reverse its direction of rotation, and as the left side of the window keeps coming towards us (see Figs. 3 and 4, Row *I*, Chart I), it appears to be going farther away (see Fig. 3 and 4, Row *II*, Chart I). A similar apparent reversal is seen to take place when the trapezoidal window has revolved to a position where the short side *A* is to the right (see Fig. 9, Row *I*, Chart I). It is due to these apparent reversals that the trapezoidal window appears to oscillate instead of rotate.

The above considerations seem to furnish a reasonable explanation as to why the rotating trapezoidal window *(a)* appears rectangular in shape, *(b)* appears to oscillate instead of rotate, and *(c)* appears to move at varying rates.

But we have not yet answered the question of why the trapezoidal window appears to change in form and size. A reasonable answer to these questions seems to be based on our making use of variation in the trapezoidal characteristics of our stimulus pattern as indications to positioning of a rectangular configuration. When looking at the rotating rectangular window, the varying trapezoidal stimulus patterns have particular characteristics which give us indications of the position of the window in its rotation. For instance, when looking at the rectangular window tipped at an angle of 45° to our line of sight, the trapezoidal pattern formed on our retina will be the same shape whether the right side or the left side of the window is nearer us, and we will relate the two patterns and rectangular configurations of the same size and shape but at different inclinations.

But when we look at the trapezoidal windows, what happens is quite different. When the trapezoidal window is tipped 45° to our line of sight with the longer side *B* nearer us (see Fig. 2, Row *I*, Chart I), the shape of the trapezoidal image formed on our retina is quite different from that formed when the shorter side *A* is nearer us (see Fig. 8, Row *I*, Chart I). When the longer side *B* is nearer, there is a greater difference in the relative lengths of the sides of the trapezoid which could only be produced either by a rectangular window of the same height at a nearer distance or by a longer rectangular window at the same distance. When the shorter side *A* is nearer us, there is a lesser difference in the relative lengths of the sides of the trapezoid, which could only be produced by a rectangular window of the same length at a greater distance or by a shorter rectangular window at the same distance.

Since there are a number of indications that the distance of the window remains constant as it rotates, we translate the difference in the trapezoidal pattern on our retinas into differences in perceived length so that when it is rotating, it appears to be continually changing shape. When the indications of distance are eliminated, as was done in the preliminary experiment noted previously, we see the trapezoidal window as nearer when the longer side *B* is nearer, and farther away when the shorter side *A* is nearer (13). These considerations seem to furnish a reasonable explanation of why the rotating trapezoidal window appears to change shape (question 4) and size (question 5).

We now turn to question 6: Why does the trapezoidal window appear rectangular when the eye or eyes are at the level of the middle of the window, but of trapezium form and sometimes curved when the eye or eyes are at other levels?

The answer to this question is apparently the following: When our eyes are at the level of the middle of the trapezoidal window, the trapezoidal patterns on our retinas are identical with those that could be produced by some rectangular window at some inclination at some distance. When they are above or below, our stimulus patterns for the trapezoidal window are not trapezoids but trapeziums which, although similar to, are different from, the trapezium patterns that exist on our retinas when we look at a rectangular window from above or below.

A conclusive explanation of these appearances will be possible only when by a mathematical analysis (projective geometry) it has been determined just how the two types of trapezium patterns differ. But it seems probable that the trapezium patterns from the trapezoidal window are sufficiently similar to those from the rectangular window that we try to translate them into rectangular configurations even to the extent of seeing the window as curved. The apparent forward-and-back tipping of the trapezoidal window about a horizontal axis may be explained on the basis that the trapezium patterns are similar to those that would be produced by a rectangular window tipped about a horizontal axis.[7]

This brings us to the less significant question 7—why the trapezoidal window appears essentially the same when we use two eyes within distances at which stereoscopic vision is effective. The apparent answer is that in this situation we suppress the binocular cues and take account of the uniocular ones because uniocular cues result in perceptions which square better with what we have learned in past experience in dealing with windows. In other words, the uniocular cues have, on the basis of past experience greater prognostic reliability than do the binocular ones. This is confirmed by a number of our other demonstrations (see 1, Demonstrations 26 and 27, and 8, pp. 82 ff.). It might also be well to note here that parallax indications of distances, achieved by lateral movement of the head, do give rise to secondary alterations in the appearances of the trapezoidal window. They, however, do not aid one in seeing the trapezoidal window *as* a trapezoid rotating at a constant speed.

B. Explanation of the appearance of the small cube.[8] The appearances of the cube give rise to at least the following questions:

1. Why does it appear to rotate in a circular path quite independently of the trapezoidal window to which it is attached?

2. Why does it appear to move at a relatively constant rate when the window to which it is attached oscillates at varying speeds?

3. How is it possible for it to appear separated from the trapezoidal window to which it is attached?

To the first question an answer which may come quickly to one's mind is that we see the window move as it does for the reasons given in Chapter II, and we see the small cube rotate in a circle at relatively constant speed because that is how it is actually moving. But this answer is not quite satisfactory because the previous chapter has made it evident that the appearances we see are not determined by what we are looking at but by our interpretation of our stimulus patterns.

[7]In the apparatus as constructed, the objective factor that is varied is the trapezoidal form. The phenomena just described make it apparent that different and interesting alterations of perception would be experienced if the window were actually made in a trapezium form. Presumably, if such a form were observed with the eye or eyes at the level of the middle of the window, its appearances would be similar to those experienced when the trapezoidal window is observed with the eye or the eyes above or below the level of the window, and more exaggerated appearances would be experienced if such a window were observed from other levels.

[8]The reason for using the small cube and the tube in connection with the rotating trapezoidal window demonstration was to determine if and how the appearance and behavior of objects would appear to be altered when "put together" in different ways with an objective configuration whose form was varied so that its appearance was altered.

Perhaps a better answer for why the small cube appears as it does and seems to move as it does can be derived from the following considerations. In the previous chapter, to understand the appearance and movement of the trapezoidal window it was necessary first to understand that we saw the rectangular window appear and move as it does because we assumed it was rectangular and made use of the varying trapezoidal characteristics of our retinal images as indications of its varying positions. Our perceptions of the movement of the small cube have a similar origin and nature. Due to the characteristics of our retinal image produced by light rays reflected from the small cube, we assume its size and other characteristics. In its rotation as the cube comes towards us, its retinal image increases, and we assume it is coming nearer to us; as it goes away from us, its retinal image becomes smaller, and we assume it is going away (see 1, Chap. II, Demonstration 17). The variations in the sizes of the retinal images and the rate of their movement across our retina, although not uniform or constant in time, are nevertheless so translated, and the cube appears to be moving in a circular path at a relatively constant speed.

Let us now consider the question as to how it is possible for the small cube to appear to separate itself from the trapezoidal window to which it is attached. What has been said above explains why, if the cube were not attached to the window (i.e., if the cube were just above the window), we would see them following separate paths. That the cube does appear to separate itself from the trapezoidal window to which it is most evidently attached can only be explained on the basis that the indications causing the trapezoidal window to appear to move as it does and the cube to move as it does are accepted as definite and unequivocal, and cues indicating otherwise are suppressed.

Various three-dimensional objects were substituted for the cube and were attached in different ways. They all appeared to behave in the same manner. However, two-dimensional objects such as playing cards and small sheets of paper attached to the upper side of the shorter end of the trapezoidal window may or may not appear to move with the window, depending on how they are attached. Apparently the factors involved in these phenomena are of the same nature as those disclosed in our demonstration of Togetherness and Apartness (1, Chap. VI).

C. Explanation of the appearance of the tube. The appearances of the tube give rise to at least the following questions:

1. Why does it appear to rotate quite independently of the trapezoidal window to which it is attached?

2. Why does it appear to move at varying speeds and at speeds different from that of the trapezoidal window?

3. Why does it appear to bend and change length?

The answer to the first question has already been covered by the explanations as to why the cube appears to rotate in a circular path quite independently of the trapezoidal window to which it is attached.

The answer to the second question appears to be that the tube seems to move at varying speeds (which the cube did not) because it is seen "together" with the window in a way that causes the observer to take account of its motion in relation to the apparent motion of the trapezoidal window.

The answer to the third question involves the necessity of taking into account the phenomenon of overlay. Overlay is one of the numerous indications which we take into account in formulating our presumptions as to the distances of objects. If an object is so positioned that it overlays or cuts off part of another object, we presume that it is nearer and that the other object is farther away. As has been demonstrated, because of its high prognostic reliability, great weight is given this indication relative to the weight given other distance indications such as brightness, size, and parallax. With the rotating trapezoidal window and tube, this phenomenon of overlay comes into play.

As the window rotates we see the left half of the window overlaying the left part of the tube, and therefore in front of the tube, and the right part of the tube overlaying the right half of the window, and therefore in front of the window. As described, the tube and the window appear to be rotating about the same axis in opposite directions. When their paths cross, the observer has to make an interpretation of the happenings that are occurring to the characteristics of his retinal stimulus pattern. There are various possible interpretations he could make. He might keep the tube straight and whole and the window straight and whole, but then we would have to stop their motion; or he might ignore his overlay indications and see gaps in the mullions of the window to let the tube pass through; or he might see the window bend. If he keeps the window and the tube in motion and the window flat and whole, i.e., without gaps in it, he has to see the tube bend. It is this last interpretation that is most commonly made with this particular configuration, and this is what most observers see. With this interpretation one also sees the tube increase in length when it bends because presumably only a longer tube could fill the length of space which the apparently bent tube fills.

All of this raises the question as to just why more weight is given to certain indications than to others, or why we insist on holding to certain presumptive aspects and giving up others. Apparently the answer is that we give weight to indications on the basis of their prognostic reliability.

Some preliminary observations were made after replacing the tube with a rectangular box (a cigarette carton) with printing on it. With this setup the appearances changed. The box did not appear to bend as the tube

TABLE 1 Constancy of aspects of visual perception experienced by one observer when looking from one point of view at:

Rectangular window, cube, and tube		Trapezoidal window, cube, and tube from level of window		Trapezoidal window, cube, and tube from above or below level of window	
Constant	Altering	Constant	Altering	Constant	Altering
"Windowness"*	Inclination	"Windowness"	Inclination	"Windowness"	Rectangularity
Rectangularity		Rectangularity	Size		Inclination
			Shape		Size
Size			Motion		Shape
Shape					Motion
Motion					
Direction†		Direction		Direction	
Distance			Distance		Distance

*The word "windowness" is used for the observer's awareness (resulting from his interpretation of certain characteristics of his stimulus pattern) of "something out there" (apart from other "things") of the nature of a window.

†"Direction" refers to the subjective sense of the direction of the window from the observer's egocentric center.

does, or appeared to do so only very slightly; however, the window was still seen in the reverse of its actual position. This apparently means that the overlay indications were given no weight, or the window would be seen in its actual position. This line of investigation should be carried further.

There remains to explain why, when the tube is set at right angles to the plane of the window, it appears bent during a certain portion of its rotation when the window is rotating in one direction, but does not appear bent during the same portion of rotation when the window is rotating in the opposite direction. The only explanation that comes to mind is that we will accept the appearance of bending when it takes place gradually but will not accept seeing a straight tube suddenly bend. Observations have been made on this phenomenon, and they should be further checked. But if it is confirmed, it is an important disclosure and should be investigated.

D. Summary. Before going on to consider further questions raised by the trapezoidal window, the material presented will be briefly summarized. The presentation up to now has been an attempt *(a)* to describe to the reader the aspects of his visual experiences that would be altered when observing a rotating window whose trapezoidal form had been varied, and *(b)* to offer what appears to be a reasonable explanation of why these alterations in appearance are experienced. Table 1 may be helpful in making clear just what aspects of the observer's visual perception are not altered (remain constant) and what aspects are altered.

Briefly stated, the explanation as to why the altered aspects appear altered involves the taking into account of the characteristics of the stimulus patterns, which are essentially cryptogrammatic in nature, their translation in terms of the assumptions from past experience, the hypothesis that perceptions are not disclosures but essentially prognostic in nature, i.e., prognostic directives for action from the observer's point of view both in space and time, the weighing of "indications," sense of surety and lack of surety, value judgments.

But it should be realized that such explanations are only partial, for such questions as the following still remain to be answered: What kind of action? Action for what? If these questions are answered by saying: "Carrying out the purposes of the observer," the further questions arise: What kind of purposes? Purposes for what? The answers to these questions are beyond the scope of this paper.

3

A MICROGENETIC APPROACH
TO PERCEPTION AND THOUGHT
JOHN H. FLAVELL AND JURIS DRAGUNS

Not all that takes place during the instantiation of a stimulus can be recounted in verbal terms. Flavell and Draguns review efforts to describe the process of instantiation during that period following the presentation of the stimulus and the formulation of a verbalizable, stable cognitive response. Their review highlights the techniques available to study the cognitive process during this period. Although one would always need to question the representativeness of the experimental effort to define the process, there can be little doubt that there is induced a nonverbalizable activity that reflects the organism's effort to locate the stimulus within its existing cognitive structures. Our argument is that "microgenetic" thought or perception is the nexus of a concept of unconscious. Unconscious thought or perception is the unverbalized process of locating stimulus patterns in one's cognitive patterns.

So long as the process runs smoothly and arousal remains at approximately optimal levels, there is no verbalized sign of cognitive strain. Related to this motivational point, we would make a larger issue of the "emotionally charged character of the *vorgestalt* stage," which Flavell and Draguns mention in passing. Their description of this phenomenon is an excellent illustration of an organism being presented with stimulation that is arousing—that is, for which it cannot produce an instantaneous construction of that stimulus. Flavell and Draguns are trying to demonstrate the utility of the concept of microgenesis in discussing pathology of thought, and in doing so they theorize about the role of the unconscious in the development of unusual behaviors.

$*$ $*$ $*$

It is the purpose of this paper to present a theoretical approach to

Reprinted from Psychological Bulletin, *1957, 54, 197–217, by permission of John H. Flavell and the American Psychological Association.*

perception and thought which, although by no means entirely new, will undoubtedly seem strange and unorthodox to many. The term "microgenesis," first coined by Werner (132) as an approximate translation of the German word *Aktualgenese*, will refer here to the sequence of events which are assumed to occur in the temporal period between the presentation of a stimulus and the formation of a single, relatively stabilized cognitive response (percept or thought) to this stimulus. More specifically, the term will refer primarily to the prestages of extremely brief cognitive acts, e.g., the processes involved in immediately perceiving a simple visual or auditory stimulus, conceptually generating a word association, etc. Thus, cognitive sequences involving many seconds or minutes, such as perceptual changes resulting from prolonged fixation, will not be considered here as examples, or at least as typical examples, of microgenetic development Within this somewhat restricted conception of microgenesis or microdevelopment, one can distinguish, in terms of experimental operations, between "microgenesis of thought" and "microgenesis of perception." In the former case we refer to situations in which little attention is given to the conditions of stimulus or task presentation but careful attention is paid to the temporal development of the conceptual response. In the latter case, we refer to conditions in which considerable attention is paid to the manner of stimulus presentation but little, if any, is paid to the temporal evolution of the ensuing verbal response. The experimental paradigm of microgenesis of thought consists of presentation of a stimulus to cognition, under optimal conditions of perceptual "intake," and some sort of attempt to study, or even control, the evolution of the cognitive response to this stimulus. The paradigm of microgenesis of perception, on the other hand, usually entails the successive presentation of a stimulus under conditions of increasing clarity. Successive tachistoscopic presentation of visual stimuli with exposure times gradually increasing until complete perception is possible, considered as the experimental homologue of the everyday, near-instantaneous process of simply "seeing" an object, would perhaps be the best example of this paradigm. It should be mentioned that the distinction made here stems from a distinction between typical experimental conditions and does not imply a particular brief for or against any basic dichotomy between perception and thought.

In attempting to conceptualize processes within a microgenetic framework, at least two basic questions arise. From the evidence available, what formal principles of cognitive microdevelopment have been or could be derived to constitute a first beginning of a microgenetic theory? Of what use would such a theory be in organizing known facts of normal and abnormal perception and thought and in constructing testable hypotheses for future research? It is hoped that this paper will suggest partial answers to these questions. We shall first survey some of the theoretical and experimental work which seems to us to bear upon the first of the two questions. Following this, some tentative notions will be proposed with regard to the second question.

MICROGENESIS OF PERCEPTION

There is a fairly sizable body of literature concerned, in one way or another, with the temporal evolution of percepts. A good half of these studies emanate directly from one microgenetically oriented "school" and, in this sense, form a tightly knit whole. The remainder of the investigations differ widely among themselves as to theoretical orientation, experimental procedure, etc. In this section we will first describe the contributions of the former group of studies and then compare their findings with those of the miscellaneous remaining experiments.

In the early twenties, there arose in Germany a movement against post-Wundtian elementaristic psychology led by Felix Krueger of Leipzig. Like the better-known Berlin group, Krueger and his followers were Gestaltists and stressed the intrinsic structuredness of perception. Unlike the Berlin school, however, they were particularly concerned with the temporal development of percepts as well as with the formal properties of completed percepts. Krueger developed a complicated and somewhat esoteric general theory which is of only tangential relevance to microgenesis (59). His co-worker Sander, however, did develop an explicitly microgenetic theory of perception within Krueger's framework (94, 95) and, with his students, carried out a variety of experimental studies on the problem. He believed that perception is a developmental process consisting of a number of conceptually distinct phases. Further, he assumed that percepts obtained under inadequate stimulus conditions, e.g., brief tachistoscopic exposure, are essentially the same as the initial, transitory percepts which precede the final perceptual response under normal stimulus conditions. He granted that the precursors of the final percept are not observable in the normal, perceptual process. However, he argued that if one experimentally blocks the formation of clear, complete percepts by presenting stimuli very briefly, in bad lighting, in peripheral vision, etc., one can elicit these perceptual precursors. On the basis of experimental findings, Sander was able to offer a fairly detailed description of perceptual microgenesis or *Aktualgenese*, as he called it. Our account of the process will follow that of Undeutsch (112), one of Sander's students.

When a perceptual stimulus is presented under conditions of gradually increasing clarity, the initial perception is that of a diffuse, undifferentiated whole. In the next stage figure and ground achieve some measure of differentiation, although the inner contents of the stimulus remain vague and amorphous. Then comes a phase in which contour and inner content achieve some distinctness and a tentative, labile configuration results. Finally, the process of Gestalt formation becomes complete with the addition of elaborations and modifications of the "skeletal Gestalt" *(Gestaltgerüst)* achieved in the previous stage.

As development proceeds, external, objective characteristics more and more supplant inner, personal factors as determinants of the structure perceived. As Undeutsch puts it, the balance of endogenous to exogenous determinants changes as perceptual microdevelopment proceeds. Of particular interest to Sander and his students was the stage just preceding the formation of the final, stable percept. In this Vorgestalt or preconfiguration phase the *S* has constructed a tentative, highly labile Gestalt which is more undifferentiated internally, more regular, and more simple in form and content than is the final form which is to follow it. The construction of this initial, flux-like pre-Gestalt is said to be accompanied by decidedly unpleasant feelings of tension and unrest which later subside when a final, stable configuration is achieved. The emotionally-charged character of the *Vorgestalt* stage is stressed by many investigators (38, 40, 65, 96, 107, 116, 136) whose reports are often supplemented by colorful and dramatic verbal reports by the *S*s.

These then were the near-unanimous conclusions of Sander and his students with respect to the microgenesis of percepts. Under what experimental situations were these findings obtained? The Sander group showed no lack of imagination in their efforts to study *Aktualgenese* under all possible conditions. Some investigators presented stimuli under gradually increasing tachistoscopic exposure time. Using this technique, paintings by famous artists (65), three-dimensional geometric figures (38), and groups of everyday objects (73) were presented to *S*s and percepts elicited at each exposure time were recorded and analyzed. Sommer (107) varied this procedure by gradually decreasing, rather than increasing exposure time and was able to show, in reverse order, the usual sequence of developmental stages. Wohlfahrt (136) presented geometric designs in extreme miniature at first and gradually increased their size until *S*s were able to see them clearly and without effort. Butzmann (9) also using geometric designs, recorded perceptual alterations as stimuli were gradually moved from the extreme periphery of the visual field in towards a central fixation point. Other investigators used stimuli or arrangements of stimuli which were meaningless or disorganized and compared perceptual development under such conditions with that which occurred when meaningful, organized stimuli were used (23, 47, 48). Additional investigations conducted by the Sander group involve the microgenesis of tactile impressions (40), the temporal process of describing clearly seen objects

(116), and miscellaneous other problems (93, 96). Such was the variety of stimulus conditions employed. The perceptual responses on which the theory was based were obtained in either of two ways: (a) simple introspection, or verbal report (40, 65, 96, 107); (b) pictorial reproduction of what was perceived (9, 23, 47, 48, 73, 136), supplemented in one case by manual arrangement of concrete stimulus objects in attempted duplication of the percept (40).

It is thus apparent that Sander and his group made a vigorous and concerted attack on what they saw as an important problem in perception. In reading through the variety of parallel studies done outside of Germany one is struck by the fact that the great bulk of *Aktualgenese* research is seldom cited. Similarly, references to non-German experiments on perceptual microgenesis are equally infrequent in the work of the Krueger school. This lack of cross fertilization, however unfortunate in some ways, does make it possible to compare the experimental conclusions of scientists who are not mutually tainted by each other's theoretical preconceptions. It is therefore interesting to note that Sander's assertion that microgenesis begins with diffuse, whole percepts which subsequently become sharpened and internally differentiated receives considerable confirmation from other studies. For example, experimenters using such different stimuli as geometric figures (6), letters of the alphabet (20), Rorschach (80, 109) or self-made (31) inkblots, Rubin figure-ground cards (134), and various kinds of pictures (12, 22, 103), have also reported developmental sequences in the general direction of diffuse to specific. Further, Brigden (6) found a tendency towards simplification, completion, transposition, and increased symmetry as development progressed—a finding quite congruent with Sander's statement that percepts at the *Vorgestalt* stage tend to be made "better Gestalten" at the expense of object similarity. Brigden also lists an early tendency to complicate the percept which the Sander group did not explicitly postulate. It is, however, possible that this complication tendency is not unlike the microgenetically early overinvestment of meaning noted by Dun (23), Hippius (40), and Johannes (47, 48). As to the microgenetically late trend from specific details to integrated wholes, tachistoscopic studies using Rorschach stimuli confirm this only in part (80, 109). In these latter studies a continuous, nonreversing trend from wholes to details is found, although those whole responses which *are* given in the end stages do tend to be of the integrated, internally differentiated rather than global type. On the debit side, the intense emotionality which the Sander group reports as an invariable concomitant of *Vorgestalt* formation is certainly not stressed by most other investigators, although Douglas (22) makes explicit mention of it. There are other minor disagreements between the findings of the *Aktualgenese* group and those of other investigators. Since the experimental methods used in the studies to be compared are often only roughly equivalent, it is difficult to interpret the meaning of such disagreements with any confidence.

Before concluding our account of experimental studies of perceptual microdevelopment it must be mentioned that many of these studies would be considered quite poor by present-day methodological standards. This is especially, although not exclusively, true of the research done by Sander and his school. Few *S*s were used and these were seldom experimentally naïve, statistics were inadequate or absent, and methods of measuring and evaluating perceptual responses were informal to say the least. In addition, serious questions concerning basic assumptions can be posed, as will be seen later. Nonetheless, the existing German and non-German studies together constitute a rather extensive and exciting first assault on the truly fundamental problem of how our percepts get formed. As will soon be apparent, there has been considerably less systematic experimental work done on the equally fundamental problem of how our thoughts develop.

MICROGENESIS OF THOUGHT

If one wished to apply the term "microgenesis of thought" to all published accounts of the cognitive steps involved in solving a problem, the relevant literature would be vast indeed. Humphrey (44), Johnson (49, 50), Osgood (75), Vinacke (118, 119), Woodworth (137), Woodworth and Schlosberg (138), and others have given ample reviews of the multitude of studies which describe the temporal sequence of concept acquisition or problem solution. Likewise, there are a number of published accounts of the microdevelopment of creative thinking, most of which have been reviewed by Vinacke (119) and Woodworth (137). Wallas (122), for example, divided the development of a creative thought into four stages: preparation, incubation, illumination, and verification. Patrick (76, 77, 78) and Eindhoven and Vinacke (25) conducted laboratory studies which attempted to test Wallas' assertions. Although to define the limits of a single thought formation is admittedly a hazardous procedure, it may be fairly safe to assume that many, many thought formations occur in any solution sequence as extended as those typically involved in studies of creative thinking, formal problem-solving (24), and the like. It may be that laws of cognitive development in a solution process which extends over hours, days, or even years are of a piece with those pertaining to a "single" thought which requires seconds or fractions of a second to run its course, although at present we see no good evidence for such an identity. In any case, the present discussion will be confined primarily to those few studies which concern the nature of thought in relatively brief cognitive sequences.

As is well known, the classical controversy between the Cornell and Würzburg schools involved, among other things, a dispute as to whether images were or were not the "carriers" of mental life (4, 44). In their attempts to settle the question by means of introspection studies the members of these schools were of necessity concerned with what lay behind completed cognitive acts. Although they were not explicitly concerned with constructing microgenetic theories, some of their findings bear upon the development of thought as we are defining it. For example, despite differences in opinion as to whether or not thoughts are fundamentally imaginal in substance, both factions reported evidence that images may play a variety of roles in the microgenetic sequence. Thus, according to Humphrey's account (44, pp. 283–288), various introspective studies suggest that images sometimes seem merely to illustrate or accompany thoughts already in progress, sometimes serve as starting-points for subsequent thought microgenesis, and sometimes even constitute distractions by leading *S* to dwell upon the images instead of progressing in the thought sequence or by leading S to a thought wholly irrelevant to the cognitive task at hand. Further, Willwoll (44) found that the images which impede thinking tend to be more clear and concrete than those which do not. Although its function may be highly variable from instance to instance, it is perhaps safe to conclude that imagery, when it occurs, tends to be a phenomenon characteristic of the earlier stages of thought microdevelopment.

In addition to their studies of the role of imagery in the microdevelopmental process, these early psychologists, especially the Würzburgers, made some interesting observations about the developmental sequence as a whole. Thus Messer (70) distinguished between vague, undeveloped thoughts without words or images and fully formulated propositions with clear consciousness of meaning. For example, one of his *S*s gave the following introspection after having responded "corner" to the stimulus word "angle": "The tendency was towards the well-known proposition that the sum of the angles of a triangle equals two right angles . . . but it did not mature" (p. 178). Bühler (8) studied somewhat more complex thought problems, instructing his *S*s to "solve" a variety of proverbs, aphorisms, etc., and to report their introspections of the solution process. On many occasions the *S*s would report that they had, early in the solution sequence, vague, imageless half-thoughts or premonitions about such things as the task, the nature of the solution, the possibility or impossibility of solution, the problem's relationship to other problems, etc.[1] Bühler's data suggest that very early thoughts seem to serve somewhat as global

---

[1] For a wealth of anecdotal evidence for such microdevelopmentally early thoughts, see Wallas (122, Chap. 4).

schemata which orient the thinker as to the nature of the solution. That is, the thinker may have experiences of vaguely knowing where the solution will lie, with what problems or persons the solution is associated, how difficult the solution will be, and so on, considerably prior to possessing the fully formulated solution—prior to thinking the problem through. The S's introspections suggest that it is as if the final solution somehow differentiates out of the diffuse, generic-like, "framework" thoughts which precede it. Whether or not these microdevelopmentally immature thoughts always have an image-like composition is a question which seems less important to us today than does the question of the role these early thoughts play in the developmental process.

There have been a few psychologists, from the beginning of the century down to the present day, who have more or less explicitly theorized about the microgenesis of thought. One of the earliest of these was Jung (51), who considered the problem in the context of his studies of word association. He expressed the belief that "superficial" word association responses, such as clangs and word and phrase completions, are the initial, immediate cognitive responses to words and that they are normally suppressed in favor of the more meaningful responses which follow them in the apperceptive process.

Jung posited a temporal hierarchy of modes of word cognition which progresses, in the course of the apperceptive process, from the most superficial cognition of the physical characteristics of the word, through a cognition of the word as a member of a familiar phrase, and finally through cognition of the word's denotative and connotative meanings.

Somewhat later, Pick and Thiele (81), Van Woerkom (113, 114), and Bouman and Grünbaum (5) formulated hypotheses about thought development in the course of their work with aphasics. Pick and Thiele, drawing upon the earlier work of Bühler and Messer, suggested that the word cognition process typically goes through a series of stages which are, in part, somewhat reminiscent of Jung's formulation: *(a)* recognition of the word as a physical object, an "acoustic Gestalt," *(b)* an awareness of the general "meaning sphere" of the word, i.e., location of the word in conceptual space, *(c)* comprehension of the grammatical form of the word. Pick and Thiele state that the succession of these stages is not invariable and that more stages may be involved if S is required to make a verbal formulation of his cognition. Bouman and Grünbaum conceive of the cognition of a stimulus as beginning with a total, amorphous general impression (e.g., "good" or "bad," "right" or "wrong") which, in normal individuals, is followed by successive differentiations of the total stimulus into its component meaningful parts. Similarly, Van Woerkom insists that the developmental process typically begins with the conception of the whole idea, with a stage of analysis and synthesis following.

A more recent theoretical exposition of the course of thought development in forming word associations is given by Rapaport, Gill, and Schafer (84) and Schafer (97). They suggest that the normal process of giving a word association to a stimulus word consists of two principal microdevelopmental phases: an analytic, decompository stage in which the stimulus word is broken down into its component ideas and one of these ideas is selected as the basis for the association to come; following this, a synthetic, compository phase in which the response word is constructed from a thought associated with this particular component idea. In both phases the associative process is assumed to be guided by an over-all set to produce a response word conceptually related to the stimulus word, a set which becomes even more specific when *S* hears the stimulus word. When for any reason the thought process does not pass through both phases the resulting associative response will be atypical. Rapaport et al. designate as *close* those responses which indicate that the process has not proceeded past the first, analytic phase and as *distant* those which suggest that the synthetic process has overdeveloped in an associative sequence tangential or irrelevant to the task-induced anticipation. Thus, *close* associations include repetitions of the stimulus word, attributes, clangs, and phrase completions—associations which indicate, as Jung had suggested earlier, that the associative process has been "aborted" early in its microdevelopment. Those responses which are logically unrelated or very marginally related to their stimulus words are scored as *distant* associations, the presupposition being that intermediary associations in the synthetic phase have constituted the connecting links between the stimulus word and the seemingly irrelevant response word. Despite differences in basic theoretical orientation, Jung and the Rapaport group appear to agree, at least implicitly, on several points of importance to microgenetic theory. First, they both consider the task of giving a word association to a verbal stimulus as a simple thought problem, the study of which may shed light on cognitive processes in general. Further, they believe that producing word associations is a microdevelopmental process in which successive and perhaps conceptually distinct stages occur within a brief time span.

By far the most explicit theoretical elaboration of a microgenetic view of thought formation has been given by Schilder (98, 99). According to this theorist, thought begins with a diffuse conception of its goal, some sort of vague direction in which it is to go. The early stages of its development from this point onward he termed the *preparatory phase of thought*. In this phase a host of mental contents *(presentations* as Schilder called them) feed into the ongoing thought development. These vague *presentations* may be logically relevant or irrelevant in relation to the thought nucleus which is at this time gaining ever-increasing structure and clarity. Those ideas or images which are relevant are incorporated into the process and enrich the forming thought; those which are irrelevant normally get suppressed and at most remain only as "background music" for the evolving thought. In this early, preparatory period mental contents are said to be of a symbol- and imagelike character, very susceptible to fusions and condensations with each other and with the developing thought structure, and subject to emotional restructuring in accordance with what we would today term "primary process" influence. The logic by which certain of these primitive presentations rather than others come to the fore is not specifically described beyond stating that contiguity and similarity, especially similarity of external, superficial attributes, play major roles. Schilder further states that, as the development progresses, the thought structure normally becomes more and more reality-oriented and less and less wish-determined—Undeutsch (112) had said the same thing about perceptual development—as well as less ridden with concrete imagery, less symbolistic, less undifferentiated and unstable, etc. Schilder's theory of microgenesis can of course be roundly criticized on a number of grounds. The referents of many of his terms are highly obscure, his exposition proceeds unencumbered by restraint or caution, his thesis lacks direct evidence, and so forth. Nevertheless, it can be said that he has fashioned a series of strikingly imaginative and original hypotheses about an aspect of cognition which has sadly needed explicit theorizing, however high-flown and speculative.

At this point our rather meager history is completed and stock-taking is in order. Although the existing evidence hardly permits any kind of integrated theory of thought microdevelopment, it is at least possible to see some commonality and consistency in what has been said and to organize a series of very tentative statements about the topic—a sort of loose conceptual framework within which to think about the development of thoughts. In this hypothetical account, we will lean most heavily upon Schilder's writings but will also draw from the work of Rapaport et al., Jung, and the rest.

First of all, thought in its early stages is global, diffuse, and undifferentiated in structure (131); that is, mental contents, be they images or imageless thoughts, tend to coexist without articulation and without clearly defined interrelationships. These early thought elements may be vague, imageless thought tendencies concerning the task, the solution, the thinker's relationship to task and solution, etc. Images, when they occur in thinking, also tend to be early rather than late products and may serve as primitive and concrete anchoring-points or, as Schilder puts it (99), "symbols" for what is to come. Microgenetically early thoughts, imaginal or imageless, seem to have the quality of what Rappaport (83) has termed *drive-representations,* i.e., needs and affects are particularly sovereign in determining which thoughts push for expression, which thoughts feed into the developmental process. Moreover, the laws of combination and association of thoughts in the beginning phases likewise seem to resemble those posited for primary process thinking, i.e., association by contiguity, association by superficial, external similarity, association on the basis of common personal predicates and a prevalence of condensation and displacements (32). Thus the thought process tends first towards this, then that premature, "paleological" solution (1) and early judgments of solutions tend to be primitive, dichotomous affairs framed in terms of me-not me, good-bad, etc. (99). In the later stages of development thought ordinarily becomes differentiated into various components and these components become logically interrelated in the formation of the solution. Thought in the final phase is normally reality- rather than drive-oriented and the early non-logical thought developments have become aborted, as it were, and no longer influence the form of solution. It is very likely that, in most people under ordinary circumstances, this extraordinarily rapid developmental process does not become an object of awareness and the thinker is conscious only of the completed thought.[2]

IMPLICATIONS OF MICROGENETIC THEORY

It is proposed here that the microgenetic approach can be fruitfully applied to the cognition (perception and thought) of pathological individuals under normal conditions and of normal individuals under atypical, non-normal conditions. An attempt will be made to provide evidence that such atypical cognitions tend to manifest formal characteristics similar to those already predicated for microgenetically incomplete cognition. Such evidence would suggest the general hypothesis that most of all atypical cognitions, whether found in normal or pathological individuals, are special cases of normal, mature cognition in the sense that they are cognitive forms which have aborted prior to complete development. Thus, within this frame of reference, normal cognition is not defined simply by the absence of nonnormal attributes nor is atypical cognition viewed as a unique, qualitatively distinct formation. Normal, logical cognition is seen as a microdevelopmental achievement of the organism and deviations therefrom as developmental arrests. Such an approach, should the facts

[2] In this connection Rapaport, Gill, and Schafer (*84*) state:
"These preparatory phrases are, in the average subject, preconscious: however, in introspective and/or obsessive people, the inquiring examiner often obtains reports on what happened in the brief interval between the stimulus- and reaction-word—how definitions, images, clang and other deviant associations occurred and were rejected, though the result came quickly and as a 'popular reaction' " (p. 20).

justify it, permits one to subsume a host of cognitive phenomena under one developmental theory and, at the same time, makes the study of the normal prototypical microgenetic process something of considerable theoretical urgency.

In surveying the evidence for these beliefs, our previous major breakdown in terms of percepts versus thoughts will be abandoned; instead, we shall examine the findings topic by topic, drawing from whichever set of microgenetic hypotheses (perceptual or thought) best applies to the data at hand.

Normals under atypical conditions. Distraction constitutes one set of conditions under which normal individuals tend to produce cognitive responses which could be called atypical. There have been a few studies which have attempted to study distraction effects. Jung (51) and Speich (108), for example, both found that when Ss are asked to give word associations under distraction conditions the tendency is for superficial, external responses (clangs, word-completions, etc.) to increase. In another publication (52) Jung reports an interesting early study by Stransky on the effects of an experimental condition similar to distraction. His Ss were instructed to talk about anything for one minute without attending to what they were saying. He found that these instructions produced an abundance of immature-like processes which included substitution of superficial connections (clangs, etc.) for logical ones, numerous perseverations, and fusions of competing verbal responses which resulted in neologisms and contaminations. Not all the evidence with regard to distraction effects is in accord with microgenetic theory, however; Cameron and Margaret (11) failed to find such effects when distraction was superimposed on a task of completing incomplete sentences.

There is some evidence pertaining to the formal characteristics of thinking in dreams, daydreams, and semi-sleep. Freud (32), as is well known, characterized dream-thinking as being replete with condensations, displacements, symbolization of abstract thoughts via concrete images, prelogical thinking mediated by external and superficial or highly subjective similarity, etc. Varendonck (115), in his classical study of daydreams, has likewise stressed the lack of criticality and logical direction and the important role of nonverbal imagery which obtains in ordinary, conscious fantasy. Mintz (72), Rapaport (82), and Silberer (102) have described the hypnagogic or semisleep state in somewhat similar terms: decrease in reflective awareness, or sharply focussed self-criticality; symbolization (via images rather than words) of bodily states, attitudes, etc., as well as ordinary thought contents; and a tendency to substitute prelogical autistic thinking for logical, conventional thought. Jung (51) reports a study in which one S was given a word-association test both under normal waking conditions and under conditions of semisleep. The S, while drowsy, gave about seven times as many clang reactions as when in the waking state.

There are a variety of studies describing the effects of various drugs upon thought and perception. Smith (106) found that alcohol tends to increase the frequency of word associations of Jung's "outer" type. He did not report his results statistically but the senior author's recalculations of Smith's data suggest that this tendency was significant at about the $p <$ .15 level of confidence. Both Woodworth and Schlosberg (138) and Kohs (57) allude to old studies by Kraepelin and his students which suggest that caffeine tends to cause Ss to give more superficial word assocations. There are a number of studies describing the effects of mescaline, lysergic acid derivatives (LSD), and other "psychotogenic" drugs on cognition (28, 37, 41, 42, 43, 45, 63, 64, 69, 92, 110). Some, although by no means all, of these drug effects seem consistent with what we would consider to be the formal characteristics of microdevelopmentally early cognition. Thus Ss under the influence of LSD or mescaline have been found to show, among other things: looseness of association; rhyming and punning; inability to follow a single train of thought without interpenetration and fusions with other thought sequences; predominance of vivid imagery in thinking; and a general lability of percepts. In connection with the imagelike character of thoughts, for example, some of Meadows' Ss reported that they had to overcome the ever-present visual images in order to think abstractly (69). One of Guttman's Ss described this phenomenon as follows: "Each word I thought was connected with a picture. This hindered my thinking, as the concrete picture held me" (37, p. 213). Lindemann and Clarke (63), and Kubie and Margolin (60) have also suggested that other drugs, such as scopolamine, sodium amytal, nitrous oxide, and various barbiturates, produce cognitive states essentially equivalent to those previously described for the semisleep state.

In addition to distraction, drugs, deviations from the waking state, etc., there are several other miscellaneous conditions which deserve brief mention. According to Kohs (57), Aschaffenburg found the familiar increase in clang and completion responses when Ss were in a fatigued state. Bexton, Heron, and Scott (3) found that prolonged insulation of Ss from external stimuli caused an increase in directionless thought of the daydream type and a falling back upon extremely vivid imagery. Kline and Schneck (56) found more "associative alterations" when Ss gave word associations while under hypnosis. Although it is not altogether clear from their paper, "associative alteration" appears to include Rapaport, Gill, and Schafer's (84) *distant* and *mildly distant* categories primarily. Finally, Gellhorn and Kraines (34, 35), in another word-association study, report that experimentally induced anoxia causes an increase in perseverations and unusual, irrelevant associations—a result consistent with McFarland's earlier findings on the psychological effects of oxygen deprivation (67).

We have so far considered verbal cognitive behavior in normals under atypical organismic states. Also of interest from a microgenetic standpoint are subverbal or preverbal cognitive responses under more or less typical organismic states—namely, the kinds of cognitive responses found in studies of semantic conditioning (21, 85, 86, 87, 88, 89, 90, 91, 139) and subception (62, 66, 68, 121). In both semantic conditioning and subception studies Ss evidence some sort of "cognition" of stimuli (usually below the level of verbal report) by means of measurable electrodermal or salivary responses. It is interesting to speculate as to whether these kinds of dim cognitions which "register" only at the physiological level can be considered microgenetically early, primitive forms which do not, for one reason or another, attain conscious awareness. Some of the studies of semantic conditioning reveal curious facts which might suggest this. Razran (90), for example, reports one experiment in which a salivary response was conditioned to a given word and then S was presented with a variety of other words, each bearing a different relationship to the original stimulus word. As might be expected, synonyms, supraordinates and contrasts of the original word elicited salivary responses of fairly large magnitude. What was surprising, however, was that *homophones* (i.e., clangs) of the original word elicited salivary responses about as large as the more logically respectable coordinates, part-wholes, whole-parts, and predicates, and of greater magnitude than subordinates, a highly logical category! Common sense will assert, and Flavell (30) has demonstrated experimentally, that normals do not consciously consider words related by sound similarity to be as similar in meaning as those related in terms of any of the semantic categories mentioned above. Yet the various studies of semantic conditioning seem to indicate that we do make generalizations about verbal symbols, at the physiological level, on the basis of physical as well as semantic similarity. It may indeed be, as Jung long ago suggested, that "every apperceptive process of an acoustic stimulus begins at the stage of clang-like apprehension," and that such an apprehension somehow gets "recorded" in an immediate autonomic reaction but normally does not persist, in subsequent microdevelopment, as a conscious component of the final cognition. It may also be possible to view at least some aspects of the problem of subception in similar terms. Bruner and Postman (7) some time ago offered an interpretation of perceptual defense and subception data in terms of levels of response. They suggest that generic and diffuse affective responses may occur prior to, or at lower thresholds than, conscious cognitive responses pertaining to the specific nature of the stimulus. They also mention, in passing, the relationship of this view to the classical "stages of perception" theories we have already reviewed. More recently, Lazarus (61) has offered a somewhat similar view as one possible explanation of subception. He suggests that the autonomic nervous system may be capable of making global, all-or-none discriminations between "danger" and "no danger," "shock" and "no shock," etc., under stimulus conditions which are not adequate for precise differentiation of the more complex attributes of the stimulus.

The really intriguing question which all this poses, of course, is whether or not so-called "unconscious" thinking and perceiving can be meaningfully framed within microgenetic theory. One wonders whether the similarities which may exist between unconscious cognition, as in dreams for example, and what we have termed microgenetically early cognition are merely coincidental. May it be that unconscious, primary process cognitions are those which begin to develop, make their mark on behavior, and then, for reasons which can only be guessed at, abort below the level of conscious awareness? Conrad (15), to whose work on microgenesis we shall shortly refer, proposed a very similar explanation. The recent experiments by Smith and Henriksson (104) and Klein et al. (55) also provide some support for such a conceptualization. In these studies it was demonstrated that stimuli flashed at tachistoscopic exposure times too brief for conscious recognition definitely modified the perception of other suprathreshold stimuli presented immediately after them. Klein (54, p. 23) makes one statement, in discussing his results, which well expresses the tenor of our own musings:

> A working hypothesis in this situation is that the A figure, exposed for a few microseconds, starts a cognitive process which is interrupted or covered over so quickly by the B process that it is, in effect, aborted. Some kind of compromise formation results in the reported percept. *Such incomplete formations may provide the condition for the operation of primary process mechanisms* (italics ours).

Pathological individuals. We shall confine our discussion in this section mainly to two diagnostic groups in which atypical cognition seems especially predominant—schizophrenia and aphasia. Fairly adequate accounts of theory and research on schizophrenic cognition may be found in Arieti (1), Bellak (2), Cameron (10), Fenichel (27), Flavell (30), Goodstein (36), Kasanin (53), Wegrocki (123), and White (135). A study of the literature on schizophrenic thought and perception reveals two facts of particular relevance to a microgenetic approach. The first of these pertains to what seems to be a rather striking similarity between microgenetically immature cognition and schizophrenic cognition. The senior author, for example, has elsewhere (30) summarized some of the alleged salient features of schizophrenic thinking roughly as follows: condensations, ellipses, word salad, neologisms, clang associations, tangentiality, incoherence, word magic, "paleological" thinking based upon logically superficial predicates of either external or inner-personal origin, excessive use of concrete symbolism, and others. Secondly, the so-called "regression" theorists, i.e., Arieti (1), Von Domarus (120), Storch (111), Vigotsky (117), Werner (131), White (135) and various psychoanalysts (27), have related schizophrenic cognition to that found in normals under abnormal conditions, in children, and in people belonging to "less advanced" cultures. That is, they regard schizophrenic cognition as one instance of a more generic, *primitive* mode of cognition which is found in a variety of individuals under various conditions (30). Only Schilder (98, 99, 100) seemingly, has both stressed the formal similarities among primitive or regressive cognitive processes of various kinds and also explicitly taken the further step of viewing such processes as *themselves* possible instances of microgenetically immature cognition. It is of interest to note that Schilder focused particular attention on schizophrenia as the example par excellence of a condition in which early cognitive formations intrude into consciousness and get expressed as though they were completed thoughts. Two of the most interesting recent studies pertinent to the problem of microgenesis in schizophrenia are reported in the article by Phillips and Framo mentioned above (80). Rorschach cards were successively shown to schizophrenics and normals under increasing tachistoscopic exposure times and responses scored on a scale of amorphousness-specificity-differentiation and organization, devised by Friedman (33). As exposure time increased, the normals' percepts tended to progress from an initial amorphousness and vagueness to specificity and integration; the schizophrenics' percepts, on the other hand, tended to remain at the initial undifferentiated level. Also worthy of mention are the word-association studies by Rapaport et al. cited earlier. They found that schizophrenics exceeded normals in responses presumably indicative of an incomplete associative development, i.e., the various reactions classified as *close* or *distant*.

We have stated that Schilder is essentially the only theorist who has systematically described schizophrenic cognition in microdevelopmental terms. In this respect aphasia has fared somewhat better. As mentioned earlier, Bouman and Grünbaum, Pick and Thiele, and Van Woerkom derived their conceptions of normal microgenesis directly from studies of thought and perception in aphasia. Thus Bouman and Grünbaum, for example, found that an aphasic patient had difficulty in coping with stimuli which required analyzing parts within a whole (e.g., a design embedded within two overlapping figures) but could adequately handle perceptual and conceptual situations in which only a diffuse, over-all apprehension or a total dichotomous judgment was required. From evidence of this kind Bouman and Grünbaum, Van Woerkom, etc., drew two conclusions: first, the normal sequence of cognition has a certain characterizable developmental form; second, this developmental sequence somehow gets arrested during its early stages in aphasia. Certainly the most vocal and explicit proponent of a microgenetic interpretation of aphasic cognition has been Conrad (13, 14, 15, 16, 17, 18). Conrad has systematically applied the theoretical formulation of the *Aktualgenese* school to aphasic cognitions. He states that the normal process of cognition involves both progressive differentiation and integration of stimulus material and that in aphasia, one or both of these processes typically tends to be incomplete (14). Conrad describes four levels of disability which may occur: *(a)* normal Gestalt formation gets accomplished but with abnormal effort and tension; *(b)* the figure gets differentiated from background but does not itself become differentiated or structured; *(c)* figure and ground are not clearly articulated and the percept is vague and amorphous, as though presented tachistoscopically at very brief exposure times; *(d)* lack of any Gestalt formation of any kind (13). Conrad suggests that certain memory processes may also be considered from a microgenetic standpoint (15). For example, he elaborates upon Wenzl's (126) earlier account of the process of word-finding, suggesting that, in attempting to remember a forgotten word, we pass through successive stages structurally similar to those found in perceptual microdevelopment. The sequence of mnemonic reconstitution is the same for normals and aphasics, although, of course, the problem of searching one's memory for forgotten words may be an almost ever-present one for the aphasic. Worthy of citation here also is the extensive work of Ombredane, whose findings likewise support a microgenetic conception of aphasic disorders (74). Werner's paper (132), a revised and extended version of an earlier German publication (129), is the most recent exposition of an avowedly microdevelopmental approach to aphasia, and perhaps the only one in the literature published in English. In this study, one of a series of pioneer investigations in the area of microdevelopment (127, 128, 130), words were presented repeatedly under gradually increasing tachistoscopic exposure times and normal *S*s were asked to recount their perceptual experiences at each exposure until full recognition was achieved. Werner found that a number of his *S*s reported experiencing spheres of meaning prior to specific and complete recognition of the word stimuli. For example, some *S*s would experience "feelings" about the as yet undiscriminated stimulus word—feelings that it is "warm," "vibrating," "soft," etc. Also, *S*s would occasionally get a global impression of the domain or class within which the word belongs ("it is something shining," etc.). Werner then describes highly similar spheric experiences reported by aphasics in the course of attempting to name familiar objects, read or grasp the meaning of familiar words, and so on. He suggests that in such cases the patient's overt response is the result of a premature precipitation of spheric experiences into verbal expression, i.e., a microgenetic abortion of the kind Conrad and others have described. In the remainder of his paper, Werner discusses some interesting implications of this view for the re-education of patients with aphasic disorders.

FUTURE PROBLEMS

We have discussed some of the evidence pertaining to a microgenetic approach to cognition and some of the possible applications of this approach to various cognitive states in normal and pathological individuals. Other possible extensions could be delineated. For example, formal relationships between microgenetically immature cognition and cognitive functioning in nonaphasic brain-damaged cases, aments, depressives, manics, and normal children have not been discussed, although there is some evidence which might support some such comparisons (26, 39, 46, 79, 84, 133). Also, possible relationships between personality variables and microgenetic sequences need exploration. It is interesting to note that members of the *Aktualgenese* school were actively concerned with correlating individual differences in microdevelopmental sequence with "personality types" (23, 38, 40) and that Sander himself thought of microgenesis as a potential avenue for the exploration of the unconscious (94, 95). A recent study by Smith and Klein (105), although concerned with somewhat more extended cognitive sequences than those we have been considering, is also relevant to the problem of microgenesis-personality relationships. However, the most extensive and perhaps the most intriguing investigations in this area are those recently described by Kragh (58). This Swedish psychologist has formulated a bold and explicit personality-perceptual microgenesis theory and has reported a series of tachistoscopic experiments which purport to show relationships between the ontogenesis of personality and the microgenesis of percepts. As a final extension, one can speculate with Werner (132) as to whether such functions as memory and motor performance—as well as perceptual and conceptual developments more complex and of longer duration than the ones considered in this paper—typically undergo developmental sequences similar in formal aspects to those already described.

Such questions, however, seem somewhat premature at present in that they assume a more complete factual knowledge of the prototypical microgenetic processes than we now possess. A problem of much higher priority concerns whether, and by what means, the nature of these elusive processes themselves can be experimentally elucidated. With regard to perceptual microdevelopment, it is clear that more adequately designed studies of the formal aspects of genetic sequences are needed. For example, it would be possible to avoid the hazards of relying solely upon verbal report in tachistoscopic studies by requiring artistically trained *S*s to draw rather than describe their percepts at each exposure time level. It should then be possible to study sequences by having the drawings categorized by judges as to such formal features as diffuseness, degree of figure-ground articulation, etc. Such a study would perhaps lay claim to greater objectivity than those hitherto reported. Likewise, for the development of thoughts or concepts, a plausible experimental technique might be that of motivating *S*s to produce word associations under extreme time pressure and comparing the formal aspects of the resultant associations with those produced by *S*s who had not responded under pressure. Techniques of this type have been used with some success in the past (19, 51, 71, 101, 108). Both of the above methods, or modifications thereof, could of course also be used with nonnormal populations in order to study regressive cognition within a microdevelopmental framework.

In concluding, it is perhaps appropriate to underscore the considerable problems which confront the microgenetic approach in its current form. In the first place, the abstractness, looseness of logical structure, and general semantic imprecision which characterizes present-day microgenetic theory may be in part responsible for the ease with which it seems to subsume so many diverse cognitive phenomena. Such a criticism implies that as the conciseness and testability of the theory increases, nature will seem less cooperative and problems of generalization will arise. Likewise, at the data level, it must be apparent that the findings on the basis of which microgenetic hypotheses have been constructed are by no means gilt-edged. For example, many of the studies cited stem from an era when careful experimental control could hardly be called the rule. Perhaps a more serious criticism pertains to the nature of the typical experimental operations by which microgenesis is allegedly demonstrated. It could be argued, for instance, that the fact that an *S* might, under time pressure, produce responses classified within the theory as microgenetically undeveloped does not prove conclusively that such responses really "occur" but are suppressed in the normal, unhurried associative process. It is certainly possible to pose alternative explanations in terms of variations in set or alterations in verbal habit-family hierarchies induced by time pressure. Similarly, there is no absolute proof that the sequence of percepts found when the tachistoscopic method is used is a faithful reflection of the natural process of percept development. Pertinent criticisms of this order have been raised by Weinschenk (124, 125), and Klein.[3] It is true that one can counter such objections with logical arguments and by citing introspective evidence, such as the verbal reports of Rapaport's obsessional group mentioned earlier (Footnote 2). Nonetheless, such objections have real force and the *experimentum crucis* which would settle the matter is difficult to conceive at present. For us the microgenetic interpretation has led to a fresh, albeit highly speculative, view of a variety of cognitive phenomena and has suggested certain lines along which research might

[3]Klein, G. S. Personal communication, May 28, 1956.

proceed. We are thus inclined to tolerate its ambiguities for a time out of sheer curiosity to see what will come of it in the future.

SUMMARY

The present paper has proposed a microgenetic approach to perception and thought. Within this approach, thoughts and percepts are believed to undergo a very brief, but theoretically important, microdevelopment. Evidence was offered both to support the possibility that such microdevelopments do occur in the normal process of thinking and perceiving and to suggest some of the formal characteristics of such evolutions. Further, an attempt was made to delineate some of the possible implications of this approach for cognitive functioning in abnormal individuals and in normal individuals under atypical conditions. Finally, consideration was given to current problems and future research possibilities in relation to a microgenetic framework.

REFERENCES

1. ARIETI, S. *Interpretation of Schizophrenia.* New York: Brunner, 1955.
2. BELLAK, L. *Dementia Praecox.* New York: Grune & Stratton, 1948.
3. BEXTON, W. H., HERON, W. & SCOTT, F. H. Effects of Decreased Variation on the Sensory Environment. *Canad. J. Psychol.,* 1954, *8,* 70–76.
4. BORING, E. G. *A History of Experimental Psychology.* (2nd Ed.) New York: Appleton-Century-Crofts, 1950.
5. BOUMAN, L., & GRUNBAUM, A. A. Experimentell-Psychologische Untersuchungen zur Aphasie und Paraphasie. *Z. ges. Neurol. Psychiat.,* 1925, *96,* 481–538.
6. BRIGDEN R. L. A Tachistoscopic Study of the Differentiation of Perception. *Psychol. Monogr.,* 1933, *44,* No. 1 (hole No. 197).
7. BRUNER, J. S., & POSTMAN, L. Perception, Cognition, and Behavior. *J. Pers.,* 1949, *18,* 14–31.
8. BÜHLER, K. On Thought Connections. In D. Rapaport (Ed.), *Organization and Pathology of Thought.* New York: Columbia University Press, 1951. Pp. 39–57.
9. BUTZMANN, K. Aktualgenese im Indirekten Sehen. *Arch. ges. Psychol.,* 1940, *106,* 137–193.
10. CAMERON, N. The Functional Psychoses. In J. McV. Hunt (Ed.) *Personality and the Behavior Disorders.* Vol. 2. New York: Ronald, 1944. Pp. 861–921.
11. CAMERON, N., & MARGARET, A. Experimental Studies in Thinking; I. Scattered Speech in the Responses of Normal Subjects to Incomplete Sentences. *J. Exp. Psychol.,* 1949, *39,* 617–627.

12. CARL, H. Versuche über Tachistoscopisches Bilderkennen. *Z. Psychol.*, 1933, *129*, 1–42.

13. CONRAD, K. Uber den Begriff der Vorgestalt und seine Bedeutung für die Hirnpathologie. *Nervenarzt*, 1947, *18*, 289–293.

14. CONRAD, K. Uber differentiale und integrale Gestaltfunktion und den Begriff der Protopathie. *Nervenarzt*, 1948, *19*, 315–323.

15. CONRAD, K. Das Problem der Gestörten Wortfindung in Gestalttheoretischer Betrachtung. *Schweiz. Arch. Neurol. Psychiat.*, 1949, *63*, 141–192.

16. CONRAD, K. Uber das Prinzip der Vorgestaltung in der Hirnpathologie. *Dtsch. Z. Nervenheilk.*, 1950, *164*, 66–70.

17. CONRAD, K. Uber den Begriff der Vorgestalt Bemerkungen zu dem Aufsatz von Weinschenk. *Nervenartz*, 1950, *21*, 58–63.

18. CONRAD, K. Uber das Prinzip der Vorgestaltung Erwiderung auf die Vorstehende Arbeit von Weinschenk. *Schweiz. Arch. Neurol. Psychiat.*, 1951, *67*, 119–125.

19. CORDES, G. Experimentelle Untersuchungen über Associationen. *Philos. Stud.*, 1901, *17*, 30–77. 20. DICKENSON, C. A. The Course of Experience. *Amer. J. Psychol.*, 1926, *37*, 330–344.

20. DICKINSON, C. A. The Course of Experience. *Amer. J. Psychol.* 1926, *37*, 330–344.

21. DIVEN, K. Certain Determinants in the Conditioning of Anxiety Reactions. *J. Psychol.*, 1937, *3*, 291–308.

22. DOUGLAS, A. G. A Tachistoscopic Study of the Order of Emergence in the Process of Perception. *Psychol. Monogr.*, 1947, *61*, No. 6 (Whole No. 287).

23. DUN, F. T. Aktualgenetische Untersuchungen des Auffassungvorgang Chinesischer Schriftzeichen. *Arch. ges. Psychol.*, 1939, *104*, 131–174.

24. DUNCKER, K. On Problem-Solving. (Lynne S. Lees, Trans.) *Psychol. Monogr.*, 1945, *58*, No. 5 (Whole No. 270).

25. EINDHOVEN, J., & VINACKE, W. E. Creative Processes in Painting. *J. Gen. Psychol.*, 1952, *47*, 139–164.

26. FEIFEL, H. An Analysis of the Word Definition Errors of Children. *J. Psychol.*, 1952, *33*, 65–77.

27. FENICHEL, O. *The Psychoanalytical Theory of Neurosis*. New York: Norton, 1945.

28. FISCHER, R. Factors Involved in Drug-Produced Model Psychoses. *J. Ment. Sci.*, 1954, *100*, 623–632.

29. FLAVELL, J. H. Thought, Communication and Social Integration in Schizophrenia: An Experimental and Theoretical Study. Unpublished doctor's dissertation, Clark University, 1954.

30. FLAVELL, J. H. Abstract Thinking and Social Behavior in Schizophrenia. *J. Abnorm. Soc. Psychol.*, 1956, *52*, 208–211.

31. FREEMAN, G. I. An Experimental Study of the Perception of Objects. *J. Exp. Psychol.*, 1929, *12*, 341–358.

32. FREUD, S. The Interpretation of Dreams. In A. A. Brill (Ed.) *The Basic Writings of Sigmund Freud.* New York: Modern Library, 1938. Pp. 181–552.

33. FRIEDMAN, H. Perceptual Recognition in Schizophrenia: An Hypothesis

Suggested by the Use of the Rorschach Test. *J. Genet. Psychol.*, 1952, *81*, 63–98.

34. GELLHORN, E., & KRAINES, S. H. The Influence of Hyperpnea and of Variations in the O_2 and CO_2 Tension of the Inspired Air on Word-Association. *Science*, 1936, *83*, 266–267.

35. GELLHORN, E., & KRAINES, S. H. Word Associations As Affected by Deficient Oxygen, Excess of Carbon Dioxide and Hyperpnea. *Arch. Neurol. Psychiat.*, 1937, *38*, 491–504.

36. GOODSTEIN, L. D. The Language of Schizophrenia. *J. Gen. Psychol.*, 1951, *45*, 95–104.

37. GUTTMAN, E. Artificial Psychoses Produced by Mescaline. *J. Ment. Sci.*, 1936, *82*, 203–221.

38. HAUSMANN, G. Zur Aktualgenese raumlicher Gestalten. *Arch. Ges. Psychol.*, 1935, *93*, 289–334.

39. HEMMENDINGER, L. A Genetic Study of Structural Aspects of Perception As Reflected in Rorschach Responses. Unpublished doctor's dissertation, Clark University, 1951.

40. HIPPIUS, R. Erkennendes Tasten als Wahrnehmung und als Erkenntnisvorgang. *Neue Psychol. Stud.*, 1934, *10*, 1–163.

41. HOCH, P. H. Experimentally Produced Psychoses. *Amer. J. Psychiat.*, 1951, *107*, 607–611.

42. HOCH, P. H., CATTELL, J. P., & PENNES, H. H. Effects of Mescaline and Lysergic Acid (d-LSD-25). *Amer. J. Psychiat.*, 1952, *108*, 579–584.

43. HOCH, P. H., CATTELL, J. P., & PENNES, H. H. Effects of Drugs; Theoretical Considerations from a Psychological Viewpoint. *Amer. J. Psychiat.*, 1952, *108*, 585–589.

44. HUMPHREY, G. *Thinking: An Introduction to its Experimental Psychology*. New York: Wiley, 1951.

45. HYDE, R. W., VON MERING, O., & MORIMOTO, K. Hostility in the Lysergic Psychosis. *J. Nerv. Ment. Dis.*, 1953, *118*, 266–267. (Abstract)

46. IN DER BEECK, M. Der Begriff der Vorgestalt in der Sprachentwicklung des Kleinkindes. *Nervenartz*, 1952, *23*, 464–466.

47. JOHANNES, T. Der Einfluss der Gestaltbindung auf das Behlaten. *Arch. Ges. Psychol.*, 1932, *85*, 411–457.

48. JOHANNES, T. Der Einfluss der Gestaltbindung auf das Behalten. 2 Teil. *Arch. Ges. Psychol.*, 1939, *104*, 74–130.

49. JOHNSON, D. M. A Modern Account of Problem Solving. *Psychol. Bull.*, 1944, *41*, 201–229.

50. JOHNSON, D. M. *The Psychology of Thought and Judgment*. New York: Harper, 1955.

51. JUNG, C. G. *Studies in Word Association* (M. D. Eder, Trans.). New York: Moffat, 1919.

52. JUNG, C. G. The Psychology of Dementia Praecox. *Nerv. Ment. Dis. Monogr.*, 1936, No. 3.

53. KASANIN, J. S. (Ed.) *Language and Thought in Schizophrenia: Collected Papers*. Berkeley: University of California Press, 1944.

54. KLEIN, G. S. Perspectives to a Research Program on the Organization of Personality. Paper read at N. Y. Psychol. Assoc., New York, January, 1954.

55. KLEIN, G. S., SPENCE, D. P., HOLT, R. R., & GOUREVITCH, S. Preconscious Influences upon Conscious Cognitive Behavior, *Amer. Psychol.,* 1955, *10,* 380. (Abstract)

56. KLINE, M. V., & SCHNECK, J. M. Hypnosis in Relation to the Word Association Test. *J. Gen. Psychol.,* 1951, *44,* 129–137.

57. KOHS, S. C. The Association Method in its Relation to the Complex and Complex Indicators. *Amer. J. Psychol.,* 1914, *25,* 544–594.

58. KRAGH, U. *The Actual-Genetic Model of Perception-Personality.* Lund: CWK Leerup, 1955.

59. KRUEGER, F. The Essence of Feeling: Outline of a Systematic Theory. In M. L. Reymert (Ed.), *Feelings and Emotions.* The Wittenberg Symposium. Worcester, Mass.: Clark University Press, 1928. Pp. 58–78.

60. KUBIE, L. S., & MARGOLIN, S. The Therapeutic Role of Drugs in the Process of Repression, Dissociation, and Synthesis. *Psychosom. Med.,* 1945, *20,* 147–151.

61. LAZARUS, R. S. Subception: Fact or Artifact? A Reply to Erikson. *Psychol. Rev.,* 1956, *63,* 343–347.

62. LAZARUS, R. S., & M^cCLEARY, R. A. Autonomic Discrimination without Awareness: A Study of Subception. *Psychol. Rev.,* 1951, *58,* 113–122.

63. LINDEMANN, E., & CLARKE, L. D. Modifications in Ego Structure and Personality Reactions under the Influence of the Effects of Drugs. *Amer. J. Psychiat.,* 1952, *108,* 561–567.

64. LINDEMANN, E., & MALAMUD, W. Experimental Analysis of the Psychopathological Effects of Intoxicating Drugs. *Amer. J. Psychiat.,* 1934, *13,* 853–881.

65. MANTELL, U. Aktualgenetische Untersuchungen an Situationsdarstellung. *Neue Psychol. Stud.,* 1936, *13,* 1–96.

66. M^cCLEARY, R. A., & LAZARUS, R. S. Autonomic Discrimination without Awareness. *J. Pers.,* 1949, *18,* 171–179.

67. M^cFARLAND, R. A. The Psychological Effects of Oxygen Deprivation (Anoxemia) on Human Behavior. *Arch. Psychol.,* 1932, No. 145.

68. M^cGINNIES, E. Emotionality and Perceptual Defense. *Psychol. Rev.,* 1949, *56,* 244–251.

69. MEADOWS, A. Anxiety, Concrete Thinking and Blood Pressure Changes in Schizophrenia. Unpublished doctor's dissertation, Harvard University, 1951.

70. MESSER, A. Experimenteil-psychologische Untersuchungen über das denken. *Arch. Ges. Psychol.,* 1906, *8,* 1–224.

71. MEUMANN, E. Über Assoziationsexperimente mit Beeinflussung der Reproduktionzeit. *Arch. Ges. Psychol.,* 1907, *9,* 116–150.

72. MINTZ, A. Schizophrenic Speech and Sleepy Speech. *J. Abnorm. Soc. Psychol.,* 1948, *43,* 548–549.

73. MÖRSCHNER, W. Betrage zur Aktualgenese des Gegenstanderlebens. *Arch. Ges. Psychol.,* 1940, *107,* 125–149.

74. OMBREDANE, A. *L'Aphasie et l'Elaboration de la Pensee Explicite.* Paris: Presses Universitaires de France, 1951.

75. OSGOOD, C. E. *Method and Theory in Experimental Psychology.* New York: Oxford University Press, 1953.

76. PATRICK, C. Creative Thought in Poets. *Arch. Psychol.,* 1935, No. 178.

77. PATRICK, C. Creative Thought in Artists. *J. Psychol.,* 1937, *4,* 35–73.

78. PATRICK, C. Scientific Thought. *J. Psychol.,* 1938, *5,* 55–83.

79. PENA, C. A Genetic Evaluation of Perceptual Structurization in Cerebral Pathology: An Investigation by Means of the Rorschach Test. *J. Proj. Tech.,* 1953, *17,* 186–199.

80. PHILLIPS, L., & FRAMO, J. L. Developmental Theory Applied to Normal and Psychopathological Perception. *J. Pers.,* 1954, *22,* 465–474.

81. PICK, A. M., & THIELE, R. Aphasie. In A. Bethe (Ed.), *Handb. d. Norm. u. Pathol. Physiol.,* Vol. XV, 2. Berlin: Springer, 1931.

82. RAPAPORT, D. Consciousness: A Psychopathological and Psychodynamic View In H. A. Abramson (Ed.), *Conference on Problems on Consciousness.* New York: Josiah Macy, Jr. Foundation, 1951. Pp. 18–57.

83. RAPAPORT, D. Toward a Theory of Thinking. In D. Rapaport (Ed.), *Organization and Pathology of Thought.* New York: Columbia University Press, 1951. Pp. 689–730.

84. RAPAPORT, D., GILL, M., & SCHAFER, R. *Diagnostic Psychological Testing.* Vol. 2. Chicago: Year Book Publishers, 1946.

85. RAZRAN, G. Salivation and Thinking in Different Languages. *J. Psychol.,* 1935, *1,* 145–151.

86. RAZRAN, G. Semantic, Syntactic, and Phonetographic Generalization of Verbal Conditioning. *Psychol. Bull.,* 1939, *36,* 578. (Abstract)

87. RAZRAN, G. A Quantitative Study of Meaning by a Conditioned Salivary Technique (Salivary Conditioning). *Science,* 1939, *90,* 89–90.

88. RAZRAN, G. Semantic and Phonetographic Generalization of Semantic Conditioning to Verbal Stimuli. *J. Exp. Psychol.,* 1949, *39,* 642–652.

89. RAZRAN, G. Attitudinal Determinants of Conditioning and of Generalization of Conditioning. *J. Exp. Psychol.,* 1949, *39,* 820–829.

90. RAZRAN, G. Experimental Semantics. *Trans. N. Y. Acad. Sci.,* 1952, *14,* 171–176.

91. RIESS, B. F. Semantic Conditioning Involving the GSR. *J. Exp. Psychol.,* 1940, *26,* 238–240.

92. RINKEL, M., DE SHON, H. J., HYDE, R. W., & SOLOMON, H. C. Experimental Schizophrenia-like Symptoms. *Amer. J. Psychiat.,* 1952, *108,* 572–578.

93. SANDER, F. Uber Raumliche Rhytmik. *Neue Psychol. Stud.,* 1926, *1,* 125–158.

94. SANDER, F. Experimentelle Ergebnisse der Gestaltpsychologie. In E. Becher (Ed.), *10 Kongr. Ber. Exp. Psychol.* Jena: Fischer, 1928. Pp. 23–88.

95. SANDER, F. Structures, Totality of Experience, and Gestalt. In C. Murchison (Ed.), *Psychologies of 1930.* Worcester, Mass.: Clark University Press, 1930. Pp. 188–204.

96. SANDER, F., & JINUMA, R. Beitrage zur Psychologie des Ereoskopischen Sehens. l. Mitteilung. Die Grenzen der Binokularen Verschmeizung in ihrer Abhangigkeit von der Gestalthöhe der Doppelbilder. *Arch. Ges. Psychol.,* 1928, *65,* 191–207.

97. SCHAFER, R. A Study of Thought Processes in a Word Association Test. *Charact. Pers.,* 1945, *13,* 212–227.

98. SCHILDER, P. *Mind: Perception and Thought in Their Constructive Aspects*

New York: Columbia University Press, 1942.

99. SCHILDER, P. On the Development of Thoughts. In D. Rapaport (Ed.), *Organization and Pathology of Thought.* New York: Columbia University Press, 1951. Pp. 497–518.

100. SCHILDER, P. Studies Concerning the Psychology and Symptomatology of General Paresis. In D. Rapaport (Ed.), *Organization and Pathology of Thought.* New York: Columbia University Press, 1951. Pp. 519–580.

101. SIIPOLA, E., WALKER, W. N., & KOLB, D. Task Studies in Word Association, Projective and Nonprojective. *J. Pers.,* 1955, *23,* 441–459.

102. SILBERER, H. Report on a Method of Eliciting and Observing Certain Symbolic Hallucination-Phenomena. In D. Rapaport (Ed.), *Organization and Pathology of Thought.* New York: Columbia University Press, 1951. Pp. 195–207.

103. SMITH, F. An Experimental Investigation of Perception. *Brit. J. Psychol.,* 1914, *6,* 321–362.

104. SMITH, G. J. W., & HENRIKSSON, M. The Effect on an Established Percept of a Perceptual Process beyond Awareness. *Acta Psychologica,* 1955, *11,* 346–355.

105. SMITH, G. J. W., & KLEIN, G. S. Cognitive Controls in Serial Behavior Patterns. *J. Pers.,* 1953, *22,* 188–213.

106. SMITH, W. W. *The Measurement of Emotion.* New York: Harcourt, Brace, 1922.

107. SOMMER, W. Zerfall Optischer Gestalten Erlebnissformen und Struktur-zusammenhange. *Neue Psychol. Stud.,* 1936, *10,* 1–66.

108. SPEICH, R. Reproduktion und Psychische Activitat. *Arch. Ges. Psychol.,* 1927, *59,* 225–338.

109. STEIN, M. I. Personality Factors Involved in the Temporal Development of Rorschach responses. *J. Proj. Tech.,* 1949, *13,* 355–4l4.

110. STOCKINGS, G. T. Clinical Study of the Mescaline Psychosis with Special Reference to the Mechanism of the Genesis of Schizophrenic and other Psychotic States. *J. Ment. Sci.,* 1940, *86,* 29–47.

111. STORCH, A. The Primitive Archaic Forms of Inner Experiences and Thought in Schizophrenia. *Nerv. Ment. Dis. Monogr.,* 1924, No. 36.

112. UNDEUTSCH, U. Die Aktualgenese in ihrer Allgemeinpsychologischen und ihrer Charakterologischen Bedeutung. *Scientia,* 1942, *72,* 37–42; 95–98.

113. VAN WOERKOM, W. Sur l'Etat Psychique des Aphasiques. 1923, *L'Encephale,* 1923, *18,* 286–304.

114. VAN WOERKOM, W. Uber Störungen in Denken bei Aphasiepatienten. *Mschr. Psychiat. Neurol.,* 1925, *59,* 256–322.

115. VARENDONCK, J. *The Psychology of Day Dreams.* New York: Macmillan, 1924.

116. VIERGUTZ, F. Das Beschreiben. Experimentelle Untersuchung des Beschreibens von Gegenstanden. *Neue Psychol. Stud.,* 1933, *10* 1–92.

117. VIGOTSKY, L. S. Thought in Schizophrenia. *Arch. Neurol. Psychiat.,* 1934, *31,* 1063–1077.

118. VINACKE, W. E. The Investigation of Concept Formation. *Psychol. Bull.,* 1951, *48,* 1–31.

119. VINACKE, W. E. *The Psychology of Thinking.* New York: McGraw-Hill, 1952.

120. VON DOMARUS, E. The Specific Laws of Logic in Schizophrenia. In J. S. Kasanin (Ed.), *Language and Thought in Schizophrenia: Collected Papers.* Berkeley: University of California Press, 1944. Pp. 104–114.

121. VOOR, J. H. Subliminal Perception and Subception. *J. Psychol.,* 1956, *41,* 437–458.

122. WALLAS, G. *The Art of Thought.* New York: Harcourt, Brace, 1926.

123. WEGROCKI, H. J. Generalizing Ability in Schizophrenia: An Inquiry into the Disorders of Problem Thinking in Schizophrenia. *Arch. Psychol.,* 1940, No. 254.

124. WEINSCHENK, C. Der Bergriff der Vorgestalt und die Hirnpathologie. *Nervenartz,* 1941, *20,* 355–361.

125. WEINSCHENK, C. Conrad's neuer Begriff der Vorgestalt und die Hirnpathologie. *Schweiz. Arch. Neurol. Psychiat.,* 1951, *67,* 101–118.

126. WENZL, A. Empirische und Theoretische Beitrage zur Erinnerungsarbeit bei Erschwerter Wortfindung. *Arch. Ges. Psychol.,* 1932, *85,* 181–218.

127. WERNER, H. Studien über Strukturgesetze, IV. Uber Mikromelodik und Mikroharmonik. *Z. Psychol,* 1926, *98,* 74–89.

128. WERNER, H. Studein über Strukturgesetze. V. Uber die Auspragung von Tongestalten. *Z. Psychol.,* 1927, *101,* 159–181.

129. WERNER, H. Untersuchungen über Empfindung und Empfinden. II. Die Rolle der Sprachempfindung im Prozess der Gestaltungausdruckmassig erlebter Wörter. *Z. Psychol.,* 1930, *117,* 230–254.

130. WERNER, H. Musical "Micro-Scales" and "Micromelodies." *J. Psychol.,* 1940, *10,* 149–156.

131. WERNER, H. *Comparative Psychology of Mental Development.* Chicago: Follett, 1948.

132. WERNER, H. Microgenesis and Aphasia. *J. Abnorm. Soc. Psychol.,* 1956, *52,* 347–353.

133. WERNER, H., & STRAUSS, A. A. Pathology of Figure-Background Relation in the Child. *J. Abnorm. Soc. Psychol.,* 1941, *36,* 236–248.

134. WEVER, E. G. Figure and Ground in the Visual Perception of Form. *Amer. J. Psychol.,* 1927, *38,* 194–226.

135. WHITE, W. A. The Language of Schizophrenia. *Arch. Neurol. Psychiat.,* 1926, *16,* 395–413.

136. WOHLFAHRT, E. Der Auffassungsvorgang an kleinen Gestalten. Ein Beitrag zur Psychologie des Vorgestalterlebnisses. *Neue Psychol. Stud.,* 1932, *4,* 347–414.

137. WOODWORTH, R. S. *Experimental Psychology.* New York: Holt, 1938.

138. WOODWORTH, R. S., & SCHLOSBERG, H. *Experimental Psychology,* (Rev. Ed.). New York: Holt, 1954.

139. WYLIE, R. C. Generalization of Semantic Conditioning of the Galvanic Skin Response. Unpublished master's thesis, University of Pittsburgh, 1940.

4

PERCEPTION OF THE UPRIGHT
WHEN THE DIRECTION OF THE
FORCE ACTING ON THE BODY
IS CHANGED*
HERMAN A. WITKIN

Witkin, frequently collaborating with S. E. Asch, produced a series of studies of individual judgments of the *vertical-horizontal* continuum. The basic premise of these studies is that an individual instantiates a stimulus into the vertical-horizontal axes on the basis of integrating the multiplicity of stimuli that are recorded by the visual and intramuscular sensory apparatus. The ideal conditions for making objectively accurate determinations of verticality-horizontality are achieved when the body is in an upright position, exercising all the musculature involved in antigravity activity, at the same time that the visual field is oriented so that linear representations coincide with one's developed expectations about verticality and horizontality. Should either the body's antigravity forces or the visual field be altered so that the sensory feedback information deviates from highly developed expectation, the person will be unable to make "accurate" judgments of verticality and horizontality. If, for example, a person, while seated upright, is rotated around a circle at a substantial speed, the centrifugal force on the part of his body toward the perimeter of the circle will be greater than the force toward the center of the circle. As a result, the pressure will be greater on the sensorium associated with the outer aspect of his seat. In everyday life this condition exists when a person is seated so that he is

Reprinted from Journal of Experimental Psychology, *1950, 40, 93–106, by permission of the author and the American Psychological Association.*

*This study was carried out, for the most part, while the writer was a fellow of the National Research Council during 1943-1945. The apparatus was constructed with the aid of a grant (Grant No. 675) from the American Philosophical Society, of which grateful acknowledgment is hereby made. This grant was made to Dr. S. E. Asch and the writer; Dr. Asch, however, did not participate in this study. Gratitude is due to N. Tamber, who assisted in the investigation.

tilted away from the vertical plane, toward the side from which greater pressure is sensed. The effect, then, of being in motion around the perimeter of a circle is to perceive the body as tilted toward the perimeter of the circle. If the visual field remains upright, however, there results a contradiction of kinesthetically derived and visually derived stimulation. One of the ways that subjects can "make sense" of this combination of stimuli is to perceive the visual field as being tilted in the direction opposite to the perimeter of the circle—that is, toward the center of the rotation. Witkin's study is an attempt to quantify a person's judgmental processes during this state of conflicting kinesthetic and visual information.

With no intention of overlooking Witkin's valuable contributions to the broader study of judgmental processes, we again will focus attention on the point that subjects make the highly intricate, required judgments and are "unaware" of the process. The multitude of stimuli is integrated into a meaningful organization as an "automatic" process. There is no point at which the contradictions are so incapable of resolution as to produce an overoptimum level of arousal. We know, of course, that if one is repetitiously exposed to these kinds of visual-kinesthetic contradictions, as when one is aboard a ship in rough sea, that autonomic nervous system arousal can reach rather dramatic proportions.

*　　*　　*

I. Introduction

The direction of the perceived upright is ordinarily determined by two sets of experiences. First, visual space is filled with proper verticals and horizontals, and these provide a basis for judging the direction of the upright. Second, the gravitational pull on the body, which corresponds in direction to the true upright and which is readily detected through the postural adjustments made to it, provides another basis for judgment. Ordinarily, of course, the vertical of the visual field and the gravitational vertical coincide in direction, both forming a 90° angle with the horizon. In order to study the relative importance of each for perception of the upright, it is necessary to separate them experimentally. This separation may be accomplished in two ways: by tilting the visual field, with its main vertical and horizontal lines, while the force on the body, provided by gravity, remains unaltered; or by changing the direction of the force on the body, while the visual field remains upright. The first type of procedure, which involves radical changes in the visual determinants of perception of the upright, has already been used extensively in previous studies (1, 2, 4, 6). In extension of these studies, it is now necessary to investigate the second type of procedure.

It should be noted that modification of postural factors by simply tilting the body—a technique employed in previous studies (2, 4, 5, 6)—is basically different from their modification by altering the direction of the force that acts on the body. Tilting the body may at worst make it more difficult to detect the direction of the gravitational vector and to use it as a basis for determining the upright. The direction of the gravitational pull, of course, remains unchanged and continues to be available as a proper basis for judgment. Changing the direction of the force on the body, on the other hand, directly alters the gravitational standard for judgment. It is clear that only by changing this force is it possible to alter the postural determinants of the upright in as radical a way as the visual determinants are altered by displacing the visual field. The experiment to be described, therefore, represented a necessary extension of technique in these investigations of perception of the upright.

To change the direction of the force acting on the body is a relatively simple matter. All that is necessary is to rotate the S on a circular path, so that the effective force on the body is the resultant between the laterally-acting centrifugal force and the downward-acting gravitational force. Furthermore, it is possible, by changing the rate of rotation and thereby the magnitude of the centrifugal force, to vary systematically the direction of the effective force on the body.

Experiments utilizing this principle were performed about 75 years ago by Mach (3). He observed, while traveling on a train, that as his car went around a curve the scenery outside appeared to tilt over. He subsequently performed laboratory experiments in which some of the conditions presumably responsible for this phenomenon were duplicated. Specifically, he had himself driven about a circular track in a small fully enclosed cardboard box. Mach observed that as the box accelerated it appeared to tilt over more and more, and that after reaching a uniform speed it assumed a constant perceptual tilt. Since the shift in the perceived upright resulted from modification of the direction of the force acting on the body, Mach concluded that orientation toward the upright is based primarily upon postural experiences. This conclusion is at variance with that suggested by the results of previous studies in this series, where visual factors were found to play a primary role. In order to clarify this difference, it is necessary to investigate further the manner of perceiving the upright during rotation.

II. APPARATUS

The apparatus used to rotate the S may be seen in Fig. 1. It consisted of a totally enclosed room, five feet high by four feet wide by six feet long, which was mounted on two rubber-tired casters, and which rode on a circular hardwood track 17.2 feet in diameter. The drive consisted of a two-h.p. wound rotor induction motor, coupled through a 48-to-1 gear reducer and then through a radius arm to the room. The speed of rotation was controlled by means of a drum controller inserted in the rotor of the drive motor, which varied the circuit resistance. The speed could also be changed by varying the size of the pulley on the drive motor.

A small side door permitted entry into the experimental room. At the rear of the room, facing the direction of rotation, a comfortable leather chair, equipped with arm-rests, was attached to the floor so that it could not tip while the room was in motion. Above the chair was an adjustable headrest, which was used to hold the S's head stationary. This feature was introduced because even slight head movement during rotation were found to produce marked Coriolis reactions involving strong and unpleasant sensations of catapulting backward, to the side, and so on, depending on the nature of the head movement. The room was completely light-proof, and its interior was painted black. The front wall, facing the S, was bordered with narrow white strips emphasizing its outlines, and fixed to it were two pictures in square frames. The white strips and the frame supplied prominent vertical and horizontal lines. To illuminate the room a 6-volt 'trailer'-type bulb was mounted in each upper corner of the rear wall. Power for these lamps was provided by a storage battery placed under the S's chair. To eliminate the visual field, it was simply necessary to turn off these lights.

As in previous experiments, the S's ability to establish the V (vertical) and the H (horizontal) was measured by the accuracy with which he adjusted a rod to these positions.[1] In contrast with the earlier procedure, however, the S rather

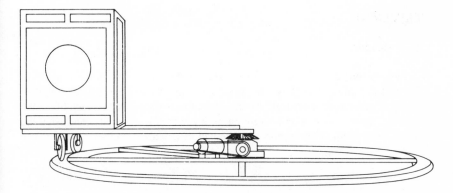

FIG. 1 *Line drawing of rotating-room apparatus.*

[1]As noted in a previous report *(4)*, the rod-adjustment procedure is most useful in the study of one aspect of perception of the upright; namely, perception of the direction of a line under various conditions. The alternative procedure, of requiring the adjustment of the whole room or of the S's body, was ruled out for the present experiments because of the extremely elaborate apparatus required. A later paper will report results of a study that measured the effects of rotation on perception of body position and position of the whole field.

than the E moved the rod, because during rotation the E was outside the experimental room. The rod was 39 in. long by one in. wide, and was coated with luminous paint to permit adjustment in the dark. It was mounted at the middle of the front wall of the room, and pivoted at its center on a shaft that ran from directly in front of the S's chair to the outside of the room. The shaft was supported on a stand rising from the floor. By turning the shaft, which had a knob on the end nearest his chair, the S was able to move the rod clockwise or counterclockwise. Outside the experimental room, on the end of the shaft that protruded through the wall, a large pointer was mounted at right angles to the shaft. The pointer was aligned with the rod inside, and moved with the rod whenever the S turned the shaft. Pasted on the outer wall, against which the pointer moved, was a large protractor, which enabled the E to determine the position of the pointer and therefore of the rod. Since the protractor and pointer were very large, the tilt of the pointer could be read off to the nearest degree, even while the room was in rapid motion. The E stood at a set position in the outer laboratory, and took readings when the room reached a certain point on the track.

With this apparatus, judgments of the upright were obtained at two different speeds of rotation, so that the direction of the force on the S's body was varied. At each speed, also, tests were conducted both in light and in darkness. In light, with the visual field present, there were available as bases for orientation an upright visual vertical and a displaced force on the body. In darkness, with the visual field absent, there remained only the displaced force on the body.

III. EXPERIMENT I

A. Procedure

Experiment Ia. The room moved around the circular track at a speed of 608 feet per min., or $67.7°$ per sec. resulting in an effective force displaced $20.5°$ from the gravitational vertical.[2] Three types of tests were given to each of 30 Ss.

Test 1. In this test the lights were on during rotation, and at its conclusion the S was simply required to report what he had experienced while the room was in

---

[2]This angle is the angle beta in the following force diagram: It was computed by

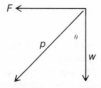

solving the formula tan $= F/W$, where F E $W(v^2/gr)$. It was also checked empirically by suspending a plumb line on the front wall of the room and determining the angle at which it was displaced during rotation.

motion. The S was blindfolded when brought into the laboratory and seated in the experimental room. This prevented him from seeing the apparatus and the circular track and thus finding out in advance the nature of the motion to which he was to be submitted. After the S was seated, the door to the room was closed, and the blindfold was removed. The headrest was then adjusted so as to prevent any head movement whatever. The S was told that the room would be set in motion, and that his task was to note everything that happened to himself and the room, so that he could give an account of it after the test was over. He was asked in particular to pay attention to the appearance of the room and to his own bodily experiences. No indication was given of the kind of motion that might take place. After this, the E stepped out of the experimental room in which the S was seated, and rotation was begun. The movement was stepped up gradually through the four speeds permitted by the control unit, until a uniform speed of 608 feet per minute was reached. The room was kept at this speed for two min. It was then slowed down through the same four speeds and finally brought to a standstill. The S was asked for a spontaneous account of his experiences; and if he failed to give a full report about the appearance of the room and his impressions of body position, he was questioned further.

Test 2. The S was now required, in addition to reporting again his experiences during rotation, to adjust the rod on the front wall to the V and the H. It was made clear at the outset that the rod was to be adjusted in relation to the outer building, rather than the experimental room. While the S watched, the rod was moved clockwise about 30° from the H position in which it had remained during Test 1. The S was told that later, at a signal from the E, he was to move the rod counterclockwise until he was satisfied that it was H. On the next signal, he was to move it counterclockwise again until it was V, then clockwise to make it H, clockwise to make it V, counterclockwise to make it H, and finally counterclockwise again to make it V. Thus he would make six adjustments of the rod, three to the H and three to the V, with H and V judgments alternating. The E left the room, which was then set in motion; and one min. after it had reached its maximum speed the E called out, "Begin," indicating that the first adjustment of the rod was to be made. When the S had completed the adjustment, and a reading of the pointer had been taken, the E called out "Next," indicating that the second adjustment of the rod was to be made. This continued until the six determinations had been made. The room was then stopped. The S was asked to give his spontaneous report, and afterwards was questioned—particularly about his method of deciding on the V and H positions.

Test 3. The procedure employed in Test 2 was repeated here in every detail, except that the experimental room was in complete darkness so that the S could see only the luminous rod.

2. Experiment Ib. The three tests of Experiment Ia were given to another group of 32 Ss, with the room rotated at a higher speed. The rate of movement was increased to 809 feet per min., or 89.9° per sec. so that the effective force on the body now formed a 33.4° angle with the gravitational vertical.

The conditions employed in Experiments Ia and Ib are summarized in Table 1.

TABLE 1 Summary of conditions employed in Experiment I.

Experiment No.	Angle of force on body	Condition of visual field	S's task
Ia (low speed)			
Test 1	20.5°	Upright field present	Observation only
Test 2	20.5°	Upright field present	Adjustment of rod
Test 3	20.5°	No field	Adjustment of rod
Ib (high speed)			
Test 1	33.4°	Upright field present	Observation only
Test 2	33.4°	Upright field present	Adjustment of rod
Test 3	33.4°	No field	Adjustment of rod

B. Results

1. Quantitative results. a. *Mean errors in adjusting rod to V and H.* Table 2 shows the average of the mean errors made by all Ss in adjusting the rod to the V and H in each of the experimental conditions.[3] Distributions of individual scores for each condition are presented in Fig. 2.

It may be seen from Table 2 that rotation of the body resulted in errors in judgment of the V and H under all conditions used: at low speed and at high speed, with and without a visual field. Moreover, the mean errors were larger at the higher speed of rotation. The same difference for the two rates of speed is seen in the individual scores (Fig. 2). In the lights-on condition the distribution for the high speed (Fig. 2c) extends farther in the direction of larger errors than the distribution for the low speed (Fig. 2a). A similar change in the distribution from the low speed (Fig. 2b) to the high speed (Fig. 2d) is found in the lights-off condition. Thus the experimental results demonstrate that the farther the effective force on the body was shifted from the gravitational vertical the farther the perceived V and H deviated from the true V and H.

Table 2 also shows that at both speeds the errors were considerably larger with lights off than with lights on. Again, the same difference is clearly indicated by the graphs for individual mean errors (Fig. 2); at both speeds the range for the lights-on condition is a very restricted one and the distribution is confined to the low-error end of the graph. Thus, it is indicated that changing the direction of the effective force on the body has a much less serious effect on perception of the V and H when an upright visual field is present.

---

[3] In computing errors, the amount by which the S's setting of the rod deviated from the true V or H was determined, without regard for the direction of the deviations. The direction of the errors in each of the conditions employed will be considered later.

When the *direction* of errors is examined, it is found that under all conditions the rod was most often tilted toward the center of rotation. This happened much more consistently when the visual field was absent than when it was present. Thus in Test 3 of Experiment 1a, with lights turned off, the rod was tilted toward the center of rotation in 93.8 percent of all

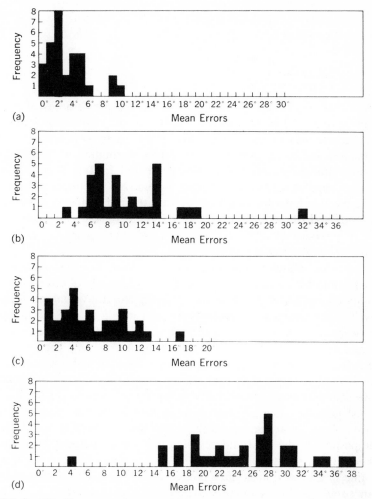

FIG. 2 *Distributions of scores for the experimental conditions used in Experiments 1a and 1b: Fig. 2a presents results for Test 2 of Experiment 1a (low speed, lights on); Fig. 2b for Test 3 of Experiment 1a (low speed, lights off); Fig. 2c for Test 2 of Experiment 1b (high speed, lights on); Fig. 2d for Test 3 of Experiment 1b (high speed, lights off). N is 30 in Figs. 2a and 2b and 32 in Figs. 2c and 2d.*

TABLE 2 Average of mean errors for all *S*s in adjusting rod to the V and H. (Errors taken without regard to sign).

Experiment		Lights on (Test 2)	Lights off (Test 3)
Ia Low speed	Mean error SD	3.1° 2.6	10.7° 5.6
Ib High speed	Mean error SD	6.3° 4.1	24.7° 7.1

settings, whereas in Test 2, with lights turned on, it was adjusted in this manner in only 67.2 percent of the settings. In the remaining settings of Test 2 the rod was brought to the true V and H in 17.0 percent of the adjustments, and tilted away from the center of rotation in 15.8 percent. The more uniform manner of adjusting the rod in Test 3 undoubtedly occurs because when the visual field is removed postural experiences provide the sole basis for judgment, so that the rod is always adjusted in accordance with these experiences. When a visual field is present, as in Test 2, it provides an additional basis for judgment, with the result that adjustments of the rod are more variable.

b. *Individual differences in magnitude of errors.* In each condition *S*s differed from one another quite markedly in magnitude of errors made in adjusting the rod to the true V and H. The range of individual mean errors for each experimental condition may be seen in Fig. 2. For the lights-on tests the range of scores is from 0° to 10° at the lower speed of rotation (Fig. 2a), and from 1° to 17° at the higher speed (Fig. 2b). The nearer the score is to zero, the more closely the settings coincide with the axes of the room. Though the spread in each case is not very great, it does indicate various degrees of conformance with the upright of the visual field. For the lights-off tests the range of scores is from 3° to 32° at low speed (Fig. 2c), and from 4° to 38° at high speed (Fig. 2d). Since in these tests judgments of the position of the rod could be based only on the perceived position of the body, these results suggest that the force acting on the body, though the same in all cases, must have produced an impression of greater body tilt in some *S*s than in others. Additional evidence that *S*s differed significantly from one another in their manner of perceiving room and body position will be presented subsequently.

2. Qualitative Results. The quantitative results given thus far do not adequately represent certain aspects of the *S*'s perception during displacement of the force acting on his body. There remain unanswered such questions as the following: How did the objectively upright room actually appear during rotation? What was the experienced position of the body? What method did the *S* use in making his judgments of the V and H? To answer these questions, some aspects of the *S*s' protocols will now be considered. This analysis is based primarily on the protocols for Experiment Ia, which are representative.

a. Effect of rotation on the perceived position of the visual field. First to be considered is the appearance of the upright room. In Test 1 of Experiment Ia, the following categories of reports were obtained. (1) Seven *S*s reported that the room remained perfectly upright throughout the test. (2) One *S* reported that the room looked tilted at the outset, while it was accelerating, but was straight during the remainder of the test. (3) Eleven *S*s reported that the room looked upright, but that because of the pressure they felt on their bodies they believe it was really tilted. (4) Ten *S*s reported that the room appeared tilted. (5) One *S* failed to take note of the appearance of the room. Thus, for 18 of the 30 *S*s the altered force on their bodies did not affect the appearance of the upright room, but for 10 of the 30 it actually caused the room to *appear* tilted. It should be added that all *S*s, regardless of how they perceived the room, perceived their bodies as tilted during rotation.

b. Modes of orientation shown by different Ss. The direction of the force acting on the body during rotation was the same for all *S*s, and all of them were placed in the same upright field. That under these identical conditions they should have differed both in manner of perceiving the situation and in method of judging the upright, points to individual differences in the emphasis assigned to visual and postural experiences. The protocols seem to indicate three different modes of orientation. (1) To some *S*s the room *looked* straight, and they therefore judged it to be straight. The postural experience of tilt was discounted, perceptually as well as intellectually, whereas visual impressions seemed to play a very dominant role. The 7 *S*s in the first category listed above were of this kind. (2) Other *S*s, although they also *saw* the room as straight, were led by the postural experience of tilt to judge it as really tilted. In these cases, postural sensations carried more weight in the final judgment, even though they did not affect perception directly. That the tilt of the room was inferred from the tilt of the body, rather than being experienced directly, is specifically indicated by the statements of some of these *S*s. One said, "The room looked straight but I knew it was tilted for I slipped to one side." Another stated, "No, the room did not look tilted; I inferred the tilt from the fact that my body was displaced," The 11 *S*s in category 3 above performed in this fashion. (3) Finally, in some cases the laterally acting force not only caused the *S*'s body to feel tilted but even had the effect of making the upright room appear tilted. The 10 Ss in category 4 above showed this kind of orientation. The apparent tilt of the upright room is very real in such cases, is it affected by knowledge of its illusory character, or by experience. Postural sensations receive much more emphasis in this kind of orientation than in the two preceding kinds. At the same time, it is significant that even on these Ss the upright visual field exerted a very strong effect. Subsequently, in adjusting the rod to the V and H, these 10 Ss had a mean error of only 4.1°, indicating that their settings were made much more in accordance with the axes of the visual field than with the direction of the force acting on the body. Had they conformed fully with the latter, their settings should have been off by 20.5°, the amount by which this force deviated from the true upright.

c. Differences between Test 1 and Test 2 in regard to apparent position of the field. In Test 2, some of the Ss gave significantly changed accounts of the situation. Of the whole group, 7 Ss reported after this test that the room looked straight and was straight, 22 that the room looked tilted and was tilted, and 1 that it looked straight but was really tilted. In other words, all but one S gave a self-consistent account: the room looked straight and was straight, or looked tilted and was tilted. This is in contrast with the results for Test 1, where more than a third of the Ss made the inherently contradictory report that the room looked straight but actually was tilted. On the whole, there was a change from Test 1 to Test 2 in the direction of bringing all of the S's experiences in the situation, and his evaluation of them, into a more consistent relationship.

The occurrence of such a shift, in the absence of a change in the structure of the situation, is probably due to two factors. First, whereas in Test 1 the S was simply asked to observe what happened, in Test 2 he was required in addition to adjust the rod to the V and H. This task certainly forced him to make a more careful estimate of his own position and the position of the room. Second, the questioning of the S at the end of Test 1 encouraged more careful attention to the situation when it recurred in Test 2. Both these features prompted a more analytical attitude in Test 2, making it less likely that visual impressions would be taken at face value or that a contradiction in experiences would go undetected.[4]

[4]The finding that a more analytical approach caused some S's to perceive the room as tilted, where previously they had perceived it as upright, points to the role of cognitive factors in perception. At the same time, it is questionable whether a genuine shift in perception was involved in every case where a change in the appearance of the room was reported. First, since room tilt, when noted at all, was most often very slight, it may simply have gone undetected under the 'free observation' conditions of Test 1. Second, although the Ss were asked about the appearance of the room, it is possible that in some cases their reports in Test 2 were based mainly on 'intellectual computations,' an approach encouraged in Test 2 for the reasons cited.

d. Experiences during Test 3. The *S*s' accounts of their experiences in Test 3, which was conducted in the dark, also contain several significant findings. Most of the *S*s reported after Test 3 that both their bodies and the room had been more tilted than in Test 2, even though the room could not be seen in Test 3. Although its supposed greater tilt was inferred mainly from the feeling of body tilt, it was also based on the reported experience that the slope of the floor underfoot had increased. The force on the body was of course the same in both tests, and the floor remained level during both periods. Specifically, 20 of the 30 *S*s reported an increased tilt of room and body in Test 3.[5] Six others reported that the tilt seemed to be about the same in the two tests, and three reported that it was less in Test 3. Each of these nine *S*s, however, showed a greater mean error in adjusting the rod in Test 3, indicating that the experienced tilt for which he was compensating in his adjustments had increased. The single remaining *S* reported that although his body felt tilted in Test 3 the room seemed to be straight; but he too showed a considerably larger mean error in adjusting the rod than in Test 2, where he had also reported that the room was straight. The general experience of increased tilt upon removal of the visual field is in keeping with the quantitative results reported earlier (Table 2). The average of the mean errors for all *S*s in setting the rod to the V and H rose from 3.1° in Test 2 to 10.7° in Test 3. The finding that with the same force acting upon it the body feels less tilted with an upright field present than when the field is removed demonstrates again the importance of visual determinants, in addition to postural ones, in the perception of body position.

e. Accuracy of perception of motion during rotation. The *S*s in the present experiment had no advance knowledge of the kind of motion to which they would be subjected; their instructions offered no information on this point, and they had no opportunity to see the apparatus. Further, being confined in the enclosed experimental room during rotation, they could not use the changing relation to objects on the outside as a basis for judging the nature of the motion. Under these conditions, their perception of the specific character of the movement could be based only on experiences induced by the rotation itself.[6] On the whole, *S*s were able to establish that some form of rotary motion was taking place at least some of the time. Thus, in Experiment Ia, all but one of the 30 *S*s reported rotation at some point during the three tests. On the other hand, the specific movement perceived very often failed to conform to the true

[5]Of these 20 *S*s, six had reported the room to be straight in Test 2.

[6]The noise of the motor and the vibration of the room during rotation undoubtedly provided cues that some movement was taking place. They were general in character, however, and probably did not help in determining the specific nature of the motion.

movement—to the extent that if, in other circumstances (in an airplane, for example), some action had been taken on the basis of the movement perceived the consequences would have been extremely serious. A number of Ss after a uniform rate of rotation had been reached, no longer experienced circular motion but reported forward movement only. One S, in fact, reported forward movement throughout, failing to perceive any rotation at all. Some of the Ss who perceived rotary motion reported rotation on the axis of the body either throughout or during part of the time. Finally, a few Ss even reported sensations of climbing and descending; these were Coriolis reactions that occurred in spite of the use of the tight-fitting headrest. It is clear that, with only the experiences produced by rotation available, gross errors in perception of the motion often occurred. Of course, if an opportunity had been provided for reference to the outer stable field (for example, through a window in the experimental room), perception would have been entirely accurate at all times.

IV. Experiment II

It has been shown that with the same force acting on their bodies and with the same visual field before them Ss differed in their perception of room position and body position, and consequently obtained different results in adjusting a rod to the V and H. This was established on the basis of a relatively small number of cases (30 in Experiment Ia and 32 in Experiment Ib). To investigate further this problem of individual differences, a modified form of Test 2 of Experiment Ib was given to a larger group of 196 Ss. This test employed the higher speed of rotation, with lights turned on. For 1½ min. after the room had reached its maximum speed, the S was permitted to observe the situation. At the end of this period, he made settings of the rod, four V and four H, in alternating sequence.

For the group as a whole the average mean error in adjusting the rod was 7.4° This is slightly higher than the average mean error of 6.3° for the 30 Ss in Test 2 of Experiment Ib. Fig. 3 gives the distribution of scores for the 196 Ss of Experiment II. As in the graphs for Test 2 of Experiment Ia and Test 2 of Experiment Ib (Figs. 2a and 2c), there is a striking concentration of scores at the lower end of the distribution. Fifty-five Ss adjusted the rod to within an average of 2° of the axes of the room; and 105, or more than half of the group, to within an average of 5°. Thus, despite the strong lateral force acting on the body, most Ss made rather small errors. At the same time, some Ss were affected to a considerably greater extent. Thus 25 Ss had errors of 15° or more, and in three extreme cases the errors exceeded 30°.

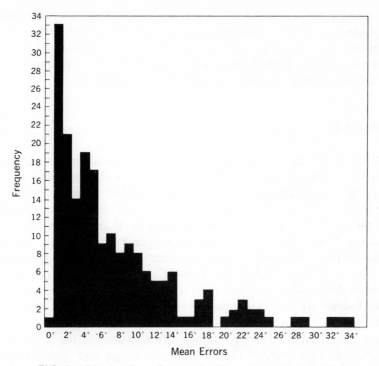

FIG. 3 *Distribution of scores for Experiment II. N is 196.*

That the wide range of errors seen in Fig. 3 was related to differences in manner of perceiving the situation is indicated in the reports obtained from the Ss about how the room appeared to them during rotation. To 61 Ss, or 31.1 percent of the group, the room continued to appear fully upright throughout rotation. Seventeen of these simply reported that the room had actually stayed upright; the other 44 stated that the room had appeared to them upright but that they believe it must have been tilted, because of the pressure they had felt. On the other hand, 135 Ss perceived the room as tilted; but most Ss brought the rod close to the axes of the upright room in making V and H settings, which indicates that even when the room was seen as tilted the magnitude of the perceived tilt was usually quite small.

To investigate the relation between judgments of the V and of the H, trials requiring V judgments were correlated with trials requiring H judgments, and r was found to have a value of $+.87$. This result indicates that the two main directions of space were judged on a common basis. This conclusion is supported by the additional finding that the average mean errors made in judging the V and in judging the H were almost identical (7.3° and 7.5° respectively), and that the distributions of individual mean error scores for the two types of judgment are very similar. Furthermore, since V judgments were made on even trials and H judgments on odd trials, the correlation obtained is a measure of odd-even reliability, and its high value indicates that each person tended to make his judgments in a consistent fashion throughout the test.

V. Experiment III

Some of the *S*s of Experiment Ia were also tested in the tilted-room situation and the frame-and-rod situation employed in earlier studies (2, 6). In the first of these, the *S* standing erect, looked through a tube which restricted his view to the interior of a tilted room. His task was to adjust a rod on the back wall of the room to the true V and H.[7] In the second situation, the *S* looked at a luminous square frame in an otherwise darkened room. Within this frame was a luminous rod, which again had to be adjusted to the V and H. The *S* made his adjustments in one series of trials while he was erect and the frame was tilted to either side; in a second series, while he was tilted to one side and the frame tilted to the same side; and in a third series, while he was tilted to one side and the frame was tilted to the opposite side. Twenty-four of the 30 *S*s of Experiment Ia were tested in the tilted-room situation, and 28 in the frame-and-rod situation. Their scores for each of these two situations were correlated with their scores for Test 2 of Experiment Ia (in which the lights were turned on and the higher speed of rotation was used). The correlation between the rotating-room and the tilted-room scores was −.69, and that between the rotating-room and frame-and-rod scores −.43. A relation between performance in the rotating room and performance in each of the other two situations is thus indicated. The probable nature of this relation becomes clearer when each of the situations is considered further. In the rotating-room situation the visual field remained upright, so that 'going along with' the field resulted in *small* errors. In the tilted-room and dark-room situations, however, the field was tilted, so that 'going along with' the field resulted in *large* errors. The finding of negative correlation between the rotating-room situation, on the one hand, and the tilted-room and frame-and-rod situations, on the other, indicates that 'going along with the visual field' is a common feature of performance in these three situations. There is thus some consistency in the way in which a given individual perceives the upright under different conditions—more specifically, in the use made of the visual field as a basis for perception. This was also indicated in a previous study (4).

[7]The test used here corresponded to Situation Gi8,a of Experiment 1 described in the report on the tilted-room experiment *(2)*.

VI. Discussion

In this study the postural determinants of perception of the upright were radically altered by changing the direction of the force acting on the body. The results make possible a further evaluation of the role of visual and postural factors in perception of the upright.

In such an evaluation, the results obtained with a visual field and without a visual field must be considered separately. It was found that *in the absence of a field* the alteration of the force acting on the body had a marked effect on perception of the upright. Not only did the *S*'s body feel tilted in every case, but also a visually presented upright line appeared tilted, again in every case. Although the shift in the perceived upright did not correspond in magnitude to the change in the effective force on the body, it was very considerable. The finding of such marked effects is not at all surprising, since when the visual field is removed postural factors alone form the basis for orientation, and changes in these factors must necessarily affect perception of the upright. This was also demonstrated in an earlier study (5) where it was found that in the absence of a field even slight changes in the position of the head or body caused an upright rod to appear tilted.

When the same change in force on the body was made *with an upright visual field present,* the effects were not so marked. Again, in every case, the *S*'s body felt tilted; and in many cases the *S* also saw the field as tilted. It is of course very significant that for some people a change in postural experiences may have this kind of effect upon visual experiences, producing an impression that does not correspond to the objective situation. However, although some *S*s' perception of the visual upright was thus affected, the magnitude of the effect was small, and with other *S*s it did not occur at all. Also, a majority of *S*s experienced less *body* tilt when the visual field was present than they did when it was absent, indicating that visual impressions even diminished the experienced force on the body.

The findings of this study may be compared with those of an earlier one (2) in which, similarly, judgments of the V and H were made under the influence of conflicting visual and gravitational standards. In that study, however, the visual field was tilted while the body remained upright, so that the conflicting visual and postural factors were in the opposite relationship to that used here. With the field tilted $22°$, *S*s erred by an average of $15.3°$ (in the direction of the tilt of the field) in setting a rod to the V and H positions, thus placing it much closer to the tilted axes of the field than to the axes of the body. In Experiment Ia of the present study, where the disparity between the visual and gravitational factors was almost the same but in the opposite relation (visual field 0°, gravitational force displaced 20.5°), the rod was again placed much closer to the axes of the visual field (average mean error, 3.3°). Together, then, the results of these two types of experiment demonstrate conclusively that perception of the direction of an external visual item is based primarily upon its relation to the surrounding field, and only in a secondary way upon postural determinants.

On the whole, the results obtained for judgments of the V and H during rotation leave no doubt that the perception of these directions is based in part upon the direction of the force acting on the body. At the same time the evidence is also clear in indicating that, when a visual field is present, the influence of this force in determining the perceived V and H is generally small. Thus, the judgment of the direction of an item within the visual field is based very much more on the observed axes of the field than on the force acting on the body. The indicated primacy of visual factors is in keeping with the results of previous studies (1, 2, 4, 6). It is especially impressive that this primacy should again be evident in the face of the very radical changes in postural factors introduced here.

As mentioned earlier, Mach (3) reached a different conclusion on the basis of somewhat similar experiments. He found that during rotation the upright chamber in which he was enclosed appeared tilted. Since for him the perceived upright seemed to correspond in direction to the resultant between the downward pull of gravity and the laterally-acting centrifugal force, he concluded that postural experiences play a primary role in perception of the upright. It is clear from the present study, however, that during rotation all people do not perceive the situation in the same manner as Mach. To some the field may appear upright; and among those who perceive it as tilted the magnitude of the tilt varies. Mach evidently based his generalizations upon too few cases, and this accounts for the discrepancy between his conclusions and those reached here concerning the relative importance of visual and postural factors in perception of the upright. In an earlier study (1), which was carried out to clarify the contradiction in results and conclusions previously reported for another experimental situation, the discrepancy was found to have a similar basis. There is thus repeated evidence of the need in perceptual studies for an adequate number of cases and for proper attention to individual performances, if valid generalizations are to be reached.

VII. Summary

As an extension of earlier studies in which the *visual* basis for perception of the upright was altered in basic fashion, the present study investigated the effect of a basic change in the *postural* determinants of the perceived upright. To accomplish such a change in postural factors, the subject was rotated about a circular path, so that the effective force acting on his body was shifted from the true upright, and now corresponded in direction to the resultant between the downward pull of gravity and the laterally-acting centrifugal force. During rotation the subject was seated in a fully enclosed room, and his task was to adjust a rod on its front wall to the true vertical and horizontal. Tests were conducted at two speeds of rotation, and at each speed the subject was tested both with a visual field and without a visual field. A total of 258 subjects served in the various experiments reported here.

It was found, first of all, that *when an upright visual field was present,* a shift in the force acting on the body had a very small effect on the perceived upright. At the lower speed of rotation, with the force on the body shifted by 20.5°, the error in adjusting the rod to the vertical and horizontal was only 3.1° (that is, the rod was off by that amount from the axes of the field, or from the true vertical and horizontal). At the higher speed, with the force on the body shifted by 33.4°, the error in adjusting the rod was only 6.3°. Thus, under conditions of conflict between visual and postural determinants of the of the perceived upright, the former proved more important. In the *absence of a visual field,* shifting the force on the body through rotation had a much greater effect on the perceived upright. At the lower speed, the mean error in adjusting the rod rose to 10.7°, and at the higher speed to 24.7°. Not only did removal of the field lead to larger errors in the setting of the rod, but in most cases it also caused the body to feel more tilted.

Marked individual differences were found among subjects in manner of establishing the upright, during rotation, both with a visual field and in its absence. With a visual field present, for example, so that a conflict existed between the visually and posturally indicated uprights, some subjects perceived the field as fully erect, and simply aligned the rod with its main axes. For other subjects, the force acting on the body had a much stronger effect, actually causing the objectively upright field itself to appear tilted, and leading to adjustments of the rod which more nearly conformed with the direction of this force. The conclusion previously reported by Mach (3), that postural factors are primary in perception of the upright, which is in contradiction to the findings of the present study, seems to be based upon the fact that he generalized from results obtained with the latter type of subject alone.

REFERENCES

1. ASCH, S. E., & WITKIN, H. A. Studies in Space Orientation: I. Perception of the Upright with Displaced Visual Fields. *J. Exp. Psychol.,* 1948, *38,* 325–337.

2. ASCH, S. E., & WITKIN, H. A. Studies in Space Orientation: II. Perception of the Upright with Displaced Visual Fields and with Body Tilted. *J. Exp. Psychol.,* 1948, *38,* 455–477.

3. MACH, E. Grundlinien der Lehre von der Bewegungsempfindungen. Leipzig: Wilhelm Engelmann, 1875, pp. 128.

4. WITKIN, H. A. Perception of Body Position and of the Position of the Visual Field. *Psychol. Monogr.,* 1949. (In press)

5. WITKIN, H. A., & ASCH, S. E. Studies in Space Orientation: III. Perception of the Upright in the Absence of a Visual Field. *J. Exp. Psychol.,* 1948, *38,* 603–614.

6. WITKIN, H. A., & ASCH, S. E. Studies in Space Orientation: IV. Further Experiments on Perception of the Upright with Displaced Visual Fields. *J. Exp. Psychol.,* 1948, *38,* 762–782.

INDEXES

AUTHOR INDEX

SUBJECT INDEX

Acceptance
 latitude, 534–546
 threshold, 107, 116, 544
Accomodation, 127, 178–180, 187, 196
Accumulative fragmentalism, 28
Achievement, 367–381
 motivation, 127, 367, 397–406, 548
 motive, 368, 378
Acquiescence, 321
 in personality, 544
Activating system, *see* Recticular arousal
 system
Activation, 15, 19, 126, 150–174
 characteristics of, 158, 173–174
 optimum level of, 126–128, 397
 pattern, 486, 488–491
 theory, 151–154
 see also Arousal
Adaptation, 420
 level, 393
 sensory, 485
Affiliation
 motive, 397–406
 need, 548–556
Aggression, 14–15, 364
 see also Hostility
Aktualgenese, see Microgenesis
Allport-Vernon Scale, 590
Alternation, *see* Behavior, alternation
Anchor, 106
 effect, 104
 stimulus, 417, 452–460
Anschauungen, 434
Anthropologists, 558–559

Anticipation, 37
 see also Expectation
Anticipatory goal response (r_g), 16, 197,
 236
Anxiety, 61, 172, 328, 362
 see also Arousal
Aphasia, 638–640
Arousal, 15, 19, 128–129, 151, 238, 532
 function, 365
 optimum, 128, 131, 465, 532, 534, 572,
 598
 reaction, 484–508
 system, *see* Reticular arousal system
 tolerance of, 548
 see also Activation
Ascending reticular arousal system. *see*
 Reticular arousal system
Assimilation, 102, 180–184, 187–191, 542–
 543
 distortion of, 543, 545
 effect, 417, 452–460
 range, 459
Associationism, 7
 stimulus-response, 14, 236, 468
 and novelty, 17–18
Associationistic learning theory, 299
Attention, 597–598
 hypothesis, 480
Attitude, 71, 572–580
 change, 534–546
 scales of, measurement, 102–120
 scaling, 103, 298, 536
 similarity, 548–556, 576–577
Attribute

84117   155.2
                          M31